Business Law

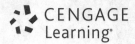

Business Law, 9th Edition
Keith Abbott, Norman Pendlebury and
Kevin Wardman

Publishing Director: Linden Harris

Publisher: Andrew Ashwin

Editorial Assistant: Lauren Darby

Production Editor: Alison Cooke

Production Controller: Eyvett Davis

Marketing Manager: Anne Renton

Typesetter: Cenveo Publisher Services

Cover design: Adam Renvoize

For product information and technology assistance, contact **emea.info@cengage.com**.

For permission to use material from this text or product, and for permission queries, email **emea.permissions@cengage.com**.

British Library Cataloguing-in-Publication Data
A catalogue record for this book is available from the British Library.

ISBN: 978-1-4080-6661-4

Cengage Learning EMEA
Cheriton House, North Way, Andover, Hampshire, SP10 5BE
United Kingdom

Cengage Learning products are represented in Canada by Nelson Education Ltd.

For your lifelong learning solutions, visit
www.cengage.co.uk

Purchase your next print book, e-book or e-chapter at
www.cengagebrain.com

Printed in China by RR Donnelley
1 2 3 4 5 6 7 8 9 10 – 15 14 13

Ninth edition

Business Law

Keith Abbott, BA (Hons), MBA, Solicitor
Her Majesty's Inspector. Former Director of Faculty of Business and Professional Studies, Hendon College

Norman Pendlebury, FCMA, MInstMgt
Former Senior Lecturer in Law, Southampton Institute of Higher Education

Kevin Wardman, LLB (Hons), LLM, ACIS, PGCE
Former Head of Postgraduate Programmes – Law, Principal Lecturer Liverpool John Moores University

Reprint incorporating

The Cancellation of Contracts Made in a Consumer's Home or Place of Work Regulations 2010
The Collective Redundancies (Amendment) Regulations 2006
The Companies (Model Articles) Regulations 2008
The Compensation Act 2006
The Consumer Protection from Unfair Trading Regulations 2008
The Corporate Manslaughter and Corporate Homicide Act 2007
The Criminal Justice and Immigration Act 2008
    The Cancellation of Contracts made in a Consumer's Home or Place of Work Regulations 2008
The EU Consumer Credit Directive 2008 and the
 • consequential 2010 Regulations on:
   – Consumer Credit
   – Total Charge for Credit
   – Disclosure of Information
   – Agreements
   – Amendments
   – Advertisements
The Employment Act 2008
The Employment Equality (Age) Regulations 2006
The Equality Act 2006
The Equality Act (Sexual Orientation) Regulations 2007
The Equality Act 2010
The Fraud Act 2006
The Gambling Act 2005
The Law Commission Act 2009
The Legislative Reform (Limited Partnerships) Order 2009
The Legal Services Act 2007
The Maternity and Parental Leave etc. and Paternity and Adoption Leave (Amendment) Regulations 2006

The Money Laundering Regulations 2007
The National Minimum Wage Regulations 1999 (Amendment) Regulations 2006
The Sex Discrimination Act 1975 (Amendment) Regulations 2008
The Transfer of Undertakings (Protection of Employment) Regulations 2006
The Tribunals, Courts and Enforcement Act 2007
The Work and Families Act 2006
The Working Time (Amendment) Regulations 2009

Continuum

The Tower Building, 11 York Road, London, SE1 7NX
370 Lexington Avenue, New York, NY 10017-6503
www.continuumbooks.com
First Edition 1982
Reprinted 1983, 1984
Second Edition 1985
Third Edition 1986
Reprinted 1986, 1987
Fourth Edition 1988
Reprinted 1989
Fifth Edition 1991
Reprinted 1991, 1992
Sixth Edition 1993
Reprinted 1994
Reprinted with amendments 1995
Reprinted with amendments 1996
Reprinted 1998
Reprinted 1999, 2000 (twice)
Seventh Edition 2002
Eighth Edition 2006
ISBN 0 8264 5916 1 (hardback)
ISBN 0 8264 5860 2 (paperback)
K. R. Abbott, N. Pendlebury and K. Wardman 2012

A CIP catalogue record for this book is available from the British Library.

Typeset by YHT, London

Printed in Great Britain by Martins the Printers, Berwick-upon-Tweed

TABLE OF CONTENTS

PART ONE   THE ENGLISH LEGAL SYSTEM

PART FIVE SOLE TRADER, PARTNERSHIP AND COMPANY

PART SIX EMPLOYMENT LAW

Answers to Reflection and Consolidation Assessment Exercises can be found on the accompanying digital resources for the book (see page xxv for details).

TABLE OF CASES

TABLE OF STATUTES

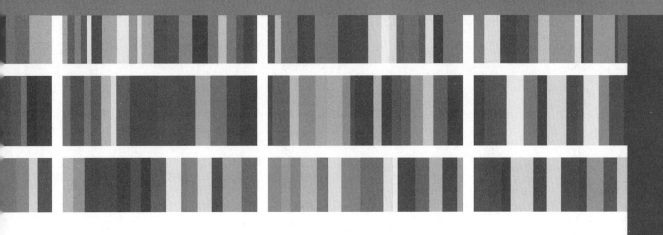

TABLE OF SECONDARY LEGISLATION/STATUTORY INSTRUMENTS

PREFACE

The bulk of the text is devoted to the presentation of legal rules in a straightforward style and format which will help students understand the subject, assimilate the necessary facts and achieve success in examinations. In addition there are introductory chapters on Learning Methods and Examination Technique and a number of past examination questions with suggested answers. To introduce each chapter there are statements of the *Learning Outcomes* which will be achieved at the end of each chapter along with *Self Test Questions* to help confirm knowledge and understanding. Also, at keys stages in the book, there are *Reflection and Consolidation* sections – which identify key elements of study and seek to develop a student's assessment skills through a series of past examination and multiple choice questions. Answers to the Self Test Questions can be found in Appendix 1; answers and guidance on the Reflection and Consolidation Exercises will be found in the book's accompanying digital support resources.

K. R. Abbott

N. Pendlebury

K. Wardman

ACKNOWLEDGEMENTS

The authors wish to express their thanks to the following for permission to reproduce past examination questions:

- Chartered Institute of Management Accountants
- Institute of Chartered Secretaries and Administrators.

Also to the Permissions Consultant Rachel Thorne for helping to secure the required permissions for this edition.

Kevin Wardman would particularly like to thank his wife Glenys and their wonderful daughters Leanne and Lauren.

WALK THROUGH TOUR

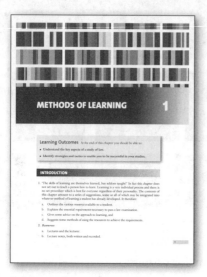

Learning Outcomes Featured at the start of each chapter to highlight to the student what they should be able to do at the end of each particular section.

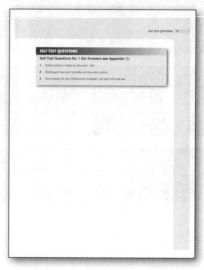

Self Test Questions At the end of each chapter designed to build student confidence through facilitating the acquisition of understanding of the key elements of law studied.

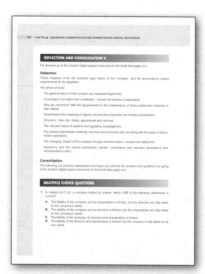

Reflection and Consolidation A fundamental part of the book which establish the vital link between student study and success in assessment; occurring at key stages in the book they direct students to the central key elements of the law and then, through a mix of multiple choice and essay style questions, prepare them for successful performance in all modes of assessment. Answers and guidance will be found on the specifically designed web site which accompanies the book.

Appendix 1 Sets out answers in a short snappy no-nonsense style to the Self Test Questions contained at the end of each chapter.

About the Website

All of our Higher Education textbooks are accompanied by a range of digital support resources. Each title's resources are carefully tailored to the specific needs of the particular book's readers. Examples of the kind of resources provided include:

- A password protected area for instructors with, for example, a testbank, PowerPoint slides and an instructor's manual.
- An open-access area for students including, for example, useful weblinks and glossary terms.

Lecturers: To discover the dedicated lecturer digital support resources accompanying this textbook, please register here for access **http://login.cengage.com**.

Students: To discover the dedicated student digital support resources accompanying this textbook, please search for Business Law 9th edition on **www.cengagebrain.co.uk.**

METHODS OF LEARNING

1

Learning Outcomes At the end of this chapter you should be able to:

- Understand the key aspects of a study of law.

- Identify strategies and tactics to enable you to be successful in your studies.

INTRODUCTION

1. 'The skills of learning are themselves learned, but seldom taught!' In fact this chapter does not set out to teach a person how to learn. Learning is a very individual process and there is no set procedure which is best for everyone regardless of their personality. The contents of this chapter amount to a series of suggestions, some or all of which may be integrated into whatever method of learning a student has already developed. It therefore:

   a. Outlines the various *resources* available to a student.

   b. Explains the essential *requirements* necessary to pass a law examination.

   c. Gives some advice on the approach to learning, and

   d. Suggests some methods of using the resources to achieve the requirements.

2. *Resources*

   a. Lectures and the lecturer.

   b. Lecture notes, both written and recorded.

    c.   Textbooks.

    d.   Past questions.

    e.   Suggested answers to past questions.

    f.   Discussions with fellow students and arranged visits, for example, to the courts.

    g.   This book.

3. *Requirements* Three qualities are necessary to pass law examinations:

    a.   Understanding the principles of law.

    b.   Learning the relevant legal facts.

    c.   Skill in applying the principles and facts to examination questions.

    This chapter suggests the best available resources for attaining the requirements of understanding and learning. Chapter 2 deals with the third requirement of application.

4. *Approach*

    a.   *Mental approach.* It is vital to neither underestimate nor overestimate your own ability or the standard of the examination. Both undue pessimism and overconfidence can be the cause of failure. The methods described below should minimize the risk of failure because of an unrealistic assessment of either personal ability or of what is expected by the examiner. The best approach is summed up in a Chinese proverb:

'That the birds of worry and care fly above your head, this you cannot change, but that they build nests in your hair, this you can prevent.'

    b.   *Physical approach*

        i.   *Timetabling.* When the course is nearing its conclusion, i.e. 6–8 weeks before the examination, it is generally advisable to prepare a revision timetable which allows roughly equal time for each paper that is to be taken. The timetable need not be complex, e.g. Mondays – Law; Tuesdays – Accounts; Wednesdays – Economics. A target number of hours should be set for each day, and if time is lost one day, it should be made good as soon as possible. Timetabling avoids time wasted deciding what to study each day, and it ensures that no subjects are neglected. The timetable may be changed occasionally if the revision time considered necessary for a particular subject changes as the examination draws near.

        ii.   *When to work.* This is mainly a matter for personal preference. It is, however, generally accepted that chances of success are not improved by working so late at night that you get less sleep than you need. A more contentious question is whether or not you should work up to the 'last minute' before an examination. The authors believe that you should do so. The evening before the examination is most usefully spent on revision rather than trying to relax watching television.

UNDERSTANDING

5. *Law is Easy to Understand!*

    a.   Such a statement by an author or lecturer may appear to reveal a lack of empathy with the problems faced by students. This is not the case. It is merely that our experience has shown that most people who fail law examinations do not do so because they are unable to understand the subject. Law is after all a human creation. It is relevant to everyday life, and the medium of expression is words. Subjects, such as mathematics, with abstract concepts and more indirect relevance are arguably more difficult to understand. All students can therefore approach law with confidence that they will not encounter insurmountable difficulties in understanding the subject.

b.   If, however, you do encounter a principle, rule, or case that you do not understand, you must never accept defeat. Read about it in several textbooks if necessary, ask your lecturer for a second explanation or discuss it with fellow students. Even if they have the same problem a discussion will almost certainly help. If a lack of understanding stems from not knowing the meaning of an individual word, then look it up in a dictionary. It seems an obvious solution, but it is rarely done.

6. *The Trap* Since law is often not difficult to understand, by its nature it lays a trap. A comparison with mathematics is again useful. If a mathematical concept is understood the answer can usually be worked out. In contrast the understanding of a legal rule does not, by itself, mean that the rule can be recalled in an examination. The trap is that understanding can be mistaken for an ability to recall, i.e. understanding can be mistaken for learning. They are related, but they are not synonymous. Understanding by itself will not enable you to succeed in a law examination, but it is the vital first step. Clearly you will not be able to learn or apply what you do not understand.

LEARNING

7. *Law is Difficult to Learn!* Inadequate learning is the main reason why many students fail law examinations. It therefore follows that learning and memory are the main things which law examinations test. A good factual knowledge of the relevant law is therefore the basis for success. Acquiring this factual knowledge can at times be boring. It may involve repetition of well understood facts, and it is usually a solitary and rather unsociable activity. Every effort must therefore be made to minimize boredom and maximize interest and enthusiasm, whilst using the limited time as effectively as possible. The best two ways to do this are:

a.   Use as many different methods of study (i.e. resources) as possible.

b.   Constantly test yourself.

8. *The Use of Different Resources* If you have allocated a particular 2-hour period for the study of law, do not spend all of the time reading notes or a book, because your concentration will soon fade. It is much more productive to select a topic and then study it using four different methods. For example in four periods of ½ hour each:

a.   Read a textbook.

b.   Read notes.

c.   Test yourself on the notes.

d.   Write a timed answer (see below).

9. *Self-Testing* The main reason for self-testing is to avoid falling into the understanding/ learning trap discussed above. If you test yourself you will find out whether or not you have

learnt what you have understood. At the end of chapters in this book (from Chapter 3 onwards) there are self-test questions which you should attempt, and obtain answers and guidance from Appendix 1. Also at key stages in the book there are sections headed 'Reflection and Consolidation'. These sections summarize and bring together knowledge and understanding covered up to that point, with comment and guidance on salient points in the text. Again, you should attempt the exercises set out here and get answers with feedback and guidance from Appendix 1.

10. *The Usefulness of Individual Resources for Learning*

    a.   *Textbooks.* It is not generally advisable to try to memorize facts from textbooks. Textbooks should only be referred to when a topic is not sufficiently understood, or when a break is needed from the other study methods.

    b.   *Lectures.* Lectures are primarily a time for the communication of the correct quantity of relevant information, and for increasing understanding by discussion and asking questions. The actual learning of this information will take place after the lecture.

    c.   *Lecture notes.* If lecture notes are adequate in detail (not excessive) and without 'gaps' they are probably the best resource for learning because they are personal to you. Read them regularly and if possible record them on cassette tapes. These cassettes should not be used as your basic learning method, but they will be useful if you feel that you need a short break from more traditional methods of study. When taking notes in lectures it is important:

        i.   To be as neat as possible – it is very difficult to learn from untidy notes.

        ii.   To space the notes out (rather like this book) – this assists the assimilation of facts.

        iii.   To only write on one side of each sheet of paper. The other side can then be used at a later date to expand on a difficult topic, or to write down a question on which a lecturer's comment is required.

    d.   *Past questions.* It is essential to obtain past questions as soon as possible after the start of the course, so that the standard of the examination can be assessed at an early date, and a good mental approach adopted. There are two main ways in which these past questions can be used:

        i.   Writing *timed answers*, i.e. without the assistance of notes, books or suggested answers, write an answer in the same amount of time as would be available in the examination. Clearly it is preferable for a lecturer to assess your answer, and even if he has not set the question he should be prepared to mark it if requested to do so. At the times when lecturer assessment is not possible (e.g. shortly before the examination) it is nevertheless useful to write timed answers. You will then have to critically assess your own answer, perhaps awarding yourself a mark, or even rewriting the answer if you consider your attempt very poor.

        ii.   Writing *model answers*. If a topic appears with regularity in the examination it is often worth writing an exam-length model answer, i.e. using all the available resources spend 1–2 hours writing the best possible answer that you can achieve. Lecturer assessment of such an answer would again be helpful. It is not suggested that you attempt to memorize every word of such an answer. It would, however, be possible to remember the structure of your answer, i.e. remember the number of paragraphs and the general point which each paragraph deals with.

e. *Suggested answers.* These are helpful only if they are used responsibly. They will be of no help if you merely read the question, then glance at the answer and either:

    i. Tell yourself (probably incorrectly) that you could write a similar answer in the examination, or

    ii. Get depressed because you know that you cannot produce such an answer.

Remember that these answers are not an indication of the standard that the examiner expects. Although they are 'examination length' each answer takes the author several hours to plan and write – a much less competent answer would still achieve a good pass.

One must nevertheless aim high. Suggested answers help to achieve this aim by serving three purposes:

    i. They illustrate the style, structure and content necessary to answer the particular question. However, they should not be regarded as the only possible correct answer. In most of the answers different cases will be just as acceptable as the cases quoted. Sometimes even a different conclusion is equally 'correct', for example if a question asks your views on the value of trial by jury. The most important advice in connection with style and content is *write in your own words*. Never try to memorize word for word sentences or paragraphs from any suggested answer. Such attempts usually fail, even one wrong word can alter the meaning of a whole paragraph.

    ii. They are a valuable means of self-testing.

    iii. They provide an incentive to practice. *Practice is* just as important as self-assessment. You would not expect to pass your driving test if all you did was read about the brakes, steering wheel and clutch in a book and then step into a car for the first time on the day of the test. Sitting a written examination is the same, practice is essential, and because suggested answers are a help in self-assessment they provide an incentive to practice, particularly at those times, e.g. shortly before the examination, when lecturer assessment is not possible.

f. *This book, Business Law,* may be used either as a study manual or as a textbook.

    i. *Use as a study manual.* If you do not have a good and adequate set of notes then use this book as a study manual, making it your basic method of study. Read it and re-read it several times (excluding the chapters which are not part of your syllabus) as you would with notes and use the coursework questions and revision questions as part of your self-testing programme.

    ii. *Use as a textbook.* If you do have good notes you may nevertheless choose to use this book as a study manual, or you may decide to use it as a textbook or a casebook referring to the text or cases when the need arises for a source of legal facts, a description of the facts of a case or clarification of a particular point of law. To facilitate use as a textbook a table of cases and an index is provided.

11. **Mnemonics** A mnemonic is an aid to memory. Some students find that a code sentence or code word is a useful memory aid. For example, a code word could be made from the seven requirements that Blackstone stated were necessary before a local custom could be accepted as law (see Chapter 4). His requirements, in the order stated in the text, are antiquity, continuity, peaceable enjoyment, obligatory force, certainty, consistency and reasonableness. The initial letters are ACPOCCR. These could be rearranged to form CCC-POAR. If this

code 'word' could be remembered it should trigger off recollection of the word which each letter represents, thus providing the basis for an answer.

12. ***Finally*** Some advice is offered to those persons for whom something goes wrong. It may be illness, or accommodation problems, or perhaps just wasted time. If you have about 4 weeks left to the examination and you seem to be heading towards certain failure but have now decided to make a late attempt to pass, then your best chance of salvation is to predict from past questions which topics are most likely to be asked. These topics should then be learnt as thoroughly as possible. It is better to have a good knowledge of a few topics than a vague knowledge of everything. You just have to hope that some of your predictions are correct.

EXAMINATION TECHNIQUE

2

Learning Outcomes
At the end of this chapter you should be able to:

- Apply a strategy and approach enabling success in your assessment.

- Apply a structure and style of answer to a typical examination question.

GENERAL POINTS

1. *Introduction* This chapter contains both 'golden rules', breach of which could mean the difference between success and failure, and useful hints which are comparatively less important, but which could nevertheless save a few vital marks. The points are dealt with in order of importance. The chapter assumes a 3-hour examination, giving a choice of 5 out of 8 questions.

2. *Answer All Parts of All Questions* Never leave a question unanswered. The first 5 marks out of 20 are the easiest to obtain, the second 5 moderately easy, the third 5 more difficult and the final 5 almost impossible. Therefore if you find that you have only 10 minutes remaining in which to answer 2 questions it is best to spend 5 minutes on each question, writing down in note form as much of the relevant law as you can remember. In such a situation it will be necessary to use the time that you would normally spend reading through your answers for this purpose.

3. *Never Leave the Examination Before the End* If you finish early check your answer paper carefully and re-read the question paper to make sure that you have not omitted part of any

of the questions. Keep reading and re-reading the question paper and your answers until the last possible moment. You may find an error or remember a case or point of law which had previously eluded you. If you do then include it at the end of the answer book and cross-reference it with the remainder of your answer.

4. *Time Allocation* The basic rule is that you should allocate equal time to each question, leaving 10–15 minutes at the end of the examination to read through your paper. If, however, you realize that you do not know enough to use all the time originally allocated to your fifth answer, whereas you could write in excess of your allocated time for your first answer, then deduct about 5 minutes from answer 5 and add it to answer 1.

5. *The First Five Minutes* As you read the examination paper for the first time underline what appear to be the key words in each question. Also write down in the margin the names of any cases, statutes or mnemonics which may be relevant. This gives you two chances of recalling these details, once at the start and again as you write each answer.

6. *Choice of Questions*

   a. Read through the whole paper 'ticking' questions which you can definitely answer and 'crossing' those which you cannot answer. If this does not produce exactly the correct amount of ticks, do not spend any further time on question choice at present – start your answers. It will be easier later in the examination to delete excess ticks, or to choose your best question out of the remaining 4 than to choose your fifth best out of 8 at the start.

   b. General essay questions for example on common law and equity or precedent result in a narrower range of marks than problem questions, i.e. there will be fewer students falling in the 0–5 and 15–20 brackets. Therefore if you are aiming for a very high mark, it is advisable to choose problem questions, although if you miss the point of the problem the result will be very serious.

7. *Order of Answering Questions* Start with the question which you are best able to answer. It is definitely very poor technique to save your best questions to the end, because if you start with your 'worst' question and make an error in timing, you may find that you have inadequate time to answer the questions on which your knowledge is greatest.

STYLE AND STRUCTURE

8. *Starting with a Conclusion* It is a bad and common error to start with a conclusion. Answers often commence, for example, 'John will succeed in his negligence claim because …'. This is a conclusion and it should therefore come at the end. If it comes at the start, and is wrong, the rest of the answer will be spent in an attempt to justify an incorrect conclusion, which often produces an answer where only one side of the argument is presented. The answer should be structured as follows:

   a. State the relevant principles of law illustrating them where applicable with decided cases. If there are two sides to a problem both of them must be discussed, and not merely the argument which supports the conclusion which will eventually be reached. The names of the characters of the problem need not necessarily be mentioned at this stage.

   b. Apply the stated principles to the facts of the problem.

c. Give your conclusion. It does not have to be 100% certain. It is acceptable to say '…
therefore John will probably succeed' if there is some reasonable doubt as to his chances. You must, however, commit yourself one way or the other, do not finish by stating
that 'John has a 50/50 chance of success.'

9. *Contradictory Conclusions* If you place your conclusion at the end this will help to avoid
the danger of self-contradiction. If, however, on reading through your answer you find contradictory statements or conclusions, you must delete one of them. If you do not do this
you will get the worst of both worlds rather than the best, i.e. even if one is correct it will
not score any marks.

10. *Repeating the Question* This is a very common fault, it never scores any marks, it wastes
time, and it spoils the structure of the answer.

11. *The Introduction* Often an answer on offer will start 'A contract is a legally binding agreement between persons. In order to make a contract there must be an offer, an acceptance of
that offer, consideration and an intention to create legal relations. An offer is …'. The whole
of this quotation, except the last three words although correct, is not sufficiently relevant to
earn any marks. An introduction (if any) should be very brief; you should get to the point of
the question as directly as possible. If you are stuck then start with the phrase 'The relevant
law is as follows …'.

12. *Format* Generally answers should be structured in un-numbered paragraphs. Occasionally
it may be suitable to make several points under headings (a), (b), (c), etc. in one particular
paragraph. Even so this should not be the basic style of the answer. If, however, you have
very little time remaining for a question it is better to write as many relevant points as possible in note form, rather than one or two paragraphs in perfect English.

13. *Balance* Answers often tend towards one of two extremes. An answer may contain a list of
principles of law, without any mention of cases, or it may consist of a number of case
descriptions apparently unconnected by legal principles. Both these extremes are very poor.
An answer should be well-balanced, containing both statements of principles of law, and
case law illustrations of those principles.

14. *Meaning* Many students fail to express what they wish to say. An example from a recent paper
stated 'Performance of a contract is only precise and exact.' The examiner will probably realize
that the student does in fact know the basic rule regarding performance of a contract. However,
the sentence, in its present form is meaningless, and probably would not obtain any marks. The
sentence should of course read 'Performance of a contract must be precise and exact.'

It is not possible to become an expert at expressing your desired meaning merely by effort
or determination, it is a very slow process. All you can do is (i) be as careful as possible, (ii)
do not try to write too fast and (iii) read through what you have written.

CONTENT

15. *Names, Dates, and Facts of Cases* Perhaps the most frequent question a law lecturer is asked
is the importance of including names, dates and facts of cases in an answer.

a. Facts without names. If you cannot remember the name of a case, but you can recall the
facts, then include the facts in your answer, but introduce them in some other way, e.g. 'In
a recent case …'. It is far better to do this than to omit the case.

b.   Names without facts. Where a principle of law is derived from a case it is acceptable for the case name alone to follow the principle. Some case names must, however, be supported by facts otherwise the answer will not be 'balanced'.

c.   Dates. Dates are comparatively less important than names. It is not worth specifically learning dates, but if you do remember the date then include it in the answer.

d.   Choice of cases. Sometimes a number of cases are equally good illustrations of a legal principle. In this situation choose the case which can be described most concisely.

16. *Jargon* Avoid the use of unnecessary 'jargon'. Do not for example start your final paragraph 'After taking all the relevant law into consideration it is submitted that …'. The simple 'In conclusion …' is far better.

17. *Latin Phrases* Wherever possible this book will avoid the use of latin phrases. However, where they are used, if you wish to say for example 'X will make a quantum meruit claim against Y' you cannot assume that the examiner knows that you know what 'quantum meruit' means. You should therefore add, perhaps in brackets, 'a payment for work done proportionate to the contract price'. The examiner then knows that you have remembered the meaning of the words as well as the words themselves.

18. *Miscellaneous Points*

a.   Never use slang, or attempt to introduce humour into your answer. For example, 'X has not got a snowflake's chance in hell of success' would not impress the examiner.

b.   Avoid the use of 'I', 'we', and 'us'. When asked in a question to 'Advise X' do not write 'You will fail in your claim,' write 'X will fail in his claim.'

c.   Never use red ink, even to underline cases. This causes confusion when two or more examiners read the script.

d.   If you wish to cross out anything that you have written use a single line drawn with a ruler. If you wish to reinstate words which you have previously crossed-out then draw a line of dots under the words deleted, and write 'stet' in the margin. This means 'let it stand'.

e.   Finally there is no need to emphasize words by underlining them or writing them in capitals. It is acceptable to emphasize case names or statutes in this way but not general words.

CONCLUSION

19. The final advice regarding the examination is 'don't panic'. This is of course easy advice to give, but it can be very difficult to put into practice. Perhaps the best antidote to possible panic is to consider the consequences of failure. Failure of an examination does not necessarily mean that you follow an inferior path through life. It may mean that you follow a different path, but it is impossible to say, at the time of the examination, whether this different path will ultimately be for the better or the worse.

PART ONE
THE ENGLISH LEGAL SYSTEM

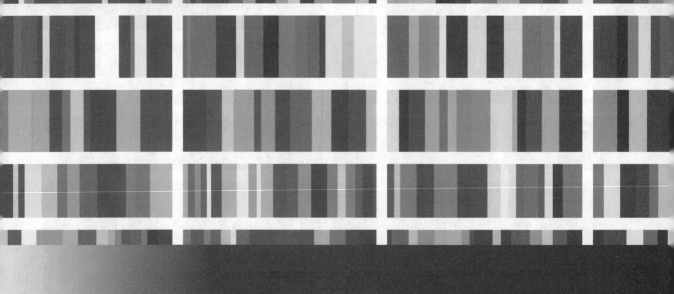

3 INTRODUCTION

Learning Outcomes At the end of this chapter you should be able to:

- Explain the difference between law, morality and justice.

- State the main differences between civil and criminal law.

WHAT IS LAW?

1. *Definition*

   a. The law of a particular state is the body of rules designed to regulate human conduct within that state. Broadly speaking there are three types of rule:

      i. Rules which forbid certain types of behaviour under threat of penalty.

      ii. Rules which require people to compensate others whom they injure in certain ways.

      iii. Rules which specify what must be done to order certain types of human activity, e.g. to form a company, to marry, or to make a will.

   b. Although it is inevitable that the courts will make some rules, Parliament is the sovereign body. It can therefore impose new rules or abolish any existing rules. The basic role of the courts is to interpret these rules, decide whether they have been broken and pass sentence or make an award of compensation.

2. *Law and Morality*

   a. The law which is enforced by the courts must be distinguished from what is sometimes referred to as 'natural' or 'moral' law. In many cases the rules of law and morality clearly coincide. For example, if a person murders another this offends both law and morality. The state will therefore punish the offender.

   b. Sometimes, however, the rules of law and morality are not the same. For example, homosexual behaviour in private between consenting adults is not illegal although some people might regard it as a breach of moral law.

   c. The term 'natural law' is sometimes used to refer to rules which although not enacted are accepted as part of the legal system. For example, the right of both sides to be heard (or to remain silent), and the principle that an accused person is innocent until proven guilty.

3. *Law and Justice* The basic aim of law is the attainment of justice in society. However, in some situations the degree of justice hoped for is not achieved. For example:

   a. Compensation for injuries usually depends on proving that someone else is at fault. If a person is injured due to his own fault, or in a 'pure' accident where no one is at fault, he will not receive compensation unless he is insured. This inequality is a result of the rules on negligence liability.

   b. The rules regarding mistake and misrepresentation in the formation of a contract often operate to determine which of two innocent parties must bear all of the loss. The loss is not divided equally, for example *LEWIS v AVERAY (1971)* (Chapter 17).

   c. Sentencing policies applied by magistrates in different areas often result in substantially different sentences for very similar offences.

4. *Conclusion*

   a. It would therefore be an oversimplification to say that most people obey the law because it is just, or because it coincides with their view of which is morally correct. Law is also closely related to force and authority and these relationships would have to be examined in order to properly explain the intrinsic nature of law, and to find out why most people obey the law.

   b. An alternative to explaining law by reference to its intrinsic nature is to explain it by reference to what it does. In the most general terms law classifies human behaviour. Human beings are capable of an infinite variety of behaviour. Some conduct is clearly acceptable, whereas other conduct is obviously wrong. In between there are numerous examples of human acts or omissions which some people would regard as acceptable, but others would regard as wrong, for example, if a man were to dress in public as a woman. The law can specify with absolute precision some activities that are regarded as unacceptable, for example driving at more than 70 miles per hour, but it would be impossible to list every example of acceptable and unacceptable conduct. Nevertheless if someone does something that is legally challenged by another person or by the State, it will have to be decided whether or not that conduct was acceptable. The legal system will therefore classify any human conduct (even things that no one has ever done before) into two basic categories: 'right' or 'wrong', i.e. in criminal cases a verdict of 'guilty' or 'not guilty' and in civil cases a finding for the plaintiff or a finding for the defendant. Law is therefore the most ambitious and complex classification system devised by man.

THE CHARACTERISTICS OF ENGLISH LAW

5. There are several features which distinguish the English Legal System from foreign systems:

    a.   *Continuity*. English law has developed since 1066 without any major changes in the system. Two factors have led to this:

        i.   England has not been conquered since 1066, and

        ii.   Acts of Parliament and case law do not become inoperative merely due to old age. For example, the *TREASON ACT 1351* was considered in ***JOYCE v DPP (1946)***.

    b.   *Absence of codification*. In some countries most of the law has been reduced to written codes which contain the whole of the law on a particular subject. Generally this is not so in England.

    c.   *The system of precedent*. This means that a judge is bound to apply rules of law formulated in earlier cases provided the facts of the case before him are sufficiently similar, and the earlier case was heard in a court of superior or (subject to exceptions) equal status.

    d.   *The judiciary*. English judges are independent of both Parliament and the Civil Service. This is evident from the fact that they often give judgement against The Crown or a Government Department. In addition a judge will be immune from liability provided he acts honestly in the belief that he is within his jurisdiction. The judiciary is important because the judges of the superior courts have a great effect on development of the law. They do not merely apply statutory rules, they *make* law when interpreting statutes and by developing the doctrine of judicial precedent.

    e.   *Common law and equity*. English law is based on two complementary systems of law known as common law and equity. Common law was the first system to develop. Its rules were rigid and sometimes harsh. Equity evolved to supplement the common law with more flexible rules based on principles of good conscience and equality.

    f.   *The accusatorial procedure*. In both civil and criminal cases the court remains neutral and hears the arguments presented by each side. In countries where an inquisitorial procedure is used the court plays a more active part, itself questioning the witnesses.

CIVIL AND CRIMINAL LAW

6. There are many ways to classify law, the most fundamental distinction being that drawn between criminal and civil law.

7. *Criminal Law*

    a.   A crime is regarded as a wrong done to the State. Prosecutions are usually commenced by the State, although they may be brought by a private citizen. If the prosecution is successful the accused person (the defendant) is liable to punishment. Some crimes, for example rape, have specific victims. Others, for example treason or speeding, can be committed without causing loss to any particular person. If there is a victim he will not usually have a say in whether or not a prosecution is brought, nor will he benefit from a conviction, since fines are payable to the State.

b. Criminal and civil hearings take place in different courts with different rules of procedure. There is also a different standard of proof. In a criminal trial the prosecution must prove the accused's guilt *beyond reasonable doubt*. In a civil action the plaintiff must prove his case on the *balance of probabilities*.

8. *Civil Law* Civil actions may be commenced by any person who seeks compensation for a loss which he has suffered. If the claimant is successful he will usually be awarded damages. The damages must be paid by the defendant. Their purpose is to compensate the claimant for his loss rather than to punish the defendant. There are many categories of civil law, for example:

a. *Contract*. This determines whether promises made by persons are enforceable.

b. *Tort*. A tort is defined as the breach of a general duty imposed by law, for example the duty not to be negligent, and the duty not to trespass on another person's property.

c. *Property law*. This includes the law relating to freehold and leasehold land, and the ownership and possession of goods.

d. *Company law*. There is a need to regulate the relationship that a company has with its directors, shareholders, creditors and employees.

e. *Commercial law*. This term covers contractual matters relating to business transactions, for example the law relating to sale of goods, consumer credit and cheques.

f. *Employment law*. This also involves contractual relationships, in this case between employer and employee. The term also includes redundancy, unfair dismissal and health and safety at work.

g. *Family law*. Marriage, divorce, nullity, guardianship and legitimacy are within the scope of family law.

9. *Crime or Civil Wrong?*

a. The distinction between a crime and a civil wrong is not found in the nature of the act itself, but in the legal consequences that follow it. Thus if a taxi driver crashes he may commit:

   i. A breach of contract, i.e. failure to deliver the passenger to his destination.

   ii. A tort, i.e. negligence if he causes damage to any person or property.

   iii. A crime, for example dangerous driving.

b. In some situations the facts will therefore indicate both a criminal offence and a possible civil action. In such cases the victim will not be able to have both actions heard in the same court. He will have to start a civil action separate from any prosecution brought by the State. However, *S.11 CIVIL EVIDENCE ACT 1968* provides that in any civil proceedings the fact that a person has been convicted of an offence shall be admissible to prove that he committed that offence. The effect is to raise a presumption that he committed the offence, unless the contrary is proved.

	Criminal Law	Civil Law
Persons affected	These are **offences** against society as a whole i.e. the **state**	These are **wrongs** taking place between private **individuals** e.g. a failure to supply goods or some service such as a breach of contract
Who brings the action?	The **state prosecutes** a **defendant**	The individual – a **claimant** – **sues** the **respondent**
Where is the case heard?	In the **criminal courts**	In the **civil courts**
What has to be proven?	The prosecution must show that the defendant committed a crime **beyond all reasonable doubt** – this is a high standard because upon a finding of guilty the defendant is **punished**	The claimant must show the respondent committed a wrong on a **balance of probabilities** – a lower standard than in criminal law, i.e. the respondent **probably** committed the wrong
Consequences of a finding of guilty or breach	**Punishment** – the defendant is fined, sent to prison, given a community service order, etc.	**Compensation** – the respondent must pay damages to the claimant for the harm caused or be subject to an injunction or specific performance

THE TITLE OF CASES

10. *Criminal Cases*

   a. Prosecutions involving the more serious criminal offences, known as indictable offences, are brought in the name of The Queen. The case will then be known as, for example, 'R v Jones', R being short for either Regina or Rex.

   b. Prosecutions for less serious offences, known as summary offences, are usually commenced in the name of the actual prosecutor (normally a police officer), for example 'Evans v Jones'.

   c. Where the offence is particularly serious or complex, for example murder or perjury, the Director of Public Prosecutions may investigate and prosecute. In addition some statutes require actions to be brought by the DPP, for example for election offences under the *REPRESENTATION OF THE PEOPLE ACT 1949*.

11. *Civil Cases*

   a. The parties' names are used, the claimant's name being placed first, for example 'Rylands v Fletcher'. This is, however, traditionally pronounced 'Rylands and Fletcher'.

   b. Sometimes there will not be a claimant and a defendant, for example if an application has been made to the court to interpret Brown's Will the case would be known as 'Re Brown'.

12. *Appeal Cases* When a party appeals he is called the appellant, and the other party is the respondent. Since the appellant's name is always placed first, when a defendant appeals the name of the case will be reversed, thus Peek v Derry in the High Court, and on appeal, became Derry v Peek in the House of Lords (now the Supreme Court).

SELF TEST QUESTIONS

Self Test Questions No. 1 (for Answers see Appendix 1):

1   Define what is meant by the term, 'law'.

2   Distinguish law and morality and law and justice.

3   Summarize the key differences between civil and criminal law.

4 THE MAIN SOURCES OF ENGLISH LAW

Learning Outcomes At the end of this chapter you should be able to:

- State where the law of England comes from and the role of custom in its creation.

- Demonstrate an understanding of judicial precedent.

- Explain the nature and role of legislation as a prime source of English law.

- Explain the nature of the impact of EC law on English law.

THE MEANING OF 'SOURCES OF LAW'

1. The previous chapter classified the law into civil and criminal by reference to the subject matter of the dispute and the legal consequences which result from the dispute. Law may also be classified by reference to its source, i.e. the means by which the law is brought into existence. There are four *legal sources* of law, namely:

   a.   *Custom.*

   b.   *Judicial precedent* – sometimes called *case law* or *judge-made law*.

   c.   *Legislation.*

   d.   *European law* – referred to as *EC Law* – (European Community Law).

2. Sometimes other meanings are attributed to the term 'sources of law':

   a. The *literary source* describes where the law is physically found, i.e. in law reports and statutes.

   b. The *formal source* describes the authority which gives force to the rules of law, i.e. the State.

   c. The *historical sources* are generally regarded as common law and equity, although the term is sometimes used to refer to the reasons behind the creation of the law, for example a report by the Law Commission.

3. This chapter concentrates on the four legal sources, but since methods of classification of law are only matters of convenience, there is an inevitable overlap between these legal sources, civil and criminal law, and common law and equity.

CUSTOM

4. *Uses of the Word 'Custom'* The word 'custom' may be used in several different senses. In one sense it is the main source of English Law since it is the original source of common law. It would, however, be wrong to equate 'common law' and 'custom' today since most common law rules owe their origins to judicial decisions rather than ancient custom. In its second sense 'custom' describes a conventional trade usage. Custom in this sense is not a source of law, but a means by which terms are implied into contracts.

5. *Local Custom* The third use of custom is to describe rules of law which apply only in a particular area for example a county or parish. In this sense custom is a distinct source of law. In addition to the characteristic of restriction to a particular locality it must be an exception to the common law. For example, under the custom of 'Gavelkind', which operated in Kent, an intestate's property (an intestate is the name given to the situation where a person dies without leaving a will) passed to his sons in equal shares, whereas over most of the country it would all pass to the eldest son. Gavelkind was abolished in 1925. A valid local custom may be limited to a class of persons within a locality such as fishermen, but it cannot apply to a class of persons throughout the country, since then it would not be an exception to common law, but a part of it.

6. *Proof of Existence of a Local Custom* Local custom also differs from common law in that if an alleged custom is to be incorporated into the law it must be proved to exist in Court. It is then said to be 'judicially noticed' and will be enforced by other courts. Thus a person who alleges the existence of a custom must prove its existence by satisfying the following tests laid down by Blackstone in 1765:

   a. *Antiquity.* Local custom must have existed since 'time immemorial'. This has been fixed by statute at 1189, the first year of the reign of Richard I. In practice proof back to 1189 is never possible, so the Court will accept proof of existence within living memory. If this is shown the person denying the existence of the custom must prove that it could not have existed in 1189.

      In *SIMPSON v WELLS (1872)* Simpson, who had been charged with obstructing a public foot-way, by setting up a refreshment stall, alleged that he had a customary right to do so deriving from 'statute sessions' (ancient fairs held for the purpose of hiring servants). It was shown that statute sessions were first authorized in the 14th century, so the right could not have existed in 1189.

b. *Continuity.* The *right* to exercise the custom must not have been interrupted. This does not mean that the custom itself must have been continuously exercised.

In *MERCER v DENNE (1905)* D owned a section of beach and wished to build on it. P, a fisherman, claimed a customary right to dry his nets on the beach and asked for an injunction to prevent the building. D's defence was that the custom was only exercised occasionally, and that before 1799 the beach ground was below the high water mark, and until recent times was unsuitable for use for drying nets.

It was held that the custom was valid. Its existence throughout living memory was proved, and the fluctuations in use were due to variations in wind and tide. However, the fisherman had always claimed the right to use such ground as was available, and so the custom extended to the additional ground now available.

c. *Peaceable enjoyment.* A custom can only exist by common consent. It must not have been exercised by the use of force, secrecy or permission.

d. *Obligatory force.* Where a custom imposes a specific duty, that duty must be compulsory, not voluntary. Blackstone said:

'A custom that all the inhabitants shall be rated towards the maintenance of a bridge will be good, but a custom that every man is to contribute thereto at his own pleasure is idle and absurd, and indeed no custom at all.'

e. *Certainty.* An alleged custom allowing tenants to take away turf 'in such quantity as occasion may require' was held void for uncertainty (*WILSON v WILLES (1806)*).

f. *Consistency.* Customs are by their nature inconsistent with common law, but they cannot, in a defined locality, be inconsistent with one another.

g. *Reasonableness.* A custom must be reasonable.

In *DAY v SAVADGE (1614)* a custom which allowed an Officer of the City of London Corporation to certify what customs were valid in matters in which the Corporation was interested was held to be invalid because it was unreasonable.

A custom cannot be reasonable if it conflicts with a fundamental principle of common law.

In *WOLSTANTON v NEWCASTLE-UNDER-LYME CORPORATION (1940)* the alleged custom allowed the landlord to undermine and remove minerals from his tenant's land without paying compensation for buildings damaged as a result. This was held to be unreasonable.

7. In recent years the tendency has been to standardize law by statute. This has led to the decline of custom as a source of law so that it is now almost extinct. The types of customary rights that do still exist are, for example, rights of way and rights to indulge in sports or pastimes on a village green.

JUDICIAL PRECEDENT (SOMETIMES REFERRED TO AS *CASE LAW* OR *JUDGE-MADE LAW*)

8. *The History of Judicial Precedent*

a. The doctrine of binding precedent did not become firmly established until the second half of the 19th century. In the common law courts the former practice was to apply the declaratory theory of common law, i.e. the law was contained in the customs of the land, and judges merely declared what it was. Thus although judges regarded precedents as persuasive they did not consider them to be binding. In **FISHER v PRINCE (1762)**, Lord Mansfield said:

'The reason and spirit of cases make law, not the letter of particular precedents.'

b. As time passed judges paid more and more attention to previous decisions and in **MIREHOUSE v RENNELL (1833)**, Baron Parke said that notice must be taken of precedents. The court could not 'reject them and abandon all analogy to them'.

c. In the Court of Chancery there was no declaratory theory, the judges merely tried to do justice in each individual case. This system lacked certainty and criticism was strong. From about 1700 the court began to pay increasingly greater respect to its previous decisions.

d. The modern doctrine of binding precedent is about 125 years old. Its present form is due to two factors. Firstly in 1865 a Council was established by The Inns of Court and The Law Society (now the Solicitors Regulation Authority) to publish under professional control the decisions of the superior courts. Prior to this, private reports were published, some were good, others were unreliable, and many cases were not reported at all. Secondly, the *JUDICATURE ACTS 1875* established a clear court hierarchy. The doctrine of precedent depends for its operation on the fact that all courts stand in a definite relationship to one another.

9. *An Outline of the Doctrine* Despite the inevitable tendency of judges to create law, binding precedent is *based* on the view that it is not the function of a judge to make law, but to decide cases in accordance with existing rules. *Two* requirements must be met if a precedent is to be binding:

a. It must be a *ratio decidendi* statement (this is the part of a judgment which deals with the interpretation of the law, see below), and

b. The court must have a superior, or in some cases equal status to the court considering the statement at a later date.

If these requirements are met, and the material facts as found are the same the court is bound to apply the rule of law stated in the earlier judgment.

10. *The Ratio Decidendi*

a. Judgments contain:

i. *Findings of fact*, both direct and inferential. An inferential finding of fact is the deduction drawn by the judge from the direct, or perceptible facts. For example, from the direct facts of the speed of a vehicle, the road and weather conditions, and the length of skidmarks, the judge may infer negligence. Negligence is an inferential finding of fact. Findings of fact are not binding. Thus even where the direct facts appear to be the same as those of an earlier case the judge need not draw the same inference as that drawn in the earlier case.

ii. *Statements of law*. The judge will state the principles of law applicable to the case. Statements of law applied to the legal problems raised by the facts as found upon which the decision is based are known as *ratio decidendi* statements. Other statements, not based on the facts as found, or which do not provide the basis of the decision, are known as '*obiter dicta*' statements. For the purpose of precedent the *ratio decidendi*, which literally means 'reason for deciding', is the vital element which binds future judges.

iii. *The decision*. From the point of view of the parties this is the vital element since it determines their rights and liabilities in relation to the action, and prevents them from reopening the dispute.

b. Sometimes it is difficult to ascertain the *ratio decidendi* of a case. For example:

i. A statement intended by the judge to be the ratio is not accepted by a subsequent court as the *ratio*, but his other reasons are accepted.

ii. In the Court of Appeal or House of Lords the different members of the court may reach the same decision, but for different reasons.

iii. A judge may intend two ratios, one of which may be treated by a later judge as an *obiter dicta* statement because it was not essential to the decision.

11. **The Hierarchy of the Courts** The doctrine of precedent depends for its operation on the fact that each court stands in a definite position in relation to every other court.

a. *The European Court*. Its decisions bind all British courts, but not its own future decisions.

b. *The Supreme Court*. Its decisions are binding on all English courts, however, since 1966, following a statement by Lord Gardiner L.C., the Court need not follow its own previous decisions.

c. *The Court of Appeal (Civil Division)*. In **YOUNG v BRISTOL AEROPLANE CO. (1944)** it was held that the court is bound by its own previous decisions unless:

i. There are two previous conflicting Court of Appeal decisions, in which case it may choose which to follow.

ii. The previous decision conflicts with a later Supreme Court judgement.

iii. The previous decision was given per incuriam. 'Per incuriam' means through lack of care because some relevant statute or precedent was not brought before the court.

d. *The Court of Appeal (Criminal Division)*. The rules are the same as the Civil Division, except that the court need not follow its own previous decisions where this would cause injustice to the appellant. The reason is that where human freedom is at stake the need for justice exceeds the desire for certainty – **R v GOULD (1968)**.

e. *The High Court (Divisional Courts)*. The High Court is bound by its own previous decisions subject to the rule in Young's Case and, in criminal cases, R v Gould.

f. *The High Court (Judges at First Instance)*. Their decisions are not binding on other High Court judges, but are of persuasive authority.

g. *Inferior Courts*. Magistrates courts, county courts and other inferior tribunals are not bound by their own previous decisions since they are less authoritative and are rarely reported.

12. **Persuasive Precedents** These are statements which a later court will respect, but need not follow. There are several kinds of persuasive precedent:

a. *Obiter Dicta*. There are two types of *obiter dicta*:

i. A statement based upon facts which were not found to exist. In **RONDEL v WORSLEY (1969)** the House of Lords (now the Supreme Court) stated an opinion that a barrister might be held liable in negligence when not acting as an advocate, and that a solicitor when acting as an advocate might be immune from action. Since the case actually concerned the liability of a barrister when acting as an advocate these opinions were obiter dicta.

    ii.   A statement which although based on the facts as found, does not form the basis of the decision, for example a dissenting (minority) judgment.

  b. *Ratio decidendi* of inferior courts.

  c. *Ratio decidendi* of Scottish, Commonwealth, or foreign courts, and statements of the Judicial Committee of the Privy Council.

13. *Overruling and Reversing*

  a. Precedents can be overruled either by statute or by a superior court. Judges are usually reluctant to overrule precedents because this reduces the element of certainty in the law.

  b. Overruling must be distinguished from reversing a decision. A decision is reversed when it is altered on appeal. A decision is overruled when a judge in a different case states that the earlier case was wrongly decided.

14. *Distinguishing, Reconciling and Disapproving*

  a. A case is distinguished when the judge states that the material facts are sufficiently different to apply different rules of law.

  b. Cases are reconciled when the judge finds that the material facts of both cases are so similar that he can apply the same rules of law.

  c. A case is disapproved when a judge, without overruling an earlier case, gives his opinion that it was wrongly decided.

15. *Advantages and Disadvantages of Precedent*

  a. *Advantages*

    i.   *Certainty*. It provides a degree of uniformity upon which individuals can rely. Uniformity is essential if justice is to be achieved. The advantage of certainty by itself outweighs the several disadvantages of precedent.

    ii. *Development*. New rules can be established or old ones adapted to meet new circumstances and the changing needs of society.

    iii. *Detail*. No code of law could provide the detail found in English case law.

    iv. *Practicality*. The rules are laid down in the course of dealing with cases, and do not attempt to deal with future hypothetical circumstances.

    v.   *Flexibility*. A general *ratio decidendi* may be extended to a variety of factual situations. For example, the 'neighbour test' formulated in **DONOGHUE v STEVENSON (1932)** determines whether a duty not to be negligent is owed to a particular person whatever the circumstances of the case.

  b. *Disadvantages*

    i.   *Rigidity*. Precedent is rigid in the sense that once a rule has been laid down it is binding even if it is thought to be wrong.

    ii. *Danger of illogicality*. This arises from the rigidity of the system. Judges who do not wish to follow a particular decision may be tempted to draw very fine distinctions in order to avoid following the rule, thus introducing an element of artificiality into the law.

    iii. *Bulk and complexity*. There is so much law that no one can learn all of it. Even an experienced lawyer may overlook some important rule in any given case.

iv. *Slowness of growth*. The system depends on litigation for rules to emerge. As litigation tends to be slow and expensive the body of case law cannot grow quickly enough to meet modern demands.

v. *Isolating the ratio decidendi*. Where it is difficult to find the *ratio decidendi* of a case this detracts from the element of certainty.

16. *The Importance of Precedent Today*

a. It may appear that since the volume of statute law is increasing rapidly as government intervention in such areas as employment and consumer affairs increases, then the relative importance of case law must be decreasing. In fact the reverse is true, since as more Acts are passed, judges will more often be called upon to create new precedents when interpreting this new law. In addition some Acts deliberately and unavoidably vest a wide discretion in the judiciary. For example, the *UNFAIR CONTRACT TERMS ACT 1977* has the underlying theme that an exemption clause must be reasonable if it is to be valid, but it is, of course, left to the judge to decide what is reasonable in each particular case.

b. In recent years the judges' jurisdiction over common law and equity has given rise to some notable developments. For example, Lord Denning's judgment in **CENTRAL LONDON PROPERTY TRUST v HIGH TREES HOUSE (1947)** has now been generally accepted as having created a new principle of equity, i.e. equitable estoppel. In **SHAW v DPP (1962)** the Court found Shaw guilty of 'conspiracy to corrupt public morals', an offence previously unknown to the criminal law. Thirdly, in **MILIANGOS v GEORGE FRANK TEXTILES (1976)** the Court effected a major reform by deciding that courts could, in future, express their judgments in foreign currency.

c. The traditional view that judges merely apply the law is useful to emphasize the fundamental feature of the constitution, namely the Sovereignty of Parliament, but it does not reflect reality, especially when a judge is faced with a 'first impression' case where there is no existing precedent and no provision in an Act of Parliament. In such cases the judge must of necessity create new law. Precedent is therefore a very important source of law, the other main source being legislation.

17. *Law Reporting* It is vital for the operation of judicial precedent to have a comprehensive and accurate system of law reporting. Prior to 1865 the quality and accuracy of law reporting varied tremendously; since 1865 the *Modern Reports* have been published by an independent body the Incorporated Council of Law Reporting for England and Wales. The Council's reports are known as the *Law Reports* and they are divided into four series. The Appeal Cases series reports on the decisions of the House of Lords and the Privy Council. The other series are known as, Queen's Bench, Family Division and Chancery Division. The facts of a case and decision are set out briefly, there then follows a detailed description of the facts and arguments of the case followed by the judgments of the various judges. The Council also publish a series called the *Weekly Law Reports*, which appear earlier than the Law Reports.

LEGISLATION

18. *Introduction*

a. The most important source of law at the present day is legislation. Statutes are passed by Parliament which is the supreme law-making body in the United Kingdom. In theory, at least, there is nothing which Parliament cannot do by statute. In practice statutes often amend, and sometimes abolish, established rules of common law or equity, overrule the effects of decisions of the courts or make entirely new law on matters which previously have not been the subject of legislation.

b.   There are two types of legislation, parliamentary and delegated legislation. The functions of Acts of Parliament are as follows:

 i.   *Law reform*. Relatively few statutes are concerned with changing substantive rules of law. Where such a change does take place it often follows from an unpopular decision of the House of Lords, or is based on a recommendation of the Law Commission.

 ii. *Consolidation*. Where existing legislation is gathered into one Act this is known as consolidation.

 iii. *Codification*. This takes place when all the law on a topic (both case law and statute law) is included in one Act.

 iv. *Revenue collection*. The annual Finance Acts which implement the Budget proposals are the main revenue collection statutes.

 v.   *Special legislation*. These Acts are concerned with the day-to-day running of society, for example the *RENT ACT 1974*.

c.   An Act will come into force on the day on which it receives the Royal Assent, unless some other date is specified in the Act itself. It will cease to have effect only when it is repealed by another Act. Whilst in force an Act is presumed to be operative throughout the United Kingdom and nowhere else, unless the Act states otherwise.

19. *The Superiority of Legislation* The rationale for the supremacy of legislation is that the will of elected representatives should prevail over that of appointed judges. The evidence for its supremacy may be summarized in three statements:

a.   No court may question the validity of an Act of Parliament. In **CHENEY v CONN (1968)** the claimant objected to his tax assessment under the *FINANCE ACT 1964* because the government was spending part of the tax collected on making nuclear weapons. He alleged this was contrary to the *GENERAL CONVENTIONS ACT 1957* and in conflict with international law. The court, however, held that the 1964 Act gave clear authority to collect the taxes and being more recent it prevailed over the 1957 Act. It was said 'It is not for the court to say that a parliamentary enactment, the highest law in this country, is illegal.'

b.   An Act of Parliament may expressly or impliedly repeal an earlier statute. In **VAUX-HALL ESTATES v LIVERPOOL CORPORATION (1932)** if compensation for compulsory purchase were assessed under an Act of 1919 the claimant's would receive £2370, whereas if it were assessed under an Act of 1925 they would only receive £1133. Furthermore the 1919 Act provided that any Act inconsistent with it would have no effect. It was held that this provision did not apply to subsequent Acts, i.e. Parliament cannot bind its successors. The 1925 Act impliedly repeals the 1919 Act so far as it was inconsistent with it, and the claimants therefore received £1133.

c.   A statute may be passed to vary or revoke the common law or even to retrospectively reverse a judicial decision. The *WAR DAMAGE ACT 1965* operated to remove vested rights to compensation from the Crown and was controversially expressed to apply to proceedings commenced before the Act came into force. It thus reversed the decision of the House of Lords in ***BURMAH OIL v LORD ADVOCATE (1965)***.

20. ***The Need for Statutory Interpretation*** Where the words of a statute are absolutely clear the need for statutory interpretation will not arise, because the persons affected by the statute will have no difficulty in conducting their affairs according to the statute. However, where there is ambiguity or uncertainty interpretation is necessary.

   a. *Ambiguity is* caused by an error in drafting whereby the words used are capable of two or more literal meanings.

   b. *Uncertainty* arises when the words of a statute are intended to apply to various factual situations and the courts have to decide whether the case before them falls within the factual situations envisaged by the Act. Uncertainty is far more common than ambiguity.

21. ***Judicial Approaches to Interpretation*** There are three recognized judicial approaches to statutory interpretation. The approach chosen will depend on the particular judge, so it is not possible to know in advance which will be used. They are known as 'rules' although they are not rules in the accepted sense of the word.

   a. *The literal rule.* This is the basic rule of interpretation. It states that the words used must be given their literal or usual meaning even if the result appears to be contrary to the intention of Parliament.

   In ***FISHER v BELL (1961)*** the *RESTRICTION OF OFFENSIVE WEAPONS ACT 1959* made it an offence to '*offer for sale*' certain weapons including 'flick knives'. A shopkeeper who displayed these knives in his window was found not guilty of the offence, since although he had displayed the goods, accepted buyers' offers, and sold the goods he had not offered them for sale, because goods on display are not an offer to sell, they are an invitation to treat. (Chapter 12.4.)

   b. *The golden rule.* This states that the literal must be followed unless to do so produces an absurd result. Where a statute permits two or more literal meanings application of the golden rule is not inconsistent with the literal rule since the literal rule cannot be applied in such cases. However, in rare cases a judge will apply the golden rule to a statute which has only one literal meaning:

   In ***RE SIGSWORTH (1935)*** the golden rule was applied to prevent a murderer from inheriting on the intestacy of his victim although he was, as her son, her only heir on a literal interpretation of the *ADMINISTRATION OF ESTATES ACT 1925*.

   The golden rule may be criticized as being subjective, since a judge who decides that a literal interpretation is absurd, and therefore contrary to the intention of Parliament, must be ascertaining the intention of Parliament from a source other than the statute itself. This is strictly speaking beyond his function.

   c. *The mischief rule.* Where an Act is passed to remedy a mischief the court must adopt the interpretation which will have the effect of remedying the mischief in question. For example, the *AFFILIATION OF PROCEEDINGS ACT 1957* refers to a 'single woman'.

   This has been interpreted to include not only unmarried women, but any woman with no husband to support her, because the mischief which the Act was passed to remedy was the possibility of a woman having an illegitimate child with no means of supporting it.

22. *Further Rules of Interpretation*

    a.   The statute must be read as a whole, and each section must be read in the light of every other section, especially an interpretation section.

    b.   The *ejusdem generis rule.* Where general words follow two or more particular words they must be confined to a meaning of the same kind (*eiusdem generis*) as the particular words. For example, 'cats, dogs and other animals' means other domestic animals.

    c.   Where a criminal statute is uncertain or ambiguous it is generally interpreted in favour of the individual.

        In *R v HALLAM (1957)* it was held that the offence of 'knowingly possessing an explosive' required the accused to know, not only that he possessed the substance, but also that it was explosive.

        Contrast *RE ATTORNEY-GENERAL'S REFERENCE (No. 1 of 1988)* where the accused received unsolicited information from an employee of a firm of merchant bankers, to the effect that there was to be a merger between two companies. He knew that if this information were generally known it would affect the price of the shares. He also knew that it was confidential information, however, within 10 minutes he had instructed his stockbroker to purchase shares in one of the companies. The merger was announced the following day and a few weeks later the accused sold the 6,000 shares that he had purchased at a profit of £3000. He was accused under *S.1 COMPANY SECURITIES (INSIDER DEALING) ACT 1985* (post Chapter 43.44) which, among other things, required him to 'knowingly obtain' price-sensitive information. He was originally acquitted on the basis that 'obtaining' meant actively obtaining the information, rather than passively obtaining it. This interpretation was rejected by both the Court of Appeal and the House of Lords on the grounds that the approach would water down the effect of the legislation and also require the courts to make almost imperceptible factual distinctions. The House of Lords recognized the importance of the general rule that in a penal statute the words would normally be given their narrower meaning, but felt that this was not appropriate in the present case.

    d.   Where a statute does not make an alteration of the law absolutely clear it will be presumed that Parliament did not intend to alter the law. For example, prior to 1898 a wife was not permitted to give evidence against her husband. The *CRIMINAL EVIDENCE ACT 1898* made her competent to do so, but in the absence of express provision it was held in *LEACH v R (1912)* that she could not be compelled to give evidence against her husband.

23. *Statutory Interpretation and Judicial Precedent* Precedent and legislation are sometimes mistakenly regarded as separate sources of law. This is not the case because once a superior court in the hierarchy has interpreted the words of an Act an inferior court is bound to adopt that interpretation if faced with the same words in the same Act. Thus statutory interpretation forms a link between the sources of precedent and legislation.

24. *Delegated Legislation*

    a.   Delegated legislation comes into being when Parliament confers on persons or bodies, particularly Ministers of the Crown in charge of Government Departments, power to make regulations for specified purposes. Such regulations have the same legal force as the Act under which they are made.

b. *Types of delegated legislation*

    i. *Orders in council.* This is the highest form of delegated legislation, many Acts of Parliament being brought into operation in this way, the power to make the Order being contained in the Act. In theory an Order in Council is an order of the Privy Council, but in fact an Order in Council is usually made by the Government and merely approved by the Privy Council. This has the effect of conferring wide legislative power on government departments.

    ii. *Rules and regulations.* A statute may authorize a minister or a government department to make a wide variety of rules and regulations. These rules, and Orders in Council, are collectively known as statutory instruments.

    iii. *By-Laws.* These are rules made by local authorities. Their operation is restricted to the locality to which they apply.

c. *Advantages of delegated legislation*

    i. It saves the time of Parliament, allowing Parliament to concentrate on discussing matters of general policy.

    ii. It can be brought into existence swiftly, enabling ministers to deal with urgent situations, such as a strike in an essential industry.

    iii. It enables experts to deal with local or technical matters.

    iv. It provides flexibility, in that regulations can be added to or modified from time to time without the necessity for a new Act of Parliament.

d. *Disadvantages of delegated legislation*

    i. Law-making is taken out of the direct control of elected representatives and is placed in the hands of employees of government departments. This is in theory less democratic.

    ii. Parliament does not have enough time to effectively supervize delegated legislation or discuss the merits of the rules being created.

    iii. A vast amount of law is created, statutory instruments outnumbering by far the amount of Acts passed each year.

e. *Control of delegated legislation*

    i. *Judicial control.* If a minister, government department or local authority exceeds its delegated power its action would be held by the court to be *ultra vires* (beyond the powers of) and therefore void.

    ii. *Parliamentary control.* There are several methods of parliamentary control. Some statutory instruments must be laid before Parliament and will cease to be operative if the House so resolves within 40 days. Others require a vote of approval from the House. In addition there is a Joint Committee of the Houses of Commons and Lords whose function is to scrutinize statutory instruments with a view to seeing whether the attention of Parliament should be drawn to the instrument on one of a number of specified grounds, for example because the instrument is obscurely drafted, or because it imposes a tax on the public.

25. **The Law Commission** The Law Commission is a major agent of law reform in England and Wales. The Commission's role is to keep the whole of the law under review with the aim of

achieving a systematic development and reform of the law programme. Proposals for reform go to the Lord Chancellor where, if approved, go forward as a Bill to be put before Parliament. The *LAW COMMISSION ACT 2009* charges the Lord Chancellor to prepare an annual report to be laid before Parliament on the implementation of any Law Commission proposals.

LEGISLATION OF THE EUROPEAN UNION

26. *The European Union and the Single Market*

    a.   The European Economic Community was set up by the Treaty of Rome 1957. The six signatories were France, Germany, Italy, Belgium, Holland and Luxembourg. On 1st January 1973 Great Britain, the Republic of Ireland and Denmark joined as a result of the Brussels Treaty of Accession. Greece joined in 1981 and Spain and Portugal in 1986. The Community was renamed the European Union in 1993. The most recent new members are Austria, Sweden and Finland, who joined on 1st January 1995. The Treaty of Nice in 2003 allowed for ten more countries to join the Union from 1 May 2004, these were Cyprus, the Czech Republic, Estonia, Hungary, Latvia, Lithuania, Malta, Poland, Slovakia and Slovenia, and Bulgaria and Romania joined in 2007. Negotiations for Turkey to join the Union are currently underway.

    b.   The object of creating a common market goes back to the Treaty of Rome in 1957. However, in 1985 EU Heads of Government committed themselves to progressively establishing a single market over a period expiring on 31st December 1992. This commitment was included in a package of treaty reforms known as the *SINGLE EUROPEAN ACT 1986 (SEA)*. The Act assisted the free movement of goods by breaking down technical barriers (for example differing national product standards) national restrictions, subsidy policies and so on. The SEA also sped up EU decision-making by extending majority voting to most major areas of the single market programme. This replaces the unanimous voting requirements which applied before the Act came into force.

    c.   In November 1993 the Treaty of European Union, signed in Maastricht, came into force. It gave the EU more powers. In particular:

        i.   It provided for the introduction of a common currency by 1999.

        ii.   It introduced European Citizenship. A number of consequences follow from this, including the right of any EU national to reside in any member state.

        iii.   It increased the powers of the European Parliament, by introducing new rights, for example the right to reject proposed legislation in certain areas if no agreement can be reached with the Council of Ministers and the right to initiate legislation by requiring the Commission to submit a proposal.

        iv.   It gave the EU a more active role in many areas, for example consumer protection, public health, industry policy, education and (with the exception of the UK) social policy.

        v.   It introduced a common foreign and security policy.

27. *European Union Institutions*

    a.   *The Commission*

        i.   This is the executive body of the EU, and consists of 20 Commissioners appointed by mutual agreement of the member governments. There must not be more than two from any country, and the present practice is for the five larger countries – France, Germany, Italy, Spain and Britain to appoint two each, and the ten smaller countries one each.

ii. The Commission is responsible for the formulation of EU policy. It acts collectively, but individual commissioners specialize in particular areas such as agriculture, transport and social affairs.

iii. The Commission has wide legislative functions. It initiates and drafts most EU legislation, and puts its proposals before the Council for enactment. The Commission also has executive functions to ensure the enforcement of Council decisions.

iv. The Commission represents the EU in negotiations with non-member states and administers certain budgets and funds. In general it acts as the day-to-day executive of the EU.

v. Each Commissioner is assisted by a small private staff whose members tend to be of the same nationality as the commissioner they serve. In addition the Commission has a staff of about 17 000, divided between various departments and auxiliary services.

b. *The Council*

i. The Council is the EU's decision-making body. It agrees legislation on the basis of proposals put forward by the Commission.

ii. Each Council meeting will deal with a particular area of policy, for example agriculture, finance or industry and will be attended by the relevant Minister from each member state.

iii. There are three methods of decision-making (a) unanimity; (b) simple majority voting i.e. at least nine member states in favour; and (c) qualified majority (weighted) voting based on the relative population of member states. Most proposals are subject to qualified majority voting.

c. *The European Parliament*

i. This directly elected body has 626 members, 87 from the UK. It has consultative and advisory functions which are exercised through 19 standing committees dealing with specialist topics, for example Agriculture, Transport, Legal Affairs and Women's Rights.

ii. Under the EU Treaties its formal opinion is required on many proposals before they can be adopted by the Council. Most proposals are subject to the co-operation procedure introduced by the SEA. This enables the Parliament to give an opinion when the Commission makes a proposal and again when the Council has reached agreement in principle (known as a 'Common Position'). Members of the European Parliament are elected for a period of 5 years.

d. *The Court of Justice.* The European Court of Justice (the ECJ) is a court of first instance from which there is no appeal. It consists of 15 judges, selected from persons whose independence can be relied on and who are either recognized legal experts or qualified for judicial office in their respective countries. The judges hold office for 6 years. They are assisted by nine Advocates General who present the cases in an unbiased manner. The decision of the Court is a single judgement, dissenting opinions are not expressed. Its decisions are binding on the national courts of member states. The jurisdiction of the Court includes:

i.   Actions brought against member states either by other member states or by the Commission on the grounds that Treaty obligations are not being fulfilled.

ii. Actions brought against EU institutions by member states, private individuals or corporate bodies.

iii. Rulings on the interpretation of the Treaties or on the validity of any of the acts of the EU institutions.

28. *The Sources of EU Law*

a.   *Treaties.* The primary sources of EU law are foundation treaties of Paris and Rome. The *TREATY OF PARIS 1951* established the European Coal and Steel Community (ECSC). The *TREATY OF ROME 1957* established the European Atomic Energy Community (EURATOM). A second *TREATY OF ROME 1957* established the European Economic Community (EEC), now contained in the *TREATY OF EUROPEAN UNION 1992*, consolidated into the *TREATY OF AMSTERDAM 1997*.

b.   *Direct effect and direct applicability* are key concepts of European Community Law. Direct applicability means that some provision of European Community Law is directly, i.e. automatically, part of the domestic (national) law of a member state of the European Union. It is not necessary for a member state to incorporate the provision in domestic legislation. Direct effect, on the other hand, means that some provision of European Community Law creates individual rights, which can be enforced in national (domestic) courts. In fact, direct effect takes two forms viz 'vertical direct effect' i.e. individual rights which can be enforced against a national (member) state and 'horizontal direct effect' i.e. individual rights, which can be enforced against other individuals. The distinction between direct applicability and direct effect forms the background to European Community 'secondary' legislation i.e. Regulations, Directives and Decisions. It is necessary, therefore, to examine each of these in turn.

c.   *EC primary legislation.* Contained in the Treaties these are mainly concerned with economic matters such as free trade, agriculture and transport. The Treaties set out in broad terms the objectives to be achieved and leave many of the details to the Council and the Commission. These bodies have law-making powers – *secondary legislation* – which they may exercise in accordance with the Treaties.

EC *secondary legislation* may be classified as:

i.   *Regulations.* These are of general application, binding in their entirety and directly applicable in all member states without the need for further legislation. They confer individual rights and duties which the national courts of the member states must protect. Their object is to obtain uniformity of law throughout the member states.

ii. *Directives.* Unlike regulations, directives do not have immediate binding force in all member states. They are addressed to member states, requiring the national Parliament to make whatever changes are necessary to implement the directive within a specified time.

iii. *Decisions.* These may be addressed either to a member state or to an individual or institution. They are a formal method of enunciating policy decisions and they are binding on those to whom they are addressed.

d.   *The legislative process*

i.   EU legislation is the result of lengthy and complex negotiations and consultations involving several Council and Commission working parties and other committees provided for by the Treaties.

ii.   Briefly the procedure is for the Commission to discuss the proposal with officials from member states and other interested parties before adopting it as a formal proposal. It is then submitted to the Council and the European Parliament. Parliament may give an opinion and, depending on the Article of the Treaty on which the proposal is based, the Council can either adopt the proposal or agree a common position by qualified majority voting. In the latter case the European Parliament may give a second opinion before the proposal is returned to the Council to be finally adopted as Community Law.

e.   *Interpretation of EU legislation.* EU legislation is drafted in terms of broad principle, the courts being left to supply the detail by giving effect to the intention of the legislature. This can be ascertained because regulations, directives and decisions are required to state the reasons on which they are based. Thus in the interpretation of EU legislation the 'golden rule' and the 'mischief rule' are applied, rather than the 'literal rule'.

29.   *Acceptance of EU Law by the UK*

a.   The *EUROPEAN COMMUNITIES ACT 1972* provides that any enactment of the UK Parliament shall have effect subject to the directly applicable legislation of the Communities. 'Directly applicable' means that a provision confers directly on individuals' rights enforceable by them in the courts of a member state without the need for further legislation by that state. Thus UK legislation is repealed by subsequent directly applicable EU legislation to the extent that the two are inconsistent. Parliament has therefore been obliged to give up sovereignty so far as EU matters are concerned. It is, however, clear that the basic principle of Parliamentary Sovereignty has not been impaired.

EU law is only enforceable in the UK because the 1972 Act so stated and it was said in *MACARTHYS v SMITH (1978)* that 'Parliament's recognition of European Community Law ... by one enactment can be withdrawn by another'.

b.   The EU is concerned primarily with economic and commercial matters, and the effect of UK entry is being felt initially in those fields. Company law is experiencing wide changes as movement is made towards a uniform set of rules applicable to business organizations throughout the EU Commercial law, particularly concerning monopolies and restrictive trade practices, is also being affected. However, criminal law, contract, tort, property law and family law will not be affected.

30.   **The European Convention on Human Rights** In the past human rights in the UK have not been contained in any written document or code; rights have been traditionally protected in two ways, one, by the courts adopting an approach which is that if the law does not prohibit an Act then it is lawful and, two, through the ability to scrutinize any institutional excesses by way of judicial review. Although the UK is a signatory to the 1951 *EUROPEAN CONVENTION ON HUMAN RIGHTS*, it was never incorporated into UK law. In 1998 Parliament passed the *HUMAN RIGHTS ACT 1998* which came into effect in 2000, and now incorporates the European Convention on Human Rights into UK law. The main provisions of the Act are: S. 3 all existing legislation must, so far as is possible, be read as being compatible with the Convention, with any new legislation before Parliament requiring that a relevant Government minister make a written

statement that the proposed legislation is compatible with the Convention. And S.7 creates the right of individuals to bring legal proceedings against public authorities for violations of the Convention.

Key rights under the Convention are:

Article 1 contracting States shall ensure that all persons within their jurisdiction be given the rights and freedoms contained in the Convention.

Article 2 all persons shall have a right to the preservation of life as afforded by law.

Article 3 no person shall be subjected to any torture, inhumane or degrading treatment or punishment.

Article 4 no person shall be held in slavery or servitude or be required to perform compulsory labour (there are exceptions here where this is the consequence of an order of the court).

Article 5(1) no person shall be deprived of their liberty except where: it is consequent upon a lawful conviction of a court, is done to stop the spread of infectious diseases or is necessary to treat the mentally ill or prevent alcohol or drug abuse.

Article 5(2) any person arrested has the right to be informed promptly of the reason for that arrest and of any charges and Article 5(3) requires that such persons be brought promptly before a judge.

Article 6 provides for the right to a fair trial in public by an independent, impartial court or tribunal and Article 6(2) provides the right to a presumption of innocence until proven guilty. Article 6(3) gives minimum rights to those charged with criminal offences; these include:

prompt information as to the details of the charge

adequate time and facilities to prepare a defence

the right to choose a lawyer and receive free legal assistance

the same right to require witnesses to attend as given to the prosecution

the right to cross-examine witnesses

to have the assistance of an interpreter free where one is needed.

Article 8 lays down that all persons have the right to respect for their private and family life, home and correspondence. Article 8(2) allows for exceptions in the interests of national security and the general public interest.

Article 9 gives the right to freedom of thought, conscience and religion.

Article 10 provides for freedom of expression.

Article 11 the right to peaceful assembly and freedom of association with others including the right to form and be a member of a trade union.

Article 12 members of the opposite sex who are of marriageable age have the right to marry and form a family.

Article 13 any individual whose rights or freedoms, as set out in the Convention, are violated has the right to an effective remedy.

Article 14 the rights stated in the Convention must be afforded without any discrimination on any grounds whatsoever.

Article 15 derogations from the Convention are allowed in time of war.

The impact of the Human Rights Act on UK law, both civil and criminal, has been and continues to be significant. For business organizations, particularly with regard to employee rights, the Act has had and continues to have, considerable impact.

SELF TEST QUESTIONS

Self Test Questions No. 2 (for answers see Appendix 1):

1   What is meant by the phrase – 'sources of law'?

2   What is 'judicial precedent' as a source of law?

3   Explain the doctrine of binding precedent in English law paying particular regard to:

   (a) The hierarchy of the courts.

   (b) The relative advantages and disadvantages of the doctrine.

4   How is legislation a source of law and how does it relate to judicial precent?

5   How can the European Union be said to be a source of UK law?

6   Within the context of EU law, explain 'direct applicability' and 'direct effect' and their significance for European 'secondary' legislation.

7   What is the European Convention on Human Rights and how is it a source of UK law?

ORIGINS OF COMMON LAW AND EQUITY

5

Learning Outcomes At the end of this chapter you should be able to:

- **Demonstrate an understanding of the nature of 'equity' and how it relates to the common law.**

THE ORIGINS OF THE COMMON LAW

1. The decisions of judges in particular cases started to form a source of English law at the end of the 13th century. Settling disputes became a lucrative source of income for the Crown and so at that time, there was established the Courts of Common Law. The judges in these Courts, known at the time as royal commissioners, travelled around the country settling disputes, often by applying local unwritten custom. Over a number of years these judges – circuit judges – began to form a source of law based upon the best customs they had come across on their travels, this became known as, the **common law**. Thus, by selecting certain customs and applying them in all future similar cases, the *common law* of England was created.

Common law is the common sense of the community, crystallized and formulated by our forefathers. It is not local law, nor the result of legislation.

THE ORIGINS OF EQUITY

2. The early common law was rigid and often harsh. This was to some extent reduced through the use of legal fictions. Fictions were used for three purposes:

   a. To reduce the severity of the criminal law. For example, stolen property in fact worth more than one shilling would be valued by the court at less than one shilling, thus classifying the offence as a misdemeanour rather than a felony and consequently reducing the severity of the sentence. Another example is the 'benefit of the clergy'. If a person could show that he was a member of the clergy he could be tried in the ecclesiastical courts where the penalties were less severe. The test to determine whether a person was a clergyman was whether he could read. To show ability to read he had only to recite a verse of Latin commonly supposed to have been Psalm 51 Verse I which most people therefore learnt by heart – just in case!

   b. To extend the scope of writs beyond their literal scope.

   c. To acquire jurisdiction from other courts. Such fictions cannot be explained by a desire to improve the common law, but by the fact that judicial salaries depended upon the number of cases heard.

2. Fictions were not, however, capable of remedying all the defects of the common law. For example:

   a. The claimant either had to fit his action into the framework of an existing writ, or show that it was similar to such a writ. If he could do neither, he had no remedy.

   b. In civil actions the only remedy which the common law courts could give was an award of damages.

   c. There were elaborate rules governing the procedure which had to be followed in bringing a case, and any slight breach of the rules might leave a claimant who had a good case without a remedy.

3. In many of these cases dissatisfied persons would petition the King, since the Curia Regis was not subject to the limitations of the common law courts, and could exercise the royal prerogative as it thought fit. For a time the King determined these petitions himself, but he later delegated this function to his Chancellor. The Chancellor was one of the most important members of the Curia Regis. He was in charge of the Chancery which was responsible for the issue of writs. Since he was already concerned with the legal process it was logical that the Chancellor should preside at hearings of petitions. Initially the Chancellor issued decrees in the King's name. In 1474 a Chancellor first issued a decree in his own name. At this point in time the Court of Chancery was created. Like the common law courts it had now become independent of the King.

THE COURT OF CHANCERY

4. The early Chancellors were members of the clergy who were very concerned to order what was, as a matter of conscience, fair between the parties. The first lawyer to be appointed Chancellor was Sir Thomas More in 1529. At first there were no fixed rules on which the Court proceeded. Gradually the Court began to be guided by its previous decisions, and

formulate general principles, known as the 'maxims of equity', upon which it would proceed. Finally the Court of Chancery evolved a body of law the principles of which were as firm as those of the common law.

5. *The Rules of Equity* These are principles which the Court of Chancery followed when deciding cases, and which are applied today when equitable relief is claimed. There are many rules, the following being some of the more well known examples:

   a. *He who seeks equity must do equity.* A person who seeks equitable relief must be prepared to act fairly towards his opponent as a condition of obtaining such relief. For example, a mortgagor who wishes to exercise his equitable right to redeem must give reasonable notice of his intention.

   b. *He who comes to equity must come with clean hands.* Not only must the plaintiff 'do equity' by making proper present concessions to the defendant, he must also have acted properly in his past dealing with the defendant. For example, **D.C. BUILDERS v REES (1966)** (Chapter 15).

   c. *Equality is equity.* For example, since equity does not allow the remedy of specific performance to be invoked against a minor (a concession to his youth), it will also not allow a minor to claim the benefit of this remedy.

   d. *Equity looks at the intent rather than the form.* For example, if an agreed damages clause in a contract is not a genuine pre-estimate of the loss that would result from a breach, equity would regard the clause as a penalty clause and treat it merely as a device to induce performance of the contract. The court would therefore enforce the contract as written, but would award the innocent party his actual loss.

6. *The Achievements of the Court of Chancery* These were considerable, in particular the Court developed the law relating to trusts and mortgages, and discretionary remedies namely:

   a. *Injunction.* An order of the court compelling or restraining the performance of some act.

   b. *Specific performance.* An order of the court compelling a person to perform an obligation existing under either a contract or trust.

   c. *Rectification.* The alteration of a document so that it reflects the true intention of the parties.

   d. *Rescission.* The restoration of the parties to a contract to their pre-contract state of affairs.

7. *The Defects of the Court of Chancery*

   a. The Court inevitably bore the characteristics of the Chancellor. This was a good feature in that excellent lawyers such as Sir Thomas More and Sir Frances Bacon were able to contribute greatly to the development of equity. It was a bad feature when the shortcomings of other Chancellors brought the Court into disrepute, for example in the 17th century the sale of offices was widespread and in 1725 when Lord Macclesfield was Chancellor, a deficiency of about £100 000 was discovered in court funds. In addition it was clear that there was a variation in the standard of justice dispensed by different Chancellors.

   b. The sale of offices resulted in an excessive number of court officials, who tended to try to extend the scope of their duties so as to increase their revenue. This meant that procedure became very slow and expensive.

c. In contrast to the excess of officials there was a scarcity of judges. At first the Chancellor was the only judge, but he was later assisted by his Chancery Masters. The chief of these was the Master of the Rolls, who was effectively a second judge. It was not until 1813 that the first Vice-Chancellor was appointed by Lord Eldon.

COMMON LAW AND EQUITY

8. *Similarities between Common Law and Equity*

a. Both common law and equity are law. In ordinary language 'equity' means natural justice, but although inspired by these ideas, equity no longer represents the flexible concept of natural justice. It is now a branch of the law.

b. Common law and equity have both developed in an English context. They are not imported systems, and have only been subject to minimal foreign influence.

c. Both have been partly embodied in statute, for example the *SALE OF GOODS ACT 1979* (common law) and the *TRUSTEE ACT 1925* (equity).

d. Since the *JUDICATURE ACTS OF 1873–1875* both have been administered in the same courts.

9. *Differences between Common Law and Equity*

a. The most important difference is that common law was constructed as a complete and independent system, whereas equity developed to remedy the defects of the common law, and would be meaningless if considered in isolation, since it pre-supposes the existence of common law. For example, the doctrine of equitable estoppel in contract developed as an exception to the arguably harsh rule of *PINNEL'S CASE (1602)* (Chapter 12).

b. Historically each system had different procedural rules since, until 1875, they were administered in separate courts. In the common law courts an action was commenced by the issues of a writ, whereas in the Court of Chancery an action was commenced by a petition, which allowed a greater scope to the plaintiff.

c. Although the administration of common law and equity has now been fused, their content nevertheless remains separate. Thus to say that a rule or remedy is 'equitable' means that it must be interpreted in an equitable atmosphere, and that the principles of equity apply. Thus the equitable remedies, for example specific performance, and rescission are discretionary, whereas the common law remedy of damages exists as a right if a wrong is proved. A recent example of the exercise of this discretion was *MILLER v JACKSON (1977)* where although the plaintiff 'won' the case the injunction he sought was refused (Chapter 25).

d. By its nature the Court of Chancery was certain to come into conflict with the Common Law courts. For example, the Chancellor would rescind a contract where the common law courts would enforce it as originally drawn. In such cases equity would have to prevail or it would be of no effect. This has been clear since 1615 when there was a dispute between Sir Edward Coke who was Chief Justice of the Common Pleas and Lord Ellesmere, the Lord Chancellor. This dispute was only resolved when King James I, after consulting the Attorney-General (Sir Francis Bacon) decided in favour of the Court of Chancery.

SELF TEST QUESTIONS

Self Test Questions No. 3 (for Answers see Appendix 1):

1   How does the common law and equity work together in establishing case law?

2   If there is a conflict between the common law and equity, which one will prevail?

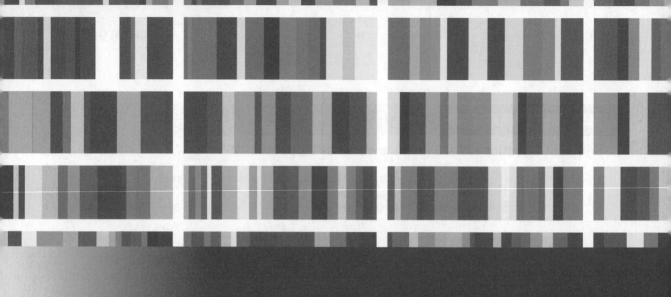

6 THE COURTS

> ## Learning Outcomes At the end of this chapter you should be able to:
>
> - Understand in outline the structure of the main civil and criminal courts.
>
> - State the advantages and disadvantages of the use of lay magistrates.

THE COURT STRUCTURE

1. The English court structure is fairly complex. It has four basic levels: the Supreme Court; the Court of Appeal; the High Court (including the Crown Court); and the Inferior Courts (including County Courts and Magistrates Courts). Within this structure there is neither a clear division into criminal and civil Courts, nor a division into first instance and appeal courts. For example, the Queen's Bench Division of the High Court hears both civil and criminal cases and operates as both a first instance and an appeal court.

2. *The Structure of the Civil Courts*

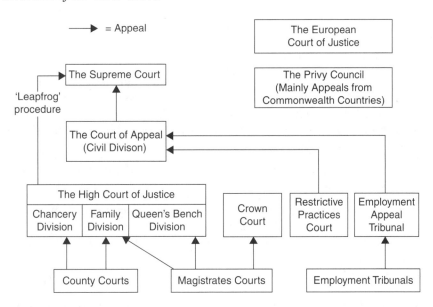

3. *The Structure of the Criminal Courts*

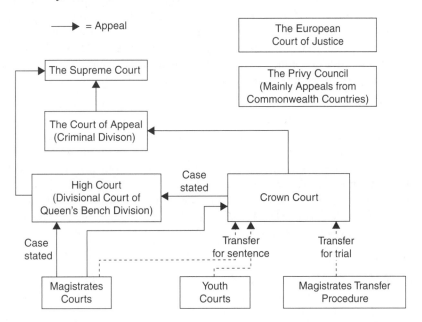

MAGISTRATES COURTS

4. *Composition*

a.   Magistrates courts are composed of Justices of the Peace (JP). The court consists of at least two, but not more than seven justices (usually three) or a stipendiary magistrate.

b. JPs (except stipendiary magistrates) are not legally qualified, but they must live within 15 miles of their commission area and they are required to undertake basic training in judicial science. Each court has a legally qualified Clerk to the Justices. He advises the justices on the law, but he does not assist them with their decision on the facts. There is no jury in magistrates courts.

c. Any person may apply, or be proposed, to be a magistrate. Selection is made by a Lord Chancellor's advisory committee, of which there is one per county. Membership of these committees is secret and the criteria which they use to make their choice is also secret. Selection criteria therefore vary from one county to another. Magistrates are unpaid, but they may claim expenses.

d. JPs keep their full-time jobs, hearing cases perhaps one day in every 2 weeks. They must retire at 70.

e. Stipendiary magistrates are full-time paid magistrates. They are appointed by the Crown on the advice of the Lord Chancellor, from barristers or solicitors with at least 7 years general advocacy experience. They are only appointed in certain urban areas and they usually sit alone.

5. *Criminal Jurisdiction*

a. *Summary offences.* The court's criminal jurisdiction exists mainly over summary offences, all of which are statutory offences. The maximum penalty that can be imposed was increased by the *CRIMINAL JUSTICE ACT 2003* to 12 months imprisonment (65 weeks for two or more offences). Most summary offenders are convicted of motoring offences. Since convictions were so numerous, the *MAGISTRATES COURTS ACT 1957* introduced a procedure enabling persons to plead guilty by post. There are over 1½ million persons a year found guilty of summary offences.

b. *Indictable offences.* The most serious indictable offences are triable only in the Crown Court, for example murder, manslaughter, rape, bigamy and conspiracy. Statute does, however, specify some offences which are both indictable and summary. In such cases, if the accused consents, the case may be tried summarily, although an accused aged 17 or over may demand the right to a jury trial in the Crown Court. If tried in the Magistrates Court and found guilty, the accused may be sent to the Crown Court for sentence if the magistrates consider that he deserves a greater punishment than they have the power to impose. The *CRIME AND DISORDER ACT 1998* gives magistrates the power to impose Anti Social Behaviour Orders on offenders aged 10 and above.

6. *Transfer Procedure*

a. The *CRIMINAL JUSTICE & PUBLIC ORDER ACT 1994* abolished committal proceedings and substituted a new procedure for transfer of cases from the magistrates court to the Crown Court for trial.

b. Cases which are triable on indictment will now automatically be transferred to the Crown Court without a hearing in the magistrates court. If a defendant considers that there is no case to answer, a written application for dismissal must be made to the magistrates court. The written representations of both prosecution and defence will be considered and a decision made to dismiss the charge, amend it, or transfer the charge or amended charge to the Crown Court for trial. A magistrates hearing will only take place if the defendant is not legally represented or if the case is particularly complex or difficult. Oral representations will then be made by both parties, but no witnesses can be called. The *CRIMINAL JUSTICE ACT 2003* limits the circumstances in which a defendant may be sent to the Crown Court for sentencing.

7. *Family Proceedings Courts and Youth Courts*

a. *Care and supervision proceedings*

i. If a person under the age of 18 is beyond parental control or in some other trouble, his situation may be considered by the Family Proceedings Court. Under S.31 *CHILDREN'S ACT 1989*, if the child is suffering or is likely to suffer significant harm because the care being given to the child is not what it would be reasonable to expect, or because the child is beyond parental control, a care order may be made. This transfers parental responsibility to the local authority and puts a duty on the authority to provide accommodation for and maintain the child. The local authority must, however, allow the child reasonable contact with parents or guardians. A care order cannot be made in respect of a married child aged 16 or 17.

ii. A supervision order provides for the supervision of the child by local authority social workers. Their duty is to advise, assist and befriend the child.

iii. If the child is not receiving full-time education suitable to his age, ability or aptitude the court may make an education supervision order on the application of the local education authority.

b. *Criminal proceedings*

i. Children (aged 10 to 13) and young persons (aged 14 to 17) will have their case heard by magistrates sitting as a Youth Court. This court will sit in private in a different building or room from that in which other courts are held. Alternatively it must sit on a different day. The court consists of three magistrates drawn from a special panel. At least one magistrate must be a woman. Children under the age of 10 are presumed to be incapable of committing a crime *(CHILDREN AND YOUNG PERSONS ACT 1963)*.

ii. Under the *CRIMINAL JUSTICE ACTS 1982* and *1988* persons under 21 years of age cannot be sent to prison for any offence. The court may impose a fine or a community order, i.e. a probation order, a curfew order, a supervision order or an attendance centre order. An attendance centre order requires a young offender to spend a specified number of hours (up to a maximum of 24) at an attendance centre. The court may also order detention in a young offenders institution. This is only available for persons aged 15 to 20. The court must not impose this custodial sentence unless it is satisfied that there is no other way of dealing with the offender. The maximum custodial sentence for an offender aged 15 to 17 is 12 months. If the person commits an offence for which the penalty is life imprisonment, the person must be sentenced to custody for life, although a person aged under 17 who is convicted of murder must be detained during Her Majesty's pleasure.

8. *Civil Jurisdiction* Magistrates' civil jurisdiction is less important than their criminal jurisdiction, but it is varied and includes, for example:

a. The recovery of certain civil debts including income tax, electricity and gas bills and council tax.

b. Domestic proceedings under the *DOMESTIC PROCEEDINGS AND MAGISTRATES COURTS ACT 1978* (see below).

c. The granting of gaming and liquor licences.

9. *Domestic Courts*

    a.   These courts are constituted under the 1978 Act (see 8.b. above) to hear domestic proceedings. 'Domestic proceedings' are defined to include, for example, affiliation, adoption, guardianship and matrimonial proceedings.

    b.   The only people allowed to be present at the hearing are the officers of the court, the parties and their legal representatives, witnesses and other persons directly concerned with the case, and other persons whom the court may permit to be present.

    c.   Under the 1978 Act either party to a marriage may apply for an order on the grounds that the other:

        i.   Has failed to provide reasonable maintenance for the applicant.

        ii.   Has failed to provide, or make a proper contribution towards, reasonable maintenance for any child of the family.

        iii.   Has behaved in such a way that the applicant cannot reasonably be expected to live with the respondent, or

        iv.   Has deserted the applicant.

    d.   If one of the above grounds is proved the court has a variety of orders available, for example:

        i.   Periodical payments and/or a lump sum (of up to £500) to or for the benefit of the applicant or any child of the family.

        ii.   Orders for custody or access.

        iii.   Orders committing children to the care of a local authority.

        iv.   Orders excluding one spouse from the matrimonial home.

10. *Advantages and Disadvantages of Lay Magistrates*

    a.   *Advantages*

        i.   Public participation in the legal process reduces the remoteness of the law from the public.·

        ii.   The system is cheap since magistrates are not paid, but it nevertheless appears to attract high quality personnel.

        iii.   Lay magistrates reduce the pressure on professional lawyers, leaving them to hear the more serious offences and most civil cases.

        iv.   Although not legally qualified, magistrates may be better qualified in other respects, for example to hear children's cases. In addition the use of lay magistrates reduces the risk of the child perceiving himself as a young criminal.

    b.   *Disadvantages*

        i.   Magistrates tend to be drawn from a narrow background. The majority are male, middle-aged and middle class. For example, less than 10% of magistrates are under 40.

        ii.   It has been argued, although not proved, that magistrates are too willing to accept police evidence.

iii. There is also evidence that sentencing policies differ widely from one area to another. A person convicted of an offence may have three or four times the chance of going to prison if he comes from an area where the magistrates prefer custodial sentences to alternative sentences such as community service, probation and fines.

THE CROWN COURT

11. *Creation* The Crown Court was created by the *COURTS ACT 1971*. It replaced the Assizes and Quarter Sessions and was made part of The Supreme Court of Judicature. The Assizes and Quarter Sessions were local courts, but in contrast the Crown Court is a single court which has buildings throughout the country and may sit anywhere in England and Wales, its jurisdiction is in no sense local. When sitting in the City of London it is known as The Central Criminal Court (The Old Bailey).

12. *Judges*

   a. Crown court judges are either:

      i. *High Court judges,* usually of the Queen's Bench Division, or

      ii. *Circuit judges,* i.e. full-time judges appointed from the ranks of barristers or solicitors of 10 years standing, or from recorders of at least 3 years standing.

      iii. *Recorders,* i.e. part-time judges who are either barristers or solicitors of 10 years standing.

   b. The judge will usually sit alone unless an appeal is being heard from a Magistrates Court, when the judge will be joined by two, three or four lay magistrates. The court, sitting in this form, also exercises a limited civil jurisdiction, mainly over appeals concerning liquor and gaming licences.

13. *Criminal Jurisdiction*

   a. The criminal jurisdiction of the Crown Court concerns all cases above the level of Magistrates Courts. The more serious offences are tried by the High Court judges and the less serious by the circuit judges and recorders.

   b. When hearing appeals from the Magistrates Courts, the court may allow the appeal, reduce the sentence or increase the sentence up to the maximum that could have been imposed by the Magistrates Court.

14. *The Jury* The court sits with a jury of 12, and a majority verdict of 10–2 will be sufficient to convict the accused.

COUNTY COURTS

15. *Introduction*

   a. County courts were created by the *COURTS ACT 1846* to try civil cases involving small sums of money. Originally the upper limit of their jurisdiction was fixed at £20. This limit has been extended on many occasions so that today they deal with the majority of the country's civil litigation.

b.   Jurisdiction is, however, limited in three respects:

    i.   It is entirely statutory, so that if in any matter statute provides no jurisdiction then none exists.

    ii.   They have no appellate jurisdiction.

    iii.   Jurisdiction is local, so there must be a connecting factor between the action and the county court district in which it is tried.

c.   There are about 400 county court districts grouped into circuits, each of which is presided over by one or more circuit judges. The term 'county court' is misleading since these circuits are not based on county boundaries.

16. *Jurisdiction*

a.   The extent of county court jurisdiction was extended considerably from 1 July 1991 by the *COUNTY COURT JURISDICTION ORDER 1991* under the provisions of the *COURTS & LEGAL SERVICES ACT 1990*. The Order abolished many existing financial limits, resulting in many cases being triable in either the county court or the High Court.

In general terms the extent of county court jurisdiction is:

    i.   Contract and tort actions for less than £25 000 shall normally be tried in a county court and actions for £50 000 and over in the High Court. Actions which fall in the middle range or have no quantifiable value can be tried in either court, depending on the complexity of the facts.

    ii.   Personal injury claims unless the claim is worth £50 000 or more.

    iii.   Equity and probate when an estate has a value of not more than £30 000.

    iv.   Mortgages – up to £30 000 amount owing.

    v.   Enforcement of payment of fines.

    vi.   Action to recover solicitors' costs up to £5000.

b.   In addition some courts outside London have bankruptcy jurisdiction which is unlimited in amount. The courts with such jurisdiction also have the power to wind up companies where the paid-up capital is less than £120 000. Some courts in coastal areas also have Admiralty jurisdiction limited to £5000 (£15 000 in salvage cases).

c.   Some county courts are designated as 'Divorce' County Courts. They have jurisdiction in undefended matrimonial matters. In addition matrimonial cases must be commenced in a divorce county court and decided there, unless they are transferred to the High Court on the application of one of the parties or on the direction of the court. Consequently most divorce proceedings take place in divorce county courts. If the case involves any dispute with regard to children, for example as to the parent with whom the child will live, the case will be heard by a nominated circuit judge who by virtue of experience and training is a specialist in family work.

17. *Composition*

a.   A county court is presided over by a circuit judge.

b.   The *COUNTY COURTS ACT 1984* contains provisions enabling judges of the Court of Appeal and High Court and recorders to sit in the county court. The judge usually sits alone, without a jury, although in some cases, for example fraud, there is provision for trial by a jury of eight.

c. Each county court also has a district judge who acts as an assistant judge and clerk to the court. He must have at least 7 years general advocacy experience. In his administrative capacity he maintains the court records, arranges for the issue and service of summonses, deals with money paid into court and a large number of similar functions. In practice much of the work is delegated to clerks and bailiffs. The district judge's function is narrower than that of the judge. He may hear undefended cases, cases where the amount at stake does not exceed £5000 and (if the judge and parties agree) any other action.

d. In most ordinary actions the district judge will conduct a pre-trial review. The purpose is to encourage the parties to settle the claim, thus avoiding the time and expense involved in going to trial. If no compromise can be reached, the district judge will fix a date for the trial.

18. *Small Claims* If a claim does not exceed £5000 (except for personal injury cases), is straightforward and does not require a substantial amount of preparation with legal costs unlikely to be large, then, under recent reforms (see below) a judge may allocate the procedure onto what is called 'the small claims track'. Legal costs are not generally recoverable under the small claims track and, from April 2000, legal aid is not available in personal injury claims; this being replaced by a scheme of 'no win no fee'.

19. *The Woolf Reforms* In 1999 significant changes were introduced with regard to procedure in the civil courts. The changes were based on the findings that the civil justice system was expensive, slow, excessively complicated and not meeting the needs of clients. Changes were introduced by the *CIVIL PROCEDURE ACT 1997*. The key thrust of the changes is to move the management of cases from litigants to judges. Initially it will be for a judge to decide which of three possible tracks a case is to proceed upon: the small claims track, the fast track or the multi-track. In addition time periods will be set by judges for the completion of certain procedures by litigants and wherever possible the parties will be encouraged to agree key points outside of the court. In this way it is hoped that cases will proceed more quickly and efficiently. New rules amend legal terminology to be in accord with more modern language; key changes are:

Old Term	New Term
Plaintiff	Claimant
Writ	Claim form
Pleading (the reason for the claim)	Statement of case
Minor/infant (person under the age of 18)	Child
Affidavit	Statement of truth
In chambers or in camera	In private
Ex parte	Without notice
Subpoena	Witness summons
Discovery (of documents)	Disclosure
Anton Pillar order (power to enter and search)	Search orders
Interlocutory injunction	Interim injunction
Mareva injunction (stopping a transfer of assets)	Freezing injunction
Next friend (an adult who acts on behalf of a child in litigation)	Litigation friend

20. ***Importance*** The practical importance of the County Courts is that they deal with the majority of the country's civil litigation. Over 1½ million actions are commenced each year, although only about 5% result in trials since most actions are discontinued or settled out of court before the trial stage is reached. Several factors may, however, prevent County Courts being as effective a means of resolving small disputes as was originally intended. These factors may be expressed as three questions:

a. Does X know that he has suffered a wrong which entitles him to a legal remedy? He may, for example, be unaware that an exemption clause is invalidated by the *UNFAIR CONTRACT TERMS ACT 1977.*

b. Does X wish to involve the law? He may see the law as a middle or upper class institution, which is 'not for me'.

c. Can X afford to risk losing his case, possibly incurring expenses in excess of his original claim?

This may be a particularly difficult decision to take if the potential defendant is an institution or company with resources to employ the best lawyers to fight the case regardless of cost.

THE HIGH COURT

21. ***Creation and Composition***

a. The High Court was established by the *JUDICATURE ACTS 1873–1875.* Prior to 1971 it sat in the Royal Courts of Justice in London, although when the judges tried a case on assize they constituted a court of the High Court. The *COURTS ACT 1971* abolished all courts of assize, but provided that sittings of the High Court could take place anywhere in England or Wales. The centres where sittings are held are determined by the Lord Chancellor.

b. The High Court is divided into three divisions, namely the Queen's Bench Division, the Chancery Division, and the Family Division. Each division has a head and a number of puisne judges.

c. High Court judges are appointed by the Queen on the advice of the Lord Chancellor. They must be barristers of not less than 10 years standing. The division to which they are appointed depends on the practice followed prior to appointment. The maximum number of High Court judges is fixed by Order in Council at 85.

d. The trial is usually before a judge sitting alone, or before two or three judges in appeal cases. A jury may sit in defamation, false imprisonment and fraud cases.

22. ***The Queen's Bench Division***

a. The jurisdiction of the Queen's Bench Division is wider than that of the other two divisions. It is both civil and criminal, and original and appellate.

b. The most important aspect of its business is its *original civil jurisdiction*, mainly over contract and tort actions. Jurisdiction over commercial matters is exercised by a Commercial Court which is part of the division. It sits in London, Liverpool and Manchester. The division also has an Admiralty Court which deals with claims for damage, loss of life or personal injury arising out of collisions at sea, claims for loss or damage to goods carried in a ship, and disputes concerning the ownership or possession of ships.

c. The *appellate civil jurisdiction* of the division is relatively minor. A single judge has jurisdiction to hear appeals from some tribunals, for example the Pensions Appeal Tribunal. A divisional court, consisting of two or more judges may hear appeals by way of 'case stated' from magistrates courts, the Crown Court and from the Solicitors' Disciplinary Tribunal. '*Case stated*' means that the magistrates write down the arguments put forward by the parties, their findings and their decision, together with reasons. This will go to the divisional court who will consider whether the decision is correct in law. If the appellant disputes an issue of fact, they may not bring an appeal by way of case stated.

d. The *criminal jurisdiction* of the High Court is exercised exclusively by the Queen's Bench Division. This is entirely appellate and is exercised by the divisional court, usually consisting of three judges, and often including the head of the division, the *Lord Chief Justice*. The jurisdiction is over appeals by way of 'case stated' from magistrates courts and the Crown Court.

e. The divisional court also exercises a *supervisory jurisdiction*. It may issue the prerogative writ of habeas corpus, and it may make orders of mandamus, prohibition and certiorari by which inferior courts and tribunals are compelled to exercise their powers properly, and are restrained from exceeding their jurisdiction.

f. Finally the jurisdiction of Queen's Bench Division judges extends to hearing trials in the Crown Court. Judges of the division spend about half their time 'on circuit' and half their time in the Royal Courts.

g. About 55 judges are appointed to the Queen's Bench Division.

23. *The Chancery Division*

a. The nominal head of the division is the *Lord Chancellor*, although he never sits in first instance cases.

b. The jurisdiction includes trusts, mortgages, bankruptcy, company law and partnership, and contentious probate business. There is some overlap of jurisdiction with the Queen's Bench Division.

c. The Chancery Division currently has about 15 judges.

24. *The Family Division*

a. This division, set up in 1970, deals with defended divorces, wardship, adoption, guardianship, legitimacy, disputes concerning the matrimonial home, and non-contentious probate cases. It also hears appeals from magistrates and county courts on family matters.

b. The head of the division is the *President*, and he is assisted by about 20 puisne judges.

25. *The Restrictive Practices Court*

a. This court was originally set up in 1956 and now deals with enforcement of the *RESTRICTIVE TRADE PRACTICES ACT 1976* and the *RESALE PRICES ACT 1976*. These acts prevent manufacturers entering into agreement which restrict free competition and fix prices with regard to their goods. However, since 1973 the court has also had the power to consider restrictive agreements in respect of services.

b. If the court considers that such agreements are contrary to the public interest it may enforce its rulings by an injunction. In practice this rarely occurs since the Restrictive Trade Practices Act 1976 requires potential restrictive trading agreements to be registered with the Director General of Fair Trading (see Chapter 19).

c. The court consists of five High Court judges assisted by ten laymen appointed by the Lord Chancellor from persons with knowledge and experience of industry, commerce or public affairs. Each case is heard by one judge and two laymen, unless it is solely an issue of law, in which the court will consist of a judge sitting alone.

THE COURT OF APPEAL

26. The Court of Appeal was split into civil and criminal divisions in 1966. The head of the civil division is the *Master of the Rolls* and the head of the criminal division is the *Lord Chief Justice*.

27. There are 28 Lord Justices of Appeal, Appeals are normally heard by three judges, but certain cases may be heard by two judges and occasionally a 'full court' of five or more judges will sit for an important case. For example, *YOUNG v BRISTOL AEROPLANE CO (1944)* (Chapter 4.11) was heard by a court of six judges. A majority decision is sufficient and a dissenting judgement is expressed.

28. The appeal takes the form of re-hearing the case by drawing on the judge's notes and the official shorthand writer's transcript and by listening to arguments from counsel. Witnesses are not heard again nor is fresh evidence usually admitted. The court may uphold or reverse the decision in whole or part, it may alter the amount of damages awarded and it may make a different order as to costs. If new evidence is discovered it may order a new trial.

29. The Civil Division hears appeals from the County Court, any Division of the High Court and from some tribunals, for example the Employment Appeal Tribunal. The Criminal Division hears appeals from the Crown Court, either against conviction or against sentence. The Home Secretary may also refer cases to the Court of Appeal. For example, in *R v MAGUIRE (1991)* the court quashed the conviction of alleged IRA terrorists who had previously been convicted of a bomb attack on a Birmingham Public House. The Attorney General may also:

a. Refer to the court for an opinion on a point of law arising from a charge which has resulted in an acquittal.

b. Refer a case for an increased sentence if he considers that the judge in the Crown Court has been too lenient.

THE SUPREME COURT

30. The *CONSTITUTIONAL REFORM ACT 2005* replaces the previous House of Lords with a Supreme Court. The Supreme Court consists of 12 members called Justices of the Supreme Court. The Supreme Court is the final court of appeal in both civil and criminal cases. A minimum of three Justices is required but in practice five normally sit. Decisions are by a majority.

31. The leapfrog procedure was introduced in 1969 because it was thought that two appeals from the High Court the Court of Appeal and then to the House of Lords were unnecessary. Appeal direct from the High Court to the House of Lords is allowed if:

   a. The trial judge grants a certificate on the grounds that the case involves a point of law of general importance, for example a matter of statutory interpretation.

   b. The parties consent.

   c. The House of Lords grants leave for a direct appeal.

Since its introduction in 1969 the leapfrog procedure has rarely been used.

32. *ARTICLE 141* of the *TREATY OF ROME* affects the jurisdiction of the Supreme Court. It provides that a court of a member state against whose decisions there is no judicial remedy under national law must refer certain questions to the European Court for a preliminary ruling, and having obtained the ruling is bound to follow it. The questions concern:

   a. The interpretation of a Treaty, or

   b. The validity and interpretation of acts of the institutions of the European Union, or

   c. The interpretation of the statutes of bodies established by an act of the Council of Ministers.

SELF TEST QUESTIONS

Self Test Questions No. 4 (for Answers see Appendix 1):

1   Draw a rough diagram of the structure of:

   a) The Civil Courts.

   b) The Criminal Courts.

2   Which of the following statements is **correct**?

   All criminal cases commence in:

   a) The County Court.

   b) The Crown Court.

   c) The Court of Appeal.

   d) The Magistrates Court.

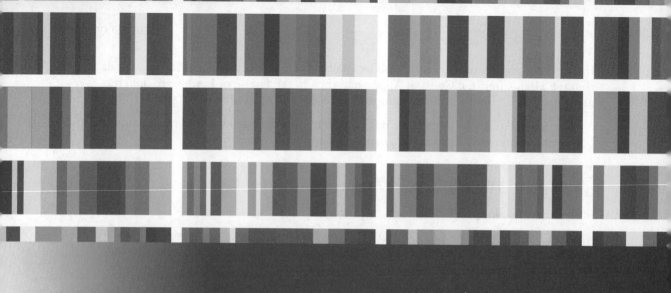

7 TRIBUNALS AND ARBITRATION

Learning Outcomes At the end of this chapter you should be able to:

- Describe the nature and form of UK tribunals.

- State how tribunals are regulated and controlled.

- Outline the main advantages and disadvantages in using tribunals.

- Explain the role of alternative dispute resolution as a dispute resolution mechanism.

1. *Statutory Tribunals*

   a. Statutory tribunals (also called administrative tribunals) are specialized courts established by statute to deal with disputes between government agencies and individuals or between two individuals in a less formal manner than is normal in a court.

   b. Tribunals have developed because the growth of social legislation in the 20th century has resulted in many new types of dispute. These disputes are often well suited to a procedure which is comparatively cheap, quick and informal. They are also far too numerous to be dealt with by the ordinary courts. Important statutory tribunals are arranged into a First Tier and Upper Tier structure; these include:

   FIRST TIER

   i. *Social entitlement.*

   ii. *General Regulatory.*

    iii.   *Health, Education and Social Care.*

    iv.   *Taxation and Land.*

    v.   *Property and Housing.*

    UPPER TIER

    i.   *Administrative Appeals.*

    ii.   *Finance and Tax.*

    iii.   *Lands.*

c.   The main difference from the ordinary courts is their composition, their members being lawyers, judges or laymen with a specialized knowledge of the field in which the tribunal operates.

d.   In recent years the control of tribunals, in particular by the courts, has increased. The *TRIBUNALS AND INQUIRIES ACT 1971* provides that in the case of certain specified tribunals the chairman is to be selected from a panel appointed by the Lord Chancellor. In addition there is a Council on Tribunals which keeps under review the working of tribunals and reports on them from time to time. Tribunals subject to the scrutiny of the council include, for example the Lands Tribunal, National Insurance Tribunals and Rent Tribunals.

    The Tribunals Service was established in 2006 to act as an executive agency for the Ministry of Justice to provide administrative support to the main tribunals. The *TRIBUNALS, COURTS AND ENFORECMENT ACT 2007*, introduced a simplified statutory framework for tribunals.

2.   Some private or professional associations have tribunals to resolve disputes between members or exercise control and discipline over them. The jurisdiction of these tribunals is based on contract in that by becoming a member of the association a person accepts the jurisdiction of the governing tribunal. In some cases the powers of the tribunal are defined by statute, for example The Solicitors Act 1974 and The Medical Act 1978 define the powers of the Solicitors Disciplinary Tribunal and the Professional Conduct Committee of the General Medical Council respectively. There is normally an appeal from such tribunals to the High Court. If the powers of the tribunal are based solely on contract, for example the tribunals of trade unions or private clubs there is no appeal to the courts, although the High Court may declare that the tribunal has acted beyond its contractual powers and that its action is void.

3.   *Tribunals of Inquiry* Parliament may, on occasions, set up a tribunal to inquire into a matter of urgent public importance. The tribunal will usually be given many of the procedural powers of the High Court, such as summoning witnesses, requiring the production of documents and examining witnesses on oath. The tribunal will sit in public unless the public interest requires otherwise. Persons appearing before the tribunal may, at the discretion of the tribunal be represented by a barrister or solicitor.

4.   *Local Statutory Inquiries* Many statutes confer jurisdiction upon Ministers to hold local inquiries. Such inquiries often arise when an order made by a local or public authority is submitted to a Minister for confirmation, for example an order for the compulsory acquisition of land. The inquiries are conducted by local inspectors but ultimate responsibility lies with the Minister. Procedure is governed by the statute under which the inquiry is held. However, the *TRIBUNALS AND INQUIRIES ACT 1958* requires the Minister to give the reasons for his decision if requested to do so.

5. *The Criminal Injuries Compensation Board* Sometimes tribunals are set up to determine an individual's right to compensation from public fund. Thus the Criminal Injuries Compensation Board was established in 1964 to provide compensation to victims of crimes of violence (or if the victim dies, his dependants). Compensation is assessed on the same basis as common law damages and is paid as a lump sum.

6. *Control by the Courts*

    a. The Donoughmore Committee in 1932 recommended four types of safeguard:

       i. Against excess of jurisdiction.

       ii. Against failure to observe natural justice, i.e. both sides must be heard, and no person may be the judge of his own case.

       iii. Through publication of reports of tribunals. (This was implemented by the *TRIBUNALS AND INQUIRIES ACT 1958.*)

       iv. Through the exercise of supervisory and appellate jurisdiction.

    b. The supervisory control of the courts over tribunals is exercised in two ways:

       i. By the issue of the crown orders:

          (a) Compelling some individual or body to perform a public duty.

          (b) Requiring a lower court to reach a particular decision due to some breach of natural justice or an excess of jurisdiction – a quashing order.

          (c) Requiring the stopping of some act being done.

       ii. By allowing an individual to bring an action against the officers of the tribunal claiming an injunction or a declaration as to his rights.

    c. *Appeals from tribunals.* The *TRIBUNALS AND INQUIRIES ACT 1971* provides for any party to appeal or to require the tribunal to state a case on a point of law to the High Court. However, there is often no right to appeal from the decision of a local inquiry.

7. *Advantages and Disadvantages of Tribunals*

    a. *Advantages*

       i. Tribunals specialize in a particular field and use personnel with specialized knowledge and experience.

       ii. They are as informal as is consistent with the proper conduct of their affairs.

       iii. They are less expensive than the courts.

       iv. They are able to meet by appointment, and therefore act more quickly than the courts.

    b. *Disadvantages*

       i. As a result of their flexibility decisions can be inconsistent and difficult to predict.

       ii. Some tribunals do not give reasons for their decisions and others hear cases in private.

       iii. In some cases there is no representation by professional lawyers.

ALTERNATIVE DISPUTE RESOLUTION

8. *Introduction*

   a. In the field of commerce in particular many parties prefer to refer their disputes to alternative dispute resolution (ADR), rather than have them resolved in court though litigation. The main advantages of these alternatives to litigation are that the proceedings tend to be; less costly, take place more quickly and are held in private; they are also much more conducive to the parties reaching a compromise agreement.

   b. An agreement to refer disputes to a form of arbitration is a contract, and is therefore subject to the ordinary law of contract. If the provision attempts to oust the jurisdiction of the courts it is void as being contrary to public policy. The parties may, however, include a '*SCOTT v AVERY (1856)* clause'. Such a clause makes reference to arbitration a condition precedent to a court action. The court may therefore stay proceedings until an arbitrator has first heard the case.

   c. The *CONSUMER ARBITRATION AGREEMENTS ACT 1988* provides that arbitration clauses in consumer contracts cannot be enforced against a non-consenting consumer if the amount involved is less than £1000. Therefore the consumer may either choose the contractual arbitration procedure or the county court small claims procedure. If the consumer's claim exceeds £1000, the court will allow the arbitration clause to be operative if to do so would not be detrimental to the consumer's interests.

9. *Procedure* The *ARBITRATION ACT 1996* allows the parties to contract out of its mandatory and non-mandatory sections. The Act lays down three principles which are to govern its application:

   a. The object of arbitration is to obtain a fair resolution of disputes by an impartial tribunal without unnecessary delay or expense.

   b. The parties should be free to agree how their disputes are resolved, subject only to such safeguards as are necessary in the public interest and the court should not intervene except as provided by the Act.

   c. An arbitrator is required to act fairly and impartially as between the parties and, in an attempt to reduce formality, the arbitrator need not follow High Court procedures but should adopt procedures suitable to the particular circumstances.

The parties are required to do all that is necessary for the proper and expeditious conduct of proceedings.

The Civil Procedure Rules require courts to encourage the use of ADR wherever possible. The exercise of such 'encouragement' was considered in two Court of Appeal cases – *HALSEY V MILTON KEYNES GENERAL NHS TRUST* and *STEEL V JOY (2004)*. The court issued guidelines stating:

   i)   A court cannot compel parties to engage in ADR, to do so may well amount to a breach of Art 6 of the European Convention on Human Rights, which gives a right of access to the courts.
   ii) The role of the court is to encourage ADR.
   iii) If a party unreasonably refuses to go to ADR, costs may be awarded against them.
   iv) The burden of showing an unreasonable refusal rests with the unsuccessful party.

10. *Other forms of ADR*

   a. *Early Neutral Evaluation.* This is where a neutral person, perhaps a lawyer or an expert in a particular field, gives a non-binding opinion on the merits of the case. This can then be used by the parties to negotiate or reach agreement.

   b. *Expert Determination.* Here an expert is agreed upon by the parties to settle the dispute which is legally binding.

   c. *Mediation.* This involves a mediator working with the parties to reach a settlement or agreed position. Mediation takes two forms: 'evaluative'; where the mediator assesses the strengths and weaknesses of the case, or 'facilitative', where his/her role is to facilitate/ broker an agreement. Mediation has significant advantages in that costs and conflict can be much reduced. If agreement is reached the parties may set out their agreement in a binding contract.

   d. *Conciliation.* This is similar to mediation with the conciliator – an outside person – actively seeking and putting forward a suggested basis for agreement between the parties. For example, ACAS (the Advisory Conciliation and Arbitration Service) has a role in relation to proceedings that may be brought before an Employment Tribunal. The procedure is that when a complaint is presented to an Industrial Tribunal, a copy is sent to the Conciliation Officer. He may try to settle the dispute if asked to do so by either party, or if in his opinion there is a good chance of a settlement. The parties should feel able to speak openly to the Conciliation Officer, since a person's statement is not admissible in evidence in an Industrial Tribunal without that person's agreement.

   e. *Med-arb.* This is a procedure that combines mediation and arbitration. Mediation is first tried, if this fails, the dispute is referred to arbitration. It is not unusual for the same independent person to act as both mediator and arbitrator.

   f. *Neutral fact-finding.* This process is commonly used in cases where there are complex technical issues to be determined. An expert in the field reviews the merits of the case and makes an assessment; this may then be used as a basis for further negotiations.

11. *Appointment of Arbitrators*

   a. Where an agreement refers a dispute to arbitration it will be presumed that this means reference to a single arbitrator, but where a specific provision is made for two arbitrators they must appoint an umpire who, if they cannot agree, will break the deadlock.

   b. The parties may appoint any person they wish to act as arbitrator. Lawyers are often appointed, but in some cases a person with relevant technical knowledge is appointed. The High Court has the power to appoint arbitrators in default of appointment by the parties, and to revoke the authority of an arbitrator on the grounds of delay, bias or improper conduct.

12. *Appeal and Enforcement* Parties to the proceedings can apply to the court challenging an award on grounds of serious irregularity, for example failure of an arbitrator to act fairly and impartially with a reasonable opportunity being given to both sides to put their case, avoiding unnecessary delay and expense. Further grounds for appeal are where the arbitrator is alleged to have exceeded his/her powers, and on a point of law.

13. *Ombudsmen* Here a formally appointed commissioner or official acts as a referee in disputes between government and the citizen. Their job is to investigate complaints of misadministration by government departments or public bodies. They have no power to impose a

remedy, but only to make recommendations. They deal with such issues as, unreasonable delay, bias, unfairness, mistakes, failure to follow correct procedures and discourtesy.

14. *Regulators* These are specially appointed individuals who deal with issues relating to the way utilities industries – gas, water, electricity, telecommunications, have dealt with complaints. Different regulators are appointed for each utility.

SELF TEST QUESTIONS

Self Test Questions No. 5 (for Answers see Appendix 1):

1   What is meant by the term 'alternative dispute resolution'?

2   Explain how arbitration, administrative tribunals and other alternative dispute resolutions can be a useful and effective alternative to the resolution of disputes by the courts. What are the advantages and disadvantages of these alternative forms of dispute resolution?

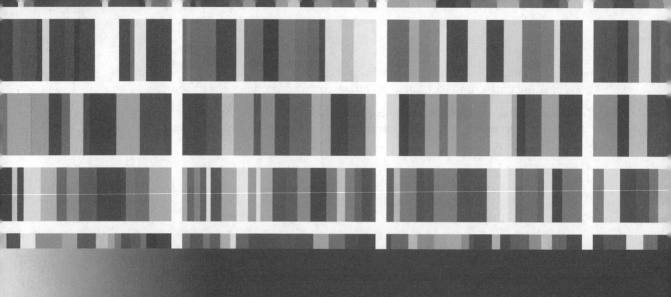

8 THE PERSONNEL OF THE LAW

Learning Outcomes At the end of this chapter you should be able to:

- Explain the key differences between the role of solicitors and barristers.

- Demonstrate an understanding of the role of the jury today and of some of its benefits and criticisms.

1. This chapter deals with solicitors, barristers, judges and juries. Both lay and stipendiary magistrates are personnel of the law, but they are discussed in Chapter 7.

SOLICITORS

2. *The Provision of Legal Services* The *COURTS & LEGAL SERVICES ACT 1990*, the *ACCESS TO JUSTICE ACT 1999* and the *LEGAL SERVICES ACT 2007* has significantly affected the traditional work of solicitors and barristers.

   The legal profession in England and Wales is divided into two distinct branches; solicitors and barristers.

3. a. The *LEGAL SERVICES ACT 2007* (the Act) – which comes fully into force in 2012 – introduces significant reforms to legal services. The Act sets out a number of important objectives for the regulation of legal services, these are:

i.   Protecting and promoting the public interest.

ii.   Supporting the principle of the rule of law.

iii. Improving access to justice.

iv. Protecting and promoting the interests of consumers.

v.   Promoting competition in the provision of services.

vi. Encouraging an independent, strong, diverse and effective legal profession.

vii. Increasing public understanding of the citizen's legal rights and duties.

viii. Promoting and maintaining adherence to the professional principles of; acting with independence, integrity and confidentiality, maintaining proper standards of work, to act in the best interests of the client, and, when acting in court, maintain the best interests of justice.

b.   The Act set up a Legal Services Board, which aims to maintain and develop standards in legal services and promote the objectives listed above.

c.   The Act allows solicitors and barristers to work together with a proportion of staff not being required to be lawyers. Alternative Business Structures (ABS) are allowed under the Act, which will facilitate legal practices to be set up as companies (see Chapter 39), partnerships or Limited Liability Partnerships (see Chapter 38). Provided the ABS has been licensed by an approved regulator – such as the Solicitors Regulation Authority – they will be able to provide a number of reserved legal activities. It now appears likely that banks, insurance companies and large retailers will become key providers of legal services in the future.

4. *Functions of Solicitors*

a.   There are about 100 000 solicitors practising in the UK. They perform a wide variety of work including conveyancing, probate, divorce, company and commercial matters and general litigation. Some solicitors, particularly in the city centres, are specialists, concentrating for example on company law or maritime law. Many others are general practitioners, deriving most of their income from conveyancing and general litigation, but prepared to undertake most work requested by their clients.

b.   If a person wishes to seek a legal remedy or use the facilities of the law for example to sell his house or make a will he will usually consult a solicitor. If a barrister's services are needed, either to present a case in court or to give an expert opinion, the solicitor will instruct the barrister. A layman cannot, in general, instruct a barrister direct.

c.   Solicitors have had a right of audience in magistrates and county courts for many years. In 1993 solicitors in private practice (but not employed solicitors) were also given the right to appear in higher courts. The decision was taken by Lord Mackay, the Lord Chancellor, under machinery set-up by the *COURTS & LEGAL SERVICES ACT 1990*. The main advantage of the change is that it widens choice for consumers and has the potential to reduce costs. The decision was welcomed by the Law Society who had been arguing for increased rights of audience for solicitors for several years.

d.   There is no legal obligation to employ a solicitor when seeking a legal remedy. A person may conduct his own case in any court in the land. He can do his own conveyancing, draw up his own will, and conduct his own divorce provided he has the time and common sense to understand and apply the basic procedures involved. Furthermore since

1985 practising solicitors have lost their monopoly on conveyancing, since this may now be done by licensed conveyancers who are not qualified solicitors.

5. *The Solicitors Regulation Authority*

    a.   The solicitors' governing body is the Solicitors Regulation Authority (previously known as the Law Society). Its main functions are:

        i.   To control entry requirements to the profession.

        ii.   To make rules governing the handling of client's money by solicitors.

        iii.   To issue practising certificates and protect the public against work by unqualified persons.

        iv.   To administer the legal aid scheme.

        v.   To run a compensation fund for persons who have suffered as a result of wrongful acts by solicitors.

        vi.   To supervize solicitors' charges and provide a complaints system.

    b.   Solicitors are liable to the general criminal law, and to a solicitors' disciplinary tribunal consisting of the Master of the Rolls, solicitor members and lay members. Solicitors, however, cannot be sued for negligence in their conduct of a case in court.

The position used to be that both barristers and solicitors could not be sued for negligence resulting from the conduct of a case.

However, now, following the case of ***ARTHUR HALL AND CO V SIMONS (2000)***, both branches of the profession can be liable in negligence for all aspects of their work.

6. *Legal Executives* Solicitors usually employ legal executives. They work under the control and authority of the solicitor, and usually specialize in a particular field, for example conveyancing. The governing body of legal executives is the Institute of Legal Executives. It sets its own examinations, however, qualification as a legal executive does not entitle a person to practise on his own account.

BARRISTERS

7. *Functions of Barristers*

    a.   Only a minority of qualified barristers practise at the bar, currently about 11 000. His/her work will then be in industry or education. Barristers' work includes advocacy in all courts, and giving written opinions on their specialist areas.

    b.   Prior to the *COURTS & LEGAL SERVICES ACT 1990* a barrister could only take instructions from a solicitor. However, S.61 now allows a barrister to enter into a contract with a client for the provision of services and payment of fees. Barristers may also make contracts with other professionals, for example accountants who are not involved in litigation, but who wish to obtain an expert opinion.

    c.   A successful barrister will usually 'take silk', i.e. become a Queen's Counsel. His work will then be exclusively advocacy. Barristers have a right to be heard in any court, but they may not form partnerships, nor may they sue for their fees.

8. *The Bar Council* This is the barristers' governing body. It was formed in 1894. Its purpose is to maintain the standards and independence of the bar. It also deals with questions of professional etiquette, but it has no disciplinary powers.

9. *Fusion of the Legal Profession*

   a. The division of the legal profession into two branches has been a topic of much discussion in recent years. In July 2003 a Consultation Paper was published asking whether the distinction between the two be abolished. In May 2004 the Government invited the Bar Council and Law Society to develop a new scheme for accrediting advocates. It seems likely that in the near future the two professions will become one.

   The main arguments for and against fusion are as follows:

   b. *Arguments against fusion*

      i. The service provided to the public. It is argued that if fusion took place the specialist barristers would join the large firms and the client's of small firms would accordingly be denied access to such specialists. This would result in the decline of small firms of solicitors.

      ii. The service provided to judges. In a judicial system that relies heavily on oral trials judges need clear argument and guidance to lead them to the correct decision. Such a service can only be provided by a select group of professional advocates.

   c. *Arguments in favour of fusion*

      i. Functions overlap in the present system, both in advocacy and in specialization in subject matter. Many solicitors are advocates and spend much of their working life in Magistrates and County Courts and, particularly in the larger firms, many solicitors are highly specialized.

      ii. The present system is inefficient since it involves duplication of effort, and the quality of work is affected because responsibility is divided. Also the custom whereby a barrister only receives his brief 1 or 2 days before the trial is seriously prejudicial to the client.

      iii. Cost. The client will usually have to pay two experts to bring his case to court, and if a Queen's Counsel is employed three lawyers would have to be paid.

   d. A number of reforms have been suggested, for example solicitors could be given a full right of audience in all courts, all barristers could be permitted to form partnerships with solicitors. Alternatively all lawyers could qualify in the same way and then practise as they please, in partnership or alone, taking instructions from lay clients or other lawyers. One class of lawyers would exist, some would be specialists and others general practitioners. Each lawyer could adjust his own practice to the needs of his clients, and his own preferences. The decisions as to which lawyers to use, and in what combinations could then be taken by the client in his own best interests. Since the passing of the *COURTS & LEGAL SERVICES ACT 1990* it is clear that no unification of the profession is likely to take place in the foreseeable future.

10. Other legal personnel include:

    a. *Public notaries.* Who are authorized to draw up deeds, prepare wills and to administer oaths and take statements of truth – an *affidavit*. Most notaries are solicitors.

    b. *Legal executives.* These are employed by solicitors to carry out routine work, such as coveyancing.

MINISTERS OF THE CROWN

11. The United Kingdom does not have a Minister of Justice. The link between Parliament and the Judiciary is provided by four ministers:

    a. *The Lord Chancellor* is the Speaker of the House of Lords, appointed by the Crown on the advice of the Prime Minister. He is chosen from eminent lawyers or judges who support the party in office and he has a seat in the Cabinet. The Lord Chancellor:

        i. Is Head of the Judiciary.

        ii. Presides over the House of Lords in both its legislative and judicial capacities.

        iii. Is responsible for advising the Crown on the appointment of High Court (puisne) judges.

        iv. Is Head of the Chancery Division of the High Court.

        v. Is responsible for the work of the Law Commission, the Land Registry, The Public Trustee and the Public Record Office.

        vi. Acts as general legal advisor to the Government and as its spokesman in the House of Lords.

        The Lord Chancellor is also the Secretary of State for Justice presiding over a department called the Ministry of Justice.

    b. *The Home Secretary* is a member of the House of Commons and of the Cabinet. His responsibilities include:

        i. The Prison, Borstal and Probation services (Borstals were replaced in 1953 by detention centres and youth custody centres).

        ii. The Police.

        iii. The administration of the Metropolitan Courts, and

        iv. Advice to the Government on the treatment of offenders and on the prerogative of pardon.

    c. *The Attorney-General* is a barrister and a member of the House of Commons. As senior law officer of the Crown he represents the Crown in important civil and criminal matters. He appoints and supervizes the Director of Public Prosecutions.

    d. *The Solicitor-General* is also a barrister and member of the House of Commons. He assists and deputizes for the Attorney-General both in the Commons and in Court.

Note: The *Director of Public Prosecutions (DPP)* is a barrister or solicitor with at least 10 years' experience. He is appointed by the Home Secretary and assisted by a staff of professional lawyers and civil service administrators. His role concerns the administration of criminal justice and his duty is to institute proceedings:

i. When the offence is punishable by death.

ii. When a case is referred to him by a government department, and

iii. In other cases where he considers that his intervention is needed.

JUDGES

12. *Appointment*

  a. Judges above puisne judges are appointed by the Crown on the advice of the Prime Minister. Two posts deserve special mention:

    i. *The Lord Chief Justice.* He is the head of the Criminal Division of the Court of Appeal and the Queen's Bench Division.

    ii. *The Master of the Rolls.* He is the head of the Civil Division of the Court of Appeal. He also has duties in connection with the admission of solicitors.

  b. High Court (puisne) judges, circuit judges and recorders are appointed by the Crown on the advice of the Lord Chancellor.

    i. *Puisne judges* must be barristers of at least 10 years standing or circuit judges who have held office for at least 2 years. They are usually appointed to the division of the High Court in which they practised, but they may sit in any division. There are 85 puisne judges. Appointment is by invitation. On retirement a knighthood is automatic.

    ii. *Circuit judges* number about 622. Any barrister of at least 7 years standing may apply to become a circuit judge, but in practice these judges are appointed from the middle ranks of barristers. Top barristers often do not apply because they are unwilling to take a drop in salary.

    iii. *Recorders* must be barristers or solicitors of at least 3 years standing. They are part-time judges who sit in the county court for about 20 days each year. At present there are about 1342 recorders.

  Judges can only be removed on an address by both Houses of Parliament. No judge has been removed from office since before 1700. Judges must now retire at 70, and circuit judges at 72.

13. *Constitutional Position*

  a. Judges are not under the control of Parliament or the Civil Service. The independence of the judiciary is a fundamental principle of constitutional law. Closely related to judicial independence is the doctrine of judicial immunity. In *SIRROS v MOORE* (1975) it was held that any judge will be immune from action provided he acts honestly and in the belief that he is within his jurisdiction.

  b. Judicial immunity extends to the parties, witnesses, advocates, the verdict of the jury and fair, accurate and contemporaneous newspaper reports.

14. *The Function of Judges*

  a. The traditional function of judges is to apply existing rules of law to the case before them. It is, however, being increasingly accepted that judges are capable of 'making law' both through the interpretation of statutes and the doctrine of precedent. Furthermore it is clear that when an Act of Parliament makes no provision for the case in question and there is no existing precedent, the judge must, of necessity, create new law.

b.   In the following notable cases the judiciary went beyond the application of existing legal rules:

    i.   In *CENTRAL LONDON PROPERTY TRUST v HIGH TREES HOUSE (1947)* Denning J. (as he then was), in the view of many writers, created a new rule of equity, namely equitable estoppel.

    ii.   In *SHAW v DPP (1962)* Shaw published a directory of prostitutes. He was found guilty of 'conspiracy to corrupt public morals', an offence previously unknown to the criminal law.

    iii.   In *MILIANGOS v GEORGE FRANK TEXTILES (1975)* the House of Lords effected an important reform by holding that English courts have power to give judgments expressed in foreign currency.

c.   Judges also exercise certain administrative functions, for example:

    i.   The Court of Protection (Chancery Division) supervizes the affairs and administers the property of persons of unsound mind.

    ii.   A rule committee chaired by the Lord Chancellor makes rules to govern procedure in the Supreme Court.

Circuit judges, district judges (who assist in the county court) and recorders do not create precedents.

JURIES

15. *The History of the Jury*

a.   The trial of criminals by jury evolved in the 13th century to replace trial by ordeal which the church condemned in 1215. Most civil cases were also tried by jury until 1854.

b.   Juries were originally summoned for their local knowledge, but by the 15th century their function had changed from witnesses to judges of fact. Nevertheless it was not until *BUSHELL v FAITH (1970)* that it was established that jurors could not be punished for returning a verdict contrary to the direction of the trial judge.

c.   Until the present century the jury was widely regarded as one of the chief safeguards of the individual against the abuse of prerogative and judicial power. However, particularly in civil cases, juries were unpredictable and liable to make errors. In 1854 the *COMMON LAW PROCEDURE ACT* therefore provided that in civil cases the trial could be heard by a judge sitting alone if both parties consented.

In 1938 the *ADMINISTRATION OF JUSTICE (MISCELLANEOUS PROVISIONS) ACT* abolished civil juries in most cases, the main exceptions being fraud and defamation. The jury has also declined in criminal cases, but the loss of faith in the criminal jury has been far less marked.

16. *The Present Day Jury*

a.   Jurors are summoned by the Lord Chancellor and selection is by random ballot. An incomplete jury may be completed by summoning any person in or near the court to serve. A juror is in contempt of court if he refuses to serve or if he is drunk. MPs, lawyers, doctors, the clergy, some ex-prisoners and the mentally unsound do not qualify for jury service. Before a juror is sworn the defence may make a challenge. Since 1988 such a challenge must be supported by reasons. The reasons must not be stated in the presence of the jurors (and the juror who has been challenged) but must be argued in private before the judge. Jurors may also be successfully challenged if they know the defendant.

b.   Juries used to be criticized because the property-ownership qualification produced a jury that was not representative of the population. However, the property qualification was abolished in 1972, and now any registered elector resident for 5 years or over, between 18 and 70, may be summoned for jury service.

c.   The jury sits in private and in general a majority verdict of 10–2 is necessary for a conviction.

17. *Criticisms of the Jury*

a.   To some people the whole idea of a jury seems absurd. Twelve individuals usually with no prior contact with courts are chosen at random to listen to evidence, often of a highly technical nature. They are given no training, they deliberate in secret, they do not give reasons for their verdict, and they are responsible to no one but themselves. After making a decision affecting the liberty of another individual they merge back into the community.

b.   More specific criticisms are:

i.   The random method of selection may produce a jury which is not intellectually capable of weighing the evidence and following the arguments presented.

ii.   Jurors are thought to be biased towards the motorist in motoring offences, and against newspapers in libel cases.

iii. Jurors can be taken in by skilled speakers, and are not experienced in weighing evidence.

iv.   The system is not popular with jurors since attendance is compulsory and unpaid.

v.   In a comprehensive study published in 1979, John Baldwin and Michael McConville found that the jury was representative of the population in terms of age and social class, but unrepresentative in terms of sex and race. Their research did not, however, find a consistent relationship between the composition of the jury and its verdict. A more important aspect of their study was to look at 'questionable' convictions and acquittals. They found that the incidence of such decisions was sufficiently high to 'shake the dogmatic and complacent attitudes that tend to characterize opinions about the jury system'.

18. *Defence of the Jury*

a.   There are many passionate defenders of the jury. They argue that it is a check upon unpopular laws, that it is the best means for establishing the truth, that it serves an important political function by involving laymen in the administration of justice, and most important that it is a safeguard of liberty. Lord Devlin wrote:

'No tyrant could afford to leave a subject's freedom in the hands of 12 of his countrymen. So that trial by jury is more than an instrument of justice and more than one wheel of the constitution: it is the lamp that shows that freedom lives.'

b.   It is also clear that in general the jury enjoys the confidence of the public, the judiciary, lawyers and the police, and although Baldwin and McConville show that its verdicts are questionable more often than was previously thought, it may well be that it reaches the right decision as often as can reasonably be expected of any tribunal.

SELF TEST QUESTIONS

Self Test Questions No. 6 (for Answers see Appendix 1):

1   What are the functions of solicitors and how do they differ in that function from barristers?

2   Define the role of a judge.

3   What is the role and function of the jury and what are the main arguments for the retaining of the jury system?

PROCEDURE AND EVIDENCE 9

'Procedure' and 'Evidence' are both topics of considerable substance and complexity. This chapter does not attempt to explain these topics in detail. It merely explains some of the basic rules, procedures and terminology. It is primarily intended to indicate that particular rules exist rather than describe their detailed content.

CIVIL PROCEDURE

1. *Introduction* The term 'procedure' covers all the steps necessary to turn a legal right into a satisfied judgment, it does not merely refer to the trial itself. The proceedings prior to trial, particularly in larger civil cases usually take many months and often result in a settlement being reached before any trial takes place. Proceedings after trial may also take many months, for example appeals procedure and the enforcement of the judgement. This section will be concerned with bringing an action in the Queen's Bench Division of the High Court, which may be regarded as the standard procedure. There are, however, many variations from this where an action is brought, for example in bankruptcy. Procedure in the Queen's Bench Division is governed by the Rules of the Supreme Court. These rules are

delegated legislation and are made by a Rule Committee under powers conferred by the *JUDICATURE ACT 1925*. It is important to note that these rules are purely procedural and will be declared ultra vires if they attempt to deal with substantive rules of law. In 1994 Lord Woolf was asked to undertake a review of the rules of procedures in the civil courts. His proposals for reform radically changed procedure in the civil courts. The *CIVIL PRO-CEDURE ACT 1997* brought in new Civil Procedure Rules in April 1999. The main changes are as follows:

a.   New terminology. For example, 'plaintiff' is now known as claimant and 'writs' are called 'claim forms'. A summary of the key changes in legal terminology are listed in Chapter 6.19.

b.   Encouragement of settlement.

Alternative Dispute Resolution is to be actively encouraged at various stages.

Pre-action protocols. These lay down a code for the parties to follow in pre-trial procedures; they include such things as timetables for the exchange of documents and use of expert witnesses.

Costs and payments into court. This gives greater discretion to the judge for the award of costs and allows for the taking into account of the conduct of the parties and the manner in which they have conducted themselves in court procedures. There is also the ability of a defendant to make an offer to settle, prior to the judge's summing up, with the effect that if the claimants case does not exceed that amount there will be no costs awarded to the claimant with the added penalty that he will have to pay part of the defendants costs also.

c.   A single jurisdiction. The High Court and County Courts become a single jurisdiction operating to common procedural rules.

d.   There are three tracks which cases may be allocated to:

   i.   A fast track – for claims between £5000 and £15 000. These cases are heard by the county court within 30 weeks.

   ii.   A small claims track – for cases up to £5000; excluding personal injury and housing cases where the limit is £1000.

   iii.   A multi-track for claims over £15 000. These are dealt with by the High Court where timetables are monitored and estimated costs agreed.

2. *Summary Procedure* The basic steps involved are as follows:

a.   The action is begun by issuing and serving a claim form.

b.   The respondent acknowledges service.

c.   An exchange of statement of case takes place.

d.   Preparation is made for the trial, including discovery and inspection of documents.

e.   The trial.

f.   If there is no appeal the matter is concluded by enforcement of the judgment.

3. *Commencement of Proceedings*

a.   *Statement of Claim.* The usual method of commencing an action is to issue a claim form. This places the matter on official record. A copy of the claim form must be served on each defendant either personally or by some other means such as service on his solicitor.

b. *Petitions.* Some actions are commenced by a petition rather than a statement of claim, for example a divorce or a company liquidation.

c. *Acknowledgement of service.* If a person on whom a statement of case is served proposes to enter a defence he must, within 14 days of service of the claim form, deliver an acknowledgement. The form of acknowledgement is served by the claimant with the claim form. After acknowledging service the defendant has a further 14 days in which to file a defence.

4. *Statement of case*

a. The object of the statement of case is to define the area of contention between the parties. A statement of case must contain a brief statement of the facts relied on, but not the evidence by which they will be proved. If a matter is not included in the pleadings it cannot usually be raised at the trial.

b. The statements are:

   i.   The *statement of claim.* This is the first statement and it is made by the claimant.

   ii. The *defence,* i.e. the defendant's answer. If the defendant has a complaint against the claimant he may include a *counterclaim* with his defence.

   iii. The *reply.* This is the claimant's answer to the defence.

c. A typical series of statement of case may appear as follows:

In the Queen's Bench Division of the High Court.

Between

        ACME BUILDERS LTD   *Claimant*

        and

        JOHN BROWN   *Respondent*

Particulars of Claim

The Claimant's claim is for the balance of the agreed price for materials supplied and work done at the Respondent's factory at 30 Newton Street, Luton, between November 2004 and June 2005.

Particulars

Agreed price of work	£20 000
Received on account	£16 000
Balance	£4000
And the Claimant claims:	£4000

Defence and Counterclaim

1. The Respondent admits that the Claimant agreed to build an extension to the Respondent's factory for the sum of £20 000 to a specification prepared by the Claimant and agreed by the Respondent in a letter dated 30th September 2013.

---

2. It is admitted that the Claimant purported to carry out the work contracted for and that the sum of £4000 is outstanding therefore. The Respondent will seek to set off his counterclaim in extinction of the sum due to the Claimant.

Counterclaim

3. It was a term of the contract that Claimant would carry out the work in a workmanlike manner.

4. In breach of contract certain work has been carried out in a defective manner and not in accordance with the agreed specification.

5. Particulars of the defects are shown on the attached schedule. The total estimated cost of rectification shown therein is £5000.

And the Respondent Counterclaims: £5000

Reply and Defence to Counterclaim

1. The Claimant admits the facts and matters set out in the Defence.

2. Paragraph 3 of the counterclaim is admitted. Paragraph 4 is denied. It is denied that any of the work is defective or fails to comply with the specification.

    d.   If either party needs more information he may ask for 'further and better particulars' of specific matters.

5. ***Default Judgments*** If the defendant fails to acknowledge service or if he fails to serve a defence the claimant may obtain a default judgment without the necessity of restoring to a trial.

6. ***Summary Judgments*** If the claimant feels that there is no defence to the action he may apply for a summary judgment. The application will be dealt with by a Master of the Court. He is an official who has most of the powers of a judge. His decision can be set aside on appeal to the judge.

7. ***Procedure from Close of Pleadings to Trial***

    a.   Between close of pleadings and trial much preparatory work must be done by the parties' solicitors.

    b.   *Disclosure and inspection of documents.* Disclosure refers to the requirements of each side to disclose to the other all documents which are relevant to the dispute. Certain privileged documents need not be disclosed, for example letters between the party and his solicitor and experts' reports.

    c.   *Summons for directions.* The interlocutory proceedings (proceedings until trial) are concluded by the taking out by the claimant of a summons for directions. A Master will hear the summons for directions. He will fix such matters as the date and venue of the trial and the numbers of expert witnesses that may be called by each side.

This would then be allocated to the *small claims track*.

8. *Payments into Court* A payment into court is a sum of money paid by the defendant (or the claimant in respect of a counterclaim) into the court office. It is allowed at any time prior to commencement of the judge's summing up in all actions for debt and damages. The purpose is to put pressure on the claimant to settle for an amount less than that originally claimed, i.e. for the amount paid in. If the claimant does not settle and goes on to be awarded less than the amount paid in the plaintiff will have to pay both his own costs and the defendant's costs incurred after the payment in. In the absence of a payment in a winning claimant would usually have his costs paid by the defendant. The judge is not told of the payment in until after he has decided the amount of damages to award. It is now also possible for the claimant to make an offer to settle which has a similar effect on costs.

9. *Trial*

   a. In the High Court the parties are usually represented by barristers although they may appear in person. Solicitors have a right of audience in the County Court and in Magistrates Courts but not in the High Court.

   b. The trial starts with the claimant's barrister outlining the issues involved and calling witnesses. The defendant's barrister then outlines his case and calls the evidence for the defence. Next the defendant's barrister and then the claimant's barrister will make a closing speech. Finally the judge gives the decision in the form of a reasoned judgement which may be delivered as soon as the case is concluded, or reserved to a later date if the judge wishes to consider the case further.

10. *Enforcement of the Judgement* The final stage is enforcement of the judgement. If the defendant does not pay a judgment debt there are several ways by which the judgement creditor can obtain payment. The most important of these is the writ of *fieri facias* (fi fa) which orders the bailiff to seize the debtor's goods and, if necessary, sell them to pay the claimant out of the proceeds. The creditor may also be able to obtain a *charging order* on the defendant's land. If the debt is not paid the creditor will eventually be able to have the land sold and recover the judgement debt from the proceeds. A *Freezing injunction* may be sought preventing the defendant from transferring assets out of reach of the court – for example, transferring money abroad.

11. Proceedings in County Courts are broadly similar to High Court actions, although rather less formal and complex.

SELF TEST QUESTIONS

Self Test Questions No. 7 (for Answers see Appendix 1):

1   Draw up a table to summarize the key changes introduced to civil procedure.

2   What mechanisms are in place to encourage out-of-court settlements?

3   Briefly summarize the procedure in a civil action.

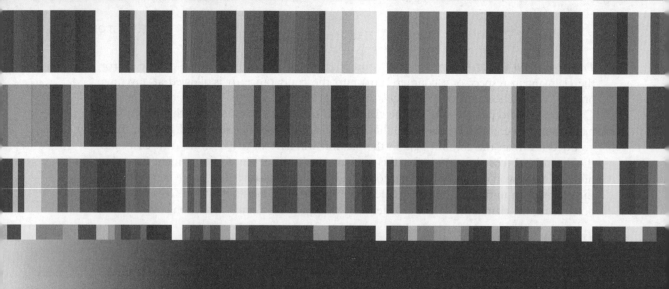

10 THE LAW OF PERSONS

Learning Outcomes At the end of this chapter you should be able to:

- Show an understanding of the differing legal statuses of the individual including nationality, domicile and residence.

INTRODUCTION

1. A legal person is a being that is regarded by the law as having rights and duties. There are two basic types of legal person – natural persons and corporations. A corporation is an artificial person which is recognized in law as a separate legal entity once the formalities for its creation have been complied with. A corporation must be distinguished from an unincorporated association, which does not have a legal identity separate from that of its members. The most significant types of corporation and unincorporated association are limited companies and partnerships respectively. These are discussed in detail in Part V.

NATURAL PERSONS

2. Human beings generally have full legal capacity, and consequently are potentially subject to any rule of law. The actual rules to which a person is subject depends on the factual situation in which he finds himself. These factual situations which affect a persons rights and

capacities are called statuses. One person may have many statuses, for example husband, father and employer. Other examples include minor, guardian, wife and mentally disordered person.

3. *Husband and Wife*

a. *Formation.* In **HYDE v HYDE (1866)** marriage was defined as the 'voluntary union for life of one man and one woman to the exclusion of all others'. The union is based on contract, but since the contract alters the legal status of the parties there are special rules for its formation and dissolution, together with a number of legal consequences.

In order to make a valid marriage:

i. Both parties must be at least 16 years old.

ii. The parties must not be within the prohibited degrees of relationship, for example a person cannot marry his sister or mother.

iii. The parties must be respectively male and female.

iv. Neither party may be already married.

v. Certain formal requirements must be complied with.

If any of the above requirements are not complied with the marriage will be void. In certain other situations a marriage will be voidable, for example if at the time of the marriage the man did not know that the woman was pregnant by another man.

b. *Consequences of marriage.* The main consequences are:

i. Both spouses are under a duty to cohabit unless separated by agreement, or by a court order.

ii. The husband normally has a duty to maintain his wife.

iii. Both have a right to occupy the matrimonial home.

iv. Both have rights regarding succession on the death of the other.

v. Either may apply to the court for the determination of any dispute arising between them as to the title or possession of property. Since 1968 one spouse may be prosecuted for stealing from the other, although the prosecution will normally require the consent of the Director of Public Prosecutions.

vi. Each can sue the other in contract and tort.

vii. A wife takes her husband's domicile.

c. *Dissolution of marriage.* The sole ground for divorce is that the marriage has broken down irretrievably. To establish this the petitioner must satisfy the court on one of the following facts:

i. That the respondent has committed adultery and the petitioner finds it intolerable to live with the respondent.

ii. That the respondent has behaved in such a way that the petitioner cannot reasonably be expected to live with the respondent.

iii. That the respondent has deserted the petitioner for a continuous period of at least 2 years immediately preceding the presentation of the petition.

iv. That the parties have lived apart for the continuous period of at least 2 years immediately preceding the presentation of the petition and the respondent consents to a
divorce.

v. That the parties have lived apart for a continuous period of at least 5 years immediately preceding the presentation of the petition.

A petition cannot normally be presented within the first 3 years of the marriage. However,
a judge may give leave to present a petition on the grounds of exceptional hardship to the
petitioner or exceptional depravity of the respondent.

4. *Minors* A minor is any person who has not reached the age of 18. In addition to the contract and tort rules applicable to minors which are dealt with in Chapters 16 and 25, there
are a number of general points that should be noted:

a. A minor cannot marry under 16, and requires his parents' consent to marry under 18.

b. A minor cannot vote and cannot become a member of parliament, or an elected council-
lor, until the age of 21.

c. A minor cannot make a will, nor can he hold a legal estate in land, but he can hold an
equitable interest.

d. A minor cannot take part directly in civil litigation, but must sue through his 'next
friend' and defend through his 'guardian ad litem'. This will usually be the mother or
father. A minor may, however, defend himself if charged with a crime.

e. There are many other rules concerning for example driving, drinking, smoking, school
attendance and work that affect minors.

f. In addition to the supervision proceedings and criminal proceedings described in Chapter 6, minors may be the subject of orders introduced in the *CHILDREN'S ACT 1989*,
to ensure their protection.

i. An *emergency protection order* removing the child from its parents can be made if
the court is satisfied that (a) there is reasonable cause to believe that the child is
likely to suffer significant harm or (b) local authority inquiries have been frustrated
by denial of access to the child or (c) the applicant (who must be an authorized person) has reasonable cause to suspect that the child is suffering, or is likely to suffer,
significant harm and their inquiries are being frustrated by lack of access.

ii. A *child assessment order* may be made if the court is satisfied that the child is suffering, or is likely to suffer, significant harm and that an assessment is needed which
requires the child to be taken away from home. Unlike the emergency protection
order this is not necessarily designed for emergencies, it may follow from professional observation of one or more suspicious or unsatisfactory circumstances.

NATIONALITY

5. Nationality is the relationship between a person and a particular state or political unit. It
is a person's political status and is important in determining the applicability of immigration law and certain other rights and duties such as the right to vote and the duty to
serve on a jury.

6. The *BRITISH NATIONALITY ACT 1981*. This Act created three new categories of citizenship to replace Citizenship of the United Kingdom and Colonies. The new categories are:

   a. *British Citizenship* i.e. persons born, registered, adopted or naturalized in the UK. This category has the right of abode in the UK and freedom from immigration control.

   b. *Citizenship of the British Dependent Territories* i.e. persons who held a UK passport before 1981 and who were born, registered or naturalized in a British dependency, for example Bermuda, Gibraltar and The Falklands. Such persons have no automatic right of entry to the UK.

   c. *British Overseas Citizenship* i.e. granted to pre-1981 passport holders in East Africa, India and Malaysia.

7. A person may acquire British Citizenship by naturalization. The conditions are as follows:

   a. Residence in the UK for the preceding 12 months plus 4 of the 7 years preceding that year.

   b. Full age i.e. 18.

   c. Good character.

   d. Ability to speak English.

   e. Intention to remain resident in the UK.

8. British citizenship may be lost:

   a. By *renunciation*. A declaration of renunciation must be made. This will be registered by the Secretary of State provided he is satisfied that the person will acquire some other citizenship or nationality.

   b. By *deprivation*. The main ground is that the Secretary of State is satisfied that registration or naturalization was obtained by fraud or misrepresentation.

DOMICILE

9. A person is domiciled in a country if he is resident in the country and has the intention of remaining there. Domicile implies a link with a particular system of law, in contrast to nationality which involves allegiance to a particular sovereign.

10. No person can be without a domicile, and no person can have more than one domicile at one time. The types of domicile are:

    a. *Domicile of origin*. This attaches to a person at birth.

       i. If he is legitimate he will take the domicile of his father.

       ii. If illegitimate, or if the father died before the child was born, it will be that of his mother.

    b. *Domicile of choice*. A person over 16 may adopt a domicile of choice. This has two elements:

       i. The fact of living in a territory, and

       ii. The intention to stay there. All relevant factors will be taken into account in determining this intention, for example whether or not a house has been purchased.

c.   *Domicile of dependence.* This type of domicile applies to children under 16. The dependent domicile of a legitimate child under 16 is that of his father, i.e. if the father's domicile of origin changes then the child's domicile also changes. Similarly if the mother of an illegitimate child takes a new domicile that domicile will become the dependent domicile of the child. If the father of a legitimate child dies the dependent domicile of the child will usually be the domicile of the mother.

The main importance of domicile is that it governs jurisdiction in many family matters, for example marriage and divorce.

RESIDENCE

11. Residence is a question of fact to be determined by the courts. The word implies a degree of permanence. The residence of a wife is prima facie that of her husband.

12. Residence is relevant in determining domicile, liability to taxation and the jurisdiction of the courts, but it is not the only factor in each case.

SELF TEST QUESTIONS

Self Test Questions No. 8 (for Answers see Appendix 1):

1   What is a natural person in-law?

2   How are a person's nationality, domicile and residence determined?

PROPERTY LAW
11

Learning Outcomes At the end of this chapter you should be able to:

- Explain difference between *real* and *personal property*.

- Explain the different forms of legal estates and legal interests in property.

- Define what a *chose in action* is and how it is assigned.

CLASSIFICATION

1. Property is anything that can be owned. It is divided into real property (realty) and personal property (personalty or chattels). Property is classified into real and personal according to the historical action necessary to recover it:

   a. If dispossessed of real property the plaintiff had a right to get back the very thing he had lost. This was known as a right in rem (a right in the thing) and was enforced by a real action.

   b. If dispossessed of anything else (including leasehold land) a person's only right was to monetary compensation from the person who had dispossessed him. This was known as a right in personam and was enforced by a personal action.

2. *Real property* consists of all freehold (as opposed to leasehold) interests in land.

3. *Personal property* is sub-divided into:

    a.   Chattels real, i.e. leasehold interests in land, and

    b.   Chattels personal (pure personalty). These are further sub-divided between:

        i.   Choses in possession, i.e. tangible, moveable objects such as a car, wristwatch or the family pet. It is possible to enjoy a right over such objects by physical possession.

       ii.   Choses in action, i.e. rights such as debts, patents and copyrights which may only be enforced or protected by bringing a legal action. Other examples are trade marks, stocks and shares, business goodwill and cheques.

LEGAL ESTATES AND LEGAL INTERESTS

4. Since the Norman conquest in 1066 it has been accepted that only the Crown may 'own' land in the absolute way that other property may be owned. Other persons hold an estate or interest in land which gives them certain rights over that land for a definite or indefinite period of time. These rights may be broadly classified as legal estates, legal interests and equitable interests. Since the *LAW OF PROPERTY ACT 1925* only two legal estates can now exist:

    a.   Fee simple absolute in possession (or freehold estate), and

    b.   Term of years absolute (or leasehold estate).

5. *Fee Simple Absolute in Possession*

    a.   The meaning of this term may be clarified as follows:

        i.   *Fee*. This means that the estate is capable of being inherited. It may devolve to any person under the deceased's will, or if he died without leaving a will it would devolve to his relatives. A fee estate would end if a person died leaving no will and no relatives. In such a case the land would revert to the Crown. A fee estate must be distinguished from a life estate. For example, land bequeathed 'to A for life re-mainder to B' is not a fee estate because A cannot bequeath the land in his will.

       ii.   *Simple*. This means without a provision as to tail. Thus a fee simple may pass to any relative or anyone else under a will, whereas a fee tail can only pass to lineal descendants. It cannot pass, for example to a brother or parent or as a gift in a will.

      iii.   *Absolute*. This means not subject to any conditions.

      iv.   *In possession*. The person is entitled to immediate physical possession, although he will still hold the freehold (i.e. be regarded as in possession) where he grants a lease of the land in return for a rental.

    b.   The distinctive characteristic of a freehold estate is that it is of uncertain duration since it cannot be known when the estate will revert to the Crown.

6. *A Term of Years Absolute*

    a.   This is an estate which, in contrast to a freehold estate, is of a certain duration, for example 99 years, 5 years or 1 month. It does not matter if the period is for less than a year provided the lease has a certain duration, nor does it matter if the estate does not take effect immediately, since there is no requirement that it must be 'in possession'.

b. A tenancy agreement made on a weekly or monthly basis is not a legal estate since there is no certainty as to duration. It is an equitable interest.

7. The *LAW OF PROPERTY ACT 1925* also provided for the creation of legal *interests*. The most important of these are easements and mortgages.

a. An *easement* is a right to use or restrict the use of another person's land in some way. For example a right of way or a right of light.

b. A *mortgage* is a form of security for a loan. It involves the transfer of an interest in land from the borrower (or mortgagor) to the lender (or mortgagee) with a provision for redemption on repayment of the loan.

EQUITABLE INTERESTS

8. The two legal estates referred to above must be distinguished from equitable interests. There are several different equitable interests. Their common factor is that they can only exist as the result of an express or implied trust.

For example, A conveys his property 'to B for the use of an in trust for C'. The common law took no notice of A's intention that B (the trustee) should hold the land for C (the beneficiary). C's only protection was in equity. Equity acknowledged that at common law the legal estate was vested in B, but as a matter of conscience compelled B to act in accordance with A's intentions.

9. The distinction between legal estates (and interests) and equitable interests is important because:

a. If a person purchases land which is subject to a legal estate or legal interest of which he is not aware he is nevertheless bound by the legal estate or interest, but

b. If he is a bona fide purchaser for value of a legal estate, which is subject to an equitable interest, he will take the estate free from the equitable interest if he had no notice (actual or constructive) of it.

   For example, A, the owner of the fee simple of 'Courtlands' grants by deed a lease to B over part of the land. (This creates a legal estate.) A also grants by means of a written contract a lease to C over another part of the land. (Since this lease is not by deed it only creates an equitable interest.) While A retains the fee simple both B and C have remedies against him, although C's remedies being equitable are discretionary. If however, A sells his fee simple to D, who is a bona fide purchaser for value without notice of C's equitable interest, or B's legal estate, then D will take the land free from C's interest, but subject to B's estate. C's interest in the land is said to be 'overreached', i.e. converted to an interest in the sale proceeds, and A must account to him with an amount of the sale proceeds equal to the value of his interest.

c. Note the meaning of 'constructive notice'. This refers to the ability to fix the whole world with notice of an equitable interest by registering it at HM Land Charges Registry. All persons are then deemed to have notice (i.e. have constructive notice) of the interest regardless of whether or not they have actual notice of it.

OWNERSHIP AND POSSESSION

10. The law has not developed concise definitions of these terms. Both, however, are relationships between persons and property.

11. *Possession* has two elements:

    a.   The means to exercise control over the thing by direct or indirect means, for example through an employee, and

    b.   The intention to exclude others.

    If a person has a) above, but not b) he has custody of the property.

12. A problem arises when considering whether or not a person can possess something which he does not know is on his person or on his land. The answer depends on the context:

    a.   If unknown to an occupier something is buried on his land, he will possess it for the purposes of the civil law of trespass and he will be able to sue any person who wrongfully disturbs it.

    b.   If, however, the thing buried is a dangerous drug, an occupier without knowledge of its presence will not be criminally liable as possessor of the drug.

    c.   It was held in ***R v HALLAM (1957)*** that the offence of 'knowingly possessing an explosive' requires knowledge on the part of the accused that the substance possessed is explosive, not merely that he possessed the substance.

13. *Ownership* has been defined by Pollock in his book 'Jurisprudence' as

    'The entirety of the powers of use and disposal allowed by law.'

    This definition illustrates that a person's rights over the property he owns are limited by law. For example:

    a.   Planning permission is necessary to build on land, or to change the use of land.

    b.   Gold and silver found under land belong to the Crown.

    c.   Adjoining land has a natural right to support.

    d.   Buildings or trees may be subject to preservation orders.

    e.   A person cannot use his land in such a way that it constitutes a nuisance.

    f.   Land may be subject to a compulsory purchase order.

14. Ownership may be acquired in the following ways:

    a.   Originally by:

        i.   Creating something, for example a painting.

        ii.   Receiving the benefit of a transaction that creates something, for example an inventor is granted a patent.

        iii. Occupation, i.e. taking possession of something that has no owner, such as a wild animal.

        iv.   Accession, i.e. something new is added to something already owned, for example a cat has a kitten.

b. Derivatively i.e. acquired from a previous owner who intends ownership to pass, for example a gift or a sale.

c. Succession i.e. by reason of the death of the previous owner.

THE ASSIGNMENT OF CHOSES IN ACTION

15. A chose in action is a personal property right which can only be protected or enforced by bringing a legal action. A chose may be legal, for example a simple debt, or equitable, for example a beneficiary's interest in a trust fund. Assignments of choses in action are possible both at law and in equity.

16. **Easements and Profits**

We noted earlier that one estate in land is the Term of Years Absolute – a leasehold estate. This gives a right to use land belonging to another for a certain fixed period in return for a payment of rent. It is also possible to own other rights in another's property.

a. Easements

These come in various forms:

i. A right of way. For example, a right to cross another's land for access.

ii. A right to light. This stops the occupier of adjoining land from building so close to another's land that light is denied to such an extent that the land affected can only gain sufficient light by artificial means.

iii. A right of support. This easement gives a right to support from another adjoining building; for example a common support wall.

b. Profits

This is a right to take from the land of another, for example fishing or mining rights. Unlike an easement these rights are not restricted to adjoining land. The *LAND REGISTRY ACT 2002* provides for profits to be registered on the Land Registry.

17. *Assignments at Law*

a. A legal assignment of a legal chose must comply with *S.136 LAW OF PROPERTY ACT 1925* if it is to be valid. This section requires:

i. That the assignment is in writing and signed by the assignor, and

ii. That it is absolute, i.e. the whole of the interest is transferred to the assignee, and

iii. That written notice is given to the debtor.

b. The effect of such an assignment is that the assignee becomes the legal owner of the chose, and can sue the debtor without making the assignor a party to the action. Consideration for the assignment is not required by *S.136*.

18. *Assignments in Equity*

a. Equitable assignments of both legal and equitable choses are possible. For example, an attempted legal assignment will take effect as an equitable assignment if it does not comply with *S.136* because, for example, only part of a debt is assigned. In general, equity looks at the intent rather than at the form and will therefore enforce an assignment provided there is:

i. Intention to assign.

ii. Identification of the chose, and

iii. Communication to the assignee.

b. Writing is not necessary for the equitable assignment of a legal chose, but by *S.53 LAW OF PROPERTY ACT 1925* an equitable assignment of an equitable chose must be in writing and signed by the assignor.

c. Notice to the debtor is not necessary to complete an equitable assignment, although it is advisable to prevent the debtor paying the assignor. The effect of the assignment is to enable the assignee to sue the debtor in his own name, except where the assignment is non-absolute, in which case equity requires the assignor to join in the action.

SELF TEST QUESTIONS

Self Test Questions No. 9 (for Answers see Appendix 1):

1   Explain the difference between *real* and *personal* property.

2   What are the possible *legal interests/estates* in land?

3   What is meant by the term *ownership* and how does this differ from *possession*?

4   What is a *chose in action* and how can they be assigned to another?

REFLECTION AND CONSOLIDATION I

For answers go to the student digital support resources for the book (see page xxv).

The aim of these sections in the book is to look back over the material we have covered so far; identify the key elements of the subject matter and, through sample coursework and examination questions, bring together a knowledge and understanding along with the development of your assessment skills. This will enable you to successfully complete any assessment appraisal.

Reflection

Key areas of study

These early chapters set the scene/context within which business law operates; areas covered include:

What is law? How the *law distinguished from morality* and what is meant by *justice*.

The *common law* – what is it and how does it work in creating new law? And, how is the *common law* distinguished from *equity*?

The structure of *the courts*.

Less formal methods of settling disputes – *tribunals and arbitration*.

Personnel involved in the administration of the law.

Rules surrounding the law of *evidence* i.e. how evidence is put before the courts and dealt with.

Who is covered by UK law i.e. *legal personalty*.

Consolidation

The following are practice assessment exercises; you will find the answers and guidance by going to the student digital support resources for the book (see page xxv).

MULTIPLE CHOICE QUESTIONS

Answers are awarded 2 marks each.

1   Which of the following statements is **correct**?

(i) In the event of a conflict between equity and the common law, the common law prevails.

(ii) An Act of Parliament can overrule any common law or equitable rule.

   A   (i) only
   B   (ii) only
   C   Neither (i) nor (ii)
   D   Both (i) and (ii)

2   All criminal cases commence in
   A   The County Court
   B   The Crown Court
   C   The Court of Appeal
   D   The Magistrates Court

CIMA, November 2001

Typical Exam Questions

3   'In English law, parliament is sovereign.' Discuss.
   (20 marks)

ICSA November 2004

4   Within the context of EU law, explain 'direct applicability' and 'direct effect' and their significance for European 'secondary' legislation.
   (20 marks)

ICSA November 2004

5   'The English legal profession is divided into two branches. This division operates for the benefit of the profession's clients.'

5   Explain and discuss. (20 marks)

ICSA November 2004

6   What is the basis of the legal distinction between real and personal property and what are the main differences between them as regards their creation and transfer?

PART TWO

THE LAW OF CONTRACT

12 WHAT IS A CONTRACT?

Learning Outcomes At the end of this chapter you should be able to:

- Distinguish a contract from agreements in general.

- Define the essential elements of a contract and briefly explain the nature of each.

- Apply the legal principles governing offer and acceptance.

- Explain the requirement of consideration and its various qualifying characteristics.

- Understand the requirement that there be an intention by the parties to create a legal relationship.

1. A contract is an agreement which legally binds the parties. Sometimes contracts are referred to as 'enforceable agreements'. This is rather misleading since one party cannot usually force the other to fulfil his part of the bargain. The usual remedy is damages.

2. The underlying theory is that a contract is the outcome of 'consenting minds', each party being free to accept or reject the terms of the other. However, to speak of consenting minds is no longer accurate because, for example:

   a. Parties are judged by what they have said, written or done, not by what is in their minds, i.e. an objective standard is applied.

b. Mass production and nationalization have led to the standard form of contract. The individual must usually 'take it or leave it', he does not really agree to it. For example, the customer has to accept his supply of electricity on the electricity board's terms – he is not likely to succeed in negotiating special terms.

c. Public policy sometimes requires that the freedom of contract should be modified. For example the *RENT ACT 1968* and the *UNFAIR CONTRACT TERMS ACT 1977*.

d. The law will sometimes imply terms into contracts because the parties are expected to observe certain standards of behaviour. A person is bound by these terms even though he has never agreed to them, or never even thought of them. For example *S.12–15 SALE OF GOODS ACT 1979*.

e. The law of agency enables the agent to bind his principal provided the agent acts within the scope of his apparent authority, even if he goes beyond his actual authority. As a result a principal may find himself bound by a contract that he did not intend to make.

3. The essential elements of a contract are:

a. That an agreement is made as a result of an offer and acceptance.

b. The agreement contains an element of value known as consideration, although a gratuitous promise is binding if it is made by deed.

c. The parties intend to create legal relations.

4. The validity of a contract may also be affected by the following factors:

a. *Capacity.* Some persons, e.g. children have limited capacity to make contracts.

b. *Form.* Most contracts can be made verbally, but others must be in writing or by deed. Some verbal contracts must be supported by written evidence.

c. *Content.* The parties may generally agree any terms, although they must be reasonably precise and complete. In addition some terms will be implied by the courts, custom or statute and some express terms may be overridden by statute.

d. *Genuine consent.* Misrepresentation, mistake, duress and undue influence may invalidate a contract.

e. *Illegality.* A contract will be void if it is illegal or contrary to public policy.

5. A contract that does not satisfy the relevant requirements may be void, voidable or unenforceable.

a. A *void* contract has no legal effect. The expression 'void contract' is a contradiction in terms since if an agreement is void it cannot be a contract. However, the term usefully describes a situation where the parties have attempted to contract, but the law will not give effect to their agreement because, for example there is a common mistake on some major term (such as the existence of the subject matter). When a contract is void, ownership of any property 'sold' will not pass to the buyer, so he will not be able to sell it to anyone else. The original seller (i.e. the owner) will therefore be able to recover the property from the person in possession.

b. When a contract is *voidable* the law will allow one of the parties to withdraw from it if he wishes, thus rendering it void. Voidable contracts include some agreements made by minors and contracts induced by misrepresentation, duress or undue influence. A voidable contract remains valid unless and until the innocent party chooses to terminate it.

Therefore if the buyer resells the goods before the contract is avoided, the sub-buyer will become the owner and will be able to keep the property, provided he took it in good faith.

c. An *unenforceable* contract is a valid contract and any goods or money transferred cannot be recovered, even from the other party to the contract. However, if either party refuses to perform his part of the contract the other party cannot compel him to do so. A contract will be unenforceable when the required written evidence of its terms is not available, e.g. the written evidence for a contract for the sale of land.

THE FORMATION OF A CONTRACT

6. The method by which the courts determine whether an agreement has been reached is to enquire whether one party has made an offer which the other party has accepted. For most types of contract the offer and acceptance may be made orally or in writing, or they may be implied from the conduct of the parties. The person who makes the offer is known as the *offeror* and the person to whom the offer is made is the *offeree*.

The **offeror** ⟶ The **offeree**
makes the offer   receives the offer

7. In addition to offer and acceptance the law imposes the additional requirement of:

a. *Consideration* i.e. something of value given or promised in return for the offer made.

b. *Intention* by the parties *to create a legal relationship*.

These elements in the formation of a contract will be dealt with in this chapter. The other requirements of:

a. *Contractual capacity.*

b. *Legality* will be considered later (see Chapter 16).

OFFER

8. *Definition*

a. An offer is a definite promise to be bound on certain specific terms. It cannot be vague as in *GUNTHING v LYNN (1831)*, where the offeror promised to pay a further sum for a horse if it was 'lucky'. However, if an apparently vague offer is capable of being made certain, either by implying terms or by reference to previous dealings between the parties or within the trade, then it will be regarded as certain. Thus in *HILLAS v ARCOS (1932)*, a contract for the sale of timber 'of fair specification' between persons well acquainted with the timber trade was upheld.

b. An offer may be made to a particular person or class of persons or to the public at large as in *CARLILL v CARBOLIC SMOKEBALL CO (1893)* (see Paragraph 9, below).

c. An offer must not be confused with the answer to a question or the supplying of information.

In *HARVEY v FACEY (1893)* P telegraphed D

'Will you sell us Bumper Hall Pen? Telegraph lowest cash price.' D telegraphed the reply

'Lowest price for Bumper Hall Pen £900.' P then telegraphed

'We agree to buy Bumper Hall Pen for £900 asked by you.'

D then decided that he did not wish to sell Bumper Hall Pen to P for £900, and P claimed that a contract had been made, the second telegraph being an offer. The court held that there was no contract, the second telegram being merely an indication of what D would sell for, if and when, he decided to sell. It was supplying of information in response to a question.

9. **Invitations to Treat** An offer must be carefully distinguished from an invitation to treat, which is an invitation to another person to make an offer. The main distinction between the two is that an offer can be converted into a contract by acceptance, provided the other requirements of a valid contract are present, whereas an invitation to treat cannot be 'accepted'. There are several types of invitations to treat:

a. *The exhibition of goods for sale in a shop.* For example *FISHER v BELL (1961)* (4.20).

   Also *PHARMACEUTICAL SOCIETY OF GREAT BRITAIN v BOOTS CHEMISTS (1953)* where by statute certain drugs had to be sold in the presence of a qualified pharmacist. Boots operated a self-service shop, with a qualified pharmacist present at the checkout, but not at the shelves on which the drugs were displayed. The precise location of the place of sale was therefore relevant to determine whether or not an offence had been committed. It was held that the display was an invitation to treat, the customer's tender of the drugs was the offer, and the taking of the money by the pharmacist was the acceptance. The sale therefore took place at the checkout, and Boots therefore did not commit an offence.

b. *General advertising of goods.* Thus a newspaper advertisement that goods are for sale is not an offer. Also in *GRAINGER v GOUGH (1896)* it was held that the circulation of a price list by a wine merchant was only an invitation to treat.

   However, advertisements of rewards for the return of lost or stolen property are offers since they clearly show an intention to be bound without the need for further negotiation. Similarly the promise to pay money in return for an act has been held to be an offer.

   In *CARLILL v CARBOLIC SMOKEBALL CO (1893)* the defendant company manufactured a patent medicine, called a 'smokeball'. In various advertisements they offered to pay £100 to any person who caught influenza after having sniffed the smokeball three times a day for 2 weeks. They also stated that they had deposited £1000 at The Alliance Bank in Regent Street to show their 'sincerity'. Mrs C used the smokeball as advertised, and contracted influenza after more than 2 weeks treatment, and while still using the smokeball. She claimed her £100. The company raised several defences:

   i.   The advertisement was too vague since it did not state a time limit in which the user had to contract influenza.

        –   The court said that it must at least protect the user during the period of use.

   ii. It was not possible to make an offer to the whole world or to the public at large.

        –   The court made a comparison with reward cases and stated that such an offer was possible.

iii. Acceptance was not communicated.

– Not necessary in such cases. A comparison was made with reward cases where no communication is necessary.

iv. The advertisement was a mere gimmick or 'puff' and there was no intention to create legal relations.

– The deposit of £1000 would indicate to a reasonable man that there was an intention to create legal relations.

v. C provided no consideration.

– It was held that the actual act of sniffing the smokeball was consideration. (The purchase price was not consideration for a contract with the manufacturer, it was consideration for the contract with the retailer.)

c. *An invitation for tenders*

i. A tender is an estimate submitted in response to a prior request. An invitation for tenders does not generally amount to an offer to employ the person quoting the lowest price.

ii. An exception may occur where tenders have been solicited from selected persons and the invitation to tender sets out a prescribed clear procedure.

In *BLACKPOOL AND FYLDE AERO CLUB v BLACKPOOL COUNCIL (1990)* the Council, who manage Blackpool Airport, intended to grant a concession to operate pleasure flights from the Airport. It sent invitations to tender to P and six other parties, all of whom were known to the Council. The invitation stated that tenders received after the last date would not be considered. P posted their tender in good time in the town hall letterbox, but this was not opened when it was supposed to be, consequently P's tender arrived late and was excluded from consideration. P sued in contract and negligence. The contract claim was that when inviting tenders the Council promised that it would consider tenders that were received in time. P succeeded, the Court of Appeal holding that it was possible to have exceptions to the rule that invitations to tender were not contractual offers. This would apply where tenders are invited from known and selected persons under a clear prescribed procedure.

iii. If tenders are invited for an indefinite amount of goods e.g. 'sugar as requested during 1994', 'acceptance' of such a tender amounts to a standing offer by the supplier to supply goods set out in the tender as and when required by the person accepting it. When the buyer places an order a contract is made for that quantity, but if the buyer does not place any orders there will be no breach. Similarly the persons submitting the tender may withdraw the standing offer at any time, except with regard to goods already ordered by the buyer under the tender.

d. *An auctioneer's request for bids.* An advertisement stating that an auction is to be held, or a request for bids is an invitation to treat, and not an offer to sell to the highest bidder. The bid is the offer, and the fall of the auctioneer's hammer is the acceptance. Until this happens the bidder may retract his bid *(S.57(2) SALE OF GOODS ACT 1979)*. However, where advertising that an auction will be held 'without reserve' means that the auctioneer must sell to the highest bidder, *BARRY v HEATHCOTE BALL & CO (2000)*.

e. *A company prospectus.* A prospectus or advertisement inviting the public to subscribe for shares or debentures is an invitation to treat, even if (as is the custom) it is described as 'an offer for sale'. The member of the public makes the offer by completing and sending in an application form. The company may then accept this offer in whole or in part. Partial acceptance is an exception to the rule that acceptance must precisely correspond to the offer, however the prospectus will make it clear that the company has the right to accept in respect of a proportion of the shares applied for.

f. In some cases it is not absolutely clear what amounts to an offer and what is an invitation to treat. For example:

   i. Buses. It is probable that the bus itself is the offer (*WILKIE v LONDON TRANSPORT (1947)*) since if the bus were an invitation to treat, and the passenger's tender of the fare an offer, then a passenger could board a bus and, not having seen the conductor, get off again without being in breach of contract.

   ii. 'Pay on exit' car parks.

     In *THORNTON v SHOE LANE PARKING (1972)* a ticket to a car park was dispensed by an unattended machine. The court held that the offer was the sign 'Parking' outside the garage, and the acceptance was the customer placing his car on the spot which caused the automatic machine to operate. In this case the precise time at which the contract was made was important, since it determined whether or not conditions printed on the ticket dispensed by the machine were a part of the contract. In this case there had been an offer and acceptance before the ticket was issued. The conditions printed on the ticket therefore come too late to be incorporated into the contract.

g. *A request for information* is not an offer capable of acceptance. In *GIBSON v MANCHESTER CITY COUNCIL (1979)* the claimant, a council house tenant, sought to 'accept' an undertaking by the local council to sell council-owned properties to tenants. The Court found that the Council had not made a legal offer capable of acceptance, only an indication to tenants that it may be prepared to sell. When the undertaking to sell was withdrawn by the Council, no contract had come into existence at that time therefore there was no legal obligation on the Council to sell. All that had occurred were initial steps towards negotiations for a sale which did not occur.

10. *Termination of Offer* An offer may be terminated in the following ways:

a. *Revocation,* i.e. withdrawal of the offer. An offer cannot be revoked once performance has commenced. In *ERRINGTON v ERRINGTON (1952)* a father told his daughter-in-law that if she took over the mortgage repayments on his house, then when the mortgage had been repaid, she could have the house. She agreed and took over the repayments. When the father subsequently died the court held that his widow could not revoke the original offer once the daughter-in-law had commenced the repayments.

Note that:

   i. A promise to keep an offer open for a fixed period does not prevent its revocation within that period. However, a person may buy a promise to keep an offer open for a fixed period, i.e. he may buy an option to purchase. The offer cannot then be revoked without breach of this 'option contract'.

   ii. Revocation is ineffective until communicated to the offeree. Thus revocation by post is ineffective until it reaches the offeree. However, if the offeree must know that the offer has been revoked he cannot accept it, even if he obtained his information through a third party.

In **DICKENSON V DODDS (1876)** D offered to sell a house to P for £800, and the offer was to be left open until 9 am Friday. On Thursday D sold the house to a Mr Allan, and a Mr Berry told P of this sale. P nevertheless wrote a letter of acceptance which he handed to D before Friday 9 am.

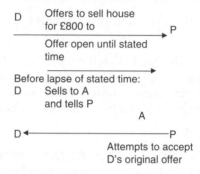

It was held that there was no contract, the offer having been withdrawn before acceptance and communication by a third party being valid. An offer to sell a particular item is withdrawn by implication if that item is sold to another person.

    iii.   Where the offer consists of a promise to pay money for the performance of an act the offer cannot be revoked once performance has commenced. For example, if a promise is made to pay £100 to the first person to swim the English Channel four times non-stop, the offer cannot be revoked once the swim has commenced.

  b. *A refusal or a counter-offer.*

    i.   In **HYDE v WRENCH (1840)** D offered his farm to P for £1000. P wrote saying he would give £950 for it. D refused this, and P then said he would pay £1000 after all. D had by now decided that he did not wish to sell to P for £1000.

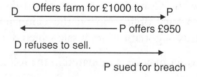

His action failed because his offer of £950 was a counter-offer which terminated D's offer of £1000, thus when P purported to accept at £1000 there was no offer in existence, and therefore no contract was formed.

    ii.   A counter-offer must be distinguished from a request as to whether or not other terms would be acceptable, since such a request does not, by itself, terminate an offer.

In **STEVENSON v McLEAN (1880)** D offered to sell iron to P for cash. P wrote and asked for 4 months credit. This inquiry was not held to be a counter-offer, but a request for information. It did not therefore terminate D's offer.

  c. *Lapse of time.* The offer will terminate at the end of the period stated in the offer, or if no period is fixed, it will terminate after a reasonable time.

In **RAMSGATE VICTORIA HOTEL v MONTEFIORE (1866)**. In June 1864 D offered to take shares in P's hotel. P did not reply to this offer, but in November he allotted shares to D, which D refused to take. It was held that the refusal was justified, since P's delay had caused D's offer to lapse.

d. *Failure of a condition subject to which the offer was made.*

In ***FINANCINGS LTD v STIMSON (1962)*** D who wished to purchase a car signed a hire purchase form on the 16th of March. This was the offer. The form stated that the agreement would only become binding when the finance company signed the form. On the 24th of March the car was stolen from the dealer's premises, and it was recovered badly damaged. On the 25th March the finance company signed the form. It was held that D was not bound to take the car. There was an implied condition in D's offer that the car would be in substantially the same condition when the offer was accepted as when it was made.

e. *Death.* The position depends on who dies.

   i.   If the offeree dies the offer lapses.

   ii. If the offeror dies the offer lapses if the offeree knows of the death at the time of his purported acceptance, or if the contract requires personal performance by the offeror, for example playing in an orchestra.

ACCEPTANCE

11. ***What Amounts to Acceptance***

a. The acceptance may be in writing, or oral, or it may be inferred from conduct, for example by dispatching goods in response to an offer to buy.

b. The acceptance must be unqualified and must correspond to the terms of the offer. Accordingly:

   i.   A counter-offer is insufficient and, as stated above, causes the original offer to lapse.

   ii. A conditional assent is not enough, for example when an offer is accepted 'subject to contract'.

c. Where it is intended to make a contract by means of sealed competitive bids, a submission by one bidder of a bid dependant for its definition on the bids of others is invalid.

In ***HARVELA INVESTMENTS v ROYAL TRUST COMPANY OF CANADA (1985)*** a seller of shares (Royal Trust (RT)) had by a telex dated 15 September agreed to accept the highest bid made by HARVELA (H) or OUTERBRIDGE (O). H bid 2 175 000 Canadian dollars. O's bid was as follows: '2 100 000 Canadian dollars or 101 000 Canadian dollars in excess of any other offer which you may receive … whichever is higher'. On 29 September RT telexed O stating that in the circumstances they were bound to accept O's offer. H objected and commenced this action. The House of Lords had to decide two issues:

   i.   Was the status of the telex of the 15 September such that a contract had been formed between RT and H?

   ii. Was there a second contract (as claimed by O) as a result of the telex of the 29 September?

It was held that the telex of 15 September was not an invitation to treat, but a unilateral offer, conditional upon the happening of a specified event. Such an event could only be done by one of the promisee's, not both. Since the intention was to create a fixed bidding sale, the court rejected the referential bid (O's bid) and held (reversing the Court of Appeal) that a binding contract existed between RT and H. Any other decision would recognize a means by which sealed competitive bidding could be wholly frustrated. Concerning the second contract it was held that no such contract had been formed because there was no intention on the part of the parties. RT's only intention, manifested in the telex of the 29 September was to perform the legal obligation that it mistakenly thought it had incurred.

d.   In complex commercial contracts which are the result of lengthy negotiations, it can be difficult to say when an offer has been made and accepted, since any draft agreement may go through several changes as new demands are made or concessions granted. In the event of a dispute the court will need to look at all the correspondence and take oral evidence to decide, on an objective basis, what was agreed by the parties.

In *TRENTHAM v ARCHITEL LUXFER (1993)* P, the main contractors on a building contract, entered into negotiations with D, who were subcontractors, to supply and install doors and windows. After D had completed the work and been paid, P tried to claim a contribution from D towards a penalty they had incurred under the main contract. D argued that no contract existed because although there had been various telephone calls and letters there was no matching offer and acceptance, nor any agreement as to whose standard terms would govern the contract. The Court of Appeal held that there was a contract, that the approach to the issue of formation should be objective (i.e. does not take account of subjective expectations and unexpressed reservations of the parties) and a precise match of offer and acceptance is not necessarily required where a contract is alleged to have come into existence, as a result of performance. It was also held that where a contract comes into existence, during and as a result of performance, it will often be possible to hold that the contract impliedly and retrospectively covers pre-contractual performance.

This case is important for two main reasons:

i.   It weakens the dominance of the 'offer and acceptance' approach to contract formation, reviving to some extent an approach advocated by Lord Denning, i.e. that you should look at the correspondence as a whole and the conduct of the parties.

ii.   It recognizes that where work is done before any formal agreement is reached, that work will generally be regarded as covered by the agreement, i.e. it will have a retrospective effect.

12. *The Communication of Acceptance – General Rules*

a.   Acceptance is not effective until communicated to and received by the offeror. Thus if an acceptance is not received because of interference on a telephone line, or because the offeree's words are too indistinct to be heard by the offeror, there is no contract.

b.   Acceptance must be communicated by the offeree or by someone with his authority.

In *POWELL v LEE (1908)* P applied for the post of headmaster of a school. He was called for interview and the managers (D being one) passed a resolution appointing him, but they did not make any arrangements for notifying him. However, one of the managers, without authority, informed P that he had been appointed. The managers subsequently reopened the matter and appointed another candidate. It was held that P failed in his action for breach of contract since acceptance had not been properly communicated to him.

c.   The offeror may expressly or impliedly prescribe the method of communicating acceptance, although there will be valid acceptance if the offeree adopts an equally expeditious method, unless the offeror has made it clear that no method other than the prescribed method will be adequate.

d.   A condition that silence shall constitute acceptance cannot be imposed by the offeror without the offeree's consent.

In *FELTHOUSE v BINDLEY (1863)* P was engaged in negotiations to purchase his nephew's horse. There was some confusion as to the price so P wrote to his nephew saying:

'If I hear no more about him I consider the horse is mine at £30 15s.' The horse was at the time in the possession of D, an auctioneer. The nephew, wishing to sell at £30 15s therefore told D not to sell the horse, but D sold the horse by mistake. P therefore sued D in conversion (a tort alleging wrongful disposal of the claimant's property by the defendant). D's defence was that the horse did not belong to P, since there was no valid contract between P and his nephew, because the condition that silence constituted acceptance was ineffective. This defence succeeded.

S.2 of the *UNSOLICITED GOODS AND SERVICES ACT 1971* makes it a criminal offence to demand payment for goods not specifically requested by a business. Also, reg. 24 of the *Consumer Protection (Distance Selling) Regulations 2000* allows for a consumer to keep unrequested goods provided three conditions are met:

i.   The goods were sent with a view to the recipient acquiring them.

ii.   The recipient must have no reasonable grounds for believing that the goods supplied were for a business purpose.

iii.   The recipient must not have either agreed to buy or return them.

The *Consumer Protection from Unfair Trading Regulations 2008*, also make it a criminal offence to demand payment for such goods.

e.   Acceptance is not effective if communicated in ignorance of the offer. However, if a person knows of the offer, the fact that he has a motive for his acceptance, other than that contemplated by the offeror, does not prevent the formation of a contract.

f.   There is no contract if two offers, identical in terms, cross in the post. For example, A offers to sell his car to B for £500 and B offers to buy A's car for £500. There is no contract because although there are 'consenting minds' there is no acceptance.

In 2002 Kodak mistakenly advertised a camera on its website for £100, the normal price was £330. A large number of people placed orders and received an automatic e-mail response confirming the model and price of £100. It was held that the automated e-mail was an acceptance at the price of £100, and Kodak were bound to supply at that cost.

In another instance, Amazon sought to avoid being contractually bound by an automated e-mail like in the Kodak case, by stating on its website that a contract would only be formed, i.e. an offer accepted, when goods were despatched to the customer. When it advertised in error, pocket computers at £7.32 instead of £274.99, it was held that Amazon did not have to honour the lower price when this was corrected before despatch of goods.

13. *The Communication of Acceptance – Exceptions*

   a. *Unilateral contracts.* These are contracts where the offer consists of a promise to pay money in return for the performance of an act. In such cases performance of the act is sufficient acceptance, however, consideration is not complete until performance has finished.

   b. *Postal rules.* Where the parties contemplate acceptance by post, acceptance is complete when the letter is posted, even if the letter is lost in the post.

   In *HOUSEHOLD FIRE INSURANCE CO v GRANT (1879)* D applied for shares in the company. A letter of allotment (the acceptance) was posted to him, but it never arrived. The company later went into liquidation and D was called upon to pay the amount outstanding on his shares. It was held that he had to do so. There was a contract between the company and himself which was completed when the letter of allotment was posted, regardless of the fact that it was lost in the post.

   Note that:

   i. If the letter is lost or delayed in the post because the offeree has addressed it incorrectly the 'post rule' will not apply.

   ii. 'Posted' means put into the control of the post office in the usual manner, and not for example, by handing it to a postman.

   iii. The post rule applies to telegrams, but where communication is instantaneous, i.e. telephone, fax and telex the general rule applies.

   iv. The parties may decide to exclude the operation of the post rule by contrary agreement. This may be wise in international sales, where the possibility of delayed communication is much greater. The post rule will also be excluded if it is clearly inconsistent with the nature of the transaction and/or the words used by the parties.

   In *HOLWELL SECURITIES v HUGHES (1974)* D granted P an option to purchase land to be exercised 'by notice in writing'. A letter exercising the option was lost in the post. It was held that the words 'notice in writing' meant that the notice must actually be received by the vendor.

CONSIDERATION

14. **Definition** A promise is only legally binding if it is made in return for another promise or an act (either a positive act or something given up), i.e. if it is part of a bargain. The requirement of 'something for something' is called consideration. It may be defined as some benefit accruing to one party, or some detriment suffered by the other. There have been several case law definitions, for example from *CURRIE v MISA (1875)*:

   'Some right interest profit or benefit accruing to one party, or some forbearance, detriment, loss or responsibility given suffered or undertaken by the other.'

15. *Executory, Executed and Past Consideration* Consideration may be executory or executed, but it may not be past.

   a. *Executory consideration.* Here the bargain consists of mutual promises. The consideration in support of each promise is the other promise and not a performed (executed) act.

For example, A orders a greenhouse from B to be paid for when it is delivered next week. There are two promises for the law to enforce, B's promise to deliver the greenhouse and A's promise to pay for it.

b.   *Executed consideration.* Here the consideration for the promise is a performed, or executed act. For example, fertilizer is ordered and paid for, and it is agreed that delivery will take place within 10 days. If delivery is late the buyer may sue, putting forward his executed act (i.e. payment) as consideration. Similarly a person who returns a lost dog, having seen an offer of reward may claim the reward. His act of returning the dog is executed consideration. The sequence of events in both examples is first the promise, and subsequently the act.

c.   *Past consideration.* If the act put forward as consideration was performed before any promise of reward was made it is not valid consideration.

For example, X promises to give Y £10 because Y dug X's garden last week. Y cannot sue because when X's promise was made Y's act was in the past.

In ***ROSCORLA v THOMAS (1842)*** P purchased a horse from D. After the sale was complete D gave an undertaking that the horse was not vicious. This proved to be wrong. P sued on this undertaking He failed since his consideration was in the past. The act put forward as consideration, i.e. the payment of the price, was complete before the undertaking was given. P therefore gave nothing new in return for the undertaking. It is not possible to sue in a 'something for nothing' situation.

In deciding whether consideration is past the courts do not always take a strictly chronological view. If the consideration and the promise are substantially the same transaction it does not matter in which order they are given. Thus manufacturers may give guarantees to persons who buy their products from retailers. The buyer then sends a card to the manufacturer to claim the benefit of the guarantee, and he usually does this after he has bought the goods.

d.   *Exceptions to the past consideration rule:*

i.   Past consideration will support a bill of exchange *(S.27 BILLS OF EXCHANGE ACT 1882)* (Chapter 35.18).

ii.   Where a subsequent promise is made to pay for services rendered at the defendant's request. The explanation is that when the request was made there was an implied understanding that there would be some payment, and the subsequent promise merely fixed the amount.

In ***LAMPLEIGH v BRAITHWAIT (1615)*** D killed a man and asked P to obtain for him a royal pardon. P did so and D then promised to pay him £100. D broke this promise and P sued him. P succeeded in this action because D's request was regarded as containing an implied promise to pay, and the subsequent promise to pay £100 was merely fixing the amount.

16.   *'Consideration Must Move from the Promisee'*

This maxim represents an alternative way of stating the basic rule of privity of contract. It means that the only person who can sue on a contract is the person who paid the price. For example, if John orders flowers to be sent to Mary, who is in hospital, and those flowers are not sent, then it is John who is entitled to a remedy against the shop. Although Mary was to have had the benefit of the flowers, she cannot sue because she did not pay the price.

17. *Consideration Must be of Some Value*

   a.   As long as some value is given the court will not ask whether it is proportionate in value to the thing given in return. In other words there is no remedy for someone who makes a bad bargain.

      In *THOMAS v THOMAS (1842)* executors agreed to convey the matrimonial home to a widow provided she paid £1 per year rent and kept the house in repair. In an action on the promise to convey it was held that the promise of payment and doing the repairs were valuable consideration.

   b.   Some acts, although arguably of some value, have been held to be no consideration:

      i.   Payment on the day that a debt is due of less than the full amount of the debt is not consideration for a promise to release the balance *(PINNEL'S CASE (1602))*. However, if the creditor agrees to take something different from what he is entitled to, or if payment is made at his request at an earlier date there is sufficient consideration.

         In *D.C. BUILDERS v REES (1965)* D owed P £482 and knowing that they were in financial trouble offered them £300 in full settlement of the debt. P accepted this cheque, but later sued for the balance of £182. P succeeded because:

         (a)   D paid P a cheque, and the court did not consider this as different from the cash to which P was entitled.

         (b)   The payment was made at D's suggestion and not at P's request.

         (c)   Equitable estoppel was not an available defence for D, because she had attempted to take advantage of P's financial difficulties and had not therefore come to equity with 'clean hands'.

      ii.   A promise to do what the promisee can already legally demand.

         In *STILK v MYRICK (1809)* P was a seaman who had agreed to work throughout a voyage for £5 per month. During the voyage two of the crew of eleven deserted, and the captain promised to divide their wages between the rest of the crew if they would complete the voyage. On completion of the voyage P requested his share, and was refused. His legal action failed on the grounds that he was already contractually bound to complete the voyage and did not therefore provide any consideration for the promise of the deserters' wages.

         Contrast *HARTLEY v PONSONBY (1857)* where 17 out of a crew of 36 deserted. The remainder were promised an extra £40 each to work the ship to Bombay. P, a seaman, had to sue to recover his £40. He succeeded, mainly because the large number of desertions made the voyage more dangerous, and this had the effect of discharging the original contract. (It was now fundamentally different from the voyage bargained for.) This left P free to enter into a new contract under which his promise to complete the voyage constituted consideration for the promise to pay £40.

         Contrast also *WILLIAMS v ROFFEY (1990)* where D engaged P to carry out carpentry work in a block of flats at an agreed price of £20 000. P soon realized that the price was too low for him to operate satisfactorily and make a profit. D was concerned that P would not complete the work on time and therefore made an oral agreement to pay P a further sum of £10 300. Seven weeks later, after D had paid P only a further £1500 P ceased work and later sued D for the additional sum promised. The Court of Appeal held that where D promised to pay P a sum of money additional to that already agreed as the contract price, in return for P's promise to perform his existing obligations on time, the resultant benefit to D was capable of being consideration for D's promise to make the additional payment (provided there was no economic duress or fraud). The court considered that this did not contravene the principle in *STILK V MYRICK (1809)*, but merely limited its application. P was therefore successful in obtaining the additional amount promised.

   iii. A promise to discharge a duty imposed by law.

In *COLLINS v GODEFROY (1831)* P was called by subpoena to give evidence in a case involving D. He afterwards alleged that D had promised to pay him six guineas for his loss of time. P failed in his action since he was bound by law to attend the trial (this is the effect of the subpoena) and he did not therefore do anything for D that he was not already bound to do. P therefore had not provided any consideration.

18. *Equitable Estoppel*

   a. Strict application of the rule in *PINNEL'S CASE (1602)* could cause hardship to a person who relies on a promise that a debt will not be enforced in full. Equitable promissory estoppel mitigates this harshness.

It may be expressed as follows:

Where a person promises that he will not insist upon his strict legal rights, and the other party acts upon that promise, then the law will require that such a promise be honoured and that he be *estopped* from going back on that promise even though it is not supported by consideration.

In *CENTRAL LONDON PROPERTY TRUST v HIGH TREES HOUSE (1947)* P leased a block of flats to D. Due to the war D was unable to sub-let the flats, and so P agreed to accept half rent. Six months after the war P claimed the full rent for the post-war period. This claim succeeded. However, the court also considered whether P would have succeeded if he had claimed the full rent back to the start of the war. Denning, J. (as he then was), said that he would not have been successful because he would have been estopped in equity from going back on his promise.

   b. Note that:

     i. The effect of equitable estoppel is suspensory, i.e. When circumstances change, so as to remove the reasons for the promise, the original rights of the promisor become enforceable again as in the High Trees case.

     ii. The principle acts as 'a shield and not a sword' – Birkett L. J. Thus it only prevents the promisor from insisting on his strict legal rights when it would be unjust to allow him to do so, it does not enable the promisee to sue on an action unless he has given consideration.

In *COMBE v COMBE (1951)* a husband during divorce proceedings promised to pay his wife an annual allowance. The wife, relying on this promise, agreed not to apply to the court for a maintenance order, and later sued to enforce the husband's promise. At first instance her claim succeeded on the authority of the High Trees case. The Court of Appeal reversed this decision because:

(a) Equitable estoppel may only be used when a person who promises not to enforce his strict legal rights goes back on this promise. It does not give effect to a new contract. Any new contract must be supported by consideration in the usual way. (It is said to operate as a *shield not a sword*.)

(b) The wife had not supplied consideration since her forbearance to apply for a maintenance order was not at the husband's request.

19. *Consideration and Existing Duties, the Modern Approach*

a.   Although consideration has always been a popular topic with examiners, problems rarely occur in practice. When they do arise it is usually because the parties to a binding contract have suffered a change in circumstances and agree to vary the original terms in a manner which confers a benefit on only one party. Then, at a later stage, the other party seeks to enforce the original terms.

b.   The modern approach to such situations, expressed by the Court of Appeal in the important case of **WILLIAMS v ROFFEY**, is that a promise to pay an additional sum to secure performance of an existing and unchanged obligation is enforceable unless it was obtained by duress (i.e. economic duress) or the promisor received no benefit. The court will, however, regard a promise that ensures the timely performance of an obligation as conferring a benefit. In **ROFFEY** the defendants had contracted to refurbish some flats for the plaintiff. Due to underestimating the costs involved Williams communicated to the defendants that he could not complete the work. The defendants then agreed to pay an extra amount per flat as they were worried that they would be subject to a heavy penalty clause for late completion with the owner of the flats. The Court held that Williams was entitled to the extra money. The carrying on of the work, though an existing obligation, brought a significant additional benefit to the plaintiff through their avoiding the penalty clause; it amounted to fresh consideration.

c.   Although the Court of Appeal claimed to distinguish **STILK v MYRICK**, most commentators believe that the court went far beyond refinement or limitation, arguably abolishing the doctrine of consideration and removing the need to resort to the complexities of equitable estoppel to enforce a change to promise.

d.   Instead the courts will consider, to a much greater extent than before, whether unfair economic pressure has been brought to bear on the defendant by a plaintiff seeking to enforce an altered agreement.

e.   Commentators have generally welcomed this more flexible approach, which allows renegotiation of contract terms in the light of changed circumstances. There is, however, some danger that it will open the door to commercial blackmail falling short of provable duress.

INTENTION TO CREATE LEGAL RELATIONS

20. Where the parties have not expressly denied an intention to create legal relations, what matters is not what the parties had in their minds, but the inferences that reasonable people would draw from their words or conduct, i.e. it is an objective test. **CARLILL v CARBOLIC SMOKEBALL CO (1893)** (see Paragraph 9, above). The decision in this case might have been different if there had been no deposit of money to show sincerity.

21. *Commercial Agreements*

a. *Agreements 'subject to contract'* where there is a commercial agreement it is presumed the parties intend to create legal relations. However, if the parties expressly deny intention by stating that negotiations are 'subject to contract' or that any agreement is to be 'binding in honour only' then there is no contract.

In *JONES v VERNONS POOLS (1938)* P claimed that he had sent D a football coupon on which the draws he had predicted entitled him to a dividend. D denied having received the coupon. They relied on a clause printed on the coupon which stated that the transaction should not 'give rise to any legal relationship … but … be binding in honour only'. It was held that this clause was a bar to an action in court.

b. *Comfort letters.* If a person has an interest in credit being allowed to another person they may write a 'comfort letter' to the lender encouraging an offer of credit. Depending on its wording the comfort letter may amount to:

    i.   A binding guarantee of the loan.

    ii. A legally binding agreement short of a guarantee, or

    iii. No agreement at all.

In *KLEINWORT BENSON v MALAYSIA MINING CORPORATION BERHAD (1989)* a holding company (D) refused to guarantee a new loan by P to one of its subsidiaries (S). D, however, wrote to P stating it is our policy to ensure that the business (i.e. its subsidiary) is at all times in a position to meet its liabilities. S later became insolvent and was unable to repay the bank. It was held that, since D had refused to give a guarantee, the comfort letter did not amount to a contract, but was only a statement of D's policy.

22. *Domestic Agreements*

a. Where there is a domestic agreement the presumption is that legal relations are not intended, For example, in a married couple an agreement by one spouse to pay the other £50 per week 'housekeeping' money. However, it is possible for a spouse to make a binding contract with the other, for example as part of a separation agreement.

In *MERRITT v MERRITT (1970)* a husband left his wife and when pressed by her to make arrangements for the future agreed that if she would pay the outstanding mortgage instalments he would, when all the payments had been made, transfer the house into her name. It was held that there was a binding contract since the presumption that legal relations are not intended does not apply if husband and wife are separated or about to separate.

b. Where adult members of a family (other than husband and wife) share a household, the financial arrangements which they make may well be intended to have contractual effect.

In *PARKER v CLARK (1960)* a young couple were induced to sell their house and move in with elderly relations by the latter's promise to leave them a share of the home. It was held that legal effect was intended, otherwise the young couple would not have taken the important step of selling their own home.

c. An agreement between persons who share a household, but which has nothing to do with the management of the household will probably be intended to be legally binding.

In *SIMPKINS v PAYS (1953)* three ladies who lived in the same house took part in a fashion competition run by a newspaper. They agreed to send their entries on one coupon and to share any prize money. The court rejected the contention that the agreement to share was not intended to be legally binding since the contract had nothing to do with the routine management of the household.

SELF TEST QUESTIONS

Self Test Questions No. 10 (for Answers see Appendix 1):

1   How is a contract different from 'other' agreements?

2   State the essential requirements for a legal offer.

3   What is an invitation to treat?

4   In what ways may an offer be terminated?

5   What amounts to a valid acceptance?

6   What is consideration in a valid contract?

7   What is meant by the statement that for a valid contract to exist there must be 'an intention to form a legal relationship'?

CAPACITY TO CONTRACT 13

In order for an agreement to be a valid contract both parties must have capacity i.e. the legal ability, to contract. In general all persons have full power to enter into any contract they wish. Different rules apply to minors, corporations, persons with mental disorder and drunks. For more detail on corporations please refer to Chapter 38.

MINORS

1. *Introduction*

   a. A minor is a person who has not yet reached his 18th birthday. When the age of majority was reduced from 21 to 18 in 1969 the practical importance of the rules governing minors' contracts was reduced since most of the decided cases concerned persons aged between 18 and 21. Problems today are most likely to arise with contracts of employment and hire purchase agreements.

b. The law governing minors' contracts shows how the law must compromise between two principles. The first, and more important is that the minor must be protected against his own inexperience. The second is that in pursuing this object the law should not cause unnecessary hardship to those who deal with minors. The compromise between these principles results in certain contracts with minors being valid, (contracts for necessaries and contracts of service), others are void or voidable, and in some cases the minor may be liable in tort or in equity. These categories are considered below.

2. Contracts for Necessaries

a. *S.3 SALE OF GOODS ACT 1979* provides that a minor must pay a reasonable price for necessaries sold and delivered. The section also defines necessaries as 'goods suitable to the condition in life of such a minor and to his actual requirements at the time of sale or delivery'.

b. Note that:

i. The term 'necessaries' is not confined to goods but also includes necessary services and, if the minor is married, necessaries for his family.

ii. The minor is only bound to pay a reasonable price, and not the contract price.

iii. If the necessaries are sold but not delivered (i.e. if the contract is executory, the adult not having performed his part) the minor is not bound.

iv. If the goods are delivered but not paid for the minor is bound because the goods are 'sold and delivered'. The time of payment is not relevant in deciding whether or not a sale has been made.

c. The burden of proving that the goods are necessaries lies on the seller.

i. Firstly, he must show that they are capable of being necessaries. Items of mere luxury, e.g. a racehorse can never be necessaries, but in *PETERS v FLEMING (1840)* it was shown that a luxurious item of utility such as a gold watch may be a necessary. This broad definition of necessaries was clearly not adopted for the benefit of the minor, but to give protection to suppliers who gave credit to young men from wealthy families.

ii. Secondly, the seller must show that the goods are in fact necessary for the particular minor in question.

In *NASH v INMAN (1908)* a tailor sued a minor for the price of clothes, including 11 waistcoats. His action failed because he could not show that the minor was not already adequately supplied. A minor is not liable if he has an adequate supply, even if the supplier did not know this.

3. Contracts of Service

a. A contract of service or apprenticeship is binding on a minor if, looked at as a whole, in the light of the circumstances when it was made, it is for his benefit. He may be bound even if some of the clauses of the contract do not turn out to be to his advantage.

In *CLEMENTS v LAND NW RAILWAY (1894)* a young porter agreed to join an insurance scheme to which his employers contributed, and to give up any claim for personal injury he might have under the Employers' Liability Act 1880. The scheme covered a wider range of injuries than the Act but the scale of compensation was lower. The minor was injured in such a way that would have entitled him to compensation under the Act, but it was held that the contract was binding on him since, looked at as a whole, in the light of the circumstances when it was made, the insurance scheme was more beneficial to him than the Act.

b. A minor will therefore not be bound if the contract is on the whole harsh or oppressive.

In *DE FRANCESCO v BARNUM (1890)* a girl was apprenticed for stage dancing by a contract which provided that she should be entirely at the disposal of her master; that she would only be paid if he actually employed her (which he was not bound to do); that she could not marry during the apprenticeship; that he could end the contract if he found her unsuitable; and that she could not accept any professional engagement without his consent. She accepted a professional engagement with D without the master's (P's) consent. It was held that P could not sue D in the tort of inducing a breach of contract since, as the contract was unreasonably harsh, it was invalid.

4. *Voidable Contracts*

a. 'Voidable' means that the contract will bind both parties, unless it is avoided by the minor before, or within a reasonable time after, reaching 18. In *EDWARDS v CARTER (1893)* 4½ years after reaching the age of majority (at that time 21) was held to be an unreasonable delay. The other party cannot avoid the contract.

b. Voidable contracts include those by which the minor acquires an interest in subject matter of a permanent or continuing nature, such as land, shares in a company or contracts of partnership.

c. When a minor avoids a contract he escapes liabilities such as rent which are not yet due, but he can be sued for liabilities (again rent is a possible example) which have accrued.

d. Avoidance will not entitle the minor to recover money paid by him under the contract unless there has been a total failure of consideration, i.e. unless he has received absolutely nothing for his money.

In *STEINBERG v SCALA (1925)* a minor purchased some shares in a company. When she was required to pay the balance of the purchase price she attempted to avoid the contract, and recover the money that she had already paid. It was held that she did not have to pay the balance, but she could not recover what she had already paid, because she had received some benefits, such as the right to vote at company meetings, and the right to receive dividends. There had not been a failure of consideration since she had received something for her money.

Contrast this with *CORPE v OVERTON (1833)* where a minor agreed to enter into a partnership to be formed in the future. He paid £100 in advance. He later changed his mind, and attempted to recover the £100. His action succeeded because, since the partnership had not yet been formed, he had received absolutely nothing for his money, i.e. there was a total failure of consideration.

e. Similarly, if a minor delivers goods under a contract which is not binding on him, he cannot get them back unless there has been a total failure of consideration.

5. *Purchase of Non-necessary Goods*

a. A minor will not be bound on a trading contract or on a contract for the purchase of non-necessary goods.

In **MERCANTILE UNION GUARANTEE CORPORATION v BALL (1937)** a minor purchased on hire purchase a lorry for use in his haulage contractor business. It was held that this was a trading contract rather than a contract for necessaries and so the infant was not bound.

b. A minor will, however, be bound if he ratifies the contract after reaching 18. No new consideration is required for the ratification.

c. The minor who purchased the goods can give a good title to a third party who takes them bona fide and for value (**STOCKS v WILSON (1913)**). The person who sold to the minor cannot recover from the third party. However, if the minor still has the property, or any property representing it, the court has the power, if it considers it just and equitable, to require the minor to return the property to the vendor (*S.3. MINORS CONTRACTS ACT 1987*). Clearly it would not be equitable to order restitution if the minor has paid for the property, although it is no longer a condition of restitution that the minor obtained the goods by fraudulently misrepresenting his age. If the minor has sold the goods it is unlikely that restitution will apply to the sale proceeds, since they will not be identifiable as 'property representing the goods'. If the goods are returned in a damaged state the vendor will not be able to obtain compensation from the minor.

6. *Loans and Guarantees*

a. Loan to minors are not binding unless ratified by the minor after reaching the age of 18. No new consideration is required for ratification.

b. By *S.2. MINORS CONTRACTS ACT 1987* a guarantee by an adult of a minor's loan or transaction will be enforceable against the guarantor despite the fact that the main transaction cannot be enforced against the minor.

7. *Liability in Tort* A minor cannot be made indirectly liable on a void contract through being sued in tort, but he can be sued in tort if his act is of a kind not contemplated by the contract.

In **BURNARD v HAGGIS (1863)** a minor hired a horse subject to a condition that he was not to use it for jumping. He broke this provision, and the horse died in a jumping accident. In this case the owner's tort action succeeded because the minor had done an act not contemplated by the contract, and had thus taken himself out of the scope of the law of contract, and the protection it affords to infants.

Contrast **JENNINGS v RUNDALL (1799)** when a minor hired a horse for 'riding' and rode it so hard that it was injured. He was held not liable in tort because all he did was an act contemplated by the contract, i.e. riding, although in an excessive manner. Since he was not liable in contract, he could not be made indirectly liable on the contract by bringing a tort action.

8. *The Effect of Equity on Minors' Contracts*

a. *Subrogation.* If an infant borrows money to buy necessaries and he actually spends money for this purpose, the lender may 'step into the shoes' of the seller and recover from the infant the reasonable price which the seller could have recovered. The lender is said to be subrogated to the rights of the seller.

b. *Specific performance.* This will not be granted to a minor, since equity will not grant it against a minor. The equitable maxim 'equality is equity' applies.

MENTAL DISORDER AND DRUNKENNESS

9. a.   If a person's property is placed under the management of the court under the *MENTAL HEALTH ACT 1983* the person will have no capacity to contract with regard to that property. However, the patient's representatives may hold the other party to the contract.

   b.   If a person is temporarily incapable of understanding what he is doing because of mental illness, drunkenness or drugs the contract will be valid unless he can prove:

       i.   That he did not understand the nature of the contract, and

       ii.   The other party knew or ought to have known of this disability.

       Such a contract will be binding if it is later ratified at a time when the person is able to understand what he is doing.

   c.   Where necessaries are sold and delivered to a person who by reason of mental incapacity or drunkenness if incompetent to contract, he is bound to pay a reasonable price. *S.3. SALE OF GOODS ACTS 1979.*

CORPORATIONS OR COMPANIES

10. There are three types of corporation or company, classified according to their mode of creation:

   a.   *Chartered corporations.* A corporation created by Royal Charter has power to do whatever an individual can do. If it makes a contract which offends the spirit of the Charter the contract is valid, although the Charter may be withdrawn.

   b.   *Statutory corporations.* They have only the powers expressly or impliedly conferred on them by the creating statute.

   c.   *Companies registered under the Companies Act 2006.*

   Here, such companies, along with all other companies registered under previous Companies Acts, have unlimited liability in contract (*S.39*) and are fully liable to all outsiders who choose to contract with them.

SELF TEST QUESTIONS

Self Test Questions No. 11 (for Answers see Appendix 1):

1 What is a 'minor' and what is the significance of the sale to minors of *necessaries*?

2 Explain what a contract of service is.

3 What are *voidable* contracts?

4 What happens where goods purchased by a minor are deemed *non-necessary* goods?

5 What is the position of a minor with regards to loans, guarantees and tort?

6 Explain the impact of mental disorder and drunkenness on a parties' ability to contract.

FORM OF CONTRACTS

14

Learning Outcomes At the end of this chapter you should be able to:

- **Explain the various requirements as to the legal form in which certain contracts have to be made.**

1. The general rule is that a contract may be in writing, or oral, or inferred from conduct, or a combination of any of these. It is a common mistake to think that a binding contract must be in writing. Writing makes it easier to prove the contents of the contract, but it is not usually necessary. There are, however, three categories of exceptions.

2. *Contracts which Must be by Deed*

   a. A conveyance or transfer of a legal estate in land (including a mortgage) or the grant of a lease for 3 or more years must be by deed. A conveyance is the document which transfers the title of unregistered land. A transfer is the document which transfers title to registered land.

   b. Consideration is not necessary for a deed. Therefore, a binding gratuitous promise can be made by deed. The essentials of a deed are:

      i. *Writing.*

      ii. *Signature.*

      iii. *Witness and Attestation.*

The *LAW OF PROPERTY (MISCELLANEOUS PROVISIONS) ACT 1989* removed the requirement that a deed must be sealed. However, it provided that the signature of the individual making the deed must be witnessed and attested. Attestation consists of a statement that the deed has been signed in the presence of a witness.

iv.   *Delivery.* This means conduct indicating that the person executing the deed intends to be bound by it. No physical transfer of possession is necessary.

v.   *Intention to create a deed.* The 1989 Act also provided that it must be clear on the face of the document that it is intended to be a deed. This requirement can be satisfied together with the requirement of attestation by using the words 'signed as a deed by AB in the presence of YZ'.

c.   By the *Companies Act 2006* there is now no requirement for a company to have a seal. Any document (including a deed) will be executed if signed by two directors or a director and the secretary, provided it is expressed to be executed by the company.

d.   The effect of non-compliance with the above is that the contract is void. Therefore any money paid or property transferred can be recovered. However, an unsealed lease operates in equity as an agreement to enter into a lease. It will therefore bind the parties. However, if it has not been registered at the Land Registry, it will not bind a third party who purchases the landlord's interest without notice of the tenant's interest. If it has been registered the purchaser of the freehold will be regarded as having notice of the lease, whatever his actual knowledge.

3. *Contracts which Must be in Writing*

a.   The main types are:

i.   The sale of disposition of land or an interest in land (other than contracts for leases of 3 years or less). By *S.2 LAW OF PROPERTY (MISCELLANEOUS PROVISIONS) ACT 1989* the contract must be in writing and must incorporate all the terms that have been expressly agreed in one document, or where contracts are to be exchanged in each contract. Both parties must sign the contract.

ii.   Consumer credit agreements (including hire purchase agreements) which are regulated by the *CONSUMER CREDIT ACT 1974*, i.e. the credit does not exceed £15 000 and the customer is not a company. These must be in writing and must contain all the terms of the agreement other than implied terms. The agreement must be signed by the customer in person and by or on behalf of the creditor or owner.

iii. Bills of exchange and cheques.

iv.   The transfer of shares in limited companies.

v.   Policies of marine insurance.

vi.   Legal assignments of choses in action.

b.   The effect of non-compliance varies, depending on the type of agreement. Usually the contract will be void, but in the case of consumer credit transactions the effect of non-compliance by the seller is to make the agreement unenforceable against the debtor unless the creditor (seller) obtains a court order – *S.127 CONSUMER CREDIT ACT 1974*. The debtor may therefore keep the goods if they are already in his possession.

4. *Contracts which Must be Evidenced in Writing* A contract of guarantee must be evidenced in writing to be legally enforceable.

   a. *Nature of the contract.* For example, if A contracts to buy goods from B, and C promises to pay B if A does not, a contract of guarantee is formed. This should be distinguished from a contract of indemnity in which the person giving the indemnity makes himself primarily liable by saying, for example, 'I will see that you are paid.' A guarantor, however, does not expect to be approached for payment. He may say, 'If he does not pay you then I will.'

   b. *Written evidence.* Any signed note of the material terms of the contract is sufficient. Besides the signature of the guarantor other evidence must include the names or identification of the parties, a description of the subject matter and any other material terms. Any consideration need not be stated. The evidence may be contained in several separate documents.

   In *ACTIONSTRENGTH LTD V INTERNATIONAL GLASS ENGINEERING & SAINT-GOBAIN GLESS UK LTD (2003)* a main contractor (IGE) fell behind with payments to a sub-contractor AS whereupon the customer, SGG, allegedly promised orally to pay any unpaid invoices owed by IGE to AS. The House of Lords held that SGG's oral guarantee was unenforceable because it had not been evidenced in writing as required by *S.4* of the *STATUTE OF FRAUDS ACT* 1677.

5. *Electronic Communications* E-commerce plays a signifcant role in transactions between organizations in the UK. With this in mind the *ELECTRONIC COMMUNICATIONS ACT 2000* was passed to help facilitate the development of electronic commerce, it provides for:

   i. A voluntary system of registration to provide cryptography support services, such as electronic signature and confidentiality services.

   ii. The legal recognition of electronic signatures.

   iii. The removal of the need for paper in other legislative provisions and the ability to modify legislation by ministerial order to facilitate the use of electronic communications and storage.

SELF TEST QUESTIONS

Self Test Questions No. 12 (for Answers see Appendix 1):

1 What contracts have to be made by *deed* and what form does a *deed* take?

2 Do contracts have to be in writing?

3 What is meant by the requirement that certain contracts must be *evidenced* in writing?

4 What are the developments in *electronic communications*?

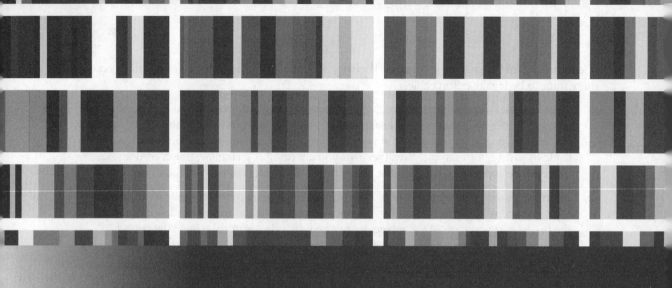

15 THE CONTENTS OF CONTRACTS

Learning Outcomes At the end of this chapter you should be able to:

- Explain the meaning and nature of express terms in a contract, namely the distinction between terms and representations and conditions and warranties.

- Understand implied terms and the role of statute.

- Demonstrate an understanding of exemption clauses and how such clauses are deemed reasonable or not under statute.

1. A contract may contain three types of clause, namely express terms (other than exemption clauses), implied terms and exemption clauses (which are always expressly agreed).

EXPRESS TERMS

2. *Contract Terms and Representations* A statement may be an express term of the contract or a representation inducing its formation. The importance of the distinction is that different remedies are available if a term is broken or a representation is untrue. Which it is depends on the intention of the parties (objectively assessed). It may be helpful to consider:

   a. The stage of negotiations at which the statement was made. The later it was made the more likely it is to be a term.

b. Whether the statement was reduced to writing after it was made. If it was it is clearly regarded as more important, and is therefore probably a term of the contract.

c. Whether the maker suggests that the other party should check the statement. If so it is likely to be a representation.

d. Whether the maker of the statement possessed special skill or knowledge as compared with the other party.

In *OSCAR CHESS v WILLIAMS (1975)* D, a private individual, sold to P, car dealers, for £280 a car honestly described as a 1948 Morris 10. It was in fact a 1939 model worth £175. The statement that it was a 1948 model was held not to be a term of the contract, since D had himself been sold the car as a 1948 model, being given a forged log book. D thus had no special knowledge as to the age of the car, whereas P, being a dealer was in at least as good a position as D to know whether the statement was true.

Contrast this with *DICK BENTLEY PRODUCTIONS v HAROLD SMITH MOTORS (1965).* A dealer sold a Bentley car stating that it had only done 20 000 miles since a replacement engine, whereas it had in fact done 100 000 miles since then. This statement was held to be a warranty since the dealer was in a better position to know the mileage than the purchaser.

3. *Conditions and Warranties*

a. There are two basic types of express term:

i. A *condition* is a vital term, going to the root of the contract, breach of which normally entitles the innocent party to treat the contract as at an end (i.e. to repudiate the contract) and to claim damages.

ii. A *warranty* is a term which is subsidiary to the main purpose of the contract, breach of which only entitles the innocent party to damages.

b. Classification as a condition or warranty depends on the intention of the parties, but in many cases their intention is not expressed and the clause will not obviously be a condition or a warranty. Such terms are called *intermediate or innominate terms.* They remain unclassified until the seriousness of a breach can be judged. If the breach goes to the root of the contract, depriving the plaintiff of the major benefits of the contract, the relevant term will be classified as a condition.

In *HONG KONG FIR SHIPPING CO v KAWASAKI KISEN KAISHA (1962)* a ship delivered under a 24-month charter party was unseaworthy, and took 7 months to repair. The court said that many contractual undertakings could not be categorized simply as 'conditions' or 'warranties', and the innocent party should be entitled to rescind only if the effect of the breach is to substantially deprive him of the benefit of the contract. Since the ship was available for 17 out of 24 months rescission was not granted.

c. The use by the parties of 'condition' or 'warranty' is not conclusive. If breach of a term expressed to be a condition can only produce a very small loss it may be held that the breach will not justify rescission.

In *WICKMAN v SCHULER (1974)* it was a 'condition of a 4-year agreement that a representative of the plaintiff should visit six named customers once a week to solicit orders'. The plaintiff failed to make some of the required visits and the defendant terminated the contract. The court held that the plaintiff could recover damages for wrongful termination. It was not likely that the parties intended that failure to make a few visits out of a total of over 1400 visits should justify rescission.

d. On occasions the parties will classify terms as conditions, which in the absence of agreement would be treated as warranties. For example, in a commercial contract a delivery date for goods is normally regarded as very important and will be assumed to be a condition. On the other hand, a deadline for payment is not regarded as so important and would normally be classified as a warranty. However, if the parties make time of payment 'of the essence' it will be a condition.

In *LOMBARD NORTH CENTRAL v BUTTERWORTH (1987)* an agreement for the hire of computers stated that prompt payment was 'of the essence'. The hirer was late paying one instalment. This was held to be a breach of condition entitling the owner to treat the contract as at an end, repossess the computers and claim damages for breach.

4. *Incomplete Contracts*

a. A legally binding agreement must be complete in its terms.

In *SCAMMELL v OUSTON (1941)* an agreement for the purchase of a van provided for the balance of the price to be paid over 2 years 'on hire purchase terms'. It was held that there was no agreement since it was uncertain what terms of payment were intended. Hire purchase terms may vary over intervals between payments, rate of interest, etc.

However, the parties may leave an essential term to be settled by specified means outside the contract. For example, it may be agreed to sell at the ruling open market price (if there is a market) on the day of delivery or to invite an arbitrator to determine a fair price. It is also possible for the price to be determined by the course of dealing between the parties.

b. In *HILLAS v ARCOS (1932)* a contract for the supply of timber in 1930 contained an option for the purchaser to buy a quantity of timber in 1931, but made no reference to the price. It was held that the missing terms of the 1931 purchase could be deduced from the conduct of the parties in their 1930 transaction when the price was determined by reference to an official price list.

c. If the parties used non-essential words, for example standard printed conditions some of which are inappropriate, such words may be disregarded.

In *NICOLENE v SIMMONDS (1953)* a contract provided that the 'usual conditions of acceptance apply'. However, there were no usual conditions of acceptance. It was held that this phrase was non-essential and meaningless. It could therefore be ignored.

5. *Standard Form Contracts* Many agreements are not individually negotiated, indeed it would be impossible for business to cope if every agreement had to be negotiated by the parties. Standard form contracts are usually used by large organizations in their contracts with consumers, for example British Telecom. They are also often used in commercial transactions. There are two main ways in which a problem with the agreed terms can arise.

a. There will be a problem of consistency when blank parts of a standard term contract are completed in a way that is inconsistent with the printed words. However, the basic rule of construction is that the particular overrides the general, thus the written words inserted in the contract override inconsistent printed words.

b.   The second problem occurs when both parties have their own standard terms. A buyer will order on his standard terms but the seller will purport to accept on his standard terms which of course will be inconsistent with those of the buyer.

In *BUTLER MACHINE TOOL COMPANY v EX-CELL-O CORPORATION (1979)* the seller offered machine tools subject to certain terms and conditions which 'shall prevail over any terms and conditions in the buyer's order'. The conditions included a price variation clause. The buyer replied by placing an order for the machine on terms and conditions which were materially different from those put forward by the seller and which, in particular, made no provision for a variation of price. At the foot of the buyer's order there was a tear-off acknowledgement of receipt of the order stating that 'we accept your order on the terms and conditions stated thereon'. The seller completed the acknowledgement and returned it to the buyer. When the seller came to deliver the machine they claimed that the price had increased by about £2900. The buyer refused to pay the increased price and contended that the contract had been concluded on his rather than the seller's terms and therefore constituted a fixed price contract. The judge found for the seller and the buyer appealed. The Court of Appeal found for the buyer because:

i.   Applying the rules of offer and acceptance, the buyer's order was a counter-offer which destroyed the offer made in the seller's quotation. The seller by completing and returning the acknowledgement form, accepted the counter-offer on the buyer's terms.

ii.   The documents comprising a 'battle of forms' were to be considered as a whole. If the conflicting terms and conditions of both parties were irreconcilable, then the acknowledgement of the order was the decisive document since it made it clear that the contract was on the buyer's and not the seller's terms.

IMPLIED TERMS

6. Terms may be implied by custom, the courts or by statute.

7. *Custom* The parties are presumed to have contracted by reference to the customs prevailing in the trade or locality in question, unless they have shown a contrary intention.

In *BRITISH CRANE HIRE v IPSWICH PLANT HIRE (1974)* both firms were in the business of hiring out cranes and heavy plant. D urgently needed a crane for work on marshy ground and agreed to hire such a crane from P. The method of payment was agreed but the hire conditions were not. P then sent D a copy of their standard conditions (which were similar to those used throughout the trade) which provided that the hirer would be liable for all expenses arising out of the crane's use. Before these conditions were signed the crane sank into the marshy ground, and P incurred expenses in recovering it. P claimed these expenses from D. Their action succeeded since both parties were in the same trade, and had equal bargaining power, and the evidence was that they both understood that P's standard conditions of hire would apply.

8. *The Courts*

a.   The courts will imply two types of terms into contracts. Firstly, terms which are so obvious that the parties must have intended them to be included. These are called terms implied in fact. Secondly, terms which are implied to maintain a standard of behaviour, even though the parties may not have intended them to be included. These are called terms implied in law.

b. *Terms implied in fact.* The implied term must be both obvious and necessary to give 'business efficacy' to the contract. The courts will not imply a term merely because it is reasonable to do so. The test used is known as the 'officious bystander' test, i.e. if when the parties were making the contract an officious bystander had asked 'Is X a term of the contract?' and if he would have received the reply 'Yes, obviously' then the term will be implied.

In **THE MOORCOOK (1889)** D, who were wharf owners, contracted to allow P to unload their ship at the wharf. The ship grounded at low water, and was damaged by settling on a ridge of hard ground. D were held to be in breach of an implied term that the wharf was safe.

In **EYRE v MEASDAY (1986)** P underwent a sterilization operation. The surgeon had advised her that the operation was irreversible and consequently P believed that she would be sterile. The fact that there was a slight risk of pregnancy after the operation was not pointed out. Later the plaintiff became pregnant and gave birth to a son. It was held that the word 'irreversible' did not amount to a guarantee of success, it merely indicated that the procedure could not be reversed, which is quite different. Applying the 'officious bystander' test the courts said that although it would be reasonable for P to assume that she was sterile, it would not be reasonable for her to think that she had been given a guarantee that she was sterile. If she had wanted such a guarantee she should have asked for it. P was therefore unsuccessful.

c. *Terms implied in law.* Terms implied in law cover many classes of contract. Thus in a contract of employment the employee impliedly undertakes, for example, to faithfully serve his employer, and that he is reasonably skilled. The employer impliedly undertakes that he will not require the employee to do an unlawful act, and that he will provide safe premises. Similarly in a tenancy agreement the landlord impliedly covenants that his tenant shall have quiet possession, and the tenant impliedly agrees not to commit waste.

In **LIVERPOOL CITY COUNCIL v IRWIN (1977)** it was held that where parts of a building have been let to different tenants, and where rights of access over the parts of the building retained by the landlord e.g. the stairs, have been granted to these tenants, then a term could be implied that the landlord would keep these parts reasonably safe.

9. *Statute*

a. The most well known examples are the terms implied by *S.12–15 SALE OF GOODS ACT 1979*:

   i. That the seller has the right to sell.

   ii. That in a sale by description the goods shall correspond with the description.

   iii. That the goods supplied are of satisfactory quality, and fit for the purpose for which they are required. 'Satisfactory quality' was substituted for 'merchantable quality' by the *SALE AND SUPPLY OF GOODS ACT 1994.*

   iv. That where the goods are sold by sample the bulk will correspond with the sample.

b. The *SUPPLY OF GOODS AND SERVICES ACT 1982* has given similar protection to persons who are supplied with (as opposed to sold) goods, and to persons who are supplied with services.

These three Acts are considered in more detail in Chapter 33.

EXEMPTION CLAUSES

10. An exemption clause is a term in a contract which seeks to exempt one of the parties from liability, or which seeks to limit his liability to a specific sum if certain events occur, such as a breach of warranty, negligence or theft of goods.

11. An exemption clause may become a term of the contract by signature or by notice.

   a. If a person signs a document he is bound by it even if he does not read it.

   In *L'ESTRANGE v GRAUCOB (1934)* P, who was the proprietor of a cafe, purchased a cigarette vending machine. She signed, without reading, a sales agreement which contained a large amount of 'small print'. The machine was defective but the vendors were held to be protected by an exemption clause contained in that small print.

   b. A person may not be bound by a signed document if the other party misrepresented its terms.

   In *CURTIS v CHEMICAL CLEANING CO (1951)* P took a white satin wedding dress, trimmed with beads and sequins to the cleaners. The assistant gave her a form to sign, and when asked about its contents said that it excluded the company's liability for damage to the beads and sequins. The plaintiff then signed the form, which in fact contained a clause excluding the company from all liability. When the dress was returned it was badly stained. The company attempted to rely on their exemption clause but it was held that they could not do so since the assistant had misrepresented (albeit innocently) the effect of the form.

   c. Where a document is not signed the exemption clause will only apply if:

      i.   The party knows of the clause, or if

      ii. Reasonable steps are taken to bring it to his notice before the contract is made.

   In *OLLEY v MARLBOROUGH COURT (1949)* P booked in at the D's hotel. When she went to her room she saw a notice on the wall stating that the hotel would not be liable for articles lost or stolen unless they were handed in for safe keeping. P left some furs in the bedroom, closed the self-locking door, and hung the key on a board in reception. The furs were stolen. It was held that the exemption clause was not effective. The contract was completed at the reception desk, and accordingly a notice in the bedroom came too late to be incorporated into the contract.

   d. The more outlandish the clause (whether it is an exemption clause, a limitation clause or an agreed damages clause) the greater the effort that must be made to bring it to the other party's attention.

   In *INTERFOTO PICTURE LIBRARY v STILETTO VISUAL PROGRAMMES (1988)* D, an advertising agency, hired 47 transparencies from P. They arrived with a delivery note requiring them to be returned by a specified date. The delivery note included nine 'small print' conditions which D never read. One of the conditions stated that if the transparencies were returned late there would be a charge of £5 per transparency per day. D returned the transparencies 14 days late and was billed for over £3500. P's claim failed since the clause imposed an unusual and exorbitant charge and they had not taken sufficient steps to bring it to the attention of a person with whom they had never previously dealt.

e. The court will not enforce an exemption clause unless the party affected by it was adequately informed of it when he accepted it. Thus the exemption clause must be put forward in a document which gives reasonable notice of the liability conditions proposed by it.

In *CHAPELTON v BARRY UDC (1940)* there was a pile of deck chairs and a notice saying 'hire of chairs 2d per session of 3 hours'. P took two chairs, paid for them and received two tickets. One of the chairs collapsed and he was injured. The Council relied on a notice on the back of the tickets by which it disclaimed liability for injury. It was held that the notice advertising chairs for hire gave no warning of limiting conditions and it was not reasonable to communicate them on a receipt. The disclaimer of liability was not effective.

Contrast *THOMPSON v LMS RAILWAY (1930)* where an elderly lady who could not read asked her niece to buy her a railway excursion ticket on which was printed 'Excursion. For conditions see back'. On the back it was stated that the ticket was issued subject to conditions contained in the company's timetables. These conditions excluded liability for injury. It was held that the conditions had been adequately communicated and therefore accepted.

A further distinction between the two cases is that in Chapelton's case the ticket was a mere receipt, it did not purport to set out the conditions for the hire of the chair, it only showed the time for which it was hired and that a fee had been paid. However, in Thompson's case it would have been obvious to a reasonable person that the ticket had contractual effect since tickets of that kind generally contain contract terms.

f. If the parties have had long and consistent dealings on terms incorporating an exemption clause, then the clause may apply to a particular transaction, even if the usual steps to incorporate it were not taken. If there are only a few transactions spread over a long period it would not be reasonable to assume that the person has agreed to the term.

In *HOLLIER v RAMBLER MOTORS (1972)* on three or four occasions over a period of 5 years H had had repairs done at the garage. On each occasion he had signed a form by which the garage disclaimed liability for damage caused by fire to customers' cars. On the latest occasion he did not sign the form. The car was damaged by fire caused by negligence of garage employees. The garage contended that the disclaimer had by course of dealing, become an established term of any contract made between them and H. It was held that the garage was liable. There was insufficient evidence to show that H knew of and agreed to the condition as a continuing term of his contracts with the garage.

12. *Limitations on the Use of Exemption Clauses*

a. In considering the validity of exemption clauses the courts have had to strike a balance between:

   i.   The principle that parties should have complete freedom to contract on whatever terms they wish, and

   ii. The need to protect the public from unfair exemption clauses in standard form contracts used by large business enterprises.

b. The use of exemption clauses by large organizations to abuse their bargaining power is clearly indefensible. Nevertheless exemption clauses do have a proper place in business. They can be used to allocate contractual risk, and thus determine in advance who is to insure against that risk.

They also make it possible for a contracting party to quote different rates according to the risk borne by him. Thus between businessmen of similar bargaining power exemption clauses are a legitimate device, but limitations on their use have been necessary in contracts involving the public. The main limitations are now contained in the *UNFAIR CONTRACT TERMS ACT 1977*, and in the past were exercised through the doctrine of fundamental breach.

13. *The Unfair Contract Terms Act 1977*

   a. The Act uses two techniques for controlling exemption clauses – some types of clause are stated to be ineffective, whereas others are subject to a test of reasonableness.

   b. The contract and tort provisions of the Act, (with the exception of *S.6*) are limited to liability which arises *in the course of a business*, and the main provisions of the Act are:

   c. *S.2 Exclusion of negligence liability.*

      i. A person cannot by reference to any contract term restrict his liability for death or personal injury resulting from negligence.

      ii. In the case of other loss or damage a person cannot restrict his liability for negligence unless the term is reasonable.

   d. *S.3 Standard term contracts and consumer contracts.* The party who imposes the standard term contract or who deals with the consumer cannot, unless the term is reasonable:

      i. Restrict his liability for his own breach, or

      ii. Claim to be entitled to render substantially different performance, or no performance at all.

   e. *S.5 'Guarantee' of consumer goods.* Where goods are of a type ordinarily supplied for private use or consumption and loss or damage arises because the goods are defective in consumer use and the manufacturer or distributer was negligent, liability for loss or damage cannot be excluded or restricted by reference to a term contained in a 'guarantee' of the goods.

   f. *S.6 Sale of goods.*

      i. *S.12 SALE OF GOODS ACT 1979* cannot be excluded.

      ii. *S.13–15 SALE OF GOODS ACT 1979* cannot be excluded in a consumer sale, but can be excluded in a non-consumer sale if the exemption clause is reasonable.

   g. *S.11 The requirement of reasonableness.* The term must be a fair and reasonable one having regard to all the circumstances which were, or ought reasonably to have been known to or in the contemplation of the parties when the contract was made. The burden of proving reasonableness lies on the person seeking to rely on the clause. In contracts for the sale of goods *Schedule 2 UNFAIR CONTRACT TERMS ACT 1977* lays down guidelines for determining reasonableness:

      i. The strength of the bargaining positions of the parties relative to each other.

      ii. Whether the customer received an inducement (such as a lower price) to agree to the term. If he did, the term is more likely to be reasonable.

      iii. Whether the customer knew or ought reasonably to have known of the existence and extent of the clause (having regard to any trade customs and any previous dealing between the parties).

iv. Where the term excludes or restricts any relevant liability if some condition is not complied with, whether it was reasonable at the time of the contract to expect that compliance with that condition would be practicable.

In *GRANVILLE OIL AND CHEMICALS LTD V DAVIS TURNER & CO LTD (2003)* a contract was entered into for the delivery of paint. The contract was subject to standard terms and conditions which required any legal action be brought within 9 months. The claimant brought a claim for damaged goods more than a year after the 9-month period arguing that the term was void under the *UNFAIR CONTRACT TERMS ACT 1977*. The Court of Appeal held that the 9-month clause was not void under the Act. The parties were both in business, they were of equal bargaining strength and the claimant might have been able to contract on different terms. Moreover, the clause had been brought to the claimant's attention. It was reasonably practicable for the claimant to comply with the clause as goods could have been checked on delivery. The clause would be effective in barring the claim.

Another case demonstrating the application of *Schedule 2 UNFAIR CONTRACT TERMS ACT 1977 (above) is BRITVIC SOFT DRINKS v MESSER UK LTD (2002)*. Here the defendants agreed to supply the claimant with a consignment of carbon dioxide used in the manufacture of drinks. The consignment was contaminated requiring the claimant manufacturer to recall a batch of drinks from customers. The defendant sought to rely on an exclusion clause limiting their liability to the claimant. The Court of Appeal upheld the original court finding that the clause was unreasonable following an application of the *Schedule 2* criteria in *UNFAIR CONTRACT TERMS ACT 1977*. It was accepted that the parties enjoyed equal bargaining status as there were other suppliers of the product which the claimant could have gone to, however, there was no discussion or negotiation of the exclusion clause; it was simply incorporated into the contract under the defendant's standard terms and conditions. The defendant was held liable.

v. Whether the goods were manufactured to the special order of the customer. If they were, the term is again more likely to be reasonable.

A common situation was considered by the House of Lords.

In *SMITH v ERIC BUSH (1989)* P wished to purchase a house. She approached the Abbey National for a mortgage and paid for a survey including a valuation report by the surveyor hired by the Building Society (Eric Bush). In view of her limited resources P did not hire her own surveyor, but relied on the building society's valuation. However, the surveyor had negligently failed to notice that the removal of the chimney breasts had left the chimneys in a dangerous state. A few months after P moved in they collapsed, causing considerable damage. Although P was allowed to see the valuation report, the mortgage application form stated that neither the Abbey National nor the surveyor gave any warranty that the report was accurate, and that it was supplied without responsibility on their part. The House of Lords held that this disclaimer of responsibility was unreasonable in circumstances where the surveyor knows that the borrower will be supplied with a copy of the report and would be likely to rely on it despite the disclaimer. P was successful in her action.

When considering all of the relevant circumstances the question for the court is limited to whether the clause satisfied the requirement of reasonableness *in relation to the particular contract*, not every contract in which it might be used.

In *PHILLIPS PRODUCTS v HYLAND (1984)* Philips hired a JCB, plus driver (Hyland) from a plant hire company. An exclusion clause in the contract stated 'When a driver or operator is supplied by the owner to work the plant, he shall be under the direction and control of the hirer. Such drivers or operators shall for all purposes in connection with their employment in the working of the plant be regarded as their servants.' Hyland nevertheless made it clear to Philips that he would not tolerate interference in the way he operated his machine. He then drove it negligently causing over £3000 of damage to Philips' buildings. It was held that the exclusion clause was not reasonable and the plaintiff hire company were therefore liable for Hyland's negligence.

h. *S.12 The definition of consumer.* A person deals as a consumer if:

    i. He neither makes the contract in the course of a business, nor holds himself out as doing so, and

    ii. The other party does make the contract in the course of a business, and

    iii. The goods are of a type ordinarily supplied for private use or consumption.

    (If the consumer is an individual then, following the *SALE & SUPPLY OF GOODS TO CONSUMERS REGULATIONS 2002*, it is no longer necessary to show that the goods are of a type ordinarily supplied for private use or consumption.)

The person who claims that the other party does not deal as a consumer must show that he does not. Where a business engages in an activity (for example buying a car) that is merely incidental to their business (for example as shipping brokers) that activity will not be 'in the course of the business unless it is an integral part of it, and it will not be an integral part unless it is carried on with a degree of regularity' (*R & B CUSTOMERS BROKERS v UNITED DOMINIONS TRUST (1988)*).

14. *THE UNFAIR TERMS IN CONSUMER CONTRACTS REGULATIONS 1999*

a. These regulations implement an EC directive on unfair contract terms.

b. They apply to terms which have not been individually negotiated in contracts for the sale or supply of goods or services to consumers. The regulations therefore cover the vast majority of consumer contracts.

c. An unfair term is defined as 'Any term which contrary to the requirement of good faith causes a significant imbalance in the parties rights and obligations under the contract to the detriment of the consumer.'

d. When deciding on 'good faith' the court will consider all relevant factors, examples of which may include:

    i. The strength of the bargaining positions of the parties.

    ii. Whether the consumer had an inducement to agree to the term.

    iii. Whether it was a special order of the consumer.

    iv. The extent to which the seller or supplier dealt fairly with the consumer.

e. The regulations give 18 examples of terms which may be regarded as unfair, including:

    i. Excluding or limiting liability of the seller when the consumer dies or is injured, where this results from an act or omission of the seller (the *UNFAIR CONTRACT TERMS ACT 1977* only covers negligent acts or omissions).

    ii.   Excluding or limiting liability where there is incomplete performance by the seller.

    iii.   Making a contract binding on a consumer where the seller can still avoid performing the contract.

f.   Two remedies are available:

    i.   The unfair term can be declared void, leaving the remainder of the contract in operation.

    ii.   An individual, consumer group or Trading Standards Department can complain to the Director General of Fair Trading or other qualifying body who can seek an injunction to prohibit use of the term. Other qualifying bodies are listed as: Director Generals of Gas, Electricity, Water and Telecommunications, the Consumers' Association, and all weights and measures authorities.

g.   The regulations overlap with the *UNFAIR CONTRACT TERMS ACT 1977*. Businesses dealing with consumers will have to have regard to both laws until consolidation takes place.

There are a number of similarities between the *1977 Act* and the *Regulations*, most notable of which is the test of *reasonableness* under the *Act* and *fairness* under the Regulations.

15. *The Requirement of Reasonableness and the End of Fundamental Breach*

a.   It has now become clear that the statutory requirement of reasonableness has replaced the common law rules on fundamental breach. The problem was that some breaches were so serious that they amounted to totally different performance or no performance at all. There used to be a rule that an exemption clause could not apply to such a fundamental breach. In 1967 this was changed by the House of Lords (now the Supreme Court) and it was said that if a clause was sufficiently well constructed it was possible to exclude liability for a fundamental breach. For example:

In *PHOTO PRODUCTIONS v SECURICOR TRANSPORT (1980)* P engaged D to provide a visiting patrol service to their factory at a charge of £8.75p per week. One night an employee of D intentionally started a fire at the factory causing damage of £615 000. D sought to avoid liability by relying on a clause which stated:

'Under no circumstances shall the company (Securicor) be responsible for any injurious act or default by any employee of the company unless such act or default could have been foreseen and avoided by the exercise of due diligence on the part of the company as his employer.'

It was not suggested that D could have foreseen and avoided the act of their employee. However, the Court of Appeal held that there was a fundamental breach to which the exemption clause did not apply. The House of Lords unanimously reversed the decision, holding that as a matter of construction, the words of the exemption clause clearly relieved D from the liability which they would have otherwise incurred.

b.   The case that finally laid to rest the doctrine of fundamental breach was decided by the House of Lords in 1983. It was the first time that the House had had to consider a statutory provision giving power to override an exemption clause.

In *GEORGE MITCHELL v FINNEY LOCK SEEDS (1983)* P, who was a farmer, ordered 30 lb of cabbage seed from D, who were seed merchants. The purchase price was about £200. D's standard term contract limited their liability for the supply of defective goods to replacement or refund of the amount paid by P. P planted the seed over a wide acreage but when the crop came up it was not fit for human consumption but consisted of unusable weeds. P claimed about £61 500 damages and about £30 500 interest. P's arguments were based both on the common law ground of fundamental breach and on the statutory ground of reasonableness. It was held that at common law the exemption clause would have protected D, but the court decided in favour of P, relying exclusively on the statutory ground. Lord Bridge said that fundamental breach had been 'forcibly evicted' from our system. Thus it will no longer be necessary to use this artificial method of analysing contract terms now that it is possible for the court to set aside the term if it does not satisfy the requirement of reasonableness. It is hoped that the application of this test will lead to less uncertainty.

Note: Since the contract in the above case was made before 1/2/78 (when the Unfair Contract Terms Act came into force) the provision which applied was *S.55 of SCHEDULE I* of the *SALE OF GOODS ACT 1979*. This applies to contracts made between 18/5/1973 and 1/2/1978 and it adopts a requirement of reasonableness very similar to the *UNFAIR CONTRACT TERMS ACT*.

SELF TEST QUESTIONS

Self Test Questions No. 13 (for Answers see Appendix 1):

1   Explain the difference between a term of a contract and a mere representation.

2   What is the difference between a *condition* and a *warranty*?

3   'A legally binding contract must be complete in its terms.' What does this mean?

4   What are *standard form* contracts?

5   What is an *implied* term in a contract?

6   Explain the nature and effect of an *exemption/exclusion*.

7   What did the *Unfair Terms in Consumer Contracts Regulations 1999*, do?

8   What is meant be the *requirement of reasonableness* in exemption clauses and the significance of a *fundamental breach*?

16 INVALIDATING FACTORS

Learning Outcomes At the end of this chapter you should be able to:

- State the significance of *mistake* in contract law and identify its various forms.

- Understand the nature, impact and forms of a *misrepresentation* in contract negotiations.

- Explain the effect of *duress, undue influence and illegality* on consent in contract.

These are factors which affect the validity of an otherwise effective contract.

MISTAKE

1. *Introduction*

   a. It is in the interest of business generally that apparent contracts be enforced. Thus most mistakes, for example as to the quality of a product, will not affect the validity of the contract. In **BELL v LEVER BROS LTD (1932)** two directors were removed by the majority shareholder LB Ltd. As there was a period of time left still to run on both directors' 5-year contracts, LB Ltd agreed to pay compensation to the directors for loss of office. It subsequently emerged that past misconduct by the directors could have rendered them liable to dismissal without compensation. LB Ltd sought to recover the money paid by arguing that the agreement to pay them compensation was void for mistake. The House of Lords ruled that both parties believed there was an entitlement to be paid and an obligation to pay (the directors' successfully arguing that they had forgotten about their previous wrongdoings). This was a mistake by LB Ltd as to the *qualities* of the directors and as such was not the kind of mistake that would invalidate a contract. This was further illustrated in *LEAF v INTERNATIONAL GALLERIES (1950)* where both the buyer and seller were mistaken as to the true identity of the artiste of a particular painting. When it was later discovered the court ruled that this was a common mistake as to quality and value of the painting and that this did not affect the validity of the contract. In a more recent case, *GREAT PEACE SHIPPING LTD v TSAVLIRIS SALVAGE INTERNATIONAL LTD (2002)* a contract was entered into to charter a vessel on the understanding, subsequently shown to be incorrect, that the vessel chartered was the nearest one to a particular location. It transpired that other vessels were nearer. The Court of Appeal held that the mistake as to distance was not such as to confound the common assumption of both parties that the vessel hired was sufficiently close to the location to carry out the service for which it had been chartered. The contract was valid and the defendants were liable to pay the hire charges. Following this case a contract will rarely be void for common mistake.

The common law rules on mistake, if applicable, render the contract *void* i.e. of no legal effect; a nullity, but these rules are exercised within narrow limits. In equity the rules have a wider scope, but their effect is less drastic. If a document is signed by mistake special rules apply.

b. It is very important to distinguish a contract which is *void for mistake* from one which is merely *voidable for misrepresentation*. The distinction is of little importance to the parties themselves, since the goods or money can be recovered from the other party to the contract if they are still in his possession. The distinction is, however, very significant if the goods have been sold to a third party. For example, if A 'sells' his car to B and then B resells the car to C, if the contract between A and B was void for mistake, then A can recover the car from C because no title passes under a void contract. C will be able to sue B for breach of the implied condition that he had a right to sell and pass title. However, in a similar situation if the contract between A and B is only voidable for misrepresentation, then provided the sale to C took place before A avoided the contract, C will obtain good title, since 'voidable' means valid until avoided. A would then have to seek a remedy for misrepresentation (innocent, negligent or fraudulent) against B.

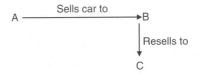

i. If contract between A and B = VOID then A can recover the car from C.

ii. If contract between A and B = VOIDABLE then if the car was sold before A's decision to end the contract, then A cannot recover the car.

It is important to realize in all of these cases that the original misled party sees no benefit in pursuing the wrongdoer, all he or she wants is to get the goods back.

2. *Common Law.* The following types of mistake render a contract void, provided the mistake actually induces the contract i.e. the claimant would not have contracted but for the mistake.

a.   *Mistake as to the existence of the subject matter*

In *GALLOWAY v GALLOWAY (1914)* a man and a woman made a separation agreement, believing that they were married. In fact they were not married because, unknown to them, at the time of their marriage ceremony the man's wife was still alive. The separation agreement was held to be void for mistake because the 'marriage' which was the basis for the agreement was void.

b.   *Mistake as to the possibility of performing the contract*

In *SHEIK BROS v OCHSNER (1957)* a contract was made for the exploitation of sisal grown on a specific plot of land. The contract provided for an average delivery of 50 tons of sisal per month. The contract was held to be void because the land was not capable of producing 50 tons per month.

c.   *Mistake as to the identity of the subject matter*

   i.   For example, A intended to buy product X, but B intended to sell product Y.

   In *RAFFLES v WICHELHAUS (1864)* P agreed to sell to D a consignment of cotton which was to arrive 'ex Peerless from Bombay'. There happened to be two ships called Peerless sailing from Bombay, one in October and one in December. P was thinking of one ship and D of the other. It was held that there was no contract.

   In *SHOGUN FINANCE V HUDSON (2004)* a rogue purchased a vehicle from a garage pretending that he was another person, a Mr Patel. He produced Mr Patel's driving licence and was checked for credit worthiness based upon the assumed identity. When the vehicle was subsequently sold by the rogue to an innocent purchaser, the garage sought to have the vehicle returned claiming the contract was void due to mistake as to identity. The House of Lords (now the Supreme Court) ruled that this was an agreement concluded in writing and that the particulars in the agreement were only capable of applying to Mr Patel, it was the intention of the rogue that the garage should identify Mr Patel as the purchaser. Before entering the agreement the garage checked that Mr Patel existed and that he was worthy of credit. On that basis they decided to contract with him and no-one else. As the agreement was concluded without his authority it was a nullity and the vehicle must therefore, be returned.

   ii.   It is important to be able to distinguish a mistake as to identity from a mistake as to quality.

   In *SMITH v HUGHES (1871)* P was shown a sample of oats by D, and thinking that they were old oats he bought them. They were in fact new oats, and he refused to accept them. It was held that his mistake did not invalidate the contract. The parties were at cross-purposes, but not to such an extent that there was no agreement at all. The mistake was only one of quality, and as such does not operate to render the contract void.

   iii.   A mistake as to quality will only invalidate the contract if it is a mistake as to the fundamental quality by which the thing is identified not if it is a mistake as to one of the various other qualities of the product.

d.   *Mistake as to the identity of the other party*

It is clear that such a mistake cannot be made when parties deal face to face; in such a situation a person can only make a mistake as to the attributes (i.e. the quality) of the other party, and not his identity. An agreement apparently made between X and Y will be void if X can prove:

i.   That at the time of the agreement he regarded the identity of the other party as of importance.

ii.   That he did not intend to contract with Y, but with a different existing person – Z, and

iii. That this fact was known to Y.

In *CUNDY v LINDSAY (1878)* Blenkarn, a rogue trader, wrote to the claimant ordering linen from an address where a highly respected business also resided in the same street. He sought to further disguise his identity through a signature that looked like that of the reputable firm. Goods were duly delivered which were then sold on to a good faith purchaser. The Court held that the contract between the claimant and Blenkarn was void for mistake and therefore title could not pass and the goods must be returned to the claimant.

Contrast *LEWIS v AVERAY (1971)* P advertised his car for sale, and was induced to accept a cheque from a crook who said he was the famous actor Richard Greene. The cheque was dishonoured. P then claimed the car from D who had bought it in good faith from the crook. The claim failed because his contract with the crook was not void for mistake since the presumption that he intended to contract with the person physically before him had not been overcome. P's mistake was as to the credit-worthiness of the other party, and not as to his identity. The contract between P and the crook was voidable for fraud. Voidable, however, means valid until avoided, and P had not avoided by the time the crook sold the car to D. The contract was therefore valid, and the crook was able to pass title to D.

In *KINGS NORTON METAL v EDRIDGE MERRETT (1897)* P received an order for wire from 'Hallam and Co'. The letterhead depicted a large factory and described Hallam and Co as a substantial firm. In fact Hallam and Co did not exist, being merely an alias for a crook named Wallis. P sent the goods to 'Hallam and Co' on credit. Wallis took possession of them and resold them to D. It was held that as Wallis and 'Hallam and Co' were the same person, P had not made a mistake as to identity, but had intended to contract with the writer of the letters. Thus the contract was only voidable for fraud, and since Wallis sold to D before P avoided the contract, D obtained title to the goods.

e.   Mistake as to the terms of the contract of which the other party is aware.

In *HARTOG v COLIN AND SHEILDS (1939)* a seller of hare skins mistakenly offered them at a price 'per pound' instead of 'per piece', there being about three pieces to the pound. The buyer, knowing of the mistake, accepted the offer, and later sued the seller for non-delivery. His action failed since he knew that the seller did not intend to contract on the terms stated.

f.   *Terminology*

Different terminology is often used to describe the various types of mistake.

i.   *Unilateral mistake.* This occurs when one of the parties is mistaken about some fundamental fact and the other party knows or should know this, for example *CUNDY v LINDSAY (1878)*.

ii. *Common mistake.* This occurs when both parties make the same mistake. Usually this will be a mistake as to the existence of the subject matter, for example *GALLO-WAY v GALLOWAY (1914)*. Note that, following *GREAT PEACE SHIPPING v TSAVLIRIS SALVAGE INTERNATIONAL LTD (2002)* (see 1.a. above) contracts will rarely be void for common mistake.

iii. *Mutual mistake.* This occurs when the two parties mean different things. It will normally be a mistake as to the identity of the subject matter of the contract, for example *RAFFLES v WICHELHAUS (1864)*.

3. *Equity* Equity will in limited situations relieve a party from the effects of his mistake where the common law would hold him to the contract. There are two equitable remedies:

a. *Rescission.* The circumstances when this remedy will be granted have never been precisely defined. In general it will only be granted if the party seeking to rescind was not at fault, and provided justice can be done to the other party by imposing conditions.

In *GRIST v BAILEY (1966)* the contract concerned the sale of a house which was occupied by a tenant. Both parties believed that the house was subject to rent control, and they agreed a price of £850. In fact the house was not subject to rent control, and so was worth £2250. The contract for sale at £850 was rescinded in equity, with the condition imposed that the vendor should give the purchaser first option to buy the house at the correct market price.

b. *Rectification.* Where there has been a mistake, not in the actual agreement, but in its reduction into writing, equity will rectify the written document so that it coincides with the true agreement of the parties provided:

i. The terms were clearly agreed between the parties.

ii. The agreement continued unchanged up to the time it was put into writing, and

iii. The writing fails to express the agreement of the parties.

In *WEEDS v BLANEY (1976)* P orally agreed with D to sell him a farmhouse and some land. P's solicitor in error prepared a contract which included further land owned by P. The error was not noticed and the land was transferred to D who became the registered owner. It was held that P was entitled to rectification of the contract and the transfer. However, in *GEORGE WIMPEY UK LTD v VI CONSTRUCTION LTD (2005)* both parties agreed that if property eventually sold above a certain base price, then a commission would be payable on that higher price to Wimpey Ltd. Though agreed, the term was never included in the final written contract. The claimant, Wimpey Ltd, sought a *rectification* of the contract to include the term omitted through mutual mistake. The Court of Appeal, in overruling a lower judgment, held that the claimant needed to show that the defendant had actual knowledge of his mistake, this they had failed to do. The fact that the defendant stood to benefit considerably by the omission of the term (prices had risen considerably) was irrelevant. Additionally, the court thought it relevant that the claimant, Wimpey, were very experienced in these types of contracts whereas the defendant was not.

The three criteria above should now have added a fourth criteria:

iv. The defendant knew of the omission – a mutual mistake – of which the claimant did not have knowledge of until later.

4. *Non Est Factum* (It is not my act)

The general rule concerning signed documents is that a person is bound even if he does not read or understand the document *(L'ESTRANGE v GRAUCOB (1934)*, Chapter 18, Paragraph 11). However, an apparent signed contract will be regarded as void if a party can successfully plead the defence of *non est factum*. Three conditions must be satisfied:

a. The signature must have been induced by fraud.

b. The document must be fundamentally different from that thought to be signed. A mistake as to the contents is not sufficient to allow *non est factum* to be raised.

c. The party seeking to avoid liability must prove that he acted with reasonable care.

In *LEWIS v CLAY (1897)* D was induced to sign two promissory notes by the fraudulent misrepresentation that his signature was required as a witness. The rest of the document apart from the space for the signature was covered by blotting paper, D being told that the documents were of a private nature. It was held that the defence of non est factum applied even though D could not say precisely what type of document he thought he had signed.

Contrast *SAUNDERS v ANGLIA BUILDING SOCIETY (1970)* The original plaintiff (a Mrs Gallie who died before 1970) wanted to help her nephew, Parkin, to raise money on the security of her leasehold house, provided she could continue to live there rent free for the rest of her life. Parkin did not want to raise the loan or become owner of the house himself as he feared this would enable his wife (from whom he was separated) to enforce a claim for maintenance against him. He therefore arranged that his friend – Lee, should raise the money on a mortgage of Gallie's house, and then give the money to him. Before Lee could mortgage the house it had to be transferred to him. An assignment was prepared under which the lease of the house was transferred to Lee for £3000 (a reasonable price was included in the assignment so as not to subsequently arouse the Building Society's suspicions). When Gallie was asked to sign the assignment she did not read it because her glasses were broken, but Lee told her it was a deed of gift to Parkin (who witnessed the document). Lee then raised money by mortgaging the property to The Anglia Building Society, but he did not pay any money to Parkin, nor did he pay the £3000 to Gallie.

It was held that *non est factum* did not apply to Gallie's signature of the assignment, since her mistake was not sufficiently serious. She believed the document would enable Parkin to raise money on the security of the house, and the document was designed to achieve this aim, though by a different method than that contemplated by Gallie. It was also stated that Mrs Gallie's carelessness prevented her from relying on *non est factum*.

MISREPRESENTATION

5. *General Definition* A misrepresentation is an untrue statement of fact which is one of the causes which induces the contract. Note that:

a. It must be a statement of fact. Such a statement may be written, spoken or made by conduct. A good example of a misrepresentation made by conduct is *SPICE GIRLS LTD v APRILLIA WORLD SERVICE BV (2000)*. Here the claimant entered into a contract to promote the Spice Girls, not knowing that one of them – Gerri Halliwell –

was to leave the group. The defendant knew of Gerri Halliwell's intention to leave the group but did not mention this at the time of the contract. The court held that in entering the contract the defendant had through their *conduct* stated that they did not know or had no reasonable grounds to believe that any of the members of the group intended to leave. This was clearly not the case and the contract would be set aside for misrepresentation – *fraudulent misrepresentation.*

i. A *statement of opinion*, for example that the goods represent good value, cannot amount to a misrepresentation unless the maker of the statement is an expert or has special knowledge.

In *BISSETT v WILKINSON (1927)* the vendor of land stated that it would support 2000 sheep. It turned out that this was not the case, but the vendor was not liable because the land had not previously been used for sheep and the purchaser knew this. The statement was therefore held to be one of opinion not fact.

A statement of opinion may by implication involves a statement of fact.

In *SMITH v LAND AND HOUSE PROPERTY CORPORATION (1884)* the vendor of a hotel described it as 'let to Mr Frederick Fleck (a most desirable tenant)'. The tenant was in fact in arrears with his rent. It was held to be statement of fact since the vendor was impliedly stating that he knew the fact that supported his opinion that the tenant was 'desirable'.

ii. A *statement of intention* is not a misrepresentation unless it can be proved that the alleged intention never existed.

In *EDGINGTON v FITZMAURICE (1885)* P was induced to lend money to a company because the directors said they intended to use the money to finance expansion. In fact this intention never existed since the directors needed the money to pay off company debts. It was held that there had been a fraudulent misrepresentation.

iii. A false statement as to the law cannot be a misrepresentation, since everyone is presumed to know the law.

b. Silence is not usually misrepresentation except:

i. When a statement made in the course of negotiations subsequently becomes false and is not corrected, or

ii. When silence distorts a literally true statement.

In *R v KYLSANT (1931)* a company when inviting the public to subscribe for its shares, stated that it had paid a regular dividend throughout the years of the depression. This clearly implied that the company had made a profit during those years. This was not the case since the dividends had been paid out of the accumulated profits of the pre-depression years. The company's silence as to the source of the dividends was held to be a misrepresentation since it distorted the true statement that dividends had been paid. However, in *SYKES v TAYLOR-ROSE (2004)* the seller of a house did not disclose to the buyer that there had been a violent murder at the house with the possibility that body parts might still be hidden there. The court held that the silence did not amount to a misrepresentation.

A case illustrating the situation where a previously made statement becomes later untrue and is not corrected is *FITZROY ROBINSON LTD v MENTMORE*

TOWERS LTD (2009). Here a previously made statement that a named individual in the defendant's employ would act as team leader on a particular project, subsequently proved untrue due to his leaving the employ of the defendant. The court held that this amounted to a misrepresentation – a *fraudulent misrepresentation* – through the failure by the defendant to inform the claimant.

   iii. Where the contract is of utmost good faith (*uberrimae fidei*).

c. The misrepresentation must induce the contract. The plaintiff therefore cannot avoid the contract if:

   i. He knew the statement was false, or

   ii. He would have made the contract despite the misrepresentation, or

   iii. He did not know that there had been a misrepresentation.

In **HORSFALL v THOMAS (1862)** the vendor of a gun concealed a defect in the gun (a misrepresentation by conduct). The buyer purchased the gun without examining it. Therefore the concealing of the defect could not have affected his decision as to whether or not to purchase it. His action therefore failed.

6. *Fraudulent Misrepresentation*

a. *Definition*. A statement which is known to be false, or made without belief in its truth, or recklessly, not caring whether it is true or false.

In **DERRY v PEEK (1889)** a company had a power conferred by a special Act of Parliament to run trams by animal power and with Board of Trade consent by steam or mechanical power. The company invited applications for shares from the public and stated in the prospectus that they had power to run trams by steam power. They had assumed that Board of Trade permission would be granted, but in the event it was not. As a result the directors were sued for fraud. The court formulated the definition of fraud stated above and held that the directors were not liable since they honestly believed their statement to be true.

b. *Remedies*. If the innocent party has suffered loss he may claim damages, based on the tort of deceit. In addition he may:

   i. Refuse to perform the contract, and

   ii. Claim rescission of the contract.

Since fraud makes a contract voidable, the innocent party may choose to affirm the contract.

c. When a contract is voidable, it will generally be valid until the other party is informed of the avoidance. However, where the seller has a right to avoid for fraud he does so if, on discovering the fraud, he takes all reasonable steps to recover the goods.

In **CAR AND UNIVERSAL FINANCE v CALDWELL (1964)** a person was induced by fraud to sell his car to a crook. The crook's cheque was dishonoured, and the crook could not be found. Immediately the cheque was dishonoured the former owner informed the police and the Automobile Association, and asked them to find his car. It was held that since he had done all he could in the circumstances he had successfully avoided the contract. It is clearly vital to avoid a contract induced by fraud as soon as possible. Since fraud makes a contract voidable, (and not void), if the crook sells the goods to a third party before avoidance he passes a good title and the original owner bears the loss. If the crook 'sells' after avoidance he cannot pass title, thus the third party to whom he has 'sold' must bear the loss.

The House of Lords stated in **STANDARD CHARTERED BANK V PARKINSON NATIONAL SHIPPING CORPORATION (2003)** that the maker of a fraudulent misrepresentation cannot raise a defence of contributory negligence.

7. *Innocent Misrepresentation*

a. An innocent misrepresentation is a statement which the maker honestly and reasonably believes to be true. The law on this topic represents an attempt to strike a balance between two innocent parties, the maker of the statement and the person who has been induced to make a contract in reliance on that statement. In such situations the law often becomes very complex. This is true of innocent misrepresentation where the rules originate from three sources, common law, equity and statute.

b. *Remedies.* The innocent party has no right to damages, but may ask the court to grant the equitable remedy of rescission i.e. restoration to the pre-contract state of affairs.

   i. Under *S.1 MISREPRESENTATION ACT 1967* the remedy of rescission is not lost if the representation is later incorporated into the contract.

   ii. Under *S.2(2)* the court has a discretion to award damages in lieu of rescission if it thinks it equitable to do so, for example if the misrepresentation is trivial it may be too drastic to rescind the contract. *S.2(2)* damages may be awarded even if the *S.2(1)* defence of reasonable belief is available (see below) but they may not be awarded in addition to rescission since the section specified 'in lieu of rescission', i.e. instead of rescission.

   iii. As with a fraudulent misrepresentation the innocent party may choose to affirm contract.

8. *Negligent Misrepresentation*

a. A negligent misrepresentation is a false statement made by a person who had no reasonable grounds for believing it to be true.

b. The innocent party has a right to damages for misrepresentation if he has suffered loss. However, if the maker of the statement proves that he had reasonable grounds for believing, and in fact did believe, up to the time the contract was made that the facts represented were true, then he has a defence (*S.2(1) MISREPRESENTATION ACT 1967*).

c. The measure of damages is the same as in a claim for the tort of deceit, i.e. the plaintiff is entitled to be put in the position which he would have been in if the representation had not been made, rather than the position in which he would have been in if the representation had been true. The deceit measure also entitles the plaintiff to recover all losses, whether foreseeable or not, provided they are not otherwise too remote.

In **NAUGHTON v O'CALLAGHAN (1990)** P purchased a racehorse (Fondu) for 26 000 guineas on the basis of a negligent misrepresentation by D as to its pedigree. At the time, if the pedigree had not been misrepresented, it would have been worth about 23 500 guineas. The misrepresentation was discovered 2 years later, during which time Fondu had been raced very unsuccessfully and was worth about £1500. P claimed the difference between the purchase price of 26 000 guineas and £1500, plus training fees and expenses. D claimed the damages were limited to the difference in value at the time of sale i.e. 2500 guineas. Normally the courts would award the difference between the value of the goods as represented and the actual value at the time of sale. However, P succeeded since there were reasons for departing from the usual position i.e.:

i.   P had purchased a completely different animal from that described in the catalogue.

ii.   The fall in value was due to Fondu's lack of success not a general fall in the value of racehorses. It probably would not have occurred if Fondu had had the pedigree described in the catalogue.

iii. The training fees and expenses were losses directly and naturally resulting from the misrepresentation.

iv.   If the misrepresentation had been discovered immediately, Fondu could have been sold for 23 500 guineas in which case damages would have been 2500 guineas.

In *F AND H ENTERTAINMENTS v LEISURE ENTERPRISES (1976)* P purchased the lease of a club premises from D for £23 100 having been told that the rent was £2400 per year, and that no rent review notices had been served. P went into occupation and spent £4000 on re-equipping and preparing the premises for use. The landlords then requested the revised rent of £6500 (valid rent review notices had in fact been served). P vacated the premises and sought rescission and damages. It was held that damages under *S.2(1)* would be awarded and that they would include compensation for expenditure properly and not prematurely incurred, i.e. the £4000. Rescission was also granted.

d.   A negligent misrepresentation may also give rise to the possibility of a negligence action under the principle in *HEDLEY BYRNE v HELLER (1964)* (Chapter 26.4). The rules for measure of damages suggest that, given the choice, a plaintiff would benefit from an action under *S.2(1)* rather than a claim for negligence. If the misrepresentation has been incorporated into the contract, and not the remoteness is an issue, it may also benefit the plaintiff to bring an action under *S.2(1)*, since the remoteness rule in contract limits losses to what may reasonably be supposed to have been in the contemplation of the parties. This is narrower than the negligence test of reasonable foreseeability, which in turn is narrower than the deceit measure described above.

9. *Bars to Rescission* The remedy of rescission will not be available in the following situations:

a.   If the innocent party, with knowledge of his rights, affirms the contract.

In *LONG v LLOYD (1958)* P was induced to buy a lorry from D after hearing representations as to its condition, and a statement that it would do 11 miles to the gallon. P then drove the lorry home from Hampton Court to Sevenoaks. The next Wednesday P drove to Rochester, and during the journey the dynamo ceased to function, an oil leak developed, a crack appeared in one of the wheels, and petrol consumption was 5 miles per gallon. He complained to D who offered to pay half the cost of a new dynamo, and this offer was accepted. The next day the lorry broke down on a journey to Middlesbrough, and P asked for his money back. A subsequent examination by an expert showed that the lorry was unroadworthy. It was held:

i.   That the representations as to the condition of the lorry were innocent.

ii.   The journey to Rochester was not affirmation because P had to have an opportunity to test the vehicle in a working capacity.

    iii. The acceptance of the offer to pay half of the cost of the dynamo, and the subsequent journey to Middlesbrough, did amount to affirmation and therefore rescission could not be granted.

If this case had been heard after 1967 P may have succeeded under *S.2(1) MISREPRESENTATION ACT 1967*. It is unlikely that D could have proved that he had reasonable grounds for believing that the lorry was in good condition.

  b. Lapse of time.

    i. Where the misrepresentation is fraudulent lapse of time does not itself bar rescission because time only begins to run from discovery of the truth.

    ii. Where the misrepresentation is innocent lapse of time may bar rescission.

In *LEAF v INTERNATIONAL GALLERIES (1950)* P was induced to buy a painting by an innocent misrepresentation that it was by John Constable. Five years later he discovered the truth and immediately claimed rescission. He could not therefore have affirmed the contract but his claim was held to be barred by lapse of time.

Two further points of interest were made in Leaf's case. Firstly, the contract was not void for mistake, the mistake being merely as to quality. Secondly, Lord Denning said that a claim to rescind for innocent misrepresentation must be barred when the right to repudiate for breach of condition is barred, i.e. when there is 'acceptance' within the meaning of *S.35 SALE OF GOODS ACT 1893. (Now S.35 SGA 1979.)*

  c. If *restitutio in integrum* is impossible, i.e. if restoration to the pre-contract state of affairs is impossible, because for example a partnership's capital has been converted into shares in a limited company as in *CLARKE v DICKSON (1858)*. A more obvious example of impossibility of restoration is where the subject matter is food which has been eaten. A modern tendency is for the courts to award rescission if the substantial identity of the property remains even though the parties cannot be precisely restored to their pre-contract position, financial adjustments being made if necessary.

  d. The intervention of third party rights. Thus a person cannot rescind an allotment of shares in a company after the company has gone into liquidation, since at this point third party rights intervene because the assets of the company have to be collected to distribute among the company's creditors.

10. *Exempting Liability for Misrepresentation* If a contract purports to take away any liability or remedy for misrepresentation that provision is of no effect unless it satisfies the requirement of reasonableness as defined by *S.11 UNFAIR CONTRACT TERMS ACT 1977*.

11. *Trade Descriptions* Note that the *TRADE DESCRIPTIONS ACT 1968* – now replaced by the *Consumer Protection Unfair Trading Regulations 2008* – which prohibits misdescriptions of goods relates to criminal law, not the law of contract.

DURESS AND UNDUE INFLUENCE

12. *Duress*

  a. This is a common law doctrine, and its effect if proved is that the contract is voidable. It is limited in scope to illegal violence or threats of violence to the person of the contracting party. To threaten a person's property is not duress, but to threaten unlawful imprisonment is duress.

In *CUMMING v INCE (1847)* an old lady was threatened with unlawful confinement in a mental home if she did not transfer certain property rights to one of her relatives. The subsequent transfer was set aside since the threat of unlawful imprisonment amounted to duress.

b.   Duress does not need to be the only factor inducing the contract, as long as it is one of the reasons.

In *BARTON v ARMSTRONG (1976)* there was a dispute between two shareholders in the same company (A and B), including a threat by A to kill B. Later B purchased A's shares on terms that were very favourable to A. The contract was set aside on the grounds of duress, even though there may have been other factors inducing B to sell his shares.

13. *Undue Influence*

a.   In developing this doctrine equity recognized that consent may be affected by influences other than physical ones. Its effect is to make the contract voidable. The burden of proof of undue influence will depend on the *relationship between the parties.*

b.   If there is no special relationship the party seeking to avoid must prove that he was subjected to influence which excluded free consent.

In *WILLIAMS v BAYLEY (1866)* a father agreed to mortgage his property to a bank if the bank would return to him promissory notes on which his son had forged his signature. The bank had hinted at prosecution and 'transportation' of the son if the father did not agree to execute the mortgage. The agreement to execute the mortgage was set aside because undue influence had been proved.

c.   Where a confidential relationship exists between the parties it is for the party in whom confidence is placed to show that undue influence was not used. Examples of such relationships are trustee/beneficiary, solicitor/client, parent/child; however, the presumption applies whenever the relationship is such that one of them is by reason of the confidence placed in him able to take unfair advantage of the other.

In *TATE v WILLIAMSON (1866)* D became financial adviser to an extravagant Oxford undergraduate. The undergraduate sold his estate to D for about half its value, and died of alcoholism at the age of 24. His executors were successful in having the sale of the estate set aside.

In *LLOYDS BANK v BUNDY (1974)* an elderly farmer, who was inexperienced in business matters, mortgaged his property to the bank to guarantee his son's business overdraft. The Court of Appeal set aside the guarantee. The farmer had placed himself in the hands of the bank and had looked to the assistant bank manager for advice. It was in the bank's interest that the farmer provided the guarantee. The Court held that the *presumption of undue influence* applied. The bank had failed to rebut the presumption since the farmer had not been advised to seek independent advice.

d.   A transaction will not be set aside on the ground of undue influence unless it can be shown that the transaction is to the manifest disadvantage of the person subjected to undue influence. Also a presumption of undue influence will not arise merely because a confidential relationship exists, provided the person in whom confidence is placed keeps within the boundaries of a normal business relationship.

In *NATIONAL WESTMINSTER BANK v MORGAN (1985)* a wife (W) signed a re-mortgage of the family home (owned jointly with her husband, H) in favour of the bank to prevent the original mortgagee from continuing with proceedings to repossess the home. The bank manager told her in good faith but incorrectly, that the mortgage only secured liability in respect of the home. In fact it covered all H's debts to the bank. W signed the mortgage at home in the presence of the manager, and without taking independent advice. H and W fell into arrears with the payments and soon afterwards H died. At the time of his death nothing was owed to the bank in respect of H's business liabilities. The bank sought possession but W contended that she had only signed the mortgage because of undue influence from the bank and therefore it should be set aside. The House of Lords (now the Supreme Court) held, reversing the Court of Appeal, that the manager had not crossed the line between explaining an ordinary business transaction and entering into a relationship in which he had a dominant influence, furthermore the transaction was not unfair to W, therefore the bank was not under a duty to ensure that W took independent advice. The order for possession was granted. This case makes *LLOYDS BANK v BUNDY (1974)* exceptional and normally the presumption of undue influence will only apply to the banker/customer relationship where it can be shown that there is some additional circumstance putting the bank in a special relationship with a customer whereby they acquire a dominant influence in the relationship.

e. Undue influence through third parties. In *BARCLAYS BANK v O'BRIEN (1993)* a husband persuaded his wife to agree to a mortgage on their house, for what he told her was £60 000 for 3 weeks, in order to secure further funds from the bank for his business of which his wife had no ownership. In fact there was no limit on the mortgage in terms of its size and duration. Employees at the bank had not followed their head office instructions that both parties should be made fully aware of the details of the mortgage. The House of Lords (now the Supreme Court) held that the wife had no access to independent legal advice, and she had suffered undue influence in agreeing to the mortgage. The bank was aware of the possibility of abuse and therefore the mortgage contract was deemed voidable. Following the case banks have become very careful in advising customers of the consequences of any contract and the importance of seeking independent legal advice. Note: advice from a customer's solicitors would be effective in this regard – *ROYAL BANK OF SCOTLAND v ETRIDGE (2001)*.

f. Where there is a commercial relationship the courts will recognize the existence of economic duress as part of the concept of undue influence.

In *THE ATLANTIC BARON (1979)* the parties reached agreement on the purchase price to be paid for a ship. There was then a currency devaluation and as a result the vendor claimed a 10% increase in price. The purchaser refused to pay. The vendor then stated that if the extra was not paid he would terminate the contract and amicable business relations would not continue. Due to this threat the purchaser agreed to the increase in price. It was later held that the threat to terminate the contract and discontinue amicable business relations amounted to undue influence. The contract was therefore voidable.

In *ATLAS EXPRESS v KAFCO (IMPORTERS AND EXPORTERS) (1989)* D made a contract with Woolworths for the delivery of its goods to about 800 Woolworths stores. D then made a contract with P, a well known company of forwarders, for carriage of the goods. P later decided that the carriage charge was too low and presented D with a revised invoice showing higher carriage charges. They also refused to accept any goods for delivery unless invoice showing the higher charges was signed.

D protested the increase, but since they were committed to Woolworths (who would probably withdraw their business if the goods were not delivered) they signed the invoice. They subsequently refused to pay the increased rate of charges. When sued by P they pleaded economic duress.

This defence was accepted by the court. It was also held that P had provided no consideration for the second agreement. Contrast this with *WILLIAMS v ROFFEY (1990)* Chapter 12.17.c.

ILLEGALITY

14. *Introduction* The law will clearly refuse to give effect to a contract if it involves the commission of a legal wrong, or if it is invalidated by statute. Also classed as illegal contracts are contracts which do not involve the commission of a crime or tort, but which are not enforced by the courts because they are contrary to public policy. The most important of these are contracts in unreasonable restraint of trade.

15. *Classification* There are many different ways to approach the classification of illegal contracts. For convenience the following categories will be used:

   a. Contracts involving the commission of a legal wrong.

   b. Contracts illegal by statute.

   c. Contracts contrary to public policy.

16. *Contracts Involving the Commission of a Legal Wrong* The following are examples only and not a complete list:

   a. Where the object is to commit a crime or a civil wrong as in *NAPIER v NATIONAL BUSINESS AGENCY (1951)*, where the contract was drawn up so as to deceive the Inland Revenue.

   b. A contract to pay money on the commission of an unlawful act.

17. *Contracts Illegal by Statute* For example:

   a. *Wagering/gambling contracts*

   The **GAMBLING ACT 2005** repealed previous law rendering such contracts null and void, now such contracts are enforceable.

   b. *Restrictive trade agreements*

   These are agreements where producers or suppliers restrict the manufacture, supply or distribution of goods by, for example, fixing a minimum selling price for goods or regulating the supply of goods. The *RESTRICTIVE TRADE PRACTICES ACT 1976* does not make such agreements automatically void, but provides machinery whereby their validity is tested. (19.c below.)

   c. *Statutes in general*

   If one party in performing a contract does an act, prohibited by statute, the act only may be illegal, or the whole contract may be illegal. It depends on whether or not the statute was intended to prohibit the whole contract.

In *ARCHBOLDS v SPANGLETT (1961)* D contracted to carry whisky belonging to P in a van which was not licensed to carry goods which did not belong to him. In carrying the whisky D therefore committed a statutory offence. The whisky was stolen on the journey and P sued for damages. D pleaded the illegality for his defence. The Court of Appeal rejected this defence because:

i.   The Act in question did not prohibit the contract expressly or by implication, and

ii.   P did not know that D did not have the correct licence.

18. *Contracts in Contravention of Public Policy* For example:

a.   *Contracts promoting sexual immorality*

In *PEARCE v BROOKS (1866)* a contract to hire out a carriage to a prostitute for the purposes of her profession was held to be illegal.

b.   Contracts which detract from the institution of marriage. For example:

i.   Marriage brokerage contracts.

ii.   Contracts in restraint of marriage.

iii. Contracts for the future separation of husband and wife.

c.   Sales of offices and honours.

In *PARKINSON v COLLEGE OF AMBULANCE (1925)* a contract to obtain a knighthood was held to be illegal since it could lead to corruption and was 'derogatory to the dignity of the Sovereign'. It has since been made a criminal offence to make such a contract.

d.   Contracts made with an enemy in wartime.

e.   Contracts which involve doing an illegal act in a friendly foreign country.

In *FOSTER v DRISCOLL (1929)* a contract was made to smuggle whisky into the USA during the period when the sale of liquor in the USA was forbidden. This contract was held to be illegal.

f.   Contracts in unreasonable restraint of trade (see below).

19. *Restraint of Trade* A contract in restraint of trade is one which restricts a person from freely exercising his trade or profession. Such contracts are on the face of it, illegal. However, some types of restraint can be justified if they are reasonable so far as the parties are concerned, and provided they are not contrary to public interest. When assessing the validity of contracts in restraint of trade the courts have had to balance the desire to allow complete freedom to contract with the fact that most restraints (especially restrictive trade practices) are contrary to public interest because they restrict the choice or bargaining power of the public. There are four types of contract in restraint of trade which may be held to be valid depending on the circumstances:

a.   *Restraints imposed on ex-employees*

i.   If the restraint is to be reasonable between the parties it must be no wider than is necessary to protect the promisee's trade secrets or business connections. Therefore a restraint imposed on an employee who has no knowledge of his employer's secrets or influence over his customers will be illegal, as it would be an attempt to prevent competition. However, if trade secrets and business connections are legitimately protected, the fact that the restraint incidentally reduces the ex-employee's power to compete does not invalidate it.

ii.   The court will also consider any time limits imposed by the restraint and/or the area it covers.

In *MASON v PROVIDENT CLOTHING (1913)* a canvasser employed to sell clothes in Islington covenanted not to enter into similar business within 25 miles of London for 3 years. The restraint was held to be void because the area of the restraint was about 1000 times as large as the area in which he had been employed.

In *FITCH v DEWES (1921)* a lifelong restraint on a solicitor's managing clerk not to practise within 7 miles was upheld. In contrast to the previous case, the main objection concerned the duration of the restraint rather than the area covered. However, a solicitor's business is one to which clients are likely to resort for a long time, thus the lifetime restraint was not unreasonable. If the business to be protected is of a more fluctuating nature, long restraints will not be upheld.

iii.   The court may grant judgement for a person against an association of employers who do not have a contractual relationship with the person concerned, but whose rules place an unjustified restraint on his liberty of employment.

In *GREIG v INSOLE (1978)* the Test and County Cricket Board sought to ban World Series cricketers from Test and County cricket by means of a change of their rules. The change of rules was held to be *ultra vires* since it was an unreasonable restraint of trade.

b.   *Restraints imposed on the vendor of a business*

The restraint will only be effective if:

i.   There is a genuine sale of the goodwill of the business.

In *VANCOUVER MALT AND SAKE BREWING CO v VANCOUVER BREWERIES (1934)* a company which was licensed to brew beer, but which did not in fact brew any, agreed to sell its business, and to refrain from manufacturing beer for 15 years. Since the company was not actually brewing beer the purchaser could only have paid for the tangible assets, because there were no intangible assets (i.e. goodwill) to sell. The purchaser had not therefore bought the promise not to brew beer, and so he could not enforce it.

ii.   The restraint must be no more than is necessary to protect the particular business bought by the purchaser. In assessing the reasonableness of the restraint the area covered, the duration of the restraint, and the type of business are again important. However, it is possible even for a worldwide restraint to be upheld.

In *NORDENFELT v MAXIM NORDENFELT (1894)* the owner of an armaments business sold it to a company and covenanted not to carry on a similar business for 25 years except on behalf of the company. The covenant was held to be valid although it prevented competition anywhere in the world.

c.   *Agreements between traders by which prices or output are regulated*

i.   Such agreements were usually valid at common law, since they were generally made between persons of equal bargaining power, and were of benefit to both parties.

They were, however, often contrary to the public interest. Parliament has therefore passed several Acts to protect the consumer.

ii.   The *RESTRICTIVE TRADE PRACTICES ACT 1976* requires certain types of restrictive trading agreements to be registered with the Director General of Fair Trading. After registration the agreement is placed on a register open to public inspection and brought before the Restrictive Practices Court to determine whether the restriction is contrary to the public interest. If it is then the offending provisions are void. Failure to register a registrable agreement also renders the restrictions in it void. Any restriction is presumed to be contrary to the public interest unless it falls within one or more of eight 'gateways' referred to in the Act, for example the agreement benefits the public because it reduces the risk of injury, or the agreement maintains export trade.

iii. The *RESALE PRICES ACT 1976* provides that if an agreement between a supplier and a dealer seeks to establish a minimum price to be charged by the dealer such a provision will be void. However, there is a power for the Restrictive Practices Court to grant exemption in certain cases.

d. *Solus agreements*

This is the name given to a contract by which a trader agrees to restrict his orders to one supplier. A solus agreement may be part of a mortgage or lease. The duration of the restraint is the most important factor in assessing the reasonableness, and thus the legality of these agreements.

In *ESSO PETROLEUM v HARPER'S GARAGE (1967)* D, who owned two garages, entered into solus agreements with P in respect of each garage. He agreed only to sell petrol supplied by P, to keep the garage open at all reasonable times, and not to sell the garage without ensuring that the purchaser entered into a similar agreement with P. One solus agreement was for a period of 4½ years, and the other (which was contained in a mortgage of his land to P) was for 21 years. The House of Lords held that the 4½-year agreement was valid, but that the 21-year agreement was invalid since it was of unreasonable duration, and was contrary to the public interest. In addition, the obligation to sell only to a purchaser who was willing to enter into a similar solus agreement made the garage unsaleable.

In *PETROFINA v MARTIN (1965)* Martin's agreement with Petrofina was almost identical to Harper's agreement with Esso. In this case, however, the duration of the restraint was 12 years. D broke the agreement by selling other makes of petrol, and P sought to enforce it by means of an injunction preventing D from doing this. It was held that the restraint was invalid because it was of unreasonable duration.

20. *Consequences of Illegality*

a. *Contracts illegal as formed*, i.e. the contract is incapable of lawful performance, or is intended to be performed illegally as in *PEARCE v BROOKS (1866)*. Such contracts are void and unenforceable. Therefore money paid or property handed over usually cannot be recovered.

b. *Contracts illegal as performed*, i.e. legal at the outset, but later used for an illegal purpose.

i.   The guilty party has no remedies.

In *COWAN v MILBOURN (1867)* D agreed to let rooms to P. He later discovered that P was going to use the rooms to give blasphemous lectures, which was an illegal purpose. D therefore refused to carry out the contract. P failed in his claim for possession since he was the guilty party.

ii.   The innocent party has his normal contractual remedies, except in respect of anything done by him after he learns of the illegal purpose.

c.   *Contracts in contravention of public policy.* Many such contracts, for example contracts in restraint of trade may not fall simply into the categories specified above, but will contain many different promises. These contracts will not be wholly void, but void in so far as public policy is contravened. The court may therefore sever the illegal part of the contract, leaving the remainder valid provided:

i.   The void promise is not substantially the whole consideration given by the party making it.

ii.   The contract can be construed as severable without destroying the main substance of what was agreed.

In *LOUND v GRIMWADE (1888)* D, who had committed a fraud making him both criminally and civilly liable, promised to pay P £3000 if P promised not to take 'any legal proceedings' in respect of the fraud. P's claim for the £3000 failed as a substantial part of the consideration for the promise to pay it was his own illegal promise to stifle a criminal prosecution.

In *GOLDSOLL v GOLDMAN (1915)* D sold his business in imitation jewellery to P, and agreed that he would not for 2 years deal in real or imitation jewellery in the UK or specified foreign countries. The restriction was held to be too wide in area, since D had never traded abroad, and in respect of subject matter since he had hardly ever dealt in real jewellery. It was, however, held that the references to foreign countries and real jewellery could be severed, so that D could be restrained from dealing in imitation jewellery in the UK for 2 years.

SELF TEST QUESTIONS

Self Test Questions No. 14 (for Answers see Appendix 1):

1   What effect will a *mistake* by either party have on a contract?

2   How does the common law define *mistake*?

3   How does equity play a role in this area of law?

4   What is a *misrepresentation* and what are its various forms?

5   What effect will *duress* or *undue influence* have on a contract?

6   What are the various forms of *illegality* in contract law and what are its consequences?

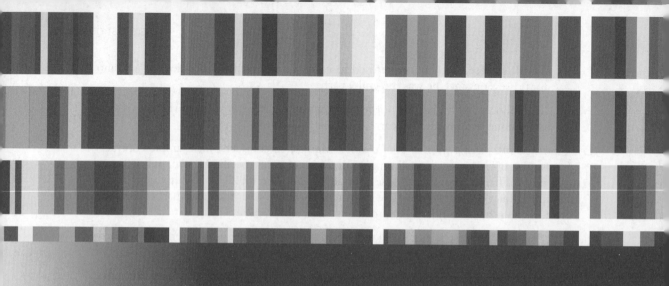

17 DISCHARGE OF CONTRACTS

Learning Outcomes At the end of this chapter you should be able to:

- Explain the rules governing when a contract may be said to have ended.
- Understand the right of consumers to cancel under statute.

1. There are four ways by which the rights and obligations of the parties may come to an end, namely performance, agreement, frustration and breach.

PERFORMANCE

2. *General Rule*

a. A person who performs a contract in accordance with its terms is discharged from any further obligations.

b. If a person's obligation is to pay money, exactly the right amount of cash must be tendered. For example, a contract will not be discharged by offering a £20 note in settlement of a £10 debt, because it is not reasonable to compel the other party to provide change. Of course if the creditor provides change without any objection the contract will be discharged. If a debtor pays by cheque, he will not be discharged until the cheque is honoured by his bank.

c. If a person's obligation is to deliver goods the goods must be tendered at a reasonable hour, not, for example in the middle of the night. The goods must also comply exactly with the contract terms. If the seller tenders too few goods, too many goods or the right amount of goods mixed with other goods, the buyer may reject all of them because performance is not exact. The same applies if the goods are not packed in accordance with the contract.

In *RE MOORE AND LANDAUER (1921)* a supplier of tinned fruit agreed to supply the goods in cases containing 30 tins each. When he delivered the goods about one half were packed in cases of 24 tins each. The correct total amount of tins were delivered, and the market value of the goods supplied was unaffected, however, there was a breach of contract *(S.13(1) SALE OF GOODS ACT 1893)* and this entitled the buyer to reject the whole consignment.

d. Many contracts state the order in which parties must perform their obligations. For example, if Fred agrees to work for Abdul for £300 per week, payable in arrears, clearly Abdul need not pay Fred until Fred has done the weeks work.

3. *Exceptions* There are six exceptions to this rule:

a. *Severable contracts.* Where a contract may be divided into several parts, payments for parts that have been completed can be claimed. Whether a contract is severable or not depends on the intention of the parties. In the absence of evidence as to intention the courts are reluctant to construe the contract so as to require complete performance before any payment becomes due.

In *ROBERTS v HAVELOCK (1832)* P agreed to repair a ship. The contract did not state when payment was to be made. It was held that P was not bound to complete the repairs before claiming some payment.

b. *Acceptance of part performance.* Where A has accepted the partial performance of B, having an option to reject, a promise to pay is implied and a *quantum meruit* may be claimed by B. A *quantum meruit* action is a claim for a percentage of the contract price in direct proportion to the percentage of work done.

In *SUMPTER v HEDGES (1898)* P agreed to build a house for D for £565. He partially erected the building, doing work to the value of £333. He then stopped the job because he ran out of funds. D, using P's materials that had been left on the site, finished the job himself. P claimed £333 for work done plus the value of his materials used by D. He failed in his claim for the £333 because although D had 'accepted' P's part performance D had no option to reject. It is impossible to reject a half-built house since the status quo cannot be restored. P, however, obtained judgement in respect of his materials that D had used to complete the house.

c. *Prevention of performance.* Where one party is prevented by the other from completely performing the contract he may bring a *quantum meruit* action to claim for the work done (Chapter 21.9).

In *PLANCHE v COLBURN (1831)* P agreed to write a book on costume and armour which was to appear in serial form in D's periodical. P was to be paid £100 on completion. After P had done some research, and written some of the book, but before he had completed it, D stopped publishing the periodical. It was held that P had been wrongfully prevented from performing the contract, and he was entitled to a *quantum meruit*.

d. *Substantial performance*. Where a contract has been substantially performed an action lies for the contract price less a reduction for the deficiencies. This exception only applies when the defect relates to the quality of performance. If the defect concerns quantity, for example of goods supplied, the general rule applies.

In *HOENIG v ISAACS (1952)* P agreed to decorate and furnish D's flat for £750. The furniture had several defects which could have been made good for £55. D argued that P was only entitled to reasonable remuneration for work done under the contract. The court, however, held that P was entitled to the full contract rate, less the cost of making the defects good, since he had substantially performed the contract.

Contrast *BOLTON v MAHADEVA (1972)* a plumber agreed to install a central heating system for £560. His work was defective in that the system did not heat adequately and it gave off fumes. The defects cost £174 to repair. The plumber failed in his action to recover the price less a reduction of £174, since he could not be said to have substantially performed the contract. He therefore recovered nothing and the defendant got a £560 heating system for £174. The decision may seem unfair. However, the court must draw the line so as not to encourage bad workmanship. It would also be unfair to allow every workman who did not complete a job to be paid pro rata for work done.

e. Where the *LAW REFORM (FRUSTRATED CONTRACTS) ACT 1943* applies (see below).

f. *Time of performance*. At common law a party who failed to perform his obligations within a given time was in breach of contract. The equitable rule, which now prevails, is that time is only of the essence of the contract if:

i. The parties expressly state, or if

ii. A party who has been guilty of undue delay is notified by the other party that unless he performs within a reasonable time, the contract will be regarded as broken.

In *RICKARDS v OPPENHEIM (1950)* a contract for the sale of a car provided for delivery on March 20. The car was not delivered on that date but the buyer continued to press for delivery. On June 29 he told the seller he must have the car by July 25 at the latest. It was held that the buyer could not have refused delivery merely because the original date had not been met, but he could do so on giving the seller a reasonable time to deliver. Here the notice did give a reasonable time, so the buyer was justified in refusing delivery after July 25.

4. *Tender of Performance*

a. Where an obligation under a contract is to deliver goods or render services, and those goods or services are offered but declined by the other contracting party, then such a refusal discharges the party tendering from further obligation and entitles him or her to sue for damages for breach.

b. Where money is tendered it must be 'legal tender' and it must be the exact sum. If such a tender is refused it does not release the debtor from his obligation to pay, but if he is sued he may pay the money into court, and the creditor will have to pay the costs of the action.

c. If the debtor sends money in the post and it is lost he will have to pay again unless:

i. The mode of delivery was requested by the creditor, and

ii. The debtor took reasonable care.

d. *Appropriation of payments.* When a debtor makes a payment to his creditor which is insufficient to discharge all amounts outstanding, the payment is appropriated as follows:

   i.   The debtor may tell the creditor which debt or debts should be discharged by the payment.

   ii. If the debtor does not do this then the creditor may appropriate the payments to debts as he chooses, including statute-barred debts.

   iii. If the debtor pays the exact amount of a particular debt, it is presumed that the payment is in discharge of the debt of that amount.

   iv. If there is a current account it is presumed that the payments are appropriated to the oldest debts first.

AGREEMENT

5. The basic rule is that an agreement to discharge a contract is binding only if it is by deed, or if it is supported by consideration. It is not necessary for this type of agreement to be reached by means of an offer from one party which is accepted by the other. The legal position depends on whether the discharge is bilateral or unilateral.

6. ***Bilateral Discharge*** i.e. The contract is executory or partly executory on both sides (both parties have obligations outstanding).

   a. The consideration requirement is automatically present since both parties will surrender something of value, i.e. the right to insist on the other party's performance.

   b. Cases of waiver, i.e. forbearance, for example of the right to insist on performance at the agreed time, fall within the principle of equitable estoppel established in ***CENTRAL LONDON PROPERTY TRUST v HIGH TREES HOUSE (1947)***. Therefore a voluntary concession granted by one party, upon which the other has acted, remains effective (i.e. binding on the promisor) until it is made clear by reasonable notice that the strict obligations of the contract are to be restored. Note also ***WILLIAMS v ROFFEY (1990)*** (Chapter 15.12).

7. ***Unilateral Discharge*** i.e. Only one party has rights to surrender.

   a. Where one party has completely performed his side of the contract, i.e. it is wholly executed on one side, any release by him of the other party must be by deed or supported by fresh consideration.

   b. Where there is a release supported by fresh consideration there is said to be 'accord' and 'satisfaction'.

   i.   The accord is the agreement by which the obligation is discharged.

   ii. The satisfaction is the consideration which makes the agreement effective.

   iii. The satisfaction may be executory.

8. There are two further ways in which a contract may be discharged by agreement.

   a. *Novation.* For example, A owes B £100 and B owes C £100. A agrees to pay C, if C will release B from his obligation to pay him. All three parties must agree to the arrangement.

b. *Condition subsequent.* Sometimes a clause in a contract will provide for its discharge if a particular event occurs in the future, i.e. subsequent to the formation of the contract.

FRUSTRATION

9. *The Basis of the Doctrine*

a. The general rule is that if a person contracts to do something he is not discharged if performance proves to be impossible.

In *PARADINE v JANE (1647)* a tenant who was sued for rent pleaded that he had been dispossessed of the land for the last 3 years by the King's enemies. His plea failed. It was said:

'When a party by his own contract creates a duty or charge upon himself, he is bound to make it good, notwithstanding any accident by inevitable necessity, because he might have provided against it by his contract.'

b. This severe rule is mitigated by the doctrine of frustration, which, if it applies, automatically discharges the contract.

c. In general if an event is to frustrate a contract it must be:

i. Not contemplated by the parties when the contract was formed.

ii. One which makes the contract fundamentally different from the original contract.

iii. One for which neither party was responsible.

iv. One which results in a situation to which the parties did not wish originally to be bound.

10. *The Application of the Doctrine* Frustration occurs:

a. If the whole basis of the contract is the continued existence of a specific thing which is destroyed.

In *TAYLOR v CALDWELL (1863)* D contracted to let a music hall to P for 4 days. Before the first day the music hall was accidentally burnt down. P claimed damages, but it was held that D was discharged from his obligation when the music hall burned down. The contract was frustrated.

b. If either party to a contract of personal service dies, becomes seriously ill or is called up for military service.

In *CONDOR v BARRON KNIGHTS (1966)* P was the drummer in a pop group. Owing to illness he was forbidden by his doctor from performing more than a few nights per week. Since the nature of the work required him to be present 7 nights a week the contract was held to be frustrated.

c. If the whole basis of the contract is the occurrence of an event which does not occur.

In *KRELL v HENRY (1903)* D hired a flat in Pall Mall for the purpose of viewing the coronation procession of Edward VII, although this was not expressly stated in the contract. He paid £25 at the time of the agreement and was to pay a further £50 2 days before the procession was to take place. Before the £50 had been paid the procession was cancelled due to the illness of the King. The contract was held to be frustrated. Performance was not physically impossible, but the court said that frustration was not limited to such cases but included 'the cessation or non-existence of an express condition or state of things going to the root of the contract, and essential to its performance'. P's claim for the balance of £50 therefore failed, as did D's counter-claim for return of the £25 already paid. D's claim would now be subject to the *LAW REFORM (FRUSTRATED CONTRACTS) ACT 1943*.

Contrast *HERNE BAY STEAMBOAT CO v HUTTON (1903)* a boat was hired 'for the purpose of viewing the naval review and for a day's cruise round the fleet'. The review was to form part of Edward VII's coronation celebrations, but it was cancelled due to his illness. The fleet was, however, still assembled. The contract was not frustrated, since it was construed merely as a contract for the hire of a boat, which could still be performed even when one of the motives of the hirer was defeated.

The above two cases are very difficult to reconcile. A clue may be found in a passage in one of the judgements from Krell v Henry. It was stated that a contract for the hire of a cab to go to Epsom on Derby day would not be frustrated if the Derby was cancelled. The contract would be construed as one to get the passenger to Epsom and not the Derby. In Krell v Henry the contract was not construed as one merely to provide a flat since it was extremely unusual for flats to be let by the day for very high rents. Contracts to carry passengers to Epsom are, however, often made on days other than Derby days.

d.   If the government prohibits performance of the contract for so long that to maintain it would impose on the parties fundamentally different obligations from those bargained for. All the circumstances are relevant, for example both the duration of the contract and the duration of the interruption.

In *TAMPLIN STEAMSHIP CO v ANGLO-MEXICAN PETROL (1916)* a ship was requisitioned by the government for use as a troopship. The charter party under which the ship was hired was for 5 years, and there were 19 months left to run. The owners claimed that the contract was frustrated so that they, and not the hirers, would obtain the government compensation (which exceeded what they would receive under the charter party). It was held that the contract was not frustrated since there may have been months during the remaining period during which the ship would be available, and because the charterers were still prepared to pay the agreed price.

e.   If the performance of the main object of the contract subsequently becomes illegal.

In *BAILY v DE CRESPIGNY (1869)* a landlord covenanted that neither he nor his successors in title would permit building on a paddock which adjoined the land let. The paddock was then compulsorily acquired for a railway, and a station was built. It was held that the landlord was not liable for breach of the covenant because it was impossible for him to secure performance of it.

11. *The Limits to the Doctrine*

a.   A contract is not frustrated if it becomes unexpectedly more expensive or burdensome to one of the parties. If the contract is to be discharged performance must become 'radically different'.

In *DAVIS CONTRACTORS v FAREHAM UDC (1956)* P agreed to build 78 houses at a price of £94 000 in 8 months. Labour shortages caused the work to take 22 months at a cost to P of £115 000. P wished to claim that the contract was frustrated so that they could then claim for their work on a *quantum meruit*. Lord Radcliffe, however, said that hardship, material loss or inconvenience did not amount to frustration, the obligation must change such that the thing undertaken would, if performed, be a different thing from that contracted for.

b.   A party cannot rely on a self-induced frustration, i.e. frustration due to his own conduct.

   i.   The doctrine of frustration clearly does not protect a person whose own breach is actually the frustrating event.

   In *THE EUGENIA (1964)* a charterer in breach of contract ordered a ship into a war zone. The ship was detained. It was held that the charterer could not rely on the detention as a ground for frustration.

   ii.   Deliberate failure to perform a condition precedent may not amount to a self-induced frustration. In each case the position must be determined in accordance with the proper construction of the contract.

   In *GYLLEHAMMER v SOURBRODOGRADEVNA INDUSTRILA (1989)* the parties had an outline agreement for the construction of a bulk carrier. The contract was subject to several conditions precedent (i.e. conditions that had to be complied with before the contract could be regarded as valid). One of these provided that the contract would be void if the shipbuilders did not obtain bank performance guarantees. When it appeared that a change in economic climate would render the building uneconomic, the shipbuilders did not seek the relevant guarantees. They then argued that their absence rendered the contract void. The purchasers claimed that it was not open to the other party to frustrate the inception of a contract by failing to take steps to allow conditions precedent to be fulfilled. The court held that this was not the case. It was clear that there would be no contract in the absence of bank guarantees and that their absence could be pleaded by the shipbuilders, whatever the reason for that absence.

   iii.   It is probable that negligence prevents a party claiming frustration. Thus if the fire in *TAYLOR v CALDWELL (1863)* had been started due to the defendant's negligence their plea of frustration would have failed.

c.   Frustration will not apply where the parties have expressly provided for a contingency which has occurred. It is a means by which risk is allocated, and loss apportioned in circumstances which neither party has foreseen.

12. *The Effect of Frustration*

a.   The contract is discharged automatically as to the future, but it is not made void from the beginning.

b.   At common law the loss lay where it fell, i.e. money paid before the frustration could not be recovered *(KRELL v HENRY (1903))* and money payable before the frustration remained payable, unless there was a total failure of consideration.

In *FIBROSA v FAIRBAIRN (1942)* a purchaser of machinery for £4800 paid £1000 on placing the order. The machinery was to be delivered in Poland. Shortly after the contract was made war broke out and Poland was occupied by Germany. It was therefore impossible to deliver the machinery. The plaintiff succeeded in his action to recover the £1000 since he had received absolutely nothing in return for his £1000, i.e. there was a total failure of consideration.

c. The position is now governed by the *LAW REFORM (FRUSTRATED CON-TRACTS) ACT 1943* whereby:

    i. Money paid before the frustrating event is recoverable and money payable before the frustrating event ceases to be payable, but if one party has incurred expenses the court may allow him to retain or be paid an amount not exceeding the amount of the expenses.

    ii. If one party has obtained a valuable benefit (other than money) because of something done by the other party in performance of the contract, he can be ordered to pay a just sum for it, not exceeding the amount of the benefit.

BREACH

13. *Definition* Breach occurs:

a. If a party fails to perform one of his obligations under a contract, for example he does not perform on the agreed date, or he delivers goods of inferior quality, or

b. If a party, before the date fixed for performance, indicates that he will not perform on the agreed date. This is an anticipatory breach.

14. *Effect of Breach* Breach does not automatically discharge the contract.

a. Breach of warranty only entitles the innocent party to damages.

b. Breach of condition entitles the innocent party to damages, and gives him an option to treat the contract as subsisting or discharged.

15. *Affirmation of the Breach*

a. If the innocent party elects to treat the contract as still subsisting, and can complete his side without the co-operation of the other, he is entitled to do so, and claim the whole sum due under the contract.

In **WHITE AND CARTER (COUNCILS) v MCGREGOR (1961)** P agreed to advertise D's business for 3 years on plates attached to litterbins. D repudiated the contract on the same day that it was made. P nevertheless manufactured and displayed the plates as originally agreed, and claimed the full amount due under the contract. A majority of the House of Lords upheld the claim, their reason being that a repudiation does not, of itself, bring the contract to an end. Its effect is to give the innocent party a choice of whether or not to determine the contract. If he chooses to affirm the contract it remains in full effect.

b. Affirmation does not of itself exclude a finding of reasonableness in relation to any exemption clause *S.9(2) UNFAIR CONTRACT TERMS ACT 1977*. This prevents the court being forced into a situation where it would feel compelled to find an exemption clause unreasonable, so as not to exclude an innocent party's remedies when he had affirmed a contract that he could have terminated.

16. *Termination*

a. If the innocent party elects to end the contract he is not bound to accept further performance, and he may sue for damages at once.

b. Where if it is to be valid, an exemption clause has to satisfy the requirement of reasonableness, it may be found to do so, and be given effect, even though the contract has been terminated by the innocent party. *S.9(1) UNFAIR CONTRACT TERMS ACT 1977*, i.e. a valid termination of a contract does not terminate an exemption clause. Clearly if it did exemption clauses would be useless in every case of a breach which entitled the innocent party to end the contract.

17. *Anticipatory Breach*

a. Where there is an anticipatory breach, and the innocent party elects to treat the contract as discharged, he can sue for damages at once.

In *HOCHSTER v DE LA TOUR (1853)* D agreed to employ P as a courier for 3 months commencing on 1 June. Before this date D told P that his services would not be required. This was to be an anticipatory breach of contract, and it entitled P to sue for damages immediately.

This decision could lead to difficulties, especially if the trial takes place before the date fixed for performance. For example, if X contracts to deliver goods to Y in 2 years time, and then indicates that he does not intend to perform, Y's damages are in general quantified by reference to the market price at the time fixed for performance. Clearly if the trial takes place before this date the market price cannot be known.

b. If the innocent party elects to treat the contract as still subsisting, he keeps it alive for the benefit of both parties, so that frustration may intervene to release the party at fault from further liability.

In *AVERY v BOWDEN (1855)* D chartered a ship from P to carry goods from Odessa. The charter allowed 45 days for loading. During this period D's agent told the captain (P's agent) that he had no cargo and that he would be wise to leave. The captain, however, remained in Odessa and pressed for performance. Before the 45 days had expired the Crimean War broke out and frustrated the contract. If P had accepted D's anticipatory breach immediately he could have sued for damages. Since he did not do so, he kept the contract alive for the benefit of both parties, so the frustration operated to relieve D from liability. P's claim for damages therefore failed.

c. The doctrine of anticipatory breach is important because:

i. It helps to minimize the total loss, because if the plaintiff could not sue immediately he would be more likely to keep himself available for performance. Whereas, since he may sue at once he has an incentive to abandon the contract and avoid the extra loss that he might have suffered had he waited.

ii. It protects a person who has paid in advance for future performance. It would be unfair if such a person could not sue until the time fixed for performance, since his advance payment may have reduced his ability to make an alternative contract.

18. *Instalment Contracts* If in an instalment contract there is a breach with regard to one or some instalments the main tests as to whether the breach entitles the innocent party to treat the contract as at an end are:

a. The ratio that the breach bears to the contract as a whole, and

b. The degree of probability that the breach will be repeated.

In *MAPLE FLOCK CO v UNIVERSAL FURNITURE PRODUCTS (1934)* the contract provided for 100 tons of rag flock to be delivered in instalments of 1½ tons at the rate of three instalments a week. The sixteenth instalment was defective and the buyers claimed to be entitled to rescind. Their claim failed mainly because the single instalment was a small quantity when compared with the contract as a whole.

19. *Consumer Right to Cancel Under Statute* As seen, the general rule under common law, is that once a contract has been concluded, both parties are bound by it. However, for purposes of protecting consumers, a number of statutes allow a consumer a right to cancel concluded contracts in certain circumstances. The Consumer Credit Act 1974 gives a right to cancel in certain circumstances (see Chapter 32.17), the Timeshare Act 1992 gives consumers who have entered into a time share agreement a 14 day period in which they can cancel the contract. In addition, there is now the *Cancellation of Contracts made in a Consumer's Home or Place of Work Regulations 2008*. These regulations allow consumers to cancel contracts if they are made during a visit by a trader to a consumer's home or place of work. (For a full discussion of the regulations see Chapter 32.17.h)

SELF TEST QUESTIONS

Self Test Questions No. 15 (for Answers see Appendix 1):

1 State the four ways in which a contract can be said to have been discharged.

2 With regard to *performance* what are the exceptions?

3 In what ways may *agreement* to discharge be shown?

4 What is the doctrine of *frustration*?

5 What are the consequences of a *breach* of a contract by one of the parties?

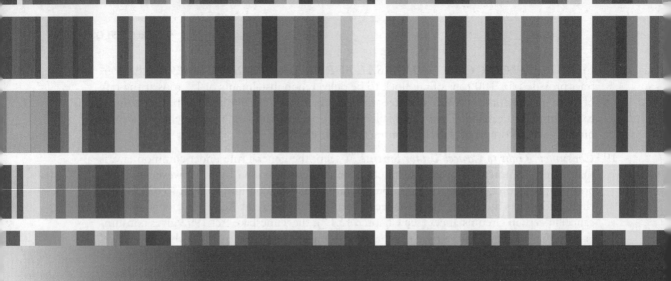

18 REMEDIES FOR BREACH OF CONTRACT

Learning Outcomes At the end of this chapter you should be able to:

- State the various forms of remedy for a breach of contract.

- Explain the principles that determine whether particular damages are too remote.

- Understand the difference between *liquidated* and *unliquidated* damages.

- Outline the equitable remedies for a breach of contract.

- Understand the rules limiting the period of time in which an action may be brought.

1. There are both common law and equitable remedies for breach of contract. The common law remedies are:

   a. Damages.

   b. An action for an agreed sum.

   c. A *quantum meruit* claim (this is a claim for work done).

   The equitable remedies are:

   a. Specific performance.

   b. Injunction.

   By far the most commonly sought remedy is damages.

DAMAGES

2. A claim for damages raises two questions:

   a. For what kind of damage should the plaintiff be compensated? i.e. Remoteness of damage.

   b. What monetary compensation should the plaintiff receive in respect of damage which is not too remote? i.e. Measure of damages.

3. Note carefully the distinction between damage and damages. Damage is the loss suffered by the plaintiff. Damages are the financial compensation awarded to him. It is very important to use the correct word. For example 'Remoteness of damages' is a meaningless phrase.

4. *Remoteness of Damage*

   a. Damage is not too remote if it is:

   'Such as may fairly and reasonably be considered either as arising naturally, i.e. according to the usual course of things from the breach itself, or such as may reasonably be supposed to have been in the contemplation of both parties at the time they made the contract, as the probable result of the breach.'

   In *HADLEY v BAXENDALE (1854)* P's mill shaft broke and had to be sent to the makers at Greenwich to serve as a pattern for a replacement. D agreed to transport the shaft to Greenwich, but in breach of contract delayed delivery causing several days loss of production at the mill. P claimed £300 in respect of lost profit. Alderson B stated the rule quoted and applied it as follows:

   i. The loss did not arise naturally since D could not foresee that his delay would stop the mill. It was quite possible that P might have had a spare shaft or been able to get one.

   ii. The loss could not have been contemplated by both parties at the time of the contract as the probable result of the breach. If D had been told that delay would stop the mill such loss would have been in his contemplation and he may then have sought to limit his liability, however he did not have this information.

   b. The above rule can be analyzed into two parts, briefly summarized as loss 'naturally arising' and loss 'in the contemplation of both parties ... as the probable result of the breach'. An example of the application of the first part is *PINNOCK v LEWIS (1923)*. The distinction between the two parts is illustrated by *PILKINGTON v WOOD (1953)*.

   In *PINNOCK v LEWIS (1923)* the seller of poisonous cattle food was held liable for the loss of the cattle to which it was fed. This loss arose naturally from his breach.

   In *PILKINGTON v WOOD (1953)* P bought a house in Hampshire, his solicitor, D, failing to notice that the title was defective. D was held liable for the difference between the value of the house with good title and with defective title – this was loss 'naturally arising'. However, P's job shortly moved to Lancashire and he wished to sell his house. The defective title made the sale difficult and meant that P was delayed in paying off his bank overdraft out of the sale proceeds. D was held not liable for this additional loss as he could not have anticipated that P would shortly want to move, nor did he know that P had an overdraft, i.e. the loss was not, and could not reasonably be supposed to have been in his contemplation.

   c.   *HADLEY v BAXENDALE (1854)*, broadly speaking, represents the law today. It was considered by the House of Lords in *KOUFOS v CZARNIKOW (1969)* when all five law lords approved the rule, although saying that the loss must be contemplated as 'a real danger' or 'a serious possibility' rather than as 'the probable result of the breach'.

       In *KOUFOS v CZARNIKOW (1969)* a ship was chartered to carry sugar from Constanza to Basrah. The charterer intended to sell the sugar immediately on its arrival. The ship owner did not know this, but he did know that there was a market for sugar at Basrah. In breach of contract the ship owner deviated and arrived 9 days late during which time the market value of the sugar had fallen by about £4000. The House of Lords unanimously upheld P's claim for this amount, approving the rule in Hadley v Baxendale subject to the qualifications mentioned above. The case is interesting in that although there was a roughly equal chance of the price of sugar rising or falling, the fact that it fell was nevertheless foreseeable as 'a serious possibility'.

   d.   When the breach of contract consists of failure to pay a sum of money the general rule is that only the sum of money, not interest or damages can be recovered (*LONDON, CHATHAM AND DOVER RAILWAY v SOUTH EASTERN RAILWAY (1893)*). This rule is considered to be unsatisfactory and there are a number of exceptions. In particular it does not apply to claims for special damages under the second limb of the rule in *HADLEY v BAXENDALE (1854)*. For example:

       In *INTERNATIONAL MINERALS AND CHEMICALS CORPORATION v HELM (1986)* a debt was due to be paid to an American plaintiff in Belgium francs. Between the due date and the judgement date the value of Belgium francs as against US dollars had fallen by 40%. It was held that the loss was recoverable since D knew that such a loss was not an improbable consequence of their default.

   e.   Note that the contract and tort tests for remoteness differ. In tort the loss must be the 'reasonably foreseeable' result of the tort. The tort test is therefore more generous to the plaintiff.

5. *Measure of Damages*

   a.   The general rule is that the plaintiff recovers his actual loss (in respect of damage which is not too remote), i.e. he is placed in the same position as if the contract had been performed. Therefore in assessing damages for breach of contract to pay a pension, or up to £10 000 damages for wrongful dismissal, (*INCOME AND CORPORATION TAXES ACT* 1970, as amended), regard must be had to the plaintiff's liability to taxation.

       In *GOLDEN STRAIT CORPORATION v NIPPON YUSEN KUBISHKA KAISHA (THE GOLDEN VICTORY) (2007)* a contract to charter a tanker, contained an express term that upon outbreak of war between certain named countries, either party could terminate the contract. The defendant breached the contract by returning the vessel early when there was still some 4 years left to run. After the breach war broke out between two of the named countries in the contract and the respondent was claiming that he should only pay damages up to the outbreak of those hostilities given that he would have been entitled to terminate the contract from that date anyway. The claimant was seeking damages for the whole of the remaining period of the charter. The House of Lords (now the Supreme Court) held that:

       i.   Damages for breach of contract are designed to compensate the injured party for the loss of his contractual bargain and he should be placed in the position he would have been in had the contract been performed. However,

ii.   If the contract would have terminated earlier (due to an event anticipated by the parties) then this has to be taken into account.

It followed that damages would be awarded up to the outbreak of hostilities and not for the entire duration of the contract. Although, as a general rule, damages should be assessed at the date of the breach (when there were no hostilities) where the parties had made express provision, this must be taken into account.

b.   *S.50-51 SALE OF GOODS ACT 1979* provide respectively that in an action for damages for non-acceptance or non-delivery, where there is an available market, the measure of damages is the difference between the contract price and the market price on the date fixed for acceptance or delivery or, if no date was fixed, at the time of refusal to accept or deliver. The provisions of these two sections are only prima facie rules and may not be applied if they would not indemnify the plaintiff for his loss.

In **THOMPSON v ROBINSON GUNMAKERS (1955)** D purchased a 'Standard Van-guard' car from P and later refused to accept delivery of it. P's profit on the sale would have been £61, but D argued that they were not liable for this amount, since the profit would still be made when the car was sold to another customer. The court rejected this argument since the supply of this model exceeded the demand. Therefore if P had found another customer he could have sold a car to him in addition to selling a car to D.

Contrast **CHARTER v SULLIVAN (1957)** D refused to accept delivery of a 'Hillman Minx' car that he had bought from P. P claimed £97 15s loss of profits. In contrast with the above case his claim failed, because the demand for Hillman Minx cars exceeded the supply. He could therefore sell every car that he could obtain from the makers and had accordingly not lost a sale.

c.   In assessing the award of damages the court may take into account inconvenience and annoyance.

In **JARVIS v SWAN TOURS (1973)** P paid £63 for a 2 week winter sports holiday. It differed vastly from what was advertised. There was very little holiday atmosphere, the hotel staff did not speak English, and in the second week he was the only guest at the hotel. P recovered £125 damages for his upset and annoyance due to having his holiday spoilt.

d.   The defence of contributory negligence under the *LAW REFORM (CONTRIBU-TORY NEGLIGENCE) ACT 1945* (Chapter 26.9) cannot be used to justify a propor-tionate reduction in damages for breach of contract (**BASILDON DISTRICT COUNCIL v LESSER (1984)**). However, the plaintiff's negligence may result in his claim being defeated.

In **LAMBERT v LEWIS (1982)** P used a trailer coupling after realizing that it was clearly defective. This negligent action relieved the supplier from contractual liability for the loss that occurred as a result of the ensuing accident.

6. *Mitigation*

a.   The above rules are subject to the limitation that the claimant must do what is reasona-ble to mitigate his loss, and cannot recover any part of it which the defendant can prove has resulted from failure to mitigate, i.e. the claimant cannot recover for a loss that he ought to have avoided.

In **DARBISHIRE v WARREN (1963)** P owned a car of which he was particularly proud. Although it was old he maintained it in excellent condition. It had a market value of about £85. The car was damaged by D's negligence and P was advised it would cost him £192 to get it repaired. P went ahead with the repairs and claimed £192 from D (less the money he had received from his insurance company, and plus the cost of hiring a car while the repairs were carried out). His claim failed. The court held that the expenditure on repairs was not justified. P should have mitigated his loss by buying a replacement vehicle on the open market.

b. *WHITE AND CARTER (COUNCILS) v MCGREGOR (1961)* (Chapter 20.15) illustrates that mitigation is only relevant to a claim for damages and not to a claim for an agreed sum.

7. *Liquidated Damages and Penalties*

a. Where no provision for damages is made in the contract then the court will assess the damages payable. These are unliquidated damages. However, the courts recognize that within the basic right of freedom to contract there is a right to specify the damages to be paid in the event of a breach. Equity, however, gives relief in circumstances where this right is abused by a party who has attempted to take an unfair advantage of his stronger bargaining position.

b. Where the parties have agreed in a contract how much is to be payable on a breach, this sum is recoverable if it is liquidated damages, i.e. a genuine pre-estimate of the loss, but not if it is a penalty, i.e. an amount fixed as a threat to prevent a breach.

c. Where it is a penalty the plaintiff can only recover his actual loss in respect of damage which is not too remote.

In *LAMDON TRUST v HURRELL (1955)* D purchased a car from P on hire purchase. The hire purchase price was £558. After he had paid £302 D defaulted and P repossessed the car, and resold it for £270. A provision in the hire purchase agreement provided that if it was terminated due to a hirer's default, the hirer must pay as compensation the difference between the sums paid (in this case £302) and £425, i.e. £123. Since P had already received £572 for the car (£302 plus £270), D objected to their claim for £123. The court held that the compensation clause was a penalty and since P had already received more than the original price of the car D was not liable to pay him any more compensation. The effect of P's clause could be more vividly seen if D had defaulted after payment of £10. D could have claimed £415 under their compensation clause and resold the car probably for at least £500, giving them a total compensation of £915. Clearly this is not a genuine estimate of loss.

d. Whether a particular sum is liquidated damages or a penalty depends on the parties' intentions. The words used by the parties are not conclusive evidence of intention, the courts will look at the following tests.

i. Is the sum stipulated extravagant in comparison with the greatest loss which could have followed from the breach? If so it is a penalty.

In *KEMBLE v FARREN (1829)*, an actor's contract provided that if either he or the theatre management broke their contract then the party in breach must pay the other £1000 as 'liquidated damages'. This was held to be a penalty clause because it was disproportionate both to the actor's daily fee of £3.69p, and to the greatest possible loss that would result from the breach.

ii. Where a lump sum is payable on the occurrence of certain events, some of which are serious and some of which are not, the lump sum is presumed to be a penalty, but where a precise estimate of the consequences of the breach is impossible the court may regard the lump sum as a genuine pre-estimate.

In *DUNLOP PNEUMATIC TYRE CO v NEW GARAGE AND MOTOR CO (1915)* P offered a trade discount to dealers who promised:

a) Not to sell below certain list prices.

b) Not to supply certain named persons.

c) Not to exhibit any of the goods, and

d) To pay £5 'by way of liquidated damages and not as a penalty' for each breach of the agreement. This clause was held to be enforceable since £5 was not an excessive figure to place on a breach the actual loss from which would be impossible to forecast.

In *ARISTON v CHARLY (1990)* P agreed to manufacture records and print sleeves for D. D entrusted P with certain metal parts, artwork, label information, negatives and lacquer necessary for the work. Since this equipment was valuable the contract provided that if P did not return the items within 10 days of D's request they would pay a penalty of £600 per day for late delivery. Following a request P returned most of the equipment within the required time. The action was commenced by P claiming amounts outstanding on their invoices, D counter-claimed £600 per day for failure to return the equipment. It was held that the clause was unenforceable because it was a penalty. £600 per day may have been a reasonable estimate of loss resulting from the failure to return all of the equipment, but under the clause the same amount was payable even if only one item were retained. It was not therefore a reasonable pre-estimate of the loss.

OTHER COMMON LAW REMEDIES

8. *Action for an Agreed Sum* A contract will often provide for the payment by one party of an agreed sum in exchange for performance by the other, for example goods sold for a fixed price. Provided the duty to pay the price has arisen the innocent party may sue the contract breaker for the agreed sum. Such action is different from an action for damages, since the plaintiff recovers the agreed sum, neither more nor less. Therefore questions of remoteness and measure cannot arise.

9. *Quantum Meruit* Where either work has been done or accepted under a void contract or where one party abandons a contract (as in *PLANCHE v COLBURN (1831)*, Chapter 20) the injured party, instead of claiming damages, may claim payment for what has been done under the contract. This is known as a *quantum meruit* claim. *Quantum meruit* means 'how much it is worth'. The claim is not based on the original contract, but on an implied promise by the other party arising from the acceptance of executed consideration.

EQUITABLE REMEDIES

10. *Specific Performance* Specific performance is a decree issued by the court which orders the defendant to carry out his obligations. It is a remedy which:

a. Is discretionary, although the discretion must be exercised within well established principles.

b. Is not normally awarded if damages would be an adequate remedy. It is most likely to be awarded in contracts for the sale of land.

c. Must be available to either party. Thus it is not available to an infant in respect of a contract not enforceable against him.

d. Is not available in respect of certain types of contract, such as those requiring personal services, for example as a butler, or contracts which require extensive supervision, for example building contracts.

11. *Injunction*

a. A *mandatory injunction* orders a person to take action to undo a breach of contract. For example, he may be ordered to take down an advertising sign erected in breach of contract.

b. A *prohibitory injunction* is an order of the court which prohibits a person from doing something. Such an injunction could be granted to prevent the breach of a reasonable restraint of trade clause.

In **WARNER BROTHERS v NELSON (1937)** D, an actress, agreed to act for P and undertook that she would not act for anyone else during the period of the agreement without P's written consent. It was held that she could be restrained by an injunction from breaking this undertaking. This did not of course force her to act for P, nor did it prevent her from obtaining different types of work.

c. A *Mareva injunction* orders a defendant not to remove specified assets from the jurisdiction of the English courts. It is a temporary injunction granted when a case is pending in court, its purpose being to prevent the defendant from nullifying the effect of a judgement which the plaintiff is likely to obtain. It is therefore ancilliary to other proceedings which must have been commenced by the time the injunction is granted. The name 'Mareva injunction' derives from the case of **MAREVA COMPANIA NAVIERA v INTERNATIONAL BULK CARRIERS (1975)**, but it is now granted by virtue of *S.37 SUPREME COURT ACT 1981*.

d. An *Anton Pillar injunction* authorizes the inspection, photographing, custody or removal of documents or property.

In **ANTON PILLER v MANUFACTURING PROCESSES (1976)** such an injunction was granted when a manufacturer of computer components feared that his agent would pass on confidential information to a competitor.

The injunctions are now granted by virtue of *S.33 SUPREME COURT ACT 1981*. They will only be granted in exceptional circumstances, the inspection or removal normally being carried out by the applicant's solicitor, accompanied by police officers.

12. Rescission and rectification are also equitable remedies. They were discussed in Chapter 19.18.

LIMITATION OF ACTIONS

13. The right to sue for breach does not last indefinitely and the parties themselves may state a time limit for any action to be brought and provided such a term is reasonable, it will be

upheld. (See previous case of *GRANVILLE OIL AND CHEMICALS LTD v DAVIS TURNER & CO LTD (2003)* Chapter 15.)

The *LIMITATION ACT 1980* lays down periods of 6 years for a simple contract, and 12 years for a deed. Time runs from the date when the breach occurred and failure to discover the breach does not usually stop time running. There are two exceptions to this rule:

a. Where the action is based on the fraud of the defendant, or the breach is concealed by the fraud of the defendant.

In *LYNN v BAMBER (1930)* P bought plum trees from D that were warranted to be 'purple Pershores'. Seven years later he discovered they were not purple Pershores and sued for damages. D pleaded that the action was statute barred. P succeeded because D's fraudulent misrepresentation and concealment of the breach of warranty were a good defence to the plea that the action was statute barred.

b. Where the action is for relief from the consequences of a mistake.

In *PECO ARTS v HAZLITT GALLERY (1983)* P purchased a drawing from D in 1970 for $18 000. In 1976 it was revalued by an expert for insurance purposes. In 1981 it was discovered that the drawing was a fake. P alleged that the contract was a void for mistake and claimed rescission and recovery of the purchase price plus interest. D's only defence was the Limitation Act. It was held that they could succeed since there was no lack of diligence on their part, i.e. they could not have been expected to obtain independent authentication at the time of purchase and they were entitled to conclude that it was original, since no doubts had been cast upon it at the time of the 1976 valuation.

This case does not contradict *LEAF v INTERNATIONAL GALLERIES (1950)* (Chapter 16.9.b) since Peco's case concerned the time limit for claiming relief from the consequences of an operative mistake, whereas Leaf's case was concerned with lapse of time following an innocent misrepresentation.

c. When there is fraud or mistake time runs from when the fraud or mistake was, or ought to have been, discovered, whichever is the earlier.

14. If at the time the cause of action accrued the plaintiff was a minor or a mentally disordered person, the action must be commenced within 6 years of the cessation of the disability. Provided there is no interval between two disabilities, for example the minor becomes mentally ill, then the two disabilities can be added together. However, if the disabilities are separated by an interval time will not be stopped from running by the second disability.

15. Where a claim is made for a contract debt time starts running afresh if before, or after, the limitation period has expired:

a. A written acknowledgement of the debt is given by the debtor to the creditor, or

b. A payment of part of the debt is made.

The Limitation Act does not apply to equitable remedies, but the maxim 'delay defeats equity' may apply.

In *POLLARD v CLAYTON (1855)* D agreed to sell P all the coal that he raised from a particular mine. In breach of the agreement he sold the coal elsewhere and 11 months later P sought specific performance of the contract. It was held that the right to this equitable remedy was barred by the unreasonable length of time that had elapsed since the breach.

SELF TEST QUESTIONS

Self Test Questions No. 16 (for Answers see Appendix 1):

1 What are seen as the two central questions when seeking to determine damages for breach of contract?

2 What is meant by the phrase, 'damage must not be too remote', as laid down in the case of *HADLEY v BAXENDALE*?

3 What factors will a court take into account when assessing the size of an award for damages?

4 'The claimant must mitigate his loss.' What does that mean?

5 What are the common law and equitable remedies for breach of contract?

6 Are there any limitations of time during which an action may be brought, and if so, what are they?

PRIVITY OF CONTRACT 19

Learning Outcomes At the end of this chapter you should be able to:

- Demonstrate an understanding of the meaning of who is bound by a valid contract.

- Explain the exceptions to the rule.

1. **The Basic Rule** The common law doctrine of privity of contract states that no one can be bound by, or take advantage of, a contract to which he is not a party. This was clearly illustrated in the following two House of Lords' decisions.

In *SCRUTTONS v MIDLAND SILICONES (1962)* a shipping company agreed to carry drums of chemicals belonging to P from America to England, the contract limiting their liability to $500 per drum. The shipping company hired a firm of stevedores (D) to unload the ship, and due to D's negligence the chemicals were damaged to the value of $1800 per drum. P were successful in their tort action against D, recovering their full loss. The court held that D could not rely on the exemption clause in the contract between P and the shipping company because they were not a party to this contract, nor were they protected by a similar exemption clause in their contract with the shipping company because P were not a party to this contract.

In *BESWICK v BESWICK (1967)* a Mr Beswick (B) entered into an agreement with his nephew (also Mr Beswick), the defendant in this case (D), whereby D was to take over B's business in return for a payment of £6.50 per week to B during his life, and after his death £5 per week to his widow. When B died D stopped the payments. B's widow sued D both in her personal capacity and in her capacity as administratix of his estate. She failed in her personal capacity, but succeeded as administratix and was awarded a decree of specific performance against D.

If a person dies leaving a will he will name an executor in the will. If a person leaves no will his affairs will be handled by an administrator who is usually his nearest relative. A female administrator is called an administratix.

2. *Exceptions*

   a. *Statutory exceptions*

      i. The *MARRIED WOMEN'S PROPERTY ACT 1882* provides that a man (or woman) may insure his (or her) life for the benefit of his wife (or husband) and children. On his death the insurance company becomes a trustee of the money due to his wife, and she as a beneficiary may sue to recover it, although she was not a party to the insurance contract.

      ii. The *ROAD TRAFFIC ACT 1972* provides that in certain cases an injured third party may proceed directly against the insurance company.

      iii. The *BILLS OF EXCHANGEE ACT 1882* provides that certain persons who come into possession of a cheque may sue the drawer of the cheque, even though they have no contract with him.

   b. *Equitable exceptions*

      Occasionally equity may confer a benefit on a third party by using the device of an implied trust.

      In *GREGORY AND PARKER v WILLIAMS (1817)* P, who owed money to both G and W, agreed with W to transfer his property to him if W would pay his (P's) debt due to G. The property was duly transferred but W refused to pay G. The common law doctrine of privity prevented G from suing on the contract between P and W. Equity, however, held that P could be regarded as a trustee for G, and that G could therefore bring an action, jointly with P against W.

   c. *Covenants*

      i. At common law the assignee of a lease takes it with the benefits of, and subject to the burdens of, the assignor. Although there is no contract between the lessor and the assignee there is 'privity of estate' and the assignee may therefore sue and be sued by the lessor.

      ii. In equity the case of *TULK v MOXHAY (1848)* established that restrictive covenants run with the land, i.e. a purchaser is bound by a covenant entered into by a previous owner if he has notice of the covenant.

      iii. Distinguish covenants in leases, which may be positive, e.g. to pay rent, or negative, for example not to keep a dog, from restrictive covenants which may apply to freehold land, for example not to build within 15 feet of the road.

   d. *Assignment*

      i. A party can assign or transfer to another person the rights contained in the contract, but cannot, without the consent of the other person, assign the burden of his contractual obligations.

ii.   By *S.136 LAW OF PROPERTY ACT 1925* a legal assignment must be in writing and signed by the assignor. The whole of the interest must be transferred to the assignee and written notice must be given to the other party.

iii. Rights that are highly personal to the original parties, for example those arising from a contract of service, cannot be assigned without the consent of the other party to the contract.

e.   *Resale price agreements.* Where a resale price agreement has been approved under provisions in the *RESALE PRICES ACT 1976* a supplier of goods may bring an action to enforce a minimum resale price against a person who was not a party to a contract with the supplier. Such resale price agreements are comparatively rare.

f.   *Collateral contracts*

i.   A collateral contract arises when a promise that is not part of the main contract is nevertheless part of another contract related to the same subject matter.

ii.   The usual situation is that a person (A) is persuaded by the statement of another (B) to enter into a contract with a third party (C). The main contract will be between A and C. The collateral contract will be between A and B based upon B's statements.

In *SHANKLIN PIER v DETEL PRODUCTS (1951)* P hired contractors (X) to paint Shanklin Pier. They specified that X use paint to be purchased from D, because D had assured P that the paint would last 7 to 10 years. X purchased and used the paint but it only lasted 3 months. P successfully sued D on the basis of their assurance that the paint would last 7 years even though the contract for the sale of the paint was from D to X. It was held that there was a collateral contract between P and D. The consideration given by P was that they caused X to make the contract with D.

The same principle applies when a person buys goods and is given a manufacturer's guarantee. The basic contract is between the customer and the retailer but the guarantee amounts to a collateral contract between the customer and the manufacturer.

3. *Conclusion*

a.   The case of *BESWICK v BESWICK (1967)* is important because in the Court of Appeal the doctrine of privity was challenged by Lord Denning. He had said that the widow could also sue in her own right because the doctrine of privity was 'at bottom … only a rule of procedure' and could be overcome if the intended beneficiary joined the promisee in the action. The House of Lords did not consider it necessary to comment on this view since they already had sufficient reason to find the widow's favour. However, the speeches all assume the correctness of the generally accepted view that a contract can only be enforced by the parties to it. Thus in *BESWICK v BESWICK (1967)* the House of Lords affirmed the continued existence of the doctrine of privity in the face of critics who have suggested that a remedy should be provided for a party who has been given specific rights under a contract, and despite Lord Denning's attempt to give effect to this suggestion.

b.   Privity has also been criticized by the Law Commission. It proposed that the general rule that a third party cannot acquire rights under a contract to which he is not a party should be substantially amended by Parliament. Its basic recommendation was that a third party should be allowed to bring an action where the parties to the contract intend to confer an *enforceable legal obligation* (not merely a benefit). This could be expressly stated or implied from the circumstances. It would not be necessary for the beneficiary to be named, although doing so would reduce doubts both over the identity of beneficiaries and the desire to create an enforceable benefit.

The recommendations of the Law Commission resulted in the *CONTRACTS (RIGHTS OF THIRD PARTIES) ACT 1999* being enacted. The Act, whilst retaining the principle of privity, gives, in certain circumstances, the right to third parties (outsiders to the agreement) to enforce the contract. S.1 lays down two circumstances where this will occur:

i.   Where the contract expressly so provides.

ii. Where a term of the contract purports to give a benefit to the third party and, upon a proper construction of the contract, the parties did not intend that it be not enforceable by the third party. This means that a presumption of third party enforceability will arise where, under the contract, a clear benefit is to be bestowed upon a person, unless evidence can be produced to rebut the presumption.

The Section goes on to require that the third party must be expressly identified in the contract. In *AVRAAMIDES v COLWILL (2006)*

```
C ———————CONTRACT——————→ B Ltd

        A term of the contract
        required C to honour
        B Ltd's existing obligations
        and liabilities
```

A third party, as a dissatisfied customer, sought to sue C under the contract with B Ltd. The Court of Appeal held that as A had not been expressly identified in the contract, he had no enforceable rights under *S.1(3)* of the *CONTRACTS (RIGHTS OF THIRD PARTIES) ACT 1999*.

Where the Act is found to apply, the third party has the same remedies as would be available if he or she had entered the contract personally; this will include the ability to seek benefits from any exclusion clauses.

The proposals if enacted would meet many of the criticisms of the present situation and would have been likely to have led to a different outcome in most of the leading cases, including *BESWICK v BESWICK (1967)*.

SELF TEST QUESTIONS

Self Test Questions No. 17 (for Answers see Appendix 1):

1 What is the rule as to privity of contract?

2 What are the exceptions to that rule?

3 What are the main provisions of the *CONTRACTS (RIGHTS OF THIRD PARTIES) ACT 1999*?

REFLECTION AND CONSOLIDATION II

For answers go to the student digital support resources for the book (see page xxv).

Reflection

Key areas of study
These chapters cover the first substantive area of business law – *the law of Contract*.

What are the necessary elements for a contract's *formation*, namely:

the finding of agreement between the parties – *offer* and *acceptance*
something of value moving between the parties – *consideration*
the minds of the parties – *intention?*

Who has the ability to contract – *capacity?*

Certain contracts need to be made in a particular way – *form*.

Some terms of a contract are more important than others – *condition* and *warranty* distinguished.

What will invalidate wholly or partially a otherwise valid contract – *mistake, misrepresentation, duress, undue influence, illegality?*

The ways in which a contract can be completed – *discharge*.

Where there has been a breach – the *remedies* available to a claimant.

Those persons affected/ bound by the contract – *privity*.

Consolidation

The following are practice assessment exercises; you will find the answers and guidance by going to the student digital support resources for the book (see page xxv).

MULTIPLE CHOICE QUESTIONS

1 The vast majority of contracts are 'simple'. What is the meaning of the word 'simple' in this context?
   A The terms of the contract are set out in writing
   B The contract does not need to be in any particular form to be binding
   C The contract contains fewer than ten provisions
   D The contract is not supported by consideration

2 A Ltd placed the following advertisement in a local newspaper:

   'We are able to offer for sale a number of portable colour television sets at the specially reduced price of £5.90. Order now while stocks last.'

   The advertisement contained a mistake in that the television sets should have been priced at £59.00. B Ltd immediately placed an order for 100 television sets.

   Which ONE of the following statements is **correct**?
   A B Ltd has accepted an offer and is contractually entitled to the 100 television sets
   B A Ltd can refuse to supply B Ltd as the advertisement is not an offer, but an invitation to treat
   C A Ltd can only refuse to sell the television sets to B Ltd if it has sold all its stock
   D As B Ltd has not yet paid for the television sets, the company has no contractual right to them

3 Which ONE of the following statements is **correct**?
   A If a person signs a contract, he/she is bound by all its terms
   B A contract which has not been signed is not binding on any of the parties
   C A person who signs a contract is deemed to have read it
   D A person who has not read a contract cannot be bound by it

4 Which ONE of the following statements is **correct**?
   A If the creditor agrees to accept less than the full amount due, the debt is discharged at common law
   B At common law, a creditor who has agreed to accept less than the full amount due, may go back on his word and recover the balance
   C Payment of less than the full amount due by a third party cannot discharge the whole debt
   D Payment of less than the amount due cannot discharge the whole debt, even if made early at the request of the creditor

5 Which ONE of the following is **not** an equitable remedy?
   A Damages
   B Specific performance
   C Rescission
   D Injunction

6 Which of the following statements is **correct**?

   (i) As a general rule, a contract will only be discharged if all its terms have been precisely performed.

(ii) If a contract becomes impossible to perform through no fault of either contracting party, the contract is frustrated and unenforceable, unless its terms provide for the frustrating event.

    A   (i) only
    B   (ii) only
    C   Neither (i) nor (ii)
    D   Both (i) and (ii)

7 In breach of contract, C Ltd refused to sell a motor car to D Ltd at the agreed price of £10 000. If the type of motor car is readily available on the market at a price of £9000, which ONE of the following is **correct**?

    A   D Ltd is entitled to an order of specific performance, forcing C Ltd to carry out its contract
    B   D Ltd is entitled to damages of £1000
    C   D Ltd is entitled to nominal damages only
    D   D Ltd is not entitled to damages

Typical Exam Questions

8 Explain how the law determines whether negotiating parties have reached agreement.

(15 marks)

CIMA, 2002

In what circumstances will frustration discharge a contract?

(20 marks)

ICSA, November 2004

10 (a) What must a claimant prove in order to satisfy a court that he has been induced to enter into a contract as a result of a misrepresentation? If he succeeds, what remedies will then be available to him?

    (14 marks)

    b. Whilst negotiating to sell his business to Ivan, Henry made a true statement which gave total figures for turnover and profits for the previous 5 years. This created an impression that the business was in a healthy state. Henry did not disclose, nor did Ivan request, a breakdown of figures which would have revealed a steady decline in profitability over this period. Ivan, having purchased the business, discovered the true state of affairs.

What remedies, if any, does Ivan have?

(6 marks)

(20 marks)

11 (a) In what circumstances will a mistake prevent the formation of a valid contract?

    (12 marks)

    (b) Victoria offers two expensive cars for sale and John and Mary call in response to the advertisement. John says that he is a well-known businessman, agrees to buy the first car and gives Victoria a cheque for the purchase price. Mary says that she merely wishes to hire the second car for a forthcoming event. Victoria agrees, accepts a cheque for the hire price and signs, without reading, what she believes to be a contract of hire; it is, in fact, a contract of sale. Both John and Mary are then allowed to drive away the cars.

The cheques have now been dishonoured and Victoria seeks your advice. Advise her as to whether she may claim ownership of the cars.

(8 marks)

(20 marks)

14 (a) When, if ever, does payment of a smaller sum discharge a debt owed to a creditor?

(10 marks)

(b) D owned a fleet of lorries.

(i) He agreed with E to deliver E's grain to his warehouse. E then asked D to deliver the grain to a different destination 50 miles away, and offered him extra remuneration. E did not pay the extra remuneration.

(ii) He agreed with F to deliver F's steel to G. G agreed to assist D with unloading the steel. When the steel was delivered G refused this assistance.
Advise D.

(10 marks)

(20 marks)

15 Explain how the courts and Parliament have sought to limit the effect of exclusion clauses in the law of contract

(20 marks)

PART THREE
THE LAW OF TORTS

20 THE NATURE OF A TORT

Learning Outcomes
At the end of this chapter you should be able to:

- Explain what is meant by a tort.

- Understand how tort differs from other 'wrongs'.

- Explain the legal requirements with regard to 'bad motive' or 'intention'.

1. A tort is a civil wrong brought about by a duty imposed by law being breached, there is no requirement for a contract to exist between a claimant and alleged wrongdoer. The law exists to provide a remedy for persons injured by the conduct of others.

2. The law of tort deals with a wide variety of wrongs, for example:

   a. Intentionally or negligently causing physical injury to another (trespass to the person and negligence).

   b. Interfering with the enjoyment of another's land (nuisance, trespass to land and the tort known as 'Rylands v Fletcher').

   c. Defamation (libel and slander).

3. A tort must be distinguished from:

  a. A *breach of contract*, where the obligation of which a breach is alleged arose from the agreement of the parties.

  b. A *breach of trust*, where the duty broken is known only to equity and not to common law and where the remedy is equitable or discretionary and not the common law right to damages.

  c. A *crime*, where the object of proceedings is to punish the offender rather than compensate his victim.

4. Each individual tort has its own particular rules governing liability, but in general the plaintiff must prove the following:

  a. That the defendant's conduct has been intentional or negligent, i.e. liability is usually based on fault. There are, however, some instances of 'strict liability', i.e. liability irrespective of fault.

  b. That the tortious act or omission caused some damage to the claimant. However, some torts are actionable 'per se' (without proof of loss), for example trespass and libel.

5. *Malice in Tort*

  a. Malice means acting from a bad motive. The general rule is that the defendant's motives are irrelevant. Therefore a good motive will not excuse a tortious act, and a bad motive will not turn an otherwise innocent act into a tortious one.

  In *BRADFORD CORPORATION v PICKLES (1895)* in an effort to induce the Corporation to buy his land, D sank a well on his land and abstracted water which would have otherwise reached the Corporation's reservoir. It was held that an injunction would not be granted to the Corporation. The right to abstract water is not (like the right to make noise on one's land) limited by the requirement of reasonableness. It is an absolute right and an element of malice could not make it a nuisance.

  b. There are several exceptions to the general rule stated above:

    i.   The plaintiff must prove malice in the torts of malicious prosecution and injurious falsehood.

    ii. In the tort of defamation if the plaintiff can prove malice this will prevent the defences of qualified privilege and fair comment.

    iii. In nuisance the plaintiff will sometimes succeed if he shows that the defendant's malice turned an otherwise reasonable act into an unreasonable one.

  In *HOLLYWOOD SILVER FOX FARM v EMMETT (1936)* D, a developer, felt that a notice board inscribed 'Hollywood Silver Fox Farm' was detrimental to his neighbouring development. When P refused to remove the notice D caused his son to discharge guns on his land to interfere with the breeding of the foxes. It was held that his action constituted a nuisance.

SELF TEST QUESTIONS

Self Test Questions No. 18 (for Answers see Appendix 1):

1   What is a tort?

2   How is tort distinguished from other 'wrongs'?

3   'Malice is not a requirement for an action in tort,' what does this mean?

GENERAL DEFENCES 21

Learning Outcomes At the end of this chapter you should be able to:

- Explain the general defences of *consent* and *remoteness of damage*.

- Outline the other general defences.

INTRODUCTION

1. A defence need only be argued by the defendant once the basic requirements of the tort have been established by the plaintiff. The general defences described in this chapter are not usually the 'first line of defence' for a defendant. Initially he will probably try to refute the allegation that he has committed the tort. For example:

   'I did not commit the tort of negligence because the plaintiff has failed to prove that I did not act as a reasonable man. I was reasonable because ....'

   If the plaintiff does establish that the tort has been committed then, and only then, need the defendant argue a defence. For example:

   'I accept that I was negligent, but the loss the plaintiff has suffered is not sufficiently closely related to my negligent act.'

   This is the defence of remoteness (see below). The distinction is illustrated by the following case.

In *WOOLDRIDGE v SUMNER (1963)* the plaintiff was a professional photographer. He was standing inside a show jumping arena when a horse ridden by D galloped off the course and into him. The judge found that whilst there was an error of judgement by D it was not sufficient to amount to a finding that D had breached his duty of care owed to P. The tort of negligence had not therefore been committed. The rider did not therefore have to argue any defence such as that P consented to run the risk of injury (see below) by standing inside the arena.

There are two main heads of defence:

Consent and remoteness of damage.

CONSENT

2. The general rule is that a person has no remedy for harm done to him if he has expressly or impliedly consented to suffer the actual harm inflicted, or if he has consented to run the risk of it. Thus, for example, a boxer could not sue as a result of a broken jaw suffered in the ring.

   a. *The Meaning of 'Consent'*

      Mere knowledge does not necessarily imply consent. The claimant must both appreciate the nature of the risk of injury and consent to run that risk.

      In *SMITH v BAKER (1891)* P, who worked in a quarry, was injured when a stone fell from a crane which his employers negligently used to swing stones above his head. When sued his employers pleaded the defence of *volenti*. They were able to show that P knew of the risk of injury, but they could not show that he freely consented to run that risk. He may have continued to work under the crane through fear of losing his job. P's action succeeded.

   b. Consent need not be expressly given. It is sufficient that the claimant voluntarily agrees to the risk of injury.

      In *ICI LTD v SHATWELL (1965)* P and his brother, who were experienced in handling explosives, disregarded their employer's instructions and tested some detonators without taking adequate precautions. P was injured due to his brother's negligence, and sued ICI (the employers) claiming that they were vicariously liable for his brother's negligence. ICI's defence of *volenti* succeeded.

      P knew the risk he was taking, but he took the risk voluntarily. Note that P could have chosen to sue his brother. If he had done so the brother could have successfully pleaded *volenti*.

   c. A consent given under protest is no consent, as where an employee has the choice between incurring a risk or giving up a job which is not normally dangerous.

      In *BOWATER v ROWLEY REGIS CORPORATION (1944)* D ordered one of their employees (P) to take out a horse which they knew was unsafe. P was injured. D's defence of *volenti* failed because P took out the horse because he was in fear of losing his job. His consent was not therefore freely given.

   d. An apparent consent may be negated by statute. For example:

      i. The *ROAD TRAFFIC ACT 1972* makes void any agreement between a driver and passenger whereby the passenger travels at his own risk since the Act makes passenger insurance compulsory.

ii. The *UNFAIR CONTRACT TERMS ACT 1977* provides that a person cannot by reference to any contract term exclude or restrict his liability for death or personal injury resulting from negligence.

3. *Rescue Cases*

a. If a respondent has placed a third party, or himself, in a position of danger is sued by the claimant in respect of injuries suffered while taking steps to effect a rescue, he cannot plead *volenti* as a defence. The claimant's moral duty to effect a rescue excludes any real consent by him.

In *HAYNES v HARWOOD (1935)* a boy threw a stone at a horse which had been left unattended, causing the horse to bolt into a crowded street. P, a policeman, was injured when he tried to stop the horse. P's action against the owners of the horse succeeded. They could not claim the defence of *volenti* since he was acting under a duty to effect a rescue, and had not therefore freely consented to run the risk of injury.

b. The general principle is similar where injuries are suffered in an attempt to rescue property, although the risks to which a claimant may reasonably expose himself are less than when life is endangered.

c. If there is no immediate danger, only inconvenience, the defence of *volenti* is likely to succeed.

In *CUTLER v UNITED DAIRIES (1933)* P attempted to catch a horse which had bolted into an empty field. In this case the owner's defence of *volenti* succeeded since, as no person was in danger, P was not effecting a rescue but was acting voluntarily.

REMOTENESS OF DAMAGE

4. *Causation and Remoteness*

a. Before the question of remoteness arises, the claimant must show that the respondent's conduct was a substantial factor in bringing about his injury. Thus if the claimant would have suffered the same injury despite the respondent's conduct he will not receive compensation.

In *BARNETT v CHELSEA HOSPITAL MANAGEMENT COMMITTEE (1969)* P went to the hospital complaining of vomiting and was sent away to see his own doctor without being given a proper examination. Shortly afterwards P died of arsenic poisoning. P's widow's negligence action failed because P would have died whatever action the hospital doctor had taken. The careless examination was not the *cause* of the death.

b. Causation and remoteness are different parts of the same series of events. For example, the causes and consequences of a car accident can be represented as follows:

Causation is concerned with factors to the left of the dotted line, and remoteness with the consequences shown to the right of the line.

5. *The Test for Remoteness*

a. When causation has been established and the basic elements to the tort have been proved, the respondent may be able to escape payment of some or all of the damages claimed by showing that there is not a sufficiently close connection between his behaviour and the damage suffered by the claimant, i.e. that the loss is too remote.

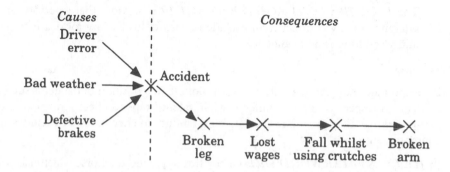

b.   The test for remoteness is '*Reasonable foreseeability*', i.e. the respondent is only liable for the consequences of his act that a reasonable man would have foreseen. This test was established in **OVERSEAS TANKSHIP (UK) v MORTS DOCKS (THE WAGON MOUND) (1961)**, which overruled **RE POLEMIS (1921)**, a case which stated that the respondent was liable for all loss which was the 'direct result' of his tort.

In **THE WAGON MOUND (1961)** an action was brought by the owners of a wharf against the owners of The Wagon Mound (a ship). The ship had discharged oil into Sydney harbour which ignited when hot metal from welding operations being carried on in the harbour fell onto a piece of cotton waste floating in the oil. The court held that damage to the wharf by fouling was foreseeable, but not damage by fire, since oil on water does not usually ignite. The ignition of the oil only occurred because the hot metal fell on to highly combustible cotton waste. Such an event was not reasonably foreseeable.

c.   Note that

   i.   The test is objective, i.e. What matters is not what the defendant actually foresaw (i.e. his subjective foresight) but what a reasonable man would have foreseen as the consequences of the tort, had he applied his mind to it.

   ii. The tort test is wider (more generous to the claimant than the contract test). In contract the loss must be foreseeable as the probable result of the breach.

d.   The following case shows that policy considerations play a part in deciding remoteness issues, i.e. even if the loss is regarded as foreseeable the claimant may not be awarded damages.

In **MEAH v McCREAMER No 2 (1986)** a negligent car driver (McCreamer) crashed, causing head injuries to his passenger (Meah). Meah underwent a personality change and 3 years later sexually assaulted and wounded two women and raped a third. He was sent to prison. In the first action resulting from these events (**MEAH v McCREAMER (1985)**) Meah received damages that compensated him for the personality change and prison sentence. The second action was a claim against Meah for damages by his victims. Liability was admitted and £17 000 was awarded. In the final action (**MEAH v McCREAMER No 2 (1986)**) Meah sought to recover this £17 000 from McCreamer. The judge regarded this as a problem of remoteness. He pointed out that:

   i.   The respondent must take his victim as he finds him even if he has an 'eggshell personality' i.e. he was the worst possible person to receive an injury of this type.

ii. The remoteness rules did not require the precise nature of the damage to be foreseeable, only the general type of damage.

iii. Policy considerations would have to be taken into account when deciding whether a particular loss should be recoverable.

Meah's barrister argued that as the claim for imprisonment was successful then it followed that he must be able to recover the damages that he had to pay to his victims. The judge, however, said that there was a distinction between imprisonment of and injuries to Meah himself, and indirect loss suffered as a result of having to compensate someone else. Furthermore it was necessary to draw the line somewhere. It would not for example be reasonable to impose on the driver (McCreamer) liability to support any child born to the victim of the rape. It was held that the damage was too remote and the case was dismissed.

6. *An intervening act*

a. When a chain of events results from a tort, sometimes the loss suffered is not within the scope of compensation merely because it is not reasonably foreseeable. For example:

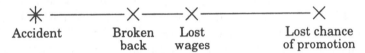

| Accident | Broken back | Lost wages | Lost chance of promotion |

Unless there was a very good chance of promotion the third consequence would probably be too remote.

b. In other cases the chain of events is said to be 'broken' by an intervening event known as a *novus actus interveniens* (a new act intervening). This may be an act of the plaintiff himself or the act of a third party over whom the defendant had no control.

In *LAMB v CAMDEN BOROUGH COUNCIL (1981)* Council workmen broke a water main, causing serious damage to L's house. In fact the house became unsafe and the tenant to whom it was let moved out pending repairs. Squatters then moved into the empty house and caused £30 000 damages. The Court of Appeal awarded P damages in respect of damage due to flooding (liability was admitted by the Council) but rejected the claim for damage caused by squatters because this was not a reasonably foreseeable result of the Council's negligence.

In *KNIGHTLY v JOHNS (1982)* D, a motorist negligently crashed his car, blocking a one-way traffic tunnel. A police inspector then told P, a police constable, to ride the wrong way down the tunnel to stop more motorists from entering. P was injured when he struck a vehicle that was entering the tunnel. It was held that D was not liable for P's injuries since P's accident was not a reasonably foreseeable result of D's negligence.

c. To refer to a new intervening act is in fact merely another way of saying that the loss is not reasonably foreseeable. In the example given in 4.b. above it could be said that the broken arm is too remote because it is not reasonably foreseeable or because the fall from crutches is a *novus actus interveniens* (a new intervening act).

d. Some intervening acts (even if not foreseeable) will not break the chain of events which links the defendant's tort with the claimant's loss. For example:

i. An act done 'in the agony of the moment' created by the respondent's tort.

In *SCOTT v SHEPHERD (1773)* D threw a lighted firework into a crowded market place. Several people threw the firework away from their vicinity until it exploded in P's face. D claimed that the onward throwing of the firework was a *novus actus interveniens.* The court, however, held that the onward throwing was an instinctive act, done in the 'agony of the moment'. It did not therefore break the link between P and D. P was awarded damages.

   ii.   Where the intervening act is a rescue.

7. *'Thin Skull' Cases*

The Wagon Mound decision does not alter the common law rule applicable in 'thin skull' cases. Thus the respondent must still take his victim as he finds him, he cannot plead the medical condition of his victim as a defence, even if this condition means that the loss suffered is not reasonably foreseeable.

In *SMITH v LEECH BRAIN (1962)* P was injured at work when due to the negligence of one of D's employees a piece of molten zinc hit him on the lip. Most people would have been burned and nothing more, but P was susceptible to cancer and the accident brought it on – P died. The court applied the rule that the respondent must take his victim as he finds him, and his estate was awarded full compensation for the loss. The loss was clearly outside the scope of 'reasonable foreseeability', but the judge made it clear that he did not think the Wagon Mound decision was intended to alter the common law rule applicable in 'thin skull cases'.

8. *Strict Liability Torts* In torts of strict liability, i.e. breach of statutory duty and 'Rylands v Fletcher' the reasonable foreseeability test does not apply. The respondent will have to compensate the claimant for all the damage which is the direct result of his tort.

OTHER GENERAL DEFENCES

9. *Mistake* The general rule is that mistake is no defence to a tort action. There are three exceptions. In each case the success of the defence depends on whether or not the respondent acted reasonably in making the mistake.

   a.   False imprisonment. If a policeman without a warrant arrests somebody who has not committed a crime when he reasonably believes that they have.

   b.   Malicious prosecution. If the person who commenced the prosecution (the respondent in the present tort action) was under the mistaken belief that the claimant was guilty of a crime.

   c.   Defamation. See Chapter 27.7.e (unintentional defamation).

10. *Inevitable Accident*

   a.   It has been said that a respondent is not liable if he can prove that damage is due to an 'inevitable accident', i.e. that he is 'utterly without fault'.

       In *STANLEY v POWELL (1891)* D fired his gun at a pheasant but the bullet hit a tree, and ricocheted into P. D was held to be completely blameless and not therefore liable in negligence.

   b.   Professor Winfield has suggested that the defence has very little relevance since the decision in *FOWLER v LANNING (1959)* which pointed out that since the burden of proving fault lies with the claimant, a defence which involves the respondent proving that he is without fault is superfluous.

c.   In any event the plea of inevitable accident cannot be raised in cases of strict liability.

11. *Act of God* This means circumstances which no human foresight can guard against. Act of God differs from inevitable accident since:

a.   It is available as a defence in strict liability cases, and

b.   The 'act' must be caused by the forces of nature without human intervention.

12. *Self-Defence* A person may use reasonable force to defend himself or his property or another person against unlawful force. What is reasonable depends on the facts of each case; however, retaliation will never be reasonable.

13. *Necessity*

a.   This defence may be used where the respondent has inflicted loss on an innocent claimant while attempting to prevent a greater loss to himself.

In *COPE v SHARPE (1912)* a fire broke out on P's land. D, a gamekeeper on adjoining land, entered P's land and burnt some of the heather to form a firebreak to prevent the fire spreading to his employer's land. When sued for trespass his defence of necessity succeeded (even though the firebreak had proved to be unnecessary), since there was a real threat of fire, and D had acted reasonably.

b.   The difference between self-defence and necessity is that self-defence is used against a claimant who is a wrongdoer, and necessity is used against an innocent complainant.

14. *Statutory Authority*

a.   Absolute statutory authority (i.e. where the statute has expressly authorized the thing done, or the thing done is a necessary consequence of what is authorized), is a complete defence, provided the respondent can prove he used all proper care.

In *ALLEN v GULF OIL (1981)* a 450-acre oil refinery dominated the small village of Waterston near Milford Haven, causing both noise and smell. P's nuisance action was one of 53 brought by local residents. D's defence was that their activities were authorized by the *GULF OIL REFINING ACT (1965)*. After some disagreement between the Court of Appeal and the House of Lords on the extent of authority granted by the statute the House of Lords (now the Supreme Court) held, that it authorized both the construction and use of a refinery together with its vast complex of jetties and railway lines. Furthermore, it operated as a complete defence to an action for private nuisance. It is perhaps unfortunate that the House did not take the view of the majority of the Court of Appeal and Lord Keith in the House of Lords. They were of the opinion that although the statute enable Gulf to make the installation and operate it (i.e. an injunction could not be granted), it did not excuse them from paying compensation for injury done to those living in the neighbourhood.

b.   Conditional statutory authority (i.e. where the injury is not a necessary consequence of what is authorized) is no defence.

15. *Illegality* It is a general principal of law that a cause of action cannot be maintained if a claimant is seeking to rely upon conduct that is illegal. In *THACKWELL v BARCLAYS BANK (1986)* T brought an action against his bank, Barclays, for refusing to cash a cheque. The cheque represented the proceeds of a fraud committed by T and his claim, therefore, was barred for illegality.

SELF TEST QUESTIONS

Self Test Questions No. 19 (for Answers see Appendix 1):

1   What is the defence of consent?

2   How does remoteness of damage constitute a defence?

3   What is the test of remoteness?

4   What are the consequences of an intervening act on the defendant's liability?

5   Explain briefly the meaning of each of the following general defences:

mistake

inevitable accident

act of God

self-defence

necessity

statutory authority

illegality.

CAPACITY IN TORT

22

Learning Outcomes At the end of this chapter you should be able to:

- State the exceptions to the general rule that any person may sue and be sued in tort.

- Explain the meaning of 'vicarious liability' as it applies to independent contracts and employees.

- Demonstrate an understanding of the principle of 'joint vicarious liability'.

PARTIES TO WHOM SPECIAL RULES APPLY

1. Generally any person can sue or be sued, but there are exceptions.

2. *The Crown*

   a. The *CROWN PROCEEDINGS ACT 1947* preserves the immunity of Her Majesty in her private capacity from any legal process, but provides machinery whereby (with some exceptions) the Crown can be sued in respect of the torts of subordinates.

   b. Actions under the Act are brought against the appropriate government department.

3. *The Post Office*

   a. No proceedings in tort lie against the Post Office for any act or omission of its servants in relation to a postal packet or telephonic communication (*POST OFFICE ACT 1969*).

b.   However, the Post Office is liable for loss or damage to a registered inland letter if caused by a wrongful act or omission of an employee or agent of the Post Office.

4. *Minors*

a.   A minor can sue in tort, although proceedings must be brought through his 'next friend', i.e. his nearest adult relative.

b.   Minority is generally no defence, however:

i.   Extreme youth may be relevant in cases where some special mental element is needed, such as malice or in considering the standard of care to be expected.

ii.   A minor cannot be sued in tort where this would be an indirect way of enforcing a contract on which he is not liable. Contrast *BURNARD v HAGGIS (1863)* with *JENNINGS v RUNDALL (1799)* (Chapter 13.7).

c.   A parent is not liable as such for his child's tort, but he may be liable on other grounds. For example:

i.   If he employs the child he may be vicariously liable as employer.

ii.   If he expressly authorizes the tort, or

iii.   If he negligently allowed his child the opportunity of causing harm, for example by allowing a young child to possess a dangerous weapon.

5. *Husband and Wife*

a.   A husband is not affected if his wife is sued and vice versa.

b.   Each may sue the other as if they were not married.

6. *Corporations*

a.   They can sue for such torts as can be committed against them and not, for example, for trespass to the person.

b.   They can be sued for the torts of an employee committed whilst he was acting in the course of his employment.

7. *Unincorporated Organizations*

a.   Such bodies have no legal existence separate from that of their members and cannot therefore sue or be sued, although members who committed or authorized the tort are liable.

b.   Where the tort arises from the use of the organization's property a representative action may be brought against one member of the organization, representing himself and the other members.

c.   There are provisions for partnerships to sue and be sued in the firm's name.

8. *Judicial Immunity* Judges, magistrates and magistrates' clerks have immunity for acts in their judicial capacity. Barristers and witnesses have immunity in respect of all matters relating to the cases with which they are concerned. This is mainly relevant to prevent actions against them for slander.

9. *Executors*

a.   At common law a personal action died with the injured person. Now under the *LAW REFORM (MISCELLANEOUS PROVISIONS) ACT 1934* (as amended) on the death of any person, all causes of action (except defamation) whether as respondent or claimant survive against the estate or for the benefit of the estate. However, the damages recoverable:

i.   Cannot be exemplary, and

ii. Where the tort caused the death, must be calculated without reference to any loss or gain to the estate resulting from the death (for example the proceeds of life assurance) except that funeral expenses may be included.

The estate may therefore claim damages for the period between injury and death, for example for pain and suffering, loss of earnings and medical expenses. However, there is no claim for loss of expectation of life or for loss of income after death.

b.   If the person is killed as a result of, for example negligence, a second separate action may be brought by dependants under the *FATAL ACCIDENTS ACT 1976*. Under this Act a person whose negligence caused the death of another will be liable to certain relatives if they have suffered financial loss because of the death. No action may be brought if more than 3 years have elapsed between injury and death. Also if the deceased was guilty of contributory negligence the damages will be reduced according to the extent to which he was at fault. In assessing damages under the *FATAL ACCIDENTS ACT 1976* any benefits arising from the death, for example insurance policies, pensions or gratuities are to be disregarded.

10. *Joint Tortfeasors*

a.   If two or more people are jointly liable in tort, either or both may be sued.

b.   If only one is sued and is required to pay damages he may usually recover a contribution from the other under the *CIVIL LIABILITY (CONTRIBUTION) ACT 1978*. The amount of contribution will be decided by the court on the basis of what is just the equitable given the responsibility of each party for the injury.

VICARIOUS LIABILITY

11. 'Vicarious liability' means liability for the torts of others, and arises because of a relationship between the parties. The relationship may be either:

a.   Employer/independent contractor, or

b.   Employer/employee (master/servant).

12. *Liability for the Torts of Independent Contractors*

a.   An independent contractor is a person who undertakes to produce a given result, and who in the actual execution of the work is not under the control of the person for whom he does it.

b.   The general rule is that an employer is not liable for the tort of his independent contractor.

In *PADBURY v HOLLIDAY AND GREENWOOD (1912)* an employee of a contractor engaged to fit windows negligently left a hammer lying on a window sill. A gust of wind caught the window which, as it moved, knocked the hammer onto P, a passer-by. D were not held liable since the tort was committed by an employee of their independent contractor.

   c.   Exceptions:

       i.   Strict liability under the rule in Rylands v Fletcher.

       ii.   Where the employer was negligent in the hiring of the independent contractor.

       iii.   Where the duty is personal, for example an employer has a duty to provide employees with reasonably safe plant and a reasonably safe system of work. If he employs a contractor in the discharge of this duty he remains liable for any negligence by the contractor.

       iv.   Where the work is 'extra hazardous'.

   For example:

   In *HONEYWILL AND STEIN v LARKIN BROTHERS (1934)* an independent contractor used magnesium flares to take pictures of the inside of a cinema. The negligence of the contractor caused a fire to start. In this case the employer of the contractor was held liable since he had ordered the performance of what was regarded as a hazardous activity.

13. *Liability for the Torts of Employees*

   a.   A person is an employee if his employer retains a right to control not only the work he does, but also the way in which he does it. The test is the right of control, not how much control was in fact exercised. This is the traditional test, but difficulties arise when applying it to professional persons such as doctors. In such cases it may be necessary to consider such criteria as payment of salaries and the power of dismissal.

   b.   The rule is that an employer is vicariously liable for the torts of his employee that are committed within the *course of his employment*. The tortious act must be a wrongful way of doing what the employee is employed to do.

   In *LIMPUS v LONDON GENERAL OMNIBUS CO (1862)* a bus driver whilst racing a bus caused an accident. His employers were held liable because he was doing what he was employed to do, i.e. driving a bus, although in an improper way.

   Contrast *BEARD v LONDON GENERAL OMNIBUS CO (1900)* a bus conductor attempted to turn a bus around at the end of its route and in doing so he caused an accident. His employers were not liable since he was employed only to collect fares and not to drive buses.

   c.   An act of violence will usually take the employee outside the scope of employment and the employer will not be liable.

   In *WARREN V HENLYS (1948)* a petrol pump attendant assaulted a customer during an argument over payment for petrol. It was held that the employer was not liable.

   d.   The employer may be liable even if the employee acts contrary to clear instructions.

   In *ROSE v PLENTY (1976)* D was a milkman. His employer did everything possible to stop the common practice of taking young children on the van and paying them to help deliver the milk. A notice at the depot said

   'Children must not in any circumstances be employed by you in the performance of your duties.'

Contrary to this instruction D employed P. While moving from one delivery point to another the boy had one leg dangling from the van so that he could jump off quickly. D drove negligently and P's foot was crushed between the van and the kerb.

It was held that D's employer was liable because D had been acting within the scope of his employment, i.e. delivering milk and collecting empty bottles, although in an improper way.

e. Sometimes a prohibition imposed by an employer on an employee will limit the scope of employment. Thus in *TWINE v BEAN'S EXPRESS (1944)* a prohibition against drivers giving lifts to hitchhikers was held to limit the scope of employment. However, this was not considered relevant to Rose v Plenty since Rose was not a mere passenger being given a lift, but he was the method by which Plenty did his job.

f. An employee may be within the course of his employment even though he has acted fraudulently.

In *LLOYD v GRACE, SMITH & CO (1912)* the respondents were solicitors who employed a managing clerk to do conveyancing. The managing clerk fraudulently induced P to convey two cottages to him by representing that this was necessary in order to sell the cottages. The clerk then resold the cottages and absconded with the sale proceeds. The solicitors were held liable on the grounds that by allowing him to perform conveyancing transactions they had given him apparent authority to act as he did. He was acting within the scope of his employment even though his act was fraudulent.

g. An employee who wrongfully uses his own property to carry on his job may still be within the course of his employment.

In *McKEAN v RAYNOR BROTHERS (1942)* an employee was told to deliver a message using the firm's lorry. Although he took his own car he was still held to be in the course of his employment.

If an employer allows an employee to use the employer's vehicle for the employee's own use, the employer will not be liable for any accident that may occur.

If an employer provides a vehicle for the employee's use, the employee may be regarded as the employer's agent if he gives another employee a lift, even though it is not within the scope of his employment to do this.

In *VANDYKE v FENDER (1970)* an employee who was provided with a company car gave other employees a lift to work. There was an accident and one of the other employees was injured. He was successful in his claim for damages against the company since Mr Fender, although not a paid driver, was driving the car as the company's agent and they were therefore liable for his negligence.

h. When an employee who is on a journey deviates from the authorized route, it is a question of degree whether he has started on a fresh journey ('a frolic of his own') which relieves the employer from liability (see *HILTON v THOMAS BURTON LTD (1961)* in Chapter 52.21).

i. Where the employer is held liable for his employee's tort, the employee is also generally liable, but if a blameless employer is held liable for his employee's tort, a term is implied in their contract that the employee will indemnify the employer (*LISTER v ROMFORD ICE & COLD STORAGE LTD (1957)*).

14. *Joint Vicarious Liability* The Court of Appeal in *VIASYSTEMS LTD v THERMAL TRANSFER (NORTHERN) LTD (2005)* recognized for the first time the possibility of more than one party being held liable for the same act. The claimant entered into a contract with Thermal, to have air conditioning installed in a factory. Thermal subcontracted the work to A who in turn contracted with B to supply labour for the installation work. B's employees worked under A's supervision during the work.

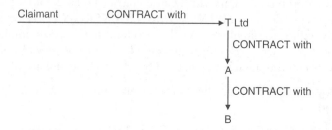

B's employees, through their negligence, flooded the factory and caused considerable damage. The claimant was seeking damages from T Ltd, A and B. (Note: the only contract was between the claimant and T Ltd, there was no contract between the claimant and A and B – so no contractual rights with A or B, the action was brought under tort.) The High Court found that T Ltd were not liable and that B was at fault; on appeal B argued that as A was supervizing B's employees, A should be liable. The Court of Appeal decided to reassess the law of vicarious liability and potential joint liability and found that A and B were each jointly liable for 50% of the loss. The case, for the first time, introduced joint vicarious liability.

SELF TEST QUESTIONS

Self Test Questions No. 20 (for Answers see Appendix 1):

1   What is meant by the term 'vicarious liability'?

2   How is vicarious liability applied to independent contractors and employees?

3   What did the VIASYSTEMS case introduce for the first time?

NEGLIGENCE

23

Learning Outcomes At the end of this chapter you should be able to:

- State and apply the test for establishing the existence of a duty of care.

- Understand the significance of 'economic loss' to a negligence claim.

- Explain the law as it applies to:

  - negligent statements

  - claims for nervous shock

  - the setting an appropriate standard of care

  - the nature of the damage suffered

  - contributory negligence

  - occupiers liability.

1. *Basic Requirements* If he is to succeed in a negligence action the claimant must prove:

   a. That the respondent owed to him a legal duty of care, and

   b. That the respondent has been guilty of a breach of that duty, and

   c. That damage has been caused to the claimant by that breach.

Note in particular that the burden of proof is placed on the claimant. Each of these requirements is now considered in turn.

THE DUTY OF CARE

2. *The Neighbour Test*

a.   The courts have always taken the view that a careless person should not have to compensate all the people who suffer as a result of his conduct. For example, when a van driver is injured due to the negligence of another driver several people may also be affected. There may be a witness to the accident who suffers nightmares as a result of his experience and a trader to whom the driver was delivering goods may lose profits because of inadequate stock. In such cases the task of the court is to consider the interests of the victims whilst being fair to the careless person.

This is achieved by asking two questions:

i.   Is there a sufficient relationship of *proximity* between the claimant and the respondent?

ii. If so, are there any *policy* reasons for negating or reducing the class of persons to whom a duty is owned?

If these questions are applied to the above example the result will be compensation for the van driver, but for policy reasons the witness and trader are unlikely to be compensated.

b.   'Proximity' does not mean physical proximity, it is based on reasonable foreseeability and is generally known as the '*neighbour test*'. The first case to establish this principle of proximity was in 1932.

In *DONOGHUE v STEVENSON (1932)* P's friend purchased a bottle of ginger beer manufactured by D and gave it to P. P drank most of the bottle, but then noticed the decomposed remains of a snail in the bottom of the bottle. P subsequently became ill and sued D in negligence. D's defence was that he did not owe a duty of care to P because there was no contract between D and P (the purchaser having been P's friend).

The court, however, held that a contractual link should no longer be the test for determining whether or not a duty of care was owed. The House of Lords (now the Supreme Court) stated that a duty of care is owed to any person who we can reasonably foresee will be injured by our acts or omissions. The court described such persons as 'neighbours'. It was held that D could reasonably foresee that somebody apart from the original purchaser may consume his product and he was therefore held liable to P.

c.   The neighbour test has been applied in numerous cases since 1932, for example:

In *KING v PHILLIPS (1952)* D carelessly drove his taxi over a boy's cycle. The boy, who was not on the bicycle, screamed. His mother (P) heard the scream and on looking out of the window saw the crushed bicycle, but not her son. As a result she suffered shock which made her ill. She failed in her action against D because it was held that a driver could only reasonably foresee that his carelessness would affect other road users and not persons in houses. He did not therefore owe a duty of care to P.

In *TUTTON v WALTER (1985)* P kept bees on land near to D's farm. D had a crop of oilseed rape which, when in flower, is particularly attractive to bees. Despite clear written instructions to the contrary D sprayed his crop while it was in flower, with a pesticide that was fatal to bees. His defence to P's action was that no duty was owed because he was doing on his own land something that he was entitled to do, and that the bees came on to the land without permission and were basically trespassers. The judge did not accept these arguments. It was held that the duty was owed under the neighbour principle and it had been broken. P therefore received compensation for the loss of his bee colony.

In *HOME OFFICE v DORSET YACHT CO (1970)* it was held that the Home Office owed a duty of care to the Yacht Club in respect of the detention of Borstal trainees who had escaped from an institution and caused damage to P's yachts. The duty to people whose property might be damaged in an escape was based on the control which the Home Office has over Borstal trainees.

d. In certain situations the courts will not apply the neighbour test without qualification. The main areas concern negligent statements, economic loss, and nervous shock, each of which are considered below (Paragraphs 3–5). In addition a claimant who is within the neighbour test may not receive compensation:

   i.   Where the respondent is guilty of an *omission* which results in foreseeable harm, for example by failing to save a small child drowning in shallow water. This exception will only apply if there is a 'pure omission', i.e. if the defendant's prior conduct gives rise to a duty, the fact that an omission is the direct cause of the harm will not save the defendant from liability – clearly a car driver cannot avoid liability by claiming that the accident was caused by his omission to apply the brake.

   ii. Where a barrister is sued for professional negligence as a result of his conduct of a case in court (*RONDEL v WORSLEY (1969)* Chapter 9.7). In *ARTHUR JS HALL & CO v SIMONS (2000)*, The House of Lords (now the Supreme Court) ruled that immunity of barristers for negligence in their work in court was no longer sustainable. This was unanimously agreed in respect of civil litigation and by a majority in respect of criminal cases.

   iii. If a person is the occupier of land and the injured person is a trespasser. (The extent of the duty is defined by the *OCCUPIERS' LIABILITY ACT 1984.*)

   iv. If the injured person is an accomplice in crime.

In *ASHTON v TURNER (1981)* D, a burglar driving a getaway car caused an accident in which P, his accomplice, was injured. Both P and D were drunk. It was held for public policy reasons that D was not liable.

3. *Economic Loss*

   a. Where negligent conduct causes economic loss (i.e. financial loss that is not consequential upon physical injury to person or property) the courts have been generally unwilling to hold that a duty of care exists.

In *MUIRHEAD v INDUSTRIAL TANK SPECIALISTS (1986)* P established a lobster farm. He intended to purchase lobsters cheaply in the summer, keep them alive until Christmas, and then sell them at a higher price. A constant supply of circulating seawater was needed to keep the lobsters alive. He installed the necessary tanks and pumps. Unfortunately the pump motor (supplied by a French firm) could not cope with the fluctuations in English voltage and a large number of lobsters were lost as a result of a pump failure. P claimed compensation for the loss of lobsters and loss of potential profit. It was held that he could recover for the loss of the lobsters and any financial loss suffered in direct consequence, but could not recover for any loss of profit.

b.   Numerous economic loss cases have concerned the liability of persons involved in the design, approval and construction of buildings. The position was reviewed by the House of Lords.

In *MURPHY v BRENTWOOD DISTRICT COUNCIL (1990)* P claimed £35 000 from D as compensation for the reduction in the value of his house which suffered as a result of defects in the design. The defective design had been approved by the Council. P relied on a 1977 case (*ANNS v MERTON LBC*) where, in a similar situation, the plaintiff had been successful. However, a 7-member House of Lords unanimously over-ruled the Anns' decision on the grounds that it did not proceed on the basis of estab-lished principles, but introduced a potentially indeterminate liability covering a wide range of situations. In Murphy's case the court held that such loss was purely economic (not physical) and was not therefore within the scope of the duty of care owed by D to P. They made it clear that the right to recover for pure economic loss, not flowing from physical injury, must be determined by the principle in Hedley Byrne v Heller (see 4. below).

In *DEPARTMENT OF THE ENVIRONMENT v THOMAS BATES (1990)* P had a 42-year lease of part of an office block constructed by D. Eleven years after the offices had been constructed it was discovered that low strength concrete had been used in var-ious supporting pillars. The building was still safe for its existing load, but the pillars were not strong enough to support the design load of the building. P carried out reme-dial work and then sued D for negligence. The court applied the decision in Murphy's case, holding that the loss was purely economic and was not recoverable in tort, because when the remedial work was carried out the building was not unsafe, but merely subject to a defect in quality which made P's lease less valuable.

c.   Hedley Byrne has been applied on many occasions. Examples include *SMITH v ERIC BUSH (1989)* (Chapter 15.13.v) and *HARRIS v WYRE FOREST DISTRICT COUNCIL (1989)*.

In *HARRIS v WYRE FOREST DISTRICT COUNCIL (1989)* P paid a valuation fee to the council in connection with a loan application. On the basis of the valuation report the Council lent P £8500 out of a purchase price of £9000. P did not personally see the valuation report. Serious settlement was later discovered which required extensive repair. The House of Lords (now the Supreme Court) held that D was liable since although P had not seen the valuation report, it was reasonable for him to assume that the surveyor conducting the valuation had not found any serious defects.

Unfortunately the *SMITH* and *HARRIS* decisions are arguably inconsistent with *MURPHY v BRENTWOOD DISTRICT COUNCIL*, in that a surveyor who carries out a negligent valuation is liable to a purchaser who suffers economic loss (the *SMITH* and *HARRIS* cases) but a surveyor who negligently approves defective plans or founda-tions will not be liable to a purchaser (*MURPHY'S* case).

d.   The cautious approach exemplified in Murphy's case has recently been applied to accountants in the leading case of *CAPARO INDUSTRIES PLC v DICKMAN (1990)* and the James McNaughton case described below.

In *CAPARO INDUSTRIES v DICKMAN (1990)* the plaintiff company sued two directors of Fidelity plc. and the accountants Touche Ross & Co, the auditors of Fidelity. The plaintiff had taken over Fidelity and alleged that the profits were much lower than shown in the audited accounts, consequently they had suffered financial loss. The House of Lords (now the Supreme Court) considered whether a duty of care is owed to persons who rely on the accounts to deal with the company or to buy and sell its shares. The House stated that the criteria for the imposition of a duty were:

(a) Foreseeability of damage.

(b) Proximity of the relationship, and

(c) The reasonableness or otherwise of imposing a duty.

To establish proximity all of the following factors will typically need to be present:

i.   The advice was required for a purpose made known to the adviser when the advice was given.

ii. The adviser knew his advice would be communicated to the recipient in order that it should be used for this purpose.

iii. It was known that the advice was likely to be acted upon without independent inquiry.

iv. It was acted on to the recipient's detriment.

The House was prepared to acknowledge that liability for negligent audit can exist, but the above factors were not present in Caparo's case. The plaintiff's action therefore failed.

In *JAMES McNAUGHTON PAPER GROUP v HICKS ANDERSON (1990)* P was known to be interested in taking over the MK Paper Group. D, who were MK's accountants had recently produced a draft profit and loss account showing a loss of £48 000. However, they told P that following a rationalization MK was now breaking even. The takeover proceeded, but it was later discovered that there were a number of errors in the accounts. P's negligence action against D failed because the Court of Appeal adopted the restrictive approach of Caparo v Dickman and held that no duty of care was owed by the accountants to P. Unlike Caparo, it was known that P was considering a takeover, however, the court was not prepared to attribute to D the knowledge that P would rely on the accounts, without further inquiry or advice, for the purpose of finalizing an agreement. The court clearly felt that P should have realized that the company was in a poor state and should have consulted its own advisers.

4. *Negligent Statements*

   a. The usual rules of liability apply when the negligent statement results in physical injury. For example, in *CLAY v CRUMP (1963)* D, an architect, stated that a wall on a demolition site was safe and could be left standing. It later collapsed injuring P. P succeeded in his action against D for his negligent statement.

   b. Where the negligent statement results in financial loss different rules of liability apply. The difference concerns the persons to whom a duty of care is owed. Instead of the 'neighbour test' laid down in *DONOGHUE v STEVENSON (1932)* the courts initially formulated in *HEDLEY BYRNE v HELLER (1964)*, a much narrower test based on a 'special relationship' between the parties.

In *HEDLEY BYRNE v HELLER (1964)* D were bankers and P were advertising agents. They had a mutual client E Ltd who wished to place advertisements on television. E requested credit from P, so P asked D for references. D stated that E was a respectably constituted firm and was considered good, although the statement was made without responsibility on their part. P therefore incurred personal liability on several advertising contracts. E then went into liquidation and P were unable to recover over £17 000 owed to them. P therefore sued D on his negligent statement. It was held that he did have a possible action, and he would have succeeded, but for the disclaimer of responsibility. In order to succeed in such a case the plaintiff must show a special relationship by proving that:

i.   He relied on the special skill and judgement of the defendant, and

ii. The defendant knew or ought to have known of this reliance and thus accepted responsibility for making the statement carefully.

In *ROYAL BANK OF SCOTLAND PLC v BANNERMAN JOHNSTONE MACLAY (2003)* RBS lent money to a customer who subsequently went into liquidation. RBS claimed that it had lent the money based upon accounts audited by the defendants, BJM, for the customer. BJM argued that they did not owe a duty of care to RBS because it was not possible for RBS to show that they relied on the accounts when making the loan decisions. The Court held that a duty would be owed to RBS if BJM knew that the accounts would be passed to third parties and were likely to be relied upon. BJM knew that the accounts were likely to be so used and therefore owed a duty of care to the end user, RBS. If they had wished to disclaim liability they should have included a disclaimer which they did not do. Following the case the Institute of Chartered Accountants in its guidance to members (*Audit 01/03*) has pointed out that unless a disclaimer is attached to audited accounts, member auditors may well find themselves liable to third parties.

c.   In some exceptional situations a claimant may succeed even if he does not rely on any statement by the respondent, although in such cases there must be close proximity between the claimant and the respondent.

In *ROSS v CAUNTERS (1979)* D was a solicitor. One of his clients bequeathed some property to the claimant. At the time the will was executed D had failed:

i.   To tell the testator that the will must not be witnessed by the spouse of any beneficiary.

ii. To check that the will had been properly executed.

iii. To notice that P's husband had witnessed the will, and

iv. To draw the testator's attention to this fact. (It was admitted that if the testator had been told of the error he would have put it right.)

As a result of iii. above P was prevented from inheriting under the will. She was, however, successful in her negligence action against D, despite the fact that she clearly had not relied on any statement by D. The judge did not adopt the 'reasonable foreseeability' test or the 'special relationship' test. He chose a point between the two, in effect there must be a *close proximity* between P and D – P *individually (or as a member of a specific and limited class) must be in the defendant's direct contemplation as someone likely to be closely and directly affected by his acts.*

This requirement was satisfied in ***ROSS v CAUNTERS (1979)*** because:

i.   P was named in the will.

ii.   The proximity was in no way accidental or unforeseen, but arose out of D's duty to his client. In fact the aim of the transaction between D and his client was to confer a benefit on P.

d.   If there is a subsequent contract between the claimant and the respondent, based wholly on a negligent statement made by the respondent, the claimant will not be confined to contractual remedies, but may also have a remedy in tort.

In ***ESSO PETROLEUM v MARDON (1976)*** Esso found a site for a filling station on a busy main road. A company executive with 40 years experience of the petrol trade estimated that sales would be 200 000 gallons per year by the third year, (assuming access to the main road), so Esso bought the site. However, planning permission was then refused for direct access to the main road, thus reducing potential sales. Despite this the executive later represented to M that sales would be 200 000 gallons per year. Even though M's own estimate was 100 000–150 000 gallons per year he accepted a tenancy relying on the accuracy of the executive's statement. His rent was based on expected sales of 200 000 gallons per year. In the first 15 months sales were only 78 000 gallons and M could not therefore pay the rent. He was sued by Esso. In return he brought a counter-claim against Esso, claiming damages in contract for breach of warranty and damages in tort for a negligent statement. It was held by the Court of Appeal:

i.   On the contract point: That since the party making the statement had expertise it could be interpreted as a warranty (i.e. a term of the contract rather than a mere representation inducing the contract) breach of which entitled the innocent party to damages.

ii.   On the tort point: That if a person professing to have special knowledge or skill makes a representation which induces the other to contract with him he is under a duty to take reasonable care to see that the representation is correct. Esso were therefore liable in damages. Esso's defence to the tort claim was that ***HEDLEY BYRNE v HELLER (1964)*** could not apply since it was concerned solely with liability in tort, and not where a pre-contract statement made in negotiations later resulted in a contract – in which case the law of contract provides the plaintiff's only remedies. This defence clearly failed.

e.   A disclaimer of responsibility by the defendant (as in Hedley Byrne v Heller) will be sufficient to exclude the duty of care. However, since the *UNFAIR CONTRACT TERMS ACT 1977*, the exemption clause must satisfy the requirement of reasonableness. See ***SMITH v ERIC BUSH (1989)*** (Chapter 15.13.v).

5. *Nervous Shock*

a.   Nervous shock occurs when a person is so affected by a horrifying event that they suffer an identifiable psychiatric illness. Ordinary grief and sorrow, which is reasonably foreseeable, does not amount to nervous shock. The courts have been very reluctant to regard a duty as owed to persons who suffer nervous rather than physical injuries. There are several reasons for this:

i.   Fear of fraudulent claims.

ii.   The difficulty of fixing a monetary value to such loss.

     iii. Unfairness to defendants if damages become out of proportion to the negligent conduct complained of.

b. It used to be thought that to claim for nervous shock the claimant must fear injury to himself or a near relative and that the shock must result from actually seeing the accident itself rather than the aftermath. However, decided cases have extended the basis for a claim.

In ***CHADWICK v BRITISH RAILWAYS BOARD (1967)*** the Board were held liable in negligence for a serious railway accident in which 90 people died. P was a voluntary rescue worker who worked all night in the wreck. As a result he later suffered from neurosis which necessitated hospital treatment. P succeeded in his action against the British Railways Board. It was held that in the circumstances injury by shock to volunteer rescue workers was foreseeable. Accordingly a duty was owed to such persons and damages could be awarded even though the shock did not arise from fear of injury to himself or his family.

In ***MCLOUGHLIN v O'BRIEN (1982)*** P's husband and three children were injured in a car accident caused by D's negligence. One of the children died almost immediately. At the time of the accident P was at home about two miles away. About an hour later the accident was reported to her by a neighbour who said that he thought her son was dying. The neighbour then drove her to hospital where her fourth child (who was not in the accident) told her that her youngest daughter aged 3, was dead. At the hospital she saw through a corridor window her other daughter (aged 7) crying, with her face cut and covered in dirt and oil, she could also hear her son (aged 17) shouting and screaming. As a result of seeing these injuries and the distressing way in which she learned of them P suffered a severe shock, depression and a change of personality. The House of Lords (now the Supreme Court) awarded damages since the loss was reasonably foreseeable and the injury was an illness rather than 'normal' grief and sorrow. The House was not impressed by the public policy argument that such a decision 'would open the floodgates'.

c. More recently the Supreme Court has laid down more restrictive principles for nervous shock cases.

In ***ALCOCK v CHIEF CONSTABLE OF WEST YORKSHIRE (1991)*** the case resulted from the disaster at Hillsborough Football Ground in Sheffield when too many people were allowed into the ground. Nearly 100 people were killed and many more injured as they were crushed against railings and barricades. The scenes were witnessed on nationwide television. The House of Lords (now the Supreme Court) established the principle that the person at fault owes a duty of care to a person who is not actively involved in the accident only if:

     i. There is a close tie of love and affection with the primary victim such that it is reasonably forseeable he will suffer nervous shock, and

     ii. There is proximity in time and space i.e. the claimant must see or hear the accident for its immediate aftermath with his own unaided senses.

It was therefore held that only the parents or spouses of the victims could recover damages for nervous shock, provided they had actually seen the accident by being at the ground or as a result of identifying bodies afterwards. Parents or spouses who had only seen the disaster by viewing live television could not get damages.

d. It has been held that damages for nervous shock can be recovered as a result of witnessing damage to property.

In *ATTIA v BRITISH GAS (1987)* P suffered a nervous shock when, on returning home, she saw that the whole of her house was on fire as a result of D's negligence.

THE STANDARD OF CARE

6. The defendant will discharge his duty if he takes reasonable care. This is an objective test, i.e. the test is 'Did the defendant exercise the care that a reasonable man would have exercised?' It is not 'Did he do his best?'

The care which a reasonable man would show varies with the circumstances. Some relevant factors may be:

a. The magnitude of the foreseeable risk.

In *LATIMER v AEC (1953)* a thunderstorm flooded D's factory, making the floor slippery. D did all they could to clear the water and make the factory safe. P nevertheless slipped and was injured. P alleged negligence, claiming that the factory should have been closed. It was held that the risk of injury did not justify such a drastic measure. P's claim failed.

b. The known characteristics of the party exposed to the risk.

In *PARIS v STEPNEY BOROUGH COUNCIL (1951)* P, who only had one eye, worked for the council as a vehicle welder. He was blinded completely when a spark flew into his one good eye. He sued his employers for negligence claiming that he should have been supplied with goggles. The evidence was the goggles were not thought necessary for two-eyed welders. However, since the loss of a person's only good eye is far more serious that the loss of one of two good eyes, goggles should have been supplied to P. The council had broken their duty of care.

In *SIMONDS v ISLE OF WIGHT (2003)* a 5-year-old child was injured after falling off a swing. The Local Council were held not liable, the Court finding that the swing presented an inherent and obvious risk which a parent should appreciate when they allowed their child to use it. And in *POPPLETON v TRUSTEES OF THE PORTSMOUTH YOUTH ACTIVITIES COMMITTEE (2008)* the Court of Appeal held that where a risk is obvious and removal of it impracticable, there will be no liability. Here the claimant was paralyzed when he fell from a climbing wall; the Court found that no amount of matting could have provided complete protection from an awkward fall. The risks were inherent and obvious and the claimant had clearly consented to exposing himself to those risks.

An interesting case illustrating how the courts assess foreseeable risk is, *ABOUZAID v MOTHERCARE (UK) (2000)*. The claimant, a 12-year-old boy, was seeking compensation for injuries he received when helping his mother to attach a bag to his brother's pushchair which helped keep legs and feet warm. The bag attached to the pram by means of elasticated straps and a metal buckle. One of the straps slipped from his hand and the buckle injured his eye. On the degree of foreseeablity of harm by the manufacturer, the court found (i) there were no previous comparable accidents; (ii) elasticated tape was a commonly used material on these products and there was no pre-existing evidence to suggest its use might cause injury; (iii) although there was a potential for harm to occur, the likelihood of injury occurring was small. The manufacturer was found not liable.

c.   Whether the respondent was faced with an emergency.

In *WATT v HERTFORDSHIRE C.C. (1954)* P, a fireman, was injured when a jack slipped in a lorry while going to an accident. The lorry was not equipped to carry the jack, but it had been used because the fire brigade were faced with an emergency. P's action failed, the council had not broken its duty of care.

d.   Whether a special relationship exists, such as that of competitor to spectator as in *WOOLDRIDGE v SUMNER (1963)* (Chapter 21.1).

e.   The state of health of the respondent. If the respondent causes a road accident he will only escape liability if his actions at the relevant time were wholly beyond his control, as in a case of sudden unconsciousness.

In *ROBERTS v RAMSBOTTOM (1980)* D collided head on with a parked vehicle, causing injury to its occupants. D claimed that he was not liable because 20 minutes earlier he had unknowingly suffered a stroke.

This affected his mind so that he could not drive properly. It also meant that he could not appreciate the he was unfit to drive. He did, however, have sufficient awareness of his surroundings and traffic conditions to continue to control the car, although in an inadequate way. It was held that where a driver retains some control, even if imperfect, he must be judged by the objective standard of a reasonable driver. In this case, even though D was not morally to blame because of the nature of the disabling symptoms, D had fallen below this objective standard and was liable.

f.   In addition to any statutory and contractual duties owed by an employer to his employee an employer has a common law duty to act with reasonable care towards his employees. To assess whether he has discharged this duty it will be necessary to consider, among other things, whether he has provided:

i.   A competent staff.

ii. Proper tools, machinery and premises, and

iii. A safe system of work and supervision.

Where work is done on another person's premises the employer's duty is less onerous, although he must still show reasonable care.

In *WILSON v TYNESIDE WINDOW CLEANING CO (1958)* the employer discharged his duty of care by telling window cleaners employed by him to take reasonable care, and not to clean windows if it was dangerous to do so.

g.   In order to counter what the Government saw as a 'compensation culture' whereby otherwise desirable acts, e.g. a doctor or nurse coming across an accident in the street, were being discouraged from doing something by the fear of potential litigation, the *COMPENSATION ACT 2006* was passed. The Act allows a court to take into account, when assessing, whether a defendant had, 'done enough' and met the duty owed, the extent to which action or inaction on his part, might deter or prevent an otherwise desirable activity from being undertaken. The considerations to be taken into account when assessing the requisite steps a defendant could have taken are two-fold; would such steps:

   i.   Prevent a desirable activity from taking place at all?

   ii.   Discourage persons from undertaking functions in connection with a desirable activity? (*S.1*).

The Act further provides that an apology, an offer of treatment or other redress, shall not of itself amount to an admission of negligence (*S.2*). In the past a defendant apologizing was often seen as an admittance of 'guilt'.

The provisions of the Act are well illustrated in: ***PERRY v HARRIS (2008)***. In this case parents had hired a bouncy castle for their children's party. A child was injured when another child, engaged in a somersault on the castle, accidently kicked and seriously injured another child. The parent, defendants, accepted that they owed a duty of care to the children in allowing them to play on the equipment, the question was whether they had 'done enough' to meet that duty of care owed. One of the parents was supervizing the activities but was distracted by another child calling for attention. The Court of Appeal held that such activities were desirable for young children, and that it would be against public policy for parents to stop such activities from taking place and that whilst some surveillance and supervision was required, it need not be constant. The required standard of care would be identified on the basis of the facts which the defendant parents know or ought to have known. The chances of severe injury were not reasonably foreseeable, constant surveillance was not required against those less foreseeable risks. The claimants had met the requisite standard of care and were not liable. (Note the potential harshness of the tort of negligence's requirement for a degree of 'fault' on the part of the defendant – an innocent, severely injured child gets no compensation.)

7. ***Res Ipsa Loquitur*** (the facts speak for themselves)

   a.   In some situations the claimant will not need to prove a breach of the duty of care. This is where the maxim *res ipsa loquitur* applies.

   b.   The maxim applies when:

      i.   The 'thing' is under the control of the respondent.

      ii.   The respondent has knowledge denied to the claimant, and

      iii.   The damage is such that it would not normally have happened if proper care had been shown by the respondent.

   c.   If these requirements are fulfilled there is prima facie evidence of a breach of duty. The burden of proof is then shifted to the respondent, who must prove that he did show reasonable care.

   d.   The maxim does not apply when the facts are sufficiently known because it depends on an absence of explanation.

   e.   *Res Ipsa Loquitur* was considered in the following four cases. In the first two it was held to apply, in the latter two it did not apply. However, even when it does apply (i.e. b.i–iii are present), it does not guarantee success for the claimant. It merely shifts the burden of proof to the respondent, who may be able to show that despite the facts he acted as a reasonable man at all times.

In *BYRNE v BOADLE (1863)* a barrel of flour fell from D's warehouse injuring P, a passer-by. No explanation could be given by D for the incident and P was in no position to prove a breach of duty by D. The court therefore placed the burden of proof on D, who had to show that he had not broken his duty of care. He was unable to do this and P therefore succeeded in his action.

In *MAHON v OSBORNE (1939)* a swab was left in a patient's body after an operation. Clearly the patient could not prove a breach of duty, since he was under an anaesthetic. However, the presence of the swab raised the inference of a breach of duty (*res ipsa loquitur*). The surgeon was unable to show that he had used reasonable care and was accordingly held liable.

In *FISH v KAPUR (1948)* P's jaw was found to be broken after D, a dentist, had extracted a tooth. It was held that this was not a *res ipsa loquitur* situation since there were reasons other than the dentist's breach of duty which could have accounted for the broken jaw. For example, P may have had a weak jaw. P was therefore compelled to prove the three requirements of negligence in the usual way.

In *TURNER v MANSFIELD CORPORATION (1975)* P was a driver of a corporation dustcart. For some reason, which was never explained, the movable body of the cart rose and hit a bridge, causing the cab section to rise from the ground and jamming the dustcart under the bridge. P jumped from the cab and was injured in his fall to the ground. The Court of Appeal held that this was not a case to which *res ipsa loquitur* applied. It was for P who was in control of the dustcart to give an explanation of the accident. Since he could not do this, his action failed.

DAMAGE

8. The claimant must show that as a result of the breach of duty he has suffered some damage. If a person's unreasonable conduct fortunately injures no one then that person cannot be liable in negligence (although he may be guilty of a criminal offence, e.g. careless driving). The rules on damage have already been covered, but are summarized below:

   a. The damage must be *caused* to a substantial extent by the respondent's conduct.

   b. The damage must be sufficiently closely related to the negligent act, i.e. it must not be too *remote*.

   c. In most cases the damage must be either physical injury to the claimant's person or property or economic loss consequential upon physical injury, e.g. lost wages as a result of a broken leg.

   d. In cases of identifiable psychiatric illness the courts may award damages if such illness is reasonably foreseeable, but considerations of public policy limit the scope of such damages.

   e. If the damage is economic loss unaccompanied by any injury to person or property a 'special relationship', based on reliance, must exist between the claimant and the respondent (*HEDLEY BYRNE v HELLER (1964)*).

CONTRIBUTORY NEGLIGENCE

9. a. At common law if the claimant was guilty of any negligence which contributed to the cause of the accident, he recovered nothing.

   b. Since 1945 by virtue of the *LAW REFORM (CONTRIBUTORY NEGLIGENCE) ACT 1945* where a person suffers damage partly as a result of his own fault, and partly due to the fault of another, the damages recoverable will be reduced according to his share of responsibility.

   c. A person can be guilty of contributory negligence if his conduct while in no way contributing to the accident itself, contributed to the nature and extent of his injuries.

      In *O'CONNELL v JACKSON (1971)* D, a car driver, knocked P off his moped, the accident being entirely D's fault. P suffered severe head injuries which the evidence showed would have been less serious if he had been wearing a crash helmet. It was held that the plaintiff's damages would be reduced by 15%.

   d. The court does not approach the problem by saying 'What injuries would he have suffered if he had been wearing a crash helmet – we shall compensate him for such injuries?' The court says, 'Given that he has suffered injuries X, Y and Z, what was his percentage of fault either in causing the accident or contributing to such injuries – his damages shall be reduced by this percentage?'

   e. To prove contributory negligence it is not necessary for the respondent to show that the claimant owed him a duty of care, only that he failed to take reasonable care for his own safety. For example:

      In *FROOM v BUTCHER (1976)* it was held that failure to wear a seat belt amounted to contributory negligence.

      In *OWENS v BRIMMELL (1977)* P's damages were reduced by 20% because he accepted a lift in D's car knowing that D was drunk.

      In *BADGER v MINISTRY OF DEFENCE (2006)* the claimant had his award of damages reduced by 20 per cent when, after contracting lung cancer through exposure to asbestos through the negligent act of his employer, he failed to stop smoking.

OCCUPIERS' LIABILITY TO LAWFUL VISITORS

10. The duty of occupiers of premises towards lawful visitors is governed by the *OCCUPIERS' LIABILITY ACT 1957.*

   a. An '*occupier*' is a person who has some degree of control over the premises. He need not necessarily be the owner. It is also possible for there to be more than one occupier.

   b. '*Premises*' includes land, buildings, fixed, or movable structures such as pylons and scaffoldings; and vehicles, including ships and aeroplanes.

   c. '*Visitors*' are persons lawfully on the premises, such as customers in shops and factory inspectors. A trespasser will be deemed to be a lawful visitor for the purposes of the Act if the occupier has granted him implied permission by habitual acquiescence in his known trespass.

11. The extent of the duty is laid down in *S.2(2)* of the Act:

'A duty to take such care as in all the circumstances of the case is reasonable to see that the visitor will be reasonably safe in using the premises for the purpose for which he is permitted by the occupier to be there.'

This duty is merely an enactment of the common law duty to act as a reasonable man (see 6. above). The Act states that all the circumstances of the case are relevant in determining the duty owed. Therefore the occupier:

a. Must be prepared for children to be less careful than adults. In the case of very young children the occupier is entitled to assume that they will be accompanied by an adult.

b. May expect a person who is doing his job to guard against the ordinary risks of his job.

In *ROLES v NATHAN (1963)* the claimants, who were chimneysweeps, were employed by D to block up holes in the flues of a coke-fired heating system. Despite a warning from D they attempted to do this while the coke fire was lit, and they were both killed by carbon monoxide gas. Their executor's action failed since it was a risk incidental to their job which they should have foreseen and guarded against.

Contrast *SALMON v SEAFARERS RESTAURANTS (1983)* when a fire broke out at D's fish and chip shop due to the negligence of one of the employees. The fire melted a seal of a gas meter, gas escaped and there was an explosion. P, a fireman, was injured. D contended that they were only liable if a fireman was injured as a result of some foreseeable but nevertheless exceptional risk, not risks ordinarily incidental to the job of a fireman. It was held that the duty was not limited in this way, the duty owed was the same as that owed to any other visitor. In this case it was foreseeable that firemen would be needed and that such an explosion might result from the fire. D was therefore liable.

c. Will not be liable if the injury results from the faulty work of an independent contractor, provided the occupier took reasonable steps to ensure that the contractor was competent, and that the work was properly done.

d. May be able to escape liability by giving an adequate warning of any danger. However, it must be remembered that under the *UNFAIR CONTRACT TERMS ACT 1977* an occupier of business premises cannot exclude liability for causing death or personal injury through negligence and cannot exclude liability for other loss or damage unless the exclusion clause satisfies the Act's requirement of reasonableness (Chapter 15.13).

12. The Act preserves the right of the occupier to plead the defence of *volenti non fit injuria* in respect of risks 'willingly accepted' by the visitor.

13. The *DEFECTIVE PREMISES ACT 1972* provides that any person who undertakes work for, or in connection with, the provision of a dwelling owes a duty of care to:

a. The person who orders the work, and

b. Any person who subsequently acquires an interest in the dwelling.

OCCUPIERS' LIABILITY TO TRESPASSERS

14. The *OCCUPIERS' LIABILITY ACT 1984* has replaced the common law rules governing the duty of occupiers of premises to persons other than visitors. The Act covers not only trespassers but also persons using rights of way who fall outside the meaning of 'visitor' under the *OCCUPIERS' LIABILITY ACT 1957*.

In *TOMLINSON v CONGLETON BOROUGH COUNCIL and CHESHIRE COUNTY COUNCIL (2004)* the claimant was severely injured when he dived into a shallow lake in a park owned by the Council. Warning signs existed around the lake and the Council had an active policy of policing the lake to remove swimmers. The claimant accepted that he was a trespasser – through his ignoring of the signs – but sought damages under the *OCCUPIERS' LIABILITY ACT 1984* claiming that the duty owed to him as a trespasser had not been discharged in that the Council should have done more to prevent swimmers entering the water. The House of Lords held that although a duty was owed to him as a trespasser it had been met, the danger was perfectly obvious.

15. For several years prior to 1984 the occupier's duty to trespassers was to act with common sense and humanity. This required all the surrounding circumstances to be considered, for example the seriousness of the danger, the type of trespasser likely to enter and in some cases the resources of the occupier.

In *BRITISH RAILWAYS BOARD v HERRINGTON (1972)* BRB's electrified railway ran near a park used by children. The fences on each side of the railway were in poor condition and BRB knew that people used to climb through the broken fence to take 'short-cuts' across the railway. H, aged 6, got through the fence and was seriously injured when he touched the live rail. The House of Lords (now the Supreme Court) held that the old rules relating to liability towards trespassers no longer applied, and although an occupier does not owe the same duty of care to a trespasser as he owes to a visitor, he must act by standards of common sense and humanity and warn or exclude, within reasonable limits, those likely to be injured by a known danger. BRB were therefore held liable.

16. The main provisions of the 1984 Act are:

a. *Duty owed.* The occupier owes a duty if:

    i. He is aware of the danger or has reasonable grounds to believe that it exists, and

    ii. He knows, or has reasonable grounds to believe, that someone is in (or may come into) the vicinity of the danger, and

    iii. The risk is one against which in all the circumstances of the case he may reasonably be expected to offer that person some protection.

b. *Duty broken.* The duty is to take such care as is reasonable in all the circumstances to see that the person to whom the duty is owed does not suffer injury on the premises by reason of the danger concerned.

c. *Damage.* The occupier can only be liable for injury to the person. The Act expressly provides that the occupier incurs no liability in respect of any loss of, or damage to, property.

d. *Warnings.* The duty may be discharged (in appropriate cases) by taking reasonable steps to give warning of the danger. The Act also preserves the right of the occupier to plead the defence of *volenti*.

17. The Act does not significantly change the law, all the circumstances remain relevant, including what the occupier does know and ought to know both about the existence of the danger and the likelihood of trespassers. It is therefore very unlikely that Herrington's case or the other cases described below would be decided differently under the Act, and it will still be rather difficult to predict the outcome of many cases, contrast for example the cases of Penny and Harris.

In *HARRIS v BIRKENHEAD CORPORATION (1975)* P, aged 4, fell from the upper window of a derelict vandalized house. The house had been acquired for demolition by the council. Due to an administrative oversight the doors and windows had not been boarded up in the usual way. It was held that the council were liable because the house was a dangerous and tempting place for young children, therefore a humane and commonsense person should take precautions.

In *PENNY v NORTHAMPTON BOROUGH COUNCIL (1974)* a trespasser threw an aerosol can into a fire started by boys on a council tip. The can burst and injured an 8-year old trespasser. It was held that the council were not liable.

In *PANNETT v MCGUINNESS (1972)* D, who were demolition contractors, were burning rubbish on a demolition site. They appointed three workmen to supervise the fire and keep a lookout for children. P, aged 5, fell into the fire while the men were away and was badly burned. Although P was a trespasser, and the men had on many occasions in the past chased children away, D was held liable since he had failed to keep a proper lookout.

Contrast *WESTWOOD v THE POST OFFICE (1974)* P, an adult employee of the post office, was injured when he entered an unlocked room which had warning of danger on the door. Although the room should have been locked P's claim failed since a notice of danger is regarded as adequate warning to an adult.

SELF TEST QUESTIONS

Self Test Questions No. 21 (for Answers see Appendix 1):

1   What are the essentials of an action in negligence?

2   What is the 'neighbour test' and how is it used to establish a duty of care is owed?

3   What is 'economic loss'?

4   How can negligent statements amount to an actionable claim in negligence?

5   What is the legal position relating to 'nervous shock'?

6   How is the 'standard of care' assessed?

7   What did the Compensation Act 2006 introduce?

8   What is meant by the phrase, '*res ipsa loquitur*'?

9   What are the rules relating to the nature of any 'damage' caused?

10 What is meant by 'contributory negligence' and how will it affect a claim?

11 What are the rules applicable to occupiers of land?

12 Is a duty owed to trespassers?

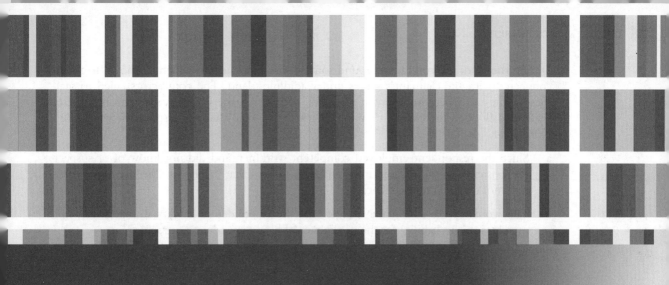

STRICT LIABILITY

24

Learning Outcomes At the end of this chapter you should be able to:

- **Explain and apply the law of 'strict liability' and the Rule in** *Rylands v Fletcher*.

- **Understand breach of statutory duty with particular reference to the** *CONSUMER PROTECTION ACT* 1987.

1. Strict liability is liability which arises without fault. There are two torts dealt with in this chapter. The first is known as the tort of 'Rylands v Fletcher' the second is 'Breach of Statutory Duty'. The chapter also deals with the strict liability and criminal liability imposed by the *CONSUMER PROTECTION ACT 1987*.

RYLANDS V FLETCHER

2. The rule stated by Blackburn J. is

'The person who for his own purposes brings on his lands and collects and keeps there anything likely to do mischief if it escapes, must keep it at his peril, and if he does not do so is *prima facie* (on the face of it) answerable for all the damage which is the natural consequence of its escape.'

In *RYLANDS v FLETCHER (1868)* the respondent, a mill owner, employed independent contractors to build a reservoir on his land for the purpose of supplying water for his mill.

During the work the contractors found some disused mine shafts which unknown to them connected with the claimant's mines under adjoining land. The contractors failed to seal these shafts and when the reservoir was filled with water, the water escaped through these shafts and flooded the claimant's mine. Blackburn J. held that the respondent was liable. Note that:

a. Since the respondent employed competent workmen and did not know of or suspect the existence of the disused mine shafts, it follows that liability is absolute (strict) and does not depend on negligence.

b. The words of the rule make it clear that the respondent's liability was personal, not merely vicarious liability for the negligence of his independent contractor.

3. The rule applies to water, animals, chemicals, filth, industrial use of gas or electricity, and exceptionally humans.

In *ATTORNEY-GENERAL v CORKE (1933)* D allowed gypsies to occupy his land, living in caravans and tents. The gypsies fouled and caused damage to adjoining land. It was held that Rylands v Fletcher applied since although it was lawful to allow gypsies onto land, it was not a natural use of land, and therefore the owner had to bear the risk of damage due to this non-natural use.

Following *PAGE MOTORS v EPSOM BOROUGH COUNCIL (1980)* it is clear that where gypsies are concerned an action in nuisance is more appropriate (Chapter 25.4).

4. There must be a non-natural use of land, i.e. some special use bringing with it increased danger to others. The rule does not therefore apply to:

a. Damage due to things naturally on the land, although in such cases an action may lie in nuisance (see *LEAKEY v NATIONAL TRUST (1980),* Chapter 25.2).

b. Damage due to a natural use of the land, for example domestic gas, electricity or water.

In *RICKARDS v LOTHIAN (1913)* D was the occupier of business premises and P was the lessee of the second floor. One evening an unknown person deliberately blocked a sink on the fourth floor and turned on the tap. Consequently P's stock was found next morning badly damaged. P's Rylands v Fletcher action against D failed because:

i. Domestic water was not a non-natural use of the land, and

ii. Because the escape was caused by the deliberate act of an unknown person.

In *TRANSCO PLC v STOCKPORT METROPOLITAN BOROUGH COUNCIL (2004)* the claimant was seeking the recovery of costs involved in repairing a gas main, which had broken through the collapse of an embankment. The cause of the collapse was water leakage from a water pipe supplying a number of houses owned by the Council. The leakage in the pipe had gone undetected for a considerable time with water finding its way to the embankment and, over a period of time, weakening it. The claim was based on strict liability under the rule in Rylands v Fletcher. The House of Lords (now the Supreme Court) held the Council not liable because:

i. It had not brought onto the land anything likely to cause damage if it escaped.

ii. Piping water to the houses was an ordinary use of the land.

c. It has been held that the storage of chemicals by a firm based in an 'industrial village' was a natural use of the land.

In *CAMBRIDGE WATER COMPANY v EASTERN COUNTIES LEATHER (1991)* the judge rejected P's claim with regard to pollution of a nearby public water supply borehole because the storage of chemicals by firms involved in the local tanning industry was a natural use of the land for the purposes of the rule in *RYLANDS v FLETCHER (1868)*. This decision represents a significant relaxation of the rule.

5. There must be an escape beyond the boundaries of the defendant's land.

In *READ v J. LYONS (1947)* P was employed as an inspector of munitions factories. She was injured by a shell which exploded while being manufactured. She claimed under the rule in Rylands v Fletcher, but failed because there had been no escape of the dangerous thing over the boundaries of the defendant's land.

6. *Defences*

   a.   The escape was caused by:

      i.   The claimant.

      ii.   Act of God.

      iii.   The deliberate act of a third party over whom the respondent had no control as in *RICKARDS v LOTHIAN (1913)*.

   b.   The accumulation was made:

      i.   With the claimant's express or implied consent.

         In *PETERS v PRINCE OF WALES THEATRE (BIRMINGHAM)* (1943) D leased to P a shop in the same building that contained the theatre. The theatre had installed (and P knew this) a sprinkler system as a fire precaution. During a frost the water in the sprinkler system's pipes froze, cracking the pipes. In the following thaw P's shop was flooded and his stock damaged. There was no liability under Rylands v Fletcher because the sprinkler system was for the common benefit of both the theatre and P's shop, and because P had impliedly consented to run the risk of accidents involving the system.

      ii.   With absolute statutory authority.

BREACH OF STATUTORY DUTY

7. Whether or not a tort action is possible by a person injured due to a breach of statutory duty depends on the construction of the particular statute.

Generally an action will lie, unless it is clear from the statute, or the pre-existing law that this was not intended. However, no action will lie if:

   a.   It is clear that the penalty provided by the Act was intended to be the only remedy.

         In *ATKINSON v NEWCASTLE WATERWORKS (1877)* P's timber yard was destroyed by fire because there was insufficient water pressure in the mains to put it out. The *WATERWORKS CLAUSES ACT 1874* provided a £10 penalty if a waterworks company allowed the pressure to fall below a specified minimum. The pressure was below this minimum. However, P's action to recover his full loss did not succeed, since the statute did not disclose a cause of action by individuals for damage of this kind, because this would amount to the waterworks company providing a gratuitous fire insurance service. It was clear that the £10 penalty was the only penalty intended to be imposed by the Act.

b.   The Act was passed for the benefit of the public generally rather than particular individuals, for example the *TRADE DESCRIPTIONS ACT 1968*.

c.   The Act was passed for the benefit of a section of the public of which the plaintiff is not a member.

In *HARTLEY v MAYOH AND CO (1954)* P, a fireman, was electrocuted while fighting a fire at D's premises. His electrocution was due to D's breach of statutory regulations. P, however, failed to recover compensation because the regulations were expressed to be for the benefit of 'employees' and he was not a member of this class of persons.

d.   The claimant suffered damage different from that which the statute was intended to prevent.

In *GORRIS v SCOTT (1874)* sheep were swept from the deck of a ship in a storm because they were not in pens. However, the purpose of the statutory requirement of 'penning' sheep was to prevent the spread of infection and not to stop them being washed overboard. The claimant therefore recovered nothing.

e.   If the claimant suffers *economic loss* caused by a highway authority's breach of its statutory duty to repair a highway.

In *WENTWORTH v WILTSHIRE COUNTY COUNCIL (1992)* P's dairy farm was served by a road which fell into disrepair. As a result, from January 1980, Milk Marketing Board tankers could not use the road to collect milk. Initially the Council denied that the road was maintainable at public expense, but at a Crown Court hearing in November 1981 it was established that it was a public highway and that the Council had the statutory duty to maintain it. Nine months later it was repaired, but this was too late to save the farm. P claimed approximately £77 500 damages for economic loss due to breach of statutory duty. The Court of Appeal (reversing the High Court) held that Parliament's intention, based on the construction of the *Highway Act 1959*, was that compensation for economic loss was not payable. The remedy for breach of the Act is to obtain a court order that the highway be put into proper repair. No other means of enforcement was indicated by the Act. P's claim was unsuccessful.

8.   The statutory duty may be absolute, or to take reasonable care, depending on the construction of the statute. If it is absolute (i.e. liability is strict), then contributory negligence is an available defence, but it will be no defence to plead:

a.   *Volenti non fit injuria* (see Chapter 21.2).

b.   That the duty has been delegated to a competent person, or

c.   That reasonable care was taken.

9.   The fact that the statutory penalty is applied for the benefit of the injured party does not exclude a remedy in tort.

In *GROVES v LORD WIMBORNE (1898)* P, a factory employee, was injured when he caught his hand in machinery which by statute should have been fenced. The statute provided that an employer must pay a fine for breach of this statutory duty, and also provided that the fine may be applied for the benefit of the injured party. P therefore received 'double 'compensation' he was awarded damages in tort for breach of statutory duty (he ~~~~, of course, have to prove fault only that the statute had been broken and that ' ~~~~ injured) and he had the fine imposed by the criminal law given to him.

PRODUCT LIABILITY

THE CONSUMER PROTECTION ACT 1987

10. *Introduction*

    a. Consumer groups have argued for some time that the law governing civil liability for damage due to defective goods is unfair. For a consumer to sue a manufacturer he must either proceed via a chain of contractual actions (possibly being defeated by an exemption clause) or he must sue for negligence and prove fault. This means that the law often fails to regulate the conduct of those responsible for the damage.

    b. Industrial groups have opposed strict product liability on the ground that insurance would be prohibitively expensive and some smaller businesses could be forced to close.

    c. After many years of deliberation the EC issued a directive on product liability in July 1985. This has been implemented in the *CONSUMER PROTECTION ACT 1987*. The Act has three main parts dealing with product liability, consumer safety and misleading price indications.

11. *Part I. Product Liability. Basic Rule. S.2*

    a. To succeed in a product liability claim against a manufacturer the plaintiff must show four things:

        i. That the product contained a defect.

        ii. That the claimant suffered damage.

        iii. That the damage was caused by the product, and

        iv. That the respondent was a producer, 'own brander' or importer of the product.

    b. A supplier will also be liable if he fails to identify the producer or importer when requested to do so.

    c. The effect of this section is that in future liability will no longer be decided by reference to the fault of the manufacturer or some other person, but by reference to the state of the product in question, i.e. strict liability is introduced. Even so the claimant may experience some difficulty proving that the defect in the product caused the injury.

    d. A 'product' must be moveable and industrially produced, e.g. cars are products, buildings are not. Products of the soil, stock farming and fishing are not products unless subjected to industrial process, e.g. potatoes are not, but potato crisps are products.

12. *The Meaning of 'Defect'*

    a. There are three types of product defect:

        i. A *manufacturing defect* occurs when a product fails to comply with the manufacturer's product specifications and consequently deviates from the norm. The frequency of such defects can be calculated fairly accurately and the producer will be able to spread the risk via insurance and pricing.

    ii. A *design defect* occurs when the product specifications are themselves at fault and present a hazard. This type of defect is far more serious and has led to major claims for compensation, particularly in defective drug cases, for example the Thalidomide case.

    iii. A *duty to warn defect* refers to the producer's responsibility to provide appropriate warnings and instructions to enable the consumer to use the product safely.

  b. *S.3* lays down the criteria for judging defectiveness. There is a defect in a product if the safety of the product is not such as persons generally are entitled to expect, taking all circumstances into account, including:

    i. The presentation of the product, including instructions and warnings.

    ii. The use to which it could reasonably be expected to be put.

    iii. The time when the product was supplied.

For an illustration see the case of ***ABOUZAID v MOTHERCARE UK (2000)*** (see Chapter 23.6.a)

  c. The above test is satisfactory in respect of manufacturing and duty to warn defects, but it is less appropriate for design defects. This is because it is based on consumer expectations and consumers will not know what to expect because they will not usually know how safe it is possible to make the product.

  d. The omission of 'reasonably' from the phrase 'entitled to expect' suggests a stricter standard than that normally applied in tort. However, reasonableness is retained in the factors that the court must take into account.

In ***A& OTHERS V NATIONAL BLOOD AUTHORITY & OTHERS (2001)*** the NBA were held liable for damage done to recipients of blood infected by Hepatitis C following blood transfusions. The Court found that the danger was known in 1988 but the NBA did not introduce screening tests until 1991. Blood and blood products contaminated with the virus were 'defective products' under *S.3* of the *CONSUMER PROTECTION ACT 1987.*

13. **Defences** (*S.4*)

  a. Any person has a defence if he can show:

    i. That the defect is attributable to compliance with any enactment.

    ii. That he did not at any time supply the product.

    iii. That the supply was otherwise than in the course of a business.

    iv. That the defect did not exist in the product at the time of supply.

    v. That the state of scientific and technical knowledge at the relevant time was not such that the producer might be expected to have discovered the defect.

    vi. That the defect constituted a defect in a product in which the product in question had been comprised and was wholly attributable to the design of the subsequent product.

    vii. More than 10 years has elapsed since the product was first supplied.

b.   The most important defence is v. above, since it directly challenges the basic concept of strict liability for product defects. It is known as the '*state of the art*' defence. It is particularly significant in the area of drugs where new products are constantly being developed on the boundaries of medical and scientific knowledge. A defect in a new drug could affect thousands of users but they would not be compensated if the defect was unknowable at the time of the product's circulation.

c.   The impact of the 'state of the art' defence will depend on the attitude of the courts. There are two possible approaches:

   i.   The stricter approach is based on the assumption that the producer will be aware of all the available information and technology relating to his product at any given time. There will be two issues for the court. Firstly, was the knowledge available? Secondly, whether the producer applied the knowledge.

   ii. The second approach pays more regard to the practicalities of the situation and would allow the producer to escape liability if the product was as safe as possible bearing in mind cost, utility, consumer expectations, the availability of safe alternatives and so on. Thus a producer would not be expected to make a product safe if to do so would be prohibitively expensive or if it would reduce the product's utility.

14. *Part II. Consumer Safety* Part II is intended to provide the public with better protection from unsafe consumer goods. It primarily imposes criminal sanctions, but will also assist the plaintiff in a civil action for negligence since, if a manufacturer has been found guilty under the Act, the claimant will be able to rely on the breach of statutory duty, rather than have to prove a breach of the duty of care. The main provisions are:

   a.   A person is guilty of an offence if he supplied consumer goods which are not reasonably safe *(S.10)*.

   b.   The Secretary of State may make safety regulations (for example with regard to flammability or toxicity) governing the making and supplying of goods. Such regulations cover for example children's nightdresses and electric blankets.

   c.   The Secretary of State may serve a 'prohibition notice' upon a supplier, prohibiting him from supplying goods which are unsafe. A 'notice to warn' may also be served requiring the supplier to publish, at his own expense, a warning to customers about unsafe goods.

15. *Part III Misleading Price Indications*

   a.   *S.20* provides that a person commits an offence if, in the course of a business, he gives consumers an indication which is misleading as to the price at which any goods, services, accommodation or facilities are available.

   b.   Examples of misleading price indications include:

      i.   An understatement of the price.

      ii.   Failing to make it clear that some other additional charge will be made.

      iii. Falsely indicating that the price is expected to be increased, reduced or maintained.

      iv.   Making a false price comparison, for example by falsely stating that the price has been reduced.

c.   The Office of Fair Trading has issued a code of practice on misleading price indications. Compliance or non-compliance with the code may be taken into account by the court when determining whether or not an offence has been committed (*S.25.*).

d.   The Act provides various defences, for example:

i.   That the respondent took all reasonable precautions and exercised all due diligence to avoid the commission of an offence (*S.39.*).

ii.   That the respondent was an innocent publisher or advertising agency who was unaware, and who had no ground for suspecting, that the advertisement contained a misleading price indication (*S.24.*).

e.   The courts have tended to interpret the 'due diligence' defence fairly strictly, although less rigorous precautions are expected of small firms.

In *RILEY v WEBB (1987)* the respondent's supplied pencils containing poisonous substances contrary to the *PENCILS AND GRAPHIC INSTRUMENTS (SAFETY) REGULATIONS 1974.* The respondent's order to their suppliers included a general condition requiring conformity with statutory safety requirements. It was held that this was insufficient, since the defendants should have brought the particular regulations to the attention of their suppliers and obtained a positive assurance that they would comply with them.

SELF TEST QUESTIONS

Self Test Questions No. 22 (for Answers see Appendix 1):

1   What is meant by the term 'strict liability'?

2   What is the rule in Rylands v Fletcher?

3   What do you understand by the phrase, 'breach of statutory duty' within the context of 'strict liability'?

4   How does the Consumer Protection Act 1987 impose 'strict liability' on manufactured goods?

5   State the necessary ingredients for the Act's application.

6   What are the remedies under the Act?

NUISANCE 25

Learning Outcomes At the end of this chapter you should be able to:

- Explain the nature of private and public nuisance having regard to:
  - those factors to be taken into account in assessing its existence
  - who may sue
  - any defences available
  - remedies.

PRIVATE NUISANCE

1. A private nuisance is an unlawful interference with the use or enjoyment of another person's land. It will not usually be an unlawful activity. The interference may consist of:

   a. Actual injury to property, for example fumes killing shrubs, or roots undermining a wall.

   b. Interference with health or comfort, for example noise, smoke or smell.

   c. Interference with easements or natural rights.

2. Whatever the type of harm it does not follow that any harm constitutes a nuisance. Regard must be had to the rule of 'give and take' between neighbours. It may therefore be relevant to consider:

    a.   *How far the act complained of is unusual or excessive.*

        In *FARRAR v NELSON (1885)* D bred and kept pheasants on his land. Had he kept only a reasonable number the inconvenience caused to his neighbour would not have constituted a nuisance. D, however, kept an excessive amount of pheasants and this was held to amount to a nuisance.

    b.   *Duration.* The longer the duration of an interference the more likely it is to be a nuisance. An isolated act cannot be a private nuisance.

        In *BOLTON v STONE (1951)* D hit a cricket ball out of the ground hitting P. The evidence was that on only about eight occasions had balls been struck out of the ground in 35 years. P sued in negligence and nuisance.

        P's negligence action failed because she was not owed a duty of care. Injury to passers by was only foreseeable as a remote possibility, it was not reasonably foreseeable.

        It was held not to be a nuisance because it was an isolated act. A private nuisance must be a continuing state of affairs.

    c.   *The respondent's intention.* An act that would not otherwise be actionable may become a tort if it is done with intention to injure or annoy as in *HOLLYWOOD SILVER FOX FARM v EMMETT (1936)* (Chapter 23.5).

    d.   *The character of the neighbourhood.* A person in a town cannot expect silence and clean air. Thus the standard of comfort protected by the law varies from place to place. However, the character of the neighbourhood is only relevant where the interference is to health and comfort and not where actual damage to property is caused. If actual damage is caused it is a nuisance regardless of the neighbourhood.

    e.   *Sensitivity.* The law gives no special protection to abnormally sensitive persons or property. Thus no remedy lies if sensitivity is the sole reason for the damage.

        In *ROBINSON v KILVERT (1889)* Heat which rose from D's flat damaged exceptionally sensitive paper stored by P in the above flat. There was no suggestion that the heat was excessive. P did not receive compensation because the paper was only damaged because it was very sensitive.

    f.   *The respondent's lack of care.*

        i.   If lack of care allows an annoyance to become excessive the respondent may be liable.

            In *ANDRAE v SELFRIDGE (1938)* P, a hotel owner, recovered damages from D, who was demolishing the adjoining premises. Although building and demolition do not usually constitute a nuisance, since they are socially desirable, if the amount of noise and dust created is unnecessarily great, as in this case, a nuisance will be committed.

        ii.   If a landowner's lack of care allows his land to encroach upon his neighbour's land he may be liable in either nuisance or negligence.

            In *LEAKEY v NATIONAL TRUST (1980)* soil and tree stumps had fallen onto P's land from a natural mound on D's land, the movement being caused by natural subsidence due to weather and soil conditions. It was held that an occupier of land owes a general duty of care to neighbouring occupiers to take reasonable steps to prevent the natural or non-natural state of the land from causing damage to neighbours. In such cases it does not matter whether the action is brought in negligence or nuisance. It was suggested by D that the rule in Rylands v Fletcher indicated that there was no liability for the natural state of the land. It was, however, held that although liability under Rylands v Fletcher is restricted to non-natural use of the land it does not exclude or deny liability for natural hazards.

3. *Persons Who Can Sue*

a. Since the interference must be with the enjoyment or use of land it follows that the only person who can usually sue is the occupier of the land, not his lodger, guest or wife.

In **MALONE v LASKEY (1907)** M occupied a house which was leased by D to his (M's) employers. M's wife (the claimant) was injured when a lavatory cistern fell on her due to being loosened by vibrations from D's electric generator which was in adjoining premises. P's nuisance claim failed since she was not D's tenant, and in nuisance it is the tenant who must sue and no other persons on the premises.

b. A reversioner can also sue if there is a permanent injury to his interest in the property. (A reversioner is an owner of freehold property who has granted a lease. His interest is called the freehold reversion. He may also be called a lessor or landlord.)

4. *Persons Who Can be Sued*

a. The person who created the nuisance may be sued even if he has vacated the land.

b. The person in possession may be sued unless:

  i. The nuisance was caused by an independent contractor, *except* where the work necessitated special precautions by the occupier.

  In **BOWER v PEATE (1876)** P and D owned adjoining houses, each having a right of support from the other. D hired an independent contractor to pull down and rebuild his house, and the contractor undertook to support P's house while the work was in progress. The contractor was, however, negligent, and P's house was damaged. D was held liable because the duty to support his neighbour's house could not be delegated by D. If D wished to work on his house then he must himself accept the risk of damage to P's house. (The nuisance in this case was the interference with an easement, i.e. the right of support that each could expect from his neighbour.)

  ii. The nuisance was caused by a trespasser, or

  iii. The nuisance existed before the occupier acquired the property, except where the occupier failed to take reasonable steps to abate it.

c. An occupier will be liable for a nuisance committed by a trespasser if he adopts the nuisance:

In **SEDLEIGH-DENFIELD v O'CALLAGHAN (1940)** a trespasser (the county council) entered D's land and laid a drainage pipe in a ditch. The council protected the end of the pipe with grating so that it would not get blocked with leaves. The grating was unsatisfactory and every few months one of D's employees used to unblock the grating. On one occasion a blockage caused the flooding of P's land (which adjoined

D's land). Usually proof that a nuisance was caused by a trespasser is a defence. However, in this case D had, on finding out about the nuisance, acquiesced in its presence and continued it himself. He was therefore held liable.

In **PAGE MOTORS v EPSOM BOROUGH COUNCIL (1980)** D leased P land for use as a car showroom and garage. At the start of the lease there were a few gypsies on D's adjoining land, but the number rapidly increased. D had a statutory duty to provide adequate sites for gypsies in the area, but they did not do so. P alleged that the gypsies were a nuisance – there was smell from bonfires, uncontrolled dogs, obstruction of access and customers and suppliers had become reluctant to visit the garage. Eventually, over 3 years after the lease was granted, sites were established and the gypsies left the area. It was held that although D had not caused the nuisance they had allowed it to continue for far too long and were liable for any loss suffered by P. The judge appreciated that the council had difficulties because of the lack of alternative sites and pressure from the Department of the Environment not to move gypsies needlessly. However, he pointed out that his decision was just in that it had the effect of sharing the burden of a local problem among the whole community on whose behalf the council was acting rather than allowing it to fall on one individual.

    d.   A landlord out of possession is not liable, unless he permits his tenant to commit the nuisance.

5. *Defences*

    a.   *Volenti non fit injuria* (see Chapter 21.2).

    b.   Absolute statutory authority.

    c.   The nuisance was caused by a stranger and the respondent could not possibly have known of it.

    d.   Long use, i.e. 20 years, provided the nuisance is capable of forming the subject matter of an easement. An *easement* is a right to use or restrict the use of another person's land in some way, for example a right of way or a right of light.

    e.   It may be a defence to establish that commission of a nuisance is in the public interest. There are, however, two conflicting Court of Appeal cases on this point.

In **MILLER v JACKSON (1977)** the Court of Appeal held that a cricket club were guilty of negligence and nuisance in allowing cricket balls to be struck out of the ground into P's adjoining premises, but refused an injunction and awarded damages on the basis that the greater interest of the public in being able to play cricket on a ground where it had been played for over 70 years should prevail over the hardship of a few individual householders, who had recently purchased their houses, and were deprived of the use of their gardens while the game was in progress.

Contrast this with **KENNAWAY v THOMPSON (1980)** where the nuisance complained of was noise from motorboat racing and water-skiing. The Court of Appeal held that a nuisance existed and they granted an injunction which limited the number of days on which large-scale activities could take place and limited the noise level on other occasions. They refused to follow Miller v Jackson, feeling that it was wrong to allow a nuisance to continue merely because the wrongdoer is willing and able to pay for any injury he may inflict. The court felt that the two reasons for refusing to grant an injunction in Miller v Jackson (i. the public interest and ii. that the plaintiff 'came to the nuisance') were contrary to earlier authority and were not binding on the court.

6. *Ineffective Defences*

a. That the claimant came to the nuisance.

In ***STURGES v BRIDGEMAN (1879)*** D had for many years been manufacturing sweets in premises adjoining P's garden. P, a doctor, then built a consulting room that adjoined the manufacturing premises. He then sued D in nuisance, due to the noise and vibrations caused by D's machinery. D's defence was in effect 'I was here first.' However, this defence is ineffective, and particularly in view of the area (Wimpole Street) the noise and vibrations were held to constitute a nuisance. D also claimed that he had acquired a right to commit the nuisance through long use. It was held that this was not possible – any right acquired through long use (20 years) must be capable of forming the subject matter of an easement.

b. That reasonable care has been taken.

In ***RAPIER v LONDON TRAMWAYS (1893)*** D kept about 200 horses in stables adjoining P's land. Although D took reasonable measures to minimize any nuisance a certain amount of noise and smell was caused by the horses. D were held liable in nuisance – it was no defence to say that they had done everything possible to prevent it.

c. That the respondent's conduct would not have amounted to a nuisance had it not been for the contributory acts of others.

7. *Abatement of Nuisances* In addition to the usual remedies of damages and/or an injunction the law will sometimes allow the remedy of abatement, i.e. removal of the nuisance.

a. If there are two ways of abating a nuisance the less mischievous must be selected.

b. Entry onto the land of a third party is not permissible.

c. Notice should be given to the occupier of the land in which the nuisance arises except:

   i.   Where abatement is possible without entry, or

   ii. In cases of emergency, such as a fire.

d. Abatement allows a person to cut off the branches of his neighbour's trees which overhang his land.

e. Abatement is also applicable to public nuisance.

PUBLIC NUISANCE

8. A public nuisance is an unlawful act or omission which endangers the health, safety or comfort of the public (or some section of it) or obstructs the exercise of a common right, for example selling contaminated food or obstructing a highway. For example ***AB AND OTHERS v SOUTH WEST WATER SERVICES (1992)*** (Chapter 28.4).

9. It differs from private nuisance in that:

a. It is a crime as well as a tort.

b. An isolated act may be a public nuisance.

c. It need not involve an interference with the use of enjoyment of land.

d. Several people at least must be affected.

In *R v MADDON (1975)* D dialled 999 and informed the telephonist that there was a 200 lb bomb at the local steelworks. The call was a hoax and D was charged with the offence of committing a public nuisance. The only people who knew of the call and its contents were the telephonist, eight security guards, and the police – who conducted an hour-long search until the hoax was discovered. It was held that the offence of public nuisance had not been committed since not enough people were affected.

 e. A right to commit a public nuisance cannot be acquired by long use.

10. Potentially the same people may sue and be sued as in private nuisance, except that a private individual may only sue if he has suffered some special damage different from that suffered by the class of persons affected.

In *CAMPBELL v PADDINGTON CORPORATION (1911)* the Council erected a stand in Burwood Place, London so that council members could view King Edward VII's funeral procession. P owned a flat in Burwood Place which she often let for the purpose of viewing public processions. The Council's stand obstructed this view, so that she could not let her flat. Since the stand was a public nuisance, and since she had suffered special damage in excess of that suffered by the public at large, she was successful in her action against the Council.

11. If the same act is both a public and private nuisance the right of a private individual to sue for private nuisance is not affected.

12. *Highway Nuisances* Common examples of public nuisances are obstructions on highways or dangerous premises adjoining the highway. Principles of 'give and take' also apply to public nuisance. Thus a temporary obstruction, if reasonable in its size and duration, may be permissible. However:

 a. Liability is strict for the collapse of an artificial projection over the highway, for example a lamp. If the projection is natural the occupier will be liable only if he knew or ought to have known of the danger.

  In *NOBLE v HARRISON (1926)* the branch of a tree on D's land that overhung the highway suddenly fell and damaged a passing coach. The owner of the land was not held liable, because a reasonable examination would not have revealed the tree's defect.

 b. If something projects above the highway this will not constitute a public nuisance if no obstruction is caused.

 c. If a local authority allows a highway to become dangerous it may be liable unless it can be shown that reasonable care has been taken having regard to various matters such as the expected volume of traffic, and the standard of maintenance appropriate to such a highway.

13. *Remedies*

 a. Criminal aspect – a prosecution or an application for an injunction by the Attorney General.

 b. Civil aspect – an application for an injunction and/or damages by the person suffering loss. (An injunction is an order of the court instructing a person to either – stop doing something, or do something – in the sense of putting right some wrong e.g. repair a fence or drain; see Chapter 28.8.)

It now appears, following two House of Lords decisions – *R v RIMMINGTON (2006)* and *R v GOLDSTEIN (2006)* – that public nuisance will become obsolete in that most kinds of conduct coming under common law nuisance are now regulated under statute, for example, the:

ENVIRONMENTAL PROTECTION ACT 1990 and the *WATER RESOURCES ACT 1991,* which cover respectively, pollution from noise, smoke and fumes and water pollution

NOISE AND STATUTORY NUISANCE ACT 1993

NOISE ACT 1996

ANTI-SOCIAL BEHAVIOUR ACT 2003

CLEAN NEIGHBOURHOODS AND ENVIRONMENT ACT 2005.

All provide alternative avenues for alleged nuisance activities. Local authority environmental health officers have the power to serve abatement notices requiring the person or persons responsible for a statutory nuisance to stop or restrict its occurrence or recurrence. Failure to comply with such a notice is a criminal offence and could lead to a maximum fine of £20 000. The *ENVIRONMENTAL PROTECTION ACT 1990* also allows an individual to initiate proceedings in a magistrates' court to obtain a court order to stop the nuisance.

SELF TEST QUESTIONS

Self Test Questions No. 23 (for Answers see Appendix 1):

1   What is private nuisance?

2   The need for 'give and take' requires that certain factors be taken into account; what are they?

3   Who may sue and be sued?

4   What are the defences to an action for private nuisance?

5   What is public nuisance?

6   What remedies are available where a private or public nuisance is shown to have occurred?

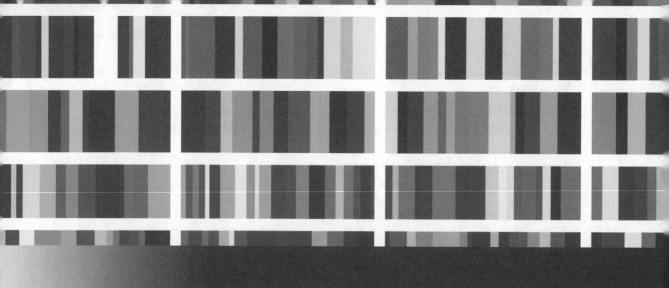

26 TRESPASS AND CONVERSION

Learning Outcomes At the end of this chapter you should be able to:

- Define the forms of trespass to the person.

- Explain what trespass to land and trespass to goods consists of, the defences and remedies.

- Explain the meaning of 'conversion' and what is entailed in its committal.

TRESPASS TO THE PERSON

1. *Definition* A trespass to the person is an intentional interference with the person or liberty of another. It was formerly thought that an action for trespass to the person could be brought where personal injuries were caused negligently though directly. However, since *LETANG v COOPER (1965)* it has been clear that the phrase 'trespass to the person' is restricted to intentional acts. Where an unintentional act causes physical injury the correct action is negligence. Trespass to the person is actionable *per se* (without proof of loss) unless the defendant establishes that his act was justified. It may take three forms – assault, battery and false imprisonment.

2. *Assault*

   a.   An assault is an act of the respondent which causes the claimant reasonable fear of an immediate battery on him by the defendant.

b. Words are no assault, but they may prevent the act that they accompany from being an assault.

In *TUBERVELL v SAVAGE (1669)* during an argument D brandished his sword saying, 'If it were not assize time I would not take such language from you.'

However, since it was assize time (i.e. the local criminal courts were in session), these words prevented the brandishing of the sword from being an assault.

c. It has been suggested that if a person rounds a corner and is confronted by a motionless gunman, the gunman may commit an assault if he does not move the gun barrel away from the other person. However, it is generally accepted that some movement is necessary to commit an assault.

In *INNES v WYLIE (1844)* a policeman stood motionless in order to block a doorway. This was held not to be an assault.

3. *Battery*

a. Battery is the intentional application of force to another person. The amount of harm inflicted is relevant to the amount of damages awarded, but not to the determination of liability.

b. It is a battery to throw something, e.g. water, at the plaintiff so that it hits him; or to remove a chair from under him; or to set a dog on him; or to drag him away from something for his own good.

c. Consent is a defence to battery, but the defence will not apply if the defendant does some act which was not contemplated by the plaintiff.

In *NASH v SHEEN (1953)* P went to the hairdresser for a permanent wave, but was instead given a tone-rinse which changed the colour of her hair and caused a rash over the rest of her body. The hairdresser was held to have committed a battery.

d. It is not a battery to touch a person to attract his attention.

4. *False Imprisonment*

a. This is the infliction of bodily restraint not authorized by law.

b. The restraint must be total.

In *BIRD v JONES (1845)* D closed off the public footpath over one side of Hammersmith Bridge, and charged people admission to his enclosure to watch the Boat Race. P climbed into the enclosure from one side, and was prevented from leaving from the other side. He was, however, told that he could go out the same way that he came in. It was held that there was no false imprisonment since the restraint was not total.

c. The claimant need not know that he is being detained.

In *MEERING v GRAHAME – WHITE AVIATION CO (1919)* P was suspected of thefts from his employers, although he did not know that he was a suspect. When he was asked to answer some questions concerning the thefts he voluntarily agreed – he still did not realize that he was a suspect. He later found out that while he was being questioned there were two of the works security guards outside the door who would have prevented him leaving if he had attempted to do so. He succeeded in his false imprisonment action, not on the grounds of his discomfort, but because of the injury to his reputation caused by his employer's action.

d. It is no tort to refuse to allow a person to leave premises when he does not fulfil a reasonable condition subject to which he entered them.

In **ROBINSON v BALMAIN NEW FERRY CO (1910)** the terms of a contract to travel on a ferry provided that the passenger must pay one penny on entering the wharf and a further penny on leaving. P paid his penny to enter, but just missed the ferry. He attempted to leave without paying another penny, but was restrained from doing so until he had paid. He failed in his false imprisonment action. The court said there was no duty on a person to make exit from his premises gratuitous, where a person had entered on the basis of a definite contract which involved their leaving in another way.

e. In addition to the usual remedy of damages the remedies of self-help (i.e. breaking out) and an application for a writ of habeas corpus are available. *Habeas corpus* is a writ designed to provide a person, who is kept in confinement without legal justification, with a means of obtaining release. An application may be made, for example, by the parents of a child who is being kept in an institution against their wishes.

5. *Justification of Trespass to the Person*

a. Defence of person or property. Reasonable force may also be used to remove a trespasser.

b. Parental authority. Reasonable and moderate punishment may be administered.

c. Lawful arrest. A person arrested without warrant must be told of the reason for the arrest, and taken to a magistrate or police station as soon as possible.

d. Judicial authority.

e. Necessity.

In **LEIGH v GLADSTONE (1909)** P who was on hunger strike in prison was forcibly fed by warders in order to save her life. The defence of necessity was successfully raised against her action for battery.

f. Inevitable accident (see **STANLEY v POWELL (1891)** Chapter 21.11).

TRESPASS TO LAND

6. Trespass to land is the *direct interference* with the *possession* of another person's land without lawful authority. It is a tort actionable per se, i.e. without proof of loss.

7. *Possession* Since trespass is a wrong done to the possessor only he rather than the owner can sue. Possession includes not only physical occupation, but occupation through servants and agents. Mere use, for example as a lodger, is not possession.

8. *Interference*

a. This must be direct, either by:

i. Entering on land, or

ii. Remaining on land after permission to stay has ended. An exception is a lessee, who if he remains at the end of his lease retains possession and therefore does not become a trespasser.

iii. Placing objects on land.

b. If a right to enter is abused this may be a trespass.

In *HARRISON v THE DUKE OF RUTLAND (1893)* the Duke owned a grouse moor. A road led across this moor which he allowed the public to use. P, however, abused this right of entry by deliberately frightening the grouse just as the Duke and his party were about to shoot. P was physically restrained by members of the shooting party and he brought an action for false imprisonment. His action failed because proportionate and reasonable force may be used to restrain or eject a trespasser and P, because he had abused his right of entry, was a trespasser.

c. Entry below the surface is a trespass, as is entry into airspace, if it takes place within the area of ordinary use.

In *KELSEN v IMPERIAL TOBACCO CO (1957)* P and D occupied adjoining premises, D, however, occupied a taller building than P. D attached an advertising sign to their wall which projected a few inches into the airspace about P's premises. P was successful in obtaining a court order compelling D to remove the sign since it was a trespass.

d. *S.76 CIVIL AVIATION ACT 1982* exempts civil aircraft flying at a reasonable height from liability for trespass, but it imposes strict liability on the owner of the aircraft for all damage caused by things falling from it.

e. If a person enters in exercise of a common law or statutory right and abuses the right by a positive act he is deemed to be a trespasser from the moment he entered the premises, i.e. a trespass *ab initio* (from the beginning).

In *THE SIX CARPENTERS CASE (1610)* six carpenters entered a public house and consumed a quantity of wine and bread. They then refused to pay the price. They were not held to be trespassers *ab initio* since their act was a non-feasance (an omission) and not a misfeasance.

9. *Defences*

a. The general defences of *volenti* (see Chapter 21.2), necessity, inevitable accident, self-defence and statutory authority all apply, but mistake is no defence.

b. Entry to exercise a common law right. For example, A enters B's land to repossess his goods that B has wrongfully taken onto his land.

c. Entry by licence, for example theatre guests. When the licence expires the person becomes a trespasser when he does not leave, in contrast to a lessee who remains in possession.

d. There is a rule which states that a person claiming land from another who is in possession of it can succeed only by showing a stronger title than the person in possession. If the land rightfully belongs to neither of them, but to a third party, the person in possession will have the defence of *jus tertii*.

In *DOE d. CARTER v BARNARD (1849)* P was wrongfully turned off certain land by D. In her action to recover possession it became evident that neither P nor D were entitled to the land. P's action to recover the land therefore failed since she could not show a better title than D. D could therefore claim the defence of jus tertii.

10. *Remedies* The remedies available to the claimant depend on whether or not he is in possession of the land. If an owner has been wrongfully dispossessed he cannot sue for trespass since he is not in possession.

a. Remedies available to the person in possession:

    i. Damages, nominal or compensatory.

    ii. Injunction.

    iii. Ejection of the trespasser. Reasonable and proportionate force may be used (i.e. proportionate to the amount of force that the trespasser is using to prevent ejection).

b. Remedies available to an owner who has been wrongfully dispossessed:

    i. Re-entry, however the re-entry must be peaceful.

       In *HEMMINGS v STOKE POGES GOLF CLUB (1920)* P refused to leave his cottage when his tenancy had been lawfully ended by notice to quit. The landlords, using reasonable force, removed P and his furniture and re-entered the premises. It was held that they were entitled to do this. (The law regarding tenants has now been changed so that it is illegal to remove a tenant without first obtaining a court order. Reasonable force may, however, be used to remove a licensee remaining on premises after the termination of his licence.)

    ii. An action for the recovery of land. The limitation period for this remedy is 12 years.

    iii. Having recovered possession as above, such person is deemed by the doctrine of Possession by Relation to have been in possession since the moment his right to possession accrued. He can therefore maintain an action for *mesne profits*, i.e. profits lost to the claimant while the defendant was wrongfully in possession.

11. *Criminal Liability*

a. *Squatters.* The fact that trespass is not usually a crime has led to problems with persons who trespass and take up residence on other people's property.

    i. *S.6 CRIMINAL LAW ACT 1977* created the offence of using or threatening violence to secure entry to premises on which there is another person who opposes entry. This offence, however, cannot be committed by a displaced residential occupier or someone acting for him.

    ii. By *S.7 CRIMINAL LAW ACT 1977* it is an offence for a trespasser to fail to leave premises when required to do so by a displaced residential occupier.

b. *Travellers. S.39 PUBLIC ORDER ACT 1986* gives senior police officers the power to direct trespassers to leave land. The officer must reasonably believe that two or more trespassers intend to reside there, that reasonable steps have been taken by the occupier to ask them to leave and that either:

    i. Damage has been caused to property.

    ii. The trespassers have used threatening, abusive or insulting words or behaviour towards the occupier, or

    iii. That the trespassers have brought at least 12 vehicles onto the land.

Failure to comply with the police officer's direction is a criminal offence.

TRESPASS TO GOODS

12. A trespass to goods is the direct interference with the possession of goods. The interference must be direct and not consequential, although in some cases physical contact is not necessary, for example to chase cattle is a trespass to goods. Generally the interference will take one of three forms:

    a. Taking the goods.

    b. Damaging goods or altering their physical condition.

    c. Interfering with goods, for example moving them about.

13. Only persons in possession (i.e. having immediate physical control) can sue. Some persons not in actual possession are deemed to have possession for this purpose. For example, a master who has given custody of his goods to his servant, or the personal representative of a deceased person, is deemed to be in possession.

14. Defences include:

    a. Inevitable accident.

       In *NATIONAL COAL BOARD v EVANS (1951)* in the course of excavating the foundations of a building D damaged a cable belonging to the NCB. It was held that since the presence of the cable was unforeseeable D was not liable, having the defence of inevitable accident.

    b. Reasonable defence of person or property. For example injuring a dog which is attacking somebody.

    c. Pursuance of a legal right or legal process. For example levying distress for rent.

    d. In addition trespass to goods or land will not be unlawful if it is by police following procedures laid down in the *POLICE AND CRIMINAL EVIDENCE ACT 1984*, for example if the police enter premises without a warrant to make an arrest, or if the police enter premises with a search warrant the police may take articles found on premises if they reasonably believe that they are evidence in relation to an offence.

CONVERSION

15. *Definition* Conversion is some dealing by the respondent in relation to the claimant's goods which is a denial of the claimant's right to possess and use those goods. It is the main method by which rights in personal property are protected.

16. *The Wrongful Act*

    a. The respondent may be liable in conversion even if he never possessed the goods provided his dealing constituted an unjustifiable denial of title.

       In *VAN OPPEN v TREDEGARS* (*1921*) P delivered goods by mistake to a firm. D purported to sell the goods to the firm. The firm disposed of the goods in the course of their business. D was held liable.

    b. The respondent will not be liable if he merely moves goods without any denial of title.

In *FOULDES v WILLOUGHBY (1841)* D moved P's horses from D's ferry, hoping that this would also induce P to leave. P remained and was ferried across the river. It was held that there is no conversion since there had been no denial of P's title to the horses.

c. The usual form of conversion is an abuse of existing possession by for example:

    i.   Destroying goods.

    ii.   Altering their nature.

    iii.   Wrongfully refusing to return them.

    iv.   Selling and delivering them to the third party, even if the respondent dealt innocently with the goods. (Note the exceptions in *S.22, 24* and *25 SALE OF GOODS ACT 1979* (Chapter 33).

        In *HOLLINS v FOWLER (1875)* D, a broker, sold and delivered cotton belonging to P. He was acting on behalf of a crook although he did not know this at the time. He was held liable in conversion because he had sold and delivered goods in denial of P's title.

d. Involuntary receipt of goods is not conversion, although the recipient must not wilfully damage or destroy them unless they become a nuisance. However, a person who receives unsolicited goods will be entitled to deal with them as if they were a gift if the sender fails to take them back within 6 months, or at some earlier date if the recipient gives notice to the sender (*UNSOLICITED GOODS AND SERVICES ACT 1971*).

e. Conversion may arise in situations where a seller of goods includes a term in his contract reserving title until payment.

    In *CLOUGH MILL v MARTIN (1985)* a contract for the sale of yarn had a reservation of title clause stating that the ownership of the yarn remained with the seller until the seller had received payment in full, or the yarn was sold by the buyer in a bona fide sale at full market value. When a receiver was appointed, the seller claimed a quantity of the yarn. The receiver refused to return it. The seller's claim was upheld and the receiver was held personally liable in conversion.

17. *The Claimant's Rights*

a. At the time of the conversion the claimant must have been in possession of the goods, or have had a right to immediate possession.

b. Where the claimant has been deprived permanently of the goods the measure of damages is their market value at the time of the conversion unless:

    i.   The respondent has the goods and refuses to deliver them, in which case it is their value at the time of refusal.

    ii.   The value has increased since the date of the conversion, in which case the measure may be the value at the date of judgement (provided the claimant sues promptly).

SELF TEST QUESTIONS

Self Test Questions No. 24 (for Answers see Appendix 1):

1   What is trespass to:

the person

land

goods?

2   Explain the wrongdoing involved in 'conversion'.

27 DEFAMATION

Learning Outcomes At the end of this chapter you should be able to:

- Define the meaning of defamation.

- Distinguish 'libel' from 'slander'.

- Explain how attribution to the claimant is shown.

- State the defences to an action in defamation and the significance of an 'unintentional act' and any 'mitigation' shown by the claimant.

1. A defamatory statement is a false statement that tends to injure the claimant's reputation, or causes him to be shunned by ordinary members of society. There are two forms of defamation namely libel and slander.

2. *Distinctions Between Libel and Slander*

   a. A defamatory statement is libel if it is in permanent form, or if it is for general reception. For example writing, pictures, films, radio, television, the theatre, records or waxworks. If the statement lacks permanence it will be slander. For example spoken words or gestures.

   b. Libel is a crime as well as a tort, whereas slander is only a tort.

   c.   Libel is actionable per se, slander is not unless:

      i.   It imputes a crime punishable by imprisonment.

      ii.   It imputes certain existing diseases, such as venereal disease or AIDS.

      iii.   It imputes unchastity, adultery or lesbianism in a woman.

      iv.   It is calculated to damage the claimant in any office, trade or profession held or carried on by him.

3. If the claimant is to succeed in a defamation action he must show three things:

   a.   That the statement is defamatory.

   b.   That it refers to the claimant.

   c.   That it has been published by the respondent.

In addition to the above requirements in most cases of slander (i.e. where it is not actionable per se) the claimant must prove damage, i.e. Material loss capable of monetary evaluation, such as loss of employment, and not mere loss of friends or reputation.

Each of the three main requirements is now considered in turn.

4. *The Meaning of 'Defamatory'*

   a.   A useful guide was laid down by Lord Atkin in *SIM v STRETCH (1936)*. He said,

'Would the words tend to lower the claimant in the estimation of right thinking members of society generally?'

In *SIM v STRETCH (1936)* a housemaid left P's employment, and went to work for D, for whom she had worked in the past. D then sent P the following telegram.

'Edith has resumed her services with us today. Please send her possessions and the money you borrowed, also her wages.'

P alleged this telegram was defamatory in that it implied he was in financial trouble, having to borrow off a housemaid, and not having paid her wages. The House of Lords (now the Supreme Court) held that the telegram was not defamatory, since if a statement has a number of good interpretations, it is unreasonable to seize upon a bad one to give a defamatory sense to the statement.

   b.   A statement would satisfy Lord Atkin's test if it:

      i.   Reflects on a person's trading or professional ability.

      ii.   Imputes dishonesty, criminality or immorality.

      iii.   Imputes insanity, certain diseases or that the claimant has been raped.

In *YOUSSOUPOFF v M.G.M. PICTURES LTD (1934)* M.G.M. made a film about the life of Rasputin. In the film Rasputin was represented as having raped a Princess Natasha. In the film Princess Natasha was also represented as being in love with the man who was eventually to murder Rasputin.

In real life the claimant, a Russian Princess (whose name was not Natasha) was married to a man who was undoubtedly concerned with the murder of the real-life Rasputin. P alleged that because of her marriage reasonable people would think it was she who had been raped. P succeeded in her libel action.

It appears rather illogical that it is defamatory to accuse a person of something, which if it had happened, would have been actively resisted by that person, for example rape or the catching of certain diseases. It does, however, probably reflect the reality of life in that so-called 'reasonable people' may in fact shun a person who has been raped or who is ill.

c. A statement is not defamatory if the claimant's reputation suffers in the eyes of only a section of the community in circumstances where the majority of the community would approve of his action.

In *BYRNE v DEANE (1937)* D was the proprietor of a golf club and P was a member. There were some illegal gaming machines in the clubhouse, P informed the police of this and the machines had to be removed. A few days later a poem appeared on the wall near where the machines had been. The poem referred to the machines and ended as follows:

'But he who gave the game away, May he Byrne in hell and rue the day.'

P alleged that this was defamatory, in that it showed that he was disloyal to his fellow members. It was held that the words were not defamatory because 'right-thinking members of society' would not think less of a person who upheld the law. It was not sufficient that he was shunned by the members of the golf club.

d. A problem may arise if the words used are not prima facie defamatory. In this case an innuendo is required if the claimant is to succeed. An innuendo is a statement by the claimant of the meaning that he attributes to the words.

In *TOLLEY v J.S. FRY AND SONS LTD (1931)* D, a chocolate manufacturer, published an advertisement showing a picture of P, and a poem including P's name and D's name. P was a well known amateur golfer and he had not given his consent for his name and picture to be used in this way. The picture and poem were not by themselves defamatory. However, P brought a libel action alleging an innuendo. He alleged that reasonable people would think that he had been paid for the use of his name and that he therefore was not a genuine amateur golfer. It was held that this was a reasonable inference. He succeeded in his libel action.

In *CASSIDY v DAILY MIRROR (1929)* D published a picture of Cassidy and a young woman with a statement that their engagement had been announced. This information was given to the paper by Cassidy himself. Cassidy was, however, already married and his wife brought a libel action claiming that the photograph and statement contained an innuendo to those who knew her that she was not married to her husband, and was accordingly 'living in sin' with him. The evidence was that some people who knew her were given this impression. She therefore succeeded in her action. Note that:

i. The young woman would probably have succeeded if she had brought an action. The innuendo would have been that she was the type of person who went out with married men. This would have been the thoughts of people who knew Cassidy was already married.

ii. If the case had occurred after 1952 the paper may have been able to succeed in the defence of unintentional defamation (see below).

e. The statement must also be false. The legal presumption is that it is false. Thus the respondent has to prove its truth, rather than the claimant its falseness.

5. *Reference to the Claimant*

   a. The claimant need not necessarily be named.

   In *J'ANSON v STUART (1789)* a newspaper, speaking of a swindler (without naming him) described him as follows: 'He has but one eye, and is well known to all persons acquainted with the name of a certain noble circumnavigator.'

   The claimant was able to succeed in his defamation action because he only had one eye and a name similar to that of a famous admiral.

   b. Except where a plea of unintentional defamation succeeds, it is no defence to say:

   i. That the respondent did not intend to refer to the claimant.

   In *HULTON v JONES (1910)* a humorous newspaper article described the immoral life of a fictitious churchwarden from Peckham called Artemus Jones. There existed, however, a real Artemus Jones, who was a barrister. The evidence was that the people who knew him thought the article referred to him. Artemus Jones was awarded damages of £1750.

   ii. That the words were intended to refer to a third person of whom they were true.

   In *NEWSTEAD v LONDON EXPRESS (1939)* the newspaper published a statement that Harold Newstead a 30-year old Camberwell man had been convicted of bigamy. Unfortunately there were two 30-year-old Harold Newsteads in Camberwell, and whilst the statement was true in respect of one of them it was untrue of the other. The Harold Newstead who had not been convicted of bigamy therefore recovered damages.

6. *Publication by the Respondent* The claimant must prove that the statement was published i.e. communicated to at least one person other than himself. However:

   a. A person is not liable if publication occurs only as a result of an act which is not reasonably foreseeable by him, for example a letter being opened by the claimant's butler. (It is, however, reasonably foreseeable that a letter will be opened by the claimant's wife.)

   b. Two or more persons may be responsible for the same publication, for example the author, printer, publisher and bookseller. The bookseller will have a defence if he did not know of the libel and could not be expected to know of it.

7. *Defences*

   a. *Justification.* The defence of justification is available if the statement is true in substance. Small inaccuracies do not defeat this defence.

   In *ALEXANDER v N.E. RAILWAY CO (1865)* P had been convicted of failing to pay his rail fare. The railway published a poster stating that his sentence was a fine or 3 weeks imprisonment. In fact the alternative was 2 weeks imprisonment. It was held that this small inaccuracy did not defeat the defence of justification. Note that:

   i. A respondent can plead inconsistent defences. For example, if an innuendo is alleged, the defendant could plead firstly that there is no possible innuendo, and secondly that if there is then it represents the truth.

   ii. If, for example, A says, 'B said C is a thief.' Then to succeed in the defence of justification he must prove that C is a thief, and not just that B said C is a thief.

   iii. An honest belief that the statement is true is no justification.

   iv. By *S.5 DEFAMATION ACT 1996* where the words complained of contain two or more distinct charges against the claimant the defence does not fail merely because the truth of each charge is not proved if the charge not proved to be true does not materially injure the claimant's reputation having regard to the true charges. For example, if A calls B 'a thief and a murderer' and B is a murderer, but not a thief, B would be unlikely to succeed in a defamation action against A since a murderer's reputation can hardly be lowered by being called a thief, albeit incorrectly.

  b. *Fair comment.* This defence will apply where the statement is a fair comment made in good faith on a matter of public interest. Note that:

   i. The subject matter must be of public interest, for example the conduct of politicians, or crime reporting.

   ii. The statement must be opinion not fact.

   iii. The comment must be based on facts which, if stated with the comment, must be true.

   iv. The comment must be fair, i.e. an honest expression of the respondent's opinion. It cannot therefore be motivated by malice.

   v. An example of fair comment would be 'Mr X raped Miss C; he is a disgrace to the community.' The second part of the quotation is a comment on the first, it is also opinion. Since crime is a public interest, if Mr X did rape Miss C the defence would be available to the maker of the statement.

  c. *Absolute privilege.* No action lies for defamation however false or malicious the statement, if it is made:

   i. In Parliament.

   ii. In parliamentary papers.

   iii. In the course of state communications.

   iv. In judicial proceedings.

   v. In newspaper reports of judicial proceedings, provided they are fair, accurate and contemporaneous. 'Newspaper' in this context includes weekly but not monthly publications.

  d. *Qualified privilege.* The defence will be available in the following situations, provided the statement was not published more widely than necessary, and provided it was not motivated by malice:

   i. Where A makes a statement to B about C and A is under a legal, social or moral duty to make the statement to B, and B has an interest in receiving it.

     In *WATT v LONGSDON (1930)* D, a company director, received allegations of drunkenness, dishonesty and immorality by P, who was an employee of the company. He showed these allegations to the chairman of the company and to P's wife. The communication to the chairman was held to be subject to qualified privilege since both the duty to make the statement, and an interest in receiving it were present.

It was held, however, that he had no legal, social or moral duty to communicate the allegations to P's wife. Thus in respect of the communication to her the defence of qualified privilege failed.

ii.   Where A makes a statement to B about C and A has an interest to protect and B has a duty to protect it.

In **SOMERVILLE v HAWKINS (1851)** D told two servants that he had dismissed P for robbing him. D could plead the defence of qualified privilege because he had an interest to protect, i.e. his own property.

iii. For fair and accurate reports of judicial or parliamentary proceedings, whether or not they are in a newspaper, and whether or not they are contemporaneous.

iv.   For fair and accurate reports in a newspaper or broadcast on various matters, such as public meetings (*S.7 DEFAMATION ACT 1996*). The *S.7* definition of 'newspaper' includes monthly publications.

v.   For professional statements between solicitor and client.

e.   *Unintentional defamation (S.4 DEFAMATION ACT 1996)*. This defence only applies to words published innocently, i.e. where:

i.   The publisher did not intend to refer to the claimant, and

ii.   The words were not prima facie defamatory, and the publisher did not know of any possible innuendo, and

iii. The publisher was not negligent.

Where the above conditions are satisfied the publisher may make an 'offer of amends', i.e. an offer of a suitable correction and apology, and an offer to take reasonable steps to notify persons who have received copies of the alleged defamatory words. If the offer is accepted, the matter is closed. If the offer is refused, the publisher has a defence if he can prove:

i.   That the words were published innocently.

ii.   That the offer was made as soon as possible, and

iii. That the author wrote them without malice.

The *DEFAMATION ACT 1996* provides that the assessment of damages will be done by the judge, not a jury.

8. *Mitigation* The respondent may mitigate his payment of damages by:

a.   Apology.

b.   Proof of provocation.

c.   Evidence of the claimant's bad reputation prior to the publication of the defamation.

SELF TEST QUESTIONS

Self Test Questions No. 25 (for Answers see Appendix 1):

1   What is the legal definition of defamation?

2   How is *slander* and *libel* distinguished?

3   What is the meaning of the word *defamatory*?

4   How is the defamatory statement linked to the claimant?

5   'A defamatory statement must be published', what does that mean?

6   Name the defences to defamation.

7   What is the position regarding an unintentional defamation?

8   What is required for a respondent to mitigate the payment of damages?

REMEDIES AND LIMITATION PERIODS

28

Learning Outcomes At the end of this chapter you should be able to:

- State the remedies for a victim of tort.

- Explain the workings of the limitation periods for the bringing of legal actions in tort.

REMEDIES

1. *Damages* It will be clear from the previous chapters that the main remedy for the victim of a tort is an award of damages. Damages are a sum of money payable by the respondent. The respondent may, however, choose, or be required by law, to insure against the payment of damages. Tort damages are always unliquidated, i.e. they clearly cannot be fixed by prior agreement between the parties. There are three main types of damages:

2. *Compensatory Damages*

   a. Their purpose is to put the claimant, so far as money can do, in the position that he would have been in if the tort had not been committed. This sum must take into account future loss, since usually only one action may be brought. The damages awarded will be itemized under several 'heads', for example:

      i.   Loss of amenity.

      ii. Pain and suffering.

    iii.   Loss of expectation of life.

    iv.   Loss of income, both actual and prospective.

b.   The relationship between iii. and iv. has been reviewed by the House of Lords (now the Supreme Court).

In **PICKETT v BRITISH RAIL ENGINEERING (1980)** the court held that a claimant, (provided he survived the tort), could recover damages for loss of income on the basis of his pre-accident life expectancy. This overrules the Court of Appeal decision in **OLIVER v ASHMAN (1962)** which decided that damages for future loss of income should be awarded only for the period during which the claimant is expected to remain alive.

c.   Where damages are awarded for loss of earnings, the fact that the claimant would have paid tax on his earnings must be taken into account, thus reducing the award of damages (**BRITISH TRANSPORT COMMISSION v GOURLEY (1955)**). The notional tax reduced is not paid to the Inland Revenue, it could therefore be argued that this represents a benefit to the defendant or to his insurance company.

d.   Social security benefits, for example for sickness or disablement are also deducted, although if the claimant failed to make a national insurance claim, and had not acted unreasonably in failing to claim, the sum will not be deducted. Insurance benefits receivable because of the claimant's private payment of premiums are not deductable, nor is a disability pension received as of right.

e.   Compensatory damages may be ordinary or special:

    i.   Ordinary damages are assessed by the court as compensation for losses which cannot be positively ascertained, and will depend on the court's view of the nature of the claimant's injury. Such damages, e.g. for pain and suffering, need not be quantified in the statement of claim.

    ii.   Special damages can be positively ascertained, for example damage to clothing, costs of repairs to cars. Special damages must be specifically claimed.

3. *Nominal Damages* If a tort is actionable per se, and the claimant proves the elements of the tort without showing actual loss, he will be awarded a small sum of money, for example £1 in recognition of the fact that he has suffered a wrong.

4. *Exemplary Damages* These are granted in rare cases, their purpose being to punish the respondent in addition to compensating the claimant. They may be awarded for:

a.   Oppressive, arbitrary or unconstitutional acts of public officials.

In **AB AND OTHERS v SOUTH WEST WATER SERVICES (1992)** the claimants suffered ill effects as a result of drinking contaminated water from D's water system which had been polluted in July 1988 when 20 tons of aluminium sulphate was accidentally introduced into the system at a water treatment works. D was subsequently prosecuted and convicted for contamination of the water supply, for which they as the water authority were responsible. The claimants brought a number of actions against D, i.e. under the Consumer Protection Act 1987, under the rule in **RYLANDS v FLETCHER (1868)**, for breach of contract, in nuisance and in negligence. They also claimed exemplary damages because D acted in an arrogant and high-handed manner in ignoring complaints and deliberately misled the complaint by sending a circular letter to all customers asserting that the water was safe to drink, when it was known to be unfounded as no adequate tests had been carried out. They further failed to give any proper information to public health authorities, hospitals, doctors and customers as to any precautions that should be taken to minimize the effects of consumption of contaminated water. Finally they failed to close down the treatment works or provide clean water from an alternative source, but continued to supply contaminated water for a longer period than they would have done had they been properly informed.

The Court of Appeal held that exemplary damages are not limited by the cause of action sued on but by the status of the respondent and the quality of his conduct. Exemplary damages may therefore be awarded in a claim of public nuisance against a water authority which has deliberately interfered with a person's rights as a member of the public.

b. When the respondent's conduct has been calculated to make a profit for himself.

In *CASSELL v BROOME (1972)* D published a book, knowing that it was defamatory of P, because they thought that any damages awarded to P would be less than the profits of the book. The court, however, awarded exemplary damages against D, awarding P more than his actual loss to ensure that D did not profit from his tort.

5. *Injunction*

a. An injunction is an equitable remedy. It may be an order of the court commanding something to be done (a *mandatory injunction*) or it may forbid the respondent from doing something (a *prohibitory injunction*). Like other equitable remedies, the award of an injunction is at the court's discretion. An example of the exercise of this discretion is *MILLER v JACKSON (1977)* (Chapter 25.5) when although the claimant 'won' the case he was not granted the injunction that he wanted.

b. A valuable feature of this remedy is the power of the court to grant an *interlocutory* (until trial) *injunction*. Thus a temporary remedy may be obtained within days or even hours of the complaint arising. The matter must, however, be serious, and the judge must consider that there would be a high chance of success for the claimant at a full hearing of the case.

6. *Other Remedies* Other remedies may be appropriate for particular torts, for example:

a. Abatement of nuisance.

b. Escape from false imprisonment.

c. Ejection of trespassers.

d. Application for a writ of habeas corpus.

LIMITATION OF ACTIONS

7. Time limits for action in tort are governed by the *LIMITATION ACT 1980* and the *LATENT DAMAGE ACT 1986*.

a. An action for the recovery of land must be brought within 12 years (*S.15 LIMITATION ACT 1980*).

b. An action for damages in respect of personal injury caused by negligence, nuisance or breach of duty must be brought within 3 years (*S.11 LIMITATION ACT 1980*).

    c.   An action under the Fatal Accidents Act 1976 must be brought within 3 years (*S.12 LIMITATION ACT 1980*).

    d.   An action for a claim not involving personal injury may not be brought later than 6 years from the date on which the cause of action accrued or 3 years from when the claimant knew or ought to have known about the damage. There is an overriding time limit of 15 years from the date of the respondent's breach of duty.

    e.   There is a special 3-year time limit in cases of libel and slander (subject to an extension of 1 year by the High Court (*ADMINISTRATION OF JUSTICE ACT 1985*).

8. *The Point When Time Starts to Run*

    a.   Where a tort is actionable per se, time runs from the moment of the wrongful act.

    b.   Where a tort is actionable only on proof of damage, time runs from the moment damage was first suffered. Problems have occurred in cases of 'latent damage' i.e. damage which does not manifest itself until some time after the act or omission which causes it. In such cases time does not begin to run until such time as the claimant discovers the damage, or ought, with reasonable diligence, to have discovered it.

    c.   Where a cause of action is based on or concealed by fraud, time does not begin to run until the claimant discovers the fraud, or could with reasonable diligence have done so.

    d.   Where a tort is of a continuing nature, for example nuisance or false imprisonment, a fresh cause of action arises daily, and an action lies for such instances of the tort as lie within the statutory period.

9. *Discretion to Exclude Time Limits*

    a.   By amended *S.14A* of the *LA 1980* the period of limitation may be extended by 3 years from when the claimant had relevant 'knowledge' to bring an action for damages. What constitutes relevant 'knowledge' was considered in *HAWARD v FAWCETTS (A FIRM) (2006)*. H acquired a company and undertook significant future investments in the company relying upon accounts supplied by F. The initial purchase and investments took place from 1994 up until 1998 when the company went into liquidation. H was seeking to commence an action against F in 2001 (now outside the 6-year limitation period) claiming that he did not realize the questionable soundness of F's accounts until he sought specialist financial advice in 1999; he was arguing that, under *S.14A*, the limitation period should run from when he had 'knowledge' of F's negligence, in 1999. The House of Lords held that the requisite knowledge was knowledge of facts constituting the essence of a claim, not when H first realized that he might have a right of action. Based on the facts the Court found that H had sufficient knowledge to justify investigating a claim earlier than 1998, the scale of losses and substantial injections of capital should have alerted H to the possibility that F had been negligent. The action would be time barred.

SELF TEST QUESTIONS

Self Test Questions No. 26 (for Answers see Appendix 1):

1   What are 'damages'?

2   State the four heads of compensatory damages.

3   What is meant by, 'nominal' and 'exemplary' damages?

4   What are the characteristics of an injunction?

5   What are the periods of limitations in civil actions?

REFLECTION AND CONSOLIDATION III

For answers go to the student digital support resources for the book (see page xxv).

Reflection

Key areas of study
These chapters cover the large area of civil law called – *torts,* i.e. civil wrongs.

Of these the tort of negligence is by far the most commonly resorted to tort; it covers those situations where one person has caused loss or damage to another by their actions or failures to act. Main areas of study include:

defining a tort

defences: *consent*, *mistake*, *act of God*, *self-defence*, *necessity*,

statutory authority, *illegality*

causation and *remoteness of damage*

vicarious liability

the basic requirements of the tort of negligence

occupiers' liability and *strict liability*

other torts – *nuisance*, *trespass* and *defamation*

limitation periods in which to bring an action.

Consolidation

The following are practice assessment exercises; you will find the answers and guidance by going to the student digital support resources for the book (see page xxv).

MULTIPLE CHOICE QUESTIONS

1   Which of the following is a correct statement of the law?

In the tort of negligence, if a claimant is partly responsible for his/her own injuries, then:

A   No compensation can be recovered from the defendant
B   The defendant is fully liable if he/she was mainly responsible for the injuries
C   If the defendant was negligent, he/she remains fully liable for all the injuries caused
D   The compensation will be reduced to take account of the claimant's share of the responsibility

2   In the tort of negligence, damages are payable in respect of:

A   Reasonably foreseeable losses
B   Losses which are a direct consequence of the breach of duty
C   All the losses caused by the breach of duty
D   Losses which are within the contemplation of the parties

3   Which ONE of the following is correct?

A   Professional advisers cannot be liable in respect of negligent advice in the tort of negligence, but may be liable for breach of contract
B   Professional advisers cannot be liable for breach of contract in respect of negligent advice, but may be liable in the tort of negligence
C   Professional advisers may be liable in respect of negligent advice in either contract or tort
D   Professional advisers cannot be liable in respect of negligent advice in either contract or tort

Typical Exam Questions

4   The rule in 'The Wagon Mound (1961)' governs remoteness of damage in the tort of negligence. Discuss.

(20 marks)
ICSA, November 2004

5   (a)   What is meant by *res ipsa loquitur* in the law of tort?

(b)   Harry is driving his car when suddenly the brakes fail. He is unable to stop and crashes into a motorcycle ridden by Susan damaging the motorcycle and injuring Susan. Advise Harry as to his civil liability.

6   a.   Define public nuisance and distinguish it from private nuisance.

b.   The noise and vibrations from the Acme Plastics Ltd's factory annoy all the residents of Park Road. One of the residents, Mr Evans, is particularly annoyed because on one occasion a piece of hot plastic waste material from one of the factory chimneys fell on to his house causing damage to the roof. Advise the residents and Mr Evans.

7   Advise Thomas whether an action for negligence is likely to succeed against each of the parties in the following cases, explaining the relevant principles of law involved.

a. Albert, a practising accountant, upon whose advice Thomas made an investment which proved to be worthless.

b. Bernard, a barrister, who represented Thomas in a recent case and who conducted the case badly.

c. Charles, a car driver, whose car skidded and crossed on to the wrong side of the road where it collided with Thomas's car.

d. David, a demolition worker, who carelessly injured a fellow worker thereby causing Thomas, who was passing at the time to suffer nervous shock.

8 a. What is the distinction between libel and slander, and why is it important?

b. Mike, a radio journalist, recorded a private interview on his tape recorder with one Quip, a prominent politician, in which Quip accused Red, a political opponent, of being a traitor to his country and that he had 'sold out to the Russians'. Is this statement defamatory, and if so, is it libel or slander? Would your answer be the same if Mike broadcast the interview from the radio station for which he works?

9 (a) In what circumstances is an employer liable for the wrongful acts of his employees?

(14 marks)

(b) Eric, an accountant, is sent by his employer to audit the accounts of a client. Eric's instructions prohibit him from giving any advice on the investment of surplus funds. However, he does give such advice carelessly and, in acting upon it, the client suffers loss. To what extent is the employer liable for this loss?

(6 marks)

(20 marks)

10 Mr Adams and Mrs Barker are neighbours. Mr Adams has, in the last 2 years, done the following things on Mrs Barker's land without her permission:

a. He has allowed the roots of his tree to extend into Mrs Barker's garden, where they have undermined the foundations of Mrs Barker's house.

b. He has moved the boundary fence which he shares with Mrs Barker one metre into Mrs Barker's land.

c. He has dug a hole in Mrs Barker's garden, and taken soil from it for his own garden.

What torts, if any, has Mr Adams committed?

11 (a) What is meant in the law of torts by a '*novus actus interveniens*'?

(b) Arthur is employed by A B Ltd. Because of his employer's negligence Arthur sustains a broken leg.

Consider A B Ltd's liability if:

i. Arthur is left with a severe limp because of an error made by the surgeon who set his leg in plaster.

ii. Arthur's workmates, believing that he has merely dislocated a joint attempt to manipulate his leg back into place. This makes Arthur's injury much worse and it becomes necessary to amputate his leg.

12 To what extent is a supplier of goods liable in civil law (both for negligence and under the *CONSUMER PROTECTION ACT (1987)*) for injuries caused by those goods to people with whom he has no contractual relationship?

(20 marks)

13 a. Explain the meaning and effect of the following defences which may be put forward to an action in tort:

    i.   Consent.   (4 marks)

    ii. Contributory negligence.   (4 marks)

    iii. Statutory authority.   (4 marks)

   b. What remedies may follow a successful tort action?

(8 marks)
(20 marks)

14 a. An occupier owes a common duty of care to lawful visitors who enter his premises. Explain this statement.

(12 marks)

   b. Walter, the owner of a warehouse, spreads rat poison on slices of bread with the intention of putting it down to attract and destroy vermin.

   Simon, an employee with learning difficulties, who has forgotten his lunch, finds the bread and eats a slice, as does Young, a small boy who has wandered into the warehouse.

   Both Simon and Young become seriously ill.

   Discuss the possible liabilities of Walter.

(8 marks)
(20 marks)

PART FOUR
COMMERCIAL LAW

29 AGENCY

Learning Outcomes
At the end of this chapter you should be able to:

- Understand
  - the nature of the agency relationship
  - the ways in which an agent may be appointed
  - the duties of the agent.
- State the authority of the agent.
- Explain who can sue and be sued.
- Outline the various types of agent.
- Explain how an agency may be terminated.

INTRODUCTION

1. An agent is a person who is used to effect a contract between his principal and a third party. The agent may be an employee of the principal, for example a salesman in a shop, or he may be an independent contractor, for example an estate agent. Whatever the type of agent the distinctive

characteristic of the relationship is that the agent has the power to make a binding contract between a principal and a third party without himself becoming a party to the contract.

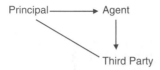

Principal ⟶ Agent ⟶ Third Party

2. There are several different types of agent, the more important being considered later. However, all agents will fall into one of three general categories:

   a. A *special agent's* authority is limited to the performance of a specific act, such as buying a particular car.

   b. A *general agent/commercial agent* has authority to perform any of the duties which are normally within the scope of the business entrusted to him, for example a solicitor or a partner within a partnership (see Chapter 38.5).

   c. A *universal agent* is appointed by a deed known as a 'power of attorney'. He has unlimited authority and may perform any acts that his principal could have performed including the execution of a deed on his behalf.

3. Since an agent does not contract on his own behalf he need not possess full contractual capacity – he may, for example, be a minor. The principal, however, must have full capacity to make the contract in question.

4. In everyday language the word 'agent' is often used to describe anybody who buys and sells goods. For example, a car dealer may be described as the 'sole agent' for a particular make of car. This does not mean that the dealer acts as the legal agent of the manufacturer when he sells the car to a customer. In practice the dealer acts on his own account when he buys from the manufacturer and sells to the customer. This wider use of the word 'agent' must be distinguished from the narrow legal usage. In law an agent is someone whose purpose is to make a contract between his principal and a third party.

APPOINTMENT OF THE AGENT

5. Agency may be created in the following four ways.

6. *Express Agreement* The agent may be appointed verbally or in writing, unless he is authorized to execute a deed, in which case the appointment must be by deed.

7. *Implication – through apparent or ostensible authority*

   a. Agency will arise when, although there is no specific agreement, a contract can be implied from the conduct or relationship of the parties.

   It is possible, under general principles of agency law, for an agency relationship to be found to exist *without an express agreement*. This is where there is found to be some *apparent or ostensible authority* for one person to act on behalf of another. This can be brought about where two parties, who are alleged to be agent and principal, agree to a situation being present where; to an outside party, one is acting on behalf of the other. If the outsider reasonably understands this to be the case *and* as a consequence decides to contract with the party he understands to be acting for that other, then an agency relationship will be deemed to exist and the party who appears to be being represented, will become a principal and the other his agent. As a consequence, the principal will incur liability for the acts of his agent to the outside person – the third party.

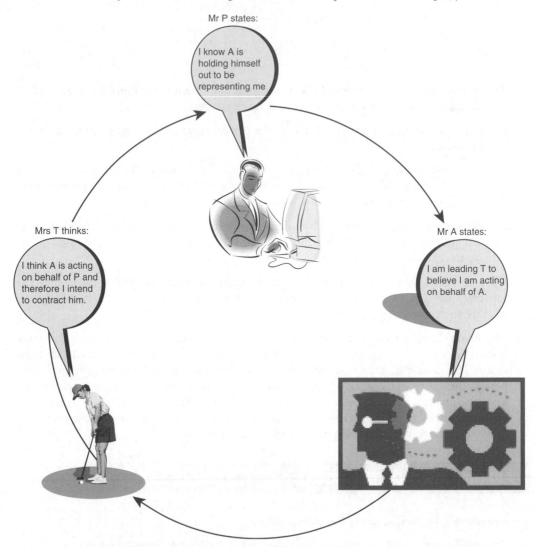

In **HELY-HUTCHINSON v BRAYHEAD LTD (1968)** a managing director of B Ltd often committed the company to contracts without the knowledge of fellow directors – the board and reported such agreements to the board later. When the director entered into a contract to guarantee the debts of a company that went into liquidation, the company sought to deny liability arguing that the director did not have the authority to provide such a guarantee. The Court held that the actual authority of the director to act may be expressed or implied and where, as here, he was appointed to act on behalf of the board, the board impliedly authorized him to do all such things as fall within the usual scope of that office. The contract was binding on the company and was enforceable by the third party.

b. The test is objective and agency may therefore be implied even if the principal and agent did not recognize the relationship themselves (**GARNAC GRAIN CO. v H.M. FAURE (1967)**).

c.   If an alleged agent is a partner in a firm, he will be held to be acting as the agent of his co-partners if the contract that he made is within the usual scope of the partnership business.

d.   Cohabitation (rather than marriage) raises a presumption that the woman has authority to pledge the man's credit for necessaries. In defining necessaries regard is had to the man's style of living rather than to his actual means. The presumption can be rebutted by evidence that, for example, the trader had been told not to supply goods to the woman on credit, or that the woman had sufficient funds to purchase necessaries.

e.   An implied agency may arise by estoppel. Thus if a person by his words or conduct represents another as having authority to make contracts on his behalf, he will be bound by such contracts as if he had expressly authorized them, i.e. he is *estopped* (meaning, not allowed to assert an otherwise enforceable legal right) by his conduct from denying the existence of an agency.

In *PICKERING v BUSK (1812)* a broker was employed by a merchant to buy hemp. After he had completed the purchase the broker retained the hemp at his wharf, at the request of the merchant. He then sold the goods. The purchaser was held to have obtained a good title to the goods because the broker was apparently an agent to sell, and the merchant was not allowed to assert his legal rights to the goods because of an apparent agency relationship exited.

8.   *Necessity* Agency of necessity is formed by operation of law (i.e. automatically). Thus the principal may be bound to a contract made on his behalf without authority and which he refuses to ratify. Three conditions must be satisfied:

a.   There must be an emergency, making it necessary for the agent to act as he did.

In *PRAGER v BLATSPIEL (1924)* A bought skins as agent for P but was unable to send them to P because of prevailing war conditions. Since A was also unable to communicate with P he sold the skins before the end of the war. It was held that A was not an agent of necessity, because he could have stored the skins until the end of the war. There was no real emergency.

b.   It must be impossible to get instructions from the principal.

In *SPRINGER v GREAT WESTERN RAILWAY (1921)* a consignment of fruit was found by the carrier to be going bad. The carrier sold the consignment locally instead of delivering it to its destination. It was held that the carrier was not an agent of necessity because he could have obtained new instructions from the owner of the fruit. He was therefore liable in damages to the owner.

c.   The agent must have acted in good faith, and in the interests of all the parties.

In *GREAT NORTHERN RAILWAY v SWAFFIELD (1874)* a horse was sent by rail and on its arrival at its destination there was no one to collect it. GNR incurred the expense of stabling the horse for the night. It was held that GNR was an agent of necessity who had implied authority to incur the expense in question.

9.   *Ratification*

a.   If a duly appointed agent exceeds his authority, or a person having no authority purports to act as agent, the principal is not bound.

b. The principal may, however, adopt the contract at a later date, provided:

    i. The agent named his principal and specifically informed the third party that he was contracting as agent.

    ii. The principal had contractual capacity at the date of both the contract and the ratification, and if the principal is a company, it must have been incorporated at the time of the contract.

    In *KELNER v BAXTER (1866)* P sold wine to D who purported to act as agent for a company which was about to be formed. When it was formed the company attempted to ratify the contract made by D. It was held that it could not do so, since it was not in existence when the contract was made. D was therefore personally liable to pay for the wine.

    iii. The principal had full knowledge of all material facts, or was prepared to ratify in any event.

c. A void contract cannot be ratified. Similarly a forged signature cannot be ratified because forgery is an illegal act, and because a forger does not purport to act as an agent.

In *BROOK v HOOK (1871)* a man forged his uncle's signature on a promissory note. When a third party came into possession of the note and discovered the forgery, he intended to bring proceedings against the forger. The uncle then purported to ratify his nephew's act by signing the note, but later refused to honour it. It was held that the ratification was ineffective and the promissory note was therefore void.

d. If A, who has no authority to do so, contracts with X, on behalf of P, any ratification by P relates back to the making of the contract by A.

In *BOLTON PARTNERS v LAMBERT (1888)* the managing director of a company acting as an agent of the company, but without authority to do so, accepted an offer by the defendant for the purchase of company property. The defendant later withdrew his offer, but the company then ratified the manager's acceptance. It was held that D was bound by the contract as the ratification was retrospective to the time of the manager's acceptance.

THE RELATIONSHIP BETWEEN PRINCIPAL AND AGENT

10. *The Duties of an Agent*

a. He must carry out his principal's lawful instructions, unless he is acting gratuitously.

In *TURPIN v BILTON (1843)* an insurance broker, in return for a fee, agreed to effect insurance on P's ship. He failed to do so and the ship was lost. The broker was held liable to P.

b. He must exercise reasonable care and skill in the performance of his duties. The degree of skill expected of him depends on the circumstances. More skill is expected of a professional person than of a layman who merely advises a friend. If a payment is made this will also be taken into account in assessing the care and skill expected but even an unpaid agent may be liable in tort for negligence if he gives bad advice (*HEDLEY BYRNE v HELLER (1964)*) (Chapter 26).

c. He must act in good faith and for the benefit of his principal.

   i. He must not let his own interests conflict with his duty to his principal. It does not matter that the contract is made without intent to defraud, for example if an agent appointed to buy sells his own property to the principal at a proper market price. The reason for the rule is to prevent the agent from being tempted not to do the best for his principal.

   In *ARMSTRONG v JACKSON (1917)* P employed D, a stockbroker, to buy some shares for him. In fact D sold his own shares to P. It was held that P could rescind the contract. The agent's interest as seller was to sell at the highest possible price, whereas his duty as agent was to buy at the lowest possible price – clearly a conflict of interest and duty.

   ii. He must not make a secret profit, i.e. he must not use his position to secure a benefit for himself.

   In *LUCIFERO v CASTEL (1887)* an agent appointed to purchase a yacht for his principal bought the yacht himself and then sold it to his principal at a profit, the principal being unaware that he was buying the agent's own property. The agent had to pay his profit to the principal. (This case also illustrates i. above.)

   The agent must pay the profit to the principal even if the principal could not have earned the profit himself.

   In *READING v ATTORNEY GENERAL (1951)* a sergeant in the British Army in Egypt agreed to accompany lorries carrying illicit spirits. He was paid £20 000 so that his presence in uniform would ensure that the vehicles were not searched. It was held that as he made his profit through the use of his position, he had to account to the Crown as his employer. (The sergeant was not strictly an agent, but he was held to have a fiduciary relationship with his employer similar to a principal/agent relationship.)

   iii. He must not misuse confidential information regarding his principal's affairs. If the principal fears that the agent will destroy or dispose of confidential information the principal may apply for an *Anton Piller injunction*, authorizing the principal's representative to enter the agent's premises to remove the confidential material. An Anton Piller injunction is an ex parte injunction, i.e. it is granted on the application of the principal without the agent being represented. The name derives from the case *ANTON PILLER KG v MANUFACTURING PROCESSES (1976)* where it was first granted.

   iv. Certain employees owe fiduciary duties to their employer, e.g. the managing director of a company. Sometimes senior managers are also regarded as having an agency type of relationship with their employer. Such persons generally have a duty to disclose their own breaches of duty and any breaches by other employees.

   In *CYBRON CORPORATION v ROCHEM (1983)* a 'European Zone Controller' received on retirement a generous package of benefits. It was then discovered that he had, with other employees, set up a rival business and participated in large scale commercial fraud. The company sued to recover the money paid to him on his retirement. The court held that even if the person concerned had no duty to disclose his own breach (this was not made clear) he was under a duty to disclose breaches by other employees. Such a duty does not apply to all employees in all situations, it depends on the particular employee and the circumstances in general, however, it clearly applies to a zone controller who is responsible for a large section of his employer's business. The company was therefore successful and the agreement concerning payments on retirement was voidable for non-disclosure.

v.   A breach of duty by the agent may result in the agent losing his right to remuneration, but this will not be the case if the right to remuneration accrued before the principal exercised his right to terminate the contract for breach.

In *ROBINSON SCAMMELL v ANSELL (1985)* an estate agent had been engaged to sell P's house. The agent found purchasers, but when P's own house purchase fell through A informed the purchasers that the sale might not proceed and suggested alternative properties for them to look at. On discovering this P informed A that the agency was terminated. They then contacted the original purchasers and successfully completed the sale to them. The agents claimed their fee and their client refused to pay. It was held that the right to remuneration accrued before the breach. The estate agents were therefore awarded their commission. The Court of Appeal based their decision on *KEPPEL v WHEELER (1927)* where although the plaintiff was awarded damages for breach, the agent received his commission because the breach was not sufficiently serious to justify termination of the agency agreement.

d.   He must not delegate the performance of his duties, unless the principal expressly or impliedly authorizes the agent to appoint a sub-agent. An agent does not, however, 'delegate' by instructing his own employees to do necessary acts in connection with the performance of his duty.

e.   He must not mix his own financial affairs with those of his principal, for example by paying money received on behalf of his principal into his own account. In addition he must render accounts to the principal when required.

11. *Duties of the Principal*

a.   He must pay the agent the commission or other remuneration that has been agreed. If nothing has been agreed the agent is entitled to what is customary in the particular business, or in the absence of custom, to reasonable remuneration. The exact point in time at which the right to commission arises depends on the terms of the contract between the principal and the agent. This has given rise to difficulty, particularly in cases concerning estate agents.

In *LUXOR (EASTBOURNE) v COOPER (1941)* the contract provided that the vendor of land should pay the estate agent his commission 'on completion of sale'. A prospective purchaser was introduced by the agent. He was ready, willing and able to buy, but the sale did not take place because the owner refused to deal with him. It was held that the agent was not entitled to commission.

Contrast this with *SCHEGGIA v GRADWELL (1963)*. A similar contract provided that the vendor should pay commission as soon as 'any person introduced by us enters into a legally binding contract to purchase'. It was held that an agent was entitled to his commission when the purchaser signed a binding contract, although the vendor later rescinded the contract because of the purchaser's breach.

b.   He must indemnify the agent for losses and liabilities incurred by him in the course of the agency.

In *ADAMSON v JARVIS (1827)* an auctioneer sold goods on behalf of his principal, being unaware that the principal had no right to sell. The auctioneer was held liable to the true owner in conversion, but was entitled to an indemnity from the principal.

It has been held that an agent may be indemnified when he makes a payment on behalf of his principal which is not legally enforceable by the third party, but which is made as a result of some moral or social pressure.

In *READ v ANDERSON (1884)* an agent was employed to bet on a horse. The horse lost and the agent paid the bet. It was held that he was entitled to an indemnity from the principal since if he had not paid he would have been recorded as a defaulter.

12. *Commercial Agents*

a. The *COMMERCIAL AGENTS (COUNCIL DIRECTIVE) REGULATIONS 1993* were passed to clarify the relationship between commercial agents and their principals.

b. A *commercial agent* is a self-employed intermediary who has the authority to negotiate the sale or purchase of goods on behalf of another person. The necessary status of the 'agent', required for the relationship to come within the Directive, was examined in *TAMARIND INTERNATIONAL LTD v EASTER NATURAL GAS (RETAIL) LTD (2000)*. For a person to become a commercial agent of another and thereby be regulated by the Regulations, his function must be a *primary role* for the 'principal', not a *secondary role* (*Reg.2(4)*). In this case the court held that the correct test was:

> 'To enquire into the primary purpose of the agency agreement to determine whether the agent had been appointed to develop goodwill in the principal's business i.e. giving the principal a commercial advantage.'

Definition of goodwill

Goodwill in a business is the benefit a business has built up from its reputation and trade connections. It is an asset of the business. Often, upon an insolvency where a buyer is being sought, the only substantial asset worth selling is the goodwill. (The tort of *passing-off*, see Chapter 34.22 relates to the protection of goodwill attached to a business.)

In the *TAMARIND CASE*, applying the test, it showed that the 'agent's' activities were not secondary they were primary and sought to develop the goodwill of the 'principal's' business; the agreement was regulated by the Regulations and the termination of the contract entitled the agent to compensation.

In relation to these commercial agents the regulations state that the duty of good faith (*Reg 3(1)*) specifically includes:

i. A duty of the *agent* to make proper efforts to negotiate and conclude transactions and to communicate all necessary information to the principal.

ii. A duty of the *principal* to provide the agent with necessary documentation and information, and to notify the agent if he expects the volume of transactions to be significantly lower than anticipated.

In *CURETON v MARK INSULATIONS LTD (2006)* the duty of good faith owed by the agent to his principal was breached when the agent approached existing customers of the principal to sell insulation to them in direct competition with the principal. The agent would be liable.

THE AUTHORITY OF THE AGENT

13. *Express, Implied and Apparent Authority*

    a. Where the agent is given *express authority* an act performed within the scope of this authority will be binding on the principal and the third party.

    b. Where an agent is employed to conduct a particular trade or business he has *implied authority* to do whatever is incidental to such trade or business. This is the case even if the principal told the agent that he did not have such authority, unless the third party knew of the lack of authority.

        In *WATTEAU v FENWICK (1893)* the manager of a public house was instructed by D, the owner, not to purchase tobacco on credit. P, who was not aware of this restriction sold tobacco to the manager, and the manager was unable to pay for it. P then successfully sued D. It was held that the purchase of tobacco was within the usual authority of a manager of a public house, and it was this authority upon which the seller was entitled to rely.

    c. If a person's words or conduct lead another to believe that an agent has been appointed and has authority, he will usually be estopped from denying the authority of the agent, even though no agency was agreed between the principal and agent. The agent is said to have *apparent authority.*

14. *Breach of Warranty of Authority*

    a. A person who professes to act as agent, and who either has no authority from the alleged principal, or has exceeded his authority, is liable in an action for breach of warranty of authority at the suit of the party *with whom he professed to make the contract.*

    b. The agent is not liable if the third party knew of his lack of authority at the time the contract was made.

    c. The agent is liable whether he acted fraudulently or innocently. For example, where his authority is terminated without his knowledge by the death or insanity of his principal.

        In *YONGE v TOYNBEE (1910)* a solicitor was conducting litigation on behalf of a client who went insane. After this happened, but before the solicitor heard of it, he took further steps in the action. As a result the other party to the litigation incurred further costs. It was held that he could recover these costs from the solicitor since the solicitor had continued the action after the agency had been ended by the client's insanity. It made no difference that the solicitor had acted in good faith and with reasonable care.

WHO CAN SUE AND BE SUED?

15. The question of whether or not the agent can sue or be sued by the third party depends on the parties' intention. If their intention is not clear, the following rules apply:

16. *If the Agent Names the Principal* The agent generally incurs neither rights nor liabilities, and drops out as soon as the contract is made. Only the principal can sue and be sued.

17. ***If the Agent Discloses the Existence but not the Name of the Principal*** Again the general rule is that the agent can neither sue nor be sued, but a contrary intention is more easily inferred than when the principal is named. Regardless of whether or not the principal is named, in the following exceptional cases the agent may be personally liable:

    a.   If he signs his own name to a deed in which his principal is not named.

    b.   If he signs a negotiable instrument in his own name without adding words indicating that he is signing as agent.

    c.   If the custom of the particular trade makes him liable.

    d.   If he agrees to be liable.

18. ***If the Agent Does Not Disclose the Existence of the Principal***

    a.   The agent may sue and be sued on the contract.

    b.   The undisclosed principal may also sue on the contract provided:

        i.   The agent's authority to act for him existed at the date of the contract, and

        ii.   The terms of the contract are compatible with agency.

            In ***HUMBLE v HUNTER (1842)*** an agent entered into a charter-party and signed it as 'owner'. It was held that the word 'owner' was incompatible with an agency relationship. Evidence was not admissible to show that another was principal. The principal could not therefore sue on the contract.

    c.   On discovering the principal, the third party may choose to sue him instead of the agent. The commencement of proceedings against either the principal or agent does not necessarily amount to a conclusive election so as to bar proceedings against the other (***CLARKSON, BOOKER v ANDJEL (1964)***). A judgement against one is, however, a bar to an action against the other.

19. ***Torts of the agent*** The principal is liable together with the agent, for a tort committed within the scope of the agent's actual or apparent authority.

    In ***UNITED BANK OF KUWAIT v HAMMOND (1988)*** a solicitor signed guarantees and undertakings, without actual authority. The result was that the bank lent money to a fraudulent third party. It was held that the bank was reasonable in its belief that the solicitor was acting with the firm's authority. The firm was therefore held liable.

TYPES OF AGENT

The following are examples of the more important types of agent.

20. ***Auctioneers***

    a.   An auctioneer is an agent to sell goods at a public auction.

    b.   He has authority to receive the purchase price and can sue for it in his own name.

    c.   He has a lien on the goods for his charges.

    d.   He has implied authority to sell without a reserve price and even if he sells below a reserve price specified by the owner the contract will be binding. If, however, he declares that the sale is 'subject to a reserve', then a sale below the reserve price is not binding on the owner.

21. *Mercantile agents or Factors*

 a. A factor is an agent 'employed to sell goods or merchandise consigned or delivered to him by or for his principal for a compensation'. Factors are also known as mercantile agents.

 b. His powers are:

 i. To sell in his own name.

 ii. To give a warranty, if it is usual in the course of the business.

 iii. To receive payment for goods sold, give valid receipts and grant reasonable credit.

 iv. To pledge the goods under the Factors Acts. (To pledge means to deposit as security.)

 c. In addition a factor has a lien on the goods for his charges, and he has an insurable interest in the goods.

22. *Brokers* A broker has been defined by Story as 'An agent employed to make bargains and contracts in matters of trade, commerce or navigation between other parties for a compensation commonly called brokerage.' In contrast with a factor:

 a. He rarely has possession of goods and therefore has no lien on them.

 b. He does not buy and sell in his own name, unless there exists a trade custom enabling him to do so.

 c. He has no power to pledge the goods.

23. *Stockbrokers* A member of the Stock Exchange has an implied authority to make contracts for his principal in accordance with the rules of the Exchange. These rules bind the principal even if he is not aware of them, provided they are neither illegal or unreasonable.

24. *Del Credere Agents* Is an agent for the sale of goods who, in consideration of a higher reward than is usually given, guarantees to his principal, the due payment of the price of the goods sold by him to a third party.

25. *Commercial Agents* The *COMMERCIAL AGENTS (COUNCIL DIRECTIVE) REGULATIONS (1993)* was introduced to harmonize rules governing contracts between agents and their principals across Member States. Its aim was to improve the position of agents. Under the *Regulations* commercial agents are defined as self-employed intermediaries who have continuing authority to negotiate the sale or purchase of goods on behalf of a principal. The *Regulations* lay down minimum requirements to protect the agent, such as; minimum periods of notice, when commission is due and the right to claim compensation on the termination of the contract.

TERMINATION OF AGENCY

25. *By the Act of the Parties*

 a. The parties may at any time mutually agree to terminate the agency.

b. The principal may revoke the agent's authority at any time, subject to the following restrictions:

   i. If the agent is also an employee then proper notice must be given to terminate his contract of employment.

   ii. The principal should give notice of the revocation to third parties with whom the agent has dealt, otherwise he will be estopped from denying the capacity of the agent, should the agent make subsequent contracts with these third parties.

   iii. A termination in breach of contract will entitle the agent to damages.

      In ***TURNER v GOLDSMITH (1891)*** G, a shirt manufacturer, employed T as an agent to sell such goods as should be forwarded to him. The agency was for 5 years, determinable by either party at the end of that time by notice. After 2 years G's factory was burned down and he ceased business. T's action for loss of commission succeeded since there was a definite agency agreement for 5 years and this contract was not frustrated merely because the factory in which G manufactured shirts was burnt down.

   iv. Where the principal has given the agent an authority coupled with an interest he cannot revoke. For example, if the agent is authorized to collect debts on behalf of his principal and retain a part of the sum collected.

c. If an agent commits a serious breach of an express or implied duty, for example making a secret profit by failure to disclose the correct selling price of the principal's goods, the principal may terminate the agency agreement without notice and sue for damages. If the agent has made a secret profit the principal is entitled to it even if he could not have made the profit himself.

26. *By Operation of Law*

a. On the death or insanity of either the principal or the agent.

b. On the bankruptcy of the principal.

c. If the subject matter or the operation of the agency agreement is frustrated or becomes illegal, for example if the principal becomes an alien enemy.

27. *By Completion of the Agency Agreement*

a. Either the period fixed for the agreement comes to an end, or

b. The purpose for which the agreement was created is accomplished.

SELF TEST QUESTIONS

Self Test Questions No. 27 (for Answers see Appendix 1):

1   What is the nature of an agency relationship?

2   What are the different ways in which an agent may be appointed?

3   Explain the nature of the relationship between agent and principal.

4   What is the source of an agent's authority to act?

5   Who can sue and be sued should things go wrong?

6   What are the different types of agency?

7   How may an agency relationship be terminated?

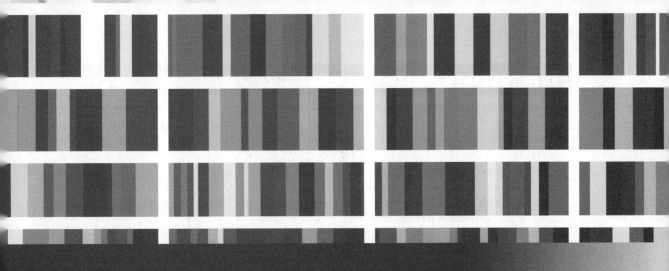

SALE OF GOODS

30

INTRODUCTION AND DEFINITIONS

1. A sale of goods is the most common type of commercial transaction. Most of the common law relating to the sale of goods was first codified by the *SALE OF GOODS ACT 1893*. This was amended by the *SUPPLY OF GOODS (IMPLIED TERMS) ACT 1973* and the law has now been consolidated by the *SALE OF GOODS ACT 1979* (the Act) the most recent amendment to the Act being the *SALE AND SUPPLY OF GOODS TO CONSUMERS REGULATIONS 2002*. References in this chapter to sections are to sections of the 1979 Act, unless otherwise stated.

   The *SALE AND SUPPLY OF GOODS TO CONSUMERS REGULATIONS 2002* introduced some significant changes to the legal framework for the sale and supply of consumer goods. These are:

   a. Where a seller, in the course of a business, delivers consumer goods which do not conform with the contract of sale, for example, they do not meet a satisfactory level of quality or performance, it is presumed that any lack of conformity existed at the time of delivery if discovered within the first 6 months. This in effect reverses the burden of proof onto the seller for a period of 6 months from the date of delivery, that is, *he* must show to the satisfaction of the court that at the time of delivery the goods did comply with the contract.

   b. A hierarchy of remedies is set where there is a lack of conformity.

       i.   The consumer is entitled to a repair or replacement free of charge within a reasonable period and without major inconvenience to the consumer. If this is impossible or disproportionate, or the seller has not remedied the defect within a reasonable time or without major inconvenience to the consumer.

       ii. The consumer will be entitled to either, a reduction in price, or rescission of the contract (unless the shortcoming is minor).

   c. The Regulations introduce an automatic legally binding consumer guarantee.

2. The *UNFAIR CONTRACT TERMS ACT 1977* is also very important to contracts for the sale of goods. In addition to the statutory rules the ordinary principles of contract law are also applicable, for example the rules relating to mistake, misrepresentation, offer, acceptance and agency.

3. *Contract of Sale Distinguished From Other Transactions*

   a. 'A *contract of sale of goods* is a contract whereby the seller transfers or agrees to transfer the property in goods to the buyer for a money consideration called the price' (*S.2(1)*).

   b. A *mortgage* is the transfer of the general property in the goods from the mortgagor to the mortgagee to secure a debt.

   c. A *pledge* is the delivery of goods by one person to another to secure payment of a debt. It differs from a mortgage because a mortgagee obtains the general property in the goods whereas a pledgee only obtains a special property necessary to secure his rights, i.e. only possession passes, coupled with a power to sell. By *S.62(4)* the Act does not apply to a transaction in the form of a contract of sale which is intended to operate by way of mortgage, pledge or other security.

   d. A contract for *work and labour* is sometimes difficult to distinguish from a sale of goods. The test is whether the substance of the contract is the skill and labour exercised for the production of the item. Contracts for work and labour are governed by *THE SUPPLY OF GOODS AND SERVICES ACT 1982*.

In *ROBINSON v GRAVES (1935)* it was held that a contract with an artist to paint a picture was not a sale of goods because the substance of the contract was the skill and experience of the artist and it was immaterial that some paint and canvas would also pass to the purchaser. Similarly a contact for the repair of a car is not a sale of goods even if the repairs involve fitting some new parts.

e. A sale presupposes a 'price'. Therefore if the consideration is goods alone the contract is one of *exchange* and the Act will not apply. A part exchange, for example where a second-hand car plus cash is given in return for a new car, is a sale of goods.

4. *Sale and Agreement to Sell Distinguished*

a. The term 'contract of sale' in the Act includes both actual sales and agreements to sell (*S.61(1)*).

   i.   Where under a contract of sale, the property in goods is passed from the seller to the buyer, the contract is called a '*sale*' (*S.2(4)*).

   ii. Where the transfer of the property in the goods is to take place at a future time or subject to some condition later to be fulfilled the contract is called an '*agreement to sell*' (*S.2(5)*).

   iii. An agreement to sell becomes a sale when the time elapses or the conditions are fulfilled subject to which the property in the goods is to be transferred (*S.2(6)*).

b. The distinction is important because several consequences follow from the passing of property:

   i.   Unless otherwise agreed the risk passes with the property (see 25. below).

   ii. If the property has passed to the buyer the seller can sue for the price.

   iii. If the seller resells the goods after the property has passed to the buyer, the second buyer acquires no title unless he is protected by one of the exceptions to the '*nemo dat*' rule (see 27. below). Similar principles apply if the buyer resells goods before the property has passed to him.

c. '*Property*' means the right of ownership. It is of course possible to transfer possession of goods without transferring the ownership of them, for example hire purchase contracts and contracts whereby the seller has reserved his title as in *ALUMINIUM INDUSTRIE B.V. v ROMALPA (1976)* (see 22. below).

5. *Goods*

a. '*Goods*' means 'All chattels personal other than things in action and money'. The definition includes industrial growing crops, and has been held to include a ship and a coin sold as a collector's item.

b. The Act also distinguishes between:

   i.   '*Specific goods*', i.e. 'goods identified and agreed upon at the time a contract of sale is made' e.g. 'My Ford Escort M123 ABC'.

   ii. '*Future goods*', i.e. 'goods to be manufactured or acquired by the seller after the making of the contract of sale' e.g. A wedding cake.

    iii. *'Unascertained goods'*, i.e. goods defined only by a description applicable to all goods of the same class or goods forming part of a larger consignment e.g. six bottles of Chateau Laffite 1961 or e.g. half of that lorry load of sand.

  c. The distinction between specific and unascertained goods is important because, for example *S.6–7* only apply to specific goods (see 26. below) and because the rules governing the passing of property are different.

CAPACITY, FORM, SUBJECT MATTER AND PRICE

6. *Capacity*

  a. Capacity is regulated by the general law concerning capacity to contract, but where necessaries are sold and delivered to a minor, or a person who by reason of mental incapacity or drunkenness is incompetent to contract, he must pay a reasonable price for them (*S.3*).

  b. 'Necessaries' are goods suitable to the condition of life of the minor or other incompetent person, and to his actual requirements at the time of sale and delivery (Chapter 13.2).

7. *Form* Subject to various statutory provisions a contract of sale may be in writing, by word of mouth or implied from conduct (*S.4*).

8. *Subject Matter* The goods may be existing goods, owned or possessed by the seller, or future goods (*S.5*).

9. *The Price*

  a. The price must be in money. It may be:

    i. Fixed by the contract.

    ii. Left to be fixed in the manner agreed in the contract, or

    iii. Determined by the course of dealing of the parties.

  b. If it is not determined as above the buyer must pay a reasonable price (*S.8*), however, the absence of agreement as to price may render the contract void for uncertainty.

  c. Where the contract specifies that the price shall be fixed by the valuation of a third party and the third party does not make the valuation the contract is avoided. If, however, the goods or part of them have been delivered to and appropriated by the buyer he must pay a reasonable price for them. If the failure to value is the fault of the buyer or seller that party is liable to pay damages (*S.9*).

THE TERMS OF THE CONTRACT

10. The following questions, which were considered in Chapter 15, are also relevant to sales of goods:

  a. Is a statement made in negotiations a mere representation inducing the contract, or a term which is part of the contract?

  b. If it is a term, is it a condition or a warranty?

c. If a term has not been expressly agreed, can it be included in the contract by implication?

d. Are any exemption or limitation clauses valid?

11. *Conditions and Warranties*

a. Of the four questions stated above, that relating to conditions and warranties merits revision and further discussion.

b. A *condition is* a vital term, going to the root of the contract, breach of which normally entitles the innocent party to repudiate the contract and claim damages.

c. A *warranty* is a subsidiary term, breach of which only entitles the innocent party to damages.

d. The intention of the parties determines whether a clause is a condition or warranty, but in the absence of evidence of intention the courts will consider the commercial importance of the term, or less usually, the effects of the breach as in *HONG KONG FIR SHIPPING v KAWASAKI KISEN KAISHA (1962)*.

e. In the above case it was stated that many contracted undertakings could not be categorized simply as 'conditions' or 'warranties'. It has since been held that the division into conditions and warranties is not exhaustive. A term may be an 'intermediate term' in which case the remedy would depend upon the nature of the breach rather than the status of the term. If the breach goes to the root of the contract repudiation is justified, in other cases repudiation is not justified.

In *CEHAVE NV v BREMER (1975)* the buyers (B) agreed to purchase for £100 000 a shipment of animal feed. The contract between the sellers (S) and B provided that the goods should be 'shipped in good condition'. When the shipment arrived at its destination it was unloaded into containers. It was then discovered that some of the goods had been damaged in transit and B refused to accept delivery. The container owners applied to court and it was ordered that the goods be sold. In 'somewhat strange circumstances' they were sold to an importer for £30 000 who then resold them to B the same day for £30 000. The Court of Appeal held that there was a breach of the term that the goods be 'shipped in good condition' but this term was neither a condition nor a warranty, but an 'intermediate term'. Since breach of this term did not go to the root of the contract B was not entitled to reject the goods. The Court also decided that B could not reject for breach of the implied condition as to merchantable quality, it being concluded that the goods were merchantable.

12. *The Treatment of Conditions as Warranties*

a. By *S.11(2)* a buyer may waive a breach of condition by the seller, or elect to treat it as a breach of warranty.

b. By *S.11(4)* a 'buyer *must* treat a breach of condition as a breach of warranty where the contract is *non-severable* and he has *accepted* the goods or some of them'. Note that:

i. *S.11(4)* does not apply to a breach of *S.12(1)* (see below).

ii. The meaning of non-severable contracts and acceptance is discussed below – *S.31* and *S.35*.

iii. *S.11(4)* must be read subject to the amended *S.35*.

13. *Stipulations as to Time*

    a.   By *S.10* unless a different intention appears from the terms of the contract, stipulations as to *time of payment* are not deemed to be of the essence of the contract. Whether any other stipulation as to time is of the essence of the contract depends on the terms of the contract.

    b.   Where a party has waived a stipulation, for example as to the time for delivery, which was of the essence of the contract, he may again make that stipulation of the essence by giving the other party reasonable notice of his intention to do so (***RICKARDS v OPPENHEIM (1950)***) (Chapter 27.3).

14. The implied terms of the Act were outlined in Chapter 15. They will now be considered in more detail.

15. *Title*

    a.   By *S.12(1)* there is an implied *condition* that the seller has the right to pass good title to the goods.

        In ***NIBLETT v CONFECTIONERS' MATERIALS CO (1921)*** cans of condensed milk were labelled in a way that infringed the trade mark of a third party. The third party could therefore have restrained the sale by S to B by obtaining an injunction. It was held that S were in breach of the implied condition that they had the right to sell the cans. This case shows that *S.12* will be broken not only where the seller lacks the right to pass the property in the goods to the buyer, but also where he can be stopped by process of law from selling the goods.

    b.   By *S.12(2)* there is an implied *warranty* that the goods are free of any encumbrance not made known to the buyer, and the buyer will enjoy quiet possession of the goods except so far as it may be disturbed by the owner or other person entitled to the encumbrance disclosed.

        In ***MICROBEADS v VINHURST ROAD MARKINGS (1975)*** S sold to B road marking equipment. At the time of the sale, unknown to S, a third party had applied for a patent in respect of the equipment. At the time of the sale the third party could not have objected to B's use of the equipment. Two years after the sale, the third party, who had now been granted patent rights informed B that he was infringing a patent. B then sued S for breach of *S.12(1)* and *S.12(2)*. It was held that there was no breach of *S.12(1)* since at the time of sale S could not have been prevented by injunction from selling the goods. However, there was a breach of *S.12(2)*. The activities of the third party amounted to an infringement of B's quiet possession of the goods. S was therefore liable even though he did not know of the patent application.

    c.   Since the essence of a contract is the transfer of property, if the seller breaks *S.12(1)* there will be a total failure of consideration and the buyer will be entitled to recover the whole price with no deduction for his use.

        In ***ROWLAND v DIVALL (1923)*** B purchased a car from S for £334. Both B and S dealt in good faith. Four months later it was discovered that the car was stolen and B had to return it to the true owner. B sued to recover the price paid to S. S argued that since B had accepted the car he was limited by *S.11(4)* to a claim for damages for breach of warranty, and that in assessing these damages an allowance should be made for his use. Both these arguments failed. Atkin L.J. said that there could not be acceptance if there was nothing (i.e. no title) to accept, and that since B had paid for the property in the car and not merely the right to use it, there had been a total failure of consideration, entitling him to recover the whole purchase price without any set off for the use of the car. This has been criticized in that it is unrealistic to say that consideration has failed totally when B had 4 months use of the car before he had to return it.

16. *Description*

a. Where goods are sold by description there is an implied *condition* that:

   i. The goods will correspond with the description (*S.13(1)*), and

   ii. If the sale is by sample, as well as by description, the bulk of the goods will also correspond with the sample (*S.13(2)*).

   In *GRANT v AUSTRALIAN KNITTING MILLS (1936)* a buyer of underpants contracted dermatitis because of an excess of sulphite in the garment he purchased. It was held:

   a) A sale may be 'by description' even if the buyer has seen the goods before buying them provided he relied essentially on the description, and any discrepancy between the description and the goods is not apparent. There was therefore a breach of *S.13*.

   b) Reliance on the seller's judgement is readily inferred in retail sales because a buyer will go into a shop with confidence that the seller has selected his stock with skill.

   c) The buyer did not need to specify his purpose because it is obvious and therefore may be implied. *S.14* was therefore also broken.

   In *HARLINGDON & LEINSTER ENTERPRISES LTD v CHRISTOPHER HULL FINE ART LTD (1990)* the respondent sold a painting to the claimant which turned out to be a fake. The respondent believed that the painting was by a named artist – *Munter* – and described the painting as such during negotiations. However, the respondent made it clear to the claimant that he was not an expert in this field. The claimant, also no expert, examined the goods and satisfied himself that it was by *Munter* and bought it. The invoice for the sale described the painting as 'a *Munter*'. Upon subsequently discovering that the painting was a fake, the claimant sought a remedy under *S.13(1)* claiming that it was a 'sale by description'. The Court of Appeal held that:

   i. The respondent had made it clear to the claimant that his attribution to *Munter* could not be relied upon, and that the claimant should exercise his own judgement.

   ii. A contract will not be a sale by description merely because the seller made some statement about the goods. *The buyer must show that the description influenced his decision to buy.* The claimant was unable to show this and the action failed.

b. A sale of goods is not prevented from being a sale by description solely because goods being exposed for sale are selected by the buyer (*S.13(3)*).

   The Section does not therefore require written or verbal descriptions to be given by the seller, for example goods selected by the buyer from a supermarket shelf may be sold by description. On the other hand even if the seller does describe the goods, it will not be a sale by description if there is no reliance whatsoever by the buyer on that description.

   In *LIENSTER ENTERPRISES V CHRISTOPHER HULL FINE ART (1990)* S informed B that he had two paintings by Gabriele Munter of the German impressionist school, however, S had no expertise in German impressionist paintings and B knew this.

B later visited S, inspected the paintings and bought them. It was later found out that the paintings were not by Munter. It was held that B had not relied on S's statement as to the artist, but had relied entirely on his own skill and judgment. It was not therefore a sale by description. The court also rejected B's claim that the painting was not of merchantable quality.

c. A sale by description may include such matters as measurements and methods of packing, for example *RE MOORE AND LANDAUER (1921)* (Chapter 20.2).

d. It is possible to be in breach of *S.13*, without being in breach of *S.14*, since goods that are of merchantable quality and/or fit for their purpose may nevertheless not comply with the seller's description.

17. *Satisfactory Quality and Fitness for Purpose*

a. By *S.14(1)* there is no implied condition or warranty as to quality or fitness for a particular purpose of the goods sold, except as provided by the following sub-sections, or by *S.15*. This sub-section preserves the basic rule of caveat emptor (let the buyer beware).

b. *Satisfactory Quality*

i. This is defined under the Act – see iii. below.

ii. *S.1 SALE AND SUPPLY OF GOODS ACT 1994* inserts a new *S.14(2)* in the 1979 Act, it states that where goods are sold in the *course of a business* there is an implied *term* that the goods *supplied* under the contract are of *satisfactory quality*.

The new section uses the word '*term*' to include both conditions and warranties and it refers to goods *supplied* under the contract, not just goods sold. It would therefore cover the quality of a 'free gift' offered as an inducement to purchase goods.

iii. Goods are of a satisfactory quality if they meet the standard that a reasonable person would regard as satisfactory, taking into account any description, the price (if relevant) and all other relevant circumstances. This definition makes it clear that defects which would render new goods unsatisfactory will not necessarily be unacceptable if they occur in second-hand goods, it is a matter of degree. In this respect it is similar to the old *S.14(2)*. For example, in *SHINE v GENERAL GUARANTEE FINANCE (1988)* it was held that a 20-month-old second-hand car was not of merchantable quality at the time of sale when the buyer later discovered that 8 months earlier it had been written off by insurers, since it had been totally submerged in water for over 24 hours.

iv. The new section differs from the old in that examples are given of aspects of quality of goods. The list is not exhaustive and the court may, of course, consider any relevant aspect of quality when deciding whether quality is satisfactory. The Act's guidelines include:

state and condition

fitness for all the purposes for which goods of the kind in question are commonly supplied

appearance and finish

freedom from minor defects

safety, and

durability.

v.   The implied term does not extend to any matter making the goods unsatisfactory which is specifically drawn to the buyer's attention before the contract is made where the buyer examines the goods and the examination ought to reveal the matter which, in a sale by sample, would have been apparent on a reasonable examination of the sample.

c.   *Fitness for Purpose*

i.   By *S.14(3)* where goods are sold in the *course of a business* and the buyer makes known to the seller the purpose for which the goods are being bought there is an implied *condition* that the goods are reasonably fit for that purpose, except where the circumstances show that the buyer does not rely, or that it is unreasonable for him to rely, on the skill or judgement of the seller.

In *ASHINGTON PIGGERIES v CHRISTOPHER HILL (1972)* B asked S to compound food for minks in accordance with a recipe supplied by B. The recipe included herring meal, which is toxic to minks. S compounded the food, which was later fed to the minks with the result that many died. S argued that they were not liable because B had supplied the recipe, and B and themselves were in the same line of business. S were, however, held liable. The court said that reliance on the seller's skill and judgement need not be total but it must be substantial and effective.

ii. Where the purpose for which the goods are required is obvious, it need not be made known expressly because it is clearly implied.

In *GODLEY v PERRY (1960)* a 6-year-old boy purchased a toy plastic catapult. The catapult broke whilst being used and the boy lost an eye. His action against the shopkeeper who sold it to him was successful. There was no need for the boy to make known the purpose of his purchase since it was known by implication.

iii. This section also applies to second-hand goods, but the standard of fitness expected is lower. Like *S.14(2)* it does not apply to a private seller who does not sell in the course of a business.

The relationship between *S.14(2)* and *S.14(3)* was well illustrated in *JEWSON LTD V KELLY (2003)*. Here the buyer purchased a number of boilers from Jewson for installation into some newly converted flats. When he failed to pay for the goods and the Jewson brought proceedings, the buyer counterclaimed for damages for breach of *S.14(2)* and *(3)*. The buyer claimed that the boilers were not of satisfactory quality in that they did not meet the particular energy efficiency ratings required for the flats and that this was causing problems in finding buyers. The Court of Appeal held that it was the function of *S.14(3)* to impose any special obligation on the seller based upon the particular circumstances of the buyer, not *S.14(2)*. There had been no argument by the buyer that the boilers were unsatisfactory in themselves, *S.14(2)*, the issue was whether the particular circumstances of the buyer in needing them to help meet certain energy efficiency targets, rendered them unsatisfactory. The buyer did not provide Jewson with any special information about the particular nature of the purchase – the need to achieve key energy saving ratings – as such he could not show that he relied upon their skill and judgment with regard to the boiler's particular suitability for the particular purpose required. The buyer could only show reliance on the seller as to the intrinsic qualities of the boilers under *S.14(2)* and here they were reasonably fit for their purpose. The seller was not liable.

18. *Sale by Sample*

    a. *S.15* provides that where there is a sale by sample, *conditions* are implied that:

        i. The bulk will correspond with the sample.

        ii. The buyer will have a reasonable opportunity of comparing the bulk with the sample, and

        iii. The goods shall be free from any defect making their quality unsatisfactory, which would not be apparent on reasonable examination of the sample.

    b. If a sale is by sample and description the goods supplied must correspond with both the sample and the description.

    In *NICHOL v GODTS (1854)* the seller sold 'foreign refined rape oil warranted only equal to sample'. When it was delivered the bulk did correspond with the sample but the sample was not 'foreign refined rape oil'. It was held that both *S.13* and *S.15* were broken because if the sale is by sample and description there is an implied condition that the goods correspond with both sample and description.

19. *Exemption Clauses* The acceptability of exemption clauses is governed by the *UNFAIR CONTRACT TERMS ACT 1977*. This was considered in more detail in Chapter 18. *S.6* of the Act (as amended) refers to contracts for the sale of goods and states that:

    a. *S.12 SGA 1979* cannot be excluded.

    b. *S.13–15 SGA 1979* cannot be excluded in a consumer sale, but can be excluded in a non-consumer sale if the exemption clause is reasonable.

    c. The regulations made under *S.22 FAIR TRADING ACT 1973* make it a criminal offence for someone in the course of a business to display at a place where consumer transactions take place a notice of an exemption clause which is void under *S.6 UNFAIR CONTRACT TERMS ACT 1977*.

THE TRANSFER OF THE PROPERTY IN THE GOODS TO THE BUYER

20. Property (ownership) and possession must be distinguished since the property in goods sold may pass to the buyer although the seller retains possession of the goods. The moment property passes is important for several reasons (see 4.b. above).

21. By *S.16* where there is a contract for the sale of *unascertained goods* (i.e. goods defined by description only, and not identified until after the contract is made), no property passes to the buyer unless and until they are ascertained. Thus if a large consignment of goods are handed to a carrier who is directed to set aside the contractual goods, no property passes until the carrier has done so because until then the goods are unascertained.

In *HEALY v HOWLETT AND SONS (1917)* B ordered 20 boxes of fish from S. S consigned 190 boxes by rail and directed railway officials to set aside 20 boxes for B's contract. The train was delayed and the fish had deteriorated before 20 boxes had been appropriated for B. It was held that since property did not pass until appropriation for B, it was held that since property did not pass until appropriation the fish were at S's risk at the time of deterioration and B was not therefore liable to pay the price.

THE TRANSFER OF THE PROPERTY IN THE GOODS TO THE BUYER

22. By *S.17* if the contract is for the sale of *specific or ascertained* goods the property passes when the parties intend it to pass. Intention is ascertained from the terms of the contract, the conduct of the parties, and the circumstances of the case. This section enables the parties to agree to 'reserve title' to the goods until the buyer's outstanding debts are paid.

    In ***ALUMINIUM INDUSTRIE BV v ROMALPA (1976)*** the claimants, who were sellers of aluminium provided in their conditions of sale that 'The ownership of the material to be delivered by AIBV will only be transferred to the purchaser when he has met all that is owing to AIBV no matter on what grounds.'

    After having taken delivery of a consignment of aluminium the purchaser went into liquidation. S who had not received the purchase price sought to enforce the above provision so as to secure payment prior to the distribution of B's assets to the general creditors. It was held that S could recover the consignment.

    This decision created a remedy for an unpaid seller in addition to those provided by *S.39. SGA.* This remedy of possession is wider than the remedy of lien since a lien is for the price only, whereas the Romalpa remedy may be exercised until 'all that is owing' has been paid. It is also wider than stoppage in transit since the right to stop in transit ends when transit ends, whereas the Romalpa remedy may be exercised after delivery of the goods. However, a Romalpa clause will not apply where the material is subjected to a manufacturing process. For example, in ***RE PEACHDART (1983)*** leather was sold on reservation of title terms. The intention was that it be used in the manufacture of handbags. It was held that the supplier's title ceased to exist when the leather had been made into handbags.

    To increase the protection afforded by a reservation of title clause it is advisable for the supplier:

    a. To require that the material in question be kept separate from the buyer's other stock, and

    b. To reserve a right of access to the buyer's premises.

23. Where the parties have not shown a definite intention at the time of contracting *S.18* states that the following 'rules' shall be applied to decide the time at which property shall pass.

    a. *Rule 1.* Where there is an unconditional contract for the sale of specific goods in a deliverable state the property passes when the contract is made, and it is immaterial whether the time of payment or delivery or both are postponed.

        In ***TARLING v BAXTER (1827)*** B purchased a haystack. Before he took it away it was destroyed by fire. B was held liable to pay for the haystack because the property passed when the contract was made.

        Note that:

        i. If, after the contract has been made, the parties agree that the property will pass at a certain time, the agreement will be ineffective if the property has already passed under Rule 1.

            In ***DENNANT v SKINNER & COLLOM (1948)*** a crook purchased a car at an auction. He was allowed to take the car away on payment of a cheque on condition that he signed a document whereby it was agreed that the property would not pass until the cheque had cleared. The crook then resold the car to the defendant. The cheque was later dishonoured. It was held that the defendant got good title to the car because property had passed to the crook under Rule 1 before the agreement was signed. The agreement was therefore of no effect.

LIVERPOOL JOHN MOORES UNIVERSITY
LEARNING SERVICES

ii.   'Deliverable state' means such a state that the buyer would under the contract be bound to take delivery of them (*S.61(5)*).

b.   *Rule 2.* Where the contract is for specific goods and the seller is bound to do something to the goods to put them into a deliverable state, the property does not pass until this has been done and the buyer has notice thereof.

In *UNDERWOOD v BURGH CASTLE BRICK AND CEMENT SYNDICATE (1922)* the contract was for the sale of an engine, weighing 30 tons. At the time of sale it was imbedded in a concrete floor. Whilst being detached from its base and loaded into a railway truck the engine was damaged. The seller nevertheless sued for the price. It was held that the goods were not in a deliverable state when the contract was made so that the property did not pass under Rule 1. Also property would not pass under Rule 2 until the engine had been safely loaded into the truck.

c.   *Rule 3.* Where the specific goods are in a deliverable state but the seller has still to do something, such as weighing, measuring or testing the goods, the property does not pass until such act has been done and the buyer has notice thereof.

i.   For example B purchases a sack of potatoes from S. The price of potatoes is 25 pence per pound, but the total weight of the sack is not known. If it is agreed that the seller will weigh the potatoes to ascertain the total price payable property does not pass until this is done and the buyer has notice of it.

ii.   Both Rule 2 and Rule 3 are confined to acts done by the seller. If the buyer is to do the act, the property would pass on making the contract.

d.   *Rule 4.* Where goods are delivered on approval or on sale or return the property passes:

i.   When the buyer signifies his approval or acceptance to the seller, or

ii.   When he does any other act adopting the transaction, such as pawning the goods, or

iii.   If he does not signify approval or acceptance, property passes when he retains the goods beyond the agreed time or, if no time was agreed, beyond a reasonable time.

In *POOLE v SMITH'S CAR SALES (BALHAM) LTD (1962)* P left his car with D on 'sale or return' terms in August 1960. After several requests D returned the car in November 1960 in a badly damaged state due to use by D's employees. It was held that since the car had not been returned within a reasonable time the property in the car had passed to D and he was accordingly liable to pay the price agreed.

e.   *Rule 5(1).* Where there is a contract for the sale of unascertained or future goods by description the property passes when the goods of that description and in a deliverable state are unconditionally appropriated to the contract by one party with the express or implied assent of the other.

In *PIGNATARO v GILROY (1919)* S sold 140 bags of rice to B. Fifteen bags were appropriated by S for the contract and B was told where he could collect them. The bags were then stolen through no fault of S before B was able to collect them. B failed in his action to recover the price paid for the 15 bags. It was held that S's appropriation of the bags for the contract, without any objection by B, constituted transfer of title to those bags. They therefore belonged to B when they were stolen.

f.   *Rule 5(2).* A seller who delivers goods to the buyer or to a carrier for transmission, without reserving a right of disposal, is deemed to have unconditionally appropriated the goods to the contract.

In *EDWARDS v DDIN (1976)* S filled B's petrol tank and B drove off without paying. It was held that B was not guilty of theft because the property had passed to him. It was impossible for the seller to reserve a right of disposal to petrol which at the point of delivery is mixed with the petrol already in B's tank. At that point the petrol is unconditionally appropriated to the contract with the consent of both parties. (B would now be guilty of the offence of making off without payment (*S.3 THEFT ACT 1978*).)

Note that:

i.   Rule 5 must be considered in conjunction with *S.16.* Under *S.16.* no property passes until the goods are ascertained. Rule 5 shows when goods are ascertained.

ii.   An example of an implied assent to appropriation would be where B orders goods to be sent by post. When S dispatches the goods this amounts to appropriation by S with B's consent.

24. By *S.19* the seller may reserve the right of disposal of the goods until certain conditions are fulfilled and the property will not then pass until the conditions imposed by the seller are fulfilled.

25. Risk (*S.20*).

a.   The general rule has already been stated, i.e. that the risk 'follows' the property. Thus the owner must bear any accidental loss.

b.   This rule may be varied by trade usage or by agreement.

In *STERNS v VICKERS (1923)* S agreed to sell 120 000 gallons of spirit out of a tank containing 200 000 gallons which was on the premises of a third party. A delivery warrant was issued to B, but he did not act on it for some months, during which time the spirit deteriorated. It was held that although no property had passed (because there had been no appropriation) the parties must have intended the risk to pass when the delivery warrant (i.e. the authority requiring the third party to release the spirit to B) was issued to B. B therefore remained liable to pay the price.

c.   If delivery is delayed through the fault of either party the goods remain at the risk of that party as regards any loss which might not have occurred but for the delay.

In *DEMBY HAMILTON v BARDEN (1949)* S agreed to send 30 tons of apple juice by weekly consignments to B. B delayed in taking delivery of some of the juice which as a result went bad. B was held liable to pay the price since the loss was his fault.

26. *Perishing of Goods*

a.   Where there is a contract for the sale of *specific* goods, and the goods without the knowledge of the *seller* have perished at the time the contract is made, the contract is void *(S.6)*. The section is limited to specific goods, but also applies where part of a specific consignment of goods has perished before the contract is made.

In *BARROW LANE AND BALLARD v PHILLIPS (1929)* S sold 700 bags of nuts. Unknown to the sellers 109 bags had already been stolen at the time of sale. It was held that the specific consignment of 700 bags had perished because a substantial part of it was missing.

b. Where there is an agreement to sell *specific* goods and subsequently the goods, without any fault on the part of the seller or buyer, perish before the risk passes to the buyer, the agreement is thereby avoided (*S.7*).

c. Note that:

   i.   *S.6* is a partial enactment of the common law rules relating to mistake in the formation of a contract.

   ii. *S.7* is an enactment of the common law rule relating to frustration when there is a sale of specific goods. *S.7* cannot apply if the risk passes to the buyer at the time of sale, i.e. if *S.18*. Rule 1 applies.

   iii. *S.6–7* do not apply to sales of unascertained goods.

SALE BY A PERSON WHO IS NOT THE OWNER

27. The basic common law rule is that where the seller does not own the goods sold, ownership cannot pass to the buyer, this is sometimes referred to as the *nemo dat quod non habet* rule, which literally translated means, 'no man gives that which is not his own'. A thief, for example, can never own the goods he sells and if found, they must be returned to the rightful owner. The buyer may of course sue the seller for breach of *S.12(1)*, but is not entitled to any compensation from the true owner unless money was spent improving the goods before the buyer discovered they were not his. It is a general tenet of commerce that where goods are 'sold' to another and, for whatever reason, ownership in the goods has not passed, all the original owner wants is to get his goods back, no one wants to sue the seller thief or bankrupt business.

The basic *nemo dat* rule is enacted in *S.21* which provides that where goods are sold by a person who is not the owner, the buyer acquires no better title than the seller unless:

a. The seller had the authority or consent of the owner, or

b. The owner is precluded by his conduct from denying the seller's authority to sell. For example:

   In *EASTERN DISTRIBUTORS v GOLDRING (1957)* M owned a van and he wanted to buy a car from C. However, he did not even have enough money for a hire purchase deposit. M and C therefore devised a scheme whereby C would pretend to a finance company (ED) that he owned both the car and the van – he would sell them both to ED, and then buy both back on hire purchase. In order to convince ED that C owned both the car and the van M signed a form to this effect. C then sold the van to ED, but ED did not accept the car. However, C told M that the *whole deal* had fallen through. Neither C nor M paid any of the hire purchase instalments for the van. M, who had been in possession of the van all the time, then sold it to G (M believed he was the owner since C had told him that the deal had fallen through). ED then sued to recover the van from G. It was held that since M had acted as if C was the true owner of the van (by signing a form to this effect so as to trick ED) he was *estopped* (meaning, as a consequence of his actions, he was denied the enforcement of what otherwise would have been an enforceable legal right) from denying C's right to sell. ED therefore acquired a good title to the van from C. M therefore had no title to pass to G. ED therefore succeeded in their action to recover the van from G.

Note that:

i.   Where there is an estoppel the effect is to pass title to the buyer.

ii.   The mere fact that the owner gives possession of the goods to a third party does not estop him from denying that person's authority to sell.

In **CENTRAL NEWBURY CAR AUCTIONS v UNITY FINANCE (1957)** A agreed with B that A would sell a car to a finance company, which would then let it to B on hire purchase. A then handed the vehicle and registration book to B before the arrangements with the finance company had been completed. The finance company then refused B's application for hire purchase. B, however, was a crook and he had in the meantime sold the car to C. It was held that C did not get title to the car because B had no title to pass to him, and A's conduct in handing over the car and its registration book did not *estop* (see above) him from disputing B's authority to sell.

28. Apart from the two general exceptions contained in *S.21* there are several other exceptions (see 29.–33. below).

29. *Sale Under a Voidable Title*

a.   Under *S.23* where a seller of goods has a *voidable title*, but this title has not been avoided at the time of sale, the buyer acquires a good title provided he buys in good faith without notice of the seller's defect in title.

b.   This provision only applies to contracts which are voidable, for example for fraud, and not those which are void for mistake. Contrast **LEWIS v AVERAY (1971)** with **CUNDY v LINDSAY (1878)**. Note also **CAR AND UNIVERSAL FINANCE v CALDWELL (1964)** (Chapters 16.2 and 16.16).

30. *Mercantile Agents*

a.   Under *S.2 FACTORS ACT 1889* any sale, pledge or other disposition by a mercantile agent in possession of goods or documents of title with the consent of the owner, and in the mercantile agent's ordinary course of business to a bona fide purchaser for value without notice of any defect in his authority is as valid as if expressly authorized by the owner.

b.   A mercantile agent is an agent having in the customary course of his business authority to sell goods, or raise money on the security of goods. This definition includes an auctioneer or broker, but not a clerk or warehouseman.

c.   It has been held that in the case of second-hand vehicles to be within 'the ordinary course of business' the sale must be accompanied by delivery of the registration book (**PEARSON v ROSE AND YOUNG (1951)**).

31. *Dispositions by a Seller who Remains in Possession After a Sale*

a.   By *S.24* where a person having sold goods continues in possession of them or documents of title to them, the delivery or transfer by him, or by a mercantile agent acting for him, of the goods or documents under any sale, pledge or other disposition, is as valid as if authorized by the owner, provided the second buyer takes in good faith without notice of the previous sale.

b.   The usual sequence of events would be:

i.   A sale by X to Y under which the property passes, but X remains in possession.

ii.   A second sale by X to Z and delivery to Z.

c. For the section to apply the seller must continue in actual physical possession of the goods after the first sale, but not necessarily as seller. He may retain possession as, for example, a hirer or a trespasser.

In *WORCESTER WORKS FINANCE v COODEN ENGINEERING (1971)* A sold a car to B, B paying by cheque. B resold the car to C but remained in possession of it. When B's cheque was dishonoured A went to B to repossess the car and B allowed A to take it away. When C discovered this he sued A in conversion. It was held that although B was not a seller (since he never had title to the car) but a trespasser, the section nevertheless applied to him since continuity of physical possession was the vital factor, not the character of that possession. Note also that 'other disposition' was widely construed so as to include a retaking of the goods with the seller's consent. This case clearly does not follow the usual sequence referred to above.

d. Consider the following example:

X, who wishes to raise some money, sells his car to a finance company for £1000, and then takes it back on hire purchase, paying a deposit and the balance by instalments. Throughout the transaction X keeps possession of the car. X then sells the car to Y for £900. Advise Y. *S.24* is the correct advice and Y may keep the car. The finance company could have avoided this result by requiring the car to be delivered to them, and then immediately delivering it back to X. X would not then have 'continued in possession'.

e. *S.24* gives no protection to the seller, he remains liable to the first buyer.

32. *Dispositions by a Buyer Who Obtains Possession After an Agreement to Sell*

a. By *S.25* where a person having bought or agreed to buy goods obtains possession of the goods or documents of title with the seller's consent the delivery or transfer by that person or by a mercantile agent acting for him of the goods or documents under any sale, pledge or other disposition to a person receiving them in good faith and without notice of any lien or other right of the original seller has the same effect as if the person making the delivery or transfer were a mercantile agent in possession of the goods or documents with the owner's consent.

b. The usual sequence is:

i.   X agrees to sell to Y and Y is given possession of the goods although the property in the goods has not yet passed.

ii. Y 'sells' and delivers the goods to Z who takes them in good faith.

c. The person making the disposition must have bought or agreed to buy the goods, the section does not apply to someone who only has an option to purchase as in a hire purchase agreement (*HELBY v MATTHEWS (1895)*), nor does it apply to someone who has taken the goods on approval or on sale or return.

d. The disposition must have been one which could have been made by a mercantile agent acting in the ordinary course of business (*NEWTONS OF WEMBLEY v WILLIAMS (1964)*).

e. The section is not intended to take title away from an owner from whom goods have been stolen.

In *NATIONAL MUTUAL AND GENERAL INSURANCE ASSOCIATION v JONES (1988)* thieves stole a car. They sold it to A, who sold it to B, who sold it to C, who sold it to D, who sold it to Jones. All the parties (A, B, C, D and Jones) were innocent and unaware of the defect in title. C and D were car dealers. It was held that Jones did not obtain title to the car because A did not make a contract of sale with B, and A and B could not properly be described as 'seller' and 'buyer'. Thus A did not deliver the goods to B 'under a sale' as required by the section, because a contract of sale supposed that the seller had, or was going to have, a general property in the goods.

f.   In 1985, there was an interesting case involving both *S.25* and reservation of title clauses.

In *FOUR POINT GARAGE v CARTER (1985)* Carter purchased a new car from X Limited. X Limited did not have the car in stock so it arranged to buy the car from Four Point who delivered it direct to Carter (who was unaware of Four Point's involvement). The contract between Four Point and X Limited reserved title to the car until the price had been paid. A few days after Carter had taken delivery X Limited went into liquidation without having paid Four Point. Four Point claimed that they were entitled to recover the car under their reservation of title clause. Carter claimed the protection of *S.25*. As regards *S.25* it was held that there was no difference between a delivery direct to a sub-purchaser and a delivery to a buyer who then delivered to a sub-purchaser. X Limited would be regarded as having taken constructive delivery, therefore Four Point delivered to Carter as X Limited's agent. Concerning the reservation of title clause it was held that the basic form of clause used did not preclude implication of a term authorizing the garage to sell the car in the ordinary course of business. Carter was therefore successful on both arguments.

33. Where there is a disposition under a common law or statutory power of sale, or under a court order.

34. *Sale of motor vehicles on hire purchase – HIRE PURCHASE ACT 1964* If a vehicle which is subject to a hire purchase agreement is sold by the hirer to a private person who buys in good faith and without notice of the hire purchase agreement, the buyer acquires good title in the vehicle, even as against the owner. Note: businesses such as motor dealers and finance companies cannot claim this benefit, it must be innocent private individuals. In *GE CAPITAL BANK LTD v RUSHTON AND JENKINS (2005)* a respondent bought cars from a company which subsequently went into liquidation. The purchase of the vehicles was linked to a loan made to the company. The claimant was a previous lender to the company which held title/ownership in the cars. The respondent sought to rely on the *HIRE PURCHASE ACT 1964* and so gain good title. The Court of Appeal found that although the respondent was not in business as a motor dealer, he was a trade purchaser and not a private buyer and as such could not claim under the Act.

35. *Conclusion* The reasons for the general rule and its exceptions were summed up in Bishopgate Motor Finance v Transport Brakes (1949) when the Court stated:

'In the development of our law two principles have striven for mastery. The first is the protection of property. No one can give a better title than he himself possesses. The second is the protection of commercial transactions. The person who takes in good faith for value without notice should get a good title. The first principle has held sway for a long time, but it has been modified by common law itself and by statute so as to meet the needs of our times.'

PERFORMANCE OF THE CONTRACT

36. *Delivery*

   a.   Delivery is the physical transfer of possession from one person to another. It does not necessarily mean transportation. Delivery may be actual or constructive, for example when the keys to a warehouse in which the goods are stored are handed to the buyer.

   b.   It is the duty of the seller to deliver the goods and the buyer to accept and pay for them (*S.27*).

   c.   Payment and delivery are concurrent conditions unless otherwise agreed, for example if the sale is on credit (*S.28*).

37. *Place of Delivery* (*S.29*)

   a.   Except where there is a provision in the contract the place of delivery is the seller's place of business, unless the contract is for specific goods, which to the knowledge of the parties are in some other place, in which case that other place is the place of delivery.

   b.   If the goods are in the possession of a third party there is no delivery until the third party acknowledges to the buyer that he holds the goods on his behalf.

   c.   If goods are to be sent, the seller must send them within a reasonable time, and demand or tender of delivery must be made at a reasonable hour to be effective.

38. *Incorrect Delivery* (*S.30*)

   a.   If the seller delivers a larger or smaller quantity of goods than ordered the buyer may

      i.   Reject the whole, or

      ii.   Accept the whole, or

      iii.   Accept the quantity ordered and reject the rest.

   b.   If he chooses ii. or iii. above he must pay for the goods at the contract rate. He cannot accept the incorrect goods. He will only be able to accept them if the seller first offers to sell them to him.

39. *Instalment Deliveries* (*S.31*)

   a.   The buyer is not bound to accept delivery by instalments unless so agreed.

   b.   Where a contract provides for delivery in stated instalments which are to be separately paid for, and the seller makes defective deliveries, or the buyer fails to take delivery of, or pay for one or more instalments, it is a question of construction whether this amounts to a repudiation of the whole contract or to a severable breach giving a right to compensation, but not a right to treat the whole contract as at an end. The tests to be used in applying this section were laid down in *MAPLE FLOCK CO v UNIVERSAL FURNITURE PRODUCTS (1934)* (Chapter 17) as follows:

      i.   The ratio quantitatively which the breach bears to the contract as a whole, and

      ii.   The degree of probability that the breach will be repeated.

   c.   If instalments are to be separately paid for the contract is more likely to be construed as severable.

S.11(4) is relevant to severable and non-severable contracts. As a result of this section if an instalment contract is non-severable and the buyer accepts the first instalment this will prevent his rejection of later defective deliveries, and will limit his remedy to damages for breach of warranty.

40. *Acceptance*

a. By *S.35* (as amended by the *SALE AND SUPPLY OF GOODS ACT 1994*) the buyer accepts the goods when he:

i.   Intimates to the seller that he has accepted them, or

ii. Does any act to the goods which is inconsistent with the ownership of the seller, such as subselling and delivering the goods, or

iii. Retains the goods, after the lapse of a reasonable time without intimating to the seller that he has rejected them.

In ***CLEGG v OLFE ANDERSON (2003)*** C agreed to buy a yacht from A 'in accordance with the manufacturer's standard specifications', it was delivered on the 25 July. On 8 August C realized that the boat was not to the manufacturer's specifications – the bottom section was heavier than it should have been. Discussions took place between buyer and seller up until 6 March when C stated that he was rejecting the boat and wanted a refund of the purchase price. The Court of Appeal held that the boat was not of satisfactory quality and that A was in breach of condition under *S.14(2)* of the *SALE OF GOODS ACT 1979*. A claimed that C had accepted the goods under *S.35* and had therefore lost his right to reject the goods. The Court found that C had not indicated to A that he had accepted the goods nor had he done anything in relation to the boat which could be deemed inconsistent with A's ownership. In deciding whether a 'reasonable time' had elapsed under *S.34(4)* the Court held that account could be taken of the time required to modify or repair goods. C had requested information in August and September but did not receive a response until the following February. The 3-week period from receiving that information until early March did not exceed a reasonable time under *S.35(4)*. C was entitled to reject the goods. In ***J&H RITCHIE LTD v LLOYD LTD (2007)*** the buyer purchased a piece of farm machinery which after a couple of days use was found to have a section that vibrated badly. By agreement the machinery was taken back by the suppliers who, upon inspection, found that two bearings were missing. The repair was carried out and the buyer informed that the machinery was now ready for collection. The buyer requested details of the repair and documentation confirming that it was now up to a satisfactory specification: the supplier refused to provide this information, thereupon the buyer sought to reject the goods and claim a refund. The supplier was contending that the goods had been accepted by the buyer. The House of Lords (now the Supreme Court), in applying *S.35* held that a buyer:

(i) Has the right to reject goods up to the point when the goods are accepted.

(ii) Is not taken to have accepted goods merely by agreeing to a repair.

Given the nature of the machinery – a complex piece of equipment – the buyer was entitled to the information requested in order to make an informed choice of whether to accept or reject the goods. The buyer, in this case, was entitled to reject the goods and receive a refund.

b.   Where goods are delivered to a buyer which he has not previously examined, he is not deemed to have accepted them until he has had a reasonable opportunity of examining them to ascertain conformity with the contract. The seller is bound to afford this opportunity if so requested. In the case of a contract for sale by sample the buyer must have a reasonable opportunity of comparing the bulk with the sample.

c.   The buyer is not deemed to have accepted goods merely because:

   i.   He asks for, or agrees to, their repair by or under an arrangement with the seller, or

   ii. The goods are delivered to another under a sub-sale or other disposition.

d.   *Right of partial rejection.* If a seller supplies some goods which are in breach of contract together with others which are unaffected by the breach, a new section *(35A)* inserted by the 1994 Act gives the buyer a right to accept the goods which were unaffected by the breach without losing his right to reject the rest. This effectively replaces *S.30(4)* which is repealed.

THE RIGHTS OF THE UNPAID SELLER

41. *Lien (S.41–43)*

a.   A lien is the right to retain possession of goods (but not to resell them) until the contract price has been paid.

b.   The unpaid seller's lien is for the price only. When the price is tendered it does not enable him to retain possession for any other purpose, for example to recover the cost of storing the goods during the exercise of the lien.

42. *Stoppage in Transit* (*S.44–46*)

a.   After the seller has parted with the possession of the goods to a carrier for transmission to the buyer he can stop the goods and retake possession on the buyer becoming insolvent (i.e. if the buyer is unable to pay his debts as they fall due).

b.   The period of transit operates from the time when the goods are handed to the carrier until the time when the buyer takes delivery of them. Transit is also terminated if:

   i.   The buyer obtains delivery before the arrival of the goods at the agreed destination, for example because the carrier hands them to the buyer's agent during transit, or

   ii. If, on reaching the agreed destination, the carrier acknowledges to the buyer that he is holding the goods to the buyer's order, or

   iii. If the carrier wrongfully refuses to deliver the goods to the buyer.

43. *Resale of Goods* The general rule is that lien and stoppage in transit do not give the unpaid seller any right to resell the goods. By *S.48* the exceptions are:

a.   Where they are of a perishable nature, or

b.   Where the buyer, after being given notice by the seller that he intends to resell, does not pay for them within a reasonable time, or

c.   Where the seller has expressly reserved the right to resell if the buyer defaults in payment.

44. *Repossession of Goods*

   a.   If the seller has reserved title to the goods until the contract price, or any other debt owing to him by the buyer is paid, then he may repossess the goods if the buyer, being a company, goes into liquidation or receivership (*ALUMINIUM INDUSTRIE BV v ROMALPA (1976)*) (see 22. above).

   b.   The right to repossess from a buyer who is a private individual would arise:

   i.   If he were adjudged bankrupt, or

   ii. If it were intimated in some other way that the goods would not be paid for.

45. *Remedies Against the Buyer* The above remedies are all enforced against the goods. The remedies against the buyer are:

   a.   An action for the contract price, provided the property in the goods has passed to the buyer.

   b.   An action for non-acceptance. *S.50* provides that in an action for damages for non-acceptance, where there is an available market the measure of damages is, *prima facie*, the difference between the contract price and the market price on the date fixed for acceptance, or if no date was fixed, at the time of refusal to accept. Note: *THOMPSON v ROBINSON GUNMAKERS (1955)* and *CHARTER v SULLIVAN (1957)* (Chapter 20.5).

THE REMEDIES OF THE BUYER

46. The buyer may:

   a.   Sue for non-delivery. *S.51* provides that in an action for damages for non-delivery, where there is an available market the measure of damages is, *prima facie*, the difference between the contract price and the market price on the date fixed for delivery, or if no date was fixed, at the time of refusal to deliver.

   b.   Sue to recover any money paid to the seller.

   c.   Repudiate the contract for breach of a condition by the seller, unless:

   i.   He has waived the breach, and elected to treat it as a breach of warranty, or

   ii. The contract is non-severable and he has accepted the goods or part of them (*S.11(4)*).

   d.   In respect of a breach of warranty:

   i.   Set up the loss in diminution of the price, or

   ii. Sue for damages.

   e.   Sue for specific performance. This equitable remedy is at the discretion of the court and will not normally be granted when damages are an adequate remedy. The goods will need to be specific or ascertained and not readily available elsewhere in the market. The remedy is appropriate for goods which have a special value or which are unique, for example a classic car or a painting.

f. Seek a compensation order for 'any personal injury, loss or damage', where a trader is convicted of a criminal offence under the provisions of the *POWERS OF CRIMINAL COURTS (SENTENCING) ACT 2000*. Magistrates can award up to £5000, there is no limit in the Crown Court. This can be a useful remedy where the consumer has, for example, suffered minor harm with a stand alone civil action not worth bringing or where the consumer has no civil remedy.

Remedies under the Sale of Goods Act

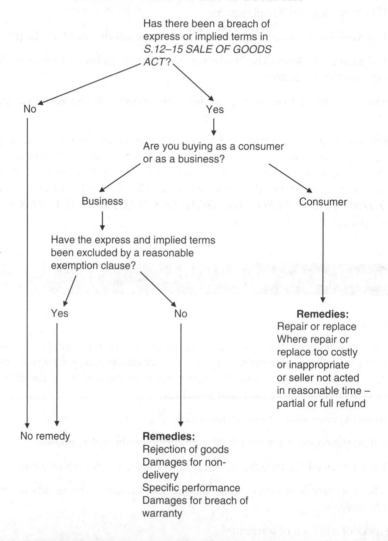

AUCTION SALES

47. By *S.57* the following rules apply to auction sales:

a. Each lot is deemed to be the subject of a separate contract of sale.

b. The sale is complete when the auctioneer announces its completion by the fall of the hammer or in other customary manner. Until this happens the bidder may retract his bid or the seller may withdraw the goods. Generally an auction sale will be an unconditional contract for the sale of specific goods within the meaning of *S.18 Rule 1*. Property will therefore pass when the contract is made i.e. on the fall of the hammer.

In ***DENNANT v SKINNER (1948)*** P sold a car by auction to X. Later X gave P a cheque for the price and signed an agreement that ownership would not pass until the cheque had cleared. Before the cheque cleared X sold to D. It later became apparent that the cheque would not be honoured. It was held that P could not recover the car from D since X had acquired title when it was knocked down to him. The subsequent agreement that ownership would not pass until the cheque was cleared did not transfer title back to P.

c. A sale may be subject to a reserve price i.e. a minimum price below which the goods cannot be sold.

d. A seller may expressly reserve the right to bid, provided this is notified at the sale.

e. Where a sale is not notified to be subject to a right to bid on behalf of the seller, it is not lawful for the seller to bid (or employ any person to bid) nor is it lawful for the auctioneer to knowingly take any such bid. Any sale contravening this rule may be treated as fraudulent by the buyer.

THE SUPPLY OF GOODS AND SERVICES ACT 1982

48. *THE SUPPLY OF GOODS AND SERVICES ACT 1982* (referred to in this section as 'the Act') has two main parts. Part I amends the law with respect to terms implied in certain contracts for the supply of goods. Part II codifies the common law rules applicable when a person agrees to carry out a service.

49. *Part I*

a. Many modern commercial transactions where property is transferred do not fall within the definition of a sale of goods. For example:

i. Contracts for work and materials e.g. building, car repair, and contracts to install central heating or double-glazing.

ii. Contracts of exchange or barter. Provided there is no money consideration these are not sales of goods. A contract of part-exchange is a sale of goods (see 3.e above).

iii. 'Free Gifts'. If a buyer is given a gift of 'product x' if he buys 10 units of 'product y', he will own product x although it was not sold to him.

iv. Contracts for the hire of goods.

b. The problem was that Sale of Goods Act protection did not apply to goods supplied under such contracts. This could be unfair. For example, when someone supplied work and materials his obligations in respect of the materials were those implied at common law, but if he only supplied the materials he would be subject to the more stringent requirements of the Sale of Goods Act.

c. This anomaly has been remedied by the 1982 Act. The Act applies to 'contracts for the transfer of property in goods' and 'contracts for the hire of goods'. *S.2–5* provide for statutory implied terms on the part of the seller similar to those in *S.12–15 SALE OF GOODS ACT 1979*. Thus:

    i.   By *S.2* there is an implied condition that the transferor has the right to transfer the property in the goods.

    ii. By *S.3* there is an implied condition that the goods will correspond with their description.

    iii. By *S.4* there are implied conditions relating to quality and fitness for purpose.

    iv. By *S.5* there is an implied condition that where the transfer is by reference to sample the bulk will correspond with the sample.

  d. Contracts for the hire of goods are defined in *S.6*, and *S.7–10* provide for statutory implied conditions similar to *S.12–15 SALE OF GOODS ACT 1979*.

50. *Part II.*

  a. The purpose of the Act is to codify the common law relating to the three areas mentioned above, namely skill, time and price.

  b. The Act applies to contracts 'under which a person agrees to carry out a service'. However, it does not apply to contracts of employment, apprenticeships, services rendered to a company by a director and the services of an advocate before a court or tribunal.

  c. By *S.13* there is an implied term that where the supplier is acting in the course of a business he will carry out the service with reasonable care and skill.

  d. By *S.14* there is an implied term that where the supplier is acting in the course of a business and the time for the service to be carried out is not fixed by the contract or determined by the course of dealings between the parties, the supplier will carry out the service within a reasonable time.

  e. By *S.15* there is an implied term that where the consideration is not determined by a contract or in a manner agreed in the contract or by the course of dealing between the parties, the party contracting with the supplier will pay a reasonable price.

51. *Exclusion of Liability S.7 UNFAIR CONTRACT TERMS ACT 1977* (as amended by the *SUPPLY OF GOODS AND SERVICES ACT 1982*) (*UCTA*) deals with contracts for the supply of goods other than contracts of sale or hire purchase. *S.2* of the 1977 Act is relevant to Part II of the 1982 Act.

  a. If the exclusion clause relates to title it will be void (*S.7(3A) UCTA 1977*).

  b. If the exclusion clause relates to description, quality, fitness or sample:

    i.   If the buyer deals as a consumer the clause is void (*S.7(2)*).

    ii. If the buyer does not deal as a consumer the exclusion clause must satisfy the requirement of reasonableness (*S.7(3)*).

  c. If the exclusion clause relates to poor quality work, i.e. a breach of *S.13* the clause must satisfy the requirement of reasonableness (unless the negligent work causes personal injury or death, in which case it is void) (*S.2 UCTA 1977*).

  d. If there is a complaint in a consumer contract for work and materials it will be necessary to discover the exact nature of the complaint. If it concerns defective materials the exclusion clause will be void. On the other hand if the materials are acceptable but the workmanship is negligent the exclusion clause will have to satisfy the reasonableness test. *S.2* of the 1977 Act does not distinguish between consumer and non-consumer contracts, however, recent cases have shown that it is becoming more difficult for a trader to exclude liability for negligence when he deals with a consumer. For example, in *WOODMAN v PHOTO TRADE PROCESSING (1981)* (a test case supported by the Consumers Association), P took some film of a friend's wedding to a shop for developing. The shop displayed a notice limiting their liability to the cost of the film. Due to the processor's negligence the film was ruined. It was held that the exemption clause in the shop was unreasonable and P was awarded £75 to compensate him for his disappointment.

SELF TEST QUESTIONS

Self Test Questions No. 28 (for Answers see Appendix 1):

1   What are the key changes introduced by the *SALE AND SUPPLY OF GOODS TO CONSUMERS REGULATIONS 2002*?

2   How is a 'contract of sale' distinguished from other contracts?

3   What is meant by 'goods'?

4   How does 'capacity' relate to a sale of goods?

5   What is meant by the term 'title' or 'ownership' in goods?

6   What is a 'sale by description'?

7   Explain the requirements for 'satisfactory quality and fitness for purpose' of goods – what does this mean?

8   Go through and distinguish the *Rules* governing a 'transfer of ownership'.

9   What is the position where goods are sold by someone who is not the owner?

10 How is performance of the contract of sale determined?

11 What are the rights of the unpaid seller?

12 What remedies exist for the buyer?

13 Explain the key parts of the *SUPPLY OF GOODS AND SERVICES ACT 1982*.

31 CONSUMER PROTECTION

Learning Outcomes At the end of this chapter you should be able to:

- Explain the source and aims of the *CONSUMER PROTECTION FROM UNFAIR TRADING REGULATIONS 2008*.

- State and explain the definitions of

  - unfair commercial practice

  - misleading actions

  - misleading omissions

  - aggressive commercial practices.

- Outline the nature and content of the listed unfair commercial practices.

- Summarize the offences under the Regulations and the defence of due diligence.

- State how enforcement of the Regulations takes place.

CONSUMER PROTECTION FROM UNFAIR TRADING REGULATIONS 2008

1. The Regulations create criminal offences relating to unfair commercial trader-to-consumer practices. They seek to harmonize the law in this area across the European Union (EU). It is important to note two limitations of the Regulations:

   i. In creating criminal offences they do not give rights to individual consumers to enforce. Enforcement is through the Office of Fair Trading and local authority trading standards officers.

   ii. They do not cover practices in commercial relationships between businesses.

   Scope of the Regulations Various terms require defining, these are commercial practice, trader and product and unfair commercial practice.

   a. *Commercial practice.* The Regulations seek to regulate *commercial practice* that is business dealings between a trader and a consumer. *Commercial practice* is defined as

   'any act, omission, course of conduct, representation or commercial communication (including advertising) by a trader, which is directly connected with the promotion, sale or supply of a product to a consumer.' (reg.2(1).)

   Note: there is no requirement for a contract to have been concluded between trader and consumer, it is simply *practices* that are regulated. The advertising of products to consumers would constitute a *practice* for purposes of the Regulations even though no goods may have been sold. The definition of *commercial practice* is also very wide and is likely to cover just about anything a trader might do or omit to do in the course of business. It would cover, for instance, after-sales service or the buying of part-exchange goods by a trader from a consumer. In **FLETCHER v BUDGEN (1974)** a motor dealer was convicted of an offence when he made statements to a customer to the effect that the car he was seeking to trade in as part-exchange, was virtually valueless. This resulted in the customer selling the car to the trader at a 'knock-down' price. Today under these Regulations, this would amount to *an unfair commercial practice* leaving the trader guilty of an offence.

   b. *Consumer.* A consumer can include another business where that business is dealing with a trader *as a consumer* for goods which are not connected with the business of the consumer, e.g. ordering office furniture would be acting as a consumer if the business is not trading in office furniture. Whilst sole traders and partnerships can be classed as consumers when seeking to acquire goods not connected with their businesses, *a company cannot be a consumer.*

   c. *Trader and product.* The definition of who is a *trader* is wide including all who engage in regular forms of business trading: it would include everyday sellers on the Internet, for instance. And *product* will include any goods or services, including immovable property, rights and obligations. This means that, goods, services, downloaded software, sales of land, premium telephone calls and membership of clubs, etc would all be products.

   d. *Unfair commercial practice.* This is at the core of the Regulations and is defined as being 'that which contravenes the requirements of *professional diligence*, and *materially distorts* or is likely to distort the *economic behaviour of the average consumer* with regard to the product.' (reg.3(3).)

   Three key elements of this definition require further examination in order to understand the meaning of this key definition:

(i) *Professional diligence*. This is defined as:

The standard of special skill and care which a trader may reasonably be expected to exercise towards consumers which is commensurate with either:

an honest market practice in the trader's field of activity, or

the general principle of good faith in the trader's field of activity.

(a) *Honest market practice* would be the standard of care and skill which a consumer might reasonably expect to receive from a similar trader, e.g. where the alleged unfair practice complained of is say, a motorcar dealer. Here, the assessment of *honest market practice* would involve comparing the car dealer in question, with that of what might reasonably be expected of a similar car dealer in general. (Note: it is the same test for assessing the standard of care owed in the tort of negligence – see Chapter 23.6)

(b) The alternative *general principle of good faith* is not defined in the Regulations. However, it would be likely to give enforcement officers the scope to look at overall business practice in a particular field, e.g. taking the motor trader example above; although a number of similar traders might be adopting certain common practices and so meet the requirements of the first definition (a), there may be significant developments within the motor traders' industry to adopt better practices e.g. the promotion of some new code of practice.

(ii) *Materially distort economic behaviour* means, in relation to the average consumer, to 'Significantly impair his or her ability to make an informed decision (a transactional decision), thereby resulting in a decision being taken which would otherwise not have been taken.'

Such *transactional decisions* by consumers could be to act or refrain from acting e.g. to buy or not to buy, sell or not to sell.

However, it is important to note that this impairment of a consumer's decision with regard to a particular transaction, is not just confined to decisions taken at the commencement of the relationship with the trader. They may be impaired decisions taken *during* that relationship, e.g. a decision to pay off a debt early, or cancel a contract, or use or not use, after-sales services etc.

Average consumer. There is no specific definition of this term within the Regulations. Other parts of the Regulations however, refer to the *average consumer* as being 'reasonably well informed, observant and circumspect.'

The *average consumer* may also be formed from a particular group of consumers. Reg.2(5) provides that if a clearly identifiable group of consumers is particularly vulnerable to the commercial practice or product in question, on account of being mentally or physically infirm, or on account of their age or credulity, the effect on the *average consumer* shall be the effect on an average member *of that group*. However, for this to apply the trader would have to have reasonably foreseen this particular vulnerability and that the average consumer within that group would be likely to make an impaired transactional decision and thus distort the economic behaviour of that identified group.

In summary, in order for a commercial practice to be unfair, it must:

i.   Contravene the requirements of *professional diligence*, and

ii. *Distort*, or be likely to distort, *the economic behaviour of the average consumer*.

e. ***Specific instances of unfair commercial practice.*** The Regulations also list a number of specific instances of unfair commercial practice:

(i) *Misleading actions.* A commercial activity is misleading if it is untruthful and deceptive, and it causes or is likely to cause the average consumer to make a transactional decision he would not otherwise have made. (reg.5.)

Reg.5, lists matters which an untruthful or deceptive commercial practice relates to with regard to a product. The list is extensive and contains amongst others 'matters': its description, price, any risks associated with its use, availability, benefits, etc. (These are fully listed in regs.5(4) and 5(4)(b).)

It is also possible for a trader to commit the offence of *misleading actions*, in the way he describes himself. Again reg.5 lists the various aspects of a false or misleading description relating to the status of a trader. These include amongst others, assets, qualifications, affiliations or connections, etc. (A full list is contained in reg.5(4)(j).)

Mr Jones bought a washing machine from an online advert which described the goods as:

'Low energy saving, made by a leading named manufacturer, with goods readily available from stock, free delivery.'

The supplier also described himself as being a member of the *British Washing Machine Retailers' Federation.*

It subsequently transpired that:

the product was not low energy saving

was not produced by the named manufacturer

there was a 6-month waiting time for delivery

a £50 delivery charge was payable

the supplier/trader was not a member of the stated federation.

Here there would be: an *unfair commercial practice* in that the various statements made would *materially distort the economic behaviour of the average consumer* (like Mr Jones) in that it would have *impaired* his *ability to make an informed decision, thereby causing him to take a transactional decision that he would not have otherwise taken*. And, when applying the criteria listed in reg.5 to the particular product, the finding would likely be based upon:

characteristics of the product – 'low energy and made by a leading named manufacturer'

availability – '6-month waiting time'

price – 'additional delivery charge'

affiliations or connections – 'member of a named federation'.

It is also possible to commit an offence under a *misleading action* by *creating confusion* in marketing the product. This is confusion relative to a similar competitor product e.g. by naming a product with a similar sounding name to that of a rival product.

(ii) ***Misleading omissions.*** This is where a trader commits an unfair commercial practice by omitting information on the product. Again the Regulation lays down an extensive list of matters likely to be regarded as *material omissions* with regard to a product. They include amongst others: information provided which is unclear, unintelligible, ambiguous or untimely, is information which the average consumer needs, to take an informed transactional decision etc. (Fully listed under reg.6.)

An example is the advertising of the price of a product, with no mention of a charge being incurred where payment is made using a credit card.

(iii) *Aggressive commercial practices.* This is an offence committed by a trader where he engages in unfair commercial practice through behaviour which could be seen as *harassment, coercion* or *undue influence*, in that it *significantly impairs or is likely to significantly impair the average consumer's freedom of choice or conduct in relation to a product.* (reg.7.)

Again, like for *misleading action* and *misleading omission*, the Regulations provide an extensive list of criteria against which to assess whether a particular practice is *aggressive*. These include, where it significantly impaired consumer choice, the nature of any threatening, abusive language or force, when it occurred, whether legal action was threatened which could not legally be taken etc. (A full list is contained in reg.7.)

Mrs Smith, in responding to an advertisement for cheap holidays, attends a local hotel. Once there she is coerced and bullied into not leaving until she books a holiday. At the time she felt threatened and intimidated.

The allegation of *aggressive commercial practice* Mrs Smith was subjected to would be assessed against the criteria listed in reg.7. It would be likely to be found to have constituted an aggressive practice when applying such criteria. The consequence being, that an average consumer, like Mrs Smith, would have had their ability to make an informed decision – a *transactional decision* – significantly impaired, thereby resulting in a decision being made – to book a holiday – which otherwise would not have been taken.

Practices deemed automatically unfair. Schedule 1 of the Regulations lists some 31 commercial practices which are always to be considered unfair. Unlike other commercial practices there is no requirement that an average consumer might have been induced to act differently – having their economic behaviour distorted to engage in these acts will have caused a trader to commit an offence under the Regulations (reg.12). A sample from the list includes:

claiming to be a signatory to a code of conduct when the trader is not

claiming a product or the trader has been approved by some public body when this is not the case

inviting a purchase of goods knowing that there are reasonable grounds that they cannot be supplied etc. (A full list is given under Schedule 1.)

f. *The requirement for a guilty mind –* **mens rea.** In order for a trader to be guilty of an offence under the Regulations, there is a requirement that the trader:

knew or recklessly i.e. without regard as to whether the practice contravenes the requirements of professional diligence (as stated in reg.3(3), see d. above) *or not.* (reg.8).

In order to avoid being found to have acted recklessly, a trader must positively and consciously ask himself the question, 'Does the practice I am about to engage in contravene the requirement upon me to show professional diligence?' To do nothing, or simply not care, is not an option.

Although, as seen (b. above), a company cannot act as a consumer, it can obviously act as a trader, and if found guilty under the regulations, its officers can be found personally guilty if they partook in the commission of the offence or if their negligence caused the offence to be committed.

Prosecutions must be brought within 3 years of the commission of the offence or within 1 year of its discovery, whichever is the earlier. The maximum penalty is *an unlimited fine or 2-years' imprisonment.*

g.   *The defence of due diligence.* Reg.17(1) provides a defence where a trader can show that the commission of the offence was due to:

   i.   A mistake.

   ii.   Reliance on information supplied by another.

   iii. The act or default of another person.

   iv.   An accident.

   v.   Some other cause beyond his control, and

   vi.   He took all reasonable precautions and exercised all due diligence to avoid the commission of the offence.

h.   *Enforcement.* Responsibility for enforcement rests with the Office of Fair Trading and local authority Trading Standards Services. They have powers to investigate breaches of the regulations and make test purchases, enter premises, copy documents, seize and detain goods.

SELF TEST QUESTIONS

Self Test Questions No. 29 (for Answers see Appendix 1):

1   What is an unfair commercial practice?

2   What is meant by the phrase, 'misleading actions'?

3   What are 'misleading omissions'?

4   Explain the nature of 'aggressive commercial practices'.

5   Summarize the provisions relating to automatic, 'unfair commercial practices'.

6   What *mens rea* is required, and what are the offences under the Regulations?

7   Explain the defence of, 'due diligence'.

8   How are the Regulations enforced?

32 COMPETITION POLICY

Learning Outcomes
At the end of this chapter you should be able to:

- Explain the general nature of competition law with particular reference to *Articles 81* and *82*.

- State the role and function of the Competition Commission.

Open and fair competition is seen as being vital to a fair and efficient market with the best possible prices amongst producers and suppliers. However, unfettered competition leads to unfair practices with monopolies and unfair agreements being reached between manufacturers and service providers; such as price fixing or practices which deter other competitors from entering the market. It can lead to relationships between producers and suppliers being cooperative rather than competitive. It is thus necessary to regulate the market.

The key legislative provisions in this area are the *COMPETITION ACT 1998* and the *ENTERPRISE ACT 2002*.

1. As a member of the European Union the UK is subject to EC law on regulating competition between member states; these are principally, *Articles 81* and *82* of the *TREATY OF ROME (1957)*. *Article 81 prohibits agreements between organizations that restrict or distort competition*: these include price fixing, market sharing, restricting competition. The European Commission will grant certain exemptions and gives block exemptions for certain categories of agreement. In **CREHAN V INNTREPRENEUR PUB COMPANY (IPC) AND BREWMAN GROUP LIMITED (B) (2003)** C was a tenant of two public houses. As a part of the tenancy agreement he was required to buy all of his beer from B. This led to

C going out of business because other untied public houses could buy their beer from who-ever they chose which had the effect of them being able to gain much lower prices for their beer. C complained that the tied agreement was a breach of *Article 81*.

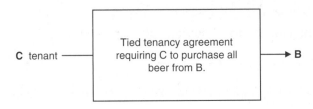

The High Court held that two conditions had to be satisfied for a successful claim under *Article 81*:

(i) Having regard to the legal and economic context of the lease, whether it was diffi-cult for other businesses to enter the market or increase their market share, and

(ii) Whether there existed a network of similar leases that had the effect of sealing off the market.

The Court found that a significant number of estates had been sold recently following UK legislation (the *SUPPLY OF BEER (TIED ESTATES) ORDER* 1989), and it was not diffi-cult for newcomers to enter the market or existing participants to increase their market share, there was no infringement of *Article 81*.

Article 82 prohibits abuse of a dominant position; this is where a small number of suppliers or produces have in effect a monopoly in the market, this might include imposing unfair buy-ing or selling prices. In **PUBLISHERS' ASSOCIATION V COMMISSION OF THE EC (1992)** UK publishers were seeking to continue enforcing a minimum resale price on books sold in the UK and other EC member states (the Net Book Agreement). The European Commission found the agreement contrary to *Article 81* and required its abolition. This was subsequently confirmed by the European Court of Justice.

The European Commission also has power to control mergers and takeovers with a view to ensuring that they do not impede effective competition.

2. UK competition law is contained in the *COMPETITION ACT 1998*. The Act mirrors the two *Articles 81* and *82*. Organizations may apply to the Office of Fair Trading for individual or block exemptions. Individual exemptions are granted where it can be shown that any agreement leads to improving production or distribution or promotes developments which will ultimately benefit the consumer. Any restrictions in such agreements must be indispens-able to achieving these aims and the agreement must not lead to the elimination of competi-tion. Block exemptions are based on the same criteria as individual agreements but apply automatically to certain sections of the market. The Competition Commission was estab-lished under the *COMPETITION ACT* and its role is to:

i. Hear appeals against decisions of the Office of Fair Trading.

ii. Investigate specific markets or the conduct of companies or mergers, here it reports to the Secretary of State with recommendations for any course of action.

The *ENTERPRISE ACT 2002* introduced a number of changes to UK competition law set-ting up new statutory bodies such as the Competition Appeal Tribunal and a new system for market investigations. Also individuals who dishonestly engage in cartel agreements may be prosecuted and lastly there is a new power to allow the Office of Fair Trading to apply for a disqualification order for directors who have committed breaches of competition law.

SELF TEST QUESTIONS

Self Test Questions No. 30 (for Answers see Appendix 1):

1   What does UK competition law seek to achieve?

2   What do Articles 81 and 82 state and where can these EC laws be found in UK law?

3   What is the role and function of the Competition Commission?

CONSUMER CREDIT
33

Learning Outcomes At the end of this chapter you should be able to:

- Find the source statutory materials regulating consumer credit and understand the context of such regulation.

- Distinguish a 'consumer hire agreement' from a 'consumer credit agreement'.

- Understand what a 'debtor–creditor–supplier agreement' is, and the obligations placed upon the parties.

- State the features of 'hire purchase agreement' and the obligations on the hirer and borrower.

- Explain the provisions governing 'advertising' of consumer credit.

- State the information requirements and format for pre- and post-regulated agreements.

- Understand the courts' powers to intervene in an 'unfair' credit relationship.

INTRODUCTION: THE CONSUMER CREDIT ACT 1974 (AS AMENDED)

1. The consumer credit industry is regulated by the *CONSUMER CREDIT ACT 2006* (the Act).

2. The purposes of the Act are:

   a.   To introduce a uniform system of statutory control over the provision of credit. (The *CONSUMER CREDIT ACT 2006* amends the *CONSUMER CREDIT ACT 1974.*) In addition, the *EU CONSUMER CREDIT DIRECTIVE 2008/48/EC*, which sought to build on a unified system of control over credit provision, was introduced into UK law through delegated legislation (see Chapter 4.24) using a number of statutory instruments/regulations. It is useful, at this point, to list those statutory instruments/regulations, and they are:

     Consumer Credit (EU Directive) Regulations 2010 (SI 2010/1010) (EU Directive) Regulations)

     Consumer Credit (Total Charge for Credit) Regulations 2010 (SI 2010/1011)

     Consumer Credit (Disclosure of Information) Regulations 2010 (SI 2010/1013)

     Consumer Credit (Agreements) Regulations 2010 (SI 2010/1014)

     Consumer Credit (Amendment) Regulations 2010 (SI 2010/1969)

     Consumer Credit (Advertisements) Regulations 2010 (SI 2010/1970).

     These regulations came into force on 1st February 2011.

   b.   To protect the interests of consumers by introducing a new system of licensing those who offer credit, and by increasing the protection of purchasers of credit by redressing bargaining inequality, controlling trading malpractices and regulating the remedies for default.

3. Previous credit legislation has imposed different rules according to the status of the creditor and the type of lending. The Act treats all lenders alike and regulates in the same way, so far as possible, all forms of credit, for example a cash loan, a sale of goods on credit, a credit card transaction or a hire purchase deal. It provides hirers of goods with similar protection to credit purchasers of goods, recognizing that hire is often an alternative to credit. It also recognizes that:

   a.   Prior to entering into an agreement the consumer needs an adequate supply of information to make an informed choice.

   b.   The imposition of trading standards and the provision of consumer protection is needed at every stage of the transaction, and

   c.   The credit industry is not made up of creditors only but also a wide range of ancillary businesses, for example debt collectors, debt counsellors, credit reference agencies and brokers – either a 'broker' in the traditional sense or a retailer offering the financial services of a creditor in order to sell his goods.

4. The responsibility for the operation of the Act rests with the Director General of Fair Trading, whose duties include:

   a.   Supervision of the working and enforcement of the Act, and

   b.   Administration of the licensing system.

5. The Act reforms the consumer credit industry within a framework of new and different terminology. The Act applies to '*regulated agreements*'. A regulated agreement may be either a *consumer credit agreement* or a *consumer hire agreement*.

6. ***Regulated Consumer Credit Agreements*** There are two types of consumer agreement regulated under the *Act*: consumer *credit agreements* and *consumer hire agreements*.

a. A consumer credit agreement is – as from April 2008 – a credit agreement by which the creditor (a lender, who may be an individual, sole trader, partnership or a company) provides the debtor (a borrower, who must be an individual or partnership but NOT a company, see Chapter 38) with credit of any amount. Before April 2008, the credit advanced to a borrower, must not have been more than £25 000. The term 'individual' is defined to include partnerships and other unincorporated bodies even though they are not usually thought of as 'consumers'. Companies cannot be debtor/borrower 'individuals'.

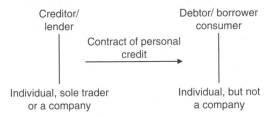

Personal credit is given a wide definition to include 'a cash loan or any form of financial accommodation' (*S.9*). For instance this definition will include:

hire purchase

conditional sale

credit sale

credit cards

loan

overdrafts

shop budget accounts.

Definitions. Hire purchase (see 8. below) is where a customer pays regular amounts to the seller in order to *hire* the goods, which he then purchases at the end of the term by exercising *an option to buy*.

Conditional sale is where the customer gets immediate possession of the goods in return for regular payments, with ownership passing (see chapter 30) to the buyer when all the payments have been made.

Credit sale is where ownership and possession immediately pass to the buyer and he is given time to pay. The key difference between a credit sale and a conditional sale and hire purchase agreements, is that as ownership has passed to the buyer he may sell the goods to another at any time. This means that the lender cannot reclaim goods and must sue to borrower for any unpaid payments.

Credit cards/tokens allow the holder to pay for goods and services using the card up to a set limit and also to obtain cash by producing a plastic personalized card.

Loans are where customers of a bank are lent money for a particular purchase e.g. to build an extension to property, refit a kitchen, buy a car, etc. The money is lent for a set period of time with repayments being made from the customer's current account with interest charged and sometimes security for the loan being required (security is where the borrower agrees that if he fails to repay, the borrower can take and sell certain goods or property e.g. a house).

Overdrafts are where a bank agrees for a customer to spend up to a set amount over and above that actually in the customer's account at any particular time. Interest is usually charged on the overdraft on a daily basis.

Shop budget accounts are offered by large retail outlets where the customer agrees to pay a regular set amount to the store in return for the ability to spend a multiple of that amount, for example, agreeing to pay say £20 per month might allow a customer to spend at any one time up to ten times that amount. These type of agreements are often referred to as 'revolving or running credit accounts'; more purchases can be made provided they do not exceed the set limit. Interest is usually charged on a balance outstanding at the end of any given month.

b. *S.10* provides that credit may be either:

   i. '*Running Account*' credit, i.e. credit up to an agreed limit, for example a bank overdraft or a credit card, or

   ii. '*Fixed Sum*' credit, i.e. credit of a definite amount, for example a bank loan or a hire purchase agreement.

c. *S.11* provides for the classification of credit agreements according to the purpose for which the credit is given. It refers to:

   i. *Restricted-use credit*. The credit facility may be used for a stipulated purpose only, for example a hire purchase agreement or a shop budget account.

   ii. *Unrestricted-use credit*. The debtor may use the loan as he pleases, for example an overdraft facility or a credit card if it is used to obtain cash.

d. *S.12–S.13* provide a further type of classification based on the relationship between the creditor and the supplier:

   i. *Debtor–creditor–supplier* agreements, i.e. where credit is provided to finance a transaction between a debtor and a supplier. If the supplier of the goods also supplied the credit it is still a debtor–creditor–supplier agreement. The usual type of hire purchase transaction involving a consumer, a dealer and a finance company is a debtor–creditor–supplier agreement (see below), sometimes referred to as a *linked credit agreement*.

   ii. *Debtor–creditor* agreements. In effect any agreement to supply credit which is not a debtor–creditor–supplier agreement, for example a personal bank loan.

   iii. The categorization between debtor–creditor–supplier and debtor–creditor agreements is necessary because under the Act the creditor under a debtor–creditor agreement does not incur any liability for the quality of goods supplied, whereas the creditor who finances sales of goods directly, or in the course of an agreement with the supplier, does have such liability.

e. The Act also regulates *credit card or credit-token* agreements. A credit-token is, for example, a cash dispenser card or a credit card issued by a retailer. The extent of the credit card holder's liability is defined in the Act (*S.66 and S.84*). The card holder is not liable for another person's use of the card unless he has previously accepted the card or the use by another person amounted to acceptance. A card holder accepts the card when he (i) signs it; (ii) he signs a receipt for it or (iii) it is first used, either by the card holder himself or a person he authorizes to use it.

8. *Regulated Consumer Hire Agreements* A consumer hire agreement is an agreement where goods are hired, leased, rented or bailed to an individual. Goods are *bailed* where possession of the goods is transferred to the consumer, but not ownership (see Chapter 31) with the goods having to be returned when the purpose for which they are *bailed* is completed. The period over which the hire agreement covers has to be 3 months or more, and if the goods have been hired before April 2008, the amount charged for the hire has to be no more than £25 000, after this date the amount charged can be of any amount. A House of Lords judgment (now the Supreme Court) shows how the framework of regulation applies in practice. In *DIAMOND V LOVELL (2000)* a Mrs Diamond hired a replacement car following an accident of which she was not responsible. Mr Lovell's insurance company paid for the repairs to Mrs Diamond's car but refused to pay the hire fee. The insurance company put forward two lines of defence. Firstly, the agreement between Mrs Diamond and the hire company was a regulated consumer credit agreement and was unenforceable because it did not comply with the Consumer Credit Act. Secondly, Mrs Diamond had not mitigated her loss; she could have hired a car at a much lower rate, the particular hire company specialized in accident repair hire vehicles requiring no payment from the hirer simply a claim on the final settlement. The House of Lords held that the agreement was a consumer credit agreement and unenforceable because it did not contain all the terms 'prescribed' in regulations made under the Consumer Credit Act. As to mitigation of loss, Mrs Diamond acted reasonably in engaging the services of the hire company but this did not mean she was entitled to recover the full amount. She had obtained additional services – not having to pay or pursue a claim for car hire, benefits which she would not be entitled to claim for under English law; any claim would have been limited to a general market hire rate.

There are certain consumer hire agreements which are exempt from the regulations; these are agreements for the hire of meters to consumers for metering the use of gas, electricity and water where the hirer is an organization authorized by statute.

HIRE PURCHASE – PRELIMINARY MATTERS

8. Probably the most common method of obtaining the possession and use of goods before making full payment is to enter into a hire purchase agreement. A hire purchase is a bailment of goods (i.e. a delivery of possession of goods) plus the grant of an option to purchase the goods. The consumer does not 'agree to buy' the goods at the time of the contract. Therefore if he sells the goods before he has exercised his option to purchase he does not pass title to them.

In *HELBY v MATTHEWS (1895)* the owner of a piano hired it to a bailee. The agreement provided that the bailee should pay monthly instalments, he could terminate by delivering the piano to the owner, and if he paid all the instalments punctually he would become the owner of the piano, but until such time the piano would be the property of the owner. Before paying all the instalments the bailee pledged the piano with a pawnbroker as security for an advance. It was held that the owner could recover the piano from the pawnbroker because the bailee had not 'agreed to buy' the piano, he merely had an option either to purchase the piano by paying all the instalments, or to return the piano. Consequently he could not pass title to the pawnbroker.

9. *The Role of the Finance Company* Usually when a consumer wishes to purchase goods on hire purchase the dealer himself does not provide the credit. The dealer sells the goods to a finance company for cash. The finance company (now the owner) then hires the goods to

the consumer, the rights and obligations being between the finance company and the consumer, rather than between the dealer and the consumer.

10. *The Prescribed Form for Credit or Hire Agreements* There are certain requirements which must be met.

Prior to the agreement a debtor or hirer must be given details of the agreement he is about to sign, and the agreement must be:

i.   Readily legible.

ii.   Contain all the terms.

iii. Comply with regulations as to its form and content e.g. correctly stating the amount of the loan or hire.

iv.   Where appropriate, give details of any right to cancel.

v.   Be signed personally by the debtor or hirer.

In *WILSON V SECRETARY OF STATE FOR TRADE AND INDUSTRY (2003)* W, a borrower, was charged a 'document fee' of £250 which, because she did not pay it immediately, was added to the loan. W claimed under *S.127* of the *CONSUMER CREDIT ACT* that the agreement was unenforceable as it did not correctly state the amount of the loan. The House of Lords (now the Supreme Court) confirmed the Court of Appeal's view that the 'document fee' was not credit and as a result one of the prescribed terms was incorrect rendering the agreement unenforceable.

11. *Obligations in Relation to Hire Purchase Contracts*

   a. *Obligations of the creditor (owner)*

      i.   The *SUPPLY OF GOODS (IMPLIED TERMS) ACT 1973* imposes obligations relating to title, description, quality and fitness for purpose, and sample very similar to those imposed by the *SALE OF GOODS ACT 1979*. The lender also has an obligation to deliver the goods at the agreed time, or if no time is agreed, within a reasonable time.

      ii.   The restrictions on the use of exemption clauses imposed by the *UNFAIR CONTRACT TERMS ACT 1977* apply to hire purchase in the same way as they apply to sale of goods.

      iii. If the lender breaks an express or implied *condition of* the contract the bailee can treat the contract as at an end and claim damages. He is entitled to repayment of all the instalments that he has paid, but he must allow the lender to repossess the goods. If the lender breaks a *warranty* the bailee may claim damages.

      iv.   By *S.56* if a dealer arranges with a consumer for goods to be sold to a finance company the dealer is deemed to have conducted the negotiations as agent for the creditor. Thus the lender will be liable for any representations or contractual promises made by the dealer.

   b. *Obligations of the dealer (credit-broker)*

      i.   Although the usual type of hire purchase contract will create a contractual relationship between the finance company (the owner) and the consumer, the dealer may be liable on an implied collateral contract.

         In *ANDREWS v HOPKINSON (1956)* a car dealer said of a second-hand car 'It's a good little bus; I would stake my life on it; you will have no trouble with it.' A hire purchase agreement was entered into. A week later P was injured in a collision caused by a serious defect in the car. P could not sue the finance company because of an effective exemption clause, but he was successful in his action against the dealer, the court holding that there was an implied contract between P and D and express term of which was 'you will have no trouble with it'. Since this term was broken P received damages. This case is not affected by *S.56* (above) since that section also preserves the personal liability of the dealer.

    ii.   The dealer is deemed to be the agent of the lender for the purposes of receiving any notice of revocation, cancellation or rescission, and where such notice or payment is received he is deemed to be under a contractual duty to transmit the notice or payment to the creditor.

  c. *Obligations of the borrower*

    i.   To take delivery of the goods.

    ii. To take reasonable care of the goods.

      The borrower is not liable for fair wear and tear, but he will be liable for damage caused by his own negligence, or if he deals with the goods in a manner which is clearly unauthorized by the lender. If the goods are stolen the agreement will be discharged by frustration and both parties will therefore be free from further liability.

    iii. To pay the instalments, unless the borrower has exercised his option to terminate (see below).

12. ***Hire Purchase, Conditional Sale, and Credit Sale Agreements*** In addition to the more common hire purchase agreements the Act also regulates conditional sale and credit sale agreements.

  a. A *conditional sale* is an agreement for the sale of goods whereby the price is payable by instalments and ownership remains with the seller until fulfilment of all conditions governing payment of instalments and other matters specified in the agreement. The 'buyer' under a conditional sale agreement is not regarded as a person who has bought or agreed to buy the goods. Thus he will be treated the same way as a borrower under a hire purchase agreement and will not be able to pass good title to the goods.

  b. A *credit sale* is an agreement for the sale of goods, the purchase price being payable by five or more instalments, not being a conditional sale agreement. Under such agreements the ownership of the goods passes to the buyer at once, and he may therefore pass on good title to another person.

FORMATION OF THE AGREEMENT

13. *New categories* of consumer credit and hire agreements, which require the provider to hold a consumer credit licence, were introduced by the *CONSUMER CREDIT ACT 2006*. The following business agencies require a consumer licence; these are providers of:

  a. *Consumer credit* e.g. finance companies, banks and moneylenders.

  b. *Consumer hire* e.g. car rental, TVs.

  c. *Credit brokerage* – these businesses that work on behalf of a credit, loan or hire providers, e.g. estate agents, car dealers.

  d. *Debt adjustment* – these businesses work with consumers and credit providers to rearrange payment of existing debts in a manner or amount that differs from the original agreement.

e. *Debt counselling* – this type of business helps consumers reduce their overall debt with creditors in the most effective way.

f. *Debt collection.*

g. *Debt administration* – these deal with general debt matters linked to administration orders made under the *INSOLVENCY ACT 1986* (see Chapter 47.23).

h. (from October 2008) *Credit repair* – this is a service where the business works with a consumer to improve their credit rating (that is, how they are rated in terms of risk of non-repayment). This service is particularly important to people who are trying to get better credit options including more competitive rates.

i. *Credit reference* – these businesses compile reports for credit providers to allow them to evaluate the financial stability of the subject of the report.

j. *Brokers* e.g. arranging credit for a customer with a finance company.

The Office of Fair Trading (OFT) determines the fitness or otherwise of applicants for a licence. In exercising its judgement, the OFT has regard to:

> any offences or wrongdoings committed by the applicant

> whether an applicant's business practices appear deceitful, unfair or improper.

Any person who carries on any of the above activities without a licence commits a criminal offence (see Chapter 3.6). The OFT has the power to impose a civil penalty (see Chapter 3.8) of up to £50 000, where a category of business listed above, has not complied with any OFT requirement. There is a Consumer Credit Appeals Tribunal which deals with any appeals from a decision of the OFT, after which there is an appeal route to the Court of Appeal and Supreme Court (see Chapter 6.2).

14. *Seeking Business*

a. *Advertising of credit.* An advertisement must give a fair and reasonably comprehensive picture of the credit offered, for example the 'true' rate of interest. An offence is committed if the advertisement:

i. Gives information which is false or misleading in a material respect.

In **METSOJA v NORMAN PITT (1989)** a car dealer advertised a new car with a 0% credit facility. The dealer also operated a part exchange facility, however, the part exchange allowance was lower if a new car was bought on credit than it would be if the car were purchased for cash. It was held that the lower allowance on part exchange for persons purchasing on credit was a hidden charge for credit contrary to the Act.

ii. Fails to comply with the regulations that are from time to time in force.

iii. Advertises restricted-use credit where the person offering the credit does not hold himself out as prepared to sell the goods or services for cash.

The aim of regulating advertisements is to promote 'truth in lending' and thus allow consumers to shop around for the best deal. The *CONSUMER CREDIT (ADVERTISE-MENTS) REGULATIONS 2010* are supplemented by more general rules contained in the *CONSUMER PROTECTION FROM UNFAIR TRADING REGULATIONS 2008.* Credit advertisements for businesses are exempt from the regulations. The regulations apply to all forms of advertising including Internet, TV, radio, teletext and telephone. Where an advertisement refers to any interest rate charged or cost of credit, there must be an example illustrating that charge in the advertisement itself. The following illustrates the information required to be contained in credit advertising:

> a. the rate of interest
>
> b. fees charged to be included in the total credit charge
>
> c. total amount of credit
>
> d. representative APR (actual percentage rate)
>
> e. the cash price and amount of any advance payment
>
> f. duration of agreement
>
> g. total amount payable
>
> h. amount of each repayment of credit.

It is a criminal offence for an advertisement not to meet the regulations, with the advertiser, publisher and anyone who devised the advert or arranged for its publication being potentially guilty of the offence. There is defence where a person can show that he had no knowledge or grounds to suspect that publication of the advertisement would be an offence.

b. *Canvassing.* It is an offence:

  i. To solicit entry by an individual into a regulated debtor-creditor agreement *off trade premises*, unless in response to a written request.

  ii. To send an unsolicited credit-token.

  iii. To send a circular to a minor soliciting the use of credit or hire facilities.

c. *Quotations.* The *CONSUMER CREDIT (CONTENT OF QUOTATIONS) (AMENDMENTS) REGULATIONS 1999* sets out certain information that must be included in any quotation –

  If applicable, that security is or may be required and a statement that 'Your home is at risk if you do not keep up repayments on a mortgage or any loan that uses your house as security.'

d. *Assessment of creditworthiness.* The *CONSUMER CREDIT (EU DIRECTIVE) REGULATIONS 2010* require that creditors assess the creditworthiness – the ability to repay – of a borrower, before entering a new agreement for credit or where in an existing credit agreement, the amount borrowed is significantly increased. The Regulations do not stipulate how the process of assessing the creditworthiness of a borrower is to be achieved, but requires that such an assessment must contain information from the borrower and from a credit reference agency where necessary.

e. *Explanation of terms.* The *DISCLOSURE REGULATIONS 2010* requires that certain explanations be given to a borrower in all regulated consumer credit agreements before the contract is entered into. This requirement does not apply to:

  i. Agreements secured against land.

  ii. Agreements where the credit exceeds £60 260.

  iii. Agreements entered into wholly or mainly for business purposes.

The creditor is required to:

provide borrowers with adequate explanations of *certain matters* (see below)

advise the borrower to consider all pre-contractual information and, where the borrower is there in person, allow the information to be taken away

give the borrower an opportunity to ask questions concerning the credit agreement

provide a point of contact for the borrower to ask for further information.

f.   *Matters requiring explanation.*

  i.   Features of the agreement which may make the particular credit provided unsuitable e.g. short term credit being used where a longer term loan would be more suitable.

  ii.   How much the borrower will have to pay periodically and where in the agreement that amount is determined e.g. where on a credit card the borrower only pays the minimum monthly amount, the method of calculating further interest payments.

  iii. Any features of the agreement which may operate in a manner which would have a significant effect on the borrower in a way which the borrower is unlikely to foresee e.g. 0% balance transfers on credit cards.

  iv.   Consequences for the borrower arising from a failure to make repayments e.g. loss of home, charges incurred for late payment.

  v.   The effects of the exercise of any right to withdraw from the agreement and how and when this right may be exercised e.g. details of any charges that may be incurred through early withdrawal.

A borrower cannot waive the right to have this information and the creditor can choose how explanations are to be given, for example oral, face to face, in writing.

15. *Pre-Contractual Information* The *DISCLOSURE REGULATIONS 2010* require that certain information be given to the borrower before the contract is entered into. This requirement does not apply to:

a.   Agreements secured against land.

b.   Agreements where the credit exceeds £60 260.

c.   Agreements entered into wholly or mainly for business purposes.

The information must be provided in good time with the borrower having adequate time to consider it before entering the contract. This information is provided on a standard form: Pre-contract Credit Information (PCI) form. The lender must also provide information relating to:

  i.   Where credit is refused based upon information provided by a

        credit reference agency and the particulars of the credit

        reference report.

  ii.   The borrower's right to request a copy of the draft agreement.

  iii. The period of time the lender is bound by information contained

  iv.   in the PCI form.

16. *Formal Requirements*

    a. The agreement itself must:

        i. Be in writing.

        ii. Contain all express terms in a clearly legible form.

        iii. Be signed by the borrower personally and by or on behalf of the creditor or owner.

        iv. Comply with the current regulations as to form and content (these are set out in the *AGREEMENT REGULATIONS 2010*).

        Certain terms are called *prescribed terms* and if these terms are not included in the agreement the contract will not be executed properly and the lender cannot enforce the agreement without a court order. The *prescribed terms* are:

        the amount of credit or credit limit

        the rate of interest

        the timing of repayments.

        v. In the case of a cancellable agreement, contain a notice in the prescribed form indicating the right of the debtor to cancel the agreement, including how and when the right is exercisable and the name and address of a person to whom notice of cancellation may be given.

    b. *Copies of the agreement.* The borrower must receive:

        i. Immediately upon signing – a copy of the form that the debtor signs.

        ii. Within 7 days – a second copy of the completed agreement. This second copy is only necessary if the agreement was not completed by the borrower's signature (i.e. if the creditor has not previously signed it). In the case of a cancellable agreement this copy must be sent by post and must contain details of the borrower's right to cancel.

        iii. Within 7 days (if no second copy is required) – a notice sent by post giving details of rights concerning cancellation of cancellable agreements.

    c. Non-compliance with the required formalities renders the agreement unenforceable against the borrower except on a court order. In some situations, for example if the creditor fails to give notice of the right to cancel, the court must refuse to enforce the agreement.

17. *The Borrower's Right to Cancel*

    a. Borrowers have a right to withdraw from a credit agreement within 14 days from the date of the agreement.

    b. Notice of cancellation must be given before the end of the fifth day following the day on which the consumer received the second copy (where necessary) or, if there was no second copy, notice of his cancellation rights. Thus if the borrower signs an unexecuted agreement (i.e. not yet signed by the lender) on 1st May, and receives his second copy on 7th May, the cancellation or 'cooling off' period will expire at midnight on 12th May.

    c. Notice of cancellation must be in writing and may be served on either:

        i. The lender.

        ii. The credit broker (for example a garage in a tripartite hire purchase agreement for the sale of a car) or supplier who negotiated the agreement, or

        iii. Any person specified in the notice of cancellation rights.

d.   Notice of cancellation is effective when posted, even if it is lost in the post. Where electronic notice is given e.g. fax, e-mail, it is effective from the time of transmission.

e.   The effect of cancellation is that the agreement is treated as if it had never been entered into. Therefore any deposit paid, or goods handed over in part exchange by the consumer must be returned to him, and he has a right to hold the goods in his possession until this is done. The consumer need not send the goods back himself, but he must retain them and permit their collection in response to a written request. He has a duty to take reasonable care of the goods for 21 days, but thereafter owes no duty of care unless he has unreasonably refused to comply with a request to permit collection, in which case the duty continues until such request is complied with.

f.   Non-cancellable agreements include non-commercial restricted-use credit arranged to finance the purchase of land, or arranged in connection with a bridging loan (i.e. a loan to enable the purchase of a house prior to the sale of the purchaser's previous house).

g.   The borrower's right to cancel was extended by the *CANCELLATION OF CONTRACTS MADE IN A CONSUMER'S HOME OR PLACE OF WORK REGULATIONS 2008*, which allow consumers to cancel contracts of *any kind* which are made during a visit by a trader to a consumer's home or place of work, or made at another's home or place of work. Key features of the Regulations are:

   i.   They apply whether the visit was requested by the consumer or not.

   ii.   They apply where a trader has organized an excursion away from business premises.

   iii.   Goods or services provided must be of a price exceeding £35.

   iv.   The trader cannot enforce the contract unless, at the time of the contract, the consumer was given written notice of the right to cancel within 7 days.

   v.   The notice of cancellation given by the consumer must be in writing.

   vi.   Once notice is given any goods supplied to the consumer must be made available for collection by the trader.

   vii.   The consumer gets back any money already paid and does not have to pay any money remaining due under the cancelled contract.

MATTERS ARISING DURING THE AGREEMENT

18.   The main obligations of the lender and borrower have already been considered. However, there are a number of other matters which may arise during the period of a regulated consumer credit agreement.

19.   *Additional Information* The borrower is entitled to receive, in return for a request in writing and a payment , another copy of his agreement and a statement of the current financial position of his account. The *CONSUMER CREDIT ACT 2006* introduced new rights to post-contract information. Lenders in regulated fixed-amount credit agreements must provide borrowers with an annual statement of their borrowings. If the lender fails to do this then he will be unable to enforce the agreement nor charge interest over the period of the default. The *EU CONSUMER CREDIT DIRECTIVE 2008* also gives rights to borrowers to request a statement of account showing instalment payments where repayment is by instalments. The request can be made at any time during the agreement and must be

provided as soon as is reasonably practicable. The *EU CONSUMER CREDIT DIRECTIVE 2008*, also requires lenders to inform borrowers in writing prior to any changes in the rate of interest.

20. **Credit Intermediaries** The *EU CONSUMER CREDIT DIRECTIVE 2008* requires that credit intermediaries – that is persons who facilitate agreements between a borrower and lender – disclose the extent to which they are acting independently or working for one or more creditors. Failure to disclose is a criminal offence punishable by a fine.

21. **Appropriation of Payments** A borrower might have two or more agreements with the same lender and so tender a payment insufficient to discharge the total amount due under all the agreements. In such a case:

   a. The borrower may allocate his payment between the various agreements as he thinks fit.

   b. In the absence of allocation by the borrower the lender must appropriate the payment towards the various sums in due proportion that they bear to one another. He cannot appropriate them to the agreements that would best serve his interests.

22. **Early Payment by the Borrower** The borrower is entitled, at any time, by notice to the lender and payment of all the amount outstanding, to discharge his indebtedness.

23. **Variation of Agreements** Where, under a power conferred by the agreement, the lender varies the agreement, for example by increasing the rate of interest payable, the variation does not take effect until notice of it is given to the borrower in the prescribed manner.

24. **Death of the Borrower**

   a. If the agreement is fully secured the lender may not take action.

   b. If it is unsecured or partly secured the lender may take action on an *order of the court* provided he can prove that he has been unable to satisfy himself that the present and future obligations of the borrower are likely to be discharged.

25. **Liability of Lender for Supplier's Default**

   a. In the usual triangular hire purchase agreement where a customer requires goods or services from a supplier and is provided with credit from a lender, the lender will be liable for the supplier's default if the lender has contracted with the customer to supply the goods or services. The lender will be personally liable for breach of implied conditions as to title, quality, fitness for purpose and so on. He will also usually be liable for misrepresentations made by the dealer to the customer, since under *S.56* the dealer is deemed to have conducted negotiations as agent for the creditor.

   b. In a debtor–creditor–supplier agreement where the lender has not personally contracted to supply goods or services to the customer, *S.75* provides that if the borrower (customer) has a claim against the supplier for misrepresentation or breach of contract, the borrower has a similar claim against the lender. For example, if the borrower uses a credit card to pay for goods then he may choose to bring a claim against the lender (the credit card company) rather than the supplier, provided the cash price for the goods is more than £100, but less than £30 000.

   In **UNITED DOMINIONS TRUST v TAYLOR (1980)** a car dealer introduced the customer to UDT. UDT lent the customer the money to enable him to purchase the car from the dealer. Taylor did not make loan repayments and was sued by UDT. His defence was that he had purchased the car because of misrepresentations by the dealer as to its condition and that the dealer was in breach of contract i.e. the contract by which he bought the car. Taylor therefore claimed he had a right to rescind the contract with the dealer and, by virtue of *S.75*, a similar right to rescind the loan agreement. It was held that this was the effect of *S.75* and judgment was given in Taylor's favour.

c. The *EU CONSUMER CREDIT DIRECTIVE 2008* introduced a new *S.75A* regarding a lender's liability to the customer for any misrepresentation or breach of contract by the supplier. This law covers those agreements not covered by *S.75*:

i. The cash price of the goods and services is more than £30 000.

ii. The amount of credit does not exceed £60 260.

iii. Goods or services are purchased under a *debtor–creditor–supplier agreement* (sometimes referred to as a *linked credit agreement*) (see 6.d.ii above).

iv. There has been a breach of contract and the borrower/customer has been unable to get satisfaction from the supplier.

The general view is that, unlike *S.75*, *S.75A* will not apply to credit cards. Also, *S.75* gives an option to the borrower to sue either the credit provider – the lender – or the supplier of the goods and services, *S.75A* requires that the supplier be pursued first with an option to sue the lender if this proves impossible – e.g. the supplier becomes insolvent.

26. *Liability for Loss or Misuse of Credit Cards*

a. *S.66* and *S.84* of the Act, lay down the extent of a borrower's liability where a credit card (sometimes referred to as a *credit token*) is misused. There are two points in time which need to be distinguished:

i. Misuse of the card at the time of initial acceptance by the borrower (governed by *S.66*, and

ii. Misuse following acceptance of the card by the borrower (governed by *S.84*).

For the borrower to incur any liability in i., it has to be shown that the use by the other person constituted an acceptance by the borrower.

Acceptance by the borrower here is when he:

signs the card

signs a receipt for it

first uses the card by himself or by a person he authorizes to use it.

With regard to any borrower liability following acceptance, i.e. ii., the borrower is required to notify the creditor/card issuer as soon as possible where the card has been lost, stolen or liable to misuse. The borrower will then be not liable for any loss arising after notice has been received by the creditor. Notice can be given orally but some agreements state that notice has to be made in writing with notice being effective only if it is received by the creditor within 7 days.

The extent of any liability on the part of the borrower before notice is effective will depend on the circumstances; if the person who misuses the card obtained possession of it with the borrower's consent, then the borrower will be liable without limit. If the borrower did not consent i.e. the card was lost or stolen, liability will be limited to £50 or lower if the credit limit on the card is lower.

b. *Distance selling*

Where the card is used in connection with distance selling contracts, such as on the Internet or by mail order, the *CONSUMER PROTECTION (DISTANCE SELLING) REGULATIONS 2000* comes into play. Here, if the card is used fraudulently, the consumer/borrower is entitled to:

i. Cancel payment, or if the payment has already been made,

ii. A re-credit, with all sums returned to the borrower/card user.

The Regulations also, with regard to distance selling contracts, remove the card-holder liability for the first £50 of any loss arising.

DEFAULT AND TERMINATION

27. *Default Notices* Whenever a borrower defaults on the credit agreement, the lender is stopped from taking any action to enforce the agreement unless he has first served on the borrower a 'default notice' which must specify:

a. The alleged breach.

b. The action required to put it right if it is capable of remedy, and if not

c. What sum, if any, is required to be paid as compensation, and

d. The date by which such action must be taken, which must be not less than 7 days after the service of the default notice.

In *WOODCHESTER LEASE MANAGEMENT SERVICES LTD v SWAIN & CO 1999* a firm of solicitors entered into an agreement to hire a photocopier. Regular payments were made for a number of years when the firm of solicitors – the hirer – stopped paying. The claimant hire company, sent a default notice to the hirer, which contained an error in the calculation of the owed. The Court of Appeal held that a default notice must contain an accurate statement on the amount owed, and as this was an important part of the notice, it made the claimant's default notice invalid. Minor errors might be overlooked by the court, but not one as important as this.

If the debtor carries out the requirements of the default notice, the breach is treated as if it never happened. The *CONSUMER CREDIT ACT 2006* requires that lenders give borrowers or hirers notice of any arrears within 14 days after the default, and at 6-monthly intervals thereafter. This is called a sums in arrears notice and failure to comply with the notice requirements will prevent an action being brought during the period of non-compliance and the borrower or hirer will not be liable for any interest payments during that period.

28. *Further Restriction on Remedies for Default*

a. Where goods are bought on hire purchase *S.90* provides that once one-third or more of the total price of the goods has been paid the lender cannot recover possession of them except on an order of the court. Such goods are known as 'protected goods'.

b. The section does not apply if the borrower voluntarily surrenders the goods.

c. If goods are recovered by the lender in contravention of *S.90.* the agreement will terminate and the borrower is released from all liability. In addition he is entitled to recover from the lender all sums paid under the agreement.

    d. Entry on to any premises by the lender to take possession of goods subject to hire purchase, conditional sale or consumer hire agreements is prohibited except by court order. Clearly this is of importance if the goods are not protected under *S.90.*

    e. The charging of default interest at a higher rate than the basic rate of interest is prohibited.

29. *Termination*

    a. The borrower may, at any time before the final payment falls due, terminate a *hire purchase* or *conditional sale agreement* by giving notice in writing to any person authorized to receive the sums payable under the agreement.

    b. The borrower's liability is to pay the sums which have accrued due, plus the amount, if any, by which one half of the total price exceeds the total of the sums paid, or such lesser amount as may be specified in the agreement. He is also liable to compensate the lender for any damage to the goods if he has failed to take reasonable care of them.

    c. If any contract term is inconsistent with these provisions, for example a term which imposes additional liability on the borrower, such term is void. The contract may, however, grant the borrower more favourable terms for termination than those provided by the Act.

    d. Different rules apply to the termination of a *consumer hire agreement.* Termination does not affect any liability which has already accrued. The right to terminate does not arise until the agreement has been in existence for 18 months, unless the agreement itself provides for a shorter period. The period of notice which must be given is one instalment period or 3 months, whichever is less. The right to terminate a consumer hire agreement does not apply:

        i. Where the total hire payments exceed £1500 per year, or

        ii. Where the goods are hired for a business, and are freely chosen by the hirer from a supplier, and the hiring arrangement is not made until the goods have been chosen, or

        iii. Where the hirer obtained the goods so that he could in turn hire them out in the course of his business.

JUDICIAL CONTROL

Judicial control over the provisions of the Act is exercised by the County Court.

30. *Enforcement Orders*

    a. In several situations, for example if the agreement is 'improperly executed' the Act provides that, before he can enforce the agreement, the lender must obtain a court order, i.e. an *'enforcement order'*.

    b. As a general rule the court must dismiss the application if in all the circumstances justice appears to require this. In some cases the court has no choice but to dismiss the application, for example where the agreement was a cancellable one, but the borrower was not given proper notice of his right to cancel it.

31. *Time Orders* On an application for an 'enforcement order', or on an application to recover possession of goods after service of a default notice, the court may grant a *'time order'*. This

gives the borrower more time to pay, or to do something else he should have done, such as maintaining any security in good repair. While a time order is in force the consumer is protected against the consequences of his default, thus a security cannot be enforced, and the goods cannot be recovered by the lender.

32. ***Return and Transfer Orders***

    a.   Where a lender seeks to recover, because of a breach by the consumer, goods which he has let on hire purchase, the court may order the borrower to return the goods under a '*return order*'. Where it thinks fit, the court may suspend the return order so long as the borrower keeps up revised payments under a 'time order'.

    b.   As an alternative (in cases where goods may be divided up) the court may make a '*transfer order*' giving ownership of part of the goods to the borrower and returning the rest to the lender, depending on how much the borrower has already paid in respect of the total price of all the goods.

33. ***Unfair Credit Relationship Test***

S.19–22 of the *CONSUMER CREDIT ACT 2006,* amends the 1974 Act in allowing the court to examine alleged unfair credit agreements by taking account of all relevant factors over the entire duration of the agreement and not simply those relevant at the time the agreement was made (as was the case under the previous *CONSUMER CREDIT ACT 1974*). *S.140A(1)* gives power to the court to make an order if it finds that an agreement between lender and borrower unfair. In taking account of all relevant circumstances this may include one or more of the following:

    a.   Any terms of the agreement or of any related agreement.

    b.   The way in which the lender has exercised or enforced any of his rights under the agreement.

    c.   Any other thing done (or not done) by, or on behalf of, the lender.

The Act also allows borrowers to access an alternative dispute resolution scheme rather than having recourse to the courts. It provides borrowers with free access to a quick and efficient resolution of consumer credit disputes. Lenders will have a duty to refer complaints to the Financial Ombudsman Service.

Another factor in assessing fairness might be European legislation; the *UNFAIR COMMERCIAL PRACTICES DIRECTIVE 2005/29/EC.* This will apply to consumer credit and has a non-exhaustive list of commercial circumstances that may be considered unfair.

31. ***Interest on Trade Debts*** Small businesses have traditionally suffered from late payment for goods and services supplied to larger companies; their weak bargaining position making it difficult for them to include in their contracts to supply late payment interest charge clauses. The *LATE PAYMENT OF COMMERCIAL DEBTS (INTEREST) ACT 1998* now gives to small businesses a statutory right to claim interest on late payment of commercial debts for the supply of goods and services to other businesses and public bodies. A small business is defined as one with fewer than 50 full-time employees, a large business is one where there are over 50 full-time employees. Interest becomes payable the day after the 'relevant date', this is either the date agreed by the parties or 30 days after the supplier has performed his obligations. Any attempt to exclude the Act will be subject to there existing some other substantial remedy within the contract, otherwise such terms will be of no effect.

SELF TEST QUESTIONS

Self Test Questions No. 31 (for Answers see Appendix 1):

1   What are the main statutory source materials regulating consumer credit?

2   What are the two types of agreement regulated and how are they defined?

3   Explain what each of the following terms means:

conditional sale

credit sale

credit card/ token

loan

overdraft

shop budget.

4   What is a 'debtor creditor supplier agreement'?

5   What is a 'regulated' consumer agreement?

6   What are the features of a 'hire purchase agreement'?

7   What are the obligations on a hire purchase lender/hirer?

8   What is a credit broker

9   What are the obligations placed upon a borrower/hirer of goods?

10   What are the main provisions governing the advertising of consumer credit?

11   What is meant by the phrase; 'assessment of creditworthiness'?

12   What is required to be disclosed by way of information before a regulated agreement is entered into?

13   Outline the implications of a borrower's right to cancel.

14   Once a regulated agreement has started, what additional information is required in the agreement?

15   What are the liabilities on a credit card holder upon its misuse?

16   What are 'enforcement' and 'time' orders?

17   What are the unfair credit relationship provisions?

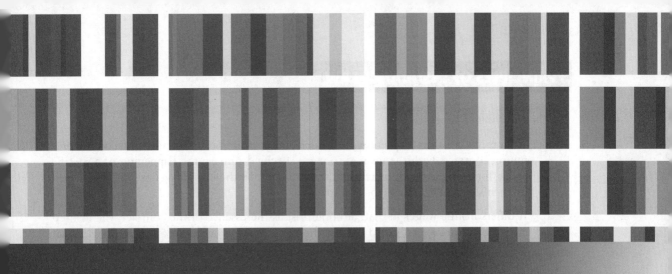

INSURANCE

34

Learning Outcomes At the end of this chapter you should be able to:

- Explain what a contract of insurance is.

- State what is meant by the terms:

  - good faith

  - insurable interest

  - indemnity

  - subrogation

  - contribution

  - risk.

- Understand the key elements of *life, fire, motor vehicle, theft* and *accident* insurance.

PRINCIPLES OF INSURANCE LAW

1. *The Contract of Insurance*

   a.   Insurance is a contract whereby the insurer, in return for a sum of money called the premium, contracts with the insured to pay a specified sum on the happening of a specific event, for example death or accident, or to indemnify the insured against any loss caused by the risk insured against, for example fire.

   b.   It differs from a wager in that, although risk is the essence of the contract, the insured takes out insurance to guard against the risk of loss, whereas in a wager the contract itself creates the risk. In insurance the insured must therefore have some interest apart from the contract, i.e. an insurable interest.

   c.   Many insurance contracts provide that the answers submitted by the insured in his proposal form are 'the basis of the contract'. This has the effect that all the terms of the contract are treated as conditions and the insurers will be able to avoid liability if the proposal form is incorrect, even if the wrong answer was given innocently and does not relate to a material fact.

   For example, in *DAWSONS v BONNIN (1922)* in response to a question on a proposal form as to where a lorry would be garaged, the proposer inadvertently inserted the wrong address. The lorry was later lost due to fire and a claim was made under the policy. It was held that since the proposal form was expressed to be 'the basis of the contract', all answers were conditions, the inaccuracy of which entitled the insurer to avoid the policy, even if, as in this case, the answer to the question did not affect the premium charged.

2. *The Principle of Good Faith*

   a.   All contracts of insurance are *uberrimae fidei*. They are therefore voidable at the option of the insurer for non-disclosure of any material fact which was known, or ought to have been known, to the insured at the time of making the contract.

   b.   A fact is material if it would influence the judgement of a prudent insurer in deciding whether to accept the risk, and if so at what premium and on what conditions.

   In *LONDON ASSURANCE v MANSEL (1879)* D failed to disclose that several insurance companies had declined proposals to insure his life. This was held to be a material factor which should have been disclosed. Rescission of the contract was therefore granted.

   c.   A policy of insurance, like any other contract is voidable for misrepresentation, whether innocent or fraudulent. The insurer, however, can only avoid if the misrepresentation is materially and substantially false. Where an insurer avoids a voidable contract, they need not return any premiums paid.

3. *Insurable Interest*

   a.   Insurable interest means that the insured must be so circumstanced in relation to the subject matter of the insurance as to benefit by its existence or be prejudiced by its destruction (*LUCENA v CRAUFURD (1806)*). Thus, for example a person has an insurable interest in his property and in his own life or in that of his wife.

b.   The common law does not require the insured to have an insurable interest. However:

   i.   If the contract is one of indemnity (see below) an insured who has no interest at the time of the loss will have no claim – he loses nothing, therefore no indemnity is necessary.

   ii.   Any policy in which the insured, at the time of the policy has no insurable interest and no expectation of acquiring one is a wager, and void under the *GAMING ACT 1845.*

   iii.   The *LIFE ASSURANCE ACT 1774* provides that any insurance on the life of a person is void unless the person taking out the policy has an insurable interest in the life insured. Despite its name this Act also applies to personal accident and fire insurance policies.

   The effect of i.–iii. above is that an insurable interest must be present in all contracts of insurance. What 'insurable interest' means in relation to specific types of insurance contract is considered below under the appropriate heading.

4. *Indemnity*

   a.   An indemnity policy is one under which the insured will be compensated (i.e. indemnified) for his actual loss so far as it does not exceed the sum insured. For example, if X insures his house for £20 000 and it is burnt down, if £5000 will restore it, then he may claim £5000 and no more. If it will cost £40 000 to restore it, then he may claim £20 000.

   b.   A 'valued policy' may, however, agree the measure of indemnity at the time when the policy is issued instead of waiting until the time of the loss. Such a contract is valid unless the overvaluation is so gross as to amount to a wager. The insured can recover the agreed value if the loss is total. If the loss is partial he can recover such proportion of the agreed value as is represented by the depreciation in the actual value. For example:

   In *ELCOCK v THOMSON (1949)* a house was insured against fire. In the policy its value was agreed at £106 850. The house was damaged in a fire. In fact its actual value before the fire was £18 000 and after the fire was £12 600, i.e. the depreciation in actual value was £5400. The court therefore held that the insured was entitled to recover:

$$\frac{5400}{18\,000} \times 106\,850 = £32\,055$$

   c.   The insured can never recover more than the sum for which the property is insured. For example:

   In *DARRELL v TIBBITTS (1880)* a house was damaged by a gas explosion. The landlord recovered £750 from insurers. The tenant was, however, obliged under the terms of his lease to repair the damage. He did this with money received from the local authority (whose negligence caused the explosion). It was held that the insurers could recover the £750 paid to the landlord because clearly he had suffered no loss. To allow him to keep the money would be to award him double compensation.

   d.   Provided the policy is not a 'valued policy' the measure of indemnity:

   i.   In the event of total loss, not the cost price, but the market value of the property at the time and place of the loss. For example, in *LEPPARD v EXCESS INSURANCE CO (1979)* a cottage was insured for £10 000, this sum being stated to be the amount necessary to replace the property in its existing form if it was completely destroyed. When the cottage was destroyed the insured claimed £10 000. The Court of Appeal, however, only awarded him the market value of the cottage at the time of its destruction, namely £3000.

  ii. In the event of partial loss, the cost of repairs.

e. If the property is under-insured, (i.e. insured for less than its market value), the insurer is still liable for a partial loss up to the full limit of the sum insured. Some policies guard against this by including a 'subject to average' clause, whereby if the amount insured is less than the value the insurers are only liable for that proportion of the actual loss which the sum insured bears to the value of the property. For example, the market value of X's house is £20 000, but it is only insured for £10 000. If X suffers fire damage to the extent of £5000, he can only recover £2500 from the insurer.

f. All contracts of insurance are contracts of indemnity except:

  i. Life assurance.

  ii. Insurance against accident to, or illness of, the insured himself.

5. *Subrogation*

a. If the contract is one of indemnity the insurers have a right of subrogation, i.e. having paid the insured his compensation, they are permitted to take over any rights that the insured has against the person who caused the loss. The insurers bring the action in the name of the insured, who must lend his name in return for a promise that he will not be liable for costs. The insurers are said to 'step into the shoes' of the insured, i.e. they are subrogated to his rights. For example, A has insured his property against damage by fire with X Ltd. A fire is caused by B's negligence. X Ltd must pay A under the policy, but they are then entitled to sue B in negligence. If they recover the damages from B which exceed the amount they have had to pay to A, the excess received belongs to A.

b. If the insured renounces or compromises any right of action he has against a third party, he must repay to the insurers the benefit of which he has thereby deprived them.

In *PHOENIX ASSURANCE v SPOONER (1905)* D's premises were insured against fire with P. The Local Authority then issued a compulsory purchase notice, but before the purchase had been completed the premises were destroyed by fire. The Local Authority then completed the purchase having agreed with D to pay a sum which reflected the fact that D had received some money from P. In addition it was agreed that the Local Authority would indemnify D against any claim brought by P. When P did claim it was held that, since fire insurance is a contract of indemnity, P was entitled to all the rights that D had against the Local Authority, and this included a right to the full market value of the property. Since D had accepted less than the market value (because she had received some insurance money) she had deprived P of their opportunity to obtain the market value from the Local Authority. D therefore had to pay compensation to P, but could reclaim the amount paid from the Local Authority under her agreement with them.

6. *Contribution*

a. Where there is more than one policy enforceable at the time of loss covering the same subject matter, risk and interest the insured may recover the total loss from either insurer.

b. Any insurer who pays more than his share may claim a contribution from the others in proportion to the sum insured with each.

7. *Risk*

a. Loss resulting from negligence is covered.

In *HARRIS v POLAND (1942)* the insured deliberately hid her jewellery in the grate of her fireplace. Later, having forgotten this, she lit the fire, and damaged her jewellery. Her claim succeeded even though she had been negligent and despite the fact that the fire had not escaped from its usual boundaries.

b. Clearly loss resulting from negligence is precisely what motor vehicle insurance is designed to cover. A claim will in fact lie even if the driving is so negligent that it amounts to a criminal offence.

c. A loss will not be covered if it is a loss of profits or if it is caused by:

    i. The insured's own wilful misconduct. (The burden of proving this lies on the insurer.)

    ii. Ordinary wear and tear.

TYPES OF INSURANCE CONTRACT

8. *Life Assurance*

a. A life assurance contract is one by which the insurer in return for either a lump sum or annual payments over a specified period, undertakes to pay the person for whose benefit the insurance is made, a sum of money on the death of the person whose life is insured. The term '*assurance*' is used where the event concerned must occur, in this case death. The term '*insurance*' is used when the event may occur, for example an accident or theft.

b. *Insurable interest*

    i. The interest must be a pecuniary interest, and must exist at the date of the contract but need not continue until the date of the death. Thus a man may take out a policy on the life of his wife, and even if they divorce he may claim under the policy when his former wife dies.

    ii. A person may insure his own life for his own benefit for any sum he wishes, even though he intends when insuring to assign the policy to another person.

    iii. Spouses have an unlimited insurable interest in each other's lives, but other relatives, such as father and son, have no insurable interest in the lives of each other.

    iv. A creditor has an insurable interest in the life of the debtor up to the amount of the debt at the date of insurance.

    v. An employee has an insurable interest in his employer's life to the extent of his wages, and an employer may insure against the loss of his employee's services through death.

c. *Suicide*

    i. If the insured is insane when he commits suicide the insurance money is recoverable unless the policy otherwise provides.

    ii. If the insured is sane the position is unclear. Prior to 1961 suicide was a crime, and since it is contrary to public policy to allow a person to profit from his crime the insurance money could not be recovered by his personal representatives. Suicide is no longer a crime, however, it is probable that the money is irrecoverable, because money is not generally payable under a policy when the insured deliberately brings about the event insured against.

d. *Assignment*

  i.   Assignment means that the right to receive the policy money is transferred from the person originally entitled to the asignee.

  ii. The assignee need not have an insurable interest in the policy.

  iii. The assignee must protect his interest in the policy by notifying the insurers.

  iv. The assignee has a right to sue the insurers, if necessary, for the policy money.

9. *Fire Insurance*

a. A fire insurance contract gives the insured an indemnity covering loss caused by fire during a specified period.

  i.   'Fire' means ignition and not merely overheating.

  ii. 'Loss caused by fire' does not merely include items burned, it could include damage caused by the water used to fight the fire.

b. Clearly the insured cannot recover if he deliberately starts the fire, but if the loss is merely caused by his negligence this does not defeat his claim – *HARRIS v POLAND (1942)* (see 7. above).

c. In contrast to life assurance, since the contract is one of indemnity, the insurable interest must exist not only when the contract is made, but also when the loss occurs. Any legal or equitable interest in the subject matter suffices as an insurable interest. For example, an interest as an owner, tenant, mortgage, trustee, beneficiary or personal representative. However, a shareholder has no interest in and cannot insure the property of a company, even if it is a 'one-man' company – *MACAURA v NORTHERN ASSURANCE CO (1925)* (Chapter 43).

d. Restoration of the building.

  i.   At common law the insured was not bound to use money received from the insurance company to reinstate the property. He was entitled to be indemnified in cash which he could use as he wished.

  ii. However, the *FIRES PREVENTION (METROPOLIS) ACT 1774*, which despite its name applies throughout the country, provides that any person, (for example a tenant), interested in a building destroyed by fire can require the insurer to spend the insurance money on the reinstatement of the building.

10. *Motor Vehicle Insurance*

a. Under the *ROAD TRAFFIC ACT 1988* a motorist must insure against any liability he may incur as a result of causing the death or injury of a third party. The third party has a right to sue the insurers direct despite the general privity of contract rule.

b. If the user of a motor vehicle is not insured against liability for causing injury to third parties both the owner and the user have committed a criminal offence. In addition to their criminal liability any person who does not have the required compulsory insurance is liable to pay damages for breach of statutory duty if there is no other remedy available to the injured party.

In *MONK v WARBEY (1935)* D lent his car to a friend. The friend's driver drove negligently causing injury to P. The friend was not covered by insurance and D's policy only applied when the owner was driving it. D was therefore liable to pay damages to P for breach of statutory duty.

c. A provision in the policy which purports to exclude the insurer's liability to indemnify the insured because of his age, physical or mental condition, the condition of his vehicle or the number of passengers carried is void. However, a limitation as to user, for example for 'private' purposes only, will prevent a third party from recovering damages from the insurer if he is injured while the car is being used in another way, for example as a taxi.

d. *Unsatisfied judgements.* In 1946 motor vehicle insurers agreed to set up the Motor Insurers Bureau (M.I.B.). The M.I.B. will satisfy a judgement where the driver does not have the compulsory cover, because for example he had not taken out a policy, or the insurers have gone into liquidation. The conditions are:

   i. Notice of proceedings is given to the M.I.B. before, or within 7 days after their commencement, and

   ii. The liability is one that is required to be covered by the *ROAD TRAFFIC ACT* 1988

e. The M.I.B. has also agreed to compensate 'hit and run' victims if:

   i. Neither the owner nor driver can be traced.

   ii. On the balance of probabilities the owner or driver would be liable to compensate the victim.

   iii. The victim was a compulsory risk within the meaning of the Road Traffic Act.

   iv. The accident was not a deliberate attempt to run down the victim, and

   v. The claim is made in writing within 3 years of the accident.

11. *Insurance Against Theft*

   a. The principles applicable to life and fire insurance also apply to theft. For example:

   In *ROSELODGE v CASTLE (1966)* when insuring their stock against theft diamond merchants failed to disclose that the sales manager had a previous conviction for smuggling diamonds. It was held that this amounted to non-disclosure of a material fact, and the insurers could avoid the claim, even though the sales manager was not the thief.

   b. The insurer may avoid the contract if, for example:

   i. The property has been deliberately overvalued, or

   ii. The stolen property was illegally imported, with the intention of evading customs duty. The rationale here is that if the insured was indemnified for the theft, he would profit from his illegal act of importing the goods.

12. *Accident Insurance*

   a. Life assurance policies usually also cover personal injury to the policy holder.

   b. A person who does not have life assurance may either insure himself against personal injury or insure against liability arising from injuries to third parties. He will not, however, be able to claim under a liability policy in respect of a deliberate unlawful act by himself.

In **GRAY v BARR** *(1971)* D shot and killed Gray in a fight. He was acquitted of both murder and manslaughter but Gray's personal representatives made a claim against him under the *FATAL ACCIDENTS ACT 1976*. D sought an indemnity under his accident liability policy in respect of any damages he might have to pay. It was held that even if the death was an 'accident' within the terms of the policy, the policy would not cover accidents which occurred as a result of threatening unlawful violence with a loaded gun.

   c.   An injured third party may sue the insurer direct if the insured is bankrupt, or if the insured is a company which has gone into liquidation.

13. ***Employers' Compulsory Insurance*** The *EMPLOYERS' LIABILITY (COMPULSORY IN-SURANCE) ACT 1969* makes it compulsory for every employer (except nationalized industries and local authorities) to insure himself against liability for injury or disease sustained by his employees and arising in the course of their employment.

SELF TEST QUESTIONS

Self Test Questions No. 32 (for Answers see Appendix 1):

1   What is a contract of insurance?

2   Explain what is meant by each of the following insurance terms:

   the principle of good faith

   insurable interest

   indemnity

   subrogation

   contribution

   risk.

3   What are the essential elements of contracts for:

   life insurance

   fire insurance

   motor vehicle insurance

   insurance against theft

   accident insurance?

PATENTS, COPYRIGHT, TRADE MARKS AND PASSING-OFF

35

Learning Outcomes At the end of this chapter you should be able to:

- Understand the meaning of a design right.

- Define what is meant by a patent and the process for its application.

- Explain the meaning of copyright and the nature of the protection it gives.

- Explain what trade marks are; the requirements as to its establishment; and the nature of any infringement.

- Explain what is 'passing-off' and the requirements for it to be shown to have occurred.

INTRODUCTION

1. In order to encourage new inventions and original works and to protect the goodwill of those who have built up a business the law gives statutory protection to patents, designs, copyright and trade marks. These rights are governed by the *COPYRIGHT, DESIGNS AND PATENTS ACT 1988* and the *PATENTS ACT 1977* (as amended). In addition the economic tort of 'passing-off' prevents a person from conducting himself so that customers

will mistake his goods, services or business for that of someone else. This branch of law is known as intellectual property law.

DESIGNS

2. *Design Right*

   a. A *design right* is a new property right created under the 1988 Act. Hardware is automatically protected and does not need to be registered. The right subsists in an original design. It does not apply to the following:

      i. Method of construction.

      ii. Interface (enabling the article to be placed in or against another article in order that either article may perform its function).

      iii. Surface decoration.

   b. *Duration*. The design right expires 15 years from the end of the calendar year in which first recorded in a design document or an article was made to the design. If the design was made available for sale or hire within 5 years from first being recorded or an article being made, expiry is 10 years from the end of the year in which this occurred. Designs registered with the Registered Designs Act 1949 expire 10 years from the 12th January 1988 (commencement date of the 1988 Act).

   c. *Remedies for infringement*. The following remedies are available:

      i. Damages.

      ii. Order for delivery-up. The articles delivered up would be disposed of by forfeiture to the design right owner or by destruction.

PATENTS

3. *Definition* A patent is the name given to a bundle of monopoly rights which give the patentee the exclusive right to exploit the invention for a given period of time. It is a right to stop others, an inventor does not need a positive right to exploit his own invention.

4. *Applying for a Patent*

   a. An application is made to the Patent Office. If the invention has been made by an employee in the course of his employment, the employer owns the invention and may apply for a patent with the inventor's consent. Alternatively a joint application may be made, or the employee may apply, in which case the grant will be subject to the employer's interest.

   b. At the Patent Office a document called a '*Complete Specification*' is filed. This contains a description of the article, process or machine, including working instructions and a statement of 'claims' which define the scope of the invention for which the inventor seeks his monopoly. It is against these claims that any infringement is judged.

c. The Patent Office carries out '*research*' to test for novelty. According to the result of this search the applicant may decide to abandon or modify his application or request an *examination* by a qualified Patent Office examiner. The main task of the examiner is to see that the claims of the specification describe things that are not only new, but also inventive. Once the examiner is satisfied the specification is published and for 3 months afterwards any interested party can object by notice to the Patent Office.

A bagless cyclonic vacuum cleaner invented and patented by Dyson was held to have been infringed subsequently by Hoover (***DYSON APPLIANCES LTD V HOOVER LTD (2000)***).

d. In the event of no opposition or failure of objections the '*Letters Patent*' will be sealed and the patentee can sue in the High Court (or in some cases the County Court) for any infringement.

e. Once granted the patent covers the UK and is in force for 4 years, and it can be renewed annually for a further 16 years, after which it can be extended by an application to the High Court for a further 5 or 10 years.

5. *International Application Procedure* An application at the British Patent Office will only result in the grant of a British Patent. Until recently an applicant who wanted protection in other countries had to file applications in each country for which a patent was required. This was costly and resulted in the application being examined with varying degrees of thoroughness in each country. Two systems now exist to minimize the need for separate national applications.

a. The *PATENTS CO-OPERATION TREATY* (in operation since 1978) provides for the filing of a single application designating the countries for which the applicant seeks protection. A single search is carried out and the application is then sent to each of the designated countries for separate examination as a national application according to their local laws.

b. The *EUROPEAN PATENT CONVENTION* (in operation since 1978) to which EU member states and some other European countries belong, provides for an application to be filed at the European Patent Office in Munich. The application is searched and examined at the European Patent Office and if the invention satisfies the requirements of the Convention separate national patents are granted for the specified countries.

6. *Patentability* Patents must fulfil the following requirements specified in the *PATENTS ACT 1977*:

a. It must be a patentable invention which is capable of industrial application. The Act does not define what is patentable, instead it lists a number of things that are not patentable inventions, for example:

   i. Discoveries, scientific theories or mathematical methods.

   ii. Literary, dramatic, musical or artistic works.

   iii. Schemes, rules or methods for performing a mental act, playing a game, doing business or programming a computer.

   iv. The presentation of information.

b. *Novelty.* The invention must be new, i.e. it must not have been made available to the public anywhere in the world by written or oral description, by use or in any other way.

c.   *Inventive steps.* An invention involves an inventive step if it is not obvious to a person skilled in the art, having regard to state-of-the-art knowledge.

7. **Employee Inventions** Since most inventions are made by company employees, the question of rights to the invention are important. The Act provides that an invention made in the course of employment shall belong to the employer, but it also establishes a statutory award scheme to compensate employees for inventions made on behalf of their employers. The award will ensure a fair share to the employee having regard to the benefit derived by the employer. Any contract term which diminishes the employee's rights under the Act is void.

8. *Ownership, Assignment and Licensing*

   a.   A patent, or an application for a patent, is personal property, but it is not a chose in action.

   b.   An assignment must be in writing and signed by both parties, otherwise it is void.

   c.   Licensing is a method of developing a patent whereby the patentee gives permission for the sale or manufacture of the patented article, subject to express conditions.

9. *Licences of Right for Drugs* The 1988 Act brings in legislation in respect of 'licences of right' for drugs. The intention is to bring the law in Great Britain into agreement with the laws of nearly all other countries. It was considered in the public interest that there should be the right of free use of inventions for the manufacture of food and medicine. Patents may be taken out for these purposes but the patents would not be used to restrain manufacture of them.

   In the case of a patent for drugs, without waiting for the 3-year period applicable to other patents, a licence could be had by any person interested on such terms as the comptroller thought fit to secure that drugs should be available to the public at the lowest prices consistent with the patentees deriving a reasonable advantage from their patent rights. The applicant for a licence of right of this nature may make his application in the 16th year of the patent.

10. *Infringement*

    a.   There are two questions in relation to infringement:

         i.   Does the scope of the invention as defined in the claims cover the product or process concerned?

         ii.   Is the defendant's conduct prohibited by the Act?

    b.   The Act provides that a person infringes a patent if he does any of the following:

         i.   If the invention is a product, he makes, disposes of, uses or imports the product, or keeps it for disposal or otherwise.

         ii.   If the invention is a process, he uses it or offers it for use, when he knows or should know that there would be an infringement, or if he disposes of, uses, imports or keeps any product obtained by means of that process.

         iii. Supplies means essential for putting an invention into effect to a person not entitled to work the patent, when he knows, or should know, that the means are suitable and that they are intended to be used to put the invention into effect.

    c.   An inventor whose patent is infringed is entitled to an injunction, delivery of the infringing articles and damages, which may be assessed on a loss of profits or royalty basis. He will also be given a 'certificate of contested validity' which entitles him to larger costs in any future infringement action. If the patentee loses, the grant of the patent may be revoked or the specifications may be found not wide enough to cover the defendant's product or process.

The *PATENTS ACT 2004* was passed to assist, particularly small businesses, to enforce patent rights. It enables the Patent Office to provide an independent non-binding opinion on patent validity or alleged infringement thus limiting recourse to litigation. The legislation encourages the out of court settlements of disputes and deters patent owners from making unreasonable allegations of infringement. There is also provision for a European Community patent to be granted with a centralized Community Patent Court with jurisdiction over invalidity and infringement proceedings.

COPYRIGHT

11. **Definition** Copyright protects the independent skill, labour and effort which has been expended in producing work and prevents others from helping themselves to too large a portion of that skill, labour and effort. Unlike a patent, a copyright is not a monopoly, it is a right of protection against copying. Copyright is acquired by bringing a work into existence. There is no requirement of, nor provision for, registration.

12. **Statutory Protection**

    a. *Subsistence of copyright.* Works eligible for copyright protection are put into three groups:

        i. Literary, dramatic, musical or artistic works.

        ii. Sound recordings, films broadcasts or cable programmes.

        iii. Typographical arrangement of published editions.

    A computer programme is treated as literary work.

    b. *Artistic works.* The following are protected:

        i. Paintings, drawings, sculptures, engravings and photographs, *irrespective of artistic quality.*

        ii. Works of architecture, being either buildings or models of buildings.

        iii. Works of artistic craftsmanship, not included in the above categories.

    The phrase 'irrespective of artistic quality' has enabled the courts to hold that engineering production drawings are entitled to copyright.

    c. *Ownership.* The 1988 Act simplifies the previsions regarding ownership of copyright, the only case where the case in a literary, dramatic or musical work does not initially rest in the author is where the work is made by an employee in the course of his employment in which case the employer is the first owner of the copyright unless there is some agreement to the contrary. The Act also introduces a concept of literary, dramatic, musical or artistic work which is computer generated in circumstances in which there is no human author. The author is taken to be the person by whom arrangements necessary for creation of the work are undertaken.

d.   *Duration.* The present term of copyright protection is the life of the creator plus 70 years.

e.   *Right of the copyright owner.* The copyright in a work is the exclusive right to do the following acts in the UK:

    i.   Copy the work. (Copying includes storing in any medium by electronic means.)

    ii.   Issue copies to the public.

    iii.   Perform, show or play the work in public.

    iv.   Broadcast or include in a cable programme service.

    v.   Make an adaptation of the work.

Copyright in the typographical arrangement of a published edition includes not only the right to copy the work but also the right to issue copies to the public.

The 1988 Act introduces the moral rights of an author as follows:

    i.   *Paternity right.* An author of a literary, dramatic, musical or artistic work, or the director of a film has a right to be identified as author or director in certain circumstances.

    ii.   *Right of integrity.* An author has the right not to have his work subjected to derogatory treatment amounting to distortion or mutilation of the work or which is otherwise prejudicial to the honour or reputation of the author or director.

    These two rights subsist throughout the duration of the copyright.

    iii.   *Privacy.* A person who commissions a photograph or film for private or domestic purposes has a right not to have:

    a) Copies issued to the public.

    b) The work exhibited in public.

    c) The work broadcast or included in a cable programme.

An entitled person may waive the above rights.

13.   *Indirect Copying* Copying a product which has been manufactured from drawings amounts to indirectly copying the drawings and is an infringement of copyright.

In *BERSTEIN v SIDNEY MURRAY (1981)* a dress designer saw P's design at an exhibition and later marketed dresses which were a copy of P's both in materials and design. It was held that although the dresses themselves were not protected by copyright D had indirectly copied the sketches made by P.

Contrast *BRITISH LEYLAND v ARMSTRONG PATENTS (1986)* where D declined to obtain a licence from P to produce spare parts for BL cars, but nevertheless produced replacement exhaust pipes by copying the shape and dimensions of the original. P alleged that D had by indirect copying infringed the copyright in P's original drawings of the exhaust system. The High Court and Court of Appeal granted an injunction in favour of P, but the House of Lords reversed this decision. It was held that although exhaust pipes were purely functional articles which were neither patentable nor a registerable design, the replacements produced by D were clearly recognizable as copies of P's drawings in which artistic copyright subsisted. Therefore D had infringed P's copyright but car owners had an inherent right to repair their cars in the most economical way possible and must have access to a free market for spares. P was not entitled to derogate or interfere with that right by asserting their copyright against a person manufacturing parts solely for repair.

Manufacturers have protested that this decision amounts to a 'pirates charter' in that it allows a producer of spares to copy the original design of an article and sell it at a cheaper price than the manufacturer.

14. *Restricted Acts*

   a. The acts restricted by copyright in artistic work are:

      i. Reproducing the work in any material form, including converting a two-dimensional work into a three-dimensional work and vice versa.

      ii. Publishing the work, including television broadcasts.

      There will be no infringement with regard to drawings if the article is not regarded by non-experts as a reproduction.

   b. There is no copyright in a name because of the improbability that a name could amount to an original work.

15. *Infringement*

   a. Infringement occurs when a person, without the consent of the copyright owner, contravenes the rights of the copyright owner. Secondary infringement will occur if:

      i. A person, without permission, transmits a work by means of a telecommunication system if he knows that infringing copies will be made on reception.

      ii. A person supplies a copy of a sound recording or film, knowing or believing that the recipient will make infringing copies.

   b. *Electronic infringement of copyright.* The 1988 Act introduces measures for copyright protection in respect of the latest forms of technology which have an impact on the copyright system.

      Where copies of a protected work are issued to the public in an electronic form which is 'copy protected' any person who makes or trades in, or advertises any device specifically designed to circumvent the copy protection or who publishes information intended to help persons to circumvent it commits an infringement of copyright.

      Copyright is also infringed by a person who dishonestly receives a programme either broadcast or distributed by cable transmitted from the UK with the intention of avoiding payment.

   c. *Remedies for infringement.* The following remedies are available:

      i. Injunction.

      ii. Damages.

      iii. Order for delivery-up.

      iv. Account for profit.

      The 1988 Act makes it a criminal offence if a person knew or had reason to believe that copyright would be infringed in the event of making or dealing with infringing articles.

The TRADE MARKS (OFFENCES AND ENFORCEMENT) ACT 2002 should aid enforcement in that the Act gives police the power to obtain warrants to search and seize property from any business that they believe is using unlicensed software and to subsequently prosecute.

The COPYRIGHT AND RELATED RIGHTS REGULATIONS 2003 have been introduced to help the music and film industries from unauthorized downloading of their works on the Internet. It makes it a criminal offence for those making infringing copies or illicit recordings who communicate them to the public.

16. *Licensing*

   a. The 1988 Act renames the Performing Rights Tribunal – the Copyright Tribunal and gives the Secretary of State additional powers of supervision over, and regulation of, the licensing of right.

   b. The new regime of control will operate where rights are either licensed pursuant to a licensing scheme or licensed by a licensing body. A licensing scheme is defined as a scheme setting out:

      i. The classes of case in which the operator of the scheme is willing to grant copyright licences, and

      ii. The terms on which licences would be granted in those classes.

   c. A licensing body is a society or other organization which has as a main object the negotiation or granting of copyright licences and whose objects include the granting of licences covering works of more than one author.

   d. A copyright licence means a licence to do or authorize the doing of any of the acts restricted by copyright.

   The following disputes may be referred to the Tribunal:

      i. Over the terms of a scheme proposed to be operated by a licensing body.

      ii. Over the terms of a scheme already in operation.

      iii. In respect of a scheme already subject to an order by the tribunal.

      iv. Between a person who claims to be covered by a scheme but complains that the operator of the scheme has either refused a licence or offered one on unreasonable terms.

   The Tribunal's jurisdiction over licences from licensing bodies is with respect to disputes concerning licences proposed, granted or withheld by a licensing body but not pursuant to a licensing scheme, e.g. a dispute between the Performing Rights Society and the BBC would be appropriate in this case.

17. *Performances* The 1988 Act states:

   a. *Persons Protected*. The following persons are protected:

      i. Those who act, sing, deliver, declaim, play in or otherwise perform literary, dramatic, musical or artistic works.

      ii. Those having recording rights in relation to a performance.

   b. *Rights of action*. Performers and persons having recording rights have civil rights of action for damages, an injunction, that illicit recordings be delivered up or the seizure of illicit recordings exposed for sale or hire. The seizure remedy is subject to the safeguards that the police must be given advance notice, only premises with public access may be entered and force may not be used. In addition to civil remedies performers are also protected by penal provisions.

c. *The Copyright Tribunal.* The Tribunal is given a limited jurisdiction with respect to performances, i.e. a person wishing to make a recording from an existing recording may apply to the Tribunal where:

    i.   The identity of the performer cannot be ascertained, or

    ii.   The performer unreasonably withholds consent.

d. *Extent of rights.* The rights last for 50 years from the day when the performance took place.

TRADE MARKS

18. *Definition*

a. A trade mark is a mark used in relation to goods or services so as to indicate a connection in the course of trade between the goods and some person having a right to use the mark.

b. The commercial purpose of a trade mark is to distinguish the goods or services of a company from those of its competitors. Many trade marks indicate quality and induce customers to buy the goods.

c. The legal purpose of a trade mark is to prevent others from using the mark and thus benefiting from the goodwill attached to the mark.

d. Like patents, trade marks constitute 'industrial property'. However, trade marks are concerned with commercial features and sales, rather than the technical features which are crucial to patents. While the life of a patent is limited to 70 years a trade mark can be renewed indefinitely. Another difference is that the cost of registering, renewing and enforcing trade mark rights is much less expensive than for patents.

e. Trade marks are defined in the *TRADE MARKS ACT 1994*, which was passed to implement the EU directive on trade marks. A trade mark is defined as '*Any sign capable of being represented graphically which is capable of distinguishing goods or services of one undertaking from those of another.*' Trade marks can consist of words (including personal names), designs, letters, numerals or the shape of goods or their packaging.

In *NESTLE SA'S TRADE MARK APPLICATION (HAVE A BREAK) (2003)* the High Court ruled that registration of these words would not be granted because the phrase was not distinctive.

In ***BECKHAM V PETERBOROUGH FOOTBALL CLUB (2003)*** Victoria Beckham failed to get an injunction to restrain the football club from using the word 'Posh' a registered trade mark. The term had been used by the club for a number of years. The Court found that the use of the term in the particular context would not lead to any public confusion.

f. The shape of goods can be a trade mark, however there is no protection if the shape:

    i.   Results from the shape of the goods.

    ii.   Is necessary to obtain a technical result, or

    iii.   Adds substantial value to the goods.

g. Smells, colours and sounds can be protected if they can be represented graphically. Geographic names can be protected where the mark acquires a distinctive character.

In **SHIELD MARK BV V KIST (2004)** a mark consisting of the first five notes of a Beethoven composition were held to be capable of being the subject of a trade mark.

h. The 1994 Act also introduces *collective marks* which are marks which can be used by anyone who is a member of a certain association owning a mark.

19. *Registration* Registration at the Trade Mark Registry confers a statutory monopoly on the use of the mark and a registered owner may sue for infringement. The Registry has issued guidelines on the treatment of Internet domain names. Signs such as: http://, www., co., gov., org. and words such as 'web' and 'net' are not distinctive enough to stand as trade marks for goods and services offered via the Internet. Trade mark examiners will examine a domain name and decode whether it has a sufficient distinctive element to be considered as a trade mark in the electronic information services class or in the software class.

20. *Infringement*

a. Infringement occurs when any person, without permission, uses in the course of a trade, a mark identical to the registered mark or so similar as to be likely to deceive or cause confusion. Infringement also occurs if a person compares his goods with those of a trade mark owner and refers to the latter's goods by the trade mark, for example a comparative price list setting out the trader's brand and comparing it with a famous name product.

In **ARSENAL FOOTBALL CLUB PLC V REED (2003)** the case arose out of two registered trade marks, the words, 'Arsenal' and 'Arsenal Gunners' along with its cannon and shield emblems. The marks were used on a wide variety of goods. Mr Reed sold unofficial Arsenal souvenirs outside the club's ground. Mr Reed had a notice by his stall indicating that his products were not official club merchandise. Upon referral to the ECJ the court ruled that the function of a trade mark is to avoid confusion as to the origin of goods and that the disclaimer did not remove the confusion. The Court of Appeal ruled that on the facts, Mr Reed was infringing the Arsenal trade mark in spite of his disclaimer.

b. When considering whether marks are similar the idea conveyed by the mark must be looked at as well as any physical similarity.

In **TAW v NOTEK (1951)** P used a drawing of a car in the shape of a cat's body with the eyes as headlamps as their trade mark. D used the head of a cat with the eyes as car headlamps. It was held that although the drawings were visually dissimilar the idea was the same, so P's trade mark had been infringed.

c. When infringement occurs the plaintiff is entitled to an injunction and damages on an account of profits and to an order for destruction or modification of the offending goods.

d. Where goods are sold that infringe a trade mark title to those goods will not pass and the seller will be in breach of the implied condition in *S.12 SALE OF GOODS ACT 1979.*

21. *The Community Trade mark* This is a single trade mark right which extends throughout the EU. It is available to any member of the EU or person domiciled in a EU country. It may consist of any distinctive sign capable of being represented graphically. Applications

can be made to the UK Registry in London or directly to the CTM office in Spain, known as the Office for Harmonisation in the Internal Market.

PASSING-OFF

22. ***Definition*** Passing-off is a tort. X will commit a tort, against Y if he passes off his goods or business as those of Y. Y need not prove that X acted intentionally, or with intent to deceive. Nor does he have to prove that anyone was actually deceived, if deception was likely. There is also no requirement for Y to prove damage.

In ***ASPREY & GARRARD LTD V WRA (GUNS) LTD (2002)*** the respondent, an ex-employee of the claimant, set up a rival company using his own name – William R. Asprey Esq. The High Court granted an injunction restraining the use of his own name for passing-off and infringement of trade mark. The use of one's own name is an exception to the passing-off rules and must not, as it did here, cause confusion.

23. ***Types of Passing-Off***

a. Passing-off is usually committed by imitating the appearance of the claimant's goods, or by selling them under the same or a similar name. If the name used by the claimant merely describes his goods then generally no action will lie. However, it is possible for a name that was originally only descriptive to come to signify goods produced by the claimant It is also possible for a word to lose its trade meaning and become merely descriptive.

b. The tort may be committed by applying the name of the locality in which the claimant produces goods to the respondent's goods.

In ***BOLLINGER v COSTA BRAVA WINE CO (1961)*** P, who manufactured champagne, brought an action against D who were describing their product as 'Spanish champagne'. It was held that the word 'champagne' was generally regarded as referring exclusively to wine produced in the Champagne region of France and even with the prefix 'Spanish' purchasers could be misled. An injunction was granted to prevent D using the name.

c. A person may usually carry on business under his own name, unless he does so fraudulently. But he must not mark his goods with a name (even his own name) if this will have the effect of passing-off those goods as goods of another.

d. Passing-off may be committed by using another person's name or trade name.

In ***HINES v WINNICK (1947)*** P broadcast with a band called 'Dr Crock and the Crackpots'. After he left the programme D gave the same name to a replacement band. It was held that the public were likely to be misled and an injunction was granted.

e. It is not necessary for the defendant's trade to be identical to that of the plaintiff if there is sufficient similarity to mislead the public.

In ***HARRODS LTD v R. HARRODS LTD (1923)*** the famous Knightsbridge store successfully prevented a money-lending company from trading under the Harrods name. Although the nature of their business was different there was sufficient likelihood that the public would assume that they were connected.

In contrast there have been many cases where a claimant has failed to prevent the use of a similar name because the likelihood of confusion or loss of business did not exist. For example, the owners of 'Wombles' books and television programmes could not prevent a company from leasing 'Wombles' rubbish skips and a Mr Albert Edward Hall was allowed to continue to use the name the 'Albert Hall Orchestra' despite an objection from the proprietor of the Royal Albert Hall.

f. False advertising is not generally passing-off, but it may be in exceptional circumstances.

In *MASSON SEELEY v EMBOSSOTYPE MANUFACTURING (1924)* D copied P's catalogue in such a way that the public would believe that the goods offered were P's goods. D's goods were, however, inferior to P's goods. It was held that this was passing-off.

'Switch selling' does not amount to passing-off.

In *RIMA ELECTRIC v ROLLS RAZOR (1965)* D advertised so as to lead the public to believe that they could buy 'Magicair' hairdryers for 5 guineas. However, they had no Magicair hairdryers so they offered other makes to enquirers. It was held that this was not passing-off.

g. *Reverse passing-off.* Usually passing-off occurs when the defendant holds out his goods as being those of the plaintiff. However, passing-off may also occur when the respondent holds out the claimant's goods as being his own, hence the 'reverse' passing-off.

In *BRISTOL CONSERVATORIES v CONSERVATORIES CUSTOM BUILT (1989)* D showed prospective customers photographs of P's ornamental conservatories, which they held out as being examples of their own goods and workmanship. If the customer placed an order, he would then be supplied with a conservatory manufactured by D. In this case the Court of Appeal was concerned only with D's motion to strike out P's statement of claim as disclosing no reasonable cause of action. However, on the facts as alleged the Court held that there was a triable issue.

24. *Remedies* The plaintiff may obtain an injunction and/or damages. Damages will reflect lost profit (if any) plus loss of goodwill and reputation.

SELF TEST QUESTIONS

Self Test Questions No. 33 (for Answers see Appendix 1):

1 What is a design right?

2 Explain the definition and essential elements of: patents, copyright and trade marks, and what has to be shown to establish infringement.

3 What is 'passing-off'?

DATA PROTECTION

36

Learning Outcomes At the end of this chapter you should be able to:

● For purposes of applying the *DATA PROTECTION ACT 1998*:

– define the meaning of 'data'

– identify 'persons' covered by the *Act* and the rights conferred on individuals

– explain the key principles underpinning the *Act*

– understand the application of the *Act* to employees and the impact of the *HUMAN RIGHTS ACT 1998*

– explain the law regarding 'computer misuse'.

1. The *DATA PROTECTION ACT 1998* builds upon previous legislation to give rights to individuals whose 'personal data' are stored on computers and certain manual files.

2. *Data Covered* The Act defines 'data' as information which is:

   a. Being processed by means of equipment operating automatically in response to instructions given for that purpose.

   b. Is recorded with the intention that it should be processed by means of such equipment.

   c. Is recorded as part of a relevant filing system or with the intention that it should form part of a relevant filing system, or

    d.   Though not falling within a, b, or c, forms part of an accessible health, educational or publicly accessible record.

3. ***Persons*** The Act defines specific persons associated with regulated data; these are: a *data controller* who is a person who determines the manner and purpose for which personal data are to be processed; a *data processor* who is any person (other than an employee of the data controller) who processes the data on behalf of the data controller; a *data subject* is an individual who is the subject of personal data.

    Personal data have to relate to a living individual identifiable from the data already in the possession of the data controller or from data likely to come into his possession. In ***DOUGLAS v HELLO! LTD (2003)*** when a magazine published unauthorized wedding photos it was held that the photos were *personal data* and the magazine a *data controller* and that their publication was a breach of the Act in causing damage and distress to the claimants (see Chapter 51.2.i.)

    The Data Protection Registrar is renamed the Data Protection Commissioner and the process of 'registration' with the Commissioner is renamed 'notification'.

4. ***Rights Conferred*** Under *S.7* of the Act individuals have the right of access to their personal data. A data subject has the right to be told whether personal data are being processed by, or on behalf of, a data controller and of the nature of such data, the purpose for which it is being processed, and those to whom it will be disclosed. In addition an individual is entitled to a copy of any personal data and information the data controller has as to the source of that data. The obligation of a data controller to supply the above is conditional upon a request being made in writing by the data subject with payment of a fee. An individual has the right to instruct a data controller, upon giving reasonable notice, to cease processing his personal data for purposes of direct marketing.

    Where a decision, which will significantly affect an individual, is to be made by a data controller based solely upon personal data being processed automatically, an individual has the right to prevent such a decision being taken by the giving of notice in writing; further, even where the data subject serves no such notice, a data controller, in such circumstances, must as soon as is reasonably practicable, inform the data subject that a decision was made on that basis. The individual then has 21 days to require the data controller to reconsider the decision and the data controller has 21 days in which to notify the individual of the steps taken to comply with the request.

5. ***Rights*** A data subject may apply to a court to have inaccurate personal data rectified, blocked, erased or destroyed. A data controller who wishes to process personal data must first make a notification to the Commissioner to be included on the register.

6. ***Data Protection Principles*** The Act lays down a number of principles which will govern personal data processing, these are that such data be:

    a.   Processed fairly and lawfully.

    b.   Obtained only for lawful purposes.

    c.   Adequate, relevant and not excessive in relation to the purpose for which it is to be processed.

    d.   Accurate and kept up-to-date.

    e.   Not kept for longer than is necessary for the stated purpose.

    f.   Processed in accordance with the rights given under the Act to data subjects.

g.   Subject to measures of security to prevent unauthorized or unlawful processing, accidental loss, destruction or damage; not transferred to a country or territory outside of the European Economic Area unless that country or territory ensures an adequate level of protection for the rights and freedoms of data subjects.

7. ***Sensitive Data*** Certain data are termed 'sensitive personal data'; this is defined as information relating to a person's racial or ethnic origin; political or religious beliefs; membership of a trade union; physical or mental health or condition; sexual life; alleged commission or commission of any offence or proceedings relating to such an offence. Here, when assessing compliance with principle a. above i.e. that data be processed fairly and lawfully, certain specific conditions are stated as being relevant, these are whether:

a.   The data subject has given explicit consent to the processing of his/her personal data.

b.   The processing was necessary in order for the data controller to perform a right or obligation imposed on him in connection with employment.

c.   The processing is necessary to protect the vital interest of the data subject.

d.   The processing is carried out in the legitimate course of a non-profit-making body's activities; the information has been made public as a result of a deliberate act of the data subject.

e.   Processing was necessary for the purposes of legal proceedings or the administration of justice; processing is necessary for medical purposes and is undertaken by a health professional or some other person who owes a duty of confidentiality equivalent to that of a health professional; in the field of racial or ethnic origin processing is necessary to ensure that unequal treatment in these areas does not occur; processing is necessary for purposes set out by the Secretary of State.

There are exemptions from the data protection principles, data protection rights and the need to register in relation to: national security; crime and taxation; health education and social work; journalism, literature or art; and domestic purposes.

8. ***Monitoring of Employee Communications*** Article 8 of the *HUMAN RIGHTS ACT 1998* (see Chapter 4.29), giving the right to privacy, has raised particular concerns for employers. In ***HALFORD V UNITED KINGDOM (1997)*** complaints by an Assistant Chief Constable that her telephone calls made from the office were monitored in contravention of Article 8 were upheld. The Government argued that telephone conversations at work fell outside of the Convention and that employers should in principle be able to monitor calls made by employees on telephones owned by the employer. The European Court of Human Rights did not accept this argument and stated that an employee had a reasonable expectation of privacy. This raises the question of the extent to which employers can monitor employee's e-mails and Internet access. Is there any reason why e-mails should be treated differently from telephone calls giving employees the right to a reasonable expectation of privacy? *S.1* of the *REGULATION OF INVESTIGATORY POWERS ACT 2000* makes it unlawful for any person, without lawful authority, to intentionally intercept a communication in the course of its transmission by way of a public or private telecommunications system. However, it will be lawful where the interceptor believes that both parties have agreed to such monitoring. Also the Act gives powers to the Secretary of State to introduce regulations where it is felt to be a reasonable and legitimate practice for the purpose of carrying on any business. Obvious instances of this will be where the employer is required to monitor communications for purposes of national security or ensuring compliance with regulatory or self-regulatory practices or to detect or prevent crime.

9. *Computer Misuse* The *COMPUTER MISUSE ACT 1990* creates three criminal offences to deal with the misuse of computers. These are:

a. *Unauthorized access to computer material.* This makes it an offence to perform any function with the intention of gaining unauthorized access to programmes or data held on a computer. This is aimed at *hackers* both internal and external to an organization. Internal *hacking* occurs where a person within an organization knowingly exceeds the limits of their authority in order to gain unauthorized computer access. External *hacking* is where a person outside of an organization, using public telecommunications systems, seeks to gain unauthorized computer access. The penalty is a maximum of 6-months imprisonment, or a fine not exceeding £5000.

b. *Unauthorized access to commit or facilitate the commission of an offence.* The offence committed or facilitated is one where the penalty is fixed by statute or where a maximum sentence could be 5 years or more imprisonment; examples of such offences might be serious fraud, theft or blackmail, for instance, an unauthorized transferring of funds from the account of an individual. The maximum penalty for this offence is 5-years imprisonment or an unlimited fine.

c. *Unauthorized modification of computer material.* This offence is committed where an individual seeks to intentionally modify the contents of a computer in order to impair a computer's operation or hinder access to its data. This offence would cover such acts as introducing computer viruses. Here the maximum penalty is 5-years imprisonment or an unlimited fine.

The Act also allows a UK court to extradite an offender from the UK to another country for trial as well as hear offences committed outside of the UK where there is a connection between the activities of the offender and the UK.

10. *Enforcement* Where the Commissioner can show reasonable grounds for believing that a data controller has or is about to contravene any data protection principles or commit or has committed an offence under the Act, he or she may apply to a circuit judge for a search warrant. Main offences created under the Act are:

a. Failure to specify changes in contravention of a notice to do so by the Commissioner.

b. Deliberately or recklessly making a false statement while purporting to comply with an enforcement notice.

c. Unlawfully obtaining, selling or offering to sell personal data.

11. *Freedom of Information Act 2000* The Act requires that public authorities have in place an approved publication scheme. The scheme identifies information available from the authority and how it can be obtained. Individuals can request this and other information which must be made available within 20 days, subject to certain exemptions such as information relating to national security and information given in confidence. There is an approved fee payable. Public authorities is a wide term which covers, central and local government, police and prosecution services, the health service and education which includes colleges and universities. There is an appointed Commissioner to deal with complaints. He has the power to issue notices:

a. A *decision notice*; requiring that a public authority responds as to whether a request has been dealt with.

b. An *information notice*; requiring a public authority to provide specified information.

c. An *enforcement notice*; requiring a public authority to provide the information requested.

SELF TEST QUESTIONS

Self Test Questions No. 34 (for Answers see Appendix 1):

1 Under the *DATA PROTECTION ACT 1998*; explain how each of the following terms are defined:

data

rights conferred

the data protection principles.

2 What are the problems for an employer seeking to monitor computer misuse under the Act?

3 What is 'computer misuse' under the *COMPUTER MISUSE ACT 1990*?

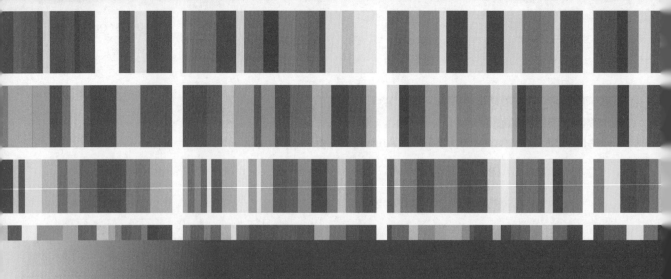

37 REGULATORY BODIES

Learning Outcomes At the end of this chapter you should be able to:

- Outline the application of the *FINANCIAL SERVICES AND MARKETS ACT 2000* to financial regulation.

- Explain the nature and function of the Securities and Investments Board.

- Appreciate financial self-regulation.

- Explain the nature of the Stock Exchange.

- Show an understanding of the offences of *fraud* and *malpractice* as defined in the *FRAUD ACT 2006*.

THE FINANCIAL SERVICES AND MARKETS ACT 2000

1. *Historical Context*

   a. Prior to statutory intervention (initially through the *FINANCIAL SERVICES ACT 1986*) the regulation of financial services was on a piecemeal basis, combining government measures with a large element of self-regulation. Self-regulation was provided by the Stock Exchange, and various accountancy, legal and other professional bodies which regulated the conduct of their own members.

b.   The rapidly changing markets of the 70s and 80s opened up loopholes in the regulatory system. In particular there was no regulation of investment management or of advice in areas other than securities. Also an increasing number of private investors were becoming involved in high risk investments, that were previously the preserve of professional investors.

c.   The *FINANCIAL SERVICES and MARKETS ACT 2000* gives authority to regulate financial services to the Financial Services Authority (FSA), now. The Act has wide effect, bringing sole practitioners and substantial investment firms within one framework. The guiding principle is basically one of self-regulation within a statutory framework. The Act is largely concerned with protecting the private investor by trying to ensure that he is not cheated or misled. It cannot, of course, provide a remedy if he simply makes a poor investment decision.

2. *Coverage*

a.   One of the main provisions allowed for the establishment of an agency to which most of the powers under the Act could be delegated This is called the Securities and Investments Board (SIB). However, not all of the regulatory powers in the Act have been transferred to the SIB. Excluded from its responsibilities are provisions concerning:

i.   Listing requirements for public issues.

ii.   Takeovers and mergers.

iii. Insider dealing investigation and prosecution (see 18. below).

b.   The regulatory structure for investment business is headed by the SIB, which is assisted by several self-regulating organizations (SROs) and recognized professional bodies (RPBs). These must be recognized by the SIB, on the basis that their methods of regulating their members provide a sufficient level of investor protection.

c.   In some cases the FSA confers authority on firms to carry out investment business, although those firms are responsible to another regulator for their mainstream business. For example:

i.   Banks continue to be supervised by the Bank of England so far as their banking business is concerned.

ii.   Insurance companies are regulated by the Department for Business Innovation & Skills (DTI), except for the marketing of life assurance and unit trusts.

iii. Building societies are regulated under the FSA for investment business, but their traditional lending and borrowing activities are regulated by the Building Societies Commission.

3. *Investments*

a.   The basic principle underlying the regulatory framework is that no one may carry on an investment business unless they are either authorized or exempt. Any person in contravention will have committed a criminal offence and any investment agreement entered into will be unenforceable The Act provides detailed definitions of 'investments' and 'investment business' which are briefly summarized below.

b.   *Investments*. This is defined very widely to cover any right, asset or interest in the following categories:

    i.   Company shares, including shares of foreign companies.

    ii.   Debentures, and any other instrument creating or acknowledging indebtedness, including cheques, bills of exchange, bankers drafts and bank notes.

    iii.   Government, local authority or other public authority securities.

    iv.   Warrants or other instruments entitling the holder to subscribe for investments in the above categories. Warrants give the holder the right to purchase or subscribe for a security at a predetermined price on one or more of a number of future dates.

    v.   Certificates or other instruments conferring rights to acquire, dispose of, underwrite or convert investments. For example, a depository receipt permitting trading in a security, where the security does not fulfil the requirements for listing on the Stock Exchange.

    vi.   Units in collective investments schemes, for example units in unit trusts.

    vii.   Options to acquire or dispose of certain investments, for example options on currencies, gold or silver. Options give the holder a right to buy (a call option) or sell (a put option) the investment at a fixed price. The option may normally be exercised at any time before the maturity date.

    viii.   Futures for investment purposes. These are defined as rights under a contract for the sale of a commodity, or of property, under which delivery is to be made at a future date and at a price agreed when the contract is made. Futures are excluded from regulation if the contract is made for commercial rather than investment purposes.

    ix.   Contract for differences. These are contracts designed to secure a profit, or avoid a loss, by reference to fluctuations in the value of property, any description in an index, or any other factor.

  c.   *Investment Business.* This includes:

    i.   Dealing in investments i.e. buying, selling, subscribing for or underwriting investments either as principal or as agent.

    ii.   Arranging deals in investments.

    iii.   Managing investments.

    iv.   Advising on investments. Giving advice about the tax or legal consequences of an investment is excluded.

    v.   Establishing, operating or winding up a collective investment scheme, including acting as a trustee of a unit trust scheme.

Certain activities which would otherwise constitute investment business are specifically excluded for example:

    i.   Dealing as principal.

    ii.   Arranging an employee's share scheme.

    iii.   Supplying a financial package in connection with a sale of goods or a supply of services.

    iv.   The sale of a private company. This exemption is not restricted to the sale of the whole of the company. The shares sold may carry as little as 75% of the voting rights.

v.   Trustees and personal representatives are not carrying on an investment business in respect of investments which they manage as a trustee or personal representative unless they hold themselves out as offering investment management services or receive additional remuneration for such services in addition to remuneration as a trustee.

vi. Advice given in the course of a profession which is not investment business, provided the advice is a necessary part of other advice or services given in the course of that profession.

vii. Newspapers. Advice in financial columns of newspapers and other periodicals is excluded.

THE SECURITIES AND INVESTMENTS BOARD

4. *Introduction*

a.   As seen (2. above) The Securities and Investments Board (SIB) under the *FINANCIAL SERVICES AND MARKETS ACT 2000* is the initial regulatory body for financial services.

b.   The SIB occupies an unusual constitutional position. It is a private company limited by guarantee, financed entirely by the investment industry. Although it is not a government body it has delegated power to make rules which have legislative effect.

c.   The SIB reports annually to the Chancellor of the Exchequer, who in turn lays its report before Parliament. The SIB's authority can be removed by Parliament on a proposal from the Chancellor. Individual members may be dismissed by the Secretary of State.

d.   The SIB consists of practitioners from a wide variety of investment activities, together with independent lay members representing the users of financial services and public at large. It has a full-time executive chairman. Board members are appointed jointly by the Treasury and the Governor of the Bank of England.

5. *Authorized Investment Businesses*

a.   The main aim of the SIB is to achieve a high level of investor protection by ensuring that anyone providing any form of investment service, including those who deal in or advise on investments, meet standards of honesty, competence and solvency. Thus investment businesses, unless they fall within very limited exempt categories, must gain authorization from the SIB or from one of the other regulatory bodies set up under the Act. In order to be granted the necessary authorization a firm must satisfy its regulatory body that it is 'fit and proper' to carry on investment business. The test of this includes consideration of its financial resources, the previous record of its officers, and their level of experience and competence. The SIB maintains a list of authorized firms. This is called the central register.

b.   It is a criminal offence to carry on investment business without authorization, and the SIB can prosecute anyone who has broken this rule. The maximum penalty is 2 years imprisonment and/or an unlimited fine. It can also seek an injunction to stop such firms trading and/or a court order to restore clients' money. The SIB also has formal powers in investigation, with criminal sanctions in the event of obstruction. It can disqualify individuals from employment in the investment industry.

c. If a person, such as a solicitor or accountant is '*knowingly concerned*' with another person's (the contravener) breaches of the FSA then, in default of payment by the contravener, the person concerned may be liable to repay the investor the purchase price of the shares comprised in the investment transaction.

In ***SECURITIES AND INVESTMENTS BOARD v PANTELL S.A. (1992)*** D carried on unauthorized investment business in the UK, selling unmarketable and worthless shares in a Utah Corporation. Their solicitors were joined in the action because it was alleged that they had knowledge of their client's contravention of the Act because they operated the company's bank account, assisted in the distribution of advertisements and paid cheques for UK investors into the company's account. The Court of Appeal held that the solicitors were '*knowingly concerned*' in the contravener's breaches of the Act and were liable to repay investors the price of their shares.

6. *The Central Register*

a. Before parting with money on the basis of investment advice it is prudent to check that the adviser is legitimately carrying on investment business and is subject to the rules of one of the regulatory bodies.

b. The central register is a computerized database of investment firms. It also has an introductory section describing the regulatory system. A person consulting the register will be able to find out:

i. The name or trading name, address and telephone number of the firm's main place of business.

ii. The firm's authorization status. This is important since only investors who do business with authorized firms are eligible to make a claim on the investors' compensation fund. Also, as previously stated, any firm carrying on investment business without authorization is committing a criminal offence.

iii. Whether the firm is regulated by a Self-Regulating Organization, or a Recognized Professional Body, or the SIB itself. The regulatory body is responsible for monitoring the firm's continuing financial soundness and the way in which it handles its customers' business. It is the organization that should be contacted if any investor has a problem that cannot be resolved with the firm itself.

iv. Whether the firm can handle clients' money. Some firms are only authorized to give advice, in which case any investment cheques would need to be made out to the firm running the investment scheme, not the financial adviser.

v. The type of investment business which the firm is permitted to engage in. Firms must be authorized specifically for each type of investment business, for example business enterprise scheme management, discretionary portfolio management or options and warrants activities.

vi. Any warning messages, for example that the firm is in liquidation or suspended as a result of disciplinary action.

c. The public may access the central register:

i. By writing to the SIB, whose staff will then send the relevant information, or by telephoning the SIB, who will then pursue the individual inquiry free of charge. A member of the public may also visit the SIB and access the register personally, without charge and without the need for an appointment.

ii.   By asking a financial adviser who has direct online access to the register for a print-out of his entry in the register.

iii.   By accessing the public online service available to subscribers to Prestel or Telecom Gold. In some areas this will be available via libraries or the Citizens Advice Bureau.

7. *Rules for Regulation of Investment Businesses*

a.   In order to have a regulatory regime which encourages healthy competitive markets and enjoys the confidence of both users and practitioners, it is necessary to have rules to raise standards, maintain proper financial management and punish malpractice.

b.   These rules need to be sufficiently flexible to react to changes in the various markets. The SIB therefore has a three-tier rule structure consisting of:

i.   Core rules which have to be incorporated into the rule books of each self-regulating organization.

ii.   Rules written by each SRO for their particular members, and

iii.   Guidance notes for the interpretation of the rules.

c.   The most important rules are as follows:

i.   Investment businesses must act in the best interests of the client and must therefore do their best to make sure that they are aware of that client's circumstances. Firms must subordinate their own interests to those of the client.

ii.   Firms must comply with advertising requirements, including requirements to warn investors about the volatility or the marketability of the advertised investment.

iii.   Firms must disclose information about fees, commissions or other remuneration. If the firm manages a portfolio on behalf of the client, it must periodically send details of investment performance.

iv.   There must be separation of the status of the salesman and adviser, so that the client knows whether he is dealing with a representative tied to one company's range of products, or an independent intermediary acting as an agent of the client and advising on the full range of available investments.

v.   Investment firms must keep their money separate from the client's money.

vi.   Firms must set out the basis of their relationship with a private client in a customer agreement letter, setting out the functions or services the firm is to provide, its responsibilities and its charges.

vii.   Unsolicited visits and telephone calls to sell investments are generally prohibited. The main exceptions are calls relating to life assurance and unit trusts. However, where such a call results in a sale, the customer will have a 14-day 'cooling off period' during which the investment can be cancelled.

viii.   Firms must adhere to a proper complaints procedure, fully investigating and dealing with all client complaints and keeping records of the investigation.

ix.   All published recommendations, must be fair and not misleading, must provide appropriate information about foreseeable risks, and any predictions or forecasts must be reasonably justified.

8. *Self-Regulating Organizations* There are four SROs. Each will make rules for their members and issue guidance notes as to their interpretation. If their rules are broken they can issue warnings and reprimands or they can fine, suspend or withdraw authorization from their members. The four SROs are:

a. *The Securities and Futures Authority Limited.* SFA member firms carry on business in connection with dealing and arranging deals in for example shares, debentures, government securities, futures, options, foreign currency and commodities. They may also advise corporate finance customers and arrange deals and manage portfolios for them.

b. *Investment Management Regulatory Organization.* IMRO member firms are engaged in:

   i. The management and operation of collective investment schemes, for example authorized unit trusts.

   ii. Selling and advising on transactions in unit trusts.

   iii. Acting as a trustee of collective investment schemes.

   iv. Arranging deals in investments related to business expansion scheme legislation.

   v. In-house pension fund management and acting as pension fund trustees.

   vi. Investment advice (other than corporate finance advice) to institutional or other corporate customers.

c. *Financial Intermediaries, Managers and Brokers Regulatory Association.* FIMBRA member firms mainly advise on and arrange deals in life assurance, pensions and unit trusts. They give advice on a wide range of investments, for example life assurance shares, debentures and gilts and act as private portfolio managers.

d. *Life Assurance and Unit Trust Regulatory Organization.* LAUTRO member firms are normally insurance companies and friendly societies engaged in the retail marketing of life assurance. They may operate collective investment schemes and engage in the retail marketing of units in such schemes.

e. A review of retail regulation in March 1992 recommended that a new SRO be created to regulate investment business done with the private investor. This will be known as the *Personal Investment Authority (PIA)*. Its scope will include activities currently regulated by FIMBRA and LAUTRO.

9. *Recognized Professional Bodies*

a. Professional advisers such as accountants and solicitors provide an important source of investment advice and other investment services such as insurance broking, although this is not the main part of their activities. The system of regulation is built on the existing structure of monitoring and disciplinary arrangements that the main professional bodies already have, subject to a provision that this must provide adequate investor protection. A professional body which is recognized by the SIB will be able to issue a certificate to its members which will enable them to carry on investment business of the kind regulated by the body, without having to seek further authorization. In keeping with the idea of limited involvement of professional firms in investment business, the Act requires the professional body to have rules imposing acceptable limits on the *kind* of investment business carried on by certified persons and the circumstances in which they may carry on such business. The *scale* of such business remains a matter of judgement for the RPB, but it is intended that it is limited to business incidental to the practice of the profession. The rules of the RPB will prohibit a certified person from carrying on investment business outside those limits, unless he has separate authorization through registration with the SIB, or separate membership of an SRO. Members of professional bodies which are not RPBs must belong to an SRO, or be regulated directly by the SIB, if they carry on investment business.

b. There are nine RPBs:

    i. Chartered Association of Certified Accountants (ACCA).

    ii. Institute of Actuaries.

    iii. Institute of Chartered Accountants in England and Wales (ICAEW).

    iv. Institute of Chartered Accountants in Ireland.

    v. Institute of Chartered Accountants in Scotland.

    vi. Insurance Brokers' Registration Council (IBRC).

    vii. Law Society.

    viii. Law Society of Northern Ireland.

    ix. Law Society of Scotland.

10. *Recognized Investment Exchanges*

a. Persons running a market or exchange will fall within the definition of carrying on an investment business and will therefore need to be authorized. An RIE will provide facilities for effecting transactions in investments, although it will not be authorized for any other type of investment business. Recognition means that the exchange (but not its members) is exempt from the requirement of authorization as an investment business. Membership of an RIE is not therefore an alternative method of obtaining authorization.

b. To obtain recognition an RIE must satisfy the SIB that it meets certain basic requirements including:

    i. Sufficient financial resources to perform its functions.

    ii. Rules and practices to ensure the orderly conduct of business and afford proper protection to investors.

    iii. Dealings limited to investments in which there is a proper and reasonably liquid market.

    iv. Satisfactory arrangements for recording transactions.

    v. Effective monitoring and enforcement of rules.

    vi. Arrangements for the investigation of complaints.

    vii. Proper arrangements for the clearing and performance of contracts.

c. RIEs include:

    i. The Stock Exchange.

    ii. The London Commodities Exchange.

      iii. London International Financial Futures Exchange (LIFFE).

      iv. The London Metal Exchange.

11. *Investors Compensation Scheme*

  a. The investor protection framework cannot take the risk out of capital investment. No compensation is payable if, for example, the investment falls in value because of a fall in the market, or because an individual company collapses, or because inflation erodes the real value of the return or an investment. Compensation is only potentially available in the event of fraud or failure of the investment firm to which the investor has entrusted money.

  b. The compensation scheme may be able to help if the following conditions are satisfied:

      i. The claimant is a private investor.

      ii. The investment firm is fully authorized.

      iii. The firm cannot pay out investors' claims.

      iv. The firm owes the claimant money, or is holding shares or other investments on behalf of the claimant.

      v. The claim arises out of business regulated by the FSA.

  c. The compensation scheme is not available if:

      i. The investment firm has gone into liquidation, but was not in breach of its rules, or the law, or

      ii. The investment firm is still in business. In this case if money has been lost through mismanagement or negligent advice, the claimant will have to take up the case with the firm's regulatory body.

  d. The scheme is the responsibility of the SIB and is run on a day-to-day basis by a separate management company. The directors include representatives of the investing public and of the regulatory organizations.

FINANCIAL SELF-REGULATION

12. *The Financial Reporting Council*

  a. *Introduction*

    The Financial Reporting Council was established in 1990, following the Dearing Report i.e the report of the Review Committee on Accounting Standards. Although the FRC has the support of government it is not government controlled, but is part of the private sector process of self-regulation. This is reflected in its constitution, membership and financing. Funds are provided approximately one-third by the Department of Trade and Industry, one-third from the Consultative Committee of Accountancy Bodies and one-third from the London Stock Exchange and the banking and investment communities. The FRC is a company limited by guarantee. It has a chairman and three deputy chairmen appointed by the Secretary of State for Trade and Industry and the Governor of the Bank of England acting jointly. Council members are appointed by the chairman and deputies and include representatives from the accountancy profession, city institutions (including the Stock Exchange) and commerce generally. The Council will normally meet three times a year.

b. The main purposes of the FRC are:

    i. To provide support to its operational subsidiary bodies, the Accounting Standards Board and the Financial Reporting Review Panel.

    ii. To promote good financial reporting, from time to time making public reports on reporting standards.

    iii. To make representations to government on the current working of legislation and on any desirable developments.

    iv. To provide guidance to the Accounting Standards Board on work programmes and broad policy issues.

    v. To ensure that new arrangements are conducted with efficiency and economy and that they are adequately funded.

The Council's constitution provides for it to publish an annual report reviewing the state of financial reporting and making known the views of the Council on accounting standards and practice.

13. *The Accounting Standards Board*

a. Like the FRC, the Accounting Standards Board is a company limited by guarantee. It is a subsidiary of the FRC which acts as its sole director.

b. Its role is to make, amend and withdraw accounting standards. In doing this it will focus, so far as possible, on general principles rather than the prescription of highly detailed rules. The ASB is an autonomous body, that does not need outside approval for its actions. However, in practice it consults widely on all its proposals. Thus for all new proposals there is a formal exposure draft stage, and any comments received are normally placed on public record.

c. The ASB has a sub-committee called 'the Urgent Issues Task Force'. This assists the board where an accounting standard or Companies Act provision exists, but where unsatisfactory or conflicting interpretations have developed. It also advises on significant developments in accounting and financial reporting where no legal provision or accounting standard exists at present. The Urgent Issues Task Force also consults widely, for example by regularly circulating information sheets to approximately 3000 people, including the finance directors of all listed companies.

d. Membership of the ASB is limited to a maximum of 10. They are appointed by an appointments committee consisting of the FRC chairman and deputy chairmen, plus three council members. A majority of six out of nine (or seven out of ten) is required for any decision to adopt, revise or withdraw an accounting standard.

14. *The Financial Reporting Review Panel*

a. Like the ASB, the FRRP is a company limited by guarantee and a subsidiary of the FRC which acts as its sole director. It is autonomous in carrying out its functions, needing neither outside approval nor approval from the FRC.

b. The role of the Panel is to examine departures for the accounting requirements of the Companies Act 1985 (as amended by the Companies Act 2006) and if necessary to seek a court order to remedy them.

c. By agreement with the DTI the work of the FRRP is limited to public and large private companies, the DTI dealing with all other cases.

d. The FRRP does not scrutinize all company accounts falling within its brief. Instead it acts on matters drawn to its attention, either directly or indirectly. Its main concern is to examine material departures from accounting standards with a view to assessing whether the accounts nevertheless meet the statutory requirement to give a true and fair view. A material departure from an accounting standard does not necessarily mean that the accounts will fail the true and fair test. However, the Companies Act requires large companies to disclose in their accounts any such departures, together with reasons, thus enabling them to be readily identified and considered.

e. When a case comes to the FRRP's attention it will be considered by a group of five or more members drawn from the overall Panel membership. The group will be responsible for carrying out the functions of the FRRP for that case, without any collective involvement by the other Panel members. The group will try to discharge its function by seeking voluntary agreement from the directors on any necessary revisions to the accounts. If this approach fails, the Panel may seek a declaration from the court that the accounts do not comply with the requirements of the Companies Act and seek an order requiring the directors to prepare revised accounts. If the court grants such an order it may also require the directors to meet the costs of the proceedings and the cost of revising the accounts. If accounts are revised, either voluntarily or by order of the court, but the company's auditor had not qualified his audit report on the defective accounts, the FRRP will draw this fact to the attention of the auditor's professional body.

f. Appointments to FRRP are made by an appointments committee consisting of the FRC chairman and deputy chairmen plus three Council members. There is no upper limit to membership.

THE STOCK EXCHANGE

15. The Stock Exchange provides companies with the facility to raise capital for expansion through selling shares to the investing public.

16. *Buying and Selling Shares*

a. There are two basic ways of buying shares in public companies:

i. *Buying new issues.* Details of new issues must be disclosed in a prospectus and advertised in at least one daily newspaper. The applicant fills in an application form included in the prospectus and sends it, with a cheque, to the address given. This will usually be a merchant bank acting as an issuing house. Depending on the success of the issue and the method chosen for scaling down over-subscribed issues, the applicant may receive all, some or none of the shares applied for. The detailed rules relating to the prospectus are covered in Chapter 45.

ii. *Buying existing shares.* The main function of the Stock Exchange is to allow existing shares to be bought and sold at any time. As members of the Exchange, stockbrokers buy and sell on behalf of private individuals and institutional clients.

b. *Stockbrokers.* In addition to specialist stockbroking firms, banks and building societies also provide stockbroking functions. There are various services that stockbrokers can provide:

    i.   *Dealing only* i.e. simply carrying out the client's instructions to buy and sell the shares and arrange settlement of the deal.

    ii.   *Advisory.* The stockbroker will consider the merits of a particular company, advising whether to buy, sell or hold its shares. The broker may also suggest changes to the client's portfolio of shares.

    iii.   *Discretionary.* In this case the broker will manage the portfolio totally, informing the client on a regular basis of shares bought or sold, the value of the portfolio, and the value of dividends credited to the client's account. If a broker is appointed in this way the client will be given a 'client agreement letter'. This is a requirement of the Financial Services Act and will set out the services offered and the terms under which the broker deals for the client.

Brokers advise on a wide range of investments, not just shares. These include unit trusts, investment trusts, warrants, options, personal equity plans and so on.

When the client gives the stockbroker the order to buy shares, the broker contacts a market maker and purchases the shares at the best price at the time of the deal. From this time the client becomes the owner of the shares. The broker then draws up a contract note which is sent to the client within a few days. The share certificate will be sent later.

c.   *Payment.* The year is divided into account periods of 2 weeks each. All deals made during a particular period are bundled together and must be paid for on account day. This is the second Monday following the end of the account period. If a client purchases UK equity shares this date will appear on the contract note as the settlement date. This is all the buyer has to do. The seller will have to sign a transfer form and return it with the share certificate to the stockbroker in order to be paid for the shares being sold.

d.   *Taxation*

    i.   *Income Tax.* When a shareholder receives dividends, advance corporation tax equivalent to income tax at the basic rate will have been paid by the company. A basic rate taxpayer will therefore have no further tax to pay, but a higher rate taxpayer will have to pay additional tax at the end of the year.

    ii.   *Capital gains tax.* The difference between the purchase price and selling price of shares (after expenses) is a capital gain, or loss. Liability for capital gains tax only arises when shares are sold or otherwise disposed of. It does not apply if the shareholder continues to hold the shares. Tax will be payable if the shareholder's total capital gains (less losses) in any one year exceeds the capital gains tax threshold set by the government for that year.

17. **Fraud and Malpractice** The *FRAUD ACT 2006* aims to protect consumers and businesses against by creating a crime of fraud linked to new technology. There are three ways in which the offence can be committed:

a.   *Fraud by false representation.* This covers situations where communications are sent to a large number of individuals e.g. by e-mail, purporting to be from a legitimate source such as a bank or financial institution, asking for personal bank details. These representations can also be made orally or by conduct – as where a fraudster uses a stolen credit card to pay for goods.

b.   *Fraud by failing to disclose information.* This is where there is a *legal duty to disclose* information e.g. in medical insurance where an applicant does not disclose a pre-existing medical condition, or in a company's prospectus offering shares, where directors fail to disclose the true extent of assets and liabilities of the company.

c.   *Fraud by abuse of position.* This occurs where a person through their position owes a level of duty to another. For example, in the employment relationship, both employer and employee owe duties to the other, so this offence might be committed where an employee gives confidential information held by his employer to an outsider. Others would include trustees in charge of a trust fund, doctors, solicitors, directors of companies, etc.

For each offence it has to be shown that the defendant had an intention to benefit themselves or others, or to cause a loss or expose another to potential loss through their actions. The Act also introduces a new offence of *obtaining services dishonestly,* this allows for an offence to be committed where the defendant attempts to get some service without paying, e.g. satellite television.

SELF TEST QUESTIONS

Self Test Questions No. 35 (for Answers see Appendix 1):

1   What are the main provisions of the *FINANCIAL SERVICES ACT 2000*?

2   How are *investments* defined under the Act?

3   What is the role of the Securities and Investments Board and what is meant by *authorized investment business*?

4   What is the *Central Register*?

5   Summarize the *rules for regulation of investment businesses*.

6   What is the role of the *Financial Reporting Council*?

7   What is the nature and role of the *stock exchange*?

8   Explain the offences introduced by the *FRAUD ACT 2006*.

REFLECTION AND CONSOLIDATION IV

For answers go to the student digital support resources for the book (see page xxv).

Reflection

These chapters specifically deal with commercial law, i.e. law which has a specific application to business practice.

Key areas of study
The relationship of *agency:*

> *sale of goods* and the implied terms giving consumer rights

> law on *competition*

> *credit transactions*

> principles of *insurance*

> industrial property – *patents, trade marks, copyright* and *passing-off*

> *data protection*

> the various *regulatory bodies*.

Consolidation

The following are practice assessment exercises. You will find answers and guidance by going to the student digital support resources for the book (see page xxv).

MULTIPLE CHOICE QUESTIONS

1   Which ONE of the following is a correct statement of the law?

An agent is a person who acts on behalf of another:

A   To protect a principal's goods or services
B   To promote the sales of his principal
C   In entering into contracts
D   To improve a businesses' performance

2   A contract for the sale of goods is one where:

A   A seller gives goods to another by way of a contract, for safe keeping
B   Goods are passed to another to use in his business
C   A seller transfers or agrees to transfer, the property in goods to the buyer for a money consideration called the price
D   Goods are loaned under a contract of hire to a customer

3   Which ONE of the following is correct?

As a general rule, in a contract for the sale of goods, the goods must correspond with:

A   The expectations of the buyer
B   The description given by the seller or given on behalf of the seller
C   That recognized in the trade
D   That understood to be the description from a course of dealings with the seller

4   In a contract for the sale of goods, the goods must be:

A   Of a satisfactory size and shape
B   Satisfactory to the buyer
C   Satisfactory to all involved in its sale
D   Of satisfactory quality

5   Which ONE of the following is not correct:

A regulated consumer credit agreement is one where:

A   A bank provides a loan or overdraft
B   A consumer purchases goods on hire purchase
C   A creditor provides a personal loan to a debtor
D   A creditor provides a business with credit

Typical Exam Questions

6   Graham, a dealer, collects and sells rare books. Whilst visiting a local town he notices that Peter has three rare editions for sale in his second-hand bookshop. He negotiates and agrees a price of £500 for each of the rare editions.

On the assumption that he will have the books in his possession, he negotiates to sell the first book to Eric for £800. The second book is to be sold to Helen for £600, together with another rare book that Helen is to sell to Graham for £400 (as Graham has a buyer for this book in the sum of

£600). The third book, which is the only surviving copy, is to be sold to Richard for the sum of £1000.

Graham has now returned to collect and pay for the three books from Peter as agreed. He is shocked when Peter informs him that the sale is off because he has received an offer from Bertram in the sum of £2000 for the set of three books and has agreed to sell them to him.

Explain what remedies, if any, Graham has against Peter.

(20 marks)
ICSA, November 2004

7 Amy and Ben have recently moved into a new house together and have purchased a number of items with which they are not satisfied.

(a) Explain to Amy and Ben why the law implies terms into certain contracts for the sale of goods.

(7 marks)

(b) Advise Amy and Ben on the legal position in the following situations. They purchase:

(i) A duck down duvet from a department store but have now discovered Ben is allergic to the duvet.

(6 marks)

(ii) A desk from a second-hand dealer, which was being sold cheaply because, as the seller pointed out at the time of the sale, one of the drawers was broken. They have now discovered that the desk has woodworm.

(6 marks)

(iii) A dishwasher bought from their next door neighbour. This breaks down the first time it is used.

(3 marks)

(iv) An electric frying pan from their local electric shop, which burns out when Amy uses it to heat up hair removal wax.

(3 marks)
(25 marks)

8 (a) Explain what consumers must determine before deciding whether they have a statutory claim for breach of the implied terms under Sale of Goods Act 1979, as amended, or the Supply of Goods and Services Act 1982.

(12 marks)

(b) Explain what terms are implied into a contract regulated by the Supply of Goods and Services Act 1982, and where services only are involved and there is no formal agreement between the supplier and consumer.

(8 marks)
(20 marks)
ICSA, November 2004

9 (a) Where the buyer is in breach of contract to the seller, the seller may exercise statutory rights against the goods, subject to certain conditions.

Explain what those rights are.

(12 marks)

(b) The law provides that if a person does not have the title to the goods they cannot pass good title (the *nemo dat quod habet* rule). There are, however, a number of exceptions to this rule.

Explain how the following statutory exceptions apply in practice:

(i) Estoppel.
(ii) Common law or statutory power of sale.
(iii) Sale of a motor vehicle subject to hire purchase.

(8 marks)
(20 marks)
ICSA, November 2004

10 (a) Explain the ways in which an agency agreement can be formed, using illustrative examples to support your answer.

(10 marks)

(b) Explain in detail the ways in which an agency agreement not governed by the Commercial Agents Regulations 1993 can be terminated.

(10 marks)
(20 marks)
ICSA, November 2004

11 (a) There has been considerable concern expressed by the music industry about the downloading from the Internet of recording artists' copyrighted material.

Explain what is meant by 'copyright' in the context of intellectual property, with particular reference to how long copyright exists depending upon the 'property' involved.

(10 marks)

(b) (i) What remedies are available for the owner of copyrighted material if his rights are infringed?

(4 marks)

(i) What defences, if any, are available to a defendant in such an action?

(6 marks)
(20 marks)
ICSA, November 2004

12 (a) Explain what is meant by the expression 'extortionate credit bargain' and what action, if any, can be taken by the courts in respect of such a bargain.

(10 marks)

(b) Explain the term 'protected goods', as defined in the Consumer Credit Act 1974 (as amended). What action must a creditor follow if they wish to repossess such goods? What are the consequences of unlawful repossession?

(10 marks)
(20 marks)
ICSA, November 2004

PART FIVE

SOLE TRADER, PARTNERSHIP AND COMPANY

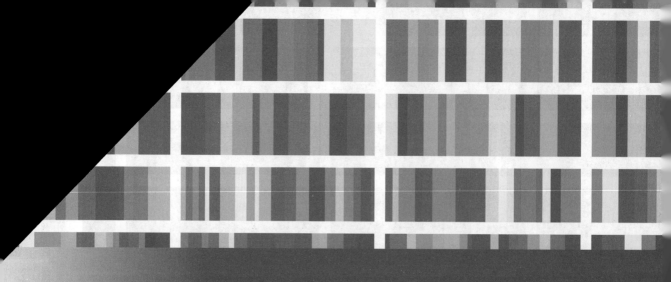

38 NON-CORPORATE BODIES

Learning Outcomes At the end of this chapter you should be able to:

- Outline the key features of the sole trader.

- Explain the nature of the partnership in terms of its:

  - definition

  - creation

  - authority and liability of partners

  - relationships between partners

  - dissolution

  - limited partnerships.

THE SOLE TRADER AND PARTNERSHIP

1. The *sole trader* can be described as an individual who carries on a business on his own account. Though he is likely to be a small business this may not be so, a sole trader could employ any number of employees. The key features of the sole trader are:

a. If he chooses not to trade under his own name he must register the name under the *BUSINESS NAMES ACT 1985*.

b. He has sole responsibility for the debts of the business and is liable personally to the ful extent of all he possesses in both business and private assets – he has *unlimited liability*. Where a sole trader business becomes insolvent – the assets no longer matching liabilities – he is said to be bankrupt brought about by the procedure known as bankruptcy laid down in the *INSOLVENCY ACT 1986* as amended by the *ENTERPRISE ACT 2002*.

c. He usually makes all the decisions and take all the profits or stands all losses.

d. There is no formalities for ending the business; he may cease trading at any time.

e. Upon the death of the sole trader the business ceases.

2. *The Partnership*

    Introduction Unincorporated associations consist of a number of persons who have come together for a matter of common interest, for example a sports club, a trade union or a *partnership*. The associations do not have a separate legal entity from their members. Thus the property of an association is regarded as belonging to the members jointly, and if a wrong is committed by a member the general rule is that he alone is liable for what he has done. There are exceptions to this rule, in particular in connection with partnerships.

    When people wish to associate for business purposes they will usually form a company or a partnership. The law of partnership is based on agency, each partner becoming an agent of the others, and is only appropriate for a relatively small number of persons who have trust in each other and who are able to provide the funds for the business from their own resources.

3. *Definition of the Partnership* A partnership is defined by the *PARTNERSHIP ACT 1890 S.1* as 'The *relation* which subsists between persons carrying on a *business in common* with a *view to profit*.'

    a. A partnership is described as a '*relation*' because, unlike a company, it is not a legal entity separate from the partners.

    b. The partners must carry on a '*business*', i.e. a trade, profession or vocation over a period of time. If they merely co-own property this does not create a partnership. However, in *KHAN v MIAH (2001)*, the House of Lords (now the Supreme Court) ruled that it is not necessary to show that the business has commenced trading:

    'Parties who agree (as in the present case) to a joint venture to find, acquire and fit out premises for business purposes, *which they intend to run as partners*, become partners from the time they embarked upon those activities.'

    In the *Khan* case, three individuals decided to set up a restaurant, the capital to do this was provided almost exclusively by only one of the partners. Before the restaurant opened and began to trade:

    i.   Premises were acquired.

    ii. Equipment and furniture bought.

    iii. Advertisements were place.

    The parties then fell out and the question arose as to whether there was a partnership between them, if there was, the property and assets purchased belonged to the partnership and – in the absence of a contrary agreement – were owned jointly by the parties.

If finding that a partnership did exist the assets were jointly owned and not the property of the single partner who had put up most of the money (see 7.e below).

c. '*In common*' means the business must be carried on for the joint benefit of the persons who are partners.

d. '*View to profit*' means the partners must intend to make a profit. It does not mean that if the actual result is a loss there is no partnership. Also, the definition in *S.1* does not require that any profits made be actually shared; there can be a partnership where one or more of the partners chooses not to share profits but take a salary instead. In *M YOUNG LEGAL ASSOCIATES LTD v ZAHID SOLICITORS (2006)* Z wanted to set up a firm of solicitors. A requirement of the Solicitors' Practice Rules states that every practice has a solicitor of at least 3 years standing, Z did not have this requirement, he therefore brought in B who did have the necessary 3 years experience. The content of the agreement with B was that he:

  i. Was named as a partner.

  ii. Received a fixed salary unrelated to profits.

  iii. Had a written assurance from Z that he would not be liable for any debts of the firm.

When the firm went into liquidation (see Chapter 48), creditors sought payment of certain debts of the firm against B as a partner. B claimed that he was not a partner as he did not share in any profits made. The Court of Appeal held that *S.1* makes no reference to a sharing of profit, just that there be an *intention* to make a profit. B was a partner and as such a claim against him could proceed.

Creation

a. No formalities are necessary, although for practical reasons writing is usually used.

b. The partners may trade under any name they please, except that the word 'limited' must not be the last word of the name.

c. Any partnership agreement will usually deal with the following matters:

  i. The firm's name.

  ii. The place and nature of the business.

  iii. The date on which the partnership is to commence and its duration. If there is no fixed period then it is a partnership at will.

  iv. The proportions in which capital is to be provided, and whether interest is to be paid on capital before profits are divided.

  v. Details of the firm's bank account, including who is allowed to sign cheques.

  vi. Whether all or only some of the partners shall manage the business and whether all partners shall give their whole time to the business.

  vii. How profits are to be shared, and provisions for drawings.

  viii. Provisions for keeping regular accounts and the preparation of an annual profit and loss account and balance sheet.

  ix. What shall happen on the death or retirement of a partner. In the absence of an agreement to the contrary the death of a partner automatically dissolves the partnership.

  x. Whether a retired partner is allowed (within limits) to compete with the firm.

xi.   A list or description of what is agreed to be partnership property.

xii. Insurance against death or sickness of a partner and for the business generally.

xiii. Any limits on the business interests of the partners outside the firm.

xiv. An arbitration clause.

5. *Authority of Partners*

a.   Every partner is an agent of the firm and therefore has *implied authority* to bind the firm by transactions entered into by him in the *ordinary course of business*. Thus an outsider who contracts with a partner within the scope of that implied authority may treat the firm as bound, despite any restriction on the authority of that partner to which the partners have agreed, unless the outsider knew of the restriction.

In *MERCHANTILE CREDIT v GARROD (1962)* A and B were partners in a firm which let garages and repaired cars. The partnership agreement expressly excluded buying and selling cars. Without B's knowledge, A, acting without the owner's consent, sold a car to a finance company for £700, paying the proceeds into the partnership account. It was held that B was liable to repay the £700 to the finance company. The prohibition on buying and selling in the partnership agreement did not entitle B (or the firm) to avoid liability since A's conduct was of a kind normally undertaken by persons trading as a garage, i.e. A apparently had authority to sell cars.

b.   In a trading partnership the following acts are within the implied authority of a partner:

i.   Borrowing money in the name of the firm and giving security by pledging its goods or by depositing title deeds to create an equitable mortgage.

ii.   Signing cheques, and drawing, accepting or indorsing bills of exchange.

iii. Employing a solicitor to defend an action against the firm. However, it is doubtful if a partner would have authority to commence any proceedings other than routine actions to recover trade debts.

iv.   Receiving payment of debts and giving valid receipts.

v.   Buying and selling goods on account of the firm.

vi.   Engaging employees to work for the firm. A partner probably does not have implied authority to dismiss employees.

c.   The following acts are outside a partner's implied authority:

i.   Consenting to a judgement against the firm.

ii.   Executing a deed.

iii. Giving a guarantee in the absence of a trade custom to do so.

iv.   Referring a dispute to arbitration.

v.   Accepting property other than money in payment of a debt.

6. *Liability of Partners*

a.   *Liability for torts.* On the usual principle of vicarious liability (since each partner is an agent of the others) all the partners are liable for a tort committed by a partner in the ordinary course of the firm's business, or with the authority of his co-partners.

In *HAMLYN v HOUSTON (1903)* a partner bribed a competitor's clerk to disclose confidential information relating to it. The partner used the information and the rival firm consequently suffered loss. It was held that the partner's firm was liable for his wrongful act since he was acting in the ordinary course of business when he obtained information about the rival.

Partners' liability in tort is *joint and several*. This means that a partner is liable jointly with the other partners and also individually liable. Thus a plaintiff may issue separate writs against each partner either at the same time or successively and judgement against one partner does not prevent an action being brought against the others.

b.   *Liability for misapplication of money or property.* Where either:

    i.   One *partner*, acting within the scope of his apparent authority, receives money or property of a third person and misapplies it, *or*

    ii.   A *firm*, in the course of its business, receives money or property of a third person and the money or property is misapplied by one or more of the partners while in the custody of the firm, then the firm is liable to make good the loss.

c.   *Liability in contract*

    i.   Every partner is liable jointly with his co-partners for all debts and obligations of the firm incurred whilst he was a partner.

    ii.   Where liability is joint it used to be the case that once a third party had sued one of the partners he could not sue the others. However, the *CIVIL LIABILITY (CONTRIBUTION) ACT 1978* removed this limit on the number of actions. It also provides that a partner who has paid a debt of the firm can claim a contribution from his partners.

d.   *Liability of a retired partner*

    i.   A partner who retires does not cease to be liable for partnership debts incurred before his retirement. These may include debts arising after his retirement from transactions during the period when he was a partner.

    ii.   A retired partner may be discharged from liability for debts incurred while he was a partner if the debts are later discharged by the new firm, or if the creditors agree to release him by novation (see below).

    iii.   A retired partner may be liable on contracts made after his retirement if he continues to be an 'apparent partner', by for example allowing his name to remain on the firm's notepaper.

e.   *Liability of a new partner*

    i.   A person admitted as a partner does not thereby incur liability for debts incurred before he became a partner.

    ii.   There may be a contract of *novation* between a retired partner, the firm as reconstituted by the entry of a new partner and the creditors. Under such a three party agreement, the creditors and the firm agree that the reconstituted firm will be liable for unpaid debts of the old firm and that the retired partner be discharged from liability.

f.   *The salaried partner*

It is common in professional partnerships, such as solicitors and accountants, to offer salaried partnerships. These partners take a salary and often do not introduce any new capital into the partnership or have any involvement in any dissolution of the firm. However, under the *PARTNERSHIP ACT 1890*, in the first instance they are fully liable as partners. They should seek indemnity for debts of the firm from the other partners because, as seen (6.a above), their liability is *joint and several*. There is a requirement that for such liability to occur, the salaried partner must be in some way in the contemplation of the outsider who is bringing the claim i.e. the partner is being 'held-out' as a full partner. In **NATIONWIDE BUILDING SOCIETY v LEWIS (1998)** a small two partner law firm – one of the partners being a salaried partner – was being sued by the society for negligent advice given on a mortgage application. The partner who had written the report containing the negligent advice went bankrupt, therefore the society pursued its claim against the salaried partner claiming he was jointly and severally liable. On appeal the court found that the society had never dealt with the salaried partner, it only learned of his existence after the report had been sent through letter headed notepaper. They had not known of his existence, nor had they relied on his existence in any way. In this case the salaried partner was not being held out as a full partner of the firm, and was, therefore, not liable.

7. *The Relationship of Partners to Each Other*

a. *Good faith.* There is duty of utmost good faith once the partnership is established. This means:

   i. Partners are bound to render true accounts and full information on all matters affecting the partnership.

   ii. A partner must account for any profit made by him without the consent of the others from using the firm's property, name or trade connections.

   iii. A partner may have a separate account unless he had agreed to the contrary, but a partner must account for any profit made in a business of the same kind as, and competing with, the firm.

b. *Management*

   i. Subject to contrary agreement every partner is entitled to access to partnership books and may take part in the management of the business.

   ii. Decisions on ordinary matters connected with the partnership business are by majority of the general partners. If there is a deadlock the views of those opposing any change will prevail, but unanimity is required for matters relating to the constitution of the firm, for example to change the nature of the partnership business or to admit a new partner.

c. *Capital, profits and losses*

   i. Profits and losses are shared equally in the absence of contrary agreement. However, if the partnership agreement states that profits are to be shared in certain proportions then, prima facie losses are to be shared in the same proportions.

   ii. No interest is paid on capital except by agreement. However, a partner is entitled to 5% interest on advances beyond his original capital.

d. *Indemnity.* The firm must indemnify any partner against liabilities incurred in the ordinary and proper conduct of the partnership business, or in doing anything necessarily done for the preservation of the partnership property or business.

   e.   *Partnership property*

       i.   The *initial* property of the partnership is that which the partners, expressly or impliedly agree shall be partnership property. It is quite possible that property used in the business should not be partnership property, but should, for example, be the sole property of one of the partners, it depends entirely on the intention of the partners.

      ii.   Property *afterwards* acquired is governed by the same principle, but clearly it will be partnership property if it is bought with partnership money.

8. *Dissolution*

   a.   Dissolution occurs:

       i.   By expiry of time, if the partnership was entered into for a fixed term.

      ii.   By termination of the adventure, if entered into for a single adventure.

     iii.   By the death or bankruptcy of a partner, unless the partnership agreement otherwise provides.

     iv.   By subsequent illegality, i.e. an event which makes it unlawful to continue the business.

      v.   By notice of a partner.

     vi.   By order of the court, for one of several reasons, for example the permanent incapacity of a partner, or because it is just and equitable to order dissolution.

   b.   *Misrepresentation.* When a partner is induced to enter into a partnership by misrepresentation he remains liable to creditors for obligations incurred while a partner, but he has several remedies against the maker of the statement including, for example, rescission and/or damages.

   c.   After dissolution the authority of the partners continues so far as is necessary to wind up the partnership affairs and complete transactions already begun.

   d.   On dissolution any partner can insist on realization of the firm's assets, (including goodwill), payment of the firm's debts, and distribution of the surplus, subject to any contrary agreement.

9. *Limited Partnerships*

   a.   Limited partnership was established by the *LIMITED PARTNERSHIP ACT 1907.* The use of this form of partnership has not been extensive due to the ease of incorporating a private company.

   b.   Under such a partnership there must be at least one general and one limited partner. The limitation on the number of partners applicable to ordinary partnerships also applies to limited partnerships.

   c.   The general partner is liable for all the firm's debts and liabilities but a limited partner is only liable to the extent of his capital contribution which may be in cash or in the form of property. Particulars of this contribution must be disclosed in the particulars registered with the Registrar of Companies and if this capital is later withdrawn, the limited partner will be liable for the firm's debts to the extent of the amount so withdrawn.

d.   A limited partnership must be registered with the Registrar of Companies. Until this is done all the partners are deemed to be general partners. The registered particulars include, for example, the firm's name, the place and nature of business, and the full name of each partner.

10. ***The Limited Liability Partnership (LLP)*** A partnership formed under the *LIMITED LIABILITY PARTNERSHIP ACT 2000*, will enjoy limited liability similar to that of the private limited company. Partners will not incur personal liability for the debts of the partnership. It is registered with the Registrar of Companies and once formed owns the assets of the business separate from the members and directors. The LLP was brought about largely through pressure from large firms of accountants and solicitors worried at the size of personal liability of individual partners for negligence e.g. auditors negligently approving accounts that are not accurate and which mislead investors. The LLP provides limited liability to the non negligent partner(s) with the negligent partner/member incurring unlimited liability. The *LIMITED LIABILITY PARTNERSHIPS REGULATIONS 2001 (S.1 2001/ 1090)* provide more details on the regulation of the LLP, broadly they apply, with appropriate amendments, company law provisions to the LLP. It is in this respect, with the consequent public disclosure requirements of an LLP, that the advantage of secrecy and privacy, an often important feature of the partnership, is lost.

11. ***Proposals for Reform*** The Law Commission (see Chapter 4.25) put forward a number of proposals for legal reform of partnership law in respect of the *PARTNERSHIP ACT 1890*. The main thrust of the proposals is to narrow the present distinction between ordinary partnerships and the limited liability partnership (see 9. above). There are three main proposals:

a.   To confer legal personality on all partnerships without registration. This was introduced by the *LEGISLATIVE REFORM (LIMITED PARTNERSHIPS) ORDER REGULATIONS 2009.*

b.   There is a transitional period to allow partners within existing partnerships to arrange their affairs to take on board separate legal entity or to opt out.

c.   Legal personality will only be granted to all partnerships, whether registered or not; all partnerships will have legal personality. One significant advantage of legal personality is that it will allow a partnership to continue even if a partner leaves or dies. The partnership having, in effect, a separate legal existence independent of its individual partners.

Another Law Commission proposal, not yet acted upon, is to remove the dissolution of a partnership under the *PARTNERSHIP ACT 1890*, when one person ceases to be a partner (see 8. above). There are also, proposals to improve the current legal provisions governing the dissolution of a solvent partnership, with regards to cost and efficiency.

Other proposals, not yet acted upon, all linked to a partnership having a separate legal existence, include:

i.   Partners should become agents of the firm and not each other.

ii. Property of the partnership should be held in the name of the firm, not individual partners. Here, the firm and not the partners would have an insurable interest in partnership property (see Chapter 34.3).

iii. Liability for debts and other obligations would fall upon the firm not individual partners, a partner's liability would be subsidiary to the firm, though unlimited. Creditors will enforce claims against the assets of the firm, as between partners liability will remain joint and several (see 6. above).

iv.   Suggestions that partners might have statutory duties owed to the firm like directors of a company (see Chapter 44.24).

v.   Partnerships should be able, unlike at the moment, to issue *floating charges* (see Chapter 42.5.b).

SELF TEST QUESTIONS

Self Test Questions No. 36 (for Answers see Appendix 1):

1   What are the key features of the sole trader?

2   How would you describe a partnership in law?

3   What are the requirements for the formation of a partnership?

4   Explain the legal authority and liability of a partner.

5   What is the nature of the legal relationship between partners?

6   In what circumstances can a partnership be dissolved?

7   What is a limited liability partnership?

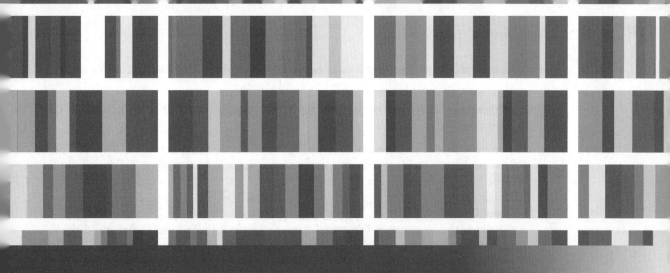

CORPORATE BODIES – THE COMPANY

39

Learning Outcomes At the end of this chapter you should be able to:

- Outline the different company forms.

- Explain the consequences of incorporation.

- Understand what is meant by the *veil of incorporation.*

- Outline the differences between *public* and *private* companies.

- Explain the registration procedure for a company.

- Understand the nature and role of *promoters.*

- Explain the law pertaining to *pre-incorporation* contracts.

1. *Companies and Partnerships* Partnerships historically were not adequate for the development of modern capitalism since (among other things) they originally did not provide any means for business people to limit their liability, and just as importantly, they did enable access to sufficient capital. These aims could only be achieved through a framework which enabled business organizations to have a separate legal personality from their members. Such a structure could be used by a small family business, but more significantly it could accommodate large and complex organizations with fluctuating membership. The framework that developed was company law. At its heart is the ability of a group of people to register a company under the Companies Acts. From the date of registration a corporate

person comes into being, having a legal personality distinct from that of its creators or members and subject to a wide range of legal rights and duties.

2. ***Types of Company*** There are three basic types of company classified according to their means of formation:

a. *Chartered companies.* A chartered company is formed by the grant of a charter by the Crown under the Royal Prerogative or under special statutory powers. This method of incorporation is no longer used by trading companies since it is far quicker and cheaper to obtain incorporation by registration. It is only used by, for example, charitable organizations, learned and artistic societies and some schools and colleges. Chartered companies include the Institute of Chartered Accountants in England and Wales, the British Broadcasting Corporation and Oxford and Cambridge Universities.

b. *Statutory companies*

   i. In the past companies were incorporated by special Act of Parliament when it was necessary for them to have special powers and monopolistic rights. This was the case when the supply of public services such as gas, water, electricity and railways was left to private enterprise. After the Second World War most of these statutory companies were nationalized and their functions taken over by public corporations. Some public services have been 'privatized' i.e. returned to public company status.

   ii. There are also other types of organization which owe their existence to statute. They include building societies, friendly societies and co-operative societies.

c. *Registered companies.* The *COMPANIES ACT 2006* provides for the registration of:

   i. Companies limited by shares.

   ii. Companies limited by guarantee (Chapter 40.22).

   iii. Unlimited companies (Chapter 40.23), and

   iv. Partnership companies (3.e below).

   The vast majority of companies are registered companies limited by shares. These companies may be public or private limited companies.

3. ***Companies and Partnerships Compared***

a. *Unincorporated associations and partnerships*

   i. Unincorporated associations consist of a number of persons who have come together for a matter of common interest, for example a sports club, a trade union or a partnership.

   ii. A partnership is defined by the *PARTNERSHIP ACT 1890* as 'The relation which subsists between persons carrying on a business in common with a view to profit.' 'Business' includes any trade, occupation or profession.

b. *The main differences between companies and partnerships*

   i. A company is created by registration under the *COMPANIES ACT 2006*. A partnership is created by the express or implied agreement of the partners, no special form being required, although writing is usually used.

   ii. A company incurs greater expenses at formation, throughout its life and on dissolution, although the fees are not excessive.

iii. A company is an artificial legal person with a legal personality distinct from its members. In contrast a partnership is not a separate legal person, although it may sue and be sued in the firm's name. The partners own the property of the firm and are liable on its contracts.

iv. Shares in a public company are freely transferable, whereas a partner cannot transfer his share without the consent of all of his partners. He may assign the right to his share of the profits, but the assignee does not become a partner.

v. Members of a company may not take part in its management unless they become directors, whereas all partners are entitled to share in management, unless the partnership agreement provides otherwise.

vi. A member of a company is not an agent of the company, and he therefore cannot bind the company by his acts. A partner is an agent of the partnership, therefore it will be bound by his acts.

vii. The liability of a member of a company may be limited by shares or by guarantee. The liability of a general partner is unlimited, although it is possible for one or more partners to limit their liability provided there remains at least one general partner. In addition, as seen, the *LIMITED LIABILITY PARTNERSHIP ACT* 2000, does provide a degree of limited liability for partnerships. The advantage of limited liability is unlikely to be real for many small companies and partnerships since lenders will usually require a personal guarantee of their loan from the directors and/or majority shareholders and partners.

viii. The powers and duties of a company are closely regulated by the Companies Acts, its constitution is specified in its Memorandum of Association, and its internal regulations are contained in its Articles of Association (although both can be freely altered by special resolution). In contrast, partners have more freedom to carry on any business they wish and to make their own arrangements with regard to the running of the firm.

ix. A company must comply with more formalities, for example certain registers must be maintained and the accounts must be audited annually.

x. Greater publicity must be given to the affairs of a company, for example to its directorate, its financial position and to charges on its assets.

xi. Company law requires maintenance of issued capital through the rule that dividends may only be declared out of profits. Partners' drawings of profit and capital are a matter of agreement.

c. *The similarity between companies and partnerships.* The main similarity is that both companies and partnerships are methods of carrying on business. Many companies are of course large and impersonal, having many institutional shareholders. Such companies bear little resemblance to partnerships. Small private companies are, however, often founded on the same basis as partnerships, i.e. a relationship of mutual trust and confidence.

d. *Conclusion.* Despite the greater degree of legal regulation affecting the registered company, the advantages of incorporation (e.g. separate legal personality, limited liability, transferability of shares and possible tax advantages) have induced many partners and sole traders to convert their businesses into corporate form. However, partnership remains important, and in many cases mutual trust and confidence are more highly regarded than the benefits of incorporation. Thus, subject to a few exceptions, partnership is the compulsory form of association for many professional persons, for example solicitors. This preserves the principle of individual professional accountability towards the client, a policy central to professional ethics.

e. *Partnership companies.* As part of the Government's policy to encourage wider individual share ownership, it has introduced legislation making it easier to set up partnership companies. A partnership company is 'A company limited by shares whose shares are intended to be held to a substantial extent by or on behalf of its employees.' The Act allows the Secretary of State to prescribe, by regulations, a model set of articles appropriate for partnership companies.

THE CONSEQUENCES OF INCORPORATION

4. *A Separate Legal Entity*

a. The most important consequence of incorporation is that a company becomes a legal person distinct from its members.

In *SALOMON v SALOMON & CO (1897)* S formed a limited company with the other members of his family, and sold his business to the company for £39 000. He held 20 001 of the 20 007 shares which had been issued by the company, and £10 000 of debentures (documents acknowledging that S was a secured lender entitled to priority of repayment in a liquidation). The balance was payable in cash.

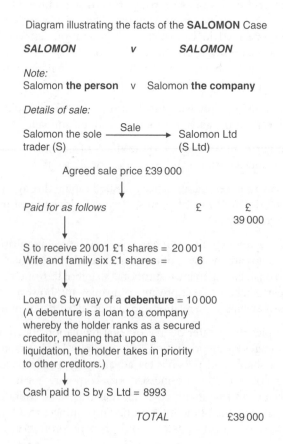

Diagram illustrating the facts of the **SALOMON** Case

SALOMON   v   **SALOMON**

Note:
Salomon **the person**   v   Salomon **the company**

Details of sale:

Salomon the sole ———Sale———▸ Salomon Ltd
trader (S)   (S Ltd)

Agreed sale price £39 000
↓

Paid for as follows   £   £
↓   39 000

S to receive 20 001 £1 shares = 20 001
Wife and family six £1 shares =   6
↓

Loan to S by way of a **debenture** = 10 000
(A debenture is a loan to a company
whereby the holder ranks as a secured
creditor, meaning that upon a
liquidation, the holder takes in priority
to other creditors.)
↓
Cash paid to S by S Ltd = 8993

TOTAL   £39 000

About a year after its formation the company was wound-up. The assets at that time were just sufficient to discharge the debentures, but nothing was left for unsecured creditors with debts of about £7500. The creditors claimed that they should have priority because S and the company were in effect the same person. The House of Lords (now the Supreme Court), however, held that S and the company were separate legal entities, the company had been validly formed, and there was no fraud on the members or creditors. S was therefore entitled to the remaining assets.

b. Salomon's case was very important because it finally established the legality of family companies where one person holds the vast majority of the shares. It also showed that incorporation was available to small businesses as well as to large enterprises. However, it caused concern because it showed that it was possible to limit liability not merely to the money put into the company, but to avoid serious risk to some of that money by subscribing for debentures rather than shares. The decision has been criticized this reason, but it can be justified on the grounds that persons who deal with a limited company know the risks, although it is not usually practical to take all the available precautions, such as a search of the company's file at the Companies Registry.

c. The fact that a company is a separate legal entity from its members is not necessarily beneficial to those members. For example, if a trader sells his business to a company he will cease to have an insurable interest in its assets though he owns most of the shares.

In ***MACAURA v NORTHERN ASSURANCE CO (1925)*** M owned a timber estate. He formed a limited company and sold the timber estate to it. Like Salomon he was basically a 'one-man company'. Before he sold the estate to the company it had been insured in his own name. After the sale to the company he neglected to transfer the insurance policy to the company. The estate was destroyed by fire. It was held that M could not claim under the policy because the assets that were damaged belonged to a different person, namely the company, and M, as a shareholder, had no insurable interest in the assets of the company.

d. The effects of separate corporate personality are further illustrated by the following case.

In ***RE ATTORNEY-GENERAL'S REFERENCE (NO. 2 OF 1982)*** the respondents were accused of theft. They had appropriated for their own private purposes funds of various companies of which they were the sole shareholders and directors. Each acted with the consent of the other. Their defence was that they had appropriated their own property. The Court of Appeal held that even persons in total control of a company were capable of stealing its property. Furthermore it was not rational to treat the accused as having transmitted their knowledge to the company, so as to regard the company as having consented to the appropriation, in fact the company should be regarded as the victim of the crime.

e. *Corporate manslaughter.* The ability to prosecute a company for the death of a person or persons caused by its negligent operations, has recently been the subject of new legal proposals. The *CORPORATE MANSLAUGHTER AND HOMICIDE ACT 2007* updates existing laws on corporate killing. This statutory criminal offence of corporate manslaughter applies where someone has been killed because the senior management of a corporation has grossly failed to take reasonable care for the safety of employees or others. This tackles the key problem with the common law; the need to show that a single individual at the very top of a company is personally guilty of manslaughter before the company itself can be prosecuted. This is a problem which favours the large public corporation with a large and diverse board and senior management, because it is almost impossible to single out one director and attribute manslaughter to him or her. The offence under the *ACT* means that courts can look at other similar companies and assess whether a particular company's management, has fallen below an acceptable general standard of care. It focuses responsibility on the working practices of the organization, as set by senior managers, rather than limiting investigations to questions of individual gross negligence by company bosses. The statutory offence will be clearly linked to the standards required under existing health and safety laws. The criminal liability of individual directors will not be affected by the proposals i.e. there is no personal liability. Corporate manslaughter is an offence committed by organizations rather than individuals and will therefore carry a penalty of an unlimited fine rather than a custodial sentence. The courts can also require that an organization take remedial steps within a defined time period to remedy any breach.

5. *Other Consequences of Incorporation* The following consequences of incorporation all flow from the fundamental consequence of separate legal personality:

   a. *Limited liability.* All companies are liable without limit for their own debts. However, companies obtain their share capital from their members. Provided a company is formed on the basis of limited liability, its members are not liable for the company's debts. Complete absence of liability is not however permitted. Each member is liable to contribute, if called upon to do so, the full nominal value of his shares so far as this has not already been paid. If he has agreed to pay more than the nominal value then his liability is limited to the amount he has agreed to pay.

   b. *Property.* An important advantage of incorporation is that the property of the company is distinguished from that of its members. In contrast the property of a partnership is jointly owned by the partners. This can cause problems when defining the true nature of the interests of the partners, which will be necessary when a partner retires. There is no similar problem when the membership of a company changes since the members do not have any direct rights to the property of the company, they only have a right to their shares. Thus when shares are transferred, the company's property remains unaffected.

   c. *Contractual capacity.* The question of contractual capacity is closely related to that of property ownership. Companies have contractual capacity and can sue and be sued on their contracts.

   d. *Perpetual succession.* The continuity of the company is not affected by the death or incapacity of some or all of its members.

   e. *Transferable membership.* Incorporation greatly facilitates the transfer of members' interests. Shares are items of property which are freely transferable provided the constitution of the company does not contain an express provision to the contrary.

   f. *Increased borrowing powers.* It is logical to assume that unincorporated traders or partnerships would find it easier to borrow money because of their personal liability. This is not the case since a company can give as security a floating charge. This is not available to an unincorporated trader or partnership. A floating charge is a mortgage over the constantly fluctuating assets of a company. It does not prevent the company dealing with these assets in the ordinary course of business. Such a charge is very useful when a company has no fixed assets such as land which can be included in a normal mortgage, but nevertheless has a large and valuable stock-in-trade.

6. *The Veil of Incorporation* The fact that the separate corporate personality of a company prevents outsiders from taking action against its members (even though the outsider can

find out who they are and how many shares they hold) has led to comparison with a veil. The corporate personality is the veil, and the members are shielded behind this 'veil of incorporation'. However, the internal affairs of the company are never completely concealed from view since publicity has always accompanied incorporation. In addition there are several situations when the law is prepared to lift the veil of incorporation either to go behind the corporate personality to the individual members, or to ignore the separate personality of several companies in a group in favour of the economic entity constituted by the group as a whole.

Veil of incorporation

7. *Examples of 'Lifting the Veil'*

a.   *If the company is being used to enable a person to evade his legal obligations*

In **GILFORD MOTOR CO v HORNE (1933)** an employee covenanted that after the termination of his employment he would not solicit his former employer's customers. Soon after the termination of his employment he formed a company, which then sent out circulars to the customers of his former employer. The court lifted the veil of incorporation, granting an injunction which prevented both the former employee and his company from distributing the circulars even though the company was not a party to the covenant. However, in a more recent case the courts' strong support for the *Salomon* principle, even where there might be some evidence of apparent wrongdoing, was shown in a Court of Appeal decision; **ORD & ANOR V BELHAVEN PUBS (1998)**. Here a respondent company pending legal action transferred its assets to another associated company. The claimant, concerned that insufficient assets remained to meet any future award of compensation, applied to have the associate company substituted as the new respondent. The Court refused stating that in the absence of evidence indicating some fraud or sham, the principle of separate legal existence as laid down in **SALOMON V SALOMON & CO (1897)** must be upheld.

b.   *Fraudulent or wrongful trading*

i.   By *S.213* of the *INSOLVENCY ACT 1986*, if in the course of winding-up it appears that business has been carried on with intent to defraud creditors, the persons responsible may be made personally liable to make such contribution to the company's assets as the court thinks proper.

ii.   A more useful provision is *S.214* of the *INSOLVENCY ACT 1986*, which enables the liquidator of an insolvent company to apply to the court to declare that a director be personally liable to contribute to the company's assets. Before making the order the court will have to be satisfied that the director knew or ought to have concluded that there was no reasonable prospect of avoiding insolvent liquidation and that he failed to take every step to minimize the creditors' loss.

c. *Groups and holding and subsidiary companies.* Significant inroads to the concept of separate corporate personality have concerned holding and subsidiary companies. For certain purposes, in particular the presentation of financial statements, the companies in a group must be treated as one.

d. The UK courts have shown a marked reluctance to lift the veil within groups of companies where one company holds shares and controls another. In ***ADAMS V CAPE INDUSTRIES PLC (1991)*** the Court of Appeal refused to lift the veil of incorporation and hold a UK parent company liable for the acts of its subsidiaries abroad even though it could be shown that the UK parent had deliberately distanced itself from its subsidiaries in light of ongoing litigation; the Court finding that the fact that one company controls the actions of another does not make it 'at one' with that other, the *Salomon* principle must be upheld. However, within the European Union, the European Court of Justice has shown itself to be far more willing to lift the veil within groups of companies for purposes of applying Community rules on competition between member states.

These instances of veil lifting will apply equally to the new Limited Liability Partnership (see Chapter 43.4).

PUBLIC AND PRIVATE COMPANIES

8. *Definitions*

a. *A public company* is a company limited by shares whose certificate of incorporation says it is (*S.4*).

b. *Private companies* are limited companies which are not registered as public companies, i.e. a company will be private unless it is specifically registered as public.

The EC directive the *COMPANIES (SINGLE MEMBER PRIVATE LIMITED COMPANIES) REGULATIONS 1992* states that a private or public company limited by shares or guarantee may be formed by one person and have one member (*S.7*).

9. *The Main Differences between Public and Private Companies*

a. *Purpose.* Public and private companies fulfil different economic purposes. The purpose of a public company is to raise capital from the public to run the enterprise. This ability to offer shares to the public is now the only advantage of a public company. The purpose of a private company is to confer separate legal personality on the business of a sole trader or partnership.

b. *Issue of Capital.* A private company may not raise capital by issuing its securities to the public. There is no restriction on the offer of securities by a public company. A public company must, however, issue a prospectus (a document which gives minimum essential information to potential members) and comply with Stock Exchange rules to obtain a listing of the securities.

c. *Transferability of Shares.* The shares of a public company are freely transferable on the Stock Exchange. A private company will, in contrast, wish to remain under the control of the 'family' or 'partners' concerned. Its articles will therefore contain a clause restricting the right to transfer shares. The restriction may be:

i.   An absolute power vested in the directors to refuse to register a transfer, and/or

ii.   A right of pre-emption (first refusal) granted to existing members when another member wishes to transfer shares.

d.   *Minimum Share Capital.* A public company must have a minimum allotted share capital of £50 000. A private company has no minimum share capital.

e.   *Company Name.* The name of a public company must end with the words 'Public Limited Company', which may be abbreviated to 'P.L.C.'. A private company's name must end with 'Limited'. This may be abbreviated to 'Ltd'.

f.   *The Memorandum.* A public company's memorandum must state that 'The company is to be a public company.'

g.   *Payment for Shares.* There are a number of differences in the rules relating to the consideration given in return for shares. For example, if a public company issues shares in return for the transfer of a non-cash asset, that asset must be independently valued to ensure that the company is receiving an asset of a value at least as great as the value of shares issued in return. In a private company there is no requirement to obtain a report on the value of non-cash consideration received as payment for shares.

h.   *Dividends.* There are detailed rules which differentiate between the ability of public and private companies to distribute their profits as dividends.

i.   *Company Administration.* The *COMPANIES ACT 1989* (now incorporated into the *COMPANIES ACT 2006*) made a number of changes designed to help small businesses by cutting the burden of regulation. Thus a private company may pass an *elective resolution* (this must be agreed by all members entitled to attend and vote at the meeting) if it wishes, for example (a) to dispense with the requirement to lay accounts and reports before the company in general meeting (b) to dispense with the requirement to hold an AGM or (c) to dispense with the requirement to appoint auditors annually.

j.   *Written Resolutions.* The 1989 Act also introduced a written resolution procedure for private companies. Anything which may be done by resolution of a private company in general meeting may now be done by a written resolution signed by or on behalf of all members.

k.   *Other Differences.* There are numerous other differences concerning, for example, directors, the secretary, commencement of business, the accounts and the minimum number of members.

REGISTRATION PROCEDURE

The law relating to registered companies is contained in the *COMPANIES ACT 2006*: all section references in this chapter are to the *COMPANIES ACT 2006*, unless otherwise stated.

10. **The Functions of the Registrar of Companies** The registrar is an official of the Department of Trade. His basic functions are:

a.   To issue certificates of incorporation and change of name.

b.   To be responsible for the registration and safe custody of documents required by statute to be filed with him and to pursue companies which fail to comply with such requirements.

c.   To issue certificates of registration of mortgages and charges.

d.   To provide facilities for the examination of filed documents by members of the public and to give copies of documents or certificates on payment of a fee.

e.   At the conclusion of the winding-up of a company the registrar will complete final dissolution by striking the company off the register.

11. *Registration/formation of New Companies* It is now possible to register and thereby incorporate a company by electronic means online.

a.   *S.7–16* of the Act, govern the requirements as to registration. To obtain registration the promoters must deliver to the registrar:

i.   Memorandum of Association;

Those persons wishing to form/incorporate a company – the *subscribers* – must put their names on the memorandum of association. This document – once key to the information on a company's constitution– is now a document only used for incorporation. Post incorporation, this document, unlike the articles of association (see below) cannot be altered. The memorandum of associations of companies existing prior to the 2006 Act, are now regarded as being within the articles of association, and as such may be altered at any time after incorporation.

ii. Articles of Association.

iii. A statement containing the name, address, nationality, business occupation, other directorships and age of each person who is to be a first director or the secretary of the company. The statement must contain the signed consent of each person named to act.

iv. Address of the registered office.

v.   A Declaration of Compliance, made by the solicitor engaged in the formation, or a person named as director or secretary, stating that the requirements of the Act have been complied with.

Where the company does not wish to adopt one of the laid down model set of articles (see Chapter 40.27) then a copy of the proposed articles must be attached.

vi. A registration fee.

The purpose of the memorandum of association is to indicate that the subscribers wish to become members of the company once formed. If the company is to be one limited by shares – by far the vast majority of registered companies – then there will also be a statement of agreement that members will take at least one share each (*S.8(1)(b)*).

The memorandum of association is now a statement that the subscribers intend to form a company. The Articles of Association are now seen as the key constitutional document of the company. Companies formed before the introduction of this new procedure (prior to 2009), will have two documents; the memorandum of association and the articles of association, however, in law, these two documents will henceforth be seen as one – the articles of association. There is nothing to stop 'old' companies, if they wish, adopting this new constitutional form.

b.   The registrar could rely on the declaration of compliance, but in practice his staff check that the documents are formally in order and that the name and objects are legal. If satisfied the registrar will issue a *Certificate of Incorporation*. The Certificate of Incorporation is *conclusive evidence* that the formalities of registration have been complied with. This means that even if it is subsequently discovered that the formalities of registration were not in fact complied with, the registration will not be invalidated. The reason for this is that once a company has commenced business and entered into contracts it would be unreasonable for either side to be able to avoid the contract because of a procedural defect in registration.

Where the above documents are sent to the registrar electronically, the need for signatures, witnesses and statutory declarations is not required; instead an electronic statement by a solicitor, or persons named as directors or secretary, will suffice.

12. *Re-registration of a Private Company as Public*

a. By *S.90–96* the company must pass a *special resolution* that it should be re-registered as public. The special resolution must:

   i. Alter the company's constitution within its new articles of association, so that it states that the company is to be a public company.

   ii. Make any other necessary changes to the articles, for example changing the name of the company so that it ends with 'Public Limited Company' or removing any previous restriction on the right to transfer shares.

b. An application to re-register must then be sent to the registrar. This must be signed by a director or the secretary and must be accompanied by a printed copy of the new articles and a number of specific documents primarily concerned with assuring that the company meets the capital requirements of public companies, for example the nominal value i.e. face value of the company's share capital must be at least £50 000.

It is common for a public company to be formed in this way, i.e. converted from an existing private company to a public company.

13. *Public Company to Re-register as Private*

a. Under *S.90–96* the company must pass a *special resolution* that it should be re-registered as private. The special resolution must, within a new articles of association:

   i. State that the company is to be a public company. The name clause must also be changed.

   ii. Make any alterations regarding the possible introduction of a restriction on the right to transfer shares.

b. The application must be signed by a director or the secretary and sent to the registrar with a printed copy of the new articles of association.

c. Within 28 days of the resolution holders of not less that 5% of the issued shares of any class *or* not less than 50 members, may apply to the court to cancel the resolution (*S.98*). The court may confirm or cancel the resolution, imposing such conditions as it thinks fit, for example that the dissenting members' shares be purchased, if necessary by the company itself.

PROMOTERS

14. A promoter is any person involved in the planning, incorporation or initial running of a company, other than persons involved in a purely professional capacity. A promoter need not necessarily be the main person behind the incorporation, but he must have

some executive function. The stereotype of a promoter may well be a city businessman, but any small trader who forms a company and sells his business to it is also a promoter.

15. **Duties of Promoters** The law has to protect shareholders from the situation where a promoter forms a company, sell shares in the company for cash and then sell his own property to the company in return for that cash, thus making a personal profit. The courts have established the principle that a promoter stands in a *fiduciary relationship* with the company which he is forming. This does not mean that he is barred from making a profit out of the promotion. It means that any profit made must be *disclosed* to the company. In this context 'the company' means existing and potential members. Thus a promoter cannot form a company and sell his own land to it at a vast profit, disclosing this only to a few of his associates who constitute the initial members, and then float off the company to the public. If the company is to be sold to the public the promoter's profit must be disclosed to potential members in the prospectus. Then, knowing what proportion of the price of their shares will go to the promoters, the public are adequately informed when making the decision of whether or not to purchase the shares.

16. **Remedies for Breach of Duty** In the event of non-disclosure of profits the company may commence proceedings for rescission or for recovery of the undisclosed profits.

   a.   The right to rescind is exercised on the usual contractual principles. Therefore:

   i.   The company must have done nothing to ratify the agreement after finding out about the non-disclosure or misrepresentation, and

   ii. Restitution must be possible although the court can order financial adjustments to be made when ordering rescission, so the restitution rule rarely operates as any real restraint.

   b.   If the contract is rescinded the promoter's secret profit will normally disappear as a result. If, however, he has made a profit on some ancillary transaction this may also be claimed by the company. A secret profit may be recovered even if the company elects not to rescind.

   c.   The company may sue the promoter for damages under the *MISREPRESENTATION ACT 1967*, or for negligence, or for fraud. This will be useful if rescission is barred.

17. **Payment for Promotion**

   a.   Promoters are not entitled to payment because:

   i.   Before incorporation the company cannot contract to pay them since it does not exist, and

   ii. After incorporation any such contract would be void since the consideration would be past.

   b.   However, the articles will provide that 'The business of the company shall be managed by the directors who may exercise all the powers of the company.' The directors may therefore pay the promoters their expenses. In practice there will be few problems since the promoters will normally be the first directors.

   c.   Another method of payment would be for the promoter to sell property to the company at an overvaluation (the difference being the 'payment'). This would be acceptable provided all the disclosure requirements are satisfied.

PRE-INCORPORATION CONTRACTS

18. *The Effect on the Company*

   a. A contract made on behalf of a company before its incorporation does not bind the company, nor can it be enforced or ratified by the company after incorporation.

   In **KELNER v BAXTER (1866)** a company was about to be formed to buy a hotel. Before the company was formed the promoters signed a contract 'on behalf of' the proposed company for the purchase of a quantity of wine. The company was formed, the hotel purchased, and the wine was delivered and consumed, but before payment was made the company went into liquidation. It was held that the promoters were personally liable to pay for the wine, any purported ratification by the company being ineffective.

   b. Therefore any pre-incorporation agreements will either have to be binding in honour only, or the promoter will have to undertake personal liability.

19. *The Effect on the Person who Purports to Contract on Behalf of the Company*

   a. By *S.51* where a contract purports to be made by a company, or by a person as agent for a company, at a time when the company has not been formed, then subject to any agreement to the contrary, the contract has effect as one entered into by the person purporting to act for the company or as agent for it, and he is personally liable on the contract. Not only can he be sued under the contract, but, following the case of **BRAYMIST LTD v WISE FINANCE CO LTD (2002)**, he can also sue the other party. In this case a solicitor signed a pre-incorporation contract for the sale of land on behalf of a – about to be formed – company, Braymist. The other party, Wise Finance, decided not to honour the contract of sale. Braymist and the solicitor representing it, sought damages from the defendant. The court held that not only could the representative of a pre-incorporation contract be sued, but also, they could sue for breach.

   b. Although *S.51* provides for an express agreement to the contrary, it does not envisage an agreement whereby the promoter incurs no liability and cannot enforce the contract since such an agreement would be invalid for lack of consideration. The Act envisages that the promoter protects himself by:

   i. Agreeing that the promoters' liability shall cease when the company, after incorporation, enters into a similar agreement, or

   ii. Agreeing that if the company does not enter into such an agreement within a fixed period either party may rescind.

20. *Contracts Made by a Public Company Before the Issue of a Certificate of Incorporation*

   a. A public company may not commence business until it has obtained a certificate of compliance with the capital requirements of public companies (sometimes known as a 'trading certificate'). In contrast a private company may commence trading from the date of incorporation.

   b. If a public company does business in contravention of the Act the transaction will be valid, but if the company fails to comply with its obligations within 21 days of being called upon to do so, the directors are liable to indemnify the other party if he suffers loss due to the company's failure to comply. This is an example of 'lifting the veil' of incorporation. In addition the company and its officers may be fined.

21. *Execution of Documents by Companies* A document will be executed if signed by two directors or a director and the secretary, provided it is expressed to be executed by the company. This relieves companies of the obligation to use seals, it does not prohibit them from continuing as before.

SELF TEST QUESTIONS

Self Test Questions No. 37 (for Answers see Appendix 1):

1   What are the main types of company?

2   What are the key differences between the company and other *unincorporated* forms?

3   What are the main consequences of *separate legal entity*?

4   What do you understand by the phrase, 'lifting the veil'?

5   Outline the main differences between public and private companies.

6   What is the registration procedure for a company?

7   Who are promoters?

8   What is the law regarding *pre-incorporation contracts*?

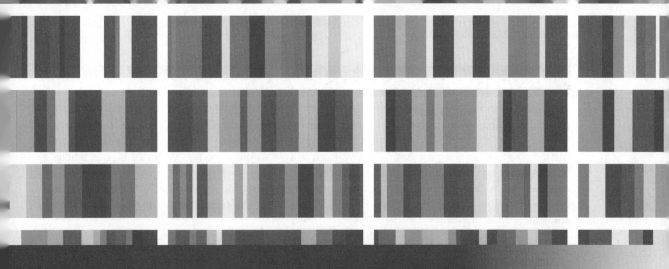

THE ARTICLES OF ASSOCIATION 40

Learning Outcomes At the end of this chapter you should be able to:

- Explain the nature and general content of the articles of association.

- Understand the rules relating to a company's choice of name.

- Explain the meaning and significance of a company's registered office.

- Understand corporate capacity and the *objects clause*.

- Explain key clauses of the articles, namely:

  – limitation of liability

  – capital clause

  – association clause.

- Outline the rules governing the alteration of articles.

- Explain the legal effect of a company's constitution once registered.

INTRODUCTION

As already noted (see Chapter 39.11) there is now, following the *COMPANIES ACT 2006*, one key document in a company's constitution, the articles of association. Companies formed before the introduction of the new Act (effective from 2009) would have two documents: the articles of association and memorandum of association. Today, these two documents will be viewed by a court as one, with the provisions of the memorandum being incorporated into the articles. The memorandum still exists but is now simply evidence that the promoters wish to incorporate a company.

1. ***The Articles*** The regulations of every company will be contained in the articles which set out its basic constitution. As this is a public document it not only lays down the internal rules of the company for those directly involved in its running, but is also a statement to the outside world. The *COMPANIES ACT 1985* sets out model sets of articles which a company could adopt in its entirety, adopt with modifications (the usual practice) or draft their own. The key set of model articles for present purposes is called Table A. The important point to note here is that if there is a dispute and a particular company's articles are unclear, the courts will look to Table A to clarify. Following the *COMPANIES ACT 2006*, the latest set of model articles is contained in the *COMPANY (MODEL ARTICLES) REGULATIONS 2008*.

2. ***Contents of the Articles***

   a. *Every company* memorandum must contain the following six clauses:

      i. Name.

      ii. Registered Office.

      iii. Objects.

      iv. Limitation of Liability.

      v. Capital, and

      vi. Association.

   b. In addition the articles of every *public company* must state that 'The company is to be a public company.'

THE NAME CLAUSE

3. ***Basic Rules*** A company, as a legal person, must have a name. The *COMPANIES ACT 2006* contains provisions which control the names of companies.

   a. By *S.59* the last word of a private company's name must be 'Limited'. This warns persons who deal with companies that they will not have access to the private funds of the members to satisfy their debts. 'Limited' may be abbreviated to 'Ltd'. A partnership name must not end with the word 'Limited'. Private companies limited by guarantee may apply to dispense with the word 'Limited' if their objects are to promote, for example, art, science or education and their articles prohibit the payment of dividends.

   b. By *S.58* a public company's name must end with the words 'Public Limited Company' or the abbreviation 'P.L.C.'.

4. *Prohibition on Registration of Certain Names (S.53)*

A company may not be registered with a name:

a. Which includes any of the following (or abbreviations thereof) *other than* at the end of the name: 'limited', 'unlimited' or 'public limited company'.

b. Which is the same as a name already appearing in the index kept by the registrar.

c. The use of which would, in the opinion of the Secretary of State, constitute a criminal offence.

d. Which in the opinion of the Secretary of State is offensive, or

e. Which would be likely to give the impression that the company is in any way connected with the Government or with a local authority.

5. *Change of Name (S.77–78)*

a. A company may change its name by *special resolution* at any time. A new certificate of incorporation will be issued and the change is effective from the date of that certificate.

b. In certain circumstances the Secretary of State may order a company to change its name, for example:

    i. If the name is too similar to a name already in the index.

    ii. If the name is so misleading as to be likely to cause harm to the public.

c. The court may also order a change of name following a successful 'passing-off' action.

In *EWING v BUTTERCUP MARGARINE CO (1917)* E, whose business was called 'The Buttercup Dairy Company' was successful in his attempt to prevent a newly registered company from using the name 'Buttercup Margarine Company' because it was considered that the public might think that the two businesses were connected.

6. *Publication of Name and Address*

a. Every company must publish its name:

    i. Outside all its places of business.

    ii. On all letters, orders, invoices, notices, cheques and receipts, and

    iii. On its seal, if it has a seal.

b. If a company does not comply with the above requirements, the company and every officer in default are liable to a fine. In addition if an officer or other person issues or signs any company letters, orders, cheques, etc. which do not bear the full name of the company he may be fined and he will be liable to any creditor who has relied on the document if the company fails to pay him.

c. The place of registration (i.e. England or Scotland), the address of the registered office and its number in the index at the registry, must also appear on all business letters and order forms.

7. *Business Names*

a. Most companies, partnerships and sole traders trade under their own names, but sometimes they prefer to use another name. This is known as a business name.

b. The *BUSINESS NAMES ACT 1985* requires any person (company, partnership or sole trader) who carries on business under a different name from his own.

i. To state its name and address on all business letters, invoices, receipts, orders and demands for payment.

ii. To display its name and address in a prominent position in any business premises to which suppliers or customers have access, and

iii. At the request of any person with whom it does business to supply a written notice of its name and address.

THE REGISTERED OFFICE

8. *The Registered Office Clause* This clause does not state the address of the registered office, it merely states that the registered office will be situated in England and Wales (or Wales alone if it is to be a Welsh company) or Scotland, thus fixing the nationality and domicile of the company.

9. *The Purpose of the Registered Office* The registered office is the official address of the company. It is also the place where writs, notices and other communications can be served, and where certain registers and documents are usually kept. It need not be a place of business of the company, in fact many companies arrange for the premises of their solicitors or accountants to be their registered office.

10. *Documents and Registers Kept at the Registered Office* The following documents and registers are usually kept at the registered office, and must be kept there unless otherwise stated:

a. The register of members, unless it is made up elsewhere in which case it can be kept where it is made up.

b. The register of directors and secretaries.

c. The register of directors' interests in shares and debentures. If the register of members is not kept at the registered office, the register of directors' interests may be kept with the register of members.

d. The register of debenture holders. If the register is made up elsewhere it may be kept where it is made up.

e. The register of charges.

f. Copies of instruments creating the charges.

g. The minute book of general meetings.

h. Directors' service contracts. These may instead be kept at the principal place of business.

i. The minute book of directors' meetings. This may be kept at any convenient place.

j. The accounting records. These may also be kept at any convenient place.

k. A copy of any contract for an off-market purchase, market purchase or contingent purchase by a company of its own shares (or if the contract is not in writing, a written memorandum of its terms) must be kept for 10 years from the date of completion of the purchase.

l. A *public company* must keep a register of interests in shares. The level at which a holding becomes notifiable is 3%. This register must be kept with the register of directors' interests.

11. ***Rights of Inspection of Documents and Registers*** The above registers and documents with the exception of d. and f. are the statutory books, i.e. the registers and documents which every company is required to keep by law. They are subject to the following rights of inspection:

   a.   Members may inspect all except i. and j. free of charge.

   b.   Creditors may inspect e. and f. free of charge.

   c.   Debenture holders may inspect d. free of charge.

   d.   Directors may inspect all of the documents and registers.

   e.   The public may inspect a., b., c., d., e., and l. on payment of a small fee. They may inspect k. only if the company is a public company.

12. ***Change of Address***

   a.   The company cannot change the clause in the memorandum which states the country in which the registered office will be situated. It may, however, move the registered office within that country. This change of address is effected by *ordinary resolution*, or if there is authority in the articles, by a resolution of the board of directors.

   b.   The company is allowed 14 days from the date of the change (i.e. the date of registration of the change) to move its registers to the new registered office. Similarly if it is necessary to move registers quickly and it has not been practicable to give prior notice, no offence will be committed as long as notice of the change is given to the registrar within 14 days. Also, for 14 days following the change, a person may validly serve any document on the company at its previous registered office.

THE OBJECTS CLAUSE

13. ***The Purposes of the Objects Clause*** The objects clause of a company relates to what the company can do – its capacity to act – e.g. manufacture certain products, provide a service, employ workers, etc. The position today is that if there is a stated objects clause, then that should be contained in the articles, where there are no stated objects, then the company's objects are unrestricted. This means that a company has the capacity to do anything provided it is legal. In some cases when a company is formed there is a wish to restrict the things it can do, e.g. where a company is formed as a charity or some social enterprise, there may well be a need to make sure the company acts within certain boundaries. However, even where a company has objects in its articles, this will not affect its ability to enter valid, enforceable contracts.

Originally the objects clause served two purposes:

   a.   Prospective members were told what kind of business they were investing in, and

   b.   Creditors were able to ensure that the funds from which they could expect payment were not used for unauthorized activities.

14. ***Brief History***

   a.   Before 1989 the basic rule was that an act outside the objects clause was *ultra vires* and void and therefore could not be enforced by the company or by an outsider. This was unpopular with companies (for whom it could be inconvenient to have restricted powers) and outsiders (who might find that their contract could not be enforced). This was generally the case even if the outsider did not actually know of the restriction on the company's power, because of the doctrine of *constructive notice*, by which, because all the registered documents are available to the public, everyone was deemed to know of the contents.

b.   Companies therefore sought to avoid the *ultra vires* rule by drafting lengthy objects clauses (often covering many pages) allowing them to do almost anything they could ever wish to do. They also usually included general powers allowing anything incidental to any of their other objects and powers. The effect of the ultra vires rule was further restricted by *S.35 CA 85* (now repealed) which stated that if an outsider dealt with the company in good faith, any transaction decided on by the directors would be deemed to be within the company's capacity, regardless of any limitations in the memorandum or articles.

c.   In 1985 the Department for Business Innovation & Skills (DTI) commissioned a report on the implications of abolishing the ultra vires rule. The report recommended complete abolition. The Government, however, took the view that total abolition would be undesirable. The 1989 Act therefore abolished the application of ultra vires in respect of outsiders, but retained the power of members to bring proceedings to restrain ultra vires acts. This ensures that commercial transactions cannot be set aside once they have been entered into, but retains some members' rights.

ARTICLES

15.   *Validity of Acts Done by Companies*

a.   By *S.39* the validity of an act done by a company shall not be called into question on the ground of lack of capacity by reason of anything in the company's memorandum.

b.   Consequently a *completed act* will have *total protection* from the ultra vires rule and will be *enforceable* by both the company and an outsider.

16.   *Members' Right to Restrain Ultra Vires Acts Beyond Stated Objects* Any member may bring proceedings to restrain an intended act which would be beyond the capacity of the company. However, this right is restricted by *S.39* which allows the company to ratify an ultra vires act by *special resolution*.

17.   *Constructive Notice*

a.   *S.39* makes it clear that an outsider is not bound to inquire as to whether an act is permitted by the memorandum or subject to any limitations on the authority of the directors. Furthermore a person shall not be taken to have notice of any matter merely because it is disclosed in registered documents or made available by the company for inspection.

b.   These sections abolish the doctrine of constructive notice subject to an exception preserved where a person taking a charge over a company's property is deemed to have notice of any matter requiring registration and disclosed on the register of charges at the time the charge was created.

18.   *Alteration of Articles*

a.   *Basic rule.* By *S.21* a company may freely amend its articles, including its objects clause, by *special* (or written) *resolution*.

b.   *Minority protection*

i.   By *S.633* holders of 15% of the issued capital may apply to the court within 21 days of the resolution to have it set aside. The court may confirm or refuse the resolution, or it may arrange for the purchase of the dissentient members' interests, if necessary by the company itself.

ii. If no application is made the company must, within 15 days after the end of the 21-day period, deliver to the registrar a printed copy of the articles as altered.

LIMITATION OF LIABILITY

19. *Contents of the Clause* Where a company is limited by shares or by guarantee this clause will merely state: 'The liability of the members is limited.'

20. *Companies Limited by Shares* The vast majority of companies, both public and private are companies limited by shares. In such a company the capital is divided into shares, for example capital of £5000 divided into 10 000 shares of 50 pence each. The members of the company are liable to pay for their shares, either in money or money's worth (i.e. non-cash assets, goodwill or know-how). Once they have paid for their shares they are under no further liability. The company is therefore said to be 'limited by shares'. It is, however, important to note that it is not the company's liability which is limited, it must discharge its debts as long as it has assets to do so. It is the members' liability to the company which is limited.

21. *Companies Limited by Guarantee*

a.   Such companies are usually formed for educational or charitable purposes. They usually raise their funds by subscription. Limitation of liability by guarantee is not appropriate for trading companies.

b.   The liability of each member is limited to the amount he has agreed to contribute in the event of winding-up. The amount (usually £1 or £5) will be specified in the memorandum. Moreover a member's liability is contingent, his money is only called-up in the event of liquidation.

22. *Unlimited Companies*

a.   There is no limit to the liability of the members of such companies. Thus although the company is a separate legal entity, the members' liability resembles that of partners, except that technically their liability is to the company itself and not to the creditors.

b.   Unlimited companies are not popular because of this personal liability. However, unlimited companies do have the advantage of greater privacy since they are not required to deliver copies of their accounts to the registrar.

OTHER CLAUSES

23. *The Capital Clause*

a.   This states amount of capital and its division into shares of a fixed amount, e.g. 'The share capital of the company is £50 000 divided into 50 000 shares of £1 each.'

b.   The capital of a public company must be not less than the authorized minimum, at present £50 000.

c.   When shares are first issued they may be issued at a *premium*, (i.e. for more than the nominal value), at *par* (i.e. at the nominal value), but not at a discount, (i.e. less than the nominal value).

d.   Once the shares have been allotted they will change hands at market value which may be above or below the nominal value. The two figures are not related. The nominal value is fixed by the promoters or directors of the company. The market value reflects the prosperity of the company and the extent of speculative dealing in the shares.

24. *The Association Clause* In this clause the subscribers to the memorandum declare that they desire to be formed into a company, and agree to take the number of shares set opposite their names. Each subscriber signs the memorandum.

25. *Alteration of the Articles Generally* Every clause of the articles may be altered except the registered office clause, i.e. the country of incorporation cannot be altered.

26. As seen (18. above) the articles may be altered by *special resolution*. Any provision which attempts to deprive the company of this power is void, for example a power given to a particular member to veto an alteration.

a.   The articles of a *private company* may also be altered by *written resolution*. Private companies may substitute the need for a meeting by a unanimous written agreement of all shareholders for any resolution passed at a general meeting. Clearly such a procedure can also be used, for example to change the company name or to alter the objects clause in the memorandum.

b.   No alteration of the articles can constitute a fraud on the minority (see below), nor overrule the general law, the memorandum, or the provisions of the Acts. For example:

i.   No increase of a member's liability is possible without his written consent, i.e. a member cannot be compelled to purchase more shares.

ii. Minority protection provisions, for example the right of a dissenting 15% to object to a change of objects, cannot be excluded.

c.   *Fraud on the minority.* The change must be for the benefit of the company, i.e. members in general. It would be improper if its purpose is primarily to injure other members.

In **BROWN v BRITISH ABRASIVE WHEEL CO (1919)** a resolution was passed adding to the articles a clause compelling a member to transfer his shares upon a request in writing by the holders of 90% of the issued shares. The change could not be for the benefit of the company as a whole, but solely for the benefit of the majority.

d.   *The effect of an alteration on outsiders.* An alteration of the articles which causes a breach of contract with an outsider is valid, and cannot be restrained by an injunction. The outsider's remedy is to claim damages for breach of contract.

In **SOUTHERN FOUNDRIES v SHIRLAW (1940)** Shirlaw had been appointed the managing director of Southern Foundries for 10 years. The articles stated that the managing director's appointment shall automatically cease if he should cease to be a director. Southern Foundries was then merged into a group called Federated Industries. All group members agreed to make certain alterations to their articles, one such change being that FI would have power to remove any director of a member company. FI then used this power to remove Shirlaw. As a result he automatically ceased to be managing director of SF, even though his contract had several years left to run. Shirlaw's claim for damages for wrongful dismissal succeeded because his contract as managing director was held to contain an implied term that the company would not do anything to make it impossible for him to continue as managing director.

27. ***The Legal Effect of the Constitution*** By *S.33* the provisions of a company's constitution when registered bind the company and the members as if they had been signed and sealed by each member and contained covenants on the part of each member to observe their provisions. The effects of this are that:

a. *The company is bound to each individual member in his capacity as member.* Thus for example it must record a properly given vote. However, it is not bound by a right given by the articles to a member acting in another capacity, for example as company solicitor.

   In ***ELEY v POSITIVE LIFE ASSURANCE CO (1876)*** the articles contained a clause appointing the claimant as company solicitor, and he acted as such for some time. The company then ceased to employ him and he brought an action for breach of contract. It was held that the articles did not constitute a contract between the company and Eley because even though he was a member they could not confer rights on him in any other capacity, including that of company solicitor.

b. *Each member is bound to the company.* Therefore a provision in the articles referring disputes between a member and the company to arbitration will be enforceable against the member provided the dispute concerns membership rights.

   In ***HICKMAN v KENT SHEEP BREEDERS ASSOCIATION (1915)*** the articles provided for disputes between members and the company to be referred to arbitration. The Association wished to expel the plaintiff from membership of the Association and the plaintiff applied for an injunction to prevent this. It was held that the Association was entitled to have the action stayed since the dispute concerned membership rights and the articles provided for such disputes to initially be settled by arbitration rather than legal action.

c. *The members are contractually bound to each other.* The main occasions when this question is likely to arise are when the articles give members pre-emption rights when another member wishes to sell his shares, or more rarely, when the articles place on members a duty to buy the shares of a retiring member. In such cases a direct action between the shareholders concerned is theoretically possible. However, a situation where members are able to sue other members may well give rise to practical difficulties. To avoid this, modern articles will make the transaction a two-stage process, each stage being a dealing with the company to which *S.33* clearly applies. The articles first require any member who intends to transfer his shares to inform the company. They then require the company to give notice to other members that they have an option to purchase the shares. If the first stage is not complied with, the company can sue the transferor. If the second stage is broken a shareholder may sue the company.

d. *Differences between the contract in S.33 and other contracts*

   i. The normal remedy of damages for breach of contract is not available because of the court's desire to maintain the capital of the company. A member may, however, obtain an injunction to prevent a breach by the company of any provision in the memorandum or articles and he may sue for a liquidated sum due to him as a member, for example unpaid dividends.

   ii. The contract does not guarantee the future rights and duties of members, since both the memorandum and articles may be altered. Thus when becoming a member a person agrees to a contract which is alterable by the other party (the company) at a future date.

SELF TEST QUESTIONS

Self Test Questions No. 38 (for Answers see Appendix 1):

1   What are the contents of the articles of association?

2   What is Table A?

3   What is meant by a company's registered office?

4   What is an *objects clause*?

5   Explain the nature of a company limited by shares.

6   How can the articles of a company be altered?

7   What is the legal effect of a company's constitution?

SHARE CAPITAL

41

Learning Outcomes At the end of this chapter you should be able to:

- Explain the processes by which a company may raise share capital.

- Outline the different types of capital and the process of its alteration.

- Explain the meaning of and requirements for dividends to be paid.

- Show an understanding of the different types of shares; their allotment and transference.

PUBLIC OFFERS FOR SHARES

1. *Raising Funds* Private companies will usually raise their funds from their own membership or from a bank. Public companies are formed when it is necessary to obtain funds from an issue of shares or debentures to the public. This has led to many provisions to protect the investing public. These are now contained in *FINANCIAL SERVICES and MARKETS ACT 2000 (FSMA – the Act).*

2. *Listed and Unlisted Securities*

   a. *Listed securities.* The Act deals with the official listing of securities, i.e. the Official List of the Stock Exchange. It provides for an application to be made to the '*competent authority'* (the Council of the Stock Exchange) by the method specified in the Listing Rules. These rules contain details of the information to be included in '*listing particulars'*.

European Union – EC law – requires that each member state create a Competent Authority to maintain and regulate the Official List and monitor adherence to the Listing Rules. In the UK this is carried out by the Financial Services Authority (FSA). The FSA can refuse an application for listing where it considers that granting it would be detrimental to investors. It can also suspend a current listing for non-compliance.

b.   *Unlisted securities.* The Act also deals with offers of unlisted securities which are to be admitted for dealing on an '*approved exchange'* for example the Unlisted Securities Market. In such cases no advertisement offering securities may be issued unless a '*prospectus'* has been approved by the FSA and delivered to the registrar of companies. The *Prospectus Regulations 2005* replaces sections of the Act relating to an offer of shares through a prospectus (a *prospectus* is a document containing financial information on a company).

3. *Private Companies* Two provisions in the Act make it clear that the Act does not apply to private companies:

a.   A private company must not apply for its shares to be listed on the Stock Exchange.

b.   A private company must not issue any advertisement offering its shares for sale.

4. *Public Issue by 'Offer for Sale'*

a.   This method may be employed when a public company wishes to raise money by issuing new shares. It involves the transfer of all the new shares to an issuing house (usually a merchant bank). The issuing house will then publish listing particulars inviting the public to purchase from it at a slightly higher price. This method is much more common than a '*direct offer'* by the company and it does not involve any risk for the company, although the issuing house will underwrite. The issuing house will not be registered as holder except in respect of shares which the public do not take. The practice is to issue renounceable letters of allotment to the issuing house. This enables it to assign its right to membership by signing forms of renunciation in favour of purchasers.

b.   The term 'offer for sale' is rather misleading, since the listing particulars are in fact an invitation to treat, not an offer capable of acceptance by the public. The offer occurs when the applicant sends in the application form, it is then up to the company to accept.

5. *Rights Issues*

a.   The modern practice when a public company wants to raise capital is to make a rights issue, i.e. new shares are created and offered to existing shareholders in proportion to their existing shareholding. It is a legal requirement that existing shareholders be given a right of first refusal when new shares are issued.

b.   To make a rights issue attractive the shares will usually be offered at 10–20 per cent less than the current market value. This can give added worth to the existing shares until they go 'ex rights' when buying them will no longer entitle the holder to participate in the rights issue. After the issue the market may mark down the price of the shares since they will have lost some scarcity value.

6. *Application and Admission to the Official List*

a.   No securities may be admitted to listing i.e. quoted, unless an application has been made to the *competent authority* in the way required by the Listing Rules. The competent authority is the Financial Services Authority (FSA). The listing rules specify the content of the listing particulars.

The information required is very detailed, but will include basic essential information, for example:

i.   The names, addresses and descriptions of the directors.

ii.   The capital to be subscribed, the amount to be paid in cash and the nature of the consideration for the remainder.

iii.   Voting and dividend rights for each class of share.

b.   In addition to any matters required by the listing rules the Act imposes a general duty to disclose information that investors and their advisors would reasonably require to make an informed decision on whether to buy the securities. It must enable them to ascertain the assets and liabilities, financial position, results and prospects of the issuer, and the rights attaching to those securities.

c.   An application may be refused if:

i.   The FSA considers that because of any matter relating to the issuer, the admission would be detrimental to investors.

ii.   In the case of shares already officially listed in another EU state, the issuer has failed to comply with his obligations in connection with that listing.

d.   The FSA may discontinue the listing of any securities if it is satisfied that there are special circumstances which prevent normal regular dealings. It may also temporarily suspend listing. This sometimes occurs at the issuer's request, for example when rumours of a takeover bid distort the normal market for the securities.

7. *Remedies for Misrepresentation and Omission*

a.   *S.90* of the Act places liability on those responsible for misstatements, omissions and misleading opinions in a company's *prospectus*. A 'person responsible' for listing particulars (which includes the company, its directors or any other person who authorized any part of the particulars) shall be liable to compensate any person who acquires the securities in question and suffers loss as a result of any untrue or misleading statement or the omission of any of the required particulars. A number of defences are possible, for example:

i.   Reasonable belief that the statement was true and not misleading, or that the matter was properly omitted.

ii.   Reliance on a statement made by an expert, provided the expert consented to the inclusion of the statement and the person responsible can show reasonable belief in the expert's competence.

iii.   That the loss resulted from the fair and accurate reproduction of a statement by an official person or contained in an official document.

iv.   The claimant acquired the securities with the knowledge that the listing particulars were false or misleading.

b.   *Damages.* There are three avenues leading to an award of damages. The action chosen will depend on several factors, including the type of misrepresentation.

    i.   By *S.2(1) MISREPRESENTATION ACT 1967* the innocent party has a right to damages for misrepresentation if he has suffered loss. However, if the maker of the statement proves that he had reasonable grounds for believing, and in fact did believe, up to the time the contract was made, that the facts represented were true, then he has a defence.

        The problem with *S.2(1)* is that the range of persons who can be sued is rather narrow. Only the other party to the contract can be sued. Thus directors and experts are excluded, as is the company, unless the securities were acquired directly from it.

    ii.   If the misrepresentation is fraudulent, damages may be recovered in tort for deceit. A fraudulent misrepresentation is a statement which is known to be false, or made without belief in its truth, or made recklessly, not caring whether it is true or false (*DERRY v PEEK (1889)*). The action will lie against all those who made the false statement, including the company.

    iii. The third possibility is that damages for negligent misrepresentation may be claimed under the rule in *HEDLEY BYRNE v HELLER (1964)*. The duty not to make negligent statements will be owed if the claimant can show that he relied on the special skill and judgement of the respondent, and the respondent knew, or ought to have known, of the reliance, thus accepting responsibility for making the statement carefully.

        The persons liable will be those who both owed and broke the duty of care. This would include directors and experts, but it probably does not include the company.

  c. *Rescission.* Since rescission is an equitable remedy its award is at the discretion of the court. In general the plaintiff will not be granted rescission in the following circumstances:

    i.   If he delays in seeking his remedy.

    ii.   If he affirms the contract, i.e. with knowledge of his right to rescind he acts in a way which is consistent with ownership of the shares, for example by voting at meetings or attempting to sell the shares, or

    iii. If the company goes into liquidation, since the rights of third parties, such as creditors and debenture holders, will then intervene.

    The remedy of rescission is affected by *S.2(2) MISREPRESENTATION ACT 1967* which gives the court a discretion to award damages in lieu of rescission if it thinks it equitable to do so.

TYPES OF CAPITAL AND ALTERATION OF CAPITAL

8. *Capital, Share Capital and Loan Capital*

  a. The word capital is generally used to describe the amount by which the assets of a business exceed its liabilities. This implies a fluctuating measure of the net worth of the business.

  b. The share capital of a limited company is not a constantly fluctuating figure. It is the minimum value of net assets which must be raised initially, and so far as possible retained in the business, i.e. it is the amount that purchasers of shares have agreed to contribute to the company in return for their shares.

c.   Share capital, which is subject to many rules of preservation and disclosure, must be distinguished from loan capital. When money is lent to a company the lender does not become a member of the company and the money raised is not subject to the same rules of preservation.

9. *Different Meanings of 'Share Capital'*

a.   *Nominal or authorized capital.* Every company must state in its articles the amount of its nominal capital. This figure shows the maximum number of shares the company is authorized to issue and the nominal value of each share. It does not indicate that any shares have been issued and paid for.

b.   *Issued capital.* Some or all of the nominal capital must be issued in return for cash or the transfer of non-cash assets. Issued capital is of far more importance than nominal capital since each shareholder is liable to pay the price of shares issued to him. It is the issued capital which, in theory, comprises a guarantee fund from which creditors can expect to be paid. It is therefore important that it is not wrongfully reduced, for example by using it to pay dividends to shareholders. However, it may of course, be quite legitimately lost in the normal course of business trading. Unless it is clear that some other meaning applies, all subsequent references to 'capital' are references to issued capital.

c.   *Called-up capital*

i.   *S.3* CA 06 provides that the liability of shareholders shall be limited to the amount, if any, unpaid on their shares. The Act therefore allows the issued shares to be partly called-up.

ii.   Called-up capital equals the aggregate of the calls made on shares, whether or not the calls have been paid, together with any share capital paid-up without being called and any share capital to be paid on a specified future date under the articles.

iii.   In practice companies usually require fairly prompt payment of the full amount of issued capital by instalments, so that issued capital and called-up capital are generally the same.

d.   *Paid-up capital.* This is the sum of the payments received by the company. Unless some shareholders refuse to pay calls the paid-up capital will equal the called-up capital. Paid-up capital is important because if a company makes a reference on its stationery to the amount of its capital, the reference must be paid-up capital.

e.   *Uncalled capital.* This is the difference between the amount already paid-up and the total nominal value of the issued shares. Uncalled capital is rare because it is unpopular with both companies and investors, companies because of the possibility that calls will not be met, and investors because of uncertainty as to when calls will be made. Where it exists, uncalled capital is a further guarantee fund for creditors. It is an asset equivalent to debtors, the debtors in this case being the members. The creditors can, however, only gain access to this fund in the event of a liquidation since they cannot compel the directors to make calls, nor can they levy execution on uncalled capital.

f.   *Reserve capital.* In order that the guarantee fund referred to above can be removed from the directors' control and made more permanent, the Act provides that a company may, by *special resolution*, determine that it shall only be called up in the event of winding-up. The special resolution creating reserve capital is irrevocable. Reserve capital, which is also known as 'reserve liability' must not be confused with 'General Reserve' or 'Reserve Fund'. These terms refer to undistributed profits.

10. *Alteration of Capital* The requirement to have an authorized share capital is abolished from 1st October 2009 – the date when the *COMPANIES ACT 2006* came fully into force. Any company registered from that date will have no restriction on the number of shares it can issue. Companies registered before that date will be subject to the authorized capital figure in their memorandum and articles until they are amended (see Chapter 39.26). There is now no statutory procedure for an increase of authorized share capital.

MAINTENANCE OF CAPITAL

11. *The Need to Maintain Capital* The acceptance of limited liability has led to a need to protect the capital contributed by the members since the members cannot be required to contribute funds to enable the company to pay its debts once they have paid for their shares in full. The capital therefore represents a guarantee fund for creditors. Companies are therefore prohibited in general from returning capital to their members, Payments to shareholders – *dividends* – must only be paid out of distributable profits. Capital is protected in two basic ways:

    a.   Provisions designed to prevent the capital being 'watered down' as it comes into the company.

    b.   Provisions designed to prevent capital going out of the company once it has been received.

12. *Underwriting Commission*

    a.   An underwriter is a person (or finance house), which, on a public issue of shares, agrees to purchase those shares which are not taken up by the public.

    b.   By *S.553* underwriters may be paid a commission not exceeding 10% of the issue price provided there is authority in the articles and compliance with any rules made by the Secretary of State under powers given in the *FINANCIAL SERVICES and MARKETS ACT 2000*. These rules include the requirement of disclosure in the listing particulars. The commission is charged on the number of shares underwritten and must be paid even if the issue is a success and the public take all the shares. The usual rate is 1¼ per cent.

    c.   When a company has been in existence for some years it will probably be able to pay underwriting commission from its accumulated profits or its Share Premium Account. In contrast when a company makes its first issue of shares these funds will not exist. Underwriting commission must therefore be paid out of the proceeds of the issue, i.e. out of capital. This is why underwriting commission is subject to statutory control.

13. *Payment for Share Capital*

    a.   It is not possible for a company to make a gift of its shares to an allottee, the shares must always be paid for.

    b.   *S.582* states that they may be paid for in money or in money's worth, including goodwill or know-how.

    c.   However, by S.582 a *public company* may not accept as payment an undertaking to do work or perform services for the company. This means that the shares of a public company must be paid up in *cash* or non-cash assets.

14. *The Issue of Shares at a Discount*

   a. By *S.580* the issue of shares at a discount is prohibited, i.e. shares may not be allotted as fully paid for a consideration of less than their nominal value. Today shares usually have a very low nominal value, for example 5 pence. Since there is no statutory obligation on a company to issue shares for the highest price it can get, it is possible for a person to obtain shares for a consideration of less than their full value.

   b. This section applies to all companies.

15. *Minimum Payment for Allotted Shares*

   a. By *S.586 a public company* may not allot shares unless they are paid-up to the extent of one-quarter the nominal value plus the whole of the premium.

   b. In practice the company will almost certainly require the shares to be paid-up to the full nominal value plus all of the premium. The *share premium* is the difference between the nominal value and the issue price.

16. *Allotment for Non-cash Consideration*

   a. By *S.585* where a *public company* allots shares which are fully or partly paid for by an undertaking to transfer to the company a non-cash asset at a future date, that asset must be transferred within 5 years of the date of allotment.

   b. *Valuation of non-cash consideration, public companies.* By *S.586* a *public company* may not allot shares for a consideration other than cash unless the non-cash asset has been independently valued by a person qualified to be the auditor of the company. The report must state that the value of the consideration (including any cash payable) is not less than the nominal value of the shares plus any premium, i.e. that the shareholders are getting value for money.

   c. *Valuation of non-cash consideration, private companies.* When a private company issues shares in return for a non-cash consideration the court will not usually inquire into the adequacy of consideration. For example, although the valuation of Salomon's business at £39 000 was described by the House of Lords as 'A sum which represented the sanguine expectations of a fond owner rather than anything that can be called a businesslike or reasonable estimate of value,' they were not prepared to set aside the transaction even though the correct valuation of the business was about £10 000 (see Chapter 39.4).

   There are three exceptional situations when the court is concerned with the adequacy of consideration:

   i.   Where the contract is fraudulent.

   ii. Where the consideration is past, and

   iii. Where the inadequacy appears on the face of the contract.

   In *HONG KONG AND CHINA GAS CO v GLEN (1914)* the company agreed to allot to the vendor of a concession to supply gas to the city of Victoria in Hong Kong, 400 fully paid shares, plus one-fifth of any future increase in capital, allotted as fully paid. It was held that the part of the agreement relating to future increases in capital was invalid because it meant that the company had agreed an unlimited value for the purchase of the concession.

17. *Serious Loss of Capital*

    a.   By *S.656* the directors of a *public company* must call an extraordinary general meeting when it becomes known to a director that the net assets have fallen to *half or less* of the company's called-up share capital.

    b.   The purpose of the meeting is to decide what action, if any, should be taken. In some cases the meeting will decide on a reduction of capital.

18. *Reduction of Capital* In the first instance, a company cannot reduce the aggregate amount of its share capital except in accordance with the procedures laid down in the Act (*S.617*). The procedure applying to all companies is that a reduction in capital requires a special resolution (a 75% majority) of the members and confirmation by the court (*S.641*).

    a.   *S.641* enables a company to reduce its capital for the stated purposes of:

        i.   Extinguishing liability on share capital not paid-up.

        ii.   Cancelling paid-up capital which is lost and no longer represented by assets.

        iii.   Repaying share capital in excess of the company's needs.

    b.   If the reduction affects creditors (i.e. i. or iii. above) the court will not confirm the reduction unless the creditors agree to it, or are paid off, or are given security.

    c.   In addition to the interests of the creditors the court will also ensure that the reduction is equitable between the various classes of shareholders involved. Note: **RE HOLDERS INVESTMENT TRUST (1971)** (Chapter 42.13).

19. *Statement of Solvency* If a private company chooses to reduce its capital under *S.641* directors are required to issue a statement of solvency (*S.642*) at least 15 days before the passing of the special resolution (a 75% majority). This has then to be registered with the Registrar of Companies. *S.643* provides that each director must state that they have formed the opinion, regarding the company's situation at the date of the statement, that there is no circumstance in which the company could be found unable to pay its debts as they fall due within 12 months. If directors make a solvency statement without having reasonable grounds for the opinions expressed in it, an offence is committed by each director (*S.643(4)*).

20. *The Issue of Shares at a Premium*

    a.   It is usual to issue shares at a price above their nominal value, i.e. at a premium. This may be because the net assets of the company exceed the nominal value of the shares, or because previously issued shares of the same class have a market value in excess of their nominal value.

    b.   By *S.610* when shares are issued at a premium (whether for cash or in exchange for property, goods or services) the premium must be paid into a *share premium account* which can only be used:

        i.   To finance an issue of fully paid bonus shares to members.

        ii.   To write off preliminary expenses.

        iii.   To write off commissions paid, or discounts allowed, or the expenses of an issue of shares or debentures.

        iv.   To provide the premium payable on the redemption of any debentures of the company.

     v.   Where redeemable shares are issued at a premium, to provide the premium payable on redemption. This is subject to conditions (see 23. below).

  c. *S.610* therefore requires that, except for the above purposes, share premiums are treated as capital, for example they cannot be distributed as dividends. In doing so it recognizes that what is important is not the arbitrarily fixed nominal value, but the actual value received for the shares when issued.

21. *The Acquisition by a Company of its Own Shares*

  a. For many years it was a fundamental case law principle of company law that a company may not purchase its own shares.

  b. The basic rule is now contained in *S.658* which states that (subject to the following provisions) a company shall not acquire its own shares. Any purported acquisition in contravention of this section is void.

  c. However, a company may purchase its own shares as long as its articles do not prohibit it. Under *S.690* a company may purchase its own shares provided:

     i.   They are fully paid-up.

     ii.   They are not unissued.

     iii. There remains some shares, other than redeemable shares, held by members.

     iv. They are paid for in full on the date of purchase.

     v.   Funds for the purchase must come out of company profits or money raised by issuing new shares.

    For public limited companies registered on a recognized stock market, this is known as a *market purchase*. For the private company it is called an *off-market purchase*.

  d. Provided the articles permit it, authority for a company to its own shares may be done by ordinary resolution (a 51% majority).

  e. There are a number of reasons why it is undesirable for a company to be able to purchase its own shares:

     i.   It is a reduction of capital, i.e. if it pays shareholder A cash for his shares, less cash is available to satisfy the claims of creditors X, Y and Z.

     ii.   If it paid shareholder A too much for his shares this would dilute the value of the remaining assets, i.e. on winding-up there would be less cash available for shareholders B, C and D.

     iii. If it paid shareholder A too little for his shares this would enhance the value of the remainder and could be used by the directors to increase the value of their own holdings.

     iv. A method of frustrating a takeover bid is to buy shares on the open market. If the directors could use the company money to do this, no doubt they would do so, thus entrenching themselves in control of the company.

  f. In recent years there has been increasing interest in relaxing the prohibition for the benefit of the company and its shareholders provided the position of creditors and other interested parties could be protected. The advantages of allowing a company to purchase its own shares are:

    i.   It facilitates the retention of 'family' control of a private company.

    ii.   It increases the marketability of a company's shares, since the company itself is a potential buyer. This in turn would increase interest in employee share schemes, and may therefore help the company to raise further capital.

    iii.   It enables both public and private companies to use surplus cash to the company's advantage. For example, if redeemable shares have a market value of less than their redemption price, they could be redeemed immediately rather than waiting to pay the higher price on the redemption date.

    iv.   It may make it easier for companies to raise venture capital from merchant banks since the banks have the possibility of 'getting out' by selling their shares back to the company.

22. *Financial Assistance for Acquisition of Shares*

a.   By *S.678* it is illegal for a public company directly or indirectly to give any financial assistance for the acquisition of any of its shares or shares in its holding company. It is irrelevant whether the financial assistance is given before, at the same time as, or after, the acquisition. The purpose of *S.678* is to extend the rule in *S.690* in an attempt to prevent evasions of it. Private companies are not prohibited from giving financial assistance to buy their own shares.

b.   '*Financial assistance*' is defined by *S.677* to include:

    i.   A gift.

    ii.   Provision of a guarantee, security, indemnity, release or waiver.

    iii.   A loan and related arrangements, and

    iv.   Any other financial assistance by a company whose net assets are as a result reduced to a material extent or which has no net assets.

c.   *S.678* can be illustrated by the following cases:

In **HEALD v O'CONNOR (1971)** the seller of the controlling shareholding in a company lent part of the price to the buyer. The loan was secured by a floating charge on the company's assets. In addition this debenture was guaranteed by the purchaser. It was held that the debenture amounted to financial assistance. Also the seller could not enforce the guarantee since it was not possible to guarantee an illegal transaction.

In **BELMONT FINANCE v WILLIAMS FURNITURE (1980)** Group 'A' wanted to buy Belmont from Group 'B' without paying for the shares with their own money. It was arranged that the purchase would be financed from Belmont's own assets, which were extracted by Group 'A' first selling to Belmont for £500 000 shares in another company which were worth only £60 000. The £500 000 was then used by Group 'A' to pay Group 'B' for Belmont's shares. It was held that the arrangement was illegal.

d.   The effects of contravention of *S.678* are:

    i.   The financial assistance, for example the guarantee or security, is void.

    ii.   The company and any officer in default are liable to a fine and/or up to 2 years imprisonment.

iii. Every director who is party to a contravention of *S.678* is guilty of a breach of fiduciary duty and is liable to recoup any losses which the company suffers as a result.

e. The exceptions to *S.678* are rather complex. Some straightforward examples include:

i. Where the lending of money is part of the ordinary business of the company, and the loan is in the ordinary course of its business.

For example, a bank may lend to its customer so that he can buy shares in the bank.

ii. Where the loan is provided in good faith in the interests of the company, for the purposes of an employees' share scheme.

For example, a company may give a guarantee or some other form of security to a bank that lends money to an employees' share scheme.

iii. Where the loan is to employees (other than directors) to enable them to purchase fully paid shares to be held by them as beneficial owners.

f. The exemption from *S.678* for private companies, allows for a '*management buyout*' to take place, i.e. the disposal of a company to its management. The management could either buy shares in the company with a loan from company funds, or more usually, the management would buy the shares with a bank loan which would be secured by company assets.

g. Payment for shares purchased by a company must be made at the time of purchase. A creditor cannot be created as a result of the purchase. Payment can be cash or part cash and property. In **BDG ROOF-BOND LTD v DOUGLAS (2000)** a court found payment to have been made by way of part cash, a piece of land and a car owned by the company.

23. *The Power to Issue Redeemable Shares*

a. By *S.684* a company may, if authorized by its articles, issue shares which are to be redeemed, or may be redeemed at the option of the company or the shareholder. The holders of redeemable shares are therefore temporary members of the company.

b. The following conditions must be fulfilled:

i. No redeemable shares may be issued unless there are shares in issue which are not redeemable.

ii. Shares may not be redeemed unless they are fully paid.

iii. The terms of the redemption must provide for payment on redemption.

iv. Except for private companies which take advantage of the power to redeem shares out of capital (see 24.h below) the shares may only be redeemed out of the company's distributable profits or out of the proceeds of a fresh issue of shares made for the purpose of the redemption *(S.690 – see 20.c above)*.

v. The terms and manner of redemption must be specified at or before the time of issue, including the date on or by which (or dates between which) the shares will be (or may be) redeemed.

c. Where shares are redeemed out of profits a sum equal to their nominal value must be transferred from profits to an account. This reserve, like the share premium account, is a statutory capital reserve.

d. If the shares are redeemed out of the proceeds of a fresh issue, capital is automatically replaced and no capital redemption reserve is needed.

e. If the shares are redeemed at a premium the basic rule is that the premium must be paid out of distributable profits. There is an exception where the shares were originally issued at a premium. In such cases the premium on redemption may be provided out of the share premium account to the extent that it does not exceed the lesser of:

i. The premiums received on the issue of the shares being redeemed, and

ii. The balance on the share premium account.

f. Shares redeemed are treated as cancelled on redemption and the amount of the company's issued capital is reduced accordingly, but the company's authorized capital is not affected.

24. *The Purchase by a Company of its Own Shares*

a. By *S.690* a company (public or private) may, if authorized by its articles, purchase its own shares (including redeemable shares).

b. The conditions that apply to the redemption of redeemable shares also apply to the purchase of own shares, for example the need for a capital redemption reserve.

c. A company may not purchase its own shares if, as a result, there would no longer be any member of the company holding shares other than redeemable shares.

d. The requirements for the authorization of purchase of own shares depend on whether the transaction is an off-market purchase or a market purchase.

e. Before a company may make an *off-market purchase*, a *special resolution* must be passed authorizing the purchase and its terms. The shares that are to be purchased *may not vote* on the resolution. Despite anything in the articles *any member* may demand a poll on such a resolution.

f. Before a company may make a *market purchase* an *ordinary resolution* must be passed. The resolution must:

i. Specify the maximum number of shares to be purchased.

ii. Specify the maximum and minimum prices which may be paid for those shares, and

iii. Specify a date, not later than 18 months after the resolution, on which the authority is to expire.

The shares to be purchased may vote on the ordinary resolution. Contrast a special resolution for the off-market purchase of own shares.

g. *All companies* must, within 28 days of a purchase of their own shares, deliver a return to the registrar stating the number and nominal value of the shares purchased and the date (or dates) of purchase. In addition a *public company* must state the aggregate amount paid by the company for the shares, and for each class of shares purchased, the maximum and minimum price paid.

h. *S.692* allow a *private company* to redeem or purchase its own shares out of *capital*. Since this potentially strikes at one of the basic functions of company law, i.e. to protect creditors by maintaining the capital fund, it is subject to extensive protective measures. Thus:

i. A *special resolution* must be passed. The shares to be purchased must not count in the special resolution vote i.e. it is a 75% special resolution of shares excluding those to be purchased.

ii. The directors must make a *statutory declaration* specifying, among other things, that they are of the opinion that the company will be able to carry on business as a going concern throughout the following year.

iii. An *auditor's report* must be attached to the statutory declaration stating that, having enquired into the company's affairs they are not aware of anything to indicate that the opinion expressed by the directors is unreasonable.

iv. Detailed *publicity requirements* must be complied with.

v. Members and creditors have statutory rights to object.

vi. If winding-up commences within 1 year, persons whose shares were purchased, or directors who signed the statutory declaration, remain liable to the extent that the payment out of capital relates to their shares.

DIVIDENDS

25. *Definition*

a. Dividends are payments made out of profits to the members of a company. Dividends paid to preference shareholders will be at a fixed rate, whereas dividends paid to ordinary shareholders will vary with the prosperity of the company. Shareholders do not have an automatic right to dividends even if profits are available. Directors may consider it more prudent to retain profits within the company. A dividend is therefore not a debt of the company until it is declared. Even then, on liquidation, it is not payable until after the outside creditors have been paid.

b. Dividends must be distinguished from interest. Interest is paid to debenture holders. It is a debt and must be paid out of capital if no profits are available.

26. *The Requirement of Solvency* Dividends cannot be paid if this would result in the company being unable to pay its debts as they fall due. All the rules are subject to this overriding condition of solvency. Clearly if a company did pay a dividend in this situation it would have to pay its debts out of capital.

27. *The Basic Rule* By S.830 no company, whether public or private, may make a distribution (i.e. pay dividends) except out of its accumulated realized profits less its accumulated realized losses. In addition unrealized profits may not be used in paying up debentures or amounts unpaid on issued shares. Note that:

a. A '*distribution*' is defined as any distribution of a company's assets to its members (including preference shareholders) whether in cash or otherwise except:

i. The issue of fully or partly paid bonus shares.

ii. The redemption or purchase of any of the company's own shares out of capital (including the proceeds of any fresh issue of shares) or out of unrealized profits.

iii. A reduction of capital.

iv. A distribution in a winding-up.

b. '*Profits*' includes both capital and revenue profits and '*losses*' includes both capital and revenue losses.

c. A provision (other than one arising as a result of a revaluation of all the fixed assets) must be treated as a realized loss. A provision is an amount set aside to meet a known liability the exact amount of which cannot be determined with accuracy.

d. To avoid a company having to translate an unrealized surplus on the revaluation of a fixed asset into a realized loss as a result of depreciating the higher value of the fixed asset, it is provided that the part of the revaluation surplus that equals the excess depreciation which has been charged as a result of the revaluation may be treated as realized profit.

For example, a company pays £10 000 for an asset and decides to write it off over 10 years (straight line method). The depreciation charge is therefore £1000. After 5 years the asset is revalued at £15 000, but its useful life does not change. In future the depreciation charge will be £3000 per year, i.e. £2000 more than if the revaluation had not been made. Thus £2000 would have to be retained from realized profits but for *S.275* which allows this £2000 to be distributed rather than retained.

e. The Act is not precise about what is to be regarded as realized profit. However, the courts will be guided by modern accounting practice. For example, a profit will be regarded as realized when a sale is completed, even if the debtor has not paid.

28. *Public Companies*

a. By *S.831* a public company may not make a distribution if its net assets are less than the aggregate of its called-up capital plus undistributable reserves, or if the result of the distribution would be to reduce its net assets below the aggregate of called-up capital plus undistributable reserves.

b. '*Undistributable reserves*' means:

i. The share premium account and the capital redemption reserve.

ii. Any other reserve which the company is prevented from distributing by law or by its memorandum or articles, and

iii. The excess of accumulated unrealized profits over accumulated unrealized losses.

c. The practical effect of *S.831* is that a public company must take into account an unrealized loss, whereas a private company need not do so. Such unrealized losses will usually arise from the writing down (other than by way of depreciation) of capital assets, since other unrealized losses will usually be charged to the profit and loss account.

29. *Relevant Accounts and Interim Dividends*

a. *S.836* requires the last annual accounts to be referred to when determining the legality and amount of any distribution.

b. *Interim dividends* are dividends which are paid between annual general meetings. Usually companies will try to make the interim dividend about the same amount as the final dividend and make the payment mid-way through the year.

c. Where a *public company* proposes to pay an interim dividend which would be unlawful if reference were made only to the last annual accounts then interim accounts will be necessary to justify the distribution. These must be properly prepared and a copy must be delivered to the registrar, but they do not have to be audited.

30. *Consequences of Unlawful Distribution*

a. *S.847* makes a dividend repayable to the company if the person receiving it knew or had reasonable grounds to believe that it had been wrongly paid. In *IT'S a WRAP (UK) LTD v GULA (2006)* the Court of Appeal held that two directors were liable to repay dividends received over 2 years when the company made a loss. It was no defence that they did not know of the provisions of the Act.

b. Where dividends cannot be recovered from shareholders, every director who was knowingly a party to the unlawful distribution must pay to the company the amount lost plus interest.

31. *The Articles*

a. The above rules must be read subject to any provision in the articles which places further restrictions on the amount available for distribution. For example, if the articles state that dividends may only be paid out of 'the profits of the business' then capital profits, i.e. realized profits on the sale of fixed assets, are not available for distribution.

b. Table A (the model set of articles – Article 30(2) for private companies, Article 69(2) for public companies) contains a number of provisions relating to dividends, for example:

    i. The company declares the dividend by *ordinary resolution*, but the declaration cannot exceed the amount recommended by the directors, i.e. the shareholders can reduce the amount of the recommended dividend but they cannot increase it.

    ii. The directors may pay interim dividends if this is justified by the profits.

    iii. Dividends shall be paid proportionate to the amounts paid-up on shares.

    iv. Instead of payment in cash the directors may direct payment of a dividend by the distribution of specific assets or paid-up shares or debentures of any other company.

    v. Any dividends payable in cash may be paid by cheque sent by post to the registered address of the holder.

    vi. Dividends do not bear interest.

32. *Capitalization Issues*

a. A capitalization issue is an allotment of fully or partly paid shares in the company to members in proportion to their existing shareholding. The money used to pay up the shares may have come from:

    i. The distributable profits of the company.

    ii. The share premium account or the capital redemption reserve, or

    iii. Any other reserve which is not available for distribution.

b. A capitalization issue is sometimes referred to as a 'bonus' or 'scrip' issue. The term 'bonus issue' is rather misleading since it implies that the shares are free. This is not the case since if the funds had not been used to pay up the bonus shares they could (if of type i. above) have been distributed as dividends.

c. If the shares are paid-up from the funds referred to in ii. or iii. above this is not a true capitalization issue since these funds must already be treated as capital. No profits have been capitalized.

   d. In order to make a capitalization issue:

      i. A company must have authority in its articles. Table A authorizes such an issue provided an *ordinary resolution* is first passed.

     ii. The nominal capital must be sufficient. If it is not, it will have to be increased.

TYPES OF SHARES

33. *The Nature of Shares*

   a. There are two basic types of company security, shares and debentures. The distinction is that a shareholder is a member of the company, whereas a debenture holder is a creditor of the company.

   b. Ownership of shares does not constitute part ownership of the assets of the company. Since the company is a separate legal entity it owns its own assets. Ownership of shares amounts to ownership of certain rights (for example the right to attend and vote at meetings) and liabilities, i.e. the liability to pay for the shares.

   c. Shares are personal property. They can be bought, sold, mortgaged or bequeathed. A fraction of a share cannot exist, but one share may be held by two or more people.

   d. A share must be distinguished from the share certificate, which is merely evidence of title to the shares.

   e. Both preference shares and ordinary shares may be issued as redeemable or irredeemable.

34. *Preference Shares*

   a. Preference shares are designed to appeal to investors who want a steady return on their capital combined with a high level of safety. As their name implies, they confer on holders preference over other classes of shareholder in respect of either dividends, repayment of capital or both.

   b. *Dividends*

      i. Preference shares have a fixed rate of dividend, for example 8 per cent. This dividend must be paid before the ordinary shareholders receive anything.

     ii. Preference shares are *cumulative* unless the articles or terms of issue state otherwise. This means that if the company cannot pay a dividend in 1 year the arrears must be carried forward to future years and all the outstanding preference dividends must be paid before the ordinary shareholders receive anything. If preference shares are *non-cumulative* and the company cannot pay a dividend the arrears are not carried forward, so the preference shareholder will not receive a dividend for that year.

    iii. Preference shares are normally *non-participating*, i.e. they are not entitled to share in the surplus profits of the company after payment of a specified dividend on the ordinary shares.

   c. *Voting*

      i. Unless the articles otherwise provide, preference shares carry the same voting rights as other shares.

    ii.   However, it is usual to restrict the preference shareholders' rights to vote to specified circumstances which directly affect them, for example when the rights of preference shareholders are being varied.

    d.   *Rights on liquidation*. Preference shareholders do not automatically have a right to prior return of their capital. If the articles are silent preference shareholders and ordinary shareholders rank equally. However, in most cases the articles will give preference shareholders priority of return of capital.

35. **Ordinary Shares** Ordinary shares are sometimes described as a residuary class, i.e. their rights are the rights that remain after the rights of the other classes of shareholders (if any) have been satisfied. Thus in good years ordinary shareholders take the major share of the profits. Also since the preference shareholders' right to vote is usually restricted, the ordinary shareholders control resolutions at general meetings. The other advantages are that they have a statutory right of pre-emption on the issue of new shares *(S.561)* and they usually take the surplus assets if a profitable company is wound up. The disadvantage is that they take the major share of the risk of failure.

APPLICATION AND ALLOTMENT

36. *Application*

    a.   When a person applies for shares he is offering to purchase new shares from the company. He is not purchasing existing shares from a previous holder.

    b.   The general law of contract applies to an application for shares:

        i.   The prospectus is an invitation to treat.

        ii.   The subscriber makes the offer when he sends in the application form.

        iii.   The company accepts the offer by resolution of the board of directors. The acceptance becomes binding when a letter of allotment is posted to the allottee.

    c.   The rules of contract are, however, modified in three ways:

        i.   By *S.561* existing shareholders usually have a statutory right to be offered new shares before they are offered to outsiders.

        ii.   The acceptance need not coincide precisely with the offer. Many issues are oversubscribed. In such cases the company will either ballot to decide to whom to allot the shares or it will allot only a proportionate part of those applied for. The company is able to do this because, on the application form, the subscriber agrees to take either the shares applied for or such lesser number as are allotted to them.

        iii.   Further modifications result from rules issued by the Stock Exchange or the Secretary of State under powers given in the *FINANCIAL SERVICES and MARKETS ACT 2000* for example an offer is irrevocable until several days after the closing date for applications. The reason for this is to inhibit '*stagging*', i.e. the revocation of an offer if it appears that the shares or debentures cannot quickly be resold at a profit.

37. **Statutory Restrictions on Allotment** There are now numerous statutory provisions relating to the allotment of shares. The following were dealt with in 15. and 16. above since they are concerned with maintenance of capital:

a. Minimum payment for allotted shares – *S.584.*

b. Allotment for a non-cash consideration – *S.585.*

c. Valuation of non-cash consideration – *S.586.*

The other main restrictions on allotment are dealt with below (see 38.–40.).

38. **Company Authority Required for the Allotment of Shares**

a. By *S.549* directors may not allot shares, except subscribers' shares or shares allotted under an employees' share scheme, without the authority of the company in general meeting or in the articles.

(Subscribers' shares are shares shown in the memorandum to be taken by the subscribers to the memorandum.)

b. The authority may be general or specific, and it must state the maximum amount of shares which may be allotted, and must limit the time during which the authority may be exercised. This time limit must not exceed 5 years.

c. An *ordinary resolution* is necessary to grant authority to the directors, and since this may have the effect of altering the articles a copy of the resolution must be delivered to the registrar within 15 days. Registration of an ordinary resolution is not normally required.

39. **Private Companies** Under the *FINANCIAL SERVICES and MARKETS ACT 2000* a private company must not issue any advertisement offering its shares for sale.

40. **Pre-emption Rights** (*S.561*)

a. A company may not allot *equity shares* unless it has made an offer to the existing shareholders to subscribe on the same or more favourable terms for such shares in proportion to their present holding.

b. By *S.560 equity shares* means shares other than:

i. Shares which have restricted rights attached to them such as rights to dividends and/or capital distribution, eg preference shares; and

ii. Shares held, or to be held, under an employees' scheme.

The definition of equity shares basically means ordinary shares, but it also includes the *right* to subscribe for, or convert to, shares.

c. Shareholders must be notified in writing and the offer must be open for at least 21 days. No allotment may be made until either 21 days has expired or every offer has been accepted or refused (*S.562*).

d. By *S.567* these provisions do not apply:

i. Where the shares are to be wholly or partly paid-up other than in cash.

ii. To *private companies* who exclude the provisions in their articles.

iii. Where the directors of *any company* have authorization to allot shares under *S.561* they may be given authority, either by the articles or by special resolution, to exercise the power without complying with the pre-emption right provisions.

iv. Where *any company* by special resolution resolves that the provisions shall not apply to a specific allotment, or shall only apply in a modified form. In such cases the directors must recommend the resolution, and circulate a written statement setting out the reasons for their recommendation.

41. *The Return of Allotments (S.558)*

   a. When *any company* allots shares (including bonus shares) it must, within 1 month of the allotment, deliver to the registrar a return of allotments. This document must state:

   i.   The number or nominal value of the shares allotted.

   ii. The names, addresses and descriptions of the allottees.

   iii. The amount paid and payable on each share, and

   iv. Details of any non-cash consideration.

   b. The return must be accompanied by a payment of capital duty at the rate of 1% of the actual value of the consideration for the shares.

   c. In the case of a public company the registrar must publish notice of receipt of the return of allotments in the Gazette.

   d. If *S.558* is contravened the allotment remains valid, but every officer in default is liable to be fined.

42. *The Share Certificate*

   a. By *S.554* a share certificate must be made out by the company and delivered to the member within 2 months of allotment or the date when a transfer was lodged for registration. If the shares are quoted on the Stock Exchange the rules of the Exchange substitute a period of 14 days.

   b. The certificate states that the person named is the holder of the shares and specifies the amount paid-up on them. It is not a negotiable instrument since an entry in the company's register of members is necessary to transfer ownership. However, by *S.768* it is *prima facie evidence of title.*

   c. Since a share certificate is prima facie evidence of title it gives rise to *estoppels* (both as to title and as to the amount paid on the shares), as against the company in favour of a person who has relied on the certificate. *Estoppel* is a rule of evidence. It arises when a person has conducted himself in such a way that reasonable inferences as to his legal position may be drawn from his conduct. He cannot then give evidence to show that his legal position is not what it appeared to be, he is estopped (i.e. barred by his own conduct) from doing so.

   d. *Estoppel* does not operate:

   i.   Where the share certificate is a forgery, or

   ii. In favour of a person who lodged a forged transfer.

TRANSFER OF SHARES

43. *Validity of Agreement to Transfer*

There must be a valid agreement to transfer, either by contract or by gift.

In *HARVELA INVESTMENTS v ROYAL TRUST COMPANY OF CANADA (1986)* the House of Lords held that if the vendor of shares in a private company invited purchasers to submit sealed bids for shares the vendor could not accept a referential bid, i.e. one expressed as the amount above that submitted by another bidder. In this case the bid was as follows:

'2 100 000 Canadian dollars or 101 000 Canadian dollars in excess of any other offer which you may receive, whichever is higher.'

It was held that such bids were unacceptable since one party cannot win and the other party cannot lose. Also if more than one referential bid were to be submitted the process would be frustrated.

44. *Transfer of All of the Shares Comprised in One Certificate*

a.   By *S.770* whenever shares are transferred a *proper instrument of transfer* must be delivered to the company, i.e. the transfer must be in writing. Thus an attempt to provide for the automatic transfer of a member's shares, for example to his wife on his death, is void.

b.   A transfer form signed by the transferor is sent by the transferee, with the share certificate and the registration fee, to the company. If the articles restrict the right to transfer shares the transfer must be submitted to the board to ensure that the restrictions are compiled with. After approval by the board the name of the transferee is entered on the register and that of the transferor deleted. The company must issue a new share certificate within 2 months, or 14 days if the company is listed on the Stock Exchange.

c.   The procedure was introduced by the *STOCK TRANSFER ACT 1982* and it applies despite anything in the articles.

45. *Transfer of Part of the Shares Comprised in One Certificate*

a.   Here a different procedure is necessary because it would be unsafe for the transferor to give the transferee the certificate in return for a consideration in respect of only part of the shares. Similarly it would be unreasonable to expect the transferee to pay for the shares whilst allowing the transferor to retain the certificate.

b.   The procedure is:

i.   The transferor executes the transfer and sends it with his share certificate to the company.

ii.   The company secretary Indorses 'certificate lodged' on the transfer and returns it to the transferor, keeping the share certificate.

iii. The transferor hands the certified transfer to the transferee who lodges it with the company for registration.

iv.   The company issues two new share certificates.

c.   The endorsement of 'certificate lodged' on the transfer is known as '*certification of the transfer*'.

i.   *S.768* provides that certification of the transfer by the company is a representation by the company that documents showing prima facie evidence of title have been produced. It is not a guarantee that the transferor has title.

ii. If the company fraudulently or negligently certifies the transfer when the transferor has not shown prima facie evidence of title the company is liable to anyone acting on the faith of it to his detriment.

iii. However, if the company merely negligently returns the old certificate to the transferor the company is not liable to persons who deal with him. Their loss would be attributed to the transferor's fraud rather than the company's negligence.

46. **Forged Transfers** The effects of a transfer of shares under a document on which the transferor's signature has been forged are as follows:

a. A forged document has no legal effect. Therefore the transferor's name must be restored to the register of members, even if he failed to reply to a letter advising him of the transfer.

b. The company is *estopped* (see 43.c above) from denying the title of a subsequent transferee who takes the transfer in good faith and for value. If such a person suffers loss due to the restoration to the register of the true owner the company must pay him compensation.

c. The person who lodged the forged transfer (the original transferee) is liable to indemnify the company for any loss it suffers as a result of having to pay compensation. The original transferee must pay this indemnity even if he was not aware of the forgery. He cannot rely on estoppel.

d. The above points were illustrated in the following case.

In **RE BAHIA AND SAN FRANCISCO RAILWAY (1868)** the holder of shares deposited the certificate with a broker. The broker forged the owner's signature and transferred them to X. When the certificate and the transfer were sent to the company for registration the secretary wrote to the owner advising of the transfer. The owner did not reply to this letter and X was registered as the new owner. X then transferred the shares to Y who was registered as owner, a new certificate being issued. When the forgery was discovered it was held:

i. That the original owner must be restored to the register.

ii. That the company was estopped from denying the validity of the certificate issued to Y, who was therefore entitled to damages.

iii. X, who lodged the forged transfer, had to indemnify the company for the loss it had incurred by compensating Y. The loss therefore fell on X, the original victim of the fraud.

47. **Restrictions on Transfer**

a. To retain control of private companies the articles usually contain either:

i. A pre-emption clause i.e. that no shares shall be transferred to an outsider as long as a member can be found to purchase them at a fair price, determined in accordance with the articles, or

ii. A power vested in the directors to refuse to register a transfer.

b. *Pre-emption clauses*

i. A member cannot exercise a pre-emption right in order to purchase the amount of shares that give voting control.

In *OCEAN COAL CO v POWELL DUFFRYN STEAM COAL CO (1932)* the claimant and respondent each held half of the shares of the Taff Merthyr Steam Co. The articles of this company stated that if a member wished to sell his shares to an outsider he must first offer them to other shareholders at the price at which it is proposed to sell to the outsider. The defendant wished to sell 135 000 shares, but the claimant only wished to buy 5000 at the proposed price. It was held that he could not do so. The claimant either had to accept or reject the offer to sell the full 135 000 shares.

    ii.   Where the pre-emption provision is disregarded the directors cannot validly register the transfer since it is breach of the articles. However, where the transfer is to a person who has paid for the shares, that person will acquire a beneficial (equitable) interest in the shares.

  c. *The power to refuse to register transfers*

The Listing Rules of the UK Stock Exchange require that there be no restriction to the transfer of shares of companies listed on the Stock Exchange. For other companies:

    i.   The directors must, in carrying out their *fiduciary duties* (see Chapter 44) act bona fide in what they consider to be the best interests of the company.

    ii.   The directors must act on grounds personal to the transferee. They cannot for example refuse to register transfers merely because small numbers of shares are involved.

    iii.   The power to refuse must be exercised within a reasonable time. *S.771* provides that the company must give notice of refusal within 2 months. This statutory period now effectively determines what is a reasonable time.

The Act requires directors to provide information about reasons for refusing to register a share transfer (*S.771*).

SELF TEST QUESTIONS

Self Test Questions No. 39 (for Answers see Appendix 1):

1   How does a company raise share capital?

2   What are the different types of capital?

3   What is meant by the phrase, 'maintenance of capital'?

4   What are the legal principles governing the maintenance of a company's capital?

5   What are dividends and how may they be paid?

6   Outline the different kinds of shares in a company.

7   Explain the rules governing the allotment and transfer of shares.

LOAN CAPITAL   42

Learning Outcomes At the end of this chapter you should be able to:

- Explain the legal implications of a company borrowing money.

- Understand the order of payment and registration process for charges.

- Explain what a *floating charge* is.

- Understand the significance of transactions conducted at an undervalue.

- Explain what a *debentureholder* is and remedies available to the holder.

1. *Borrowing by Companies*

   a. *Power to borrow*. Trading companies have an implied power to borrow and give security. *S.31* states that unless a company's articles specifically restrict the objects of the company, its objects are unrestricted. This allows the company to do all such things as are incidental or conducive to carrying on any trade or business, clearly this will include borrowing. Non-trading companies still require an express power to borrow in the articles.

   Private companies may borrow as soon as they are incorporated, but public companies must first obtain a certificate of compliance with the capital requirements of public companies *(S.536)*.

b.   *Ultra vires borrowing.* Borrowing in excess of a limit stated in the articles, or borrowing for an *ultra vires* (i.e. beyond the legal capacity of the company) purpose, is itself *ultra vires*. However, *S.39* states that, 'the validity of an act done by the company shall not be called into question on the ground of lack of capacity by reason of anything in the company's constitution.' Consequently both the lender and the company will be able to enforce the contract, and the lender will have the full range of remedies available in the event of the company's failure to repay interest or capital.

S.39 preserves members' rights to restrain ultra vires acts. Therefore any member may bring proceedings to restrain borrowing which would be beyond the capacity of the company.

c.   *Borrowing in excess of authority.* If borrowing is within the company's powers, but in excess of the authority of the person negotiating a loan on behalf of the company. *S.39* provides, in favour of a person dealing with a company in good faith, the power of the board of directors to bind the company or authorize others to do so, is deemed to be free of any limitation under the company's constitution (see Chapter 43.11).

In the unlikely event of the lender not being protected by the above provision, it would still be possible for the loan to be ratified by the company passing an ordinary resolution.

2. *The Nature of Debentures*

a.   Strictly speaking a debenture is a document by which a company acknowledges its indebtedness under a loan, although the term is also used to describe the loan itself.

b.   Debentures usually give a fixed or floating charge over the company's assets (or both) as security, although debentures may be unsecured.

However, the Stock Exchange will not allow an issue of unsecured or 'naked' debentures to be listed as 'debentures'. The listing must indicate that they are unsecured, for example 'unsecured loan stock'.

c.   A debenture may be an individual debenture evidencing a large sum lent by one person, or the company may create one loan fund known as 'debenture stock'. This is issued to create a class of debentureholders each of whom is given a debenture stock certificate evidencing the proportion of the total to which he is entitled. Whether the debenture is of the first or second type the basic rights of the holder against the company are contractual.

d.   Not every type of company indebtedness can be described as a debenture, the loan must have some permanence although the precise extent is uncertain.

3. *Differences between Shares and Debentures*

a.   A shareholder owns a bundle of rights in the company, for example the right to vote, attend meetings and receive a dividend (if declared). A debentureholder is a person who has lent money to the company. Debentureholders have a *claim against* the company rather than an *interest in* it. Shares (especially ordinary shares) carry a greater degree of risk than debentures, and ordinary shareholders may get a variable return on their investment. If profits are good this will probably exceed the fixed rate of interest paid to debentureholders. Debentures carry less risk, since interest is a contract debt and because debentures will be secured by a fixed and/or a floating charge on the company's assets.

b. The other main differences arise from the fact that debentures are not 'capital' in the company law sense. Thus:

    i. A company's purchase of its own debentures is not subject to restrictions, in contrast to a company's purchase of its own shares.

    ii. Interest on debentures may be paid out of capital, whereas dividends must be paid out of profits.

    iii. Shares cannot be issued at a discount, whereas debentures may be issued at a discount, although these debentures cannot be exchanged for fully paid shares of an equal nominal value.

4. *Similarities between Shares and Debentures*

a. The typical debenture is one of a series or 'class' similar to a class of shares.

b. Debentures are transferable, the same form being used as for a transfer of shares.

c. Debentures may be quoted on the Stock Exchange, and when debentures are issued to the public the same rules must be complied with.

d. In theory it may appear that a debentureholder is only dependent on the prosperity of the company to the same extent as any other creditor. In practice this is not the case. Since the security is generally a floating charge the debentureholder will be as concerned about the success of the company as the shareholder, because if the company is unprofitable the security is placed in jeopardy.

e. Usually a debenture is regarded as a more secure form of investment than a share. In times of high inflation this is not necessarily true. When the purchasing power of money is declining a debenture giving a fixed rate of interest and right to the future return of only the nominal value of the money advanced may well be an inadequate security. In contrast an ordinary share in a 'good' company may provide a better hedge against inflation since the nominal value of the assets is likely to appreciate as the value of money falls.

f. *Conclusion.* In practice debentures are not regarded as differing significantly from shares. Potential investors are not really concerned with the choice of whether to be a member or creditor of a company.

    They will be concerned with the potential for capital appreciation, the yield and the degree of risk. They will then make their basic choice between '*prior charges*' (i.e. debentures and preference shares) and '*equities*' (i.e. ordinary shares). From the company's point of view taxation considerations may be crucial, since debenture interest appears in the profit and loss account as an expense of running the business and therefore reduces the net profit of the company upon which corporation tax is assessed. In contrast dividends on shares are appropriations of profit after tax.

5. *Forms of Security*

a. A *fixed charge* is a mortgage of freehold or leasehold land or fixed plant and machinery, although a fixed charge may be granted over other assets, e.g. book debts or uncalled capital. It prevents the company selling the assets charged without the consent of the debentureholders.

b.   A *floating charge* is an equitable charge which has the following characteristics:

    i.   It is a charge on some or all of the present and future assets of the company.

    ii. That class is one which in the ordinary course of business changes from time to time.

    iii. The charge envisages that, until some future step is taken by or on behalf of the charge holder, the company may carry on its business in the ordinary way.

c.   A floating charge will '*crystallize*' i.e. convert to a fixed charge when:

    i.   The company defaults *and* the debentureholders take steps to enforce their security either by appointing a receiver or applying to the court to do so.

    ii. If winding-up commences.

    iii. If the company ceases business.

    iv. If an event occurs for which the charge deed provides for automatic crystallization.

d.   Advantages of floating charges (from the company's point of view):

    i.   It can charge property which is unsuitable for a fixed charge.

      This is particularly useful if it has no fixed assets, but carries a large stock-in-trade, and

    ii. It can deal with the assets charged.

e.   Disadvantages of floating charges (from the lender's point of view):

    i.   Its value is uncertain since the value of the assets subject to the charge will fluctuate.

    ii. Where a seller of goods 'reserves title' until payment, a floating charge will not, on crystallization, attach to those goods (see 6. below).

    iii. The charge may be avoided under *S.245 INSOLVENCY ACT 1986* (see 9. below).

    iv. If a creditor has levied and completed execution the debentureholders cannot compel him to restore the money, and prior to crystallization he cannot be prevented from levying execution.

    v.   The statutory preferential creditors must be paid out of assets subject to a floating charge unless there are other uncharged assets available for this purpose.

6. *Reservation of Title*

a.   '*Simple' reservation of title clauses. S.17 SALE OF GOODS ACT 1979* provides the basic rule that in a contract for the sale of specific goods property passes when the parties intend it to pass. Consequently the parties can agree that the property will not pass until the goods are paid for. (In the absence of such agreement property will usually pass when the contract is made – *S.18 Rule 1 SALE OF GOODS ACT 1979.*)

In *ALUMINIUM INDUSTRIE VAASSEN (AIV) v ROMALPA (1976)* the following clause was the main provision in a detailed reservation of title clause.

'The ownership of the material to be delivered by AIV will only be transferred to the purchaser when he has met all that is owing to AIV no matter on what grounds Romalpa went into liquidation and AIV sought to enforce the above clause by recovering a quantity of aluminium. It was held that they could do so, ownership had not passed to Romalpa, they were merely the bailee of AIV's goods (that is, holding the goods of another).'

b. *'Extended' clauses covering processed goods.* A reservation of title clause will not apply to goods which are subjected to a process under which they become a new product. The new product will be owned by the buyer, but subject to a charge created in favour of the seller by the reservation of title clause. Such a charge is not valid unless registered.

In ***BORDEN v SCOTTISH TIMBER PRODUCTS (1981)*** resin was sold on reservation of title terms. Both parties knew that the resin would soon be used to manufacture chipboard. It was held that the resin ceased to exist and the suppliers title was extinguished when the resin was made into chipboard, because this was a wholly new product.

c. *'Extended' clauses covering proceeds of sub-sales.* The situation becomes more complicated if the clause is extended to cover the proceeds of sale of goods subject to reservation of title clauses. Such an extension will be effective if it is drafted with sufficient care. The clause must make it clear that the buyer is made the agent of the seller when reselling the goods and that he holds the proceeds as trustee for the seller. The position of the seller will be even stronger if the contract requires the buyer to store the goods in such a way as they are clearly the property of the seller and keep any sale proceeds in a separate account.

7. *Registration of Charges*

a. Since most companies obtain much of their finance from debentures secured by charges, it is important that people dealing with the company are able to find out which assets are subject to charges.

b. By *S.860* almost all charges created by a company must be registered within 21 days of creation. The particulars to be delivered include:

    i. The date of creation of the charge, or of the acquisition of the property subject to the charge.

    ii. The amount secured.

    iii. Short particulars of the property charged.

    iv. The persons entitled to the charge.

c. If a charge is not registered within 21 days the security provided by the charge will only take effect in relation to events occurring after the date of registration. Under the Act, the company and its officers may be fined for failure to register in time.

d. If a charge is not delivered within the 21-day period, the charge will be void as against purchasers of an interest in, or a right over, property subject to the charge. Such protection is confined to the period before the charge is belatedly registered, i.e. once registered the charge will be valid as against persons subsequently acquiring an interest in the charged property.

e. It is the duty of the company to effect registration, but any person interested in the charge may register it. In practice, since the consequences of non-registration affect the lender rather than the company, it is usually the lender's solicitor who deals with registration.

8. *Priority of Charges*

a. Legal fixed charges rank according to their order of creation.

b. If an equitable fixed charge is created first and a legal charge over the same property is created later, the legal charge ranks before the equitable charge, unless at the time when the legal charge was created, the person to whom it was given had notice of the existing equitable charge. Notice may be given by registration of the earlier charge.

Note: An equitable fixed charge is an informal mortgage created by depositing the borrower's title deeds or share certificate with the lender.

c.   If a floating charge (always equitable) is created and a fixed charge (legal or equitable) over the same property is created later, the fixed charge will rank first since it attaches to the property at the time of creation, whereas the floating charge attaches at the time of crystallization. Once a floating charge has crystallized it becomes fixed and any subsequent fixed charge ranks after it. However, a floating charge will have priority over a later created fixed charge provided the floating charge prohibits the creation of later fixed charges with priority (known as a *negative pledge* clause).

d.   If two floating charges are created over the general assets of the company they rank in order of creation. However, if a company creates a floating charge over a particular kind of asset, e.g. book debts, that will rank before an existing floating charge over the general assets.

9.   *Avoidance of Floating Charges* (*S.245 INSOLVENCY ACT 1986*)

a.   It would be unjust to allow an unsecured creditor to obtain priority over other creditors by obtaining a floating charge when he realizes that liquidation is likely. This applies in particular to directors who may have attempted to keep the company alive by making unsecured loans to it. When they realize their attempt has failed they may well wish to cause the company to execute a floating charge in their favour.

b.   By *S.245 1A* a floating charge may be invalidated if created in certain periods before either the commencement of liquidation or the presentation of a petition for an administration order. The periods are:

i.   2 years, if the charge is in favour of a connected person, for example a director or a relative, employee or business partner of a director.

ii.   1 year, if the charge is in favour of any other person (but only if the company was insolvent at the time the charge was created, or became insolvent as a result of the transaction under which the charge was created).

iii.   At any time between the presentation of a petition for an administration order and the making of that order.

c.   *S.245 IA* does not invalidate charges to secure money paid to the company at the time of, or subsequent to the creation of the charge, and in consideration for the charge.

10.   *Transactions at an Undervalue and Preferences* (*S.238–241 INSOLVENCY ACT*)

a.   A charge may also be avoided if it is a transaction at an undervalue or a preference.

b.   A *transaction at an undervalue* occurs when the company makes a gift, or enters into a transaction for no consideration, or for a consideration worth significantly less than the value of the benefit received by the company. However, transactions made in good faith, for the purpose of the business and in the reasonable belief that the company would benefit will not be invalid.

c.   A *preference* is any act that has the effect of putting one of the company's creditors in a better position in the event of the company going into insolvent liquidation.

However, the court may not make an order unless it is satisfied that the company was influenced by a *desire* to put the creditor in a better position than he otherwise would have been.

d. A transaction may only be invalidated if the company was insolvent at the time (or if it became unable to pay its debts as a result of the transaction). The transaction must also fall within the following periods either before liquidation or the presentation of a petition for an administration order:

    i. 6 months, where the transaction is a preference (not at an undervalue).

    ii. 2 years, where the transaction is a preference (not at an undervalue), given to a connected person.

    iii. 2 years, where the transaction is at an undervalue. (If the transaction was with a connected person the company is assumed to be insolvent unless proved to the contrary.)

    iv. At any time between the presentation of a petition for an administration order and the making of that order.

e. The court has power to make any order it thinks fit, for example that:

    i. Property transferred be returned to the company.

    ii. Security given by the company be discharged.

    iii. That any person pay to the liquidator or administrator such sum as the court directs in return for the benefit received.

f. An important first case of the construction and application of *S.239 IA* (on preferences) occurred in 1990.

In **RE M.C. BACON (1990)** the company got into difficulties following the sudden withdrawal of its main trading client. At the time its overdraft was unsecured, but when the bank became aware of the situation it required a debenture as a condition of the continued overdraft facility. Eight months after the start of the crisis and 3 months after the security was given, the company went into liquidation with a deficiency of approximately £330 000 as regards unsecured creditors and an overdraft of £235 500.

The Judge found in favour of the bank (i.e. the security was not regarded as a preference) because the decision to grant the security was not influenced by a desire on the part of the directors to improve the bank's position in the event of liquidation, but by a need to avoid the calling in of the overdraft, so that the company could continue trading.

The decision will be welcomed by companies and lenders since it enables a lender to nurse a company through economic difficulties without the risk that its security will be subsequently rendered voidable. Without such a decision many otherwise viable companies would find it almost impossible to obtain the necessary funds to enable them to overcome a temporary crisis.

11. *Company's Register of Charges*

a. In addition to registration at the Companies Registry, *S.860* requires all charges given by a company to be recorded in the company's own register of charges. The register must contain:

    i.   A short description of the property charged.

    ii. The amount of the charge, and

    iii. The names of the persons entitled to the charge.

b.   Failure to register does not affect the validity of the charge, but officers of the company who knew of the omission are liable to a fine.

12. *Trustees for Debentureholders*

a.   When debentures are issued to the public the company will enter into a trust deed with trustees (usually a trust corporation). The trustees are appointed and paid by the company to act on behalf of the debentureholders. Any charge is in favour of the trustees who hold it on trust for the debentureholders.

b.   There are two main advantages of trustees:

    i.   It enables the security to be a legal mortgage of the company's land (unlike an equitable mortgagee the rights of a legal mortgagee will not be defeated by a transfer of mortgaged property to a bona fide purchaser for value). This would not be possible without trustees since under the *LAW OF PROPERTY ACT 1925* a legal estate in land cannot be vested in more than 4 persons, and

    ii. The trustees are available to exercise continuous supervision of the debentureholders' rights and take the necessary action if the company defaults.

c.   The contents of the trust deed will depend on a number of factors. For example it will:

    i.   Grant to the trustees a fixed charge over land and a floating charge over the rest of the assets.

    ii. Provide for the repayment of the principal sum borrowed plus interest.

    iii. Contain covenants by the company to insure and repair the property charged.

    iv. Specify the events in which the security becomes enforceable, and define the trustees' power to take possession of the property charged or appoint a receiver.

    v.   Define the powers exercisable by the company only with the trustees' consent, for example leasing charged property.

    vi. Provide for meetings of debentureholders, and

    vii. Provide for the remuneration of the trustees.

13. *Remedies of Debentureholders* The remedies of debentureholders are generally conferred by the trust deed. For example, it may grant the power to appoint a receiver to sell charged property. In addition the debentureholders may:

a.   Sue as creditors for arrears of interest.

b.   Petition to wind up the company on the ground that it is unable to pay its debts, and

c.   Apply to the court for the appointment of a receiver or for an order for sale if there is no power in the trust deed.

The usual first step is for the debentureholders or their trustees to secure the appointment of a receiver.

SELF TEST QUESTIONS

Self Test Questions No. 40 (for Answers see Appendix 1):

1   What is the source of a company's power to borrow money?

2   What is the difference between *shares* and *debentures*?

3   What are the main forms of security available to a company?

4   What is the process for the registration of charges?

5   What is the order of priority for the payment of charges?

6   What is a floating charge?

7   What is meant by a finding that certain transactions have been conducted at an undervalue?

8   What is a company's register of charges?

9   What legal remedies are available to the debentureholder?

43 MEMBERSHIP AND MINORITY PROTECTION

Learning Outcomes At the end of this chapter you should be able to:

- Understand the process of becoming a member of a company.

- Explain the nature, role and function of the register of members.

- Understand the *majority rule*.

- Outline the legal provisions for shareholder minority protection, with particular reference to *unfairly prejudicial conduct*.

- Explain the rule in *Foss v Harbottle*.

METHODS OF BECOMING A MEMBER

1. *The Basic Rule* A person becomes a member when:

   a.   He or she indicates that he or she has *agreed* to become a member, and

   b.   When his or her name is entered on the *Register of Members*.

2. *Methods of Indicating Agreement*

   a.   *Subscription to the memorandum*. By *S.112* the subscribers are deemed to have agreed to become members, and on registration must be entered on the register.

b. *Application and allotment.* Like subscribers, persons who have been allotted shares take them direct from the company.

c. *Transfer.* Here the member acquires his shares from an existing member, usually by purchasing them.

d. *Transmission.* This is a transfer which occurs when a member dies or becomes bankrupt.

e. *Estoppel.* If a person's name is entered on the register in error, or is not deleted when he transfers his shares, the person may be estopped from denying that he is a member if he knows of the error, but fails to take steps to rectify the register.

CAPACITY

3. *Minors* A person under the age of 18 may be a member; however:

a. If the company knows that a person is a minor it has the power to refuse to accept that person as a member.

b. Where a minor is inadvertently registered as a member, the company, provided it acts promptly, can apply to the court to have the transfer set aside and the transferor restored to the register.

c. A minor who has been registered as a member may repudiate his membership before or within a reasonable time after reaching 18.

4. *Personal Representatives*

a. On a member's death her shares vest in her personal representative who may require registration of himself as a member. If a personal representative is registered as a member he is entitled to vote and is personally liable for calls, although he may claim an indemnity out of the deceased's assets.

b. A personal representative is not obliged to become a member since *S.770* provides that he may make a valid transfer of the deceased's shares without becoming a member. If a personal representative does not register he is nevertheless entitled to all the benefits attaching to shares, such as bonuses and dividends, but the articles usually provide that he may not vote at meetings.

5. *Trustees in Bankruptcy* The position of a trustee in bankruptcy is similar to that of a personal representative in that she can transfer the shares without being registered as a member, or she can require registration. If she does not register, the bankrupt must vote as the trustee directs.

6. *Trustees and Beneficiaries* Shares may be held under a trust, and the trustee will be entered on the register of members. However, *S.125* states that no notice of a trust shall be entered on the register of members. The purpose of *S.125* is to avoid the involvement of the company in disputes where there are several equitable interests in one piece of property, and to relieve the company from liability to beneficiaries if a fraudulent trustee transfers the shares in breach of trust.

7. *Companies* A company may be a member of another company, but by *S.129* a company cannot be a member of its own holding company.

THE REGISTER OF MEMBERS

8. *Contents of the Register*

   a. By *S.112* every company must keep a register of members which must contain the following particulars:

      i. The name and address of each member.

      ii. A statement of the shares held by each member, with distinguishing numbers (if any). Where the company has more than one class of issued shares they must be distinguished by class.

      iii. The amount paid up on each share.

      iv. The date of entry on the register, and

      v. The date of cessation of membership.

   b. If the number of members falls to one a statement to that effect must be entered in the register, together with the date of the occurrence.

   c. By *S.127* the register is prima facie evidence of the matters it contains.

9. *Location of the Register S.136* requires the register to be kept at the registered office, unless it is made up at some other place in which case it can be kept at that other place. The registrar must be informed of where the register is kept and of any change in that place.

10. *Inspection of the Register* By *S.115* members may inspect the register free of charge. Non-members may inspect the register on payment of a small fee. Any person may require a copy of the register.

MAJORITY RULE

11. *The Rule in Foss v Harbottle (1843)*

    a. Where a wrong is done to a company, or there is an irregularity in the management of a company, and there arises a need to enforce the rights of the company, it is for the company to decide what action to take and it is the company which is the proper claimant in the action. For example:

       In *PAVLIDES v JENSEN (1956)* the directors sold an asset of the company to a third party at a gross undervaluation. A minority shareholder commenced an action. It was held that he could not do so as it was up to the company to decide whether to sue the directors for negligence. Alternatively the company could decide to exonerate them.

    b. The reasons for the rule are:

       i. It is the logical consequence of the fact that a company is a separate legal person. It is the company that has suffered a wrong, therefore it is the company which seeks a remedy.

       ii. It preserves the principle of majority rule.

       iii. It prevents multiple actions. If each shareholder were permitted to sue, the company might be subjected to many lawsuits started by numerous plaintiffs.

iv. It prevents futile actions. If the irregularity is one which can effectively be ratified by the company in a general meeting, it would be futile to have litigation about it without the consent of the general meeting.

12. ***Controlling Members' Duties*** The position of the controlling members (i.e. those possessing sufficient voting power to pass the appropriate resolutions at general meetings) is quite different from that of directors, since it is only directors who owe fiduciary duties to the company. In contrast shares are proprietary rights which members may exercise in their own self-interest, even to the detriment of the company. Thus directors who hold a majority of the shares may, in some cases, be able to disregard their fiduciary duties and duties of care and skill, provided they disclose what they propose to do and then pass a resolution allowing the action. Such a resolution may, for example:

   a. Ratify directors' acts in excess of the powers conferred on them.

   b. Resolve not to sue where a director has broken his duty of care and skill.

   c. Allow a director to retain a secret profit provided:

      i. The profit was not made at the expense of the minority, and

      ii. The director acted in good faith and in the interest of the company.

MINORITY PROTECTION AT COMMON LAW

13. ***Exceptions to the Rule in Foss v Harbottle*** The rule in Foss v Harbottle places the majority in such a strong position that minority shareholders would be at a serious disadvantage if the following exceptions were not allowed:

   a. Where the company does an illegal or ultra vires act. However under *S.39*:

      i. If a company is required to carry out an ultra vires act in pursuance of an illegal obligation arising from a previous act of the company, the members cannot restrain the act.

      ii. A company may ratify an ultra vires act by special resolution.

   b. Where the company acts on a resolution which has not been properly passed.

      In ***BAILLE v ORIENTAL TELEPHONE CO (1915)*** a company was successfully restrained from acting on a special resolution of which inadequate notice had been given.

      This exception has been severely curtailed by *S.40(1)* which provides that in favour of a person dealing with a company in good faith, the power of the board of directors to bind the company, shall be deemed to be free of any limitation under the company's constitution. 'Constitution' includes any resolution of the company and any agreement between the members, as well as the constitutional documents.

   c. Where the individual rights of the plaintiff as a shareholder have been infringed, for example shareholder's right to vote.

   d. Where the majority is committing a fraud on the minority. The word 'fraud' in this context does not mean deceit in the criminal sense as the following examples show:

i. *Expropriation of the company's property.*

In **COOK v DEEKS (1916)** the directors, whilst negotiating a contract on behalf of the company, took the contract in their own names. Then at a general meeting they used their votes to pass a resolution declaring that the company had no interest in the contract. It was held that the resolution was a fraud on the minority and was ineffective.

ii. *Expropriation of other members' property.*

In **DAFEN TINPLATE v LLANELLY STEEL (1920)** P was a member of D and used to purchase steel from them. When P started to purchase steel elsewhere a new article was inserted which conferred on the majority an unrestricted power to buy out any shareholders they might think proper. It was held that this power of expulsion went further than was necessary to protect the company's interests.

iii. *An issue of shares designed to harm the minority.*

In **CLEMENS v CLEMENS LTD (1976)** the claimant held 45% of the issued shares and her aunt, who was one of the directors of the company held 55%. The aunt's shares were used at a general meeting to pass resolutions to issue further shares to directors and to trustees of an employees' share ownership scheme. The resolutions were carefully designed to reduce the claimant's holding from 45% to about 24.5%. This deprived her of her power to block a special or extraordinary resolution. It also reduced the value of her rights under a pre-emption clause in the articles (a clause entitling her to first refusal if another member wished to sell shares). The court set aside the resolutions on the ground that they were oppressive to the claimant, since they were specifically designed (i) to ensure that she could never get control of the company and (ii) to remove her negative control.

iv. *A reduction of capital designed to harm a class of shareholders.*

In **RE HOLDERS INVESTMENT TRUST (1971)** a capital reduction scheme was not confirmed by the court because a resolution of the preference shareholders was only passed because trustees, who held a substantial number of ordinary shares, voted in favour of the scheme because it would be advantageous to their beneficiaries due to their larger holding of ordinary shares. It was held that the resolution had not been effectively passed because the majority had not considered what was best for the class of preference shareholders as a whole.

v. *A negligent act which benefits the majority at the expense of the company.*

In **DANIELS v DANIELS (1978)** the controlling directors and shareholders (Mr and Mrs Daniels) caused the company to sell a piece of land to Mrs Daniels at an undervalue. The claimant, a minority shareholder, did not allege fraud because he did not know all that had happened. His action was nevertheless successful and Mrs Daniels had to account for the profit. The strongest case against the claimant was **PAVLIDES v JENSEN (1956)**, but this case was distinguished because the directors had not there benefited from their breach of duty since the sale had been to a third party.

14. *Personal, Derivative and Representative Actions*

a. *Personal actions.* Such an action can be brought when a person has been deprived of his individual rights as a shareholder.

b.   *Derivative actions.* Where there is a dispute between the company and third parties (whether they are its directors or its controlling shareholders) and any person other than the company is allowed to appear as claimant on behalf of the company, then the action is called a *derivative action*. In such cases the right to sue is derived from the company since it is the company which has suffered as a result of the action of the majority. Where an action is successful the damages awarded belong to the company. Usually a derivative action is only appropriate where the wrongdoers have voting control and therefore prevent the company from making a claim.

c.   *Statutory derivative actions.* The *COMPANIES ACT 2006 S.260* introduced a new procedure under which shareholders can bring proceedings on behalf of the company against a director for damage caused through negligence or breach of fiduciary duty. Whilst any legal costs will be met by the company, any compensation awarded by a successful claim will go to the company. There are a number of safeguards against frivolous actions being brought; *S.261* of the Act requires that a claimant obtains permission to proceed with the claim, and the court must refuse permission where in its view:

   i.   Continuance would not accord with the duty to promote the success of the company, or

   ii.   The act or omission has been authorized or ratified by the company, or

   iii. The act or omission is likely to be ratified by the company.

   In *STAINER v LEE (2010)* S applied under *S.261* for permission to continue a derivative action against two directors of the company. S, a minority shareholder, alleged that the directors were in breach of their fiduciary duties to the company in allowing the company to make an interest free loan to a linked company. The Court found that the failure to obtain interest over a period of almost 9 years on loans amounting to £8.1 million, were strong grounds for a claim that the directors were in breach of their fiduciary duties (see Chapter 44.24) and the application to continue the action would be granted.

   Also, under *S.262,* where a company has brought a claim and the cause of action is one which could be brought as a statutory derivative action, a member of the company may apply to the court for permission to continue the claim as a derivative action if:

   i.   The manner in which the company commenced or continued the claim amounts to an abuse of process of the court.

   ii.   The company has failed to prosecute the claim diligently, and

   iii. It is appropriate for the member to continue the claim as a derivative claim.

   S.263 deals with whether permission to continue a derivative claim brought in respect of a director's breach of duty should be granted. Again, criteria is laid down governing where a refusal by the court should be made; this is when:

   i.   Any person acting in accordance with the duty to promote the success of the company would not seek to continue the claim.

   ii.   The cause of action arises from an act or omission that has yet to occur, and the act or omission has been authorized by the company.

   iii. Where the act or omission has occurred, has been ratified by the company since its occurrence.

Under *S.239* members are allowed to pass a resolution saying that the company is ratifying conduct of a director, however under the section, the director in question and any person associated with him, cannot vote on the resolution.

d. *Representative actions.* Where individual shareholders have suffered personal loss in addition to the injury to the company one shareholder may bring a *representative action* on behalf of himself and all the other shareholders who have suffered similar injury. If a representative action is successful the plaintiff will obtain a declaration that the improper conduct has been proved. Each injured party may then claim damages without further need to prove improper conduct.

S.994 UNFAIR PREJUDICE

15. *Basic Rule*

a. By *S.994 a member* may petition the court for an order on the ground that the affairs of the company are being or have been conducted in a manner which is *unfairly prejudicial* to the interests of its members generally or some part of the members (including at least himself) or that any proposed act or omission of the company is or would be so prejudicial.

b. Petitions under *S.994* have been successful in the following situations:

i. Where directors of a private company made incorrect statements to their shareholders regarding acceptance of an offer for their shares made by another company owned by the directors.

ii. Where the majority made a rights issue with a view to altering the voting balance, because they knew that the minority shareholder could not afford to exercise his right to purchase.

iii. Where the majority made a rights issue with a view to depleting the funds of a shareholder engaged in litigation with the company or with the majority shareholders.

iv. Where the majority acted contrary to a person's 'legitimate expectation' to take part in the long-term management of a quasi-partnership company.

In **RE A COMPANY** (No. 00477 of 1986) the petitioners (directors of A Ltd) sold their shares in A Ltd to O plc, relying on promises that O plc would develop A Ltd's business and that A Ltd's managing director (S) would be a director of O plc. In fact O plc sold A Ltd's assets to support its own business. S was also replaced as managing director of A Ltd and asked to resign from the board of O plc. The petitioners were successful and obtained an order that their shares be purchased at a price equivalent to the value of their shares in A Ltd at the date of the sale.

16. *The Powers of the Court* The court may make any order it thinks fit. Thus it can:

a. Regulate the future conduct of the company's affairs.

In **RE HARMER (1959)** a successful family company was controlled by Mr H. He and his wife (who always voted with him) could control both ordinary and special resolutions at general meetings. The directors were Mr and Mrs H and their two sons. Mr H was the chairman and had a casting vote. The two sons brought an action under *S.210CA 1948* (similar, but narrower, previous legislation) on the ground that their father repeatedly abused his controlling power, particularly with respect to the appointment and dismissal of staff, and the opening of a branch in Australia. (This was opposed by the sons and proved to be an unsuccessful venture.) Mr H was generally intolerant of views contrary to his own, whether held by his sons or other shareholders. At the time of the hearing Mr H was 89 years old.

The court granted an order that removed Mr H from the board and made him 'president' of the company for life at a salary of £2500 per year. This post gave him no rights, and imposed no duties on him. It was directed that he should not interfere with the affairs of the company except in accordance with the decisions of the board.

b. Require the company to do or refrain from doing any act. Thus the court may require the company not to make any alteration either to its memorandum or articles, or to make a specific alteration.

c. Authorize civil proceedings to be brought in the name of, and on behalf of, the company by such persons and on such terms as it directs. This is important because if the court authorize proceedings a minority shareholder can sue a director on behalf of the company even if he cannot bring his claim within one of the exceptions to the rule in Foss v Harbottle.

d. Provide for the purchase of the shares of any member by other members or by the company.

In *RE BIRD PRECISION BELLOWS (1984)* the petitioners held 26% of the shares in a small 'quasipartnership' company. They suspected that the managing director was concealing bribes paid to secure contracts. After an unsuccessful attempt to secure the appointment of DTI inspectors the petitioners were removed from the board by the votes of the managing director, his wife and one other shareholder. The petitioners alleged unfair prejudice in that they had been wrongfully excluded from the company's affairs and they sought an order that the majority purchase their shares. It was held that exclusion from participation in the affairs of a 'quasi partnership' company was unfairly prejudicial and that in such companies a fair price for the purchase of the minority's shares should be calculated on a pro rata basis, not discounted because it was a minority shareholding.

17. *S.994 and Foss v Harbottle*

a. The rule in Foss v Harbottle and its exceptions have created several problems, in particular:

   i. The extent of the 'fraud on the minority' exception, and

   ii. The procedural problems of personal, representative and derivative actions.

b. *S.994* has undoubtedly helped in both cases:

   i. It has the potential to supersede the concept of 'fraud on the minority' and replace it with the more flexible concept of fairness, and

   ii. It provides a simpler procedure than the common law since the court can give authority for legal proceedings in the company's name. It is likely that a dissatisfied minority shareholder would proceed in this way rather than attempt to sue under the common law rules.

c. *S.994* provides a practical and flexible remedy. They may be used, for example, to curtail excessive directors' remuneration, or to request an order that a dividend be declared. *S.994* also provides a remedy for an individual member. There is no minimum percentage of shares which must be held, nor minimum number of members who must join in the action. The conduct must, however, be unfairly prejudicial to members in their *capacity as members* and not, for example, in their capacity as directors, creditors or employees.

SELF TEST QUESTIONS

Self Test Questions No. 41 (for Answers see Appendix 1):

1 Explain how a person becomes a member of a company, dealing in particular with capacity.

2 What is the register of members?

3 Explain the *Majority Rule.*

4 What is the rule in *Foss v Harbottle*?

5 What minority protections are exceptions to the rule in *Foss v Harbottle*?

6 What is *conduct unfairly prejudicial* and how does this give minority protection?

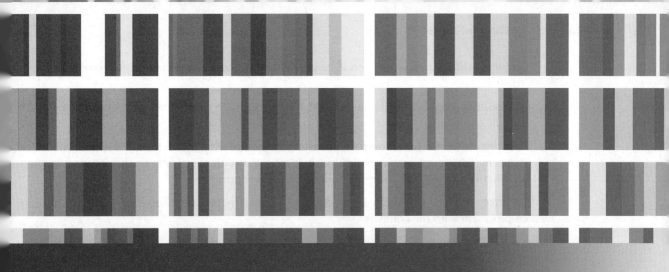

DIRECTORS AND THE SECRETARY

44

Learning Outcomes
At the end of this chapter you should be able to:

- Explain the general nature of directors and their appointment.

- Understand the power of directors in the company's affairs.

- State the disclosure requirements for the exercise of directors powers.

- Explain the fiduciary duty placed upon directors and the statutory general duties.

- Explain the nature and role of the company secretary.

- Understand and apply the legal rules governing *insider dealing*.

APPOINTMENT AND REMOVAL OF DIRECTORS

1. *Position of Directors*

   a. Directors are the persons to whom management of a company is entrusted. Together with the managers and the secretary they are the 'officers' of the company. It is not necessary that a natural person be appointed, a director may be another company. A person who acts as a director, e.g. by attending board meetings and taking part in board decisions will be a director even if he is called by another name such as 'governor' or 'trustee'.

b. The position of a director is similar to that of an agent in that he can bind his principal (i.e. the company) by his acts without incurring personal liability.

c. Directors have also been compared to trustees because they owe fiduciary duties to the company. However, they are not true trustees because the legal title to the company's property is vested in the company and not in the directors.

d. Directors are not servants of the company unless they have a separate contract of employment with the company.

2. *Number of Directors*

a. By *S.155* every company must have at least one director, who is a natural person, i.e. an individual, so the board of a company cannot consist of companies represented by corporate representatives. (Note: as a separate legal entity, companies can be shareholders and directors of other companies.)

b. *Executive and non-executive directors.* Executive directors devote substantially the whole of their working time to the running of a company. They are usually made employees through entering into a contract of employment (see Chapter 50). Non-executive directors do not devote the whole of their time to running a company; they have only an occasional involvement. In practice, non-executive directors tend to be of three kinds:

   i. Retiring directors, whom the board wish to retain for occasional help and advice.

   ii. Persons with some public status, e.g. politicians, lords and dukes, leading entrepreneurs (this type of non-executive are seen as having a key role to play in attempts to regulate the conduct of boards of the larger public company listed on the Stock Exchange) (see Chapter 46.34).

   iii. Specialists in a particular field e.g. finance, marketing.

   Note: All directors, whether executive or non-executive, in the first instance, owe the same duties and can be liable to the same extent, as the executive director (see below).

c. By *S.270* private companies may, at their discretion, have a company secretary, public companies must have a company secretary.

3. *Methods of Appointment*

a. *First directors.* By *S.12* a statement of the first directors and secretary must be delivered with the application to register the company. The statement must contain their signed consent to act in the relevant capacity. These persons are, on the company's incorporation, deemed to have been appointed as its first directors and secretary.

b. *Subsequent directors.* The usual method of appointment is by the company in a general meeting, i.e. by *ordinary resolution*. Retiring directors are eligible for re-election and, if Table A is adopted, a retiring director who offers himself for re-election will be automatically elected unless a resolution not to fill the vacancy is passed or a resolution for his re-election is lost.

c. *Casual vacancies*

   i. A casual vacancy is one that occurs between general meetings, for example because of the death or resignation of a director.

    ii.   Table A empowers the board to fill casual vacancies, and also to appoint additional directors up to the maximum specified in the company's articles.

    iii.   A person appointed by the board holds office until the next Annual General Meeting. He will then be eligible for re-election. His appointment will not be taken into account for determining who shall retire by rotation (see 5. below).

4. *Persons Who May Not be Appointed*

    a.   *Undischarged bankrupts.* By *S.11 COMPANY DIRECTORS DISQUALIFICATION ACT 1986* an undischarged bankrupt commits a criminal offence if he acts as a director without the permission of the court.

    b.   *Persons disqualified by the court* under *S.2–4 COMPANY DIRECTORS DISQUALIFICATION ACT 1986.* Where a disqualification order is made the person concerned may not (without permission of the court) act as a liquidator, director, administrator, receiver or manager, nor may he take part in the promotion, formation or management of a company. A court of summary jurisdiction may make a disqualification order of up to 5 years, other courts up to 15 years. A disqualification order may be made in the following circumstances:

        i.   Where a person is convicted of an indictable offence in connection with the promotion, formation, management or liquidation or receivership of a company. (The maximum period for disqualification is 15 years.).

        ii.   Where a person has been persistently in default in relation to filing documents with the registrar. (Maximum period 5 years.).

        iii.   Where, in the course of a winding up, it appears that a person has been guilty of fraudulent trading *(S.993)* or, while an officer, liquidator, receiver or manager of a company, has been guilty of fraud or breach of duty to the company. (Maximum period 15 years.).

    c.   *A person disqualified by the court* under *S.6–9 COMPANY DIRECTORS DISQUALIFICATION ACT 1986*, because his conduct as a director, either considered in isolation or taken together with his conduct as a director of any other company, makes him unfit to be concerned with the management of a company. These sections are considered in more detail in 33.–34. below.

5. *Vacation of Office* The office of director may be vacated by:

    a.   *Death of the director.*

    b.   *Dissolution of the company.*

    c.   *Retirement by rotation.* Table A states that at each AGM one-third of the directors shall retire. Those to retire are those who have been longest in office. Retiring directors are eligible for relection.

    d.   *Removal*

        i.   By *S.168* despite anything in the articles or any agreement between the company and the director, a company can remove a director by *ordinary resolution*.

        ii.   *Special notice* must be given of any resolution to remove a director *(S.168(2))*.

        iii.   On receipt of this notice the company must send a copy to the director. He may then make written representations to the company which must be sent to the members with notice of the meeting unless they are an attempt to gain needless publicity for defamatory matter. If the company receives the representations too late to send out with notice of the meeting the director may demand that his statement be read out at the meeting. In any case he may speak on the resolution at the meeting *(S.169)*.

iv. Removal under *S.168* does not deprive the director of his right to damages for loss of appointment as managing director should such a post be automatically terminated, see **SOUTHERN FOUNDRIES v SHIRLAW (1940)** (Chapter 39.26.d). A director will not, or course, be entitled to damages if he was removed as a result of his own breach of duty or breach of contract.

v. *S.168* does not prevent the company from attaching weighted voting rights to a director's shares on a resolution for his removal.

In **BUSHELL v FAITH (1970)** a company had an issued capital of 300 fully paid shares divided equally between F and his two sisters. The company's articles contained a provision that if a resolution were proposed to remove a director the shares held by that director would carry three votes each. The sisters wanted to remove F from his post as director, but he invoked the above article. The sisters disputed its validity. The House of Lords (now the Supreme Court) held that the article was not inconsistent with the terms of the Act and was therefore valid, although Lord Morris dissented on the grounds that the article made 'a mockery' of *S.168*.

vi. The removal of a director of a 'quasi-partnership' company may be so unfair that the court will grant a petition to wind the company up on the 'just and equitable' ground – *S.122 INSOLVENCY ACT 1986 (g)*, **RE WESTBOURNE GALLERIES (1973)** (see Chapter 48.5.iii).

e. *Disqualification.* Table A provides that a director shall vacate office in the following circumstances:

i. If he ceases to be a director by virtue of a provision of the Act or if he becomes prohibited by law from being a director.

ii. If he becomes bankrupt or makes a composition arrangement with his creditors.

iii. If he becomes of unsound mind.

iv. If he resigns by notice in writing, or

v. If he is absent from board meetings for more than 6 months without permission.

6. ***Directors' Remuneration*** Since directors are not servants of the company they are not entitled as of right to remuneration. Table A empowers the company in a general meeting to fix directors' remuneration. Directors cannot therefore vote remuneration to themselves, but if they appoint one of their number as managing director his remuneration may be fixed by the board. Once fixed, remuneration is a debt and must be paid out of capital if there are no profits. (For director remuneration see Chapter 46.34.)

POWERS OF DIRECTORS

7. *Relationship between the Board and the Company*

a. The extent of directors' powers is defined by the articles. Table A provides that 'The business of the company shall be managed by the directors who may … exercise all the powers of the company.' Also 'No alteration of the memorandum or articles and no such direction shall invalidate any prior act of the directors.'

b. Thus if the shareholders do not approve of the directors' acts they must either remove them under *S.168* or alter the articles to regulate their future conduct. (The alteration cannot have a retrospective effect.) They cannot simply take over the functions of the directors. For example:

In **SCOTT v SCOTT (1943)** the company in a general meeting resolved, firstly to pay dividends to preference shareholders, and secondly that the financial affairs of the company be investigated by a firm of accountants. It was held that the resolutions were invalid as they usurped the powers which the articles had vested in the directors.

Table A, makes the directors' powers 'subject … to any direction given by special resolution'.

c. If directors exceed their powers, or exercise them improperly, their acts can be ratified by an *ordinary resolution* of the company.

In **BAMFORD v BAMFORD (1970)** in order to prevent a takeover bid the directors allotted 5000 shares to another company. The articles provided that all unissued shares were to be at the disposal of the directors. Two shareholders sought a declaration that the allotment was void because it was not made bona fide for the benefit of the company. Soon afterwards an ordinary resolution approving the allotment was passed at a general meeting. Proceeding on the assumption that the directors had not acted for the benefit of the company, and had therefore acted improperly, the court had to decide whether the ordinary resolution had cured the irregularity. It was held that it had, and the allotment was valid.

8. *Board Meetings*

a. Subject to the provisions of the articles the powers conferred on the directors are conferred on them collectively as a board. Prima facie therefore their powers can only be exercised at a properly constituted board meeting. However, Table A provides that a resolution in writing signed by all the directors will be valid.

b. *Notice.* A board meeting may be summoned by a director at any time and directors must be given a reasonable period of notice. This may be days, hours or even minutes, depending on the circumstances.

c. *Quorum.* The quorum will be fixed by the articles. Table A provides that the quorum shall be fixed by the directors, and if it is not so fixed, shall be two. If a director has an interest in a contract to be considered at the meeting he does not count towards the quorum.

d. *Voting.* This is also governed by the articles. Usually directors have one vote each and a majority decision will prevail. If voting is equal the resolution is lost unless the chairman has a casting vote and exercises it in favour of the resolution.

e. *Delegation.* The board may, of course, appoint agents or servants of the company, but it must not delegate the exercise of its discretion. It is an application of the rule of agency that a person to whom power is delegated must not delegate further without the consent of his principal. This rule is usually modified in two ways:

i. The directors may delegate any of their power to committees consisting of one or some of the directors, and

ii. The board may appoint and delegate to a managing director. Today most companies are run by a managing director rather than by the board.

9. *The Managing Director*

  a.   Table A provides that the directors may appoint one of their number as managing direc-
       tor on such terms as they think fit. He therefore has no settled functions. His powers
       and duties depend on his service agreement.

       In *CADDIES v HOLDSWORTH (1955)* the service agreement of the managing
       director of a holding company provided that he should perform the duties in relation to
       the business of the holding company and its subsidiaries as should be assigned to him by
       the board of the holding company. After policy disagreements the board directed him
       to confine his attention to the business of one of the subsidiaries. It was held that this
       was not a breach of his service agreement even though he had been deprived of the
       power of the company which was employing him.

  b.   It is usual to provide that the managing director is not subject to retirement by rotation,
       but that his appointment as managing director will automatically end if he ceases for any
       reason to be a director.

       In *SOUTHERN FOUNDRIES v SHIRLAW (1940)* (see Chapter 40.26.d) it was
       held that a managing director's service contract contained an implied condition
       that the company would not make it impossible for him to act by removing him
       as a director. When he was removed damages for breach of contract were therefore
       payable.

10. *Unauthorized Acts by Directors* Sometimes a company may wish to avoid a contract on the
    ground that either:

  a.   It was made by a person who was not a director (but who acted as such), or

  b.   It was made by the board, but in excess of the directors' collective authority as a board,
       or

  c.   It was made by an individual director without the required delegated authority of the
       board.

  In such cases the outsider will be protected if he can persuade the company to ratify the
  contract. If the company will not ratify, the outsider may be able to rely on *S.39* or on the
  rules of agency.

11. *Power of Directors to Bind the Company*

  a.   *S.39* provides that in favour of a person dealing with a company in good faith, the power
       of the board of directors to bind the company, or authorize others to do so, shall be
       deemed to be free of any limitation under the company's constitution.

  b.   '*Constitution*' is defined to include any resolution of the company and any agreement
       between the members as well as the constitutional documents.

  c.   The Act also makes it clear that even a person dealing with a company with knowledge
       that the transaction is beyond the directors' powers will be protected. Such knowledge,
       by itself, does not amount to 'bad faith'. Bad faith will, however, exist if the person deal-
       ing with the company assists the directors in the abuse of their powers, or is party to
       fraud.

  d.   To prevent the new provisions being used as a vehicle for fraud *S.181* contain meas-
       ures invalidating certain transactions where directors have exceeded limitations
       placed upon their powers to bind the company. (These are discussed in 18. below.)

12. *The Rules of Agency* Under the normal rules of agency where a person without actual authority contracts on behalf of a company, the other party can hold the company bound if he can show:

   a. That he was induced to make the contract by the agent being represented as occupying a certain position in the company.

   b. That the representation was made by persons with actual authority to manage the company, and

   c. That the contract was one which a person in the position which the agent was held out as occupying would usually have authority to make.

   In *FREEMAN & LOCKYER v BUCKHURST PARK PROPERTIES (1964)* a director who had never been appointed managing director assumed powers of management with the company's approval. He entered into a contract with the claimants, who were architects. The company denied liability to pay the claimants' fees, but were held bound to the contract because the act of engaging architects was within the scope of the authority of a managing director of a property company and the claimants were not obliged to enquire whether the person was properly appointed. It was sufficient that under the articles there was a power to appoint a managing director, and that the board of directors had allowed him to act as such.

   d. *S.39* removes the need to rely on the rules of the agency in almost all cases, for example Freeman's case, since the Act refers to the 'power of the Board of Directors to bind the company, or authorize others to do so'. There may, however, still be a few situations where a valid 'holding out' is done by someone other than the directors.

ENFORCEMENT OF FAIR DEALING BY DIRECTORS

13. *Introduction* The Act deals with specific aspects of a company's relationship with its directors. It deals with situations where the interests of a director and his company may conflict, concerning for example employment contracts, property transactions and loans. Before proceeding it is necessary to define several terms used in Part X.

   a. *Shadow directors*

      i. For the purpose of Part X the term 'director' generally includes a shadow director.

      ii. A shadow director is a person in accordance with whose instructions the directors are accustomed to act unless the directors act on that person's advice only when it is given in a professional capacity.

   b. *Connected persons.* Where the Act refers to 'a person connected with a director' the following are included (unless they are already directors):

      i. The director's spouse.

      ii. The director's child (whether legitimate or not) or stepchild, so long as in either case the child is aged under 18.

      iii. A company where the director, either by himself or in concert with others, controls more than 20% of the voting power or equity share capital.

iv. A person acting in the capacity of trustee of any trust, (except one operating as an employees' share scheme or pension scheme), the beneficiaries of which include the director or any person in i., ii. or iii. above, and

v. A person acting in his capacity as partner of the director or of any person in i., ii. or iii. above.

c. *Relevant company.* A relevant company is either a public company or a private company in a group which contains a public company.

d. *Quasi-loan.* A quasi-loan is basically a payment or an agreement to pay a third party on behalf of a director or connected person where the company will be reimbursed in due course. For example, where the company provides the director with credit card facilities, or pays for goods and services used by a director on terms that the director reimburses the company at some future date.

e. *Credit transaction.* A credit transaction may take any one of the following forms:

i. A sale of land or a supply of goods under a hire purchase or conditional sale agreement, or

ii. A lease of land or hire of goods in return for periodical payments, or

iii. A disposal of land or the supply of goods or services where payment is deferred.

14. ***Compensation for Loss of Office*** By *S.219* it is unlawful for a company to pay a director compensation for loss of office or in connection with his retirement, unless particulars of the proposed payment (including the amount) have been disclosed to and approved by the members. If the payment is not disclosed and approved, the directors responsible for making it are liable to repay the sum misapplied.

15. ***Disclosure of Interests in Contracts***

a. By *S.177* a director who is in any way interested in a contract with the company must declare the nature of his interest at a board meeting. He must disclose his interest at the first board meeting at which the contract was discussed, or if he did not have an interest at that time, at the first board meeting after his interest arose.

b. If disclosure is not made the director is liable to a fine of unlimited amount. In addition the contract is voidable by the company unless it is too late to rescind.

16. ***Directors' Contracts of Employment***

a. *S.188* provides that a company may not enter into an agreement for the employment of a director for a period exceeding 2 years (where the company's ability to terminate is limited) unless the agreement has been approved by the shareholders in general meeting.

b. If the proper procedure is not followed the offending part of the contract is void. The remainder of the contract is valid, however, it is deemed to contain a term entitling the company to terminate the contract at any time by giving reasonable notice.

c. There is, however, nothing to stop a director entering into a contract of employment with his company making him an employee of the company. Provided all the necessary ingredients are present for creating employee status, a director may become an employee of the company (see ***SECRETARY OF STATE FOR TRADE AND INDUSTRY V BOTTRILL (1999)*** and ***CONNOLLY V SELLERS ARENASCENE LTD***

(2000)). This can have distinct advantages for a director, for example, entitlement to payment of wages as an employee upon insolvency, and a claim for unfair dismissal.

17. *Substantial Property Transactions*

   a. By *S.191* a company cannot transfer to or acquire from a director or any person connected with him any property the value of which exceeds the lesser of either £100 000 or 10% of the company's net assets without prior approval of the shareholders in a general meeting. Arrangements to transfer the property through third parties to achieve the same objectives are subject to the same requirements.

   b. Some transfers are exempt, for example transfers between companies in the same group (i.e. where the transferee company is itself a director of the transferor company) transfers by companies in liquidation and transfers of less than £2000 in value.

   c. If the transfer is not approved by the company beforehand, or affirmed within a reasonable time afterwards it is *voidable* by the company unless:

       i. Restitution of the subject matter is impossible, or

       ii. A third party who is not aware of the contravention has acquired rights bona fide and for value.

   In addition the director or connected person in question is liable to account to the company for any gain made and indemnify it against any loss resulting from the transfer.

18. *Invalidity of Certain Transactions Involving Directors*

   a. The provisions introduced by *S.39* could be used as a vehicle for fraud where directors exceed the limits placed upon their powers and bind the company in a transaction where the other parties include either a director of the company or its holding company or a person connected with, or a company associated with, such a director.

   b. By *S.181* such a transaction is voidable at the option of the company, and whether or not the transaction is avoided, any director who is a party to the transaction, or any person connected with him, or any director who authorized the transaction, is liable:

       i. To account to the company for any gain, and

       ii. To indemnify the company for any loss or damage.

   Such persons will not be liable if they can show that, at the time of the transaction, they were unaware that the directors were exceeding their powers.

   c. The basic purpose of this section is to prevent dishonest directors misusing their power to bind the company in transactions from which they can benefit. Since the company can avoid the transaction it will usually be able to recover any money or property fraudulently transferred under the transaction.

   d. By *S.181* where a private company with one member enters into a contract (which is not in the ordinary course of business) with the sole member who is also a director, the company shall (unless the contract is in writing) ensure that a written note of the contract is recorded in the minutes of the next board meeting.

19. *Loans to Directors. General Rules* It would clearly be unfair to shareholders if money invested to generate business is used personally by the directors (especially if they do not repay the loan). The prohibition (with exceptions) of loans to directors is therefore a well established principle. However, to be really effective the rules must be extended to indirect

arrangements, e.g. guarantees. There is also a need for careful anti-avoidance legislation designed to catch any scheme contrary to the general principle.

a.   *Basic rule*

   i.   By *S.197* a company may not make a loan to its directors or to a director of its holding company, nor may it enter into any guarantee or provide any security in connection with a loan made to such directors.

   ii.   Clearly a guarantee or provision of security on behalf of a director is not as directly harmful as a loan, since the company may never be called on to honour it, nevertheless it is an unacceptable risk for the company.

b.   *Anti-avoidance provisions*

   i.   By *S.197* a company may not arrange an assignment to it or assume any rights, obligations or liabilities under a transaction which contravenes these provisions. For example, if a director borrows money from a bank, with a relative acting as guarantor, and then the relative assigns the guarantee to the company *S.197* will be contravened.

   ii.   Under *S.197* a company shall not take part in any arrangement whereby:

      a) Another person enters into a transaction which if it had been entered into by the company would have contravened the above provisions, and

      b) That other person, in pursuance of the arrangement obtains a benefit from the company or another company within the group. These widely drafted provisions will prevent for example:

      A loan by X Ltd to a director of Y Ltd in return for a loan by Y Ltd to a director of X Ltd.

      A loan by a company to a director of its subsidiary, the subsidiary making up the shortfall in interest by paying the holding company 'management fees'.

      A loan by an insurance company to a director of subsidiary A on the understanding that subsidiary B will place insurance business with the company.

c.   *Relevant companies*

   The Act draws a distinction between relevant companies and other companies because, in the past, most abuses have occurred in public companies where shareholders tend to be at greater risk from the directors. There are three basic differences:

   i.   The prohibition on loans and guarantees is extended to quasi-loans and credit transactions.

   ii.   The prohibitions apply not only to transactions with directors, but with a number of persons connected with directors, for example a spouse or business partner, and

   iii.   Directors of relevant companies, but not directors of other companies, commit a criminal offence if any of these rules are broken.

20. *Loans to Directors. Exceptions*

   a.   *Loans not exceeding £10 000 (S.207).* Any company may make a loan to a director of the company or of its holding company if the amount does not exceed £10 000. Loans above £10 000 will require shareholder approval (*S.197*).

b. *Loans to holding companies (S.208).* Loans or other borrowing assistance may be given by a company to its holding company. This exception is necessary because a holding company may be a director of the company making the loan or offering borrowing assistance. Alternatively a director of a subsidiary may control more than 20 per cent of the voting power in the holding company, making the holding company a connected person. In either case prohibition of loans could interfere with proper inter-group lending.

c. *Loans etc to directors to enable them to perform their duties (S.204).*

Funds may be provided for a director to meet expenses incurred to enable him to perform his duties without shareholder approval provided it does not exceed £50 000.

d. *Loans by money-lending companies and recognized banks (S.209).* In general the loan must be in the ordinary course of business and the terms must be no more favourable than those that would be offered to an independent person of similar financial standing.

e. *Inter-group loans etc by relevant companies (S.208).* Where a relevant company is a member of a group it may lend to other members of the group despite the fact that a director of the relevant company is associated with the other members of the group. Like (b) above the reason for this exception is to prevent interference with legitimate inter-group business.

21. **Civil Remedies for Breach of S.213**

a. The transaction is *voidable* at the instance of the company unless:

    i. Restitution of the money or other asset involved is no longer possible, or

    ii. A third party who is not aware of the contravention has acquired rights bona fide and for value.

b. In addition any director or connected person who benefited from the prohibited loan or assistance and any director who authorized the arrangement, is liable to account for any gain made directly or indirectly by the arrangement, and is liable to indemnify the company for any loss resulting from it, unless such person can show that he took all reasonable steps to secure the company's compliance or was not aware of the contravention.

22. **Indemnification of Directors** The Act, *Chapter 7* and *Part 10* provides directors with a level of indemnity for personal liability in certain situations. These are:

a. For legal costs incurred through actions brought by third parties against a director, even if judgment goes against the director. Excluded are any criminal fines or fines by regulators e.g. Financial Services Authority.

b. Defence costs even where the claim is brought by the company. However, if a director's defence is unsuccessful, he may be required to repay costs to the company.

c. Where they are acting as company secretary or manager.

All indemnities must be disclosed in the durectors' annual report with any indemnity agreements available for inspection by members.

23. **Court Indemnity** Under *S.1157* of the Act, a court may excuse a director from personal liability where it can be shown that:

a. The directors acted honestly and reasonably.

b. Having regard to all the circumstances, a director ought fairly to be excused.

FIDUCIARY DUTIES AND DUTIES OF CARE AND SKILL

24. *Fiduciary Duties. Introduction*

   a. The fiduciary duties owed by directors are basically similar to those applying to any other fiduciary, for example an agent or a trustee. They are based upon the principle that since the company places its trust in the directors they must display the utmost good faith towards the company in their dealings with it or on its behalf. The duties, however, only apply to what the directors undertake without the concurrence of the company in a general meeting. For example, directors may profit from their position, but they must not make a secret profit.

   b. Note that:

   i. Although the authority of the directors to bind the company usually depends on them acting collectively as a board, fiduciary duties are owed by each director individually.

   ii. Fiduciary duties are owed to the company, not to individual shareholders (*S.170*).

   In **PERCIVAL v WRIGHT (1902)** the directors purchased some shares from a member without revealing that negotiations were in progress for the sale of all shares in the company at a higher price. In fact no sale ever took place. The plaintiff nevertheless sought to have his sale to the directors set aside for non-disclosure. It was held that the sale should not be set aside since the directors owed no fiduciary duties to individual members.

   This decision has been much criticized, and the directors involved would today be guilty of the criminal offence of insider dealing in a similar transaction involving *listed securities*. However, since **PERCIVAL v WRIGHT (1902)** was a private transaction the decision is not affected by the insider dealing legislation.

   There may, however, be occasions when directors owe a fiduciary duty to creditors, for example, where the company is insolvent or in severe financial difficulties. In **COLIN GWYER & ASSOCIATES LTD V LONDON WHARF (LIME-HOUSE) LTD (2003)** the directors, who agreed to compromise on a legal claim the company had against Colin Gwyer & Associates a compromise clearly to the detriment of the company, were found liable for breach of fiduciary duty not only to shareholders but also creditors of the company. The directors knew that the company was insolvent at the time.

25. *Directors' Duty in Relation to Employees*

   a. *S.172* states that the directors are, in the performance of their functions, to have regard to the interests of the company's employees as well as the interests of the members. The section specified that the duty is *owed to the company* and is enforceable in the same way as any other fiduciary duty owed to a company by its directors.

   b. Although directors' relationships with shareholders and employees are different they must have regard to the interests of both groups to discharge their duty to the company as a whole. Thus *S.172* allows directors to act in the interests of employees without fear of being in breach of their duty to the company. This does not mean that they can subordinate the interest of the company to that of employees by, for example, running the company at a loss to save jobs. It does, however, decrease the power of the members to object to an act which may not be beneficial to them, but would nevertheless be regarded as good industrial practice. For example, a merger would have to be arranged to minimize loss of jobs provided this could be done without undue harm to the interests of the company as a whole.

26. *Statutory Duties S.171–177*

a. The general fiduciary duties owed by a director to his or her company, is now framed under statute by way of a *Code of Conduct*. Prior to the Act of 2006, these duties were found in the common law and the Act requires that:

These general statutory duties be interpreted and applied in the same way as the established common law rules and equitable principles (*S.170(4)*).

b. There are seven general duties, these are the duty to:

   i.   Act within the powers given under the company's constitution (*S.171*).

   ii. Exercise independent judgment (*S.172*).

   iii. Promote the success of the company (*S.173*).

   iv. Exercise reasonable care, skill and diligence (*S.174*).

   v.   Avoid conflicts of interest (*S.175*).

   vi. Not accept benefits from third parties (*S.176*).

   vii. Declare any interest in proposed transactions or arrangements (*S.177*).

We now need to consider each of these *general duties* in turn.

27. *The Duty to Act within the Powers given by the Company and to Exercise those Powers for the Proper Purposes for which they were Conferred* (*S.171*)

This duty is in two parts:

   (i) *Duty to act within their* powers. This will normally be the powers laid down in the articles of association, e.g. power to issue shares, elect a chairman, etc. However *S.257* extends this to cover any special resolutions passed by members and any resolutions treated in law as being equivalent to a decision of the company. So a unanimous informal decision of the members would be regarded as part of the company's constitution.

   (ii) *Duty to use powers for a proper purpose.* If directors dishonestly use their powers for an improper purpose, for example to make a personal profit at the company's expense, they will not only have breached *S.172* (see below) in not acting bona fide – in good faith – but also the duty not use their powers for an improper purpose (*S.171*). So even where directors act honestly, in what they believe to be in the best interests of the company, they may still be liable for breach of duty in using their powers for an improper purpose.

   In **HOGG v CRAMPHORN (1967)** in order to prevent a takeover bid which they believed would be bad for the company, the directors issued shares, carrying 10 votes each, to trustees of an employee pension fund. The shares were paid for by the trustees out of an interest free loan from the company. It was held that, although the directors had acted in what they believed to be the best interests of the company and so met the duty to act in good faith (*S.172* – see below), since the proper purpose of issuing shares is to raise capital, an issue made to forestall a takeover bid was a breach of duty under *S.171*.

It is an improper purpose if shares are issued solely for the purpose of destroying the existing majority block of shares. Shares need not, however, be issued solely to raise capital, for example it may be proper to issue shares to a larger company to ensure the stability of the issuing company.

Breaches of the *improper* purpose duty can be seen in more recent instances, e.g. the so-called, 'poison pill' or 'shark repellent' strategies sometimes adopted by directors. These occur when the directors of a company put in place some defence mechanism against any unwanted or hostile takeovers, or attempts by 'others' to alter the power of the board. In *CRITERION PROPERTIES PLC V STRATFORD UK PROPERTIES (2002)* the managing director entered into an agreement with the holder of a substantial shareholding in the company, which required that the company to buy back those shares at a high price should there be any change in the control or composition of the board. The managing director was later removed and the company was asking the court to set aside the buy-back agreement on the basis of it being entered into through an improper use of the director's power. The High Court ruled that this was an improper use of the powers of the director and that the agreement would accordingly be set aside. The Court weighed up the advantages and disadvantages to the company in enforcing the agreement and found that the cost to the company in having to buy back the shares far outweighed any disadvantage caused by a shift in power within the board.

28. *The Duty to Promote the Success of the Company* (*S.172*)

A director must act in a way that he or she considers to be in good faith that would be most likely to promote the success of the company for the benefit of the members as a whole.

a. Defining *good faith* and acts *likely to promote the success of the company*.

It is clear that directors do not have to maximize economic benefit to the company whilst disregarding the interests of members, since this would mean ploughing back all the profits to the exclusion of payment of dividends. The phrase 'likely to promote the success of the company', basically means that the directors must have regard to the interests of the present and future members of the company, i.e. they must view the company as a going concern and balance this long-term view against the interests of the present members.

b. It is not for the benefit of the company if they act in their own interest or the interest of a third party, without also considering the interest of the company.

In *RE ROITH (1967)* the controlling shareholder and director of a company wished to provide for his widow without leaving her his shares. Acting on legal advice he entered into a service agreement with the company whereby on his death she would be entitled to a pension for life. Since the sole object of the transaction was to benefit the widow the agreement was not held to be binding on the company. A more recent illustration can be seen in *BRITISH MIDLAND TOOLS V MIDLAND INTERNATIONAL TRADING (2003)*. Here two directors about to resign and join a director who had previously resigned to set up a new rival company, were found to be in breach of their duty to act in good faith for the benefit of the company. They knew that the proposed new company was approaching existing employees to entice them to join the rival company (it had in fact already poached 12 employees) and they did nothing to discourage this.

c. Charitable and political donations of moderate value may be for the benefit of the company whilst it is a going concern, but if the company is about to cease then no commercial advantage can be gained by keeping outside interests happy. In such a case benefit of the company would be restricted to the economic interests of the present members.

d.   If the breach of duty is a misapplication of company property, a person who receives such property and who knows of the breach holds the property as constructive trustee and must therefore return it to the company.

e.   The Act states various factors which directors ought to consider when carrying out acts likely to promote the success of the company; these are:

 i.   The likely consequences of any decision in the long term.

 ii.   The interests of the company's employees.

 iii.   The need to foster the company's business relationships with suppliers, customers and others.

 iv.   The impact of the company's operations on the community and the environment.

 v.   The desirability of the company maintaining a reputation for high standards of business conduct, and

 vi.   The need to act fairly as between members of the company

 (*S.172(1)*).

It is worth noting at this point the likely difficulty any board of a company may well have in taking into account these, often conflicting, consequences of their actions. For example, steps taken to increase overall corporate efficiency might well lead to a requirement for fewer employees. This is likely to lead to boards of companies merely recording in the formal notes of their meetings that the above factors have been taken into account when reaching decisions on what is likely to promote the success of the company.

f.   *S.172* recognizes that there may be occasions when other interested parties may well overrule the above, e.g. where a company becomes unable to pay its debts as they fall due, the interests of creditors may well prevail (*S.214 INSOLVENCY ACT 1986* – see Chapters 47.13 and 47.14) (*S.172(3)*). And in **WEST MERCIA SAFETYWEAR v DOOD (1988)** the court stated that in a solvent company (where assets meet liabilities) the proprietary interests of shareholders entitle them **as a general body** to be regarded as the company for purposes of directors' duties. If, as a general body, they authorize or ratify a particular action of directors, there can be no challenge to the validity of what directors have done. However, where a company is insolvent (its assets no longer meet its liabilities) the interests of **creditors** intrude. They become prospectively entitled to displace the power of shareholders and directors to deal with the company's assets – here, *creditors will be owed the fiduciary duties.*

g.   The duty owed under *S.171* has to be considered jointly with the duty of good faith (*S.174*).

As noted, directors are expected to act in good faith to promote the success of the company, provided they do this they will not become liable merely because a decision turns out to be a wrong decision. However, the duty owed under *S.172* has to be considered in light of the duty to exercise care and skill in carrying out their duties (*S.174* see below), for clearly a wrong decision carried out in good faith would meet the duty under *S.172* it may well fail to meet the duty under *S.174* in that it was not carried out exercising reasonable care, skill and diligence.

Although the list of factors stated in *S.172(1)* above, is not exhaustive, it does now appear that seeking to maximize profit for shareholders alone, may now be not enough. This forms part of a more general debate currently going on about who are companies run for the benefit of – shareholders, employees, society as a whole or the environment, etc? This is referred to as the *stakeholder debate* and forms an important element of corporate governance (see Chapter 46.34).

29. ***The Duty to Exercise Independent Judgment*** (*S.173*)

   a. Directors cannot validly contract with each other or with third parties on the way which they will vote at future board meetings.

   b. Sometimes a lender will insist that, as a condition of granting a loan, his representative sits on the board of the borrowing company. In theory the duty of such directors is owed to the company and not to the person responsible for their nomination.

   c. *S.173* goes on to recognize the reality of the situation where restrictions are often placed upon directors within their respective companies e.g. a marketing director may be only allowed to act only on matters relating to marketing. In order that such commonly found restrictions on a particular director's ability to act do not amount to a breach of the duty to exercise independent judgment, *S.173* states that the duty will not be broken where:

      i. A director has entered into an agreement that restricts the future exercise of his or her discretion to act.

      ii. The restrictions are authorized in the company's constitution.

      S.173 requires of directors that they exercise independent judgment and be subservient to the wishes of others, such as fellow directors or majority shareholders.

30. ***The Duty to Exercise Reasonable Care, Skill and Diligence*** There was, historically, little obligation on directors to display any skill and diligence in carrying out their fiduciary duties. In ***RE CITY EQUITABLE FIRE INSURANCE CO (1925)*** in taking each element the Court found, as to any standard of *skill* required:

   a. A director must exhibit the degree of skill which may reasonably be expected from a person of his knowledge and experience. This standard is *objective* in that the director must act as a reasonable man, but it is *subjective* in that the reasonable man is only regarded as possessing the knowledge and experience of the individual concerned. Thus in financial matters more would be expected of a director who is a qualified accountant than a director who has no accountancy training.

   b. As to due *diligence* a director is not bound to give continuous attention to the company's affairs, his duties are of 'an intermittent nature'. Directors are not bound to attend all board meetings, but must attend when they are reasonably able to do so (***RE CARDIFF BANKING (1892)***). The degree of diligence may, however, vary depending on the facts of the case, more would be expected from a director on whom the company relies than from one director among many, or from one who is given little effective power.

   c. On a director's ability to *delegate responsibilities* to others, in the absence of suspicious circumstances directors are entitled to trust the company's officers to perform their duties properly. A director will not be liable for the acts of co-directors or other officers unless he participates in the wrong, for example by signing a cheque for an unauthorized payment.

d. Under the Act, *S.174*, there is now a statutory statement requiring that directors *exercise reasonable care, skill and diligence* along with a test to help establish the requisite standard of care, skill and diligence required in a particular case. It states:

   i.   A director must exercise reasonable care, skill and diligence, this means

   ii. A standard of care, skill and diligence that would be found by a reasonably diligent director:

      i) with the general knowledge, skill and experience that may reasonably be expected of a person carrying out the functions carried out by the director (an *objective* assessment), and

      ii) The general knowledge, skill and experience that the particular director has (a *subjective* assessment).

The two assessments work by, initially, setting a general standard that is reasonable to expect of a director when comparing him or her with a similar director of a similar company (*objective*), this will form an irreducible minimum standard; then, in looking at the qualifications and experience of the particular director in question (*subjective*), which may raise that initial standard where it is found to be reasonable to do so e.g. a director with accountancy qualifications and many years experience as a director, might well be required to meet a higher standard.

31. *The Duty to Avoid Conflicts of Interest* (S.175)

This duty relates to directors not putting themselves into a position where their personal interests conflict with those of the company. *S.175* reads as follows:

a. A director of a company must avoid a situation in which has, or can have, a direct or indirect interest that conflicts, or possibly may conflict, with the interests of the company.

   Here it is not enough for a director to avoid a situation in which he or she has a conflict of interest, he or she must also avoid a situation in which they *might* have such a conflict.

b. This no-conflict duty applies in particular to the exploitation of any property, information or opportunity which belongs to the company (and it is immaterial whether the company could take advantage of the property, information or opportunity).

   This section requires that a director must not exploit company property for his or her own ends and that information gained through their position as director, is the property of the company.

In **INDUSTRIAL DEVELOPMENT CONSULTANTS v COOLEY (1972)** the respondent was an architect who was employed as managing director of IDC. Whilst negotiating a contract with the Gas Board on behalf of IDC, Cooley realized that the contract probably would not be offered to IDC, but that if he left IDC he could obtain the contract himself. He therefore represented to IDC that he was ill and was allowed to terminate his contract. He then successfully obtained the contract with the Gas Board. IDC claimed the profit he made. It was held that Cooley was in breach of his duty as a director and must account to IDC with the profit made. It was immaterial that IDC might never have obtained the profit itself. What mattered was whether Cooley made a profit, not whether the company suffered a loss.

Thus a director must account for a profit even if it is not made at the company's expense. This is so even if the other party refused to contract with the company and even if the company is legally unable to acquire the benefit in question.

In *BOSTON DEEP SEA FISHING CO v ANSELL (1888)* directors of Boston had to pay to the company bonuses received as a result of placing contracts to purchase ice. These bonuses were only payable to shareholders who purchased ice. Boston's directors held shares in the ice-selling company, but Boston did not. The company therefore would not have been entitled to the bonus if the ice had been ordered direct.

There is Commonwealth authority for the proposition that a director does not misuse corporate opportunity if he enters into a transaction on his own account which the company has considered and rejected.

In *PESO SILVER MINES v CROPPER (1966)* (a Canadian case) the board of Peso considered and rejected the chance to purchase a number of prospecting claims near to the company's property. Peso's geologist then formed a company and it purchased the claims. Cropper, who was a director of Peso and a party to the original decision, was also a shareholder in the new company. The action was brought by Peso to claim from Cropper the profit he made on his shares in the new company. It was held that he did not have to account, he had acted in good faith and no information had been concealed from Peso's board when it made the decision not to purchase. There had not, therefore, been a misuse of corporate opportunity.

Although there is little case law on the subject it is clear that a director must not compete with the company. If he were to do so there would be an obvious conflict of personal interest and company interest.

The duty to avoid a conflict of interest does not apply to a conflict of interest arising in relation to a transaction or arrangement entered into between the director and the company.

The exemption of these potential conflict situations is because they are dealt with under a different section of the Act (*S.177* – see 33. below)

This section also exempts certain situations from the no conflict duty. These are:

i.   Where it is found that the particular conflict could not have been reasonably foreseeable, or

ii.   It has been authorized by the directors under the constitution of the company.

It goes on to set out the requirements for a proper authorization of a situation which would otherwise be a conflict of interest. It states authorisation may be given by the directors in a *private company* provided there is nothing in the company's constitution which would invalidate such an authorization, or where the company is a *public company* there must be express authorization within the company's constitution for such authorization by directors.

This means that for the *private company* the conflict is authorized provided there is no express block on this happening within the constitution and for the *public company* there has to be express authorization for directors to approve the conflict in the company's constitution.

This section continues with the requirement that for a valid authorization the director concerned or 'other interested director' must not count in any requirement for a quorum for the meeting of directors to take place – a quorum is a requirement that a minimum number of persons be present in order for that meeting to be able to conduct business – also, that directors or interested directors concerned, must not vote at such a meeting. This is a requirement for both private and public companies.

Where this process of authorization takes place, members do not need to give approval or authorization of any transaction or arrangement unless the constitution of the company requires member approval (*S.180(1)*).

32. *The Duty not to Accept Benefits from Third Parties* (*S.176*)

Third parties are persons outside of the company; this could be a human being or another company – a body corporate. It is important to distinguish this section from *S.175* the duty to avoid conflicts of interest. *S.175* is concerned with a director using company property, information or opportunity for his or her own advantage; *S.176* covers directors receiving any benefits from outsiders. This duty not to accept bribes or secret profits from outsiders continues after a director has ceased to be a director of the company (*S.170(2)(b)*).

33. *The Duty to Declare an Interest in any Proposed Transaction or Arrangement* (*S.177*)

a. If a director of a company is directly or indirectly interested in a proposed transaction or arrangement with the company, he or she must declare the nature and extent of that interest to other directors. And if any declaration under *S.177* proves to be, or becomes, inaccurate or incomplete, a further declaration must be made (*S.177(3)*).

b. The requirement to declare an interest does not apply where a director is not aware of the particular transaction or arrangement in question and that he ought not reasonably to have known of it. Also, where other directors are aware of the interest or ought reasonably to have been aware of it, there will be no requirement to declare (*S.177(6)*).

c. As already noted (see 25.b above) these general duties are owed to *the company*, therefore, any breaches may be excused or authorized by the company. This is now contained in the Act *S.180* which allows members of the company (NOT directors) to authorize any breach. Individual directors who are also shareholders and would otherwise have been in breach of one or more of the duties, must not vote on any resolutions approving or authorizing a breach (*S.239*).

d. In addition to the general requirement to declare, the Act makes it a *criminal offence* for a director not to declare an interest in any arrangement or transaction with the company (*S.182*). The same qualifications apply, as listed under the general requirement to declare contained in *S.177*, regarding:

   i. Making a new declaration if things change.

   ii. Not being required to make a declaration where it would be unreasonable to expect a director to know of the conflict.

   iii. Matters upon which fellow directors should have known.

34. *Enforcement of the General Duties* The director's duties will generally be only enforceable by the company. This means, the board of directors or shareholders in a general meeting. It is worth noting at this point that although employees are owed consideration under *S.172* – the duty to promote the success of the company – they cannot bring an action to enforce that duty or any of the others.

35. *Relief from Liability*

a. Under *S.1157* the court has the power, in an action against a director for breach of duty, to grant relief where although the director is in breach, it appears to the court that he has acted honestly and reasonably. A significant factor is assessing reasonableness will be whether legal advice was sought.

b. By *S.532*, neither the articles nor any contract may exempt or indemnify a director or other officer of the company, for the consequences of any breach; however a company may purchase insurance to cover the consequences of a breach by a director or auditor (*S.532*).

DISQUALIFICATION OF DIRECTORS

36. *Introduction* The *COMPANY DIRECTORS DISQUALIFICATION ACT 1986*, provides for a person being disqualified from acting as a director.

37. *Mandatory Disqualification* (*S.6 CDDA 1986*)

   a. A person may be subject to this procedure if he is, or has been, a director or a shadow director of a company which has gone into insolvent liquidation (whether voluntary or compulsory).

   b. The court is required to make a disqualification order if the person's conduct as a director, either considered in isolation or taken with his conduct as a director of another company, makes him unfit to be concerned with the management of a company.

   c. Since the Act came into force a number of disqualification orders have been made.

   In *RE STANFORD SERVICES LTD (1987)* a director was held to be unfit to hold office because the company owed considerable amount of PAYE, National Insurance and VAT. The director had used available funds to finance the company's business rather than arrange for the money to be set aside to meet the above liabilities. Although commercial morality may not have been infringed it was held that there had been a serious breach of the director's duties to the company's creditors and the public interest required that the misconduct should be recognized by 2 years' disqualification.

38. *Non-mandatory Disqualification* This may arise in two situations:

   a. By *S.8 CDDA 1986* an application for disqualification order may be made by the Secretary of State following a Department of Trade investigation.

   b. By *S.10 CDDA 1986* the court may make a disqualification order on its own initiative when it makes a declaration that a person is liable to make a contribution to the company's assets. This may arise under *S.213–215 IA* which deal with wrongful trading and fraudulent trading.

39. *Director Undertakings* A disqualification order can only be achieved by means of court proceedings, however, under the *INSOLVENCY ACT 2000,* the Secretary of State will have the power to accept an undertaking from a director where he or she agrees to a period of disqualification; this will achieve disqualification administratively more quickly.

40. *Acting While Disqualified* A person who concerns himself with the management of a company while disqualified, or a person who acts in the management of a company on instructions given by a disqualified person, is personally liable for all debts incurred by the company during the period in which he acts. The liability is joint and several with that of the company.

THE SECRETARY

41. *Appointment*

   a. *S.270* states that a private company may or may not have a company secretary. If there is no secretary in post, either because of a temporary vacancy or because the company has chosen, in accordance with its articles, not to have one, then the function will fall to either a director or another authorized to carry out the functions of a secretary (*S.274*). If there is a failure to authorize a director or other person, the function falls upon the board of directors.

b. A public company must have a secretary (*S.271*)

c. It is usual for the secretary to be appointed by the directors on such terms as they think fit. The directors may also remove the secretary. But the secretary may be appointed by members in a general meeting by ordinary resolution (51%).

42. **Qualifications** *S.273* stipulates minimum qualifications for secretaries of *public companies*. The directors must take all reasonable steps to ensure that the secretary is a person who appears to them to have the requisite knowledge and experience and who:

a. Already holds office as secretary, assistant secretary or deputy secretary of the company, *or*

b. For at least 3 out of the 5 years immediately preceding his appointment held office as secretary of a public company, or

c. Is a barrister, advocate or solicitor, *or*

d. Is a member of any of the following bodies:

    i. The Institute of Chartered Accountants.

    ii. The Association of Certified Accountants.

    iii. The Institute of Chartered Secretaries and Administrators.

    iv. The Chartered Institute of Cost and Management Accountants.

    v. The Chartered Institute of Public Finance and Accountancy, or

e. Is a person who, by virtue of having held any other position or being a member of any other body, appears to the directors to be capable of discharging the functions of a secretary.

43. **Powers** The secretary is the chief administrative officer of the company and on matters of administration he has ostensible authority to make contracts on behalf of the company. Such contracts include:

a. Hiring office staff.

b. Contracts for the purchase of office equipment, and

c. Hiring cars for business purposes.

    In *PANORAMA DEVELOPMENTS v FIDELIS FURNISHING FABRICS (1971)* the secretary of the defendant company entered into a number of contracts for the hire of cars. The cars were ostensibly to be used to collect important customers from Heathrow Airport, but in fact the secretary used them for his own private purposes. The Court of Appeal held that the defendant company was liable. Lord Denning M.R. said:

    'A company secretary is … an officer of the company with extensive duties and responsibilities …. He is certainly entitled to sign contracts connected with the administrative side of a company's affairs, such as employing staff, and ordering cars and so forth.'

d. Although a secretary has 'extensive duties and responsibilities' there are a number of decisions where it has been held that he does not have authority for particular acts. Thus he may not:

i. Bind the company on a trading contract.

ii. Borrow money on behalf of the company.

iii. Issue a writ or lodge a defence in the company's name.

iv. Register a transfer of shares.

v. Strike a name off the register of members.

vi. Summon a general meeting on his own authority.

44. *Duties* The secretary's duties include:

a. Ensuring that the company's documentation is in order, that the requisite returns are made to the Companies Registry, and that the company's registers are maintained.

b. Taking minutes of meetings.

c. Sending notices to members, and

d. Countersigning documents.

INSIDER DEALING

45. *Introduction* Insider dealing concerns the duties of directors, officers, some members and some outsiders when dealing in the company's securities with inside information which affects their value. It is controlled by provisions in the *CRIMINAL JUSTICE ACT 1993*.

46. *Definitions*

a. *Insider*. An insider is an individual who has information which:

i. Is inside information, and

ii. Has come from an inside source.

In each case the individual must *know* it is inside information and *know* it has come from an inside source.

b. *Inside information*. This is information which:

i. Relates to particular securities.

ii. Is specific or precise.

iii. Has not been made public, and

iv. Which would, if it were made public, be likely to have a significant effect on the price of the securities.

c. *Inside source*. A person has information from an inside source if:

i. He has it through being a director, employee or shareholder of an issuer of securities or through having access to the information because of his employment, office or profession, or

ii. The direct or indirect source of his information is one of the persons referred to in i. above.

d. *Dealing.* A person deals in securities if:

    i.   He acquires or disposes of securities either as principal or agent, or

    ii.   He procures, directly or indirectly, an acquisition or disposal of securities by another person.

    A decision not to deal, even if based on inside information, is not 'dealing'.

e. *Price-affected securities.* The price of the securities would be likely to be significantly affected if information relating to the securities were to be made public.

47. **Prohibitions** There are three offences which could be committed by an individual who has information as an insider:

a. Dealing in price-affected securities.

b. Encouraging another person to deal in price-affected securities.

c. Disclosing the information other than in the proper course of employment, office or profession.

In **R v MCQUOID (2009)** a solicitor working for a public company trading on the Stock Exchange, passed insider information regarding a takeover of the company onto a relative. When the takeover became generally known the share price tripled with the relative making a profit of around £50 000. The solicitor was found guilty of insider dealing.

48. *Defences*

a. In relation to a. and b. above (dealing and encouraging to deal) an individual has a defence if he shows that:

    i.   He did not expect the dealing to result in a profit, or

    ii.   He reasonably believed that the information had been so widely disclosed that none of those taking part in the dealing would be prejudiced by not having the information, or

    iii.   He would have dealt, even if he had not had the information.

b. In relation to c. above (disclosing the information) an individual has a defence if:

    i.   He did not expect any person, because of the disclosure, to deal in the securities, or

    ii.   Although he did expect the person to deal, he did not expect it to result in a profit attributable to the fact that the information was price-sensitive.

49. *Penalties and Remedies*

a. Insider dealing is a criminal offence, the maximum penalty being 7-years imprisonment plus an unlimited fine. Prosecutions must be brought by the Secretary of State for Trade or the Director of Public Prosecutions. The Act does not provide for civil actions.

b. Contravention of the Act does not effect the validity of the transaction. This is rather unusual since criminal acts are normally void or voidable. The rule is, however, sensible since the chain of transactions may be complex and innocent parties could be affected if the transaction were held to be void.

50. *Investigations into Insider Dealing*

a. Prior to 1986 there was no mechanism for the investigation of suspected insider dealing other than investigation by the police. This was a serious drawback to the effectiveness of the legislation.

b. The *FINANCIAL SERVICES ACT 1986* (now the *FINANCIAL SERVICES AND MARKETS ACT 2000*) empowered the Financial Services Authority to investigate suspected insider dealing offences. The FSA can require any person that may have relevant information to:

    i. Produce documents in his possession. 'Documents' includes information recorded in any form.

    ii. Attend before them.

    iii. Otherwise give all reasonable help in connection with the investigation.

They also have powers to enter and search premises for evidence.

SELF TEST QUESTIONS

Self Test Questions No. 42 (for Answers see Appendix 1):

1 What is the role of directors *vis à vis* fellow directors on the board and members?

2 How are directors appointed and removed?

3 What is the nature and source of a director's powers?

4 Outline the disclosure requirements placed upon directors.

5 What is a *fiduciary* and what are directors' fiduciaries?

6 What is *insider dealing*?

7 What are the defences and penalties for *insider dealing*?

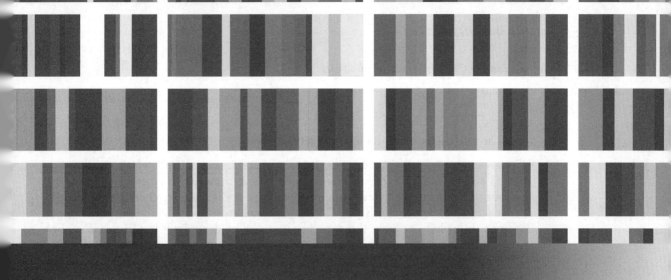

AUDITORS AND INVESTIGATIONS

45

Learning Outcomes At the end of this chapter you should be able to:

- State the law regarding the general requirement for *audit* with the exemptions.

- Explain the nature and source of the supervisory bodies.

- Understand the requirements for the appointment, removal and resignation of an auditor.

- Explain the powers, duties and liabilities of auditors.

- Outline the instigation of and processes involved in Department of Trade investigations.

THE AUDIT REQUIREMENT

1. *General Rule* All companies must have an auditor (*S.480*) and by *S.489* at each general meeting at which directors present the accounts, the company must appoint auditors to hold office from the end of that meeting until the end of the next general meeting. However, small private companies, but not public companies, are exempt from this requirement to appoint an auditor (*S.477*).

2. *Exemption for Certain Small Companies*

    a.   A company is regarded as small in any particular year if:

        i.   Its annual turnover is £5.6 million or less.

        ii. The total assets are £2.8 million or less (*S.477(1)*).

    b.   The abolition of the audit requirement is automatic for a company which satisfies the criteria and no action (e.g. resolutions) need be taken by the company. However, an exempt company may still need to have an external audit to satisfy conditions imposed by lenders who had previously placed trust in the statutory audit. In addition an exempt company must have an audit if required to do so by holders of not less that 10% of the issued shares. Such a request must be deposited in writing at the company's registered office at least 1 month before the company's year end.

    c.   The balance sheet of an exempt company must contain a statement by the directors:

        i.   That it is entitled to the exemption.

        ii. That no notice (referred to above) has been deposited by members, and

        iii. Acknowledging their responsibility for keeping accounting records and preparing accounts that give a true and fair view of the company's state of affairs.

3. *Exemptions for Dormant Companies*

    a.   A dormant company is one which has not made an accounting transaction in the preceding year or since incorporation.

    b.   A dormant company may pass a special resolution not to appoint auditors.

SUPERVISORY BODIES AND PROFESSIONAL QUALIFICATIONS

4. *Supervisory Bodies* The Act seeks to ensure that only persons who are properly supervised and appropriately qualified are appointed company auditors, and that audits are carried out properly and with integrity and independence.

5. *Types of Supervisory Body* Two types of supervisory body were established under the Act.

    a.   *Recognized Supervisory Bodies* (RSBs) of which all company auditors must be members.

    b.   *Recognized Qualifying Bodies* (RQBs) which will offer the professional qualifications required to become a member of an RSB.

    The same body can be both a RSB and a RQB. The existing professional bodies, for example the Chartered Association of Certified Accountants and the Institute of Chartered Accountants will fulfil both functions.

6. *Recognition of RSBs* By *S.30 CA 89* each RSB must be a body established in the UK (this now includes a corporate body or an unincorporated association) which maintains and enforces rules as to:

    a.   The eligibility of persons seeking appointment as company auditors, and

    b.   The conduct of company audit work.

Bodies wishing to be RSBs must apply to the Secretary of State, submitting their rules, any other written guidance and any other information that the Secretary of State may reasonably require.

7. **Rules of RSBs** (Schedule 11)

a. *Eligibility.* RSBs must ensure that only the following persons are eligible for appointment as auditors:

    i.   Individuals who hold appropriate qualifications.

    ii.   Firms controlled by qualified persons.

The RSB must ensure that such persons are 'fit and proper', taking into account the person's professional conduct, including the conduct of employees and close business associates.

b. *Professional integrity.* The RSBs' rules must ensure that audit work is carried out properly and with integrity. A DTI consultative document on the implementation of the EC Eighth Directive considers that two areas must be addressed:

    i.   The standards of performance of the audit, including compliance with approved auditing standards and guidelines, and

    ii.   General ethical standards, such as rules to cover independence, objectivity and client confidentiality.

c. *Technical standards.* The technical standards to be applied in company audits must be the subject of RSB rules. This is likely to be a reference to the need for auditing standards and guidelines rather than statements of standard accounting practice (SSAP).

d. *Maintenance of competence.* The rules of the RSB must ensure that eligible persons continue to maintain an appropriate level of competence.

e. *Investigation and enforcement.* The RSBs' rules must include provisions in respect of:

    i.   Monitoring and enforcement of compliance with its rules. The extent of monitoring is not yet clear and appropriate rules will be made after consultation between RSBs and the DTI. It may imply a regular examination of the activities of thousands of audit firms and individuals.

    ii.   Admission and expulsion of members.

    iii.   Grant and withdrawal of eligibility for appointment as an auditor.

    iv.   Disciplinary procedures.

        Note: The rules relating to ii.–iv. above must be 'fair and reasonable' and there must be adequate appeals procedures.

    v.   The investigation of complaints against members and against the RSB itself.

f. *Liability of RSBs.* RSBs and their officers, employees and governors are exempt from damages in respect of the exercise of their statutory duties, unless it can be shown that they have acted in bad faith. This prevents them from being joined in any action taken against auditors for negligence.

8. **Appropriate Qualifications** The Act makes it a requirement that auditors hold an 'appropriate qualification'. By *Schedule 10* a person will hold an appropriate qualification in the following cases:

a.   He satisfied the existing criteria for appointment as an auditor under the Act by being a member of one of the bodies recognized under that Act.

b.   He holds a recognized professional qualification obtained in the UK. In future this will be the 'appropriate qualification' for all new auditors.

c.   He holds an approved overseas qualification and satisfies any additional requirements set down by the Secretary of State.

9. *Recognized Qualifying Bodies S.32 and Schedule 12 CA 89*

a.   *Recognition.* To offer recognized professional qualifications bodies must be approved by the Secretary of State. The procedure for recognition is similar to that for recognition as a RSB. A RQB must have rules to ensure compliance with various entry, examination and training requirements.

b.   *Qualifications*

   i.   The RQB's qualification must only be open to persons who have attained university entrance level (without necessarily having gone to university) or have a sufficient period of professional experience. 'Sufficient period of professional experience' means at least 7 years in a professional capacity in finance, law or accountancy. Periods of theoretical instruction, up to a maximum of 4 years, count towards necessary experience so long as the instruction lasts for at least 1 year and is attested by an examination recognized for this purpose by the Secretary of State.

   ii. The qualification must be restricted to persons passing an examination which tests theoretical knowledge and the ability to apply it in practice, although persons may be exempted from examination in subjects in which they already hold a recognized qualification, for example a university examination of equivalent standard.

   iii. It is also a requirement that persons must have completed at least 3 years practical training, although exemption from this requirement may be possible if the person has an approved diploma evidencing practical training. The practical training must be given by persons approved by the RQB as being suitable and at least two-thirds of it must be with a fully qualified auditor. A substantial part of the training must be in company audit work.

c.   *Approval of overseas qualifications.* By *S.33 CA 89* the Secretary of State is empowered to consider professional qualifications obtained outside the UK as 'approved'. This will happen if he is satisfied that it gives a level of professional competence equivalent to a recognized professional qualification. Persons with overseas qualifications may be required to obtain additional educational qualifications to demonstrate that they have a sufficient knowledge of UK law and practice.

10. *Eligibility of Firms and Individuals*

a.   The Act provides that an individual or firm (defined to mean either a partnership or corporate body) may be appointed. Firms may only perform audits if they are controlled by qualified persons i.e. a majority of those empowered to make the decisions are qualified persons.

b.   *Appointment of partnerships.* Where a partnership is appointed the Act makes it clear that it is the firm and not the partners that has been appointed (previously appointments were, strictly speaking, of individuals). The Act also provides that the appointment will continue despite any technical dissolution of the partnership when members join and leave. When a partnership ceases the appointment may go to any eligible partnership that succeeds the practice or any individual partner who has taken over the practice.

c.   *Appointment of corporate bodies.* The Act provides that the majority of decision-makers in such bodies must be qualified persons, but it leaves many of the detailed rules to be laid down by the RSBs.

d.   *Ineligibility of auditors*

i.   A person is ineligible to be a company's auditor if he is an officer or employee of the company, or a partner or employee of such a person. The Act also provides that a person will be ineligible if he is not sufficiently independent of the company, although it leaves lack of independence to be defined by regulations.

ii.   If an auditor ceases to be eligible under the rules of the RSB of which he is a member, he must immediately vacate office and give written notice to the company. If such a person continues to act, or fails to give written notice, he is guilty of an offence.

iii.   Under the Act, if an auditor acts when ineligible the Secretary of State may direct the company to appoint another auditor to carry out a second audit or to review the first audit, stating (with reasons) whether a second audit is required.

APPOINTMENT, REMOVAL AND RESIGNATION

11. *Appointment*

a.   *First auditors.* By S.485 the first auditors may be appointed by the directors at any time before the first general meeting at which the accounts are laid. They then hold office until the end of that meeting. If the company has passed an elective resolution to dispense with the laying of accounts, the first auditors may be appointed within 28 days after the company's first annual accounts being sent to members. If the directors fail to make an appointment the general meeting may appoint.

b.   *Subsequent auditors*

i.   At each general meeting at which accounts are laid the company may appoint one or more auditors. They then hold office from the end of the meeting until the end of the next meeting at which accounts are laid.

ii.   However, if the company chooses, by elective resolution, to dispense with the annual appointment of auditors, the auditors shall be deemed to be re-appointed annually for so long as the election remains in force During this time, any member may give written notice to the company proposing that the auditors' appointment be terminated. The directors must then convene a general meeting, which must be held within 28 days of the notice being given,

iii.   If the company passes an elective resolution not to lay accounts before the general meeting, but does not elect to dispense with the annual appointment of auditors, it must still hold a general meeting each year for the purpose of re-appointing the auditors. This meeting must be held within 28 days of the dispatch to the members of the accounts. This 28-day period is defined as 'the time for appointing auditors'. Auditors appointed in this way hold office until the end of the time for appointing auditors in the next financial year.

c. *Casual vacancies* The directors or the company in a general meeting may appoint auditors to fill casual vacancies. The surviving auditor may continue to act during any vacancy. Special notice is required for a resolution:

   i.   Filling a casual vacancy, or

   ii. Re-appointing as auditor a retiring auditor who was appointed by the directors to fill a casual vacancy.

   On receipt of such notice the company must immediately send a copy to the person proposed to be appointed and (if the casual vacancy was caused by the resignation of an auditor) to the auditor who resigned.

d. *Appointment by the Secretary of State (S.486)*. If no appointment or re-appointment is made at a meeting at which accounts are laid, the company must inform the Department of Trade within 1 week. The Secretary of State may then make an appointment to fill the vacancy.

e. *Remuneration*. The term 'remuneration' includes sums paid by the company as auditors' expenses. By *S.492*:

   i.   If the directors make the appointment they fix his remuneration.

   ii. If he is appointed by the Secretary of State he fixes the remuneration.

   iii. If the auditor is appointed by the company then the company fixes his remuneration, or determines the way by which it will be fixed.

12. *Removal*

   a. By *S.510* the company may remove an auditor before the end of his period of office despite any agreement between it and him.

   b. The Registrar of Companies must be notified of the removal within 14 days.

   c. An auditor who has been removed is entitled to attend the meeting at which his term of office would have expired and any general meeting at which it is proposed to fill a casual vacancy caused by his removal. He is entitled to receive all communications relating to the meeting which a member is entitled to receive, and he may speak on any matter concerning him as a former auditor (*S.511*).

13. *Resolutions to Appoint and Remove Auditors* (S.510)

   a. Auditors may be appointed and removed by *ordinary resolution*.

   b. In the following cases *special notice* (see Chapter 45.5) is required:

      i.   To appoint a person other than a retiring auditor.

      ii. To fill a casual vacancy.

      iii. To re-appoint as auditor a retiring auditor who was appointed by the directors to fill a casual vacancy, or

      iv. To remove an auditor before the end of his term of office.

    c.   On receipt of the special notice the company must immediately send a copy to:

        i.   The person proposed to be appointed or removed.

        ii.   The retiring auditor where it is proposed to appoint another person, and

        iii.   The resigning auditor where the appointment is to fill a casual vacancy caused by his resignation.

14. *Written Representations by Auditors* (S.510)

    a.   Where (b) (i) or (b) (iv) above apply the auditor may make written representations to the company and require the company (unless it receives them too late) to send a copy of these representations to the members with notice of the meeting.

    b.   If for any reason these representations are not sent to the members the auditor can require them to be read out at the meeting. In any case he has a right to speak in his defence at the meeting.

    c.   The representations need not be sent out, or read at the meeting, if the court is satisfied, on the application of the company or any aggrieved person, that the auditor is using his rights to secure needless publicity for defamatory matter.

15. *Resignation of Auditors* (S.516)

    a.   An auditor may resign by giving written notice to the company at its registered office.

    b.   The notice will not be effective unless it contains either:

        i.   A statement that there are no circumstances connected with his resignation which he considers should be brought to the notice of the company's members or creditors, or

        ii.   A statement of such circumstances.

    c.   Within 14 days of receipt of an effective notice the company must send a copy to:

        i.   The registrar, and

        ii.   If it contains a statement of connected circumstances, to every member and debentureholder of the company.

    d.   Within 14 days of receipt of a notice containing a statement of connected circumstances the company or any aggrieved person may apply to the court if it is thought that the auditor is using the statement to secure needless publicity for defamatory matter. The court may then order that copies need not be sent to members and debentureholders. Within 14 days of the court's decision the company must send to every member and debentureholder:

        i.   A statement of the effect of the court order, if any, or if none

        ii.   A copy of the notice containing the auditor's statement of the circumstances connected with his resignation.

16. *Right of the Resigning Auditor* (S.518)

    a.   Where the notice of resignation contains a statement of connected circumstances the auditor may require the directors to convene an EGM to receive and consider the statement. This will be useful if the auditor wishes to resign mid-term.

b. The auditor may require the company to send to the members before such an EGM, or before the AGM at which his term of office would otherwise have expired, a written statement of the circumstances connected with his resignation. Unless the company receives this statement too late, it must send it to the members with notice of the meeting. *S.518* contains provisions relating to:

   i.   Reading statement at the meeting if for any reason it is not sent with the notice.

   ii. Defamatory matter.

   iii. The auditor's right to attend and receive all communications relating to the meeting.

17. *Statements to Persons Ceasing to Hold Office as Auditor* (S.519). Prior to 1989 the statement of circumstances connected with an auditor's resignation (or the statement that there are no circumstances that should be brought to the notice of members or creditors) only applied when an auditor resigned. This requirement has now been extended by the 1989 Act to all cases where an auditor ceases to hold office, for example if an auditor is removed from office or not re-appointed at a general meeting.

Where an auditor resigns or ceases to hold office, for example, is not re-appointed, a statement of circumstances to members and creditors concerning the resignation or cessation to hold office, must be made

POWERS, DUTIES AND LIABILITIES OF AUDITORS

18. *The Auditors' Report* (S.495–497A)

a. It is the duty of the auditors to report to the members on the accounts laid before the company during their term of office. 'Accounts' includes the balance sheet, profit and loss account and group accounts (if any).

b. The report must be read before the company in a general meeting, and must be open to inspection by any member.

c. The report must state whether, in the opinion of the auditors, the accounts have been properly prepared and whether a true and fair view is given:

   i.   In the case of the balance sheet, of the state of the company's affairs at the end of its financial year.

   ii. In the case of the profit and loss account, of the company's profit and loss for its financial year, and

   iii. In the case of group accounts, of the state of affairs and profit or loss of the company and its subsidiaries so far as concerns members of the company.

d. In addition:

   i.   If the accounts do not contain particulars of directors' emoluments and particulars of loan and other transactions favouring directors, the auditors must include in their report a statement giving the required particulars so far as they are reasonably able to do so.

    ii.   The auditors must consider whether the information given in the directors' report relating to the financial year in question is consistent with those accounts. If they are of the opinion that it is not consistent they must say so in their report.

  e.   The auditors' report must state the names of the auditors and be signed by them.

19. *Auditors' Duties* (S.498)

  a.   Auditors must carry out such investigations as will enable them to form an opinion as to whether:

    i.   Proper accounting records have been kept by the company, and adequate returns received from branches not visited by them, and

    ii.   The balance sheet and profit and loss account agree with the accounting records and returns.

    If they think that proper books or returns have not been kept or received by them they must say so in their report.

  b.   The auditors must also:

    i.   Acquaint themselves with their duties under the articles and the Companies Act.

    ii.   Report to the members, ensuring that the report complies with *S.495–497A*.

    iii. Act honestly and with reasonable care and skill (see below).

20. *Auditors' Powers* (S.499)

  a.   The auditors have a right of access to the books, accounts and vouchers of the company.

  b.   The auditors may require from the officers of the company such information and explanations as they think necessary for the performance of their duties. If they fail to obtain such information they must say so in their report.

  c.   The auditors may attend any general meetings, they must be sent all notices and communications relating to general meetings, and they may speak at a meeting on any matter which concerns them as auditors.

21. *Power in Relation to Subsidiary Undertakings*

  a.   Under *S.499* it is the duty of a subsidiary and its auditors to give to the auditors of the holding company such information and explanation as they may reasonably require for the purposes of their duties as auditors of the holding company.

  b.   If the subsidiary is incorporated outside Great Britain, it is the duty of the holding company, if required by its auditors, to take reasonable steps to obtain such information from the subsidiary.

22. *False Statements to Auditors* By *S.499* it is a criminal offence for an officer of the company to knowingly or recklessly make, either orally or in writing, a statement to the company's auditors which is misleading, false or deceptive in a material particular.

23. *The Standard of Care and Skill*

  a.   The Act relates the legal standard of care and skill closely to the professional standards set by the RSBs, since RSB rules must:

i. Ensure that only 'fit and proper' persons are appointed as company auditors. In determining whether someone is fit and proper the RSB has to take into account that person's professional conduct.

ii. Ensure that audits are carried out with 'professional integrity'. One component of this will be compliance with technical standards, the other will cover independence, objectivity and confidentiality.

b. To some extent this formalizes the present situation since the ICA and ACCA already require their members to act in accordance with rules enforced by disciplinary committees. However, the guidelines laid down by judicial decisions are still law and, to the extent that they are not covered by new RSB rules, they will still play a part in determining the required standard of care and skill. It has been held:

i. That they must ascertain that the books show the true financial position. To do this auditors must do more than merely verify the numerical accuracy of the accounts *(FORMENTO v SELSDON (1958))*. If entries in or omissions from the books make the auditors suspicious they must make a full investigation into the circumstances. For example:

In **RE THOMAS GERRARD (1968)** the managing director falsified the accounts by including non-existent stock and altering invoices. This caused the company's profits to be overstated. Dividends were declared that would not otherwise have been declared and too much tax was paid. The auditors became suspicious when they noticed that invoices had been altered, but they accepted the managing director's explanation and made no further investigation. The auditors were held liable to the company for the cost of recovering the excess tax paid and for dividends and tax not recovered.

ii. Auditors must check the cash in hand and the bank balance.

iii. Where payments have been made by the company, the auditors should see that they are authorized.

iv. Auditors should check that company borrowing has been authorized and is in accordance with the articles.

v. Auditors should satisfy themselves that the securities of the company exist and are in safe custody, either by making a personal inspection of the securities or checking that the securities are in the possession of a person who in the ordinary course of business keeps securities for customers, for example a bank.

vi. Auditors are not required to value stock or work in progress. They may accept the valuation of a responsible official of the company, unless they have reason to suppose it to be inaccurate. In practice auditors exceed this legal duty with regard to stocktaking.

vii. Auditors do not have a duty to comment on whether the management is running the business efficiently or profitably.

viii. If the directors do not allow auditors the time to conduct their investigations, the auditors must either refuse to make a report or make a qualified report. They must not make a report containing a statement the truth of which they have not had an opportunity to verify.

24. *To Whom are the Auditors' Duties Owed?*

a.   The auditor has a contractual relationship with the company and it is therefore the company and to the members *as a whole* to whom the basic duty is owed. Even so auditors must, on occasions, disclose facts which may harm the company.

b.   Since the decision in **HEDLEY BYRNE v HELLER (1964)** it has been clear that a person may be liable for financial loss resulting from a negligent statement even if there is no contract between the maker of the statement and the recipient (although a disclaimer of responsibility will exclude the defendant's liability).

As already noted, the duty of an auditor is owed to the company and its members as a whole, not to individual shareholders or members of the public. However, in **CAPARO INDUSTRIES PLC V DICKMAN (1990)** the House of Lords ruled that a wider duty might well be owed where the auditor is in a sufficiently close relationship with a particular person such that it can reasonably be inferred that such a person, upon receiving the information, will be likely to act upon it, here, a duty might well arise. But information put in general circulation is not, in itself, sufficient.

DEPARTMENT OF TRADE INVESTIGATIONS

25. *Types of Investigation*

a.   There are three basic types of investigation:

   i.   Investigation of the company's affairs.

   ii.   Investigation of the company's ownership, and

   iii. Investigation of share dealings.

b.   In addition there are provisions for the inspection of a company's documents, and powers under the *FINANCIAL SERVICES AND MARKETS ACT 2000* to investigate suspected insider dealing offences (Chapter 44.50).

26. *Investigation on the Application of the Members or the Company*

a.   The Secretary of State also has the power to appoint inspectors to investigate a company's affairs. This is a serious matter as the appointment of inspectors is publicly announced with their reporst often being published. The powers of investigation are contained in Part 14 of the *COMPANIES ACT 1985 (CA 85)*, they have *not* been incorporated into the 2006 Act. By *S.431 CA 85* the Department of Trade may appoint inspectors:

   i.   Where the company has a share capital, on the application of at least 200 members, or members holding at least 10 per cent of the issued shares.

   ii.   Where the company has no share capital, on the application of at least 20 per cent of the members, and

   iii. In any case, on the application of the company. (An ordinary resolution would be sufficient to authorize an application.)

b.   The applicants (or applicant) must produce evidence in support of their application. In the past *S.431 (CA 85)* has not often been used. This is because it overlaps with *S.432*

(*CA 85*). *S.432* is more flexible than *S.431* in that anyone can ask the Department to investigate and the Department may exercise their discretion to do so if there are circumstances suggesting:

i. That the affairs of the company have been conducted with intent to defraud its creditors, or in a manner unfairly prejudicial to some part of the members, or for an unlawful or fraudulent purpose, or

ii. That the promoters or managers have been guilty of fraud or misconduct, or

iii. That proper information has not been given to the members.

c. The powers conferred by *S.432* (*CA 85*) are exercisable even if the company is in voluntary liquidation. Also the word 'member' includes persons who are not members but to whom shares have been transferred or transmitted by operation of law, for example personal representatives.

d. Application for a Department for Business Innovation & Skills (DTI) investigation is a drastic step which dissatisfied shareholders will usually only consider after they have failed to obtain a remedy at a general meeting or through the courts. When an application is received the Department will call for the company to produce documents and records for internal examination by its staff. If the complaint is trivial or insubstantial it will go no further. An inspection will only be ordered if a strong case is made out since an appointment will attract publicity and cause damage to the company. If an inspection is ordered, two inspectors are usually appointed, normally a barrister and an accountant.

27. *Investigation by Order of Court S.432* (*CA 85*) also provides that the Department must appoint inspectors to investigate the company's affairs if the court order is to do so.

28. *Powers of Inspectors*

a. Inspectors have extensive powers to:

i. Require production of books and documents.

ii. Question on oath any person, and administer the oath accordingly.

iii. Obtain a warrant to enter premises and search for documents.

iv. Take copies of any documents and require any person named in the warrant to provide an explanation of documents or state where documents may be found.

v. Investigate the affairs of related companies.

vi. Inform the Secretary of State of any matters coming to his knowledge as a result of the investigation.

b. The persons referred to under ii. above must give the inspector all assistance in the investigation that they are reasonably able to give. Refusal to comply with a request for documents or information is punishable as contempt of court. Intentional obstruction of an inspector is an offence.

29. *The Inspector's Report* (S.437)

a. The inspector presents his findings in a report to the Department. In some cases the inspector will also make interim reports. The Secretary of State has a discretionary power:

    i.   To send a copy of the report to the company's registered office.

    ii.   To provide copies to specified classes of persons, for example members, auditors or persons referred to in the report.

    iii. To publish the report, unless inspectors were appointed subject to specific terms that the report would not be published (see c. below).

b.   When inspectors are appointed under a court order, the court must be sent a copy of the report.

30. *Consequences of the Report*

a.   If, as a result of the report, it appears to be in the public interest that the company be wound-up the Department may present a petition that the company be wound-up because it is just as equitable to do so. An inspector's report may also be used as evidence to support a shareholder's petition under *S.122 INSOLVENCY ACT 1986* (the 'just and equitable' ground).

b.   If it appears that there are grounds for a petition by a member under *S.994* (i.e. that the affairs of the company have been conducted in an unfairly prejudicial manner, see Chapter 43.15) the Department may, as well as, or instead of, petitioning to wind-up the company, present a petition for an order under *S.994*.

c.   The Secretary of State may bring civil proceedings on behalf of the company when it appears from any report made or information obtained that it is in the public interest to do so.

d.   The Department may also institute criminal proceedings against persons believed to be guilty of offences.

e.   It may also apply to the court for an order disqualifying a person from acting as a director *(S.8 COMPANY DIRECTORS DISQUALIFICATION ACT 1986)*.

31. *Investigation of the Ownership of a Company* S.442 *(CA 85)*

a.   i.   The Department must investigate the ownership of shares of a company on the application of 200 shareholders or holders of 10% of the issued shares, unless it considers the application is vexatious, or unless it considers it unreasonable to investigate any matter, and

    ii.   The Department may investigate share ownership if there appears to be good reason to do so.

The Secretary of State, before appointing inspectors, may require the applicants to provide security to set against costs of the investigation.

b.   The inspector has the same general powers as in the investigation of the affairs of a company.

c.   The provisions relating to the report are also similar, except that if, in the opinion of the Secretary of State, there is good reason for not divulging any part of the report, he may omit that part from the inspector's report.

d.   The Secretary of State may disclose information relating to share ownership to the following persons:

    i.   The company whose ownership was subject to investigation.

    ii.   Any member of that company.

    iii.   Any person whose conduct was investigated.

    iv.   The auditors of the company.

    v.   Any person whose financial interests appear to be affected by matters covered by the investigation.

e.   Powerful sanctions support *S.442 (CA 85)*. In particular the Secretary of State may place restrictions on shares where there is difficulty in finding out relevant facts about any shares. For example, no voting rights are exercisable in respect of the shares and any agreement to transfer the shares will be void unless approved by the court or the Secretary of State.

f.   If the Secretary of State believes that there is good reason to investigate the ownership of a company, but that it is unnecessary to appoint inspectors for the purpose, he may require any person whom he reasonably believes to have information to give such information to him.

32. *Inspection of Documents*

a.   By *S.447 (CA 85)* the Department, if it thinks there is good reason to do so, may give directions to any company requiring it to produce any specified books or papers. A similar direction may be made to any person who appears to be in possession of those books or papers. Copies or extracts of them may be taken and any person in possession of them, or a past or present officer or employee of the company, may be required to provide an explanation of them. There are also:

    i.   Provisions enabling a search warrant to be obtained in respect of premises where the documents are believed to be.

    ii.   Provisions allowing the Secretary of State to authorize 'any other competent person' (probably a lawyer or an accountant) to exercise his power to require the production of documents. The competent person will then report to the Secretary of State.

    iii.   Provisions preventing publication or excessive disclosure.

b.   It is an offence:

    i.   For any officer of the company to be a party to the destruction, mutilation or falsification of any document relating to the company's property or affairs.

    ii.   For any officer to fraudulently part with, alter or make an omission from any such document.

    iii.   For any person to knowingly or recklessly make a false explanation or statement in response to the directions of the Department.

SELF TEST QUESTIONS

Self Test Questions No. 43 (for Answers see Appendix 1):

1   What are the audit requirements for UK companies?

2   What are the exemptions?

3   Explain the processes involved in the appointment, removal and resignation of an auditor.

4   What are an auditor's powers, duties and liabilities?

5   In what circumstances might a Department of Trade investigation take place?

46 MEETINGS, RESOLUTIONS AND PUBLICITY

Learning Outcomes At the end of this chapter you should be able to:

- Explain the nature and purpose of the *Annual General Meeting* (AGM).

- Show how an AGM is convened and run.

- Explain the resolutions a general meeting of shareholders can pass.

- Explain the formalities associated with publicity and registration.

- Outline the registers which a company must maintain.

- Outline the accounting requirements for a company.

- Explain the nature and content of the *Directors' Report*.

- Outline the general purpose and requirements of *Corporate Governance*.

TYPES OF MEETING

1. *The Annual General Meeting (AGM)*

   a. Except for *private companies* every *public company* must hold an AGM within 6 months of its financial year end (*S.336*). A private company is not required to hold an AGM and is automatically entitled to have all resolutions of members taken either, by *written resolution,* i.e. without a meeting, or passed at a meeting of the members (*S.281(1)* – see 15.b below). If a member of a private company wishes to have a meeting of its members and the board is unwilling to call one – as the board always has the power to do (*S.302*) – the member requesting the meeting must hold at least 10 per cent of the company's voting shares (*S.303–306*).

b. *Unanimity rule.* For private companies there is now no need for a *written resolution* to be approved by a unanimous approval of all the members, it may be adopted by the same percentage of support as would be needed in an actual meeting e.g. an ordinary resolution (51%) or special resolution (75%) (*S.296(4)*).

These changes introduced by the *COMPANIES ACT 2006* are aimed at encouraging private companies to conduct business in a less formal, less cumbersome way.

c. *Written resolutions* are NOT permissible in the private company in two situations:

  i.   The removal of a director (*S.168*).

  ii. The removal of an auditor (*S.510*).

2. *Extraordinary General Meetings (EGM)*

  a. Any meeting which is not an AGM is an EGM. The articles usually provide that an EGM may be called by the directors.

  b. Members have a statutory right to require directors to convene an EGM. By *S.303* despite anything in the articles the directors must call an EGM if required to do so by holders – this requires that there be a minimum of two members – of at least 10% of the paid-up capital with voting rights. If the directors do not convene the meeting within 21 days the requisitionists (or more than half their number) may do so, and recover their expenses from the company, which may then recover them from the directors.

  c. By *S.306* if it is impractical to call or conduct a meeting in the manner prescribed by the Act or the articles the court may, on the application of any director or member entitled to vote, order a meeting to be called, giving such directions as it thinks fit.

  d. Note also:

  S.656, which requires the directors of a public company to call an EGM when it becomes known to a director that the net assets have fallen to half or less of the company's called-up share capital.

CONVENING MEETINGS

3. *Length of Notice*

  a. Every member is entitled to 21 days written notice of an AGM for a public company, with 14 days notice being required for all other general meetings, whether a public or private company (*S.307*). The company's articles might require longer periods of notice (*S.307(3)*). The notice may be given in electronic form.

  b. Members can require a shorter period of notice (*S.307(4)*), but this must be agreed by a majority who together, hold not less than the requisite percentage in nominal value of the shares giving a right to attend and vote at the meeting (*S.307(5)*) of:

    i.   For a private company, the required percentage is 90% or higher.

    ii.   For a public company, 95% (*S.307(6)*).

4. ***Contents of the Notice*** (*S.311*)

    a.   The notice must specify the date, place and time of the meeting. It is not necessary to give details of ordinary business, but the nature of any other business must be specified. However, where a special or extraordinary resolution is to be moved, the notice must set out the full text of the resolution.

    b.   The notice must state that a member entitled to attend and vote may appoint a proxy to attend and vote on his behalf.

5. ***Special Notice*** (*S.312*)

    a.   It is important to distinguish *special notice* from *notice of a special resolution*.

    b.   *Special notice* is required for three types of *ordinary resolution*:

        i.   To remove a director or to appoint somebody in his place *(S.168)*.

        ii.   To remove an auditor or to appoint any auditor other than the retiring auditor *(S.510)*.

    c.   Where *special notice* is required *the persons proposing the motion must give the company* 28 days notice of their intention to move the resolution. The company will then give the members notice of the resolution when it sends them notice of the meeting. If it is too late to include the resolution in the notice of the meeting it may be advertised or otherwise communicated to the members at least 21 days before the meeting.

6. ***Members' Resolutions and Statements*** (*S.314*)

Holders of at least 5 per cent of share capital with voting rights *or* at least 100 members (whether entitled to vote or not) who have paid up on average £100 each can compel the company:

    a.   By 6 weeks' requisition to give the members notice of any resolution which the requisitionists intend to move at an AGM.

    b.   By 1 week's requisition to circulate to the members a statement of up to 1000 words with respect to any proposed resolution at any general meeting.

    c.   The expenses of the company complying with a *S.314* request with regard to an AGM of a public company, do not have to be paid for by the members requesting circulation. Otherwise, the expenses – which, for the large plc on the Stock Exchange, might not be inconsiderable – must be paid for by the members who made the request, unless the company resolves otherwise (*S.316*).

7. ***Electronic Communications*** (Schedules 4 and 5 of the Act)

    a.   Notices of meetings can be sent electronically on an individual basis or posted on a website.

    b.   A proxy may be appointed electronically.

    c.   With regard to the filing of resolutions and other documents with the Registrar of Companies, the Registrar may be delivered electronically.

    d.   Table A is amended accordingly to permit this.

CONDUCT OF MEETINGS

8. *The Quorum*

    a. A quorum is the minimum number of persons who must be present to conduct a meeting.

    b. The quorum for all company meetings is two members personally present, unless the company has only one member or the court directs that the quorum shall be one (*S.318*).

    c. Table A states that if within half an hour a quorum is not present, the meeting will stand adjourned to the same day, time and place in the next week (or to such other day, time and place as the directors shall determine).

9. *The Chairman* There must be a chairman to preside over the meeting. The chairman must:

    a. Act in good faith in the interests of the company as a whole.

    b. Ensure that business is conducted in an orderly manner in the order set out in the agenda. Therefore he must ensure that members relate what they say to the items on the agenda and do not make irrelevant or provocative remarks.

    c. Allow all points of view to be adequately expressed and then put the motion to the vote and declare the result. He has a casting vote only if given one by the articles.

    d. Decide whether amendments to motions are admissible. He should reject an amendment if it is outside the scope of the business stated in the notice of the meeting.

    e. Adjourn any meeting at which a quorum is present if so directed by the meeting, and

    f. Sign the minutes of the meeting.

10. *Voting*

    a. The usual practice is to vote by a show of hands, i.e. each member present has one vote regardless of the number of shares held.

    b. However, if a poll is properly demanded, then a member's votes will depend on the number of voting shares he holds.

11. *Proxies*

    a. The term proxy is used both to refer to the person appointed to act on behalf of the member and to the *instrument* which gives him the required authority.

    b. Every member has the right to appoint a proxy to attend and vote for him. The proxy does not need to be a member (*S.324(1)*).

    c. The proxy rules under the Act are mandatory and cannot be taken away by anything in a company's articles; though the Act allows for articles to improve them (*S.331*).

    d. Where a company has share capital, the member can appoint more than one proxy, provided each proxy exercises rights attached to different shares (*S.324(2)*).

    e. Members must be informed of their statutory rights to attend, speak and vote by proxy, and of any more extensive rights contained in a company's articles, in the notice convening the meeting (*S.325*).

12. *Minutes*

    a. Every company must keep minutes of both company meetings and board meetings.

    b. When the minutes are signed by the chairman they become evidence of the proceedings. In particular they are conclusive evidence that a resolution has been carried or lost. This prevents a later argument on a point which should have been challenged at the meeting.

    c. A minute book of general meetings must be kept at the company's registered office and must be available for inspection by members for at least 2 hours on each working day.

RESOLUTIONS

13. In **RE DUOMATIC (1969)** the Court held that 'Where all the shareholders of a company assent on a matter that should be brought into effect by a resolution in a general meeting (or by a written resolution) the unanimous consent of all the shareholders without a formal meeting or written resolution is enough to satisfy the law.' This is referred to as the *Duomatic Principle*. In **DEAKIN V FAULDING (2001)** bonus payments were made to a director which should have been approved by ordinary resolution. The payment was being challenged by the new owners of the company. The High Court found that at the time of the payment there was informal consent by all the shareholders to the payment, applying the *Duomatic Principal*, the transaction was held valid.

14. The Act reduced the types of resolution which members may make to two: an *ordinary resolution* (*S.282*) and a *special resolution* (*S.283*).

    a. *Ordinary Resolution*. This is a simple majority of members present in person or by proxy entitled to vote and voting. For example, a company has ten members holding an equal number of shares. Four do not attend the meeting (or appoint proxies), three abstain, two vote for the motion and one votes against. The resolution is passed.

        i.   The period of notice depends on the type of meeting at which it is moved (21 days for an AGM and generally 14 days for an EGM).

        ii. An ordinary resolution is the type used whenever the law or the company's articles do not require a special or extraordinary resolution. In some cases the law specifies an ordinary resolution, for example *S.168* (removal of directors) and *S.510* (removal of auditors). Where a section states that 'the powers conferred by this section must be exercised by the company in a general meeting' e.g. alteration of capital, it means that an ordinary resolution is necessary.

        iii. In general, copies of ordinary resolutions which have been passed need not be filed with the registrar.

        iv. The articles may specify a higher level of approval, up to and including unanimity. (*S.281(3)*).

        v.   An ordinary resolution is to be used in all decisions required under the Act, unless the Act requires a special resolution.

    b. *Special Resolutions (S.283(1))*. These require a three-quarter majority of members present in person or by proxy entitled to vote and voting. A period of 21 days notice is required but a shorter period is acceptable if a simple majority in number holding 95%

in value of the voting shares agree. Because of this notice requirement amendments to special resolutions cannot be accepted at the meeting. A copy of every special resolution which is passed must be filed with the registrar within 15 days. Special resolutions are required for a number of important company decisions, for example:

i. To alter the objects clause of its memorandum.

ii. To alter the articles.

iii. To reduce its capital, subject to the consent of the court.

iv. To commence a voluntary winding-up.

v. To change the company name, subject to approval by the Secretary of State.

vi. To ratify an *ultra vires* act.

15. *Written Resolutions S.300*

a. *Firstly, a private company* can substitute the unanimous written agreement of its shareholders (or in the case of a company with one member a written record of the decision) for any resolution passed at a general meeting (written resolutions) (*S.281(1)*). *Secondly, a private company* can, by elective resolution, opt out of certain company law requirements, including the holding of an AGM.

b. Except as stated below, anything which can be done by resolution at a general meeting of a private company may, instead of the meeting being held, be done by a written resolution signed by or on behalf of all members of the company who would be entitled to attend and vote at such a meeting. Previous notice is not required and the signatures need not be on a single document, however each must be on a document accurately stating the terms of the resolution. The date of the resolution is the date when the last member signed it.

c. *Exceptions.* A written resolution may not be used to remove a director or auditor before their period of office has expired.

PUBLICITY

16. *Introduction* Protection by disclosure is one of the underlying principles of the Act. The theory is that if members, creditors and the public can find out relevant information about a company they will do so and then conduct their affairs with it accordingly. It has, however, always been clear that disclosure alone is not sufficient protection and extensive protective measures therefore exist, for example S.593 (which requires an independent valuation of non-cash assets received by a public company in consideration for an allotment of shares), and S.994 (which enables any member to apply for a court order if the affairs of the company are being conducted in an unfairly prejudicial manner). Publicity nevertheless remains important and is achieved in four main ways:

a. The requirement of official notification of certain matters in the Gazette.

b. The registration of certain information at the Companies Registry.

c. The compulsory maintenance of certain registers by the company, and

d. The requirement to make an annual return and disclose the company's financial position in its published accounts and directors' report.

OFFICIAL NOTIFICATION IN THE GAZETTE

17. *The Requirement of Notification* When various documents are issued by, or filed at, the Companies Registry the registrar must give notice to the public of the issue or receipt of such documents by means of a notice in the *London Gazette*. The notice merely records the name of the company, the nature of the document and the date of its receipt. The document itself is not reproduced. If a person wishes to see the document he must apply to the Registry or the company's registered office. Numerous matters require notification, for example:

    a. The issue by the registrar of a certificate of incorporation.

    b. The receipt by the registrar of:

        i. A resolution altering either the memorandum or articles.

        ii. A notice of any change among the directors.

        iii. Any documents required to be comprised in the accounts.

        iv. Any notice of a change in the situation of the registered office.

        v. Any order for the winding-up or dissolution of the company.

18. *The Effect of Official Notification* The effect of notification is that the company cannot rely, as against third parties, on the happening of certain events unless their occurrence had been officially notified or the company can show that their occurrence was actually known to the third party. The events are:

    a. The making of a winding-up order.

    b. An alteration of the articles.

    c. A change of directors, and

    d. A change of the address of the registered office.

MATTERS REQUIRING REGISTRATION AT THE COMPANIES REGISTRY

19. *Information on Record at the Companies Registry* The following information is recorded on each company's file at the Companies Registry. Any member of the public may inspect the file.

    a. The company's articles.

    b. A statement containing the names and relevant particulars of the directors and the secretary.

    c. Any notice of the appointment of a liquidator or receiver.

    d. A statement of the address of the registered office.

    e. Details of the company's nominal, issued and paid-up capital.

    f. Details of charges over the company's property.

    g. The annual balance sheet, profit and loss account, directors' report and auditors' report. (This requirement is modified in the case of certain small and medium-sized companies.), and

    h. The annual return.

20. *Resolutions Requiring Registration*

    a.   All special resolutions must be registered within 15 days of passing the resolution.

    b.   In general the fact that an ordinary resolution has been passed need not be registered. However, there are several exceptions, for example resolutions to:

        i.   Appoint or remove directors.

        ii.   Remove auditors.

        iii. Change the address of the registered office.

        iv. Increase the authorized capital.

REGISTERS WHICH MUST BE MAINTAINED BY THE COMPANY

21. a.   In addition to the various documents and registers required to be kept at a company's registered office (see Chapter 39.10), the register of directors and secretaries, the register of directors' interests in shares and debentures and the register of substantial shareholdings merit further comment.

    b.   The register of members was discussed in Chapter 42 and the register of charges in Chapters 41.7 and 47.11.

22. *The Register of Directors and Secretaries*

    a.   By *S.162* every company must keep a register of its directors and its secretary at its registered office.

    b.   The register must contain the following particulars of each director:

        i.   Name and former name (if any).

        ii.   Address.

        iii. Nationality.

        iv. Business occupation (if any).

        v.   Particulars of other directorships held, or which have been held, by him in the past 5 years, except for directorships of companies within the same group and directorships of dormant companies, and

    c.   The company must notify the registrar within 14 days of any change in the particulars on the register. When a person becomes a director the notification must be accompanied by his signed consent to act.

23. *Directors' Names on Company Stationery* A company may not state the name of any of its directors on its business letters (other than in the text or as a signatory) unless it states the given name, or initials thereof, and the surname of every director who is an individual and the corporate name of every corporate director.

24. *The Register of Directors' Interests in Shares or Debentures*

    a.   By *S.808* a director must notify the company in writing of any transaction involving his interest in the shares or debentures of the company. The notification period is 5 working days. The interest of a director's spouse or infant child must be treated as if it were the director's interest.

b.   There are detailed rules for determining when a director has an 'interest' in shares or debentures. Thus, for example a person holding a beneficial interest under a trust does have an interest in shares comprised in the trust, but the trustee (although on the register of members) does not have an interest. Also a person has an interest if shares or debentures are held by a company, and

   i.   That company or its directors are accustomed to act in accordance with his instructions, or if

   ii.   He controls one-third or more of the votes at a general meeting of that company.

c.   By *S.809* every company must keep a register of directors' interests in shares or debentures. Information must be entered in the register within 3 working days of its receipt.

25. *The Register of Substantial Shareholdings*

a.   The rules are contained in *S.792–820*. They only apply to *public companies.*

b.   A notifiable interest arises when a person knows that he has an interest in 3 per cent or more of the company's voting shares. Notification must be in writing and must be made within 2 working days from when the obligation to notify arose.

c.   Notification is necessary on cessation or acquisition of an interest and also when *any change* in a notifiable interest takes place. For example, a company may issue new shares for the purpose of an acquisition. This could dilute a shareholder's interest from, say, 6 to 2 per cent without altering the total number of shares held. He would nevertheless be under an obligation to notify the company.

d.   The rules for defining the extent of an 'interest' are very detailed.

   For example a person is deemed to have an interest if:

   i.   A spouse or infant child has an interest.

   ii.   Shares are held by a company and that company or its directors are accustomed to act in accordance with the person's instructions, or the person controls one-third or more of the votes in a general meeting of that company, or

   iii.   Another person is interested in the company's shares and the first person is *acting together* with that other person. This is discussed below.

e.   *Persons acting together*

   i.   When persons act in concert the Act attributes to each member of such a group (known as a 'concert party') the interests of the other members and places an obligation to notify on *all* members of the concert party, i.e. a person has an obligation to notify even if he does not have any shares himself but he is acting in concert with someone who has a notifiable interest.

   ii.   A concert party exists when there is an agreement (whether legally binding or not) under which at least one of the parties is to acquire an interest in the shares of a company. In addition there must be some understanding as to the way in which the interest acquired under the contract is to be used.

f.   A public company must keep a register to record within 3 days the information notified. The register must be kept at the same place as the register of directors and secretaries. The register will also contain (in a separate part) the results of any investigations carried out under *S.793* (see below).

26. *Investigation by a Company of Interests in its Shares* (*S.793*)

    a. If a *public company* knows, or has reasonable cause to believe, a person to be or have been interested in its voting shares within the past 3 years, it may make a written request of that person to indicate whether she holds or has held an interest in the shares. The request may require a written response within a specified time limit. When a company receives such information it must record it in the register of substantial shareholdings.

    b. Members holding not less than one-tenth of the paid-up voting shares may require the company to make an investigation by depositing a requisition at the registered office. The company must prepare a report on its investigation. The report must be available for inspection at the registered office within a reasonable period (not more than 15 days) after the conclusion of the investigation.

    c. If a person fails to give information when requested to do so, the company may apply to the court for an order that the shares be sold or for an order imposing restrictions on the shares in question, for example:

        i. That any transfer of the shares is void.

        ii. That no voting rights are exercisable is respect of the shares.

        iii. That (except in a liquidation) no payment shall be made in respect of sums due from the company on those shares.

    The person is also liable to a maximum of 2 years imprisonment and an unlimited fine.

THE ANNUAL RETURN

27. *Making the Annual Return* (*S.441*)

    a. *The return date.* The annual return will have to be made up to a date not later than the company's return date and filed within 28 days of the date to which it is made up. The return date will be either:

        i. The anniversary of the company's incorporation date, or

        ii. If the company's previous return was made up to a different date, the anniversary of that date.

    b. The return must be signed either by a director or the secretary.

    c. If a company does not deliver its annual return within 28 days after the return date, or delivers a return which does not contain the required information, it is liable to a fine. Every director or secretary will also be liable unless they can show that they took all reasonable steps to avoid the offence.

28. *The Contents of the Annual Return* The annual return must state the date to which it is made up and contain the following information:

    a. The address of the registered office and, if the register of members is not kept at that office, the address at which it is kept.

b.   A summary of share capital specifying for each class of share the total number of issued shares and the aggregate nominal value of those shares.

c.   The type of company and its principal business activities.

d.   A list of members on the date to which the return is made up showing individual share-holdings and changes that have taken place during the year. To avoid annual preparation of a lengthy list the company need only submit a full list of members every 3 years. In the intervening years only details of changes need be given.

e.   Particulars of directors and the secretary taken from the register, including the date of birth of each individual director.

f.   Where a private company has by elective resolution dispensed with the laying of accounts and reports before the general meeting, or with holding an AGM, a statement to that effect.

THE ACCOUNTING RECORDS AND THE ACCOUNTS

29. *Accounting Records* S.386 provides that every company shall keep records sufficient to show and explain the company's transactions, to disclose with reasonable accuracy at any time its financial position and to enable its directors to ensure that any balance sheet and profit and loss account will comply with the provisions of the Act.

a.   It is important to distinguish between the accounting records and the accounts.

   i.   The *accounting records* are the ledgers, cash book, order forms, receipts and other records maintained by the company to enable the accounts to be prepared.

   ii. The *accounts* (or financial statements) in the narrow sense consist of the balance sheet, the profit and loss account and the notes to the accounts, although other documents are comprised in the 'accounts' which are filed with the registrar.

b.   Every company must keep accounting records which must:

   i.   Show with reasonable accuracy, at any time during the financial year, the financial position of the company at that time, and

   ii. Enable the directors to ensure that any balance sheet prepared by them gives a true and fair view of the company's state of affairs and any profit and loss account gives a true and fair view of the company's profit or loss.

c.   In particular the records must contain:

   i.   A day-to-day record of money received by and spent by the company.

   ii. A record of the assets and liabilities of the company.

   iii. Statements of the stock held by the company at the end of each financial year, and

   iv. A record of goods sold and purchased, with details of the goods, buyers and sellers sufficient to enable them to be identified.

d.   The accounting records must be kept at the registered office or such other place as the directors think fit. They must be open for inspection by officers at any time.

e.   A private company must keep its accounting records for 3 years. Any other company must keep the records for 6 years from the date when they are made.

f.   Failure to keep accounting records is an offence for which officers may be fined or imprisoned for a maximum of 2 years.

30. **The Accounting Reference Period and Accounting Reference Date** By *S.394* the directors must prepare accounts based on an accounting reference period. This will commence on the day after the date to which the last annual accounts were prepared and will end on the last day of the company's financial year, known as the accounting reference date.

31. *Laying and Delivering Accounts*

a.   By *S.437* the directors, in respect of each accounting reference period, must lay before the company in a general meeting every document required to be comprised in the accounts.

b.   In respect of each accounting reference period the directors must deliver to the registrar a copy of every document required to be comprised in the accounts.

c.   The documents required to be comprised in the accounts are:

   i.   The profit and loss account.

   ii.   The balance sheet. This must be signed by one director.

   iii. The auditors' report. The copy sent to the registrar must state the names of the auditors and be signed by them.

   iv.   The directors' report.

   v.   If the company has subsidiaries, group accounts.

d.   Note that:

   i.   An unlimited company is exempt from delivering accounts provided it is not in the same group as a limited company.

   ii.   The requirements are relaxed for small and medium-sized companies. In particular a small company need not deliver a profit and loss account and a directors' report. Small and medium-sized companies are defined below.

   iii. The annual return is not annexed to the accounts, it is delivered to the registrar separately.

e.   A *small company* is a private company which in respect of a particular financial year satisfies for that year and the preceding year at least two of the following conditions:

   i.   A turnover not exceeding £6.5 million.

   ii.   A balance sheet total not exceeding £3.26 million, and

   iii. An average number of persons employed per week not exceeding 50.

f.   A *medium-sized company* is a private company which in respect of a particular financial year satisfies for that year and the preceding year at least two of the following conditions:

   i.   A turnover not exceeding £25.9 million.

   ii.   A balance sheet total not exceeding £12.9 million, and

   iii. An average number of persons employed per week not exceeding 250.

Note: Although small and medium-sized companies are permitted to file modified financial statements with the registrar, they must nevertheless prepare full financial statements for the members.

THE DIRECTORS' REPORT

32. *Introduction*

   a. Consideration of the directors' report is one of the items of *ordinary business* at the AGM.

   b. By *S.423* the balance sheet and every document which is required to be attached to it (the directors' report; the auditors' report; the profit and loss account; and group accounts, if any) must be sent to each member not less than 21 days before the AGM. They will therefore be sent to the members with notice of the AGM.

33. *Contents of the Directors' Report (DR)*

   a. *General provisions*

      i. A *business review* of the development of the business of the company during the year and of its position at the end of it. This should include not only backward-looking – called *hard* financial data, but also forward-looking – called *soft* data (*S.417*).

      ii. A statement of the principal activities of the company and any significant changes in those activities during the year.

      iii. Particulars of any important events affecting the company.

      iv. An indication of likely future developments.

      v. An indication of the activities (if any) in the field of research and development.

   b. *Dividends and reserves*

      i. The amount, if any, recommended for a dividend, and

      ii. The amount, if any, proposed to be carried to reserves.

      iii. A company whose shares are listed on a regulated market must include a corporate governance statement. That statement must deal, amongst other things, with the company's control structures, compliance with the relevant corporate governance code and contain a description of the company's internal control and risk management systems in relation to financial reporting.

   c. *Fixed assets*

      i. Any significant changes in the fixed assets during the year, and

      ii. An estimate of any substantial difference between the book value and the market value of the company's interests in land and buildings (if the directors consider this to be of significance to the members or debentureholders).

      iii. Company policies and practice on the payment of creditors.

d. *Political and charitable donations.* If such donations together total more than £200 the report must show:

    i. Separate totals for each, and

    ii. The amount of each political contribution over £200, naming the recipient.

e. *Directors*

    i. The names of persons who were directors of the company at any time during the year, and

    ii. For persons who were directors at the end of the year, the interests of each (and the interests of any spouse or infant child) in the shares or debentures of the company and other companies in the group.

    iii. Directors of public companies quoted on a stock exchange are required to produce a directors' remuneration report.

    iv. A statement by the directors about information provided to the company's auditors (*S.418*).

f. *Employees.* Except where the company has less than 250 employees the report must state the company's policy with regard to the employment, training, career development and promotion of disabled employees. Also, information about employee involvement with regard to the extent to which employees are systematically given information, consulted and encouraged to join employee share schemes.

g. *Shares purchased.* Details of any shares of the company purchased by the company during the year.

h. *Shares otherwise acquired.* Details of any of the company's shares acquired by its nominee or with its financial assistance.

i. Further requirements for the DR are to be found in *Schedule 7* to the *Accounts Regulations 2008.*

34. *Corporate Governance – Directors' Pay*

a. Over recent years there has been, and continues to be, public concern over what appear to be excessive remuneration packages for directors whilst in office, and over generous compensation packages at the end of a period in office. This is against a background of companies often performing poorly. Traditional company law sees remuneration of directors as a matter for the board alone, often with no requirement for shareholder approval. There are now two main methods of controlling directors' pay, but only for those companies listed on the Stock Exchange or Alternative Investment Market:

    i. The Combined Code of Best Practice, and

    ii. The Directors' Remuneration Report.

    Note: These are recommendations only, they do **not** form a legal requirement.

b. *The Combined Code of Best Practice.* Though not a legal requirement, the Code must be complied with in order for a company to maintain or gain listed status for its shares on the Stock Exchange or Alternative Investment Market. The Code requires companies to have a *remuneration committee*, which is independent of the board made up of non-executive directors (see Chapter 43.2.b), who then make recommendations on remuneration packages to the board. The company's annual report should also contain a statement of remuneration policy. The Code states that the contract and notice periods for directors should move towards 1 year.

c. *The Directors' Remuneration Report.* Under these regulations quoted companies should publish a report on directors' pay as part of the annual reporting cycle. The Report should be approved by the board, and a copy sent to the Registrar of Companies, and the Report should be voted on by members at the AGM. Again, note, the Remuneration Report is **not** a legal requirement.

35. **By the *Company Accounts (Disclosure of Directors' Emoluments) Regulations (1997)***

a. There are **legal requirements** for all companies, listed or unlisted, to disclose:

i. The aggregate details of directors' remuneration, with regard to:

basic salary, annual bonuses

gains made on the exercise of any share options

gains made under long-term incentive schemes

contributions to director pension schemes.

ii. Where aggregate remuneration is £200 000 or more:

figures attributable to the highest paid director

amount of his or her pension benefit.

b. *Exceptions for unlisted companies.* The above requirements must be complied with by unlisted companies, except:

i. Unlisted companies do not have to disclose the amount of gains made by directors in any exercise of share options.

ii. There is no requirement to disclose net value of assets received from long-term incentive schemes, just the number of directors in receipt of benefits under such schemes.

SELF TEST QUESTIONS

Self Test Questions No. 44 (for Answers see Appendix 1):

1 What is an AGM, and how is one convened and conducted?

2 Distinguish *ordinary* from *special resolutions*.

3 What are the requirements for publicity of a company's affairs?

4 Explain the nature and content of the registers which companies are required to keep.

5 What is an *annual return*?

6 What is the general requirement for the keeping of corporate accounts?

7 What is the *Directors' Report* and what does it contain?

8 What is *Corporate Governance*?

RECONSTRUCTIONS, MERGERS AND TAKEOVERS

Learning Outcomes At the end of this chapter you should be able to:

- Define the meaning of a *merger* as distinguished from a *takeover*.

- Explain the regulation of mergers and reconstructions under the Company and Insolvency Acts.

- Outline nature of a *voluntary arrangement*.

- Explain how *takeovers* are regulated and the role of the *City Code*.

RECONSTRUCTIONS AND MERGERS

1. *Introduction*

    a.   Several terms are used to describe the methods by which two or more companies join to form one. None of these terms have precise legal meanings. The terms are:

        i.   *Merger*. This occurs when two companies join together under the name of one of them, or as a new company formed for the purpose. A merger may also be called an *amalgamation*. Mergers generally only take place when there is agreement between the directors of both companies.

ii. *Takeover.* This term describes the acquisition by one company of sufficient shares in another company (sometimes referred to as the 'target' company) to enable the purchaser to control the target company. Sometimes takeover bids are contested by the board of the target company, and on some occasions rival bids are made for the control of the same company. A takeover differs from a merger in that both companies will remain in existence (at least for the time being). Takeovers are considered later in the chapter.

b. Sometimes a company will wish to reorganize in some way without involving other companies, it may wish for example:

i. To transfer its assets to a new company, the persons carrying on the business remaining substantially the same. This is usually referred to as a *reconstruction*.

ii. To make an *arrangement* with members and/or creditors because it is in financial difficulties, but where winding-up is not appropriate.

2. *Methods*

a. A merger, reconstruction or arrangement can be effected under *S.895* (schemes of arrangement).

b. A merger or reconstruction can be effected under *S.110 INSOLVENCY ACT 1986* (*IA*) (reconstruction by a company in voluntary liquidation). An arrangement with creditors cannot be effected under *S.110 IA*.

c. There is no particular section under which a takeover can be effected. It will, however, be seen that *S.974* enables a bidder who has purchased 90% or more of the shares in the target company to 'compulsorily purchase' the remaining shares.

3. *Mergers and Reconstructions Under S.110–111 IA*

a. *Basic procedure*

i. The members must pass a *special resolution* giving authority to the liquidator to sell the whole or part of its business or property to another company on terms that the consideration be divided among the members of the transferor company. The consideration may be cash, but it is usually shares in the transferee company.

ii. Only after the majority have ensured that there will be enough cash to pay dissentients should it pass a second special resolution, putting the company into voluntary liquidation.

iii. The effect of the scheme is that the shares in the transferee company then become the assets of the transferor company and must be distributed to its members in accordance with their rights on liquidation. The transferor company is then dissolved, its shareholders having become shareholders in the transferee company.

b. *Dissentient shareholders*

i. A dissentient shareholder is one who did not vote for the special resolution. He can require the liquidator to abstain from the sale or buy his shares. The right must be exercised by a written notice addressed to the liquidator and deposited at the registered office within 7 days of the resolution.

ii. If the parties cannot agree on a price, the matter will be referred to arbitration. The price is likely to be based on the value before reconstruction was proposed rather than after.

c. *Dissentient creditors*

The creditors are not as directly affected by a reconstruction as the members. They have their usual rights on liquidation, although the funds from which they will be paid have changed. There is no legal obligation for the transfer agreement to provide for creditors, but in practice it will usually provide either:

i. That the transferee company takes over the debts of the transferor, or

ii. That the transferor company retains sufficient funds to pay its debts.

If the creditors feel that their position is jeopardized in that the new assets received by the transferor company will not be sufficient to pay their debts they can petition for the compulsory winding-up of the transferor company on the grounds that it is unable to pay its debts.

4. *Uses of S.110 IA*

a. *For a reconstruction.* i.e. Company A transfers its assets to a new company, Company B, formed for the purpose, receiving in return shares in Company B. Companies may wish to reconstruct for several reasons, for example:

i. The reconstruction will enable the transferee company to retain and realize cash assets, paying them to its members on liquidation.

ii. It may be able to raise new capital by issuing the shares in the new company as partly paid-up.

iii. To alter the objects where there has been a successful objection by a dissentient minority.

b. *For a merger.* There are two types of merger:

i. Company A goes into voluntary liquidation, selling its assets to Company B (an established and successful company). In return the shareholders of Company A receive shares in Company B. Company A is then dissolved and the business of both companies is carried on by Company B. This is, in effect, a takeover by agreement.

ii. Companies A and B both go into voluntary liquidation. The assets of both companies are then transferred to Company C, a new company formed for the purpose, the members of A and B receiving shares in Company C. Companies A and B are then dissolved. In order to retain their goodwill Company C may change its name to A B Ltd.

5. *Schemes of Arrangement Under (S.895–900)*

a. *S.895* can be used to effect any type of *compromise or arrangement* with creditors or members, for example changing their rights in or against the company, or transferring their rights to another company which then issues shares or takes over liabilities in return for cancellation of existing rights against the first company, i.e. it can be used for both reconstructions and mergers. There must, however, be a 'compromise' or an 'arrangement':

i. A *compromise* can only be made when there has previously been a dispute.

ii. An *arrangement* has a much wider meaning and does not depend on the presence of a dispute.

b. *Procedure under (S.895)*

i. The first step is for the company, or any creditor, or any member or, if the company is being wound up, the liquidator, to ask the court to convene a meeting of creditors and meetings of each class of members.

ii. By *S.897* the company must send out with the notice of any meeting called under *S.895* statement explaining the effect of the scheme and in particular details of material interests of directors and its effect on them.

iii. The compromise or arrangement must be agreed at each meeting by a *simple majority in number* representing *75% in value* of those voting in person or by proxy.

iv. When the necessary meetings have been held and the required majorities obtained *the court must give its approval.*

c. *The role of the court*

i. It will ensure that the scheme is not *ultra vires* or an improper use of *S.895* (for example to reduce capital to which *S.641* should apply).

ii. It will check that the meetings were properly convened and that the required majority approval was obtained.

iii. Since the requirement is only for a majority of members voting rather than of all the members, the court will examine whether the class was fairly represented at the meeting. Probably the court will have already directed that a substantial percentage of the class constitute a quorum when the initial application was made to the court to hold the meetings.

iv. The court will be very careful if the majority of one class of shares also hold the shares of another class since they may vote in favour of a scheme which harms the first class of shares but benefits the second class.

v. The court will look at situations where creditors are also shareholders since a similar conflict of interest could arise.

vi. In general the court will require disclosure of all relevant information, listen to any minority objections and finally only sanction the scheme if it is one that an honest and intelligent businessman would approve. Once the court has approved the scheme it binds all parties and cannot be altered.

6. *Voluntary Arrangements Under (S.1–7 IA)*

a. The Insolvency Act contains procedures that provide an alternative to *S.895*. The procedures apply to any 'composition in satisfaction of debts' (i.e. all creditors agree to take a proportion of what is owed to them) or to a scheme of arrangement of the company's affairs.

b. Meetings of members and creditors must be held to approve the scheme (as under *S.895*) but the main difference is that although the court receives a report on the results of the meetings, it is not directly involved unless the scheme is challenged by dissenting members or creditors on the grounds that it was unfairly prejudicial to them, or that there was an irregularity at either of the meetings.

TAKEOVERS

7. ***Reasons for Takeovers*** The term takeover is usually used to describe a contested bid for the shares in one company (the 'target' company) by another company. Takeovers have become very common in recent years. They have also been the subject of increasing concern, because in some cases the interests of investors in general have suffered as directors and controlling shareholders have sought to further their own personal interests. Takeovers are not,

however, undesirable as such. It may well be that larger size brings economies of scale and better management. Takeovers often take place for one of two reasons:

a. The target company may have been badly managed so that the market price of the controlling shares has fallen to less than the potential value of the company's assets. Thus even if the offeror pays slightly more than market value for the shares it will still obtain control of the assets for less than their true value.

b. A well-managed and successful company may be sufficiently attractive to a larger company that the larger company is prepared to pay the true value for its shares to secure control of its assets.

8. *Basic Procedure*

a. The bidding company will offer to purchase all the shares in the target company either for cash or in return for its own shares. Usually the offer will be conditional on acceptance in respect of a certain percentage of the shares.

b. In some cases the dissenting minority will not wish to sell their shares even at market value. This could be inconvenient for the offeror which may wish to acquire a wholly owned subsidiary. In such a situation the Act provides for the offeror to 'buy out' the dissenting minority of the target company, provided it acquires 90% of the shares to which the offer relates and complies with certain conditions. Such a purchase will not, however, be allowed if it is being used as a means of expropriating the minority interest when there is no genuine takeover.

In **RE BUGLE PRESS (1961)** persons holding 90% of the shares in a company formed a new company. The new company then made an offer for the shares of the old company. Clearly the 90% accepted the offer and the new company then served a notice on the 10% shareholder in the old company stating that they wished to purchase his shares. He opposed the scheme on the ground that it amounted to an expropriation of his interest in that the shareholders of the new company were the persons who held 90% of the shares in the old company. His claim succeeded. This is a good example of the court lifting the veil of incorporation of the companies and basing its decision on the actual identity of the members concerned.

c. The dissenting minority also have a right to change their minds and accept the offer when it becomes clear that the offeror has a substantial majority. It applies when the shares transferred under the scheme plus those already held by the offeror amount to 90% in value of the shares or class of shares in the target company. The offeror must then give notice of this fact to the remaining shareholders and any such shareholder can then require the offeror to buy his shares.

9. *The City Code on Takeovers and Mergers*

a. The first informal city guidelines on the conduct of takeovers were published in 1959. They were not very successful and in 1968 the City Code on Takeovers and Mergers was published. The current code is the *Takeover Code, 8th edition, 2006* (the Code). The source of the relevant rules on takeovers is now found in European Community Law – *Directive 2004/25/EC (The Takeover Directive)*.

b. The operation of the Code is supervised by the *Panel on Takeovers and Mergers. S.942* confers certain statutory powers upon the Panel but does not seek to regulate its constitution. The Panel is available for consultation at any time before or during a takeover or merger. It is not, however, concerned with the merits of the bid itself, this must be

decided by the company and its shareholders. Occasionally th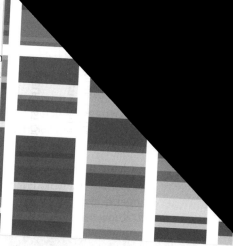
takeover, for example by asking a party to pursue a particu
investigating the conduct of an individual.

c. If the Panel discovers a breach of the Code and proposes to
appeal may be made to an *Appeals Committee* chaired by
Lords.

d. The basic purpose of the Code is to ensure that the boards
and their advisors act in the best interests of their respectiv
by providing them with full information and equal treatme
engaged in takeovers to be aware of and observe the spirit as
the code.

SELF TEST QUESTIONS

Self Test Questions No. 45 (for Answers see Appendix 1):

1 Define what is a merger and what is a takeover.

2 Explain the provisions under the Insolvency Act and the Companies Act as they apply to mergers and reconstructions.

3 What is a *scheme of arrangement*?

4 What is a *voluntary arrangement*?

5 How does statute and the City Code regulate takeovers?

48 LIQUIDATION, ADMINISTRATION (AND ADMINISTRATION ORDERS), RECEIVERSHIP AND VOLUNTARY ARRANGEMENTS

Learning Outcomes At the end of this chapter you should be able to:

- Explain the meaning of *liquidation*.

- Outline the form and nature of a *compulsory liquidation*.

- Understand the elements of fraudulent and wrongful trading.

- Explain the priority of debt satisfaction with particular reference to *ring-fencing*.

- Outline the nature and form of *voluntary liquidation*.

- Understand the process of *administration* and *administrative receiverships*.

- Explain the nature and requirements of a *company voluntary arrangement*.

LIQUIDATION – INTRODUCTION

1. *Definition*

   a. *Liquidation* is the process by which the life of a company is brought to an end and its property administered for the benefit of its members and creditors.

   b. Liquidation or winding-up (the two terms mean the same) begins either by court order (compulsory liquidation) or by the members passing a resolution to wind-up (voluntary liquidation).

   c. This chapter starts with a description of insolvency practitioners, but it must be emphasized that although most voluntary and compulsory liquidations occur because a company cannot pay its debts, companies may be liquidated for reasons other than insolvency, for example a dissatisfied minority shareholder may petition to wind up a company because he objects to the way in which the majority are running the company and he wants to recover his share of the assets.

2. *Insolvency Practitioners*

   a. Prior to 1985 neither liquidators nor receivers had to have any professional qualifications or practical experience. This no doubt contributed to some illegal and highly unethical practices by a minority of liquidators, usually to the detriment of creditors.

   b. Professional bodies must now incorporate into their rules provisions to ensure that such of their members who are permitted by its rules to act as insolvency practitioners are fit and proper persons to so act, and that they meet acceptable requirements as to education, practical training and experience. Professional bodies will be granted recognition by the Secretary of State and such recognition may be revoked if it appears to the Secretary of State that the body no longer satisfies the specified criteria.

COMPULSORY LIQUIDATION

3. *Grounds* By *S.122 INSOLVENCY ACT (1986) (IA)* there are seven grounds on which a company may be wound up by the court, although only two (f. and g. below) are of any importance:

   a. The company has resolved by special resolution to be wound up by the court.

   b. It has been formed as a public company but has not been issued with a certificate of compliance with the minimum share capital requirements.

   c. Where a company incorporated as a public company has failed within 1 year to obtain a trading certificate.

   d. It has not commenced business within a year of incorporation or has suspended business for a year.

   e. The number of members has fallen below the statutory minimum of two, except in the case of a private company.

   f. The company is unable to pay its debts, and

g.   The court is of the opinion that it is just and equitable that the company should be wound up.

4. *Inability to Pay its Debts* (*S.123 IA*)

a.   A company is *deemed* to be unable to pay its debts if:

i.   A creditor for more than £750 has served on the company a written demand for payment and within the next 3 weeks the company has neither paid the debt nor given security for its payment, *or*

ii.   Judgment (sometimes referred to as a *judgment debt*) has been obtained against the company for a debt (normally in excess of £750) and execution, i.e. payment out of the company's assets is unsatisfied, *or*

iii.   The court is satisfied, that the company is unable to pay its debts as they fall due.

iv.   The court is satisfied that the value of the company's assets is less than the amount of its liabilities, taking into account its contingent and prospective liabilities.

b.   The petition to compulsorily wind up a company will usually be presented by a creditor. The company and creditors other than the petitioner are also entitled to be heard. If some creditors oppose the petition because they feel that the continued existence of the company is their best chance of payment, the court is likely to prefer the views of the creditors to whom in aggregate the largest amount is owed.

5. *The Just and Equitable Ground*

a.   The court can make the order whenever the circumstances of justice or equity so demand. For example:

i.   When the *substratum* of the company has gone, i.e. the main purpose for which the company was formed has been fulfilled or has become incapable of achievement.

ii.   When there is *deadlock* in the management of the business because the directors cannot agree on vital matters or become personally antagonistic.

iii.   Where the company is in substance a partnership and there are grounds for dissolving a partnership, for example the basis of mutual trust and confidence has been broken.

In *RE WESTBOURNE GALLERIES (1973)* E and N had been business partners since 1945, taking an equal share in management and profit. In 1958 a private company was formed, E and N each holding one half of the shares (500 shares each). They were also the company's directors. Later it was agreed to admit N's son, G, to the business. E and N each transferred 100 shares to him and he was appointed a director. The company made good profits, but no dividends were paid, all the profit being distributed as directors' remuneration. Following a disagreement between E and N a general meeting was called and N and G removed E as a director and excluded him from management. E petitioned for an order that the company be wound up on the 'just and equitable' ground. It was held that the company must be wound up because when E and N formed the company it was clear that the basic nature of their personal business relationship would remain the same. Therefore N and G were not entitled, in equity, to use their statutory power to remove a director.

iv.   Where there is justifiable lack of confidence in the management.

In *LOCH v JOHN BLACKWOOD (1924)* the directors failed to call meetings, submit accounts or recommend a dividend. The reason was to keep the petitioners ignorant as to the value of the company, so that the directors could acquire their shares at an undervaluation. Winding-up was ordered.

b. An order to compulsorily wind up a company will not be granted merely because the directors have exceeded their powers, or because they have refused to register a transfer, where a right of refusal exists under the articles.

6. *The Petition*

a. Proceedings are commenced by the presentation of a petition by a person qualified to do so on one of the above grounds.

b. The petition should be presented in the High Court, or if the paid-up capital does not exceed £120 000 in the County Court of the district where the registered office of the company is situated.

c. A petition may be presented by:

i. The *company* or its *directors*.

ii. Any *creditor*.

iii. A *contributory*, i.e. any person liable to contribute to the assets of a company in the event of a winding-up. This includes present and certain past members.

iv. The *Official Receiver*, where the company is already in voluntary liquidation.

v. The *Secretary of State*, usually only as a result of an investigation under *S.431* or *S.432 COMPANIES ACT 1985* (sections not incorporated into the *COMPANIES ACT 2006*).

vi. The *Attorney General*, when the company is registered as a charity.

7. *Effects of a Compulsory Winding-up Order*

a. The Official Receiver becomes the liquidator and continues in office until another person becomes liquidator.

b. Any disposition of the company's property, transfer of shares or alteration in the status of members is void unless the court orders otherwise.

c. No action can be commenced or proceeded with against the company without leave of the court, and any seizure of the company's assets to satisfy a debt after the start of winding-up is void.

d. The directors' powers cease and are assumed by the liquidator. Most of their duties also cease, one exception is the duty not to disclose confidential information, which continues after the winding-up order.

e. The company's employees are automatically dismissed, but they may sue for damages for breach of contract. The liquidator may of course re-employ the employees for the time being.

f. Floating charges crystallize, and there is a possibility that other charges and transactions may be invalidated.

g. The assets remain the legal property of the company, unless the court makes an order vesting them in the liquidator. The business may continue but only with a view to its most beneficial realization.

8. *Proceedings After a Winding-up Order*

   a. A copy of the winding-up order must immediately be sent by the company to the registrar, who must publish notice of its receipt in the Gazette.

   b. The official receiver may require a *statement of affairs*. This would normally be submitted by the directors and/or the secretary, but may be required from, for example, company employees. It must contain:

      i. Particulars of assets, debts and liabilities.

      ii. Names and addresses of creditors.

      iii. Details of security held by creditors and the date when given.

      iv. Any further information which may be prescribed or which the official receiver may require.

   c. The official receiver has a duty to investigate:

      i. The causes of failure (if the company has failed), and

      ii. The promotion, formation, business, dealings and affairs of the company.

    He must make such report (if any) to the court as he thinks fit. The report is prima facie evidence in any legal proceedings of the facts stated therein.

   d. Within 12 weeks of the winding-up order the official receiver must decide whether to summon meetings of creditors and contributories. If he decides not to do so he must inform the court, the creditors and the contributories. However, he must summon meetings of both creditors and contributories if required to do so by one-quarter in value of the creditors. The purpose of the meetings is to choose a liquidator and to decide whether to appoint a *committee of creditors*. The purpose of this committee is to assist the liquidator and act as a link between him and the interests it represents. It also has a statutory power to sanction some of the liquidator's actions.

9. *General Functions of the Liquidator*

   a. To ensure that the company's assets are got in, realized and distributed to the company's creditors and, if there is a surplus, to the persons entitled to it.

   b. If the liquidator is not the official receiver he must:

      i. Furnish the official receiver with such information as he may reasonably require.

      ii. Produce and permit inspection of books, papers and other records.

      iii. Give other such assistance as the official receiver reasonably requires.

10. *Liquidator's Powers*

   a. *With the sanction* of the court or the committee of creditors he can:

      i. Bring and defend actions on behalf of the company.

      ii. Carry on the company's business to enable it to be wound up beneficially.

      iii. Pay any class of creditors in full, and

      iv. Make any compromises with creditors, contributories or debtors.

    b.   *Without sanction* he can:

        i.   Sell the company's property.

        ii.   Draw, accept and indorse bills of exchange in the company's name.

        iii.   Raise money on the security of its assets.

        iv.   Appoint an agent.

        v.   Appoint a solicitor to assist him.

        vi.   Execute deeds, receipts and other documents, using the company seal when necessary.

        vii.   Prove in the bankruptcy or insolvency of any contributory, and

        viii.   Do all other such things as are necessary to wind up the company and distribute its assets.

11. *Vacation of Office by the Liquidator* The appointment will end when the liquidator:

    a.   Is removed by order of the court, or by a general meeting of the company's creditors.

    b.   Resigns by giving notice to the court.

    c.   Ceases to be a qualified insolvency practitioner.

    d.   Is released after the conclusion of the winding-up.

12. *Dissolution* When the registrar of companies receives notice from the official receiver that the winding-up is complete, or receives notice that the final meeting of creditors has been held, he notes this fact on the company's file and 3 months later the company is dissolved.

PROVISIONS APPLICABLE TO EVERY KIND OF LIQUIDATION

13. *Fraudulent Trading*

    a.   By *S.213 IA* if in a winding-up it appears that the company has been carrying on business with intent to defraud creditors or for any fraudulent purpose, the court can, on the application of the liquidator, order that persons who were knowingly parties shall be liable to make such contributions to the company's assets as the court thinks proper.

    b.   By *S.458 IA* such persons may also be imprisoned or fined. Criminal liability may be imposed even if the company is not being wound-up, but winding-up is still a condition precedent to civil liability.

14. *Wrongful Trading* (*S.214 IA*)

    a.   If in a winding-up it appears to the liquidator that a *director* or *former director* has been guilty of wrongful trading he may apply to the court for an order that the person is liable to make a contribution to the company's assets.

    b.   The court must be satisfied that:

        i.   The company has gone into insolvent liquidation.

    ii.   At some time before the start of winding-up that person knew or ought to have concluded that there was no reasonable prospect that the company would avoid insolvent liquidation, and

    iii. That person was a director of the company at the time.

c.   The director will be deemed to know that the company could not avoid insolvent liquidation if that would have been the conclusion of a reasonably diligent person having:

    i.   The general knowledge, skill and experience that might reasonably be expected of a person carrying out that particular director's duties, and

    ii.   The general knowledge, skill and experience actually possessed by that director.

d.   The court will not make an order if it is satisfied that, after the director became aware of the condition stated in b. ii. above, he took every step with a view to minimizing the potential loss to the company's creditors as he ought to have taken in the circumstances.

In *RE PRODUCE MARKETING CONSORTIUM (1989)* the two directors of the company were aware of a serious drop in turnover and profits, and that insolvency was inevitable (despite the absence of accounts). They nevertheless continued to trade with the purpose of reducing secured indebtedness to their bank. They also ignored a warning by the auditor and made a number of untrue statements, indicating an unwillingness to acknowledge the serious state of the company's affairs. The company was eventually wound up and the liquidator claimed £108 000 compensation from the directors for wrongful trading. It was held that although there was no deliberate course of wrongdoing, the directors had not taken every step to minimize potential loss, because they allowed the company to trade for over a year after they had become (or should have become) aware of insolvency. The court held that the provisions of *S.214* were basically compensatory rather than penal, so the amount of personal liability was the loss caused to the company. The judge assessed this to be £75 000.

15. *Priority of Debts*

a.   *Winding-up costs, charges and expenses*, for example the liquidator's remuneration.

b.   *Preferential debts.* These rank and abate equally, i.e. if there are insufficient funds to satisfy all the preferential creditors, each gets an equal proportion of what is owed to him. The *ENTERPRISE ACT 2002* abolished Crown preference and so debts owed to the Inland Revenue, Customs and Excise for VAT and Social Security debts such as national insurance contributions are no longer preferential. They become unsecured creditors. Employees wages owed for the previous 4 months up to a current maximum of £800 per employee gross, are a preferential debt.

Where assets are insufficient to pay all preferential debts in full, they rank equally and receive 'so much in the pound'.

c.   *Creditors secured by floating charges.* Under the *ENTERPRISE ACT 2002* when assets of a company subject to a floating charge are realized, a certain proportion (not stated) must be set aside for the unsecured creditors; this is sometimes referred to as 'ring fencing' assets.

d.   *Ordinary unsecured creditors.* Their debts rank and abate equally.

e.   *Sums due to members* in their capacity as members, for example return of capital, and dividends declared but not paid before the commencement of the winding-up.

16. *Preferential Debts* The main preferential debts are:

    a. Any sums owed in respect of occupational or state pension schemes.

    b. Employees' arrears of wages or salary (including commission and holiday remuneration) for 4 months prior to the relevant date subject to a financial limit to be set by delegated legislation. (At present the limit is £800.)

    c. Loans by a third party e.g. a bank, to enable claims under a. and b. to be paid. This is designed to encourage banks in particular, to lend money for wages and salaries before liquidation and so encourage a company to continue trading, knowing that if the company eventually fails, the bank will be a preferential creditor.

17. *Ring-fencing* Preferential debts are paid before the floating charge holder. In order that the floating charge holder – typically banks – do not get all of the benefits, the insolvency practitioner in all situations of insolvency i.e. liquidation, administration, administrative receivership, must set aside – *ring-fence* – a certain amount to be paid to the unsecured creditor. Order 2003 under the Insolvency Act, requires the insolvency practitioner to set up a fund of £10 000 for such a purpose; if more money than this is available, then the ring-fenced amount of £10 000 is added to in the following proportions:

    50% of the first floating charge realizations

    20% of floating charge realizations after that.

    Up to a maximum ring-fenced sum for unsecured creditors of £600 000.

18. *Other Provisions* There are numerous other provisions concerning for example:

    a. The delivery of property by the company officers, advisors, employees, etc. to the liquidator.

    b. The reopening by the court of extortionate credit bargains.

    c. Transactions at an undervalue and preferences (Chapter 42.10).

    d. Avoidance of floating charges (Chapter 42.9).

    e. Disclaimer by the liquidator of onerous property, for example unprofitable contracts.

    f. Publicity requirements throughout liquidation.

VOLUNTARY LIQUIDATION

19. *Types of Voluntary Winding-up* Voluntary liquidations are far more numerous than compulsory liquidations. There are two types, *members' voluntary liquidations* (the more common type), and *creditors' voluntary liquidations*. Whether a liquidation is a members' or creditors' voluntary liquidation will depend on whether or not a declaration of solvency is filed.

20. *Members' Voluntary Winding-up*

    a. By *S.89 IA* a voluntary winding-up is a members' voluntary winding-up if, *within 5 weeks before* the resolution for voluntary winding-up (or on that date but before passing the resolution), the directors, or a majority of them made a *declaration of solvency.*

b. It must contain the latest practicable statement of the company's assets and liabilities and must state that, after inquiry, in their opinion the company will be able to pay its debts within a stated period not more than 12 months after the resolution.

c. If a director makes the declaration without having reasonable grounds for his opinion he commits a criminal offence and if, after the company is wound up, the debts are not paid in full within the specified period, it is presumed that the director did not have reasonable grounds for his opinion. He will therefore have to prove that his opinion was reasonable if he is to avoid liability.

d. If the liquidator forms the opinion that the company will be unable to pay its debts in accordance with the declaration of solvency he must call a creditors' meeting to be held within 28 days. From the date of the creditors meeting the liquidation proceeds as if the declaration of solvency had never been made, i.e. as a creditors' voluntary liquidation. The main effects of this are that the creditors can replace the liquidator with their nominee and they can appoint a committee of inspection.

21. *Creditors' Voluntary Winding-up*

a. The company must call a meeting of creditors to be held within 14 days of the resolution to wind up. One of the directors must preside over the meeting and present a statement of affairs containing:

  i. Particulars of the company's assets, debts and liabilities.

  ii. Names and addresses of the creditors.

  iii. Securities held by the creditors, with the dates when the securities were given.

b. The company meeting may appoint the liquidator, but if the creditors' meeting nominates a different person, the creditors' nominee will be the liquidator.

c. At their meeting the creditors may appoint up to five persons to a *committee of inspection*. The members then have a right to do the same, but the creditors may by resolution exclude members' nominees unless the court orders otherwise.

22. *Consequences of Voluntary Winding-up*

a. *After the commencement* of the winding-up:

  i. The company must cease business except so far as is necessary for its beneficial winding-up.

  ii. Any transfer of shares without the liquidator's sanction, or alteration in the status of members is void.

  iii. If the company is insolvent the company's servants are automatically dismissed, and

  iv. If no liquidator has been appointed or nominated by the company the directors may not exercise any of their powers except as allowed by the court. However, they may dispose of perishable goods or goods that might fall in value and they may do anything necessary to protect the company's assets.

b. *On the appointment of the liquidator* the directors' powers cease except so far as sanctioned by the company in a general meeting or the liquidator in a members' voluntary winding-up, or the committee of inspection or, if none, the creditors in a creditors' voluntary winding-up.

23. *Final Meeting and Dissolution*

   a. In a members' voluntary winding-up the liquidator presents his final accounts to a meeting of members, sends to the registrar a copy of the accounts and a return of the holding of the meeting. Three months later the company is deemed to be dissolved unless the court orders otherwise.

   b. The procedure is the same for a creditors' voluntary winding-up, except that the accounts must be presented to separate meetings of members and creditors.

ADMINISTRATION AND ADMINISTRATION ORDERS

24. *Introduction* The basic purpose of an administration order is to freeze the debts of a company in financial difficulties to assist an administrator to save the company or at least achieve the better realization of its assets. It is not a procedure designed for creditors to enforce their security. The *ENTERPRISE ACT 2002* made a number of changes to the administration procedure in order to try and make it an alternative to liquidation within the context of a rescue culture.

25. *The Power to Make an Appointment* An administrator may be appointed by:

   a. The court.

   b. An out-of-court process, by the holder of a floating charge created before September 2003, relating to the whole or substantially the whole of the company's property. A floating charge holder created after that date can no longer appoint an administrator.

   c. The company itself.

   d. The directors.

   The company itself and its directors cannot make an appointment where any insolvency or liquidation procedure is already in process (except for a voluntary arrangement) or there is a pending application.

   The administrator must perform his or her functions, *in the interests of the company's creditors as a whole*, and with three hierarchical *primary statutory purposes*:

   i. To rescue the company as a going concern, or

   ii. To achieve a better result for the company's creditors than would be achieved if the company was wound up, or

   iii. To realize i.e. sell property in order to make a distribution to one or more secured or preferential creditors.

   (Contained in *Schedule B1, paragraph 3 IA 1986*.)

   The court will only appoint an administrator where it is satisfied that the company cannot pay its debts, and is likely to achieve one or more of the primary statutory purposes above.

   The administrator is required within 8 weeks of appointment to put forward a proposal for approval of the company's unsecured creditors.

   Administration is an insolvency procedure; it can be only be sought in a situation where a company is or is likely to become insolvent. Administration is not a liquidation procedure. As noted the appointment of an administrator does not have to be through the court but any out-of-court appointment must be reported to the court.

   An administration order cannot be made after the company has gone into liquidation.

26. *The Effect of an Application*

    a.   The company cannot be wound-up.

    b.   No charge, hire purchase or retention of title clause can be enforced against the company without the consent of the court.

    c.   No other proceedings can be commenced or proceeded with against the company without the consent of the court.

27. *The Effect of the Order*

    a.   The affairs, business and property of the company are managed by the administrator.

    b.   The restrictions on winding-up and legal proceedings continue.

    c.   Any administrative receiver vacates office.

    d.   Any receiver of part of the company's property must vacate office if required to do so by the administrator.

    e.   All company documents must indicate that an administration order is in force and must name the administrator.

28. *Administrator's Powers*

    a.   He has the general power to do all things necessary to manage the affairs, business and property of the company, for example:

        i.   To carry on the business.

        ii.   To deal with and dispose of assets.

        iii.   To borrow money and grant security.

        iv.   To bring and defend legal proceedings on the company's behalf.

        v.   To employ and dismiss employees.

    b.   Further specific powers are given by the Act, for example:

        i.   To appoint and remove directors.

        ii.   To call meetings of members and creditors.

        iii.   To deal with property subject to a floating charge as if there were no charge. When property is disposed of under this power, the sale proceeds become subject to a floating charge which has the same priority as the original security.

    c.   If the administrator wishes to dispose of other charged property or of goods subject to hire purchase or retention of title agreements, he must obtain the consent of the court.

    d.   In exercising his powers the administrator is deemed to be the agent of the company and any person who deals with him in good faith does not have to inquire whether he is acting within his powers.

29. *Administrator's Duties* Although it is not referred to in the Act the administrator probably owes the same fiduciary duties to the company as a receiver. His main statutory duties are:

    a.   To take into custody or control all the property of the company.

    b.   To send notice of his appointment:

    i.   To the company – immediately.

    ii. To the registrar – within 14 days.

    iii. To the creditors – within 28 days.

c.   To require, within 21 days, a statement of affairs, from officers or employees, giving details of:

    i.   Assets, debts and liabilities.

    ii. Names and addresses of creditors.

    iii. Securities held by creditors with the dates when given.

d.   Within 3 months of the administration order, he must send to the registrar, the creditors and the members a *statement of his proposals* for achieving the purpose of the administration. He must lay this statement before a *meeting of creditors*. The purpose of the meeting is to approve the proposals.

30. *Protection of Members and Creditors*

a.   If the creditors' meeting does not approve the proposals the court may discharge the administration order, or make any other order it thinks fit.

b.   If the meeting approves the proposals (with or without modifications) it may appoint a *committee of creditors*. The committee may require the administrator to attend before it can give such information as it may reasonably require.

c.   *Any creditor or member* may apply to the court for an order on the grounds that the company is, or has been, managed by the administrator in a manner *unfairly prejudicial* to the creditors or members or that any act or omission of the administrator is or would be so prejudicial. The court may make any order it thinks fit.

31. *Discharge or Variation of the Administration Order*

a.   The administrator may apply to the court at any time to discharge or vary the order:

    i.   If it appears to him that the purpose of the administration order has been achieved or is incapable of achievement, or

    ii. If he has been instructed to apply to the court by the meeting of creditors.

b.   The court may discharge or vary the order or make any other order it thinks fit. If the order is discharged or varied the administrator must, within 14 days, send a copy of the order of discharge or variation to the registrar.

32. *A Moratorium* Under the *INSOLVENCY ACT 2000*, small companies, that is those:

a.   With a turnover of not more than £2.8 million.

b.   With a balance sheet total of not more than £1.4 million.

c.   Employing not more than 50 employees.

can if in financial difficulties, seek a moratorium to enable a voluntary arrangement with creditors to be made; this will satisfy the company's debts through a legally binding agreement. The moratorium, which initially lasts for 28 days, will give the firm's management time to put a rescue plan to creditors.

During the period of the moratorium:

a.   No petition may be presented to wind up the company.

b.   No administrative receiver may be appointed.

c.   No steps may be taken to enforce any security.

d.   No legal proceedings can be commenced or continued.

The initial 28-day period is capable of extension or reduction by the Secretary of State. Also a meeting of the company and creditors held within the initial period may agree to extend the period of the moratorium by a further 2 months.

RECEIVERSHIPS

33. *Introduction* The usual remedy for debenture-holders when debenture interest has not been paid, or when some other term of the trust deed has been broken, is to secure the appointment of a receiver to realize the assets subject to the charge and repay the debentureholders.

   a.   *Receiver.* This is a general term and it applies to any person administering any type of receivership. The powers of a receiver may include the power to manage the business, in which case the person is called a receiver and manager.

   b.   *Administrative receiver.* This term was introduced by the Insolvency Act 1986. It basically means a person appointed as a receiver or manager under a floating charge over all or most of the company's assets.

   It was found that the office of administrative receiver often inhibited any rescue attempted under an administration. This was because when a company or its creditors sought to appoint an administrator to try and save or better realize the company's assets, the holder of the power to appoint an administrative receiver under a floating charge – often a bank – would veto the application and appoint an administrative receiver whose prime interest was that of the floating charge holder and the need to manage the company in order to secure repayment of the floating charge holder. The *ENTERPRISE ACT 2002* now prevents the holder of a floating charge from appointing an administrative receiver except in certain types of company. However, as the Act only came into force on 15th September 2003, any floating charges created before that date will not be affected and will be allowed to appoint an administrative receiver.

34. *Appointment* The circumstances of the appointment of a receiver will depend on the terms of the trust deed and the nature of the security.

   a.   Where there is an appointment under a fixed charge it will indicate the circumstances when a power of sale will arise, for example if winding-up commences or if payment of interests is in arrears. In such cases a receiver can be appointed by the debentureholders to collect the income from the property from the time of default until sale.

   b.   *Appointment under a floating charge* (existing before September 2003). It will be remembered that a floating charge crystallizes i.e. becomes fixed, either when winding-up commences or when the company defaults and the debentureholders take steps to enforce their security by appointing a receiver. If the trust deed specifies the circumstances when a receiver may be appointed no application to the court will be necessary. In any other case the court must make the appointment, which it will do when:

i. The principal sum or interest is in arrears.

ii. An event has occurred on which, under the terms of issue of the debentures, the security becomes enforceable, or

iii. There has been no direct breach of the conditions under which the debentures were issued, but the security is nevertheless in jeopardy.

c. *Receiver and manager.* If it is necessary for a receiver to carry on the company's business until realization of the security he must be appointed as *receiver and manager*, since appointment merely as receiver will not confer powers of management on him.

35. *Effect of Appointment*

a. Floating charges crystallize (where charge created before September 2003).

b. The directors' powers of control are suspended, although they remain in office and are entitled to their fees. They are able to challenge the receiver's appointment. They may petition for the compulsory winding-up of the company and they may exercise their other powers provided that in doing so they do not interfere with the receiver's task of collecting in the assets.

c. If the receiver is an officer of the court (i.e. the appointment was made by the court) or if he was appointed by the debentureholders as their agent and not the company's agent, the company's servants are automatically dismissed, although the receiver may re-employ them. If he is an agent of the company all contracts of employment will continue.

36. *Receivers' Powers* A receiver will have the power conferred on him by the trust deed under which he was appointed. An administrative receiver also has the powers specified in the *INSOLVENCY ACT* 1986 although references to 'property of the company' must be construed as references to that part of the property subject to the charge.

37. *Receiver's General Duties*

a. His preliminary duty is to acquaint himself with the terms of his appointment, for example his powers of selling property and the periods for presentation of accounts. He should also ensure that charges are not invalidated by *S.860* (registration of charges), *S.238–240 IA* (transactions at an undervalue and preferences, or *S.245 IA* (avoidance of floating charges), since he may be held personally liable if he acts under an invalid charge.

b. His basic duty is to collect in the assets charged to collect rents and profits, and to exercise the debentureholders' powers of realization, and to pay the net proceeds to them. However, if a receiver is appointed in respect of a debenture secured by a floating charge, the preferential debts must be paid as soon as the receiver has assets in his hands and before any payment is made to the debentureholders.

c. Where the receiver is also appointed as manager he should take a number of practical steps to ensure that nothing is done without his authority, for example:

i. Contact the company's bankers and arrange for the bank account to be transferred into his name as receiver and manager.

ii. Notify managers of branch offices of his appointment and instruct them that no goods are to be ordered or payments made without his authority.

iii. Obtain a list of principal officers and employees, since it may be necessary in some cases to terminate their contracts of employment.

iv. Take an inventory of plant, machinery, fixtures, fittings, etc., and

v. Prepare a list of debts due to the company, noting the period of credit which has been allowed.

38. *Duties of an Administrative Receiver* (appointed prior to 2003)

a. On appointment the administrative receiver must send to the company and publish notice of his appointment.

b. Within 28 days he must notify all creditors.

c. He must immediately require a statement of affairs. This must be submitted within 21 days. The persons responsible and the contents are the same as when an administrator is appointed.

d. Within 3 months he must send a report to the registrar, secured creditors and trustees for secured creditors, containing information on the following matters:

i. The events leading up to his appointment, so far as he is aware of them.

ii. His disposal or proposed disposal of any of the company's property.

iii. His plans for carrying on the business.

iv. The amounts of principal and interest payable to the debentureholders by whom he was appointed and the amounts payable to preferential creditors.

v. The amount, if any, likely to be available to pay other creditors.

vi. A summary of the statement of affairs and his comments, if any, on it.

e. He must also send a copy of the report to unsecured creditors or publish a notice giving an address to which the creditors can write for a free copy of the report. In either case he must lay a copy of the report before a meeting of unsecured creditors summoned for the purpose. The meeting of creditors may establish a committee. Like the committee of creditors in administration it may summon the administrative receiver on 7 days notice and require reasonable information concerning the performance of his functions, but it cannot give him any directions nor is its consent required for any of his acts.

f. If the company has gone or goes into liquidation the administrative receiver must also send a copy of the report to the liquidator.

39. *The Receiver and the Liquidator*

a. In most cases when a receiver is appointed with a view to sale of assets the company will be forced into liquidation. On the other hand if the company is already in liquidation the debentureholders may seek to preserve their rights by the appointment of a receiver.

b. When the two functions are not vested in the same person the liquidator occupies the premier position since he is responsible for the interests of the creditors and contributories as well as the debentureholders. He must therefore:

     i.   See that the receiver confines his duties to the assets subject to the charge.

     ii.   See that he does not protract the receivership.

     iii. See that he discharges the preferential debts, and

     iv. Ensure that he accounts to the liquidator for any surplus after paying the debenture-holders what is due to them.

  c.   The company's books remain with the liquidator, but the receiver must be allowed such access as is necessary to enable him to perform his duties.

40. *Company Voluntary Arrangement (CVA)* (*S.895–899*)

  a.   The aim of a CVA is to avoid insolvency proceedings by seeking to put in place a satisfactory arrangement for settling the company's financial problems. For example, an arrangement may allow a creditor to be paid a percentage of the debt owed, e.g. 80p in the £1.

  b.   Directors are required to draw up proposals – a *composition* – working with an insolvency practitioner, called a *nominee*. The nominee reports to the court on the viability of the proposals and as to whether members and creditors should meet to consider them. If the court agrees, the nominee will call the relevant meetings.

  c.   At such meetings the composition is approved if:

     i.   A simple majority of members agree.

     ii.   75% in value of unsecured creditors agree.

    If passed successfully, the nominee reports back to the court and becomes *supervisor of the arrangement* and implements it. At this point creditors cannot sue for payment or petition for the company to be wound up.

  d.   Under the *INSOLVENCY ACT 2000* the CVA binds *all* creditors, whether such creditors are known or not, and whether they had notice or did not attend the relevant meeting. Such creditors can apply to the court where they can show that for whatever reason, the CVA unfairly prejudices their interests. If a creditor is deliberately excluded it will invalidate the CVA.

  e.   The rights of secured and preferential creditors are not affected; they can at any time challenge in court the decision of the supervisor. This inability to bind through a CVA, secured and preferential creditors, is seen as a major weakness of the CVA process. Also, there is no moratorium (see 32. above) against such creditors whilst CVA proposals are being drawn up and considered by members, creditors before being put to the court. However:

  f.   A moratorium linked to a CVA is available under the *INSOLVENCY ACT 2000* for small companies (see Chapter 45.31.e). Companies engaged in financial markets and those where formal insolvency proceedings are in progress or where a moratorium has been tried and been unsuccessful in the past 12 months, are excluded.

41. *Details of the CVA Process*

  a.   *Nominee's statement.* Directors appoint a nominee – usually an insolvency practitioner – and are required to provide the nominee with the following information:

     i.   The terms of the proposed CVA.

     ii.   A statement of the company's affairs detailing assets, debts and other liabilities.

    Directors are also required to provide other such information as the nominee requests.

b. *Documents to be submitted to the court.* Based upon the nominee's view that the proposal has reasonable grounds for success when put to members and creditors, and that there are sufficient funds to implement it, he or she must provide directors with a statement to that effect. The directors then apply to the court for a moratorium.

c. *Duration of moratorium.* The moratorium becomes effective as soon as the documents are filed with the court. This will last for 28 days, allowing for meetings of members and creditors to take place. The moratorium may be brought to an end by a decision of such meetings, or

   i.   By the court.

   ii. The nominee withdrawing consent.

   iii. Members and creditors deciding not to approve the CVA.

   iv. Where by the end of the 28-day period a meeting of members and creditors has not taken place.

   v.   There is no decision by the above meetings to extend it.

d. *Where views of members and creditors conflict*

   If members and creditors cannot agree, the views of creditors prevail. The court has a discretion, if petitioned, to impose the wishes of members.

e. *Requirement to notify.* The nominee is required to advertise and inform the Registrar of Companies and give formal notice to the company, the date the moratorium comes into force and ends. Also, to inform any creditor who has petitioned for a winding-up of the company.

f. *Consequences of a moratorium.* Except for a petition by the Secretary of State that a wind-up is in the public interest:

   i.   No insolvency proceedings may be commenced.

   ii. No security can be enforced.

   iii. Goods may not be repossessed.

   iv. No other legal proceedings may be enforced or continued.

   v.   Any existing winding-up petitions cannot proceed.

g. *Obtaining credit.* If the company seeks credit in excess of £250 it must first inform the potential creditor of the moratorium; failure to do so makes the company's officers guilty of a criminal offence.

h. *Disposal of assets.* While the moratorium is in force property of the company may only be disposed of, or debts paid, at the start of the moratorium; if there are reasonable grounds for believing that it will benefit the company and, where there is a moratorium committee in place (see j. below) it has been approved by that committee. Where there is no moratorium committee, approval must be given by the nominee.

   Note: this does not prevent the sale of goods in the *normal course of business* e.g. a manufacturer of washing machines selling washing machines. Breaches under this section make officers of the company criminally liable.

i.   *Sale of charged goods.* To enable corporate rescues to take place, which may involve a sale or hive down of parts of a business, charged assets and goods the subject of a hire purchase agreement, may be disposed of during the moratorium provided the charge holder, owner of goods, or court agree. The holder of a fixed charge and owner of goods is entitled to have all proceeds of sale set against amounts owing. The floating charge holder is not allowed this but retains a right of security equal to the original charge over any proceeds of sale.

j.   *A moratorium committee.* Where the period of a moratorium is extended, there is provision of the setting up of a moratorium committee which will exercise functions conferred on it by members and creditors.

k.   *The CVA binds all creditors.* Like 40.d. above, the CVA when approved binds all creditors even unknown creditors and those not served notice or relevant meetings. Also, as above there must be no deliberate exclusion of a creditor – this will invalidate the CVA – and there is a right of such creditors to apply to the court seeking a ruling that the CVA in its current form is unfair and prejudicial to their interests.

l.   *Offences.* If during the 12 months prior to the commencement of the moratorium or during its running, any officer of the company fraudulently seeks to remove property over £500 in value from the company, or who provides falsified information, they will commit a criminal offence.

SELF TEST QUESTIONS

Self Test Questions No. 46 (for Answers see Appendix 1):

1   What is meant by the term *liquidation*?

2   Who is an insolvency practitioner?

3   What are the grounds for a compulsory liquidation of a company?

4   What are the effects of a compulsory winding-up order?

5   What is *fraudulent* and *wrongful trading*?

6   State the order of payment of debts in an insolvent company.

7   What is a *voluntary liquidation*?

8   What are *administration orders*?

9   What happens in a receivership?

10   Explain what is involved in a *company voluntary arrangement.*

REFLECTION AND CONSOLIDATION V

For answers go to the student digital support resources for the book (see page xxv).

Reflection

These chapters cover the essential legal nature of the company, and the accountancy based requirements for its regulation.

Key areas of study

The general nature of the company as a separate legal entity.

A company's formation and constitution – namely the *articles of association*.

Who are members? With the requirements for the maintenance of share capital and meaning of loan capital.

Shareholders the meaning of *majority rule* and the protections for minority shareholders.

Directors – their role, duties, appointment and removal.

The role and nature of auditors and regulatory investigations.

The various shareholder meetings, how they are convened and ran along with the types of shareholder resolutions.

The changing 'shape' of the company through reconstructions, mergers and takeovers.

Insolvency and the various procedures namely: compulsory and voluntary liquidations and administration orders.

Consolidation

The following are practice assessment exercises; you will find the answers and guidance by going to the student digital support resources for the book (see page xxv).

MULTIPLE CHOICE QUESTIONS

1   In relation to E Ltd, a company limited by shares, which ONE of the following statements is correct?

   A   The liability of the company and its shareholders is limited, but the directors are fully liable for the company's debts
   B   The liability of the company and its directors is limited, but the shareholders are fully liable for the company's debts
   C   The liability of the company, its directors and shareholders is limited
   D   The liability of the directors and shareholders is limited, but the company is fully liable for its own debts

2   Adam, Ben and Carol have carried on business together in partnership since July 2001. In September 2001, they decided to enter into a formal partnership agreement. The partners agreed the terms of the agreement in October 2001 and signed the completed agreement in November 2001.

According to the law, when did the partnership commence?

A   July 2001
B   September 2001
C   October 2001
D   November 2001

3   Which of the following statements is correct?

(i) OIt is not possible to register a company limited by shares with the same name as a company already on the register.

(ii) Once on the register, a company limited by shares cannot change its registered office.

A   (i) only
B   (ii) only
C   Both (i) and (ii)
D   Neither (i) nor (ii)

4   The authorized share capital of Wye Ltd is £250 000 divided into 250 000 ordinary £1 shares. The asset value of each share is £2.

Angela and Brian are the only shareholders. Each has taken 50 000 shares and each has, so far, paid £10 000.

5   Which ONE of the following statements is correct?

A   The issued share capital of Wye Ltd is £250 000, and the paid up capital is £20 000
B   The issued share capital of Wye Ltd is £100 000, and the paid up capital is £20 000
C   The issued share capital of Wye Ltd is £250 000, and the paid up capital is £100 000
D   The issued share capital of Wye Ltd is £20 000, and the paid up capital is £20 000

6   Which of the following statements is correct?

(i) The Articles of Association of a company limited by shares contain the internal regulations of the company.

(ii) The Articles of Association form a contract between the shareholders and the company.

A   (i) only
B   (ii) only
C   Both (i) and (ii)
D   Neither (i) nor (ii)

7   Which of the following resolutions may be used to increase a company's authorized capital?

(i) Ordinary resolution.

(ii) Written resolution.

A (i) only
B (ii) only
C Both (i) and (ii)
D Neither (i) nor (ii)

8 XYZ plc has issued shares on terms that they will be bought back by the company 12 months after the date of issue. What are these shares called?

A Ordinary shares
B Bonus shares
C Preference shares
D Redeemable shares

9 Which ONE of the following statements is INCORRECT in relation to elective resolutions?

A An elective resolution may only be passed by private companies
B An elective resolution may be used to reduce the majority of votes necessary to authorize short notice to 90%
C An elective resolution may be used to authorize directors to issue shares for longer than the usual 5 years
D An elective resolution may be used to dispense with the requirement to re-elect directors annually

10 Which ONE of the following is INCORRECT?

A A public company must have at least two directors
B A private company must have at least one director
C Both public and private companies must have a qualified company secretary
D A public company must have at least two shareholders

11 Immediately before XY Ltd was placed in insolvent liquidation, Alex, the company's sole director, arranged for the company to make an early repayment of an unsecured loan of £15 000 which he had provided to the company.

Which ONE of the following is correct?

A The repayment may amount to a 'preference', and Alex may be required to hand back the £15 000 to XY Ltd
B Alex may be fined
C The repayment of the loan is valid so long as Alex was acting in good faith
D XY Ltd and Alex may be guilty of fraud

12 The court has decided that Jill, a director of Jay Ltd, has been wrongfully trading, in that she continued to carry on business at a time when she should have known that insolvency was inevitable. What are the possible consequences for Jill?

A Jill may be fined
B Jill may be imprisoned
C Jill may be required to contribute to the assets of Jay Ltd
D Jill may be required to sell her shares in Jay Ltd

13 Jack has acted in breach of his fiduciary duty as a director of JK Ltd. If the breach does not amount to fraud on the minority, which ONE of the following is correct?

A   The breach cannot be ratified by the shareholders
B   The breach may be ratified by a written or ordinary resolution
C   The breach may be ratified by a provision in the company's Memorandum of Association
D   The breach may be ratified by a resolution of the board of directors

14 Zed plc holds its board meetings on the fifteenth day of each month. At the meeting on 15 June 2001, the board discussed a potential contract with RST Ltd. On 1 July 2001, Lucy, a director of Zed plc, bought shares in RST Ltd. On 25 July 2001, Zed plc contracted with RST Ltd.

When should Lucy have declared her interest to the board of Zed plc?

A   15 June 2001
B   1 July 2001
C   15 July 2001
D   15 August 2001

Typical Exam Questions.

15 Explain the '*ultra vires*' rule as it applies to limited companies

(20 marks)
ICSA, November 2004

16 Explain the differences between fixed and floating charges.

(20 marks)

17 In relation to company law explain:

(a) The meaning of winding-up.   (3 marks)

(b) The procedures involved in:

   (i) A members' voluntary winding-up.   (3 marks)
   (ii) A creditors' voluntary winding-up.   (4 marks)

(10 marks)

18 Explain the meaning and effect of a company's articles of association, paying particular attention to the following issues:

(a) The operation of Table A model articles of association.   (2 marks)

(b) The effect of the articles on both members and non-members.   (4 marks)

(c) The procedure for altering the articles of association.   (4 marks)

(10 marks)

19 In relation to companies' loan capital explain the following terms:

    (a) Debenture   (3 marks)

    (b) Fixed charge   (3 marks)

    (c) Floating charge   (4 marks)

                                                  (10 marks)

20 In relation to a private company explain:

    (a) The power to buy its own shares.   (6 marks)

    (b) The capital redemption reserve.   (2 marks)

    (c) The permissible capital payment.   (2 marks)

                                                  (10 marks)

PART SIX
EMPLOYMENT LAW

49 EMPLOYEES AND THE SELF-EMPLOYED

Learning Outcomes At the end of this chapter you should be able to:

- Understand the importance of distinguishing an *employee* from an *independent contractor*.

- Explain the various tests used by the courts and tribunals to determine who is an *employee* and who is an *independent contractor/self-employed*.

- Outline the rights for fixed-term contract and agency workers.

1. *Distinguishing the Type of Relationship* Where there is a contract of employment there is the relationship of employer and employee. This relationship imposes certain rights and duties on each party. It is important to distinguish whether a relationship is that of employer/employee or employer/independent contractor/self-employed for several reasons. There are obligations at common law, e.g. an employer's vicarious liability for the torts of his employee. There are many statutory rights and liabilities which make the distinction important, e.g. redundancy and unfair dismissal under the *EMPLOYMENT RIGHTS ACT 1996* and social security benefits under the *SOCIAL SECURITY ACT 1975*. Over the years certain 'tests' have been incorporated into common law which have arisen from particular cases in which the relationships were distinguished.

2. *The Control Test*

   a. The first test that evolved to decide whether a person was an employee or an independent contractor was the *control test*. Under this test the greater the extent to which a person is under the direction and control of another person, the more likely he is to be an employee. Thus if a person controlled both what another did and how he did it the control test would clearly be satisfied.

b. However, as the size and complexity of businesses increased and employees became more skilled and professional, employment relationships became more impersonal. The control test was therefore less effective and even when a 'right to control' was substituted for actual control it was not possible to draw the correct distinctions with only one test. The courts therefore developed the integration test and the multiple test.

3. *The Integration Test* Under this test (also called the organization test) if the person doing the work and the work he does is an integral part of the business, rather than an accessory to it, then the person will be an employee. This test is useful in the case of professional employees, such as doctors who may be an integral part of the business without being under the direct control of their employer.

In *WHITTAKER v MPNI (1976)* a trapeze artiste engaged by a circus also performed other duties, e.g. acting as an usherette during other performances. Having fallen during her act she claimed industrial injury benefit. It was held that although the circus had no control over the artiste during the act, this was integrated into other duties and was therefore a contract of service.

Contrast *WESTALL RICHARDSON v ROULSON (1954)* where an 'outworker' in the cutlery industry who rented a workshop in a factory to polish cutlery manufactured in the factory was held to be self-employed in view of the independence he enjoyed, even though he formed an important part of the business carried on in the factory.

4. *The Multiple Test* This test (also known as the economic reality test) will take into account control and integration as well as many other relevant factors. The following factors would indicate a contract of employment:

a. Remuneration by way of payment of wages or salary, net of tax.

b. Membership of company pension scheme.

c. Holiday pay.

d. Payment when absent for illness.

e. Prohibition on working for competitors.

f. Control by employer's disciplinary code.

g. Supply of uniform and/or equipment.

h. Work done on employer's premises rather than at home.

i. Lack of personal business risk on the part of the worker.

In *READY-MIXED CONCRETE (SOUTH EAST) v MPNI (1969)* each driver of the company was financially assisted to buy his own vehicle. The vehicle had to be painted in the company's colours. The drivers had to wear the company uniform and be available for work when required. They were paid a mileage rate for work done for the company. It was held that the drivers were not employees but independent contractors as they were operating at their own financial risk.

5. *Mutuality of Obligation Test* This requirement that there exists a legal obligation on both sides to provide work and to do work in order for a contract of employment to exist, was

originally put forward in *O'KELLY* v *TRUST HOUSE FORTE (1983)*. Whilst over the years, since that case, the courts and tribunals have tended to adopt a fairly liberal approach to finding some mutuality of obligation where they thought justice required it, a recent decision in the House of Lords has brought the Trust House Forte criteria back to being a key essential ingredient. In *CARMICHAEL v NATIONAL POWER (2000)* a case involving part-time tour guides who showed members of the public around a National Power facility who sought to be treated as employees for purposes of redundancy, the House of Lords (now the Supreme Court), in overruling the Court of Appeal decision, stated that there must exist a formal legal obligation on both sides before a contract of employment and employee status can be founded. This is now firmly back as a requirement and was recently followed in *MONTGOMERY v JOHNSON UNDERWOOD (2001)*.

6. *Other Considerations*

   a. *What does the contract say?* If the employer does not want the contract to be construed as a contract of employment the contract should make it clear that the worker is an independent contractor and shall have rights and liabilities accordingly, for example personal liability to third parties for injury caused by negligent work.

   However, the parties cannot change the true relationship by putting the wrong label on it.

   In *FERGUSON v DAWSON (1978)* the worker was employed as part of the 'lump' labour force in the building industry. He gave a false name when signing on and no tax or insurance deductions were made by the contractor who engaged him. In order to claim compensation from his employer for an injury sustained at work the worker had to show that he was an employee. It was held that despite the contract which said he was self-employed, in reality he was an employee.

   In *WICKEN v CHAMPION EMPLOYMENT (1984)* a woman had an agreement with an employment agency that was described as a 'contract of service'. However, she worked as a 'temp' for the agency's clients. It was held that she was not an employee because the agency exercised minimal control over her and there was no mutual obligation to provide and accept work.

   b. *Part-time employees.* The amount of work given is not a deciding factor. A person working part-time may be an employee.

   In *MARKET INVESTIGATIONS v MINISTRY OF SOCIAL SECURITY (1969)* a woman was intermittently engaged by a market research company to act as an interviewer for a fixed remuneration. She was given detailed instructions. It was held that she was an employee.

   Contrast *WILLY SCHEIDEGGER SWISS TYPEWRITING SCHOOL (LONDON) v MINISTRY OF SOCIAL SECURITY (1968)* where a sales representative of typewriters and typewriting courses whose sole remuneration was a commission on sales with no expenses paid, was deemed to be an independent contractor.

   c. *Effect of continuous service over a period of time.* In *NETHERMERE (ST NEOTS) v TAVERNA & GARDINER (1984)* Mrs T and Mrs G were employed by N Ltd as 'homeworkers' manufacturing boys trousers. They worked whenever needed and let the company know when they were taking a holiday. They rarely refused work and gave warning when not wanting it. They submitted regular time sheets and were paid the same rate of pay as the factory workers. The work was an essential part of the factory's production. The machines used were provided by the company. It was held that there may be a contract of service if, over a continuous period of regular giving and taking of work in accordance with the parties' expectation, obligations have been established on the part of the company to provide work and on the part of the homeworker to accept it.

7. *Statutory Employment Rights and Part-time Employees* The *EMPLOYMENT PROTECTION (PART-TIME EMPLOYEES) REGULATIONS 1995* extended the same basic statutory employment rights to part-time employees as exist for full-time employees. Now part-time employees:

a. May bring a claim for unfair dismissal if employed for 1 year, and for redundancy if employed for 2 years (Chapters 56 and 57).

b. Have a right to written particulars of the terms of employment if employed for 1 month or more (Chapter 50).

c. Are entitled to a minimum period of notice after 1 month or more (Chapter 56).

d. Have a right to maternity leave (Chapter 54).

e. Have a right to an itemized pay statement (Chapter 53).

f. Have a right to time off for public duties and for trade union duties and activities (Chapter 52).

8. *Rights for Employees on Fixed-term Contracts* FIXED-TERM *(PREVENTION OF LESS FAVOURABLE TREATMENT) REGULATIONS 2002*. The Regulations' main provisions are: a right for fixed-term employees not to be treated less favourably than a comparable permanent employee, unless objectively justified. This does not require like-for-like pro rata entitlements – provided the fixed-term employee's contractual rights are as a whole at least as favourable as permanent employees' objective justification is deemed to be made out. There are also requirements that the employer advertises permanent vacancies to fixed-term employees and that a fixed-term contract will be converted to a permanent contract where the employee has been employed over 4 years (after 10 July 2002) unless the employer can demonstrate an objective justification for fixed-term employment. The ability to waive redundancy rights will be abolished.

9. *Agency Workers*

a. Judges have often had to decide which of two employers was responsible where one has lent an employee to the other. The general rule is that control remains with the original employer, because personal service contracts cannot be assigned.

In *MERSEY DOCKS & HARBOUR BOARD v COGGINS & GRIFFITH (LIVERPOOL) LTD (1946)* the Harbour Board lent the respondent company a crane plus an operator. The contract specified that the defendants would be the employer, but the Harbour Board retained ultimate right to employ, pay wages and dismiss. It was held that the Harbour Board was still the employer despite the terms of the contract. All of the circumstances should be considered.

b. The general rule can be rebutted, but the original employer must prove transfer of control. This transfer is more readily inferred when an employee is lent on his own, without equipment.

In *GARRARD v SOUTHEY & CO (1952)* G lent S two electricians for work on a factory. G retained right of dismissal and paid them. The electricians were supervised by S's foreman, a skilled electrician. One of the electricians was injured. It was held that control had passed to S who was thus responsible for provision of safe equipment.

c.   *Agency worker and a potential implied contract of employment.* In a recent court of appeal decision, ***DACUS V BROOK STREET BUREAU (2004)*** the Court of Appeal ruled that a cleaner at a council hostel was not an 'employee' of the employment agency that has assigned her to the work and as such could not bring an action for unfair dismissal against the agency. The Court gave general guidance on the employment status of agency workers who worked under the control of the client of the agency (the end-user) whilst having their salary paid by the agency who usually introduce them to the end-user. The guidance was that the employment tribunal should examine all the evidence relating to the relationships between the three parties – the worker, the agency and the end user – including any written agreements and oral statements and also the conduct of the parties. There were certain key essentials of a contract of employment which had to be found to exist; these are:

i.   A mutual obligation to provide work and do work. It was found in the present case that this was lacking. As between the cleaner and the agency; the agency was under no duty to provide her with work and she was under no duty to accept any work offered.

ii.   An obligation to remunerate the worker in return for that work – it making no difference whether the arrangements for payment were made directly or indirectly, and

iii.   A sufficient degree of control over the worker.

Such an examination might well lead to the finding of an implied contract of employment with the end-user which should have been considered in the present case.

This was followed in a more recent case, ***MUSCAT V CABLE AND WIRELESS PLC (2006)*** here the Court found that two contracts existed; a contract for services (self-employed/independent contractor contract) between agency and worker, and a contract of employment (a contract of service) between the worker and the client.

10.   ***The Importance of the Relationship between Employer and Employee*** There are numerous situations where the treatment of employees and independent contractors is different, including:

a.   *Social Security.* Entitlement to benefits and rates of contributions payable depend on whether a person is an employee or an independent contractor.

b.   *Employment protection.* The *EMPLOYMENT RIGHTS ACT 1996* (*ERA*) provides employees with statutory protection in respect of minimum periods of notice, compensation for redundancy and unfair dismissal, maternity pay and so on.

c.   *Taxation.* An employer is responsible for deducting income tax and national insurance contributions from the wages of an employee, and paying statutory sick pay.

d.   *Common law duties.* An employer has duties under common law as outlined in Chapter 52.

e.   *Employer's bankruptcy.* If an employer becomes bankrupt or, in the case of a company goes into liquidation an employee will be a preferential creditor with regard to arrears of pay.

f.   *Vicarious liability.* An employer is usually responsible for the wrongful acts of his employees, committed in the course of employment but not for the wrongful acts committed by independent contractors. Exceptions:

i.   *Negligent selection.* Where the employer is negligent in selecting the contractor, i.e. he does not ascertain the contractor's competence to do that particular job.

ii. *Negligently gives instructions.* Where an employer issues, authorizes or ratifies a negligent order or instruction, the third party has a good claim against the employer.

iii. *Strict liability.* This usually refers to the employer's statutory duty in relation to the fencing of machinery under the *HEALTH AND SAFETY AT WORK REGULATIONS 1992.* Other instances where the employer is liable for the wrongful acts of independent contractors and cannot use the defence that he did not perform the task himself are as follows:

(a) *Withdrawal of support from a neighbour's land.* Where the activities of a contractor working on the employer's land does something so as to cause subsidence on a neighbour's land.

(b) *Work carried out on or near to a highway.* Because of the obvious danger to members of the public using the highway.

(c) *The rule in Rylands v Fletcher.* Where dangerous or unpleasant substances escape onto a neighbour's land or property. In the above case water seeped onto Ryland's land through a mineshaft.

(d) *Nuisance.* Where dust and noise inevitable from an extensive building or construction operation affect neighbouring property or persons.

(e) *Acts causing fire or explosion.* Extra hazardous acts which, by their nature involve, in the eyes of the law, danger to others, e.g. where implements such as flame-bearing equipment or explosives are necessary or incidental to the work being performed.

(f) *Contractor breaks the law.* If the employer engages a contractor to perform an unlawful task he cannot evade liability for any resultant damage.

(g) *Safety of employees.* An employer cannot escape liability for a breach of his duty to provide safe working conditions by delegating this duty to an independent contractor.

SELF TEST QUESTIONS

Self Test Questions No. 47 (for Answers see Appendix 1):

1 Why is it important to distinguish an employee from an independent contractor/self-employed person?

2 What are the tests used to determine employee/self-employed status?

3 What are the particular rights afforded to the fixed-term contract and agency worker?

50 THE CONTRACT OF EMPLOYMENT

Learning Outcomes At the end of this chapter you should be able to:

- State how the contract of employment is formed.

- Outline the written particulars of the employment relationship.

- Understand the ways in which an existing contract of employment may be changed.

1. *Formation of the Contract* To be legally binding a contract of employment must fulfil all the normal contractual requirements, i.e.:

   a. *Offer and acceptance.* There must be offer and acceptance. The offer must contain the terms of the contract or indicate where they may be found. No particular form is required, the contract may be oral or in writing.

   b. *Consideration.* The consideration is the employer's promise to pay the agreed wages in return for the employee's promise to perform a particular task. Generally speaking the courts would not be concerned with the adequacy of the consideration.

   c. *Capacity.* There is some restriction on the contractual capacity of minors. Protection is given both under common law and statute. Protection is also given to women, disabled persons and ethnic minorities.

   d. *Legality.* A contract of employment must not be tainted with illegality, e.g. a contract which deliberately seeks to defraud the Inland Revenue.

In **_CORBY v MORRISON (1980)_** the employee received not only a gross wage in accordance with a wages council order but also an extra £5. This additional payment was not subject to income tax or social security deductions, neither was it shown on the pay envelope. It was held that the whole contract was illegal on the grounds of defrauding the Inland Revenue.

Contrast **_DAVIDSON v PILLAY (1974)_** where Mrs D managed a shop and each week took her wages from the till without deducting tax. It was held that D was not aware of the illegality. Only if the employer is guilty of knowingly committing an illegal act to which the employee is not a party may the employee claim under the contract.

However, a legal contract, performed illegally, e.g. where an employer contravenes the _WAGES ACT 1986_, will not be void on the grounds of illegality.

2. _Written Particulars_

a. _S.1_ of the _EMPLOYMENT RIGHTS ACT_ 1996 (_ERA_) requires an employer to provide his employees with a written statement of the terms of his employment not later than 2 months after starting work. These statements are not contracts, but are taken into account by courts and tribunals. Employees are not required by the Act to sign anything in connection with these written particulars.

b. The written particulars must include:

    i. Names of employer and employee.

    ii. Date when the employment began.

    iii. Date on which the employee's period of continuous employment began.

    Taking into account employment with a previous employer. This can be important as rights with regard to _unfair dismissal_ (covered in Chapter 56.20) and _redundancy_ (covered in Chapter 57) require a period of continuous employment for the employee in order to qualify for protection. This may be with a current employer, but where there are a number of previous employers, it is possible for periods of previous employment to count towards a continuous period of employment. The _EMPLOYMENT RIGHTS ACT 1996_, lists a number of situations where, despite a change of employer, the period of employment will continue unbroken; these are:

    (a) Transfer between associated employers e.g. between parent and subsidiary companies within the same group.

    (b) Upon the sale of a business, under the _TRANSFER OF UNDERTAKINGS (PROTECTION OF EMPLOYMENT) REGULATIONS 2006_ (covered in Chapter 56.27.d) the general rule is that continuity of employment is unbroken with the new owner taking over.

    (c) Within a partnership; where the partners change, this will not effect any continuity of employment of employees working for the partnership.

    (d) Where within an existing employment relationship, new contracts are drawn up and agreed between the parties, continuity of employment is unaffected.

    iv. Scale or rate of remuneration or the method of calculating it.

    v. Intervals at which remuneration is paid.

    vi. Terms and conditions relating to hours of work.

vii.   Terms and conditions relating to entitlement to holidays, including public holidays and holiday pay to enable these to be precisely calculated.

viii.   Terms and conditions relating to incapacity for work due to sickness or injury, including any provision for sick pay.

ix.   Pensions and pension schemes (not required if the pension rights depend on the terms of a pension scheme established under any Act of Parliament and the employee is employed by a body or authority which is required to give the new employee information concerning his pension rights or the determination of questions affecting his pension rights).

x.   Length of notice to terminate employment (both employer and employee).

xi.   Job title.

xii.   For non-permanent employment – the expected period, or if for a fixed term, the date when it is to end.

xiii.   Place of work, or an indication of the fact that the employee is expected to work at various places, and the address of the employer.

xiv.   Any collective agreements directly affecting the terms and conditions of employment.

xv.   Where the employee is required to work outside the UK for a period of more than 1 month – the length of period and the currency in which he is to be paid, any additional remuneration and benefits, and any terms and conditions in respect of his return to the UK.

c.   The statement may refer the employee to the provisions of some other document which he has reasonable opportunities of reading in the course of employment or is reasonably accessible in respect of viii. and ix. above. The statement may refer an employee to the law or the provisions of any relevant collective agreement in respect of x. above. Particulars of the other items must be included or referred to in a single document.

d.   The statement must include a note specifying any disciplinary rules applicable to the employee or referring to another document. The note should specify a person to whom the employee can apply if dissatisfied with any disciplinary decision, the person to whom he can apply for redress of grievance and the manner in which such application should be made.

In *SHERGOLD V FIELDWAY CENTRE (2006)* the Employment Appeal Tribunal took a very broad view of what can amount to a grievance requiring an employer to act. Provided the employee notifies his employer in writing and the general nature of what was complained of was the same as a subsequent claim, then that will be sufficient. There is no requirement that an employee invokes a formal grievance procedure or to state in any letter that it was a grievance.

The *EMPLOYMENT ACT 2008* requires that the ACAS *CODE OF PRACTICE ON DISCIPLINARY AND GRIEVANCE PROCEDURES* (the Code), should be followed. The Code advises employers and employees to seek to resolve disputes informally and internally, using where necessary independent third parties to help (see Chapter 56.25).

e.   An employee has the right to be given by the employer an itemized pay statement. This must include:

i.   The gross amount of wages.

ii. The amount of any deductions and the purpose of such deductions.

iii. The net amount of wages payable where different parts of the net amount are paid in different ways, the amount and method of payment.

f.   *Exemptions.* The written statement shall not apply to an employee whose employment continues for less than 1 month.

g.   *Changes to conditions of employment.* Any agreed changes to the conditions of employment must be notified to the employee within 1 month of the change taking place. The notification must be by means of a written statement. If a copy of the statement is not left with the employee the employer must preserve the statement and ensure that the employee has reasonable opportunities of reading it in the course of employment.

h.   *Employees' remedies for failure to provide written particulars.* If an employee has not been given written notice as the Act provides or thinks that his notice is incorrect he can apply to an employment tribunal. If it is necessary for the tribunal to imply a term they will consider all the circumstances particularly the way in which the parties had worked the contract since it was made. If the tribunal upholds a complaint they can state the particulars that should have been given and the employer will be deemed to have given such a statement. If the employer is in breach of any of those terms the employee can then commence an appropriate action.

S.38 of the *EMPLOYMENT ACT 2002* provides for tribunals to award monetary compensation to an employee where the particulars received are incomplete or inaccurate. Where this is so, the tribunal may increase any subsequent award made against the employer by between two and four weeks' pay.

The Court of Appeal in **ROBERTSON AND JACKSON V BRITISH GAS CORPORATION (1983)** stated that the statutory statement of particulars contained in *S.1* is neither the contract itself nor conclusive evidence of it.

3. **Part-time Employees and Fixed-Term Workers** Under the *PART-TIME WORKERS (PREVENTION OF LESS FAVOURABLE TREATMENT) REGULATIONS 2000* and the *FIXED-TERM EMPLOYEES (PREVENTION OF LESS FAVOURABLE TREATMENT) REGULATIONS 2002*, part- time workers and employees on fixed-term contracts are not to be treated less favourably than permanent employees, and as such, are entitled to the same information as permanent employees with regard to the statement of particulars required under *S.1* of the *EMPLOYMENT RIGHTS ACT 1996*. In addition such persons must not be treated less favourably than full-time permanent employees with regard to:

a.   Pay – that is normal and overtime rate. A lower rate may be justified on objective grounds other than the worker is part-time or on a fixed-term contract, for example where there is performance-related pay.

b.   Contractual sick pay and maternity pay.

c.   Occupational pensions and other benefits.

d.   Dismissal – where an employee is dismissed for reasons of being either part-time or on a fixed-term contract, this would constitute an automatic unfair dismissal with no requirement for any qualifying period of employment to be shown.

e.   Redundancy.

The Regulations also give to fixed-term employees a right to be informed of available vacancies for permanent employment and to apply for them. Also, where an employee on a fixed-term contract has had it renewed over an unbroken 4-year period then, from 10 July 2002, the renewal will convert the contract into a permanent one.

4. **Variation to the Contract of Employment** Normally a contract cannot be varied unilaterally. *S.4* of the *EMPLOYMENT RIGHTS ACT 1996* requires that changes to terms be notified to an employee within 1 month. However, this does not give an employer the right to unilaterally alter contract terms merely by giving notice. Contracts of employment have to be to some extent flexible and, in the absence of written terms the following may be implied:

a. *Implied in fact.* A term may be implied because it lends business efficacy to the contract.

In *McCAFFREY v JEAVONS LTD (1967)* an employee described as a 'travelling man' in the construction industry was deemed contractually bound to work anywhere in the UK.

In *BRISTOL GARAGE (BRIGHTON) LTD v LOWEN (1979)* it was held that there was an implication that a garage employee would not have agreed to make up cash losses due to theft from his pay. Tribunals recognize the right of an employer to introduce '*reasonable and necessary changes for the good of the organization*'. In *DRYDEN V GREATER GLASGOW HEALTH BOARD (1992)* the introduction of a no smoking policy was deemed reasonable and necessary in the interests of health and safety. And in *CRESSWELL V BOARD OF INLAND REVENUE (1984)* the need to compel retraining due to the introduction of new technology was seen as reasonable and necessary by a tribunal.

b. *Custom and practice.* These are terms implied by custom and practice in a particular trade, providing that these are well-known and reasonable.

c. *Implied by law.* Some terms may be implied at common law or statute. Implied duties of employee and employer are outlined in subsequent chapters. There is an implied 'equality' clause in the *EQUAL PAY ACT 1970* and a number of anti-discrimination clauses which are deemed to be read into all contracts of employment.

d. There may be express terms in a contract of employment that seek to give management the right to impose changes on the employee. For example, 'employees shall do whatever management from time to time deem necessary' or 'employees shall work wherever management deems necessary' – a so-called 'mobility clause'. Such terms have to withstand the test of 'reasonableness' that is, are the requests reasonable and necessary within the normal scope of an employee's existing contract?

e. *Implied through Collective agreements.* Terms in collective agreements may be incorporated into contracts of employment.

In *JOEL v CAMMELL LAIRD SHIP REPAIRERS LTD (1969)* a collective agreement related to transfers of employees between ship repair and shipbuilding. It was held to be incorporated into the contract of employment because the employees concerned had indicated that they were aware of the provision.

In *ROBERTSON v BRITISH GAS (1983)* meter readers and collectors employed by North Thames Gas received an incentive bonus of about £400 per month. The scheme was negotiated by their union and was referred to in the written statement of terms of each employee. Management gave the union 6 months notice to terminate the agreement. The union members successfully argued in the Appeal Court that this was a breach of contract.

f. *Other documents.* ***SECRETARY OF STATE FOR EMPLOYMENT v ASLEF (No. 2) (1972)***. This case involved railwaymen 'working to rule' and by strict observance of the railway rules bringing the railways to a standstill. The court held that a work to rule was a breach of the individual employee's contract of employment because:

i. There was an implied term that an employee should not wilfully disrupt his employer's undertaking.

ii. In this instance it involved refusal to work obligatory overtime.

iii. The employer's rule book contained instructions the employee was obliged by his contract to obey.

Contrast ***BRITISH LEYLAND (UK) LTD v McQUILKEN (1978)***. An agreement with trade unions on closure of a department provided that employees should be interviewed to ascertain preference for future employment. It was held that the agreement was a long-term policy plan not incorporated into individual contracts of employment.

In ***CHRISTOPHER KEELEY v FOSROC INTERNATIONAL LIMITED (2006)*** provisions as to enhanced redundancy payments, were set out in a staff handbook. The Court of Appeal held that these were contractual terms and could be relied upon.

SELF TEST QUESTIONS

Self Test Questions No. 48 (for Answers see Appendix 1):

1 How is a contract of employment formed?

2 Summarize the written particulars of employment that an employer must give to the employee.

3 What are the legal circumstances in which an existing contract of employment may be varied?

THE COMMON LAW DUTIES OF AN EMPLOYEE

INTRODUCTION

1. The duties of an employee are governed by the terms of his contract. In the absence of any express or implied terms his duties will be determined under common law. Contravention of any of these duties may give an employer the right to dismiss the employee.

IMPLIED DUTIES

2. The following are circumstances in which the courts have held employees to have implied duties towards their employers:

   a. *Indemnity.* Where the employer suffers some loss because of his liability for the wrongful act of his employee, the employee may be liable to indemnify (compensate) his employer.

In *LISTER v ROMFORD ICE & COLD STORAGE LTD (1957)* P was a driver employed by the company. His father, a driver's mate, assisted P. Due to P's negligence his father was injured and claimed damages against the company. The company in turn claimed that P should indemnify it against the loss suffered. It was held that P should indemnify the company due to his negligence.

Subsequently all members of the British Insurance Association agreed that they would not require the employer to claim indemnity from the employee unless there was evidence of collusion or wilful misconduct on the employee's part.

b.   *Misconduct*. The employee must not misconduct himself. The term misconduct includes insolence, persistent laziness, immorality, dishonesty and drunkenness. Misconduct will justify disciplinary dismissal if it directly interferes with the business of the employer, or the employee's ability to perform his services.

In *PEPPER v WEBB (1969)* a gardener who behaved in a surly manner, showed disinterest in the garden, refused to perform certain tasks in the garden and was insolent to his employer, was held to have been dismissed justifiably.

Contrast *WILSON v RACHER (1974)* a gardener was dismissed for swearing at his employer, on one occasion. It was held that this was an exceptional outburst from an otherwise competent and diligent employee who had been provoked by his employer. Therefore there were no grounds for dismissal.

c.   *Personal service*. The employee must not allow others outside the scope of his employer's control to perform his tasks.

In *ILKIW v SAMUELS (1963)* a lorry driver allowed another person to drive his lorry. He did this against express instructions from his employer and without inquiry as to the other person's ability to handle his vehicle. As a result, a third party was injured. The employer was liable because of the negligence of his own driver (the person responsible for the operation of the lorry).

d.   *Loyalty and good faith*. The employee must not accept bribes or make secret profits.

In *BOSTON DEEP SEA FISHING CO v ANSELL (1888)* whilst employed as managing director with the plaintiff company Ansell contracted with a shipbuilding company for supply of ships, taking a secret commission. It was held that Ansell's action was a breach of his duty to his employer.

e.   *Not to compete with the employer*. The employee must do nothing to harm his employer's interests, even in his spare time.

In *HIVAC v PARK ROYAL SCIENTIFIC INSTRUMENTS LTD (1946)* employees of P worked for D (a rival firm) in their spare time. It was held that P would be granted an injunction restraining them from working for D.

In *BARTLETT v SHOE LEATHER RECORD (1960)* P, an editor, worked for a newspaper and a fashion trade journal in his spare time. Although not writing on the same subject it was held that he would not be able to give of his best by reason of his spare-time activities.

However, in *NOTTINGHAM UNIVERSITY v FISHEL (2000)* the court found where an employee pursued outside activities which might affect his employer's interests, the duty of loyalty would only be broken where there is an express contractual term forbidding an employee from such conduct. As a general proposition, it was not a requirement that an employee place his employer's interests above his own.

An employee should do nothing to cause his employer to lose confidence in him:

In *SINCLAIR v NEIGHBOUR (1967)* a betting shop manager 'borrowed' £15 from the till, intending to replace it the following day, although he knew his employer would not approve. The employer discovered the employee's act and dismissed him without notice. It was held that dismissal was justified.

f. *Careful service.* An employee must exercise due care and skill in the performance of his duties. Where he claims that he has the ability to do the work undertaken, besides having the ability, he must also perform the tasks diligently and efficiently.

In *HARMER v CORNELIUS (1858)* a person who was given a job as a scene painter had never painted scenes and was incompetent. He was held to have been justifiably dismissed without notice.

In *SUPERLUX v PLAISTED (1958)* D, a vacuum cleaner salesman left his van outside his home overnight. Several cleaners were stolen. It was held that his breach of the duty of careful service justified dismissal.

An employee who is negligent can be sued for his negligence by his employer or by a third party who suffers loss as a result. However, some relief may be granted under the *LAW REFORM (CONTRIBUTORY NEGLIGENCE) ACT 1945*.

In *JONES v MANCHESTER CORPORATION (1948)* a doctor and anaesthetist, both very inexperienced, were left in charge of an emergency ward with no one to supervise them. A patient suffered an injury as a result and was awarded damages which were apportioned, 20 per cent against the doctor and anaesthetist and 80 per cent against the hospital.

g. *Account for property and gain.* An employee must account for any money or property belonging to his employer, and any gains made thereon.

READING v ATTORNEY GENERAL (1951) (see Chapter 29.10.c).

h. *Trade secrecy.* The employee must maintain secrecy over his employer's affairs during the time of his employment. If the employer wishes to extend this beyond the period of employment it would be advisable to insert a suitable clause in the contract of employment. The employee is under an obligation to his employers not to disclose confidential information obtained by him in the course of, and as a result of his employment. This duty applies both during employment and afterwards if the employee seeks to use such information to the detriment of his employer.

In *ROBB v GREEN (1895)* an employee who copied down a list of customers intending to use it after leaving employment, was restrained from doing so.

i. *Restraint of trade clauses.* Often an employer will wish to protect his trade secrets from disclosure by an employee when the employee leaves his service, and not leave it to the employee's common law duty of fidelity. The employer will do this by including in the contract of employment a clause placing some restriction on future employment, i.e. a restraint of trade clause. This important aspect of employment law is discussed in Chapter 16.19.

In *BENTS BREWERY CO LTD v HOGAN (1945)* a trade union official invited certain employees to disclose particulars of the total amount of the sales made and the wages paid at the branches of the company in which they were employed. It was held that if any employee gave that information he would commit a breach of contract, and the trade union official would be liable for inducing such breach.

However, an employee may disclose information if it is such that it is in the public interest to disclose it. Furthermore it should be disclosed to one who has a proper interest to receive it.

In *INITIAL SERVICES LTD v PUTTERILL (1968)* D was sales manager of the company which operated a laundry. He left their employment and took with him some documents relating to the company which he passed on to a national newspaper. The newspaper subsequently published articles alleging that there was profiteering in the laundry industry. The company sought an injunction against their former employee, but were unsuccessful since if the allegations were true there were arrangements in the industry which should have been registered under the *RESTRICTIVE TRADE PRACTICES ACT 1976.*

j. *A general right of confidence.* As seen above, breaches of the law of confidentiality is an accepted head of liability under the common law in the employment relationship, this right of confidentiality also extends outside of employment giving individuals a general right of confidentiality with regard to their private commercial affairs. This right of *commercial confidence* is in addition to rights of privacy contained in the *HUMAN RIGHTS ACT 1998, Article 8* (see Chapter 36). In *DOUGLAS v HELLO! LTD (2003)* two claimants, well known film stars, made a commercial contract with a magazine for them to acquire exclusive photo rights to their wedding. Unauthorized photos were taken and sold to a rival magazine – *Hello!*. This was a breach of the common law right of *commercial confidence* existing within business dealings. In addition, the Court held that the photographs were *personal data* as defined in the *DATA PROTECTION ACT 1998* (see Chapter 36.4), and *Hello!* Magazine, as a data controller (see Chapter 36.3), were liable for their processing.

k. *Whistleblowing.* The *PUBLIC INTEREST DISCLOSURE ACT 1998* prevents a worker suffering any form of detriment where he or she discloses information about the employer – a protected disclosure – believing that:

   i.   A criminal offence is being, or has been, or is about to be committed.

   ii. Some legal obligation is likely to be avoided.

   iii. A miscarriage of justice has occurred, is occurring or is likely to occur.

   iv. The health and safety of an individual is put in danger.

   v.   Damage to the environment is occurring, or is likely to occur or has occurred.

   vi. Information relating to any of the above is likely to be concealed.

This right not to suffer a detriment where a protected disclosure has occurred extends to all workers, there is no requirement for a qualifying period of employment.

In *FERNANDES V NETCOM CONSULTANTS (UK) LTD. (2000)* an employee was awarded £290 000 by an employment tribunal when he was pressured to resign after informing the parent company that his boss was submitting expense claim forms without receipts to evidence his claims. The tribunal found that the dismissal was automatically unfair under the 1998 Act.

l. *Inventions.* It is the duty of the employee to disclose all inventions made using the facilities of the employer.

In *BRITISH SYPHON COMPANY LTD v HOMEWOOD (1956)* D was employed as a technical adviser and was asked to design a soda syphon, which he did, but he patented the syphon in his own name. It was held that the patent right belonged to the employer.

Statutory provision has been made with regard to employees' inventions by the *PATENTS ACT 1977*, which largely restates the common law position. This is that an invention belongs to the employer if made in the normal course of duties under the circumstances in which it might be expected an invention to result. In addition it is deemed to belong to the employer if the invention results from special duties assigned to the employee under circumstances in which an invention might reasonably be expected to result. However, in all other cases, even where the invention occurs in the course of employment, using the employer's materials but where an invention cannot reasonably be expected it will be deemed to belong to the employee.

m. *Obedience.*

   i.   The employee must obey all lawful and justifiable orders given by his employer in the ordinary course of business, but only undertakes to perform those tasks to which he has agreed in his contract of employment. An employer may not require him to do other tasks, however reasonable, unless the contract is wide enough to permit this. This applies to both the nature of the work and to the location.

       In *PRICE v MOUAT (1862)* a lace dealer was asked to card lace. This was not a task he had undertaken and he was justified in refusing, as it would have involved a lowering of his status.

       In *O'BRIEN v ASSOCIATED FIRE ALARMS (1968)* an employee in a Liverpool factory was required to work in Barrow. It was held that such a request was outside the scope of the contract.

   ii.   In some circumstances an employee will be justified in refusing a task, even though it is in the contract of employment.

       In *OTTOMAN BANK v CHAKARIAN (1930)* D refused to move to a branch of the bank situated in a country in which his life would have been in danger. It was held that his refusal was justified.

   iii.   The duty of obedience is mitigated where the employee does not show a wilful flouting of the essential conditions of the contract.

       In *LAWS v LONDON CHRONICLE (1959)* P was secretary to an advertising manager. She followed him when he walked out of an editorial conference despite an order from the managing director to remain. It was held that P could not be summarily dismissed because her disobedience was an isolated instance and did not show an intention to repudiate her contract of service.

n. *Notice.* The employee must give proper notice of termination of his services according to the terms of his contract, the custom of the trade or statute (Employment Protection (Consolidation) Act *(EPCA) 1975*).

Note: The foregoing are examples of occasions where an employee's duties to his employer have been implied at common law. However, it is not necessarily an exhaustive list. Generally courts will not imply unreasonable terms and will justify the implication of any terms they do imply, e.g. in *SECRETARY OF STATE FOR EMPLOYMENT v ASLEF (No. 2) (1972)* Lord Denning concluded that every contract of employment should contain an obligation on the employee not to wilfully disrupt his employer's undertaking.

SELF TEST QUESTIONS

Self Test Questions No. 49 (for Answers see Appendix 1):

What are the common law duties placed upon an employee?

52 DUTIES OF AN EMPLOYER

Learning Outcomes   At the end of this chapter you should be able to:

- State and explain the common law duties placed upon the employer.

- Outline the limitations on the employer's duties.

- Explain the duties owed by the employer to persons other than employees.

- Understand *vicarious liability*.

- State the requirements for employees seeking time off work.

- State the disclosure requirements when made by a recognized trade union.

INTRODUCTION

1. This chapter is concerned with an employer's duties implied under common law and expressed in statutes. In addition, an employer's duties to persons other than employees is considered, e.g. visitors and third parties who suffer loss due to the acts of the employees.

COMMON LAW DUTIES

2. *Work* The employer is not obliged to provide work for his employees except in the following circumstances:

   a. Where employment is essential to provide a reputation for future employment. This was originally considered to be in the case of actors:

      In *CLAYTON & WALLER v OLIVER (1930)* an actor was engaged for the leading role in a show. The management engaged someone else but agreed to pay the actor for his lost wages; however, he also sued for loss of reputation. It was held that he was entitled to damages.

      This principle was also extended to journalists and skilled workers.

      In *COLLIER v SUNDAY REFEREE (1940)* P, a sub-editor was able to claim damages in accordance with the ruling given in the Clayton & Waller v Oliver case.

      In *LANGSTON v AUEW (1974)* P resigned from the AUEW in 1972 and was suspended on full pay for nearly 2 years. He succeeded in his claim, as a skilled man, for the right to work.

   b. Where remuneration depends on the amount of work, e.g. sales commission, the employer will be obliged to provide the work to enable commission to be earned –

      TURNER v GOLDSMITH (1891) (see Chapter 29.25).

      In *DEVONALD v ROSSER & SONS (1906)* the court decided that an employer was obliged to provide work for pieceworkers whose pay depended upon performance.

3. *Pay* The employer's common law duties with regard to pay are considered in Chapter 53.

4. *Indemnity* An employer must indemnify his employee where the employee has incurred a liability whilst acting on the employer's behalf, except where:

   a. The employee knew that he was doing an unlawful act.

   b. The employee knew that the employer had no right to give the order in question.

   In *BURROWS v RHODES (1899)* D were the organizers of the Jameson raid. They induced P to re-enlist in the armed forces of the British South Africa Company, this they did by means of a fraudulent statement. P believed that the venture in which he was to take part was lawful. It was held that he was entitled to damages from his employers for injuries received.

5. *Equipment and Premises (Safety)* The employer must take reasonable care to make his premises safe. Examples of unsafe premises include structural defects, bad ventilation, unsafe insulation, slippery floors or staircases, etc. Some specific areas are covered by statute, e.g. the necessity to maintain safe means of access (*HEALTH AND SAFETY AT WORK REGULATIONS 1992*).

Equipment includes plant, tools and materials, i.e. all those things with which a person may be expected to work must be of a safe nature. Many of these things are governed by various statutes, e.g. the *HEALTH AND SAFETY AT WORK ACT 1974*, and *HEALTH AND SAFETY AT WORK REGULATIONS 1992*. Plant, tools and equipment supplied by the employer must be reasonably safe and the employer fails in this duty in the following circumstances:

a. He fails to supply suitable equipment and the employee is forced to improvise:

In *LOVELLS v BLUNDELL (1944)* workers overhauling a ship's boiler needed planks, none were provided and there was not a supervisor to advise. They found a plank lying about and used it. The plank broke and they sued the firm for not providing a safe system of work. It was held that the firm was liable.

b. He provides defective equipment knowingly, or which he should have known on a reasonable examination. The onus is on the employer to inspect equipment.

In *BAXTER v ST HELENA GROUP HOSPITAL MANAGEMENT COMMITTEE (1972)* a nurse sat on a chair which collapsed due to woodworm and she suffered a back injury. It was held that the hospital was liable as the chair should have been inspected.

c. He fails to remedy defects which have been brought to his notice.

In *MONAGHAN v RHODES (1920)* a stevedore's labourer fell off an unsafe rope ladder leading to the hold of a ship. He had already drawn the foreman's attention to its danger.

d. But 'reasonableness' is all that is required:

In *LATIMER v AEC (1953)* a factory floor became flooded owing to a storm, and the water, when mixed with oil, made the floor slippery. The employer dried the floor and spread sawdust, but P slipped and was injured. It was held that the employer had taken all reasonable precautions and was not liable for the injury.

Note: The employer's failure to take reasonable steps to ensure the safety of an employee may be a breach of a fundamental term of the contract entitling the employee to resign and claim constructive dismissal.

In *BRITISH AIRCRAFT CORPORATION LTD v AUSTIN (1978)* it was held that there was an implied term in the contract of employment that the employer would not behave intolerably. In this case it was regarded as intolerable that the employer failed to investigate the possibility of purchasing special eye protectors which would accommodate the employee's own spectacles.

6. *Disciplinary and grievance procedure* We have noted that *S.1 EMPLOYMENT RIGHTS ACT 1996* provides that details of any grievance procedure be notified to employees and any failure to observe such a procedure would result in a breach of contract; however, in a recent case the duty to provide all employees with some means of redressing grievances was established as being a common law implied duty – in *WA GOOLD (PEARMACK) LTD v MCCONNELL (1995)* the claimant had suffered a reduction in salary due to changes introduced by the employer; on a number of occasions he sought to take up his grievance with management but was repeatedly put off. The Court held that the treatment he received was a breach of contract which he was entitled to treat as a breach and constructive dismissal and went on to say that the employer must reasonably and promptly afford an opportunity to employees to obtain redress of a grievance.

'REASONABLE' SAFETY

7. The employer must take reasonable care not to subject his employees to unnecessary risk. The requirements of safety on the one hand and production on the other must

sometimes conflict. By the test of 'reasonableness' judges have brought widely accepted ideas of fairness to assess the merits of a case. The standard of reasonableness indicates that there cannot be a guarantee of absolute safety. Some considerations which would be taken into account are:

a. *Inherent risk.* All work carries some risk and an employer would not be liable for events outside his control provided he had not been negligent – *MITCHIE v SHENLEY (1952)* a case involving a nurse who was injured by a mental patient.

b. *Reasonably foreseeable.* If the danger could be reduced or eliminated the question is whether or not the employer was negligent in failing to do so.

   In *DOUGHTY v TURNER MFG CO (1964)* an asbestos cover fell into a cauldron of molten metal. There was an explosion and the claimant, an employee standing by, was injured by molten metal. It was held that the explosion and hence the injuries were not reasonably foreseeable, therefore the employer was not liable.

c. *Obviousness of risk.* The more obvious the danger the more likely the law is to impose liability on the employer for failing to prevent the accident.

d. *Seriousness of risk.* This depends partly on the probability of an accident occurring but partly also on the gravity of the results if it does occur. The greater the risk the greater is the liability of the employer, and the more thorough are the precautions he should take.

e. *Cost.* The magnitude of the risk has to be weighed against other factors, particularly against the expense involved in safety measures and the necessity of carrying out the work in hand. The law would think it unreasonable to force employers to spend vast sums avoiding some slight chance of an accident.

   In *HAWES v RAILWAY EXECUTIVE (1952)* an employee was electrocuted while carrying out repair work. It was held that the only foolproof safe system was for the current to be turned off in the region, the cost of which was too great compared with the risk of injury.

A REASONABLY SAFE SYSTEM OF WORK

8. There is the requirement for an employer to provide a 'reasonably safe system of work'. Formerly just a common law duty, the duty is now incorporated into the *HEALTH AND SAFETY AT WORK ACT 1974*. A safe system consists of:

a. *Reasonably safe work-fellows.* If an employer knows or ought to know (perhaps because of complaints) that employees are a danger to others he is obliged to remove the danger. Employers are held liable for the conduct of known bullies or practical jokers.

   In *HUDSON v RIDGE MFG CO LTD (1957)* an employee of a firm was known for his practical jokes. A fellow employee suffered injury as a result of one of these practical jokes, and sued the firm for damages. It was held that the firm was liable for not providing a safe system of work.

   Contrast *SMITH v CROSSLEY BROTHERS LTD (1951)* where two apprentices, by way of a practical joke, injected compressed air into the body of a third apprentice. It was held, on the evidence, that such an action could not reasonably be foreseen, there was no failure in the duty of supervision, and the employers were not liable.

b.   *Training of employees.* Employees must be instructed in the choice of proper equipment and the correct method of working.

In **_BROWN v JOHN MILLS & CO LTD (1970)_** P was new at his job, of polishing brass nuts, which he did by the use of emery cloth wrapped around his finger whilst the nuts were secured in a lathe turning at high speed. He was injured. He had not been properly instructed in the correct method of working. It was held that the company was liable.

c.   *Effective arrangements with regard to safety apparatus.*

   i.   Arrangements must be made for the provision and use of safety apparatus which will reduce the danger to the absolute minimum. No employee, even though experienced, must be left to look after his own safety.

   In **_GENERAL CLEANING CONTRACTORS v CHRISTMAS (1953)_** a window cleaner employed by a firm fell from a ledge while attempting to clean the windows, it was normal practice to stand on the ledge to clean windows. It was held that even though normal practice, this method was not a reasonably safe system of work, and the firm was liable.

   ii.   Safety apparatus must be available at the place it is required.

   In **_FINCH v TELEGRAPH CONSTRUCTION & MAINTENANCE CO (1949)_** P was injured when metal flew into his eye from a grinding operation. Goggles were provided but the workman did not know where to find them. It was held that the company was liable.

   iii.   It is not necessary to stand over experienced workers instructed in safety systems to ensure they are used.

In **_WOODS v DURABLE SUITES LTD (1933)_** P contracted dermatitis due to working with glue. He had been instructed in the safety precautions. It was held that the employer was not liable as the employee was experienced, and the employer was not bound to stand over such a worker of full age to ensure that he took the precautions.

However, the employer must take all reasonable measures, including warning of dangers and persuasion to ensure the use of the safety equipment.

In **_QUALCAST LTD v HAYNES (1959)_** molten metal splashed onto the foot of an experienced moulder. He knew that protective clothing was available but did not wear it. It was held that the employer was not responsible for failing to bring pressure to bear on his employee.

Contrast **_BUX v SLOUGH METALS LTD (1970)_** where P, a die caster, was injured when molten metal flew into his eyes. The company had complied with statutory safety regulations in providing suitable goggles for its foundry workers, but P was not wearing goggles at the time of the accident. The court held that the company were in breach of their common law duty to take reasonable steps for P's safety. They should have made a rule, enforced by supervision, that goggles should be worn. The non-use of goggles by workers had been reported but no management action taken. There were posters in the factory, but no campaign to enforce their use.

Contrast **_JAMES v HEPWORTH & GRANDAGE LTD (1967)_** where P, who could neither read nor write, had been employed by the respondents for 4 years, the last 6 months of which he had been working at a job involving molten metal. In an accident he had molten metal splashed on his foot and claimed damages, alleging the non-provision of safety spats. A prominent notice stated that spats were available and should be used. It was held that there was no additional legal obligation upon the employers of an illiterate workman.

d. *Proper co-ordination.* When safety depends on co-ordination of the work of a number of departments the employer must ensure that such co-ordination exists.

In *SWORD v CAMERON (1839)* employees were working in a quarry in which blasting operations were being carried out. They were not given sufficient time to get clear before an explosion took place. It was held that the employer had failed in his duty to provide proper co-ordination.

e. *Suitable working conditions.* Suitable working conditions must be provided. General conditions under which work is carried out on must, so far as reasonable care can ensure, be consistent with safety.

In *McGHEE v NCB (1971)* P worked in a brick-making plant. No washing facilities were provided and he had to cycle several miles to his home after work. He contracted dermatitis. It was held that the ailment was mainly attributable to the employer's failure to provide suitable working conditions.

But the employer is not liable when he does not control the premises.

In *CILIA v H.M. JAMES & SONS (1954)* during the installation of plumbing a plumber's mate was electrocuted due to defective electrical wiring in the building. It was held that the employer was not liable as he was not in occupation of the building.

f. *Sufficient men for the task.* It is the employer's duty to ensure that there are sufficient employees to perform a task.

In *HARDAKER v HUBY (1962)* the employer was liable for not providing a plumber with a mate to help in carrying a bath upstairs.

g. *Hours of work and stress-related illness.* It is now recognized that a foreseeable risk to the health and safety of employees will include hours of work, shift patterns and how work is organized by the employer. Employees working long possibly unsociable hours with over-burdensome workloads can suffer ill-health and employers must recognize this as a risk factor in modern day work practices and plan accordingly to manage that risk.

The *WORKING TIME REGULATIONS 1998* set out broad criteria for employers as to hours and patterns of work for all employees both full-time and part-time, these include:

i.   A maximum working week of 48 hours calculated over a 17 week period.

ii.   A minimum of 4 weeks paid annual leave.

iii. Daily rest periods of at least 11 hours between each working day.

iv.   A weekly rest period of 24 hours in each 7-day period of work. This may be averaged over a 2-week period.

v.   An in work rest break of 20 minutes for employees working more than 6 hours a day.

vi.   The hours which night shift workers do should not exceed an average of 8 hours for a 24-hour period of the 17-week 'reference period'.

h. The *ASYLUM AND IMMIGRATION ACT 1996* requires that employers take steps to check the existence of certain key documents of potential employees. Failure to carry out the checks may result in a fine on the employer of up to £5000. The Act does not apply to employees under the age of 16 or to self-employed or agency workers.

LIMITATIONS ON THE EMPLOYER'S DUTIES

9. The following show the extent of the employer's duties with regard to safety provisions.

a. *Reasonable safety is all that is required.*

i. Where there are generally accepted safety measures in a particular trade there would be a prima facie breach of duty if the employer failed to take them. However, it may well be that an accepted trade practice is a bad practice and the employer may be liable if he neglects to take precautions even though trade practice has been complied with.

In *POTEC v EDINBURGH CORPORATION (1964)* P's job was to stand on a platform at a refuse depot over a deep trench keeping the refuse moving with a long pole. He fell into the trench and contended that there should have been a guard rail. Such rails were not provided at other depots because of overwhelming evidence that a guard rail would impede the use of the pole. It was held that the employer was not liable.

Contrast *CAVANAGH v ULSTER WEAVING CO LTD (1959)* where P fell whilst going down a ladder on a sloping roof. Common practice was that no hand-rail was provided. It was held that although trade practice had been complied with, it was not conclusive proof that the employer had met his obligations at law and he was liable.

ii. Where there are unusual circumstances special safety measures should be taken.

In *PARIS v STEPNEY BOROUGH COUNCIL (1951)* P a garage mechanic with one eye, lost his other eye in an accident. No goggles had been provided. It was held that whilst goggles were not usually provided, the employer should have provided them in this case because of the greater risk to eyesight involved.

Contrast *CORK v KIRBY MACLEAN LTD (1952)* P suffered injury caused partly by a breach of statutory duty by his employers and partly by reason of a fall caused by an epileptic fit. It was held that he was contributorily negligent by failing to notify his employer that he suffered from epilepsy. Consequently his damages were reduced by half.

iii. Whilst the employer must do everything reasonable to protect the employee from injury he need not go so far as to dismiss an adult worker because the work is likely to endanger him. If an employer were to conceal risk or fail to give an employee enough information for him to assess the risk, then there may be liability.

In *WITHERS v PERRY CHAIN CO LTD (1961)* P contracted dermatitis due to working in greasy conditions. She was moved to another job considered free from this hazard. However, she continued to suffer attacks of the ailment and was off work for long periods. It was held that the employer was not negligent in allowing P to continue at work as the only alternative would have been to dismiss her.

iv. The burden of proof is on the claimant who must show that:

(a) The respondent (employer) was in breach of his duty to take care, and

(b) This breach was the direct cause of the claimant's (employee's) injuries.

In *McWILLIAMS v SIR WILLIAM ARROL (1962)* the employer failed to provide safety harness for the employee who fell to his death because of the lack of a harness. Evidence was produced to show that the employee would not have worn his safety equipment even if it had been provided. The employer was not liable.

b. *Provision of tools.* Under the *EMPLOYERS' LIABILITY (DEFECTIVE EQUIPMENT) ACT 1969*, should any tools supplied to the employee prove to be defective in any way, thus causing injury to the user, the employer shall be liable to the employee. The employer's remedy is to sue the manufacturer.

c. *Protection of the employee's property.* The employer's common law duty for safety extends only to the employee's person and not his property. There may, however, be a tortious liability on the basis of a duty owed by occupiers to lawful visitors. Tucker L.J. said in *DEYONG V SHENBURN (1946)* that there is no reason why an employer knowing his servant has placed property in his care shall not be under a duty, as a neighbour, to take reasonable care of it. Furthermore there may be an express contractual duty.

In *EDWARDS v WEST HERTS HOSPITAL COMMITTEE (1957)* a resident surgeon had personal property stolen from his room at the hostel where he lived. There were no security arrangements at the hostel. It was held that the employers had no liability for the safety of employees' personal possessions.

Contrast *McCARTHY v DAILY MIRROR (1949)* where an employee had clothing stolen from a peg. It was held that this was not 'adequate accommodation' which was required to be provided for employees' clothing under the *FACTORIES ACT 1961*.

REFERENCES AND TESTIMONIALS

10. *Obligation to Give References* An employer is not obliged to give references to his employees.

In *GALLEAR v J.F. WATSON & SON LTD (1979)* a dismissed employee claimed compensation for the failure of his employers to give him a reference. It was held that there is no implied duty to provide a reference and therefore there was no entitlement to compensation.

However, if an employer does give a reference he may be liable to a charge of defamation of character if any statement tends to lower the employee 'in the eyes of right-thinking people'.

11. *Action by the Claimant and Respondent* The law relating to defamation including the action to be taken by the claimant and the defences open to the respondent, is outlined in Chapter 27. Also, there may be an alternative remedy in *negligence*. In *SPRING V GUARDIAN ASSURANCE (1994)* S failed to get a number of jobs for which he applied because of an unfavourable and inaccurate reference given to him by the respondent employer. The judge found that there was a duty of care owed to S and that a case could be based in negligence (see Chapter 24).

12. ***Qualified Privilege*** Generally an employer would claim that a reference he gave was subject to qualified privilege, i.e., being made in good faith by a person who has a legal, social or moral duty to make it, to a person who has a similar interest or duty to receive it (i.e. a subsequent employer). The success of this defence depends on the statement having been made carefully, honestly and without malice.

13. ***Untrue References***

   a.　If an employer knowingly recommends an employee in terms which he knows to be false, the subsequent misconduct of the employee may render his former employer liable for damages in the tort of deceit.

   b.　However, if the misstatement is negligent the employer may be liable to the recipient and the employee for negligent misrepresentation if either suffers consequential loss – ***HEDLEY BYRNE & CO LTD v HELLER & PARTNERS LTD (1964)***.

   In ***McNALLY v WELLTRADE INTERNATIONAL LTD (1978)*** the employer was held liable in damages for negligent misrepresentation when he led the employee to believe that the job in Libya to which the employee was being sent was within the employee's capabilities.

14. The ***EQUALITY ACT 2010*** prohibits discrimination after the end of an employment relationship e.g. an unreasonable refusal to supply a reference. Other anti-discrimination legislation deals in a similar way with regard to: age, gender re-assignment, pregnancy and maternity, race, religion and belief, sexual orientation and disability (see Chapter 55).

15. ***REHABILITATION OF OFFENDERS ACT 1974.*** Under this Act a person's convictions will not be subject to disclosure after a lapse of time. Some more serious offences are not subject to non-disclosure. The effect of this in regard to references is that an employer is not bound to disclose a spent conviction to another subsequent employer, and will therefore incur no liability.

16. The ***TELECOMMUNICATIONS (LAWFUL BUSINESS PRACTICE) (INTERCEPTION OF COMMUNICATIONS) REGULATIONS 2000*** provide employers with lawful no-consent access to their employees' use of e-mail and other communications in order to establish whether the use is related to the employers' business. In addition, the employer can record employee communications without consent where:

   a.　It is necessary to establish the existence of facts relevant to the business of the employer, for example, keeping records of transactions and other communications where it is necessary to know the specific facts of a particular conversation.

   b.　To ascertain compliance with regulatory or self-regulatory practices that apply to an employer's business.

   c.　To demonstrate that certain standards are being achieved using the telecoms system, for example, quality control and/or staff training.

   d.　To prevent or detect crime.

   e.　To detect and investigate unauthorized use of the employer's telecoms systems.

   f.　To ensure the effective operation of systems as by monitoring for viruses or other matters that threaten the system.

   The Act also allows monitoring, but not recording, without consent where:

   i.　It is necessary to determine whether or not communications are relevant to the business, for example, checking e-mail accounts.

ii.   In regard to communications that are to a confidential, anonymous counselling or support helpline.

Where an employer wishes to rely on the Act he is required to make all reasonable efforts to bring to the attention of employees that their communications might be intercepted.

EMPLOYER'S DUTY TO PERSONS OTHER THAN EMPLOYEES (SEE ALSO CHAPTERS 23.10–14)

15. The employer (as occupier of premises) has only the duty of common care to see that a visitor will be reasonably safe in using the premises for the purpose for which he is invited or permitted by the owner to be there. 'Common care' is a duty to take such care as in all the circumstances is reasonable. A 'visitor' is anyone who has expressed or implied permission of the occupier to be on the premises. This is in contrast to a 'trespasser', one who enters premises or land without permission (if continued acts of trespass are ignored it could be implied that the person was a 'visitor').

However, there is also a statutory duty under the *HEALTH AND SAFETY AT WORK ACT 1974* for an employer to give information about potential dangers on his premises to all persons working on the premises.

In *R. v SWAN HUNTER SHIPBUILDERS LTD (1981)* eight men were killed when a fire broke out on HMS Glasgow. The fire was especially intense because the vessel was badly ventilated and oxygen had escaped from a hose kit left by an employee of a firm of subcontractors. It was held that the subcontractors had not been given sufficient information about the dangers of oxygen enrichment in confined spaces, nor, such instruction as was necessary to ensure the safety of all the workers on the vessel, no matter by whom they were employed.

Note: Contravention of the *HEALTH AND SAFETY AT WORK ACT 1974* gives rise to criminal liability.

a.   The occupier is entitled to assume that the visitor will guard against the normal hazards of his own trade, i.e. where the visitor is performing work on the premises – *ROLES v NATHAN (1963)*. In this case a sweep was poisoned by dangerous fumes in a chimney.

b.   The occupier must, however, give suitable warnings of 'traps', i.e., slippery floors, steep staircases, etc.

c.   The occupier will be liable if the visitor's possessions are stolen, only where the occupier can be proved to be negligent.

d.   Where a visitor is injured through the negligence of an independent contractor working on the premises, the contractor will be liable. However, the burden of proof is on the occupier to give 'beyond reasonable doubt' facts to show that it was the fault of the contractor. In *O'CONNOR v SWAN & EDGAR (1963)* the contractors were liable when a ceiling under repair fell and injured a shopper.

e.   The position of a person other than a 'visitor' is covered by the *OCCUPIERS LIABILITY ACT 1984* (see Chapter 23.10).

VICARIOUS LIABILITY (SEE CHAPTER 22.11)

16. Where a person is injured by another the rule at common law is that the injured party may sue the actual wrongdoer. Where the wrongdoer is an employee the injured party may also have an action against the employer. This is 'vicarious liability', i.e., although the employer did not personally commit the wrong, he may be held responsible for all those who are employed by him. The third party will usually sue the employer as he is usually in a better financial position to meet a claim for damages.

17. Vicarious liability arises in two ways. Firstly, by an employer authorizing a wrongful act. Secondly, although the employer did not authorize the act the employee performed it in the course of employment. This may appear to be unfair, but the view is taken that, by employing a person, the employer makes it possible for him to commit the wrong. It is regarded as a normal business risk undertaken by the employer for which he would be wise to take out insurance.

18. *Circumstances of Vicarious Liability* The following are cases in which attempts have been made to clarify the position. Generally speaking the employer is deemed to be liable for the acts of an employee committed in the course of employment during contractual hours of work and whilst he is performing a task for which he is employed:

    a. The employee carries out an authorized task, but in a *wrongful manner*.

       In *LCC v CATTERMOLES GARAGE (1953)* an employee was employed to remove vehicles that blocked the garage entrance. As he had no licence he was instructed to push them by hand. On one occasion he drove a vehicle and caused an accident. It was held that the employers were liable for the damages as the employee had done what he was employed to do, albeit in an unauthorized manner.

    b. The employee commits a wrongful act that was *expressly forbidden* – *LIMPUS v LONDON GENERAL OMNIBUS CO (1862)*. The court found the employer liable; the employee was acting within the scope of his employment and it did not matter that the employer had expressly forbidden the wrongful act.

    c. The employee commits a *wilful wrong*, even though it was a *criminal offence* – *LLOYD v GRACE, SMITH & CO (1912)*. Here the employer would be vicariously liable even though the act was done for the benefit of the employee not his employer.

       In *LISTER V HESLEY HALL LTD (2001)* a warden employed by the defendant systematically abused children with emotional difficulties in the care of a special school. The House of Lords (now the Supreme Court) held the employer liable; the criminal acts were carried out within the scope of his employment; the employer had placed him in the position that enabled him to carry out the abuse. In so finding the House of Lords overruled an earlier decision in *TROTMAN V NORTH YORKSHIRE CC (1998)* where it was held that acts of sexual abuse were beyond the scope of employment so that the employer was not liable.

    d. The employee acts *negligently*.

       In *CENTURY INSURANCE v N IRELAND ROAD TRANSPORT BOARD (1942)* a lorry driver was smoking whilst transferring petrol from his tanker to a store. A fire resulted. It was held that the driver's employer was vicariously liable.

       Contrast *WILLIAMS v JONES (1865)* where the defendant's employee was making a signboard in a shed the floor of which was littered with wood shavings. He lit his pipe and the shed burned down. It was held that the employer was not liable as the act was not deemed to be negligent.

In the Century Insurance case there was an element of danger and lighting a cigarette amounted to negligence. In the second case lighting a pipe was not necessarily negligent in relation to the making of a signboard.

e. The employee *wrongfully permits another* to perform his duties – *ILKIW v SAMUELS (1963)*.

f. The employee makes a mistake.

In *BAYLEY v MANCHESTER, SHEFFIELD & LINCOLNSHIRE RAILWAY CO (1872)* P, a passenger, was forcibly ejected from a train onto the platform by a zealous porter who believed him (wrongly) to be on the wrong train. It was held that the company was vicariously liable for the injury caused by their employee's mistake.

19. Acts committed in an emergency, in the protection of the employers' property, are classed as being in the course of employment.

In *POLAND v JOHN PARR & SONS (1927)* an employee struck a boy whom he thought was stealing from his employer's wagon. The employer was liable. He would not have been liable if the carter's act had been so excessive as to take it out of the class of authorized acts.

20. Employers are not liable for the acts of their employees which are done outside the course of employment, even though they are closely connected with employment.

In *WARREN v HENLYS LTD (1948)* a petrol pump attendant engaged in a fight with a customer over payment. It was held that the employer was not liable as the matter had become personal, outside the course of employment.

21. When an employee uses his employer's property for purposes of his own unconnected with his employment the employer will not be liable even though he gave consent for the use of his property.

In *HILTON v THOMAS BURTON LTD (1961)* employees who were allowed to use their employer's van for reasonable purposes used it to drive to a cafe whilst awaiting their normal finishing time. On the way back there was an accident due to negligent driving. It was held that the employer was not liable as the employees were acting outside the course of employment 'on a frolic of their own'.

22. *Lifts Given in Employer's Vehicle* The following cases are examples of court decisions on this matter.

In *TWINE v BEAN'S EXPRESS (1946)* a driver employed by the defendants gave a lift to a person who was killed due to the employee's negligent driving. The employee had been expressly forbidden to give lifts and a notice to this effect was displayed in the vehicle. It was held that the employer was not vicariously liable as the driver's action was outside the scope of his employment and the injured person was deemed to be a trespasser.

In *YOUNG v EDWARD BOX & CO LTD (1951)* P was a workman employed by the defendants. He was responsible for getting himself to and from his workplace. However, due to the inadequacy of public transport on Sundays it had become the practice to get a lift in his employer's vehicle. Young was injured in the course of one of these journeys.

It was held that the employer was liable as the claimant's driver and foreman had concurred to the lifts and this was within the ostensible authority of the foreman. Thus the claimant had become a licensee and was not a trespasser.

However, Denning L.J. dissenting said

'The liability of the owner does not depend on whether the passenger was a trespasser or not; it depends on whether the driver was acting within the scope of his employment.'

Contrast *ROSE v PLENTY (1976)* (Chapter 22.13).

23. *Acts for the Exclusive Benefit of the Employee* If an act is not only forbidden but done for the exclusive benefit of the employee, the employer is not liable.

In *RAND v CRAIG (1919)* carters employed by the respondent took rubbish to land owned by the claimant and tipped it there, instead of onto a dump provided by their employer which was further off. They did this as they were paid per load.

Contrast *PERFORMING RIGHTS SOCIETY v MITCHELL & BOOKER LTD (1924)* where P accused D of infringing copyrights by performance of certain dance music in their dance hall. The band had a clause in its contract forbidding the infringement of copyright and D tried to claim that they did so for their own benefit. It was held that the band infringed the copyright in the course of employment and for the benefit of the dance hall.

TIME OFF WORK

24. *Trade Union Duties* Under the *TRADE UNION AND LABOUR RELATIONS (CONSOLIDATION) ACT 1992* an employer is obliged to permit an employee who is an official of an independent trade union recognized for collective bargaining purposes to take reasonable time off, with pay, during working hours. This is to enable the employee to carry out official duties concerned with industrial relations and to undergo relevant training in respect of these duties.

25. *Trade Union Activities* An employer is similarly obliged to allow reasonable unpaid time off for the purpose of taking part in certain trade union activities. The activities are those in which the employee takes part as a member or in his capacity as a representative, but not activities classed as industrial action.

26. *Public Duties* Under *S.50 EMPLOYMENT RIGHTS ACT 1996* an employer is obliged to permit time off, without pay, during working hours for the purpose of performing certain public duties, including Justice of the Peace, member of a local authority or a statutory tribunal, etc. The amount of time off allowed must be reasonable taking into account the length of time for the duty, time off already taken and the effect on the business of the employee's absence.

27. *To Look for Work or Make Arrangements for Training* *S.52 EMPLOYMENT RIGHTS ACT 1996* gives a right to an employee who is dismissed for redundancy, and has at least 2 years service, to reasonable time off with pay to look for new employment or to make arrangements for training.

28. *Safety Representatives* An employer shall permit a safety representative to take such time off with pay during the employee's working hours as shall be necessary to enable the safety representative to:

    a.   Perform his functions under the Act.

    b.   Undergo training to enable him to perform these functions.

29. *For Antenatal Care* An employee has a right not to be unreasonably refused paid time off during working hours to keep an appointment for antenatal care prescribed by a registered

medical practitioner, registered midwife or registered health visitor. This right is accorded to all pregnant employees irrespective of hours worked weekly or length of service. Except in the case of the first appointment the right to time off is specifically linked with attendance at appointments and the employer may require the employee to produce a certificate stating that she is pregnant and documentary evidence that an appointment has been made (see Chapter 54.21).

30. ***Complaints for Refusal to give Time Off*** In all cases where a complaint is made to an employment tribunal relating to an employer's duty to permit time off, the complaint must be presented within 3 months of the date when the alleged failure occurred, or within a reasonable time when the tribunal is satisfied that it was not reasonably practicable to present the complaint within 3 months.

DISCLOSURE OF INFORMATION

31. *Trade Union and Labour Relations (Consolidation) Act 1992*

    a. *Duty to disclose.* An independent trade union recognized by an employer for collective bargaining purposes may request either orally, or if required by the employer, in writing:

       i. Information without which the trade union representative would be materially impeded in carrying on the collective bargaining, and

       ii. Information which it would be in accordance with good industrial relations practice that the employer should disclose to the trade union representative for the purpose of collective bargaining.

    b. *Exceptions.*

       i. Against the interests of national security.

       ii. In contravention of a statutory prohibition.

       iii. Communicated to the employer in confidence.

       iv. Relating to an individual without his consent.

       v. Likely to cause substantial injury to the business.

       vi. Information concerned with legal proceedings.

    c. *Failure to disclose.* If an employer fails to disclose information the matter may be referred to ACAS. Alternatively and when the ACAS has failed in its attempt at a conciliation the CAC will hear and settle the complaint. If the CAC finds the complaint wholly or partly justified it may make a declaration, specifying:

       i. The unfounded information.

       ii. The date the employer failed to supply the information.

       iii. A period (being not less than 1 week after the declaration) within which the information must be disclosed.

32. *Health & Safety At Work Act 1974*

    a. *Employees.*

       i. To provide the employees with such information as is necessary to ensure their health and safety at work (this requirement is tested on the basis of what information could have reasonably been discovered or known by the employer and therefore disclosed), and

    ii.   To prepare, and bring to the notice of all their employees, a written statement of their general policy regarding health and safety at work of their employees and the organization and arrangements for the implementation of that policy. Moreover, any revision of this written statement must also be brought to the notice of employees.

  b. *Safety Representatives.* Additionally, safety representatives are entitled to inspect and take copies of any document which their employer is legally obliged to keep (except health records of identifiable individuals). Moreover, the employer is obliged to provide safety representatives with any information in his possession relating to health, safety or welfare which will enable the representatives to fulfil their functions except:

    i.   Any information the disclosure of which would be against the interests of national security, or

    ii.   Any information which he could not disclose without contravening a prohibition imposed by or under some enactment, or

    iii.   Any information relating specifically to an individual, unless the individual has consented to the disclosure, or

    iv.   Any information the disclosure of which would, for reasons other than its effect on health, safety or welfare at work, cause substantial injury to the employer's undertaking or, where the information was supplied to the employer by some other person, to the undertaking of that other person, or

    v.   Any information obtained by the employer for the purpose of bringing, prosecuting or defending any legal proceedings.

SELF TEST QUESTIONS

Self Test Questions No. 50 (for Answers see Appendix 1):

1   What are the common law duties owed by the employer?

2   What are the limitations on the employer's duties?

3   Explain the duties owed by the employer to persons other than employees.

4   What is *vicarious liability*?

5   What are the occasions where an employer is required to give 'time off work' to his employees?

6   What are the disclosure requirements placed upon the employer by a recognized trade union?

WAGES

53

Learning Outcomes

At the end of this chapter you should be able to:

- Outline the main provisions relating to the National Minimum Wage Act 1998.

- Explain what are the common law duties placed upon the employer with regard to pay.

- Understand what unauthorized pay deductions are.

- Outline the nature and purpose of the equal pay.

- Explain the various guaranteed payments which must be made to employees.

- State the legal requirements regarding the content of pay statements for employees.

INTRODUCTION

1. a. The contract of employment usually gives details of the amount to be paid, payment during absence from work, method of payment, etc. In the absence of express terms other terms have been implied by the courts. In addition a body of statute law has arisen

governing such things as deductions from pay etc. The *NATIONAL MINIMUM WAGE ACT 1998* (*NMWA*) empowers the Secretary of State to set a minimum wage which all employers must pay. The *EMPLOYMENT ACT 2008* amends NMWA in providing a clearer framework for enforcement.

b. *Entitlement.* Persons must be *workers* working ordinarily in the UK under a *contract of employment* (*S.1(2)* and S.*54(3)* NMWA). Part-time workers, agency workers and home workers are all covered by the Act. Self-employed and voluntary workers, and members of the armed forces, are excluded. Directors of 'one-man-companies' where the directors are also the major shareholders, *is* covered by the Act and must receive the minimum wage and the company must pay National Insurance Contributions. If the company is wound up and a sole trader or partnership business is put in its place, any former directors would become self-employed and so exempt. A spouse employed in a family business (provided it is not a company) is excluded under the 'family business' exemption provisions.

c. *Amount.* The National Minimum Wage rates are, for workers aged:

21 and over	£6.08
18 to 20	£4.98
16 to 17	£3.68
Apprentices	£2.60

Persons of compulsory school age are not entitled to the National Minimum Wage. The rate is set by the Low Pay Commission and is based upon the economic climate, it is not automatic.

d. *Wages.* Section *27* of the *EMPLOYMENT RIGHTS ACTS 1996* provides a statutory definition of the meaning of wages, it includes: any fee, bonus, commission and holiday pay.

e. *Enforcement.* Employers are required to keep records relating to pay, and workers are given a right of access to those records. Workers can require the employer to produce records for inspection which may be copied. For this to happen, a worker must show a belief based upon reasonable grounds that a breach of the NMWA has occurred. Failure by the employer to supply records to a worker can be taken to an employment tribunal who can award compensation. The burden of proof is on the employer to show that the National Minimum Wage is being paid. A worker is protected from suffering any detriment at the hands of the employer for making a complaint, any dismissal would be automatically unfair (see Chapter 56.20). The worker has a 3-month period from suspecting a breach, to bring an action; the 3-month period may be extended by a tribunal where it considers there are just grounds for doing so. Her Majesty's Revenue and Customs (HMRC) monitor wages through employer records provided for tax assessment purposes and may enforce the Act on behalf of individual workers as well as serve penalty notices on employers for failing to comply with the Act. The employer then has 4 weeks to appeal against such a notice.

PAY UNDER COMMON LAW

2. The following are the employer's duties to his employees in the absence of express provision in the contract of employment.

a. *Amount of pay.* The employer must pay the agreed remuneration or what is reasonable in the circumstances.

b. *Availability of work.* There is an entitlement to pay even though employees cannot work because no work is available. Time workers are paid for being ready, willing and able to work for their agreed hours.

    In *TURNER v SAWDON & CO (1901)* it was held that the employer had a duty only to pay wages, not to provide work to a man employed as a salesman.

c. *Pieceworkers.* Pieceworkers are also paid for being ready, willing and able. It is up to the employer to find them work (*DEVONALD v ROSSER (1906)*).

    In *MINNEVITCH v CAFE DÉ PARIS (LONDRES) LTD (1936)* musicians were employed under a contract including a clause to the effect that they would not be paid if they did not play. It was held that the clause implied that they were not entitled to receive pay for such performances their employer thought fit to cancel. This was not valid – it was up to the employer to find the musicians work to enable them to earn their remuneration.

d. If there is no work available due to circumstances outside the control of the employer, then he is under no obligation to pay his employees. Each case must be examined in the light of the circumstances.

    In *BROWNING v CRUMLIN VALLEY COLLIERIES LTD (1916)* a mine became unsafe due to flooding and work stopped. It was held that the circumstances were outside the employer's control and there was therefore no need to pay wages.

    Contrast *JONES v HARRY SHERMAN (1969)* where due to an outbreak of foot and mouth disease racing was cancelled and a turf accountant did not need so many employees. It was held that the right to 'lay-off' could not be implied into a contract of employment at fixed or guaranteed periodic wages.

e. *Overtime.* Overtime is payable when expressly agreed in the contract, or is customary. Where the overtime is expressed as obligatory the employer must provide overtime and the employee must serve it.

f. *Discretionary payments.* An employee cannot claim, as a right, a payment which has always been stated 'to be within the management's discretion' however, often and regularly it may have been paid.

    In *GRIEVE v IMPERIAL TOBACCO CO LTD (1963)* part of an annual gift was withheld from P after he took part in a strike. It was held that the company was entitled to withhold a gratuitous payment, despite the argument that it had become a term of the contract.

    However, a contractual bonus which has been earned cannot legally be withheld.

g. *Payment during illness.* Payments during periods when an employee is absent due to illness will depend on the custom of the trade or industry, or of individual firms. In the absence of any agreement or custom the following will apply:

    i. There is an implied right to receive payment.

        In *ORMAN v SAVILLE SPORTSWEAR LTD (1960)* P, a production manager, had been off work ill for 10 weeks. It was held that there was an implied term in his contract that he should be entitled to pay during sickness. It was considered that if there had been an express term that he would not be entitled. P would not have accepted the contract.

ii. The implied right can successfully be rebutted where the conduct of the employee shows that his right has been foregone.

In *O'GRADY v SAPER LTD (1940)* P, a doorman at a cinema, had never previously received pay during illness. He claimed pay after seeing the report of another case. It was held that he was not entitled, as the conduct of the parties showed that there was an implied term excluding payment during illness.

iii. An employer may expressly exclude his liability from paying wages during sickness.

In *PETRIE v MACFISHERIES LTD (1940)* a notice on the wall stated that payments made during sickness were ex-gratia payments, and indicated the amounts usually paid. It was held that the clause showed that payments were not made as of right during sickness.

h. *Suspension without pay.* The power to suspend an employee without pay must be provided for expressly or implicitly by contract. Suspension without pay in the absence of contractual power will amount to a repudiatory breach of contract of employment (i.e. constructive dismissal, see Chapter 56.22.c).

UNAUTHORIZED DEDUCTIONS FROM WAGES

3. *S.2 EMPLOYMENT RIGHTS ACT 1996* introduced new protection for employees. The Act simplified the law and put manual and non-manual workers on the same basis.

4. *Deductions from Pay* Deductions from an employee's pay will be unlawful unless:

a. Authorized by statute, e.g. income tax, national insurance contributions.

b. Agreed in the contract of employment, or

c. Agreed in advance by the employee in writing.

d. An employer may not receive payment from an employee unless in accordance with a., b. and c. above.

e. An employer may make deductions from wages or receive payments in respect of:

i. Overpayment of wages or expenses.

ii. Disciplinary proceedings in respect of a statutory provision.

iii. Payment to a third person if agreed in writing by the employee.

iv. The employee's participation in a strike or other industrial action.

v. An order by a court or tribunal.

f. 'Check-off' – authorization

An employer may not deduct union subscriptions from a worker's wages in respect of check-off arrangements unless the worker has authorized these deductions in writing within the last 3 years, and has not withdrawn his authorization. If the subscriptions are increased the employer must give at least 1-month notice before deductions are made at the higher rate. At the same time the worker must be reminded that he has the right to withdraw authorization at any time. Any contravention of these rules gives the worker the right of complaint to an industrial tribunal.

5. ***Retail Employment*** In the event of employees in the retail trade who suffer deductions from their pay on account of stock or cash deficiencies, any deduction will be limited to 10% of wages. The same limit will apply to any payment required by an employer.

6. ***Complaints to an Employment Tribunal*** An employee who considers he has been subjected to an unlawful deduction may go to an employment tribunal.

EQUAL PAY

7. ***Purpose*** The *EQUALITY ACT 2010* (*S.66–70*) (The Act) has the object of eliminating discrimination between men and women in regard to pay and other conditions of employment (e.g. overtime, bonus, output and piecework payments, holidays and sick leave entitlement). Pay is given a broad definition and includes male travel concessions not given to females; part-time employees not receiving sick pay when it was paid to full-time employees; differing redundancy payments; denial of access to compensation from a tribunal.

8. ***Persons Covered*** The Act extends to all persons under a contract of employment, full- or part-time, irrespective of age or length of service. Sex discrimination is forbidden in regard to all terms of employment, except:

   a. Where the work is wholly or mainly outside Great Britain.

   b. Members of the armed forces.

   c. Where statute law requires discrimination.

   d. A woman may enjoy privileges in respect of pregnancy and childbirth.

   e. In provisions for death or retirement.

9. ***Right to Equal Treatment*** The Act (*S.66*) imposes an equality clause into the terms of every contract of employment. This requires that terms in an employee's contract must not be less favourable than the terms in the contract of an employee of the opposite sex with regard to pay or other terms. This applies providing the work they are doing is:

   a. Like work with a man in the same employment (*S.65(1)(b)*). The work being undertaken by the comparator does not have to be identical, minor differences of no practical importance can be ignored, but there has not got to be a material difference in jobs. The approach taken by a tribunal will be to look at the nature and frequency of tasks actually being undertaken by the claimant and comparator and not confine itself to the express terms of the contract of employment. In ***CAPPER PASS LTD v LAWTON (1977)*** a female cook worked 40 hours per week preparing food for directors of the company. She received lower pay than two male chefs who worked 45 hours per week preparing 350 meals for workers. She claimed she should be paid the same hourly rate as the male chefs as her work was broadly similar and should be regarded as *like work*. The Employment Appeal Tribunal found that the jobs were broadly similar and that differences of detail were of no practical importance, she was entitled to be paid the same rate as her male comparators.

b.   Although the work is different it has been rated of equal value under a job evaluation exercise (*S.65(1)(b)*). Employers frequently carry out what are known as a job evaluation exercises where the role, skill and responsibilities of different workers are objectively assessed and pay is based upon those different levels of skill and responsibility. In this way a company driver, for example, could be assessed as being of *equal value* warranting equal pay, with say a clerical worker.

In *DUGDALE & OTHERS v KRAFT FOODS LTD (1976)* P and other women claimed unfair discrimination with regard to pay, when they received lower basic rates of pay than men who worked on a night shift and on Sundays The woman did work which was broadly similar to the men. The tribunal held that merely because the men worked at a different time did not constitute a difference of practical importance. Therefore the women should receive the same basic pay as the men.

c.   Employed on work which in terms of the demands made, is of *equal value* to that of a man in the same employment (*S.65(1)(c)*). This is an additional head of claim where there has been no job evaluation exercise carried out and work being done by a comparator is completely different. A claim for *work of equal value* can be made even if a job evaluation exercise has been carried out, provided there are reasonable grounds for believing that the exercise was not objective and was itself discriminatory on the grounds of sex.

In *HAYWARD v CAMMEL LAIRD (1984)* P was a cook employed in a shipyard. The House of Lords (now the Supreme Court) held that her work was of equal value to the company as men employed at the yard in other trades – painter, engineer and joiner – and she was therefore entitled to equal pay. This section of the Act enables claims to be made that a woman's work is equal to a male comparator where it is neither like the man's work, nor rated equivalent, but it is nonetheless equal in terms of the demands made upon her when taking account of factors such as, effort, skill, responsibility, decision-making, etc.

10. *A Comparator* The comparison of jobs may be made with an actual employee of the opposite sex employed with the same employer or another establishment owned by the same employer, or which is a member of the same group of companies or with a hypothetical comparator (*S.79*).

In *BRITISH COAL CORPORATION v SMITH (1996)* female canteen workers and cleaners employed at 47 different establishments of British Coal were allowed to compare themselves with male surface workers and clerical staff working at four different establishments; the Court finding that common terms and conditions for purposes of the Act would be found where they were substantially comparable on a broad basis. They did not have to be identical.

A not inconsiderable barrier in the past to making a claim for equal pay, is where employees are prohibited from disclosing their terms and conditions of employment to others. Some employers actively sought to pursue policies that encourage secrecy amongst the work-force. Now, under the Act, where an employee's contract of employment prohibits the disclosure or any requests for information about employment terms and conditions, insofar as this relates to a relevant pay disclosure, such a term is unenforceable (*S.77*). This should make the finding of a relevant comparator easier and so bring about more equal pay claims.

10. *Material difference defence* (*S.69*)

Where it has been established that an employee is entitled to equal treatment under a., b. or c. above, the employer would be liable unless he could prove that the variation in pay was genuinely due to a *material difference* not based on the sex of the parties. It has to be based upon a genuine need of the business and be a proportionate means of achieving that aim. For example, the higher pay may be due to longer service or higher productivity or because an employee has moved from a higher paid job to a lower one, but his higher rate of pay has been preserved (this is known as 'red circling'). As seen in a. above (when assessing whether there is *like work*), a tribunal will look at the reality of the employment relationship and not confine itself solely to the express terms of the contract of employment when seeking to assess whether there is a *material difference*. For example, if an employee is paid more for having more responsibility, the employer would need to demonstrate that those responsibilities were actual and frequently required.

In *METHUEN v COW INDUSTRIAL POLYMERS LTD (1980)* a female employee sought equality with a man who was performing the same clerical job as herself, although receiving higher pay. The employers established that the man had been transferred from the shop floor because of age and sickness but his previous income and status had been preserved. It was held that the difference was due to a 'material difference' i.e., the protection of his income and position, and nothing to do with sex.

In *COOMES (HOLDINGS) LTD v SHIELDS (1978)* the employer owned a string of betting shops. In some shops the male employees were paid more than female employees, because of anticipated trouble from customers. It was held that the deterrent function of the male staff was not a genuine difference as all males received the higher rate regardless of performance of this function.

In *CAPPER PASS LTD v LAWTON (1977)* a female cook sought equal pay with male chefs. She worked in the directors' dining room preparing up to 20 lunches a day, whilst the male chefs worked in the company's canteen preparing 350 meals a day. It was held that she was employed on 'like work' and should therefore receive equal basic pay for a 40-hour week. The Act did not intend that too minute an examination of comparative work should be done.

11. *Reference to an Employment Tribunal*

   a. A woman believing that she has a right to equal treatment for any of the reasons under the Act may refer her claim to an Employment Tribunal. If the tribunal finds the complaint well-founded, it can make an order. In addition the Secretary of State may apply for an order where it appears to him that an employee has a claim for equal treatment but it is not reasonable to expect the employee to make a complaint.

   b. Reference may be made, either during employment or within 6 months of termination.

   c. Arrears of pay may be claimed for up to 2 years before the date of reference to the tribunal. Damages in respect of non-cash benefits may be claimed for the same period.

12. *European Community Law* Article 141 of the Treaty of Rome provides that women shall be accorded equal treatment for like work with men. This is superimposed on our own legislation. Where there is a conflict or where there is a gap in our own legislation the European Community law takes precedence. The interpreter of EC law is the European Court, it is then incumbent on our own courts to apply that law.

In *McCARTHYS LTD v SMITH (NO. 2) (1980)* a female worker claimed equal pay with her predecessor, a man. The case went to the European Court which ruled that, under Article 119, provided there is not a long gap between the end of one and the beginning of the other, a woman is entitled to equal pay with her predecessor.

13. *Part-Time Workers* Discrimination against part-time workers was challenged in the European Court.

In *JENKINS v KINGSGATE (1981)* all the men in a textile factory worked 40 hours a week and all except a few women worked 30 hours. The part-timers got an hourly rate of pay 10% less than those on full-time. They claimed equality. The employers said the differential was justified based upon a material factor by the need to discourage absenteeism, increase productivity and use the plant to the full. The European Court held that working shorter hours is not itself a material difference justifying unequal pay. However, a differential can be justified if it fulfils the stated needs of the employer (productivity etc.) which are non-discriminatory.

14. *Codes of Practice* To help employers understand their legal responsibilities Codes of Practice have been created to offer practical help, these may be found at http://www.equality-humanrights.com/legal-and-policy/equality-act-codes-of-practice/.

GUARANTEE PAYMENTS *(EMPLOYMENT RIGHTS ACT 1996 (ERA); S.28–34)*

15. *Guarantee Payments* These ensure that employees who are laid-off will receive some payment during that time.

16. *Entitlement* Employees will be entitled to 5 days payment in any 3-month period at a maximum daily rate specified from time to time. This is paid when an employee is laid off work for a whole day.

17. *Eligibility* To be eligible an employee must:

    a.   Have at least 1 month continuous service when the lay-off occurs.

    b.   Be laid-off for the whole of his normal working hours.

    c.   Be laid-off because of an occurrence preventing his employer providing him with work (apart from a dispute involving employees of the same or an associated employer).

    d.   Not have unreasonably refused an offer of alternative employment.

    e.   Be available for work.

18. *Exemption* Employees who are covered by a collective agreement or a wages order with a provision for guaranteed pay may be exempted from the statutory requirements.

19. *Failure to Make Payment* Where an employer fails to make an entitled guarantee payment an employment tribunal can order him to make it.

MEDICAL SUSPENSION *(ERA S.64–65)*

20. Payment during medical suspension enables an employee to receive compensation when not actually sick or disabled.

21. *Entitlement* An employer may suspend an employee on medical grounds, (e.g. when he may be exposed to radiation or lead poisoning). During such suspension an employee is entitled to receive his pay, and may do so for a maximum period of 26 weeks.

22. *Eligibility* To be eligible an employee must:

    a. Have at least 1 month continuous service.

    b. Have not refused reasonably suitable alternative employment.

    c. Be available for work should he be required.

23. *Dismissal* If the employer dismisses an employee instead of suspending him on medical grounds the employee will have the right to a claim for unfair dismissal. He need have only 4 weeks' continuous service to qualify (not the normal 1 year).

24. *Temporary Replacements* An employer may engage temporary replacements for those medically suspended. However, he must make the temporary nature of the employment clear at the outset and offer alternative employment on termination if that is possible.

25. *Failure to Make Payment* Where an employer fails to make an entitled medical suspension payment an employment tribunal can order him to make it.

INSOLVENCY *(ERA S.182–188)*

26. The *ERA* provides protection for employees in respect of amounts owing to them at the time an employer goes bankrupt or into receivership.

27. Amounts due under the Act, e.g. time-off or medical suspension will also be regarded as wages for preferential payment.

28. If the sum owed cannot be met by the liquidator or receiver the employee may apply for payment to be made from the National Insurance Fund.

29. The maximum recoverable from the liquidator is limited to 8 weeks arrears of wages subject to a maximum of up to £800 per employee. If the amount owing cannot be met by the liquidator the excess (plus other sums, i.e. wages in lieu of notice, holiday remuneration (maximum 6 weeks) and unfair dismissal compensation) may be claimed from the National Insurance Fund up to a maximum £800 per employee (subject to review by the Secretary of State).

30. Unpaid employer contributions to occupational pensions funds up to a maximum of 12 months may be paid from the National Insurance Fund.

31. Any amount due in respect of a maternity payment may be obtained from the National Insurance Fund.

PAY STATEMENTS *(ERA S.8)*

32. The *EMPLOYMENT RIGHTS ACT 1996* gave every employee the right to a written itemized pay statement. The statement must include:

a. Gross amount of wages.

b. Deductions which vary with the wage, e.g. Income Tax.

c. Total fixed deductions, e.g. trade union subscriptions.

d. Net wages payable.

33. Failure to notify deductions makes the employer liable to pay the employee a sum equal to the amount of 13-weeks deductions, on a tribunal finding.

34. In *MILSON v LEICESTERSHIRE CC (1978)* P was advanced £111 for exam fees on the basis that if he failed or resigned within a year he would pay the money back in a lump sum. He gave notice but objected to paying back the money all at once. His employers deducted the £111 from his salary under the heading of 'miscellaneous deductions'. This was deemed not to be a properly itemized pay statement and therefore the deduction was unlawful. As P suffered no financial loss the employers were ordered to pay him a nominal sum of £25.

35. *Standing Statement* Provided that the employer has given in writing a standing statement of fixed deductions, there is no need to itemize fixed deductions on an employee's pay statement, but simply to state the total amount of the deductions. The standing statement should give the following information:

a. The amount of each deduction.

b. The intervals at which the deduction is to be made, and

c. The purpose for which it is made.

This statement must be renewed after a period of 12 months.

SELF TEST QUESTIONS

Self Test Questions No. 51 (for Answers see Appendix 1):

1 Outline the main provisions of the *NATIONAL MINIMUM WAGE ACT 1998*.

2 What are the common law duties owed to an employee with regard to wages?

3 What are regarded as unauthorized deductions from wages?

4 What is the purpose and content of the *EQUAL PAY ACT 1970*?

5 What are guaranteed payments?

6 What are the requirements for the contents of pay statements?

MATERNITY RIGHTS

54

Learning Outcomes At the end of this chapter you should be able to:

- Explain the provisions for maternity leave and its protections from dismissal.

- Understand the right to return to work.

- Explain the rights associated with suspension from work.

- Explain the provisions pertaining to antenatal care.

INTRODUCTION

1. The *EMPLOYMENT RIGHTS ACT 1996 (ERA)* gives employees the right not to be dismissed by reason of pregnancy, a right to maternity pay and leave, and a right to return to work after maternity leave. The chapter outlines the main statutory provisions.

DISMISSAL

2. Dismissal of an employee for reasons of:

   a. Pregnancy.

   b. Childbirth or maternity.

   c. Adoption leave.

   d. Parental or paternity leave.

   e. Statutory time off for dependants, or

   f. The fact that she took or asked for maternity leave.

   is an *automatic unfair dismissal* (*S.99 ERA*).

MATERNITY LEAVE

3. The *MATERNITY AND PARENTAL LEAVE REGULATIONS 1999*, as amended in 2002, provide for three types of maternity leave:

   a. Ordinary maternity leave – 26 weeks.

   b. Compulsory maternity leave – 2 weeks.

   c. Additional maternity leave – 26 weeks.

   These are periods of leave, before and after childbirth to which a pregnant employee is entitled. The dates of leave are calculated as being periods before or after the *expected week of childbirth*. The employee may choose the date on which the maternity leave period starts.

4. *Ordinary Maternity Leave* An employee may be entitled to ordinary maternity leave if she satisfies certain conditions. These are as follows:

   a. No later than 15 weeks before the expected week of childbirth, she notifies her employer:

      i. That she is pregnant.

      ii. The expected week of childbirth.

      iii. The date on which she intends to start her ordinary maternity leave.

   b. The employee must give this notice in writing if requested by her employer. She is entitled to change her mind about the date for commencement of her maternity leave provided she notifies the employer at least 28 days before the new date.

   c. The employer is entitled to request medical confirmation of the expected week of childbirth and the employee is required to provide it. Failure to provide this information will remove the right to ordinary maternity leave.

   d. As a response to the notice the employer must, within 28 days, notify the employee of the date when ordinary maternity leave will end.

   Ordinary maternity leave runs for a period of 12 months regardless of length of service.

5. *Compulsory Maternity Leave* An employer must not allow a woman who is entitled to ordinary maternity leave to work during the compulsory leave period. Compulsory leave is for 2 weeks commencing with the day on which childbirth occurs. These 2 weeks form part of the 26 week ordinary maternity leave period.

6. *Additional Maternity Leave* An employee is entitled to additional maternity leave where she can show:

   a. Entitlement to ordinary maternity leave.

   b. At the beginning of the 14th week before the expected week of childbirth, she has been continuously employed for a period of not less than 26 weeks.

   Additional maternity leave commences on the day after the last day of her ordinary maternity leave period and is for an additional period of 26 weeks.

7. *Maternity* **Pay** During the maternity leave period, the employee is entitled to all benefits contained in her terms and conditions of employment, *except wages or salary*. This means she will only be entitled to wages or salary if her contract of employment expressly so provides. However, *statutory maternity pay* is payable for 39 weeks.

   If a woman has been employed by her employer for at least 26 weeks, ending with the 15th week before the expected week of childbirth, and earns at least £95 per week, then, although she is not entitled to be paid her salary, she will receive *statutory maternity pay* (*SMP*) during the ordinary maternity leave 1-year period. There are two levels of *SMP*:

   a. *The higher rate* is paid for the first 6 weeks. This is equivalent to 90% of the woman's salary. After this she is paid;

   b. *The lower rate*, which is £128.73 per week, unless the employee does not usually earn that much. This runs for 33 weeks.

   SMP is payable by the employer; 92% of amounts paid by way of *SMP* can be recovered. For the small employer (defined as those who pay, in any 1 year, less than £45 000 national insurance contributions) 100% is recoverable plus 4.5% of each *SMP* payment, this is designed to allow the small employer to recover national insurance contributions payable on such payments.

   Maternity allowance, is payable to women who earn at least £30 a week, but who do not qualify for maternity pay from their employer. This amount is £128.73 per week, or 90% of the woman's weekly salary, whichever is the smaller, and is payable for 9 months.

   The *EQUALITY ACT 2010* puts an equality clause on pay into all contracts of employment requiring that any calculation on pay paid by the employer include any pay rises or other benefits a woman would have received but for her being on maternity leave (*S.74*).

8. *Redundancy During Maternity Leave* Where redundancy occurs during maternity leave an employee is entitled to be offered any available suitable alternative employment with her employer, his successor or associated employer. This would take effect immediately on the ending of her employment under the previous contract. The new contract must be one which is suitable and the provisions of which not substantially less favourable than if she had continued to be employed under the previous contract.

9. *Unfair Dismissal* Dismissal for reasons of pregnancy is an unfair dismissal.

RIGHT TO RETURN TO WORK

10. There is no requirement for the employee to notify her employer of her return to work after *ordinary maternity leave*, unless she wishes to return early when she must give at least 28 days notice.

   a. Where an employee is on *additional maternity leave* and wishes to return to work earlier than the 26 week period, she must give 8 weeks to her employer. Failure to do so allows the employer to postpone the return for up to 8 weeks.

   b. *Keeping in touch days.* An employee on maternity leave can agree with her employer to work (which includes training) for up to 10 days during the maternity leave period without bringing the period to an end.

   c. The employee who has 1 year's continuous employment (at the beginning of the 11th week before the expected date of childbirth) is entitled to return to the job she was previously employed to do, this means the same seniority, pension and other rights intact with terms and conditions no less favourable than those which applied before her absence.

11. *Flexible Working*

   S.80F of the *EMPLOYMENT RIGHTS ACT 1996,* makes provision for flexible working arrangements for parents with children under 16 years of age. A qualifying employee may apply to his employer for a change in the terms and conditions of employment in relation to:

   a. Hours of work.

   b. Time when work is carried out.

   c. Whether work should take place at home or in the place of business.

   No more than one application every 12 months can be made and agency workers are expressly excluded. An employee may request a contract variation where he or she has been continuously employed for a period not less than 26 weeks and be either, the mother, father, adopter, guardian or foster parent of the child, or is married to one of these. The request must be in writing. Within 28 days of the request, the employer must hold a meeting with the employee to discuss the application. The employee has the right to be accompanied by a fellow employee. After the meeting there is a further period of 14 days for the employer to notify the employee of his decision. The decision must be in writing either agreeing to the request or rejecting it. Where the request is refused, the employer must state the grounds for the refusal.

   S.80G(1)(B) of the *EMPLOYMENT RIGHTS ACT 1996,* provides the grounds for an employer refusal. There must be one or more of the following:

   a. The burden of additional cost.

   b. Detrimental effect on ability to meet customer demand.

   c. Inability to reorganize work among existing staff.

   d. Inability to recruit additional staff.

   e. Detrimental impact on quality.

   f. Detrimental impact on performance.

g.   Insufficiency of work during the periods the employee proposes to work.

h.   Planned structural changes.

i.   Such other grounds as may be specified by regulations.

The employee is entitled to appeal against any refusal by the employer. This has to be made in writing, within 14 days after the refusal, giving the grounds for the appeal. The employer then has 14 days to respond. The final step would be to make a complaint to an employment tribunal.

SUSPENSION FROM WORK ON MATERNITY GROUNDS

12. An employee is suspended from work on maternity grounds where in consequence of any requirement by statute, regulation or a code of practice issued under the *HEALTH AND SAFETY AT WORK ACT 1974* she is suspended from work on the grounds that she is pregnant, has recently given birth or is breast-feeding a child. *S.66–68* of the *EMPLOYMENT RIGHTS ACT 1996*, provide that an employee so suspended is entitled to be paid during the suspension or offered *suitable alternative work* (see 15. below). She will not be entitled to pay for any period during which she was offered suitable alternative work and unreasonably refused it.

13. She is suspended if she continues to be employed by her employer but is not provided with work or does not perform the work she normally performed.

14. The *MANAGEMENT OF HEALTH AND SAFETY AT WORK REGULATIONS 1999* requires that an employer carries out an assessment of risks to the health and safety of employees and others. The Regulations require special attention in the event of there being female employees of childbearing age.

15. ***Offer of Suitable Alternative Work*** Where alternative work is available an employee has a right to be provided with it before being suspended on maternity grounds.

16. 'Suitable' work is suitable and appropriate for her in the circumstances and the terms and conditions not substantially less favourable than those of her usual work.

17. An employee may present a complaint to an employment tribunal that she has not been offered suitable alternative work. The complaint must be submitted not later than 3 months from the first day of suspension.

18. An award of compensation may be made such as the tribunal considers just and equitable in the circumstances.

19. The amount of remuneration will be a week's pay in respect of any week of suspension.

20. A complaint that an employer has failed to pay the whole or any part of her entitlement to remuneration must be made to a tribunal within 3 months.

BRITISH AIRWAYS (EUROPEAN OPERATIONS AT GATWICK) LTD V MOORE AND BOTTERILL (2000) concerned cabin crew who could not fly during their pregnancies who were successful in their claim for full flying allowances whilst employed on ground-based work alternative work.

ANTENATAL CARE

21. ***Contractual Remuneration*** Where an employee receives any payment by way of contractual remuneration for a period when she would have received maternity payment, any sum paid reduces her entitlement to maternity pay.

22. Pregnant employees can have time off with pay during working hours to attend antenatal clinics (*S.55*).

23. Apart from the first appointment, the employer can require the employee to produce a certificate of pregnancy and appointment card.

24. If the employer fails to comply with his obligations the employee can apply to an employment tribunal which can grant her compensation. If time off has been refused the amount of compensation will be the sum she would have received if the time off had been granted. If the time off has been granted but without pay the compensation will be the pay which ought to have been paid to her.

25. This right is not dependent on the employee's length of service, i.e. she can have time off on the first day of her employment. It also does not depend on the number of hours per week that the employee works.

26. ***Parental Leave*** The *MATERNITY & PARENTAL LEAVE REGULATIONS 1999* gives to employees the right to unpaid leave, after 1 year's continuous employment, of up to 13 weeks per child, to care for their children under the age of 5 (18 for a disabled child). The employee is required to give at least 21 days notice to the employer of the intention to take parental leave. The employer can postpone the leave for up to 6 months if the needs of the business make it necessary and if it is reasonable to do so. The employee remains employed during the period of leave and has the right to return to the same job. Where the leave exceeds 4 weeks the employer may offer a similar job instead of the one previously held, so long as the terms and conditions are at least as favourable as the old job. Any complaint by an employee may be made to an employment tribunal.

27. ***Time Off for Dependants*** Employees are entitled to unpaid time off work to help a dependant who has given birth, is ill, has been injured or assaulted or who has died (*S.57A*). In addition an employee is entitled to time off to deal with an incident involving their child which occurs unexpectedly during school hours. A dependant is widely defined as being a spouse, child, parent or live-in-lover or any person who relies on the employee to make child care arrangements.

    The employee is required to inform the employer as soon as is reasonably practicable. Where an employee is denied this right a complaint can be made to an employment tribunal within 3 months of the refusal; the tribunal has the power to extend leave and/or award compensation.

28. ***Adoption Leave*** Adoption leave was introduced as part of the same legislation as paternity leave. It applies to 'An employee (whether male or female and whether married or single) who is the adoptive parent of a child newly placed for adoption.' It does not apply to stepfamily adoption or adoption by a child's existing foster carers. To qualify the employee has to meet the same requirements as for paternity leave. The leave is the same as that for maternity leave. Where a couple adopt a child, only one of them is entitled to take adoption leave.

SELF TEST QUESTIONS

Self Test Questions No. 52 (for Answers see Appendix 1):

1   What are the consequences of dismissing an employee who is pregnant?

2   Explain the provisions relating to maternity leave.

3   What is involved in the employee's right to return to work?

4   What are the consequences of a suspension from work on maternity grounds?

5   What are the employee rights associated with antenatal care?

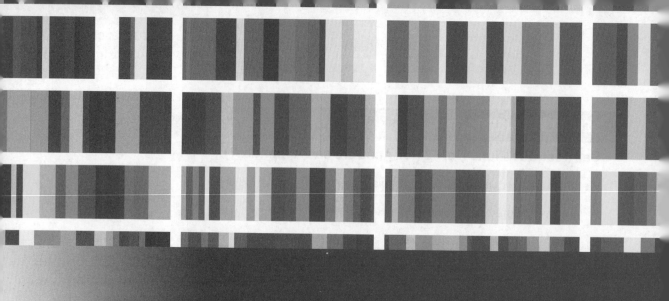

55 EQUALITY

Learning Outcomes
At the end of this chapter you should be able to:

- Understand the aims of the legislative consolidation of discrimination law through the *EQUALITY ACT 2010*.

- Explain the different forms of discrimination.

- Outline each *protected characteristic* under the Act.

- Understand the requirements of a *genuine occupational requirement*.

- Explain the liability of the employer for acts of third party harassment.

INTRODUCTION

1. To date the problems of discrimination against certain classes of employees were tackled by a number of statutes, namely:

    EQUAL PAY ACT 1970
    SEX DISCRIMINATION ACT 1975
    RACE RELATIONS ACT 1976

DISABILITY DISCRIMINATION ACT 1995
EMPLOYMENT EQUALITY (RELIGION AND BELIEF) REGULATIONS 2003
EMPLOYMENT EQUALITY (SEXUAL ORIENTATION) REGULATIONS 2003
EMPLOYMENT EQUALITY (AGE) REGULATIONS 2006
EQUALITY ACT 2006, Part 2
EQUALITY ACT (SEXUAL ORIENTATION) REGULATIONS 2007.

In addition European Community law exists in this field. Although the scope of these laws is greater than merely that of employment, this chapter outlines the main provisions of the Acts only insofar as they affect discrimination in the matter of employment.

The statutes listed above have now been replaced by the *EQUALITY ACT 2010*, a major statute, which brings together and reinstates those enactments. Having developed piece-meal over 40 years, it was felt that a single statute would make the law in this area more ac-cessible and easier to understand by establishing a single legal framework.

THE EQUALITY ACT 2010 (THE ACT)

2. *Introduction*

The Act has a number of objectives which seek to strengthen the existing law in a number of areas; it is useful to list those objectives, they are:

a. A placing of a new duty on certain public bodies to, when making strategic decisions about their functions, consider social and economic disadvantage in their area. Also, on certain listed public bodies, a more specific duty to have regard to the need to eliminate conduct which the Act forbids, in particular:

   i.   The need to advance equality of opportunity between persons who share a relevant *protected characteristic* and those who do not.

   ii. The need to foster good relations between those with a *protected characteristic* and the rest.

b. Extending the circumstances in which a person is protected from discrimination, harass-ment or victimization because of a *protected characteristic* (see below).

c. Extending the circumstances in which a person may claim if they are directly discrimi-nated against because of two relevant *protected characteristics*.

d. Allowing an employer to carry out acts of *positive discrimination* – sometimes referred to as *positive action* (see below) – to overcome or minimize a disadvantage arising from a *protected characteristic*. In this respect, the Act allows for political parties to extend the use of 'women-only' shortlists when selecting parliamentary candidates, to 2030.

e. Enabling an employment tribunal to make a recommendation to an employer to take certain steps to remedy matters not just for the benefit of the claimant (who may well have ceased employment with the respondent employer) but also for the wider workforce.

3. *Protected characteristics* (*S.4*)

The Act identifies a number of distinctive characteristics that an individual may have, and makes it unlawful for such individuals to be treated less favourably, in matters linked to employment, than others who do not have those particular characteristics. These are:

a.   Age.

b.   Disability.

c.   Gender reassignment.

d.   Marriage and civil partnership (not addressed for present purposes).

e.   Pregnancy and maternity.

f.   Race.

g.   Religion or belief.

h.   Sex.

i.   Sexual orientation.

It is important to note that treating an individual less favourably than another for reasons unconnected with the above, e.g. attitude, qualifications, experience, etc., is not unlawful discrimination.

The general rule is that to treat a person less favourably than another on grounds of any of the above will constitute an act of unlawful discrimination.

4. *Forms of Discrimination* There are four basic forms which acts of discrimination, based upon one or more of the above *protected characteristics*, can take. They are:

a.   Direct discrimination.

b.   Indirect discrimination.

c.   Discrimination by way of harassment.

d.   Discrimination by way of victimization.

Discrimination arises where an employer or prospective employer treats a person with a *protected characteristic* less favourably than he treats or would treat other persons without such a characteristic, e.g. an employer offers employment or promotes a woman because she is a woman, whilst refusing to do the same for a man.

Positive discrimination. Is an approach pioneered by the European Union. It recognizes that in certain situations it may be necessary to take action which would otherwise be unlawful discrimination, in order to redress some historical imbalance in employment e.g. too few women engineers. *Postive discrimination* occurs where an employer takes *positive action* which discriminates *in favour of* a person with a *protected characteristic* because there exists an under-representation of such persons in a particular area linked to employment, e.g. running training courses only for women employees because there are too few women in a particular level of management. Initially in *KALANKE v FREIE HANSESTADT BREMEN (1996)* the European Court of Justice ruled that for an employer to 'positively discriminate' in favour of women was unlawful. However, in recognition of the problems of redressing historical imbalances in certain job categories, the *TREATY OF ROME 1957* was amended so that Member States can maintain and adopt measures that provide specific advantages for an under-represented person in one of the *protected characteristic* groups. An example of *positive discrimination* can be seen in *APPLICATION BY BADECK AND OTHERS (2000)* where in the public service sector *positive discrimination* occurred where although there was no automatic preference for a women in that both sexes were considered equally, there was an objective assessment which considered both sexes' personal situations. If this resulted in a man and woman being equally qualified for the job, the woman was selected. This was found to be lawful.

We now need to examine the different forms which unlawful discrimination can take:

a.   *Direct discrimination (S.13)*. This has been equated with 'intentional' discrimination. Here the employer deliberately treats a person who has a *protected characteristic*, e.g. undergone gender reassignment, less favourably than a person who has not. Finding an intention on the part of an employer is often difficult. An employer will rarely admit to treating a person less favourably because of one of the *protected characteristics*. However, claimants need only provide facts upon which it appears there are grounds for forming a reasonable belief that an act of discrimination may have occurred. It is then for the employer to prove differently, e.g. at a job interview where interviewees consist of say, six women and one man, and all applicants appear to have similar qualifications, but the job is given to the one man. Here there would be, based on the particular facts, a reasonable assumption that an act of direct discrimination, based upon sex, *may* have occurred; an employment tribunal would then turn to the employer asking for an explanation, failure to do so would lead to a finding of unlawful discrimination. In ***GRIEG v COMMUNITY INDUSTRY (1979)*** a young girl applied for a job with an organization whose purpose was to relieve unemployment amongst juveniles. She was refused employment in a particular activity because she would have been the only girl in a group of men, and emotional problems were anticipated. It was held to be direct discrimination based upon the *protected characteristic* of sex, even though the motives were honourable.

As seen in the *GRIEG Case*, good intentions by the employer are irrelevant. This can be further illustrated by ***JAMES v EASTLEIGH BOROUGH COUNCIL (1990)***: the House of Lords (now the Supreme Court) ruled that discrimination was simply an objective assessment of the facts and the motives of the discriminator were irrelevant; in this case a local authority gave concessions to those in receipt of a state pension to cheaper entrance to its swimming baths, James successfully brought an action claiming sex discrimination in the provision of public services (also outlawed under the Act) in that his wife could gain cheap entry but he could not. The House of Lords ruled that the question to be asked was, 'Would a man have received the same treatment as the woman, but for his sex?' This is often referred to as the, 'but for' test, i.e., 'but for' the claimant having a *protected characteristic*, would he or she have been treated the same as others? If the answer is, yes, it is direct discrimination and unlawful.

In ***GUBALA v CROMPTON PARKINSON LTD (1977)*** P was made redundant in preference to a male colleague of the same seniority. Being made redundant and losing your job, is clearly less favourable treatment (see Chapter 57). The employer admitted that he had been influenced by the fact that the man was older (age is now also a *protected characteristic*) and had a mortgage whereas P's husband worked. It was held that this was a case of unlawful direct discrimination.

In ***BLOOMBERG FINANCIAL MARKETS v CUMANDALA (2000)*** a black employee applied for a post overseas; he expressed the wish to return home every weekend to see his wife. His application was turned down by the employer. The employer felt, given the weekly commuting, that he would not be able to give the necessary commitment to the job. In his defence the employer argued that he would have acted in exactly the same way if the weekly commuting had been to see a favourite football team. The employer also commented that in appointing a white person, he would 'fit in better'. The Employment Appeal Tribunal (EAT) held that there was no discrimination based upon the employee's marital status, but that the preference for a white person was direct discrimination on the grounds of race.

b.   *Indirect discrimination* (*S.19*). This occurs where:

i.   The same provision, criterion or practice is applied to everyone – so no apparent discrimination, everyone being treated the same – however

ii. The *effect* of such a commonly applied provision, criterion or practice is that more people within a particular *protected characteristic* group, are disadvantaged than the rest.

For example, if a height requirement for a job were fixed at 6 feet tall, there would be relatively fewer women capable of qualifying than men. What is being done by an employer appears neutral, in that it applies equally to everyone, but its *effects* are felt more deeply by persons having a particular *protected characteristic* e.g. disabled, or persons of a particular sex or age, etc.

In order to allow an employer to have genuine job requirements, unlike *direct discrimination*, there is a defence here for an employer who can show that the resultant disproportionate impact on a particular group, was for reasons unconnected with a *protected characteristic* but was a genuine requirement of the job. It was a proportionate means of achieving a legitimate aim (*S.19*).

In *STEEL v UNION OF POST OFFICE WORKERS AND GPO (1978)* women could only be 'Temporary' full-time postmen. In order to comply with the then Sex Discrimination Act, women could become full-time postmen, but walks and rounds were allocated on the basis of length of service as a full-time postman. This clearly disadvantaged women postmen who did not have the length of full-time service needed to get the best rounds. It was held that failure to make the allocation on length of service irrespective of whether it was temporary or not was discriminatory on the basis of sex.

In *PRICE v CIVIL SERVICE COMMISSION (1977)* the requirement that applicants for employment should be between the ages of 17 and 28 was held to be unlawful discrimination because, in practice, the demands of maternity prevented a considerable proportion of women from falling within that age range, and the employer could not justify the age requirement as a genuine requirement of the job.

In *POWELL v ELY-KYNOCH LTD (1981)* an agreement was in existence whereby the first employees to go if redundancies were needed would be the part-time employees. This was held to be discriminatory on the grounds of sex, as family commitments meant that all the part-time workers were women who would be unable to comply with the condition of full-time work in order to keep their jobs.

In *MacGREGOR WALLCOVERINGS LTD v TURTON (1977)* a scheme whereby employees over 60 who were made redundant received an extra 10 weeks pay was held to contravene the then Sex Discrimination Act as it precluded women (who retired at 60) from qualifying. It therefore did not give women equal rights with men to benefits. Today this would also breach the *protected characteristic* of age (see below).

In *WRIGHT v RUGBY CC (1984)* Rugby Council refused to allow P to work times which fitted in with care of her baby. It was held to be sex discrimination as it was a circumstance under which a far greater proportion of women than men would be affected.

c.   *Harassment* (*S.26*). Discrimination may also be found to have occurred where unwanted conduct related to one or more *protected characteristics*, has taken place.

In *PORCELLI v STRATHCLYDE REGIONAL COUNCIL (1986)* a female laboratory technician was subjected to continuing unpleasant behaviour of a sexual nature by her fellow male employees. The Court found that whilst a male employee who was also disliked by fellow workers would have received similar treatment, the nature of this particular treatment was of a sort that a woman would find particularly offensive and was therefore direct discrimination in the form of harassment. This subjective approach, that takes account of the particular feelings and attributes of the victim, was confirmed by the European Commission in a code it issued on protecting the 'dignity of women at work'. This requires that employers stop behaviour which an employee makes clear he or she regards as unwanted, unreasonable and offensive. Harassment happens where:

i.   Unwanted conduct related to a *protected characteristic* occurs with the purpose or effect of violating the dignity of that person, and

ii.   Takes the form of unwanted, non-verbal or physical conduct with the purpose or effect of violating the dignity of a person, in particular, by creating an intimidatory, hostile, degrading, humiliating or offensive environment (*S.26(2)* and *(3)*).

In order to give tribunals some discretion when dealing with persons who might be seen as being unreasonable or unduly sensitive, the Act states that:
Conduct shall be regarded as having the effect of violating dignity or creating an intimidating, hostile, degrading or offensive environment, only if, having regard to all the circumstances, including in particular the perception of the individual, it should reasonably be considered as having that effect.

In *DRISKEL V PENINSULAR BUSINESS SERVICES LTD (2000)* Mrs Driskel claimed that she had been harassed on the basis of sex by her boss. She alleged that she had been subject to sexual banter and comments and that at an interview for promotion he had suggested that she wear a short skirt and a see-through blouse showing plenty of cleavage. She refused to return to work unless her boss was moved elsewhere. She was then dismissed and made a claim to an employment tribunal. At the initial employment tribunal hearing, the tribunal dismissed her claim finding that each incident considered in isolation, did not amount to sexual harassment. The Employment Appeal Tribunal held that this was the wrong approach and that sexual harassment had occurred:

i.   The original tribunal should have looked at the total overall effect of the acts complained of, not each individual act.

ii.   A woman's failure to complain at times throughout the conduct should not necessarily be taken as significant.

iii. Sexual banter between heterosexual men is not the same as similar comments towards a woman.

There is other legislation relating to harassment. The *CRIMINAL JUSTICE & PUBLIC ORDER ACT 1994*, creates a criminal offence of intentional harassment – covering harassment in the workplace. The penalty on conviction is imprisonment for up to 6 months and/or a fine up to £5000. This means that an employee who is harassed at work are able to report the matter to the police. The *PROTECTION FROM HARASSMENT ACT 1997* is also relevant. The Act covers wide ranging acts of harassment and bullying at work, and provides the possibility of bringing civil proceedings against offenders.

d.   *Victimization (S.27)*. This occurs when less favourable treatment is given to a person because that person has brought proceedings under the Act, or has given evidence or made allegations with regard to any proceedings under the Act. This does not apply when the person who is victimized does not act in good faith (e.g., makes false allegations) or where the conduct of the employer was an honest and reasonable attempt to compromise the proceedings. This was shown in *ST HELENS METRO-POLITAN BOROUGH COUNCIL V DERBYSHIRE AND OTHERS (2005)*. Here the Council wrote a letter to claimants warning them of the consequences of continuing their equal-pay claims. The Court of Appeal followed an earlier House of Lords (now the Supreme Court) decision in *CHIEF CONSTABLE OF WEST YORK-SHIRE POLICE V KHAN (2001)* where it was stated that an employer may take honest and reasonable steps to safeguard its position in proceedings without infringing the victimization provisions, and found that the tribunal should have considered whether the actions of the Council were reasonable steps taken to try and persuade claimants to settle their claims. Victimization can take many forms: in *COOTE v GRANADA HOS-PITALITY LTD (1999)* victimization was held to have occurred where an employer refused to give a reference to a former employee.

e. *New forms of discrimination under the Act.*

    i. *Associative discrimination.* This allows for a person to bring an action where they have been treated less favourably, because of a *protected characteristic* held by another with whom they are associated with. In *COLEMAN v ATTRIDGE LAW (2008)* an employee had a disabled baby for which she was the main carer. When she returned from maternity leave she was treated in a way that parents of non-disabled children would not have been; she was refused flexible working and criticized for wanting time off to look after her baby. When referred to the European Court of Justice, the Court found that it was not necessary for someone who is the object of discrimination to have been treated less favourably on account of their disability, it is enough if the claimant is mistreated *on account of disability*. The employer would be, therefore, liable. This has now been enshrined in the Act.

    ii. *Perceptive discrimination.* A claim can be brought where the employer believes, wrongly, that a person has a *protected characteristic*. *Perceptive discrimination* already existed for sexual orientation (see below), age or race, this is now extended under the Act to the other *protected characteristics* i.e. sex, pregnancy, gender re-assignment (see below) and disability.

    iii. *Dual* or *combined discrimination (S.14)*. Here a claimant may bring an action where they have two or more of the protected characteristics – excluding pregnancy and maternity.

An older woman applies for a job as a driving instructor. She is unsuccessful and is told, upon requesting feedback, that she was not appointed because the nature of the job made it unsuitable for an older woman. The employer did not believe she would have the strength and agility needed to grab the steering wheel or be able to brake quickly in an emergency. She is told that she would have been appointed had she been an older man or a younger woman. Here she would not succeed on a sex or age discrimination alone, as the reason for her treatment was not her sex or age, but the combination of the two. She would be protected however, by a *combined characteristic* of the two. Note: if strength and agility were an essential requirement of the job, the employer could introduce an appropriate test to be applied to all applicants, this would not then be discrimination.

5. **Protected characteristics** It was seen in 3. above that the various forms of discrimination have to occur based upon one or more of the *protected characteristics (S.4)*. We now need to consider these more closely in order to understand their meaning:

a. *Age.* A*geism* is the term given to an act whereby an employer treats a person less favourably on the grounds of their age. The Act makes it unlawful for an employer to; directly or indirectly discriminate or harass a person in the employment sphere on the grounds of their age. Enforcement will be through tribunals and compensation potentially will have no maximum limit. Under age discrimination law, there will be an employer defence of *justification*, if he can show that the action was a proportionate means of attaining a legitimate aim. It is important to note that the protection given from being treated less favourably because of age, applies to all age groups, not just old people; e.g. for an employer not to give a job to an applicant because they are too young, is just as discriminatory and unlawful as to not give the job because they are too old.

b. *Disability.* The purpose behind *disability* being a *protected* characteristic is to enable disabled people to live independently in society by enjoying equal opportunities at work, in access to goods and services and by way of educational facilities. The Act also imposes a duty on public authorities to have regard to the need to eliminate disability discrimination in the carrying out of their functions. The Disability Rights Commission (DRC) was set up to give practical guidance on prevention of disability discrimination and to promote equality of opportunity.

The DRC have issued a Code of Practice to guide employers and others.

Disability is defined in the Act as a physical or mental impairment which has a substantial and long-term effect on a person's ability to carry out normal day-to-day activities (*S.6*).

The determination of disability involves a four-stage test:

i.   A finding of a physical or mental impairment.

ii. That impairment must have a substantial adverse effect.

iii. It must have a long-term adverse effect.

iv. The adverse effect must relate to the ability to carry out normal day-to-day activities.

Certain addictions and conditions are not to be treated as impairments for purposes of the Act. These include:

i.   Addictions to alcohol, nicotine or any other substance, unless the addiction was originally the result of medically prescribed drugs or treatment.

ii. A tendency to set fires, to steal or to physically or sexually abuse other persons.

iii. Exhibitionism and voyeurism.

iv. Seasonal allergic asthma, although this may be taken into account where it aggravates other conditions.

v.   Severe disfigurement which results from tattooing or piercing.

It is unlawful for an employer to discriminate against a disabled employee:

i.   In the terms of employment and in opportunities for promotion, transfer, training or other benefits, or

ii. By dismissal or any other disadvantage.

This could be *direct discrimination*, where a disabled person, on the grounds of their disability, is treated less favourably than another person not having that particular disability, and the relevant circumstances, including the abilities of the person being used as the comparator, are the same as, or not materially different from those of the disabled person. Or, *indirect discrimination* where less favourable treatment is given to a disabled person for a reason related to his or her disability, and the employer cannot show that the treatment can be justified. So there is unlike for *direct discrimination*, a defence of justification. Any justification must be material to the circumstances and substantial. The justification defence cannot be used for failures to make reasonable adjustments (see below). The employer would need to show that material and substantial circumstances would have applied even if the adjustments had been made.

The Act (*S.20*) places a duty on employers to make *reasonable adjustments* in relation to the disabled persons. The employer has to take all reasonable steps to ensure that no provision, criterion or practice employed on his behalf or any physical feature of premises occupied by him, leads to discrimination against a disabled person. The obligation applies to not only existing employees but also applicants for employment. There is no obligation placed upon the employer if the employer does not know, or could not have reasonably been expected to know, that the applicant or employee had a disability.

Provision criteria or practice includes arrangements for:

i.   Determining who should be offered employment.

ii.   Any term, condition or arrangements on which employment, promotion, transfer, training or any other benefit offered.

In *NOTTINGHAM COUNTY COUNCIL V MEIKLE (2004)* a local authority school teacher experienced a deterioration in her sight to the point where she lost sight in one eye and some vision in the other. She made a number of requests to her employer for adjustments to be made in her workplace; these included a different classroom location; an increase in time allowed for preparation; and enlarged notices and written materials. There were delays in response from the employer and eventually she resigned. The Court of Appeal found that the continuing failure of her employer to make the requested adjustments amounted to disability discrimination causing a fundamental breach of contract leading to a constructive dismissal (see Chapter 56).

In *ARCHIBALD v FIFE COUNCIL (2004)* an employee road sweeper had an accident and became unable to walk. She was allowed to apply for other positions that did not involve walking; she did so and was unsuccessful and eventually dismissed for lack of *capacity* to do the job – as road sweeper (see Chapter 56.23.a) The House of Lords (now the Supreme Court) held that where an employee has become disabled and can no longer do the job, but is capable of doing other jobs within the organization, the employer is under a duty to take reasonable steps/adjustments to prevent any less favourable treatment on the employee. Allowing the employee to apply for other posts without competition from other applicants, would be a reasonable step to take.

There is a defence here, where the employer can show that the less favourable treatment based upon disability, was a proportionate means of achieving a legitimate aim; that is, some objective reasons that were appropriate, such as the fact that it is a small organization with no scope for offers of alternative jobs.

The Act (*S.60*) allows an employer limited conditions on which questions of health may be raised of a job applicant before a job offer is made. These are questions with regard to:

i.   Any reasonable adjustments that may be required for the person to do the job and attend interviews.

ii.   Determining an applicant's ability to perform an essential part of the job.

iii.   Monitoring equality and diversity information for the organization.

iv.   Enabling positive action policy (see 4. above) to be pursued.

v.   Demonstrating an occupational requirement (see below) of the person required for the job.

vi.   Matters of national security.

Note: this ability of the employer to ask pre-employment questions is important, for once employment commences an employer is entitled to ask health questions when seeking to meet the obligations under health and safety (see Chapter 60).

c.   *Gender reassignment* (*S.7*). Gender reassignment is:

i.   A process which is undertaken under medical supervision for the purpose of reassigning a person's sex by changing physiological or other characteristics of sex.

The Act provides that a person unlawfully discriminates against another by treating them less favourably on the grounds that they intend to undergo, is undergoing or has undergone gender reassignment. In *CHESSINGTON WORLD OF ADVENTURE LTD V REED (1997)* an individual announced a change of gender from male to female and, as a result, was subjected to continuous harassment from fellow workers. She eventually was absent through sickness and was dismissed. The Employment Appeal Tribunal held that the employer, who had known of the harassment, was directly liable for the obviously, less favourable discriminatory treatment that had taken place.

The Act also protects a person who wishes to live permanently as a member of the opposite sex but does not wish to undergo any medical procedures.

Note: permanency is required, so a person wishing to dress up as a man or a woman – a cross-dresser – would not be protected.

d.   *Pregnancy and maternity* (see Chapter 54).

e.   *Race* or *Sex* (*S.9*). Under the Act it is an offence for an employer to discriminate against an employee, that is – treating them less favourably through, direct or indirect discrimination, by harassment or victimization – on account of their colour, race, nationality or ethnic or national origins, or sex.

The Act covers discrimination in advertising for an employee, engaging or dismissing him or in his conditions of employment (e.g. opportunities for training and promotion).

In *ZARCZYNSKA v LEVY (1978)* a white student got a part-time job in an East London public house. She was told not to serve blacks. She objected to this and was sacked. She complained to the CRE which supported her appeal. The EAT said she was treated less favourably than a person who went along with the colour bar and was therefore discriminated against on racial grounds.

6.   *Exceptions* Where race is a genuine occupational requirement; it is lawful in certain circumstances to discriminate, these are:

a.   Where authenticity in drama or other entertainment requires a person of a particular racial group.

b.   Where the production of visual imagery in art or photography requires a person from a particular racial group for reasons of authenticity.

c. Where the job involves working in a place where food and drink is served to the public and membership of a racial group is required for authenticity.

d. Where the job holder provides persons of that racial group with personal services promoting their welfare, and where those services can be most effectively performed by a person of that racial group.

In *TOTTENHAM GREEN UNDER FIVES' CENTRE V MARSHALL (NO.2) (1991)* it was held that the desirability of having a nursery worker who could read and talk in a dialect of children and parents was sufficient to justify a genuine occupational qualification exception.

There is a statutory duty on public authorities to promote racial equality and to prevent racial discrimination.

Genuine Occupational Qualification (GOQ). With regards to the *protected characteristic* of sex, like race and sexual orientation (see below) the Act provides a defence where the particular sex of a person, is a genuine occupational qualification for a job. A person's sex is regarded as a genuine occupational qualification where:

a. The essential nature of the job calls for a man (or woman) for reasons of physiology (excluding physical strength or stamina), e.g., modelling clothes, bunny-girls.

b. Considerations of decency or privacy, e.g., because of likely physical contact (clothing sales assistant), or because it involves use of sanitary facilities (lavatory attendant).

c. The nature of location of the establishment makes it impracticable, e.g., on an oil rig, or ship where separate sleeping and sanitary facilities do not exist.

d. In a single-sex establishment, e.g., a single-sex hospital. It is reasonable to restrict employment to persons of the same sex as that of the establishment.

e. The jobholder provides a personal service, e.g., where a person of a particular sex is more acceptable, e.g., social worker, masseuse.

f. Where the law requires it, e.g., the restriction on a woman resuming work within 4 weeks of giving birth, and exposure to lead.

In *PAGE v FREIGHT HIRE (TANK HAULAGE) LTD (1981)* the applicant, a 23-year-old divorcee was removed by her employer from haulage work involving the chemical dimethylformide on the grounds that the substance was a danger to women of child-bearing age. The employer claimed that he was required to do this under the general duty to safeguard the health and safety of his employees imposed by *S.2* of the *Health and Safety at Work Act 1974*. The EAT held that the employer had acted lawfully.

g. *Religion or belief (S.10)*. The Act protects employees from being discriminated against because of their choice of *religion*, religious *beliefs* (or non-belief), or other similar philosophical belief – be that a real or perceived belief. *Religion* means any religion and lack of religion. *Belief* means: any religious or philosophical belief or lack of belief (*S.10*).

The case of *LILLIAN LADELE v ISLINGTON BOROUGH COUNCIL (2008)* illustrates the problems a service provider might easily encounter where the service they are required to provide, conflicts with an individual employee's *protected characteristic*. Here an employee of the council required to carry out registrations of births, marriages and deaths, refused to register a single sex marriage, arguing that it conflicted with her Christian religious beliefs. The Employment Appeal Tribunal and the Court of Appeal ruled that the provision of public services without discrimination overrode an individual employee's need of protection of religious belief.

h. *Sexual orientation (S.12).* The Act outlaws direct or indirect discrimination, harassment or victimization on grounds of actual or perceived sexual orientation. Sexual orientation is given a broad definition to include heterosexual, homosexual and bisexual preferences. However, the Act does not extend protection to those discriminated against because they have a particular type of sexual preference, for example, paedophilia. The words 'on grounds of' means that the Act would protect third parties discriminated against – *associative discrimination* (see e.i above), for example, a man harassed at work because his son is homosexual, or someone is discriminated against because they have gay friends. As noted, the Act includes *perceptive discrimination* (see e.ii above) with regard to sexual orientation; so if an employer believes a particular employee is bisexual and discriminates against them for that reason, it does not matter if the employee is in fact not bisexual. To bring an action a claimant does not have to declare his sexual orientation; all he has to show is that he was treated less favourably than a heterosexual person by his employer because the employer believed the claimant to be bisexual or homosexual.

In *DITTON v CP PUBLISHING LTD (2007)* a gay employee was subjected to offensive comments about his sexual orientation by a company director for the first 8 days of his employment. He was then dismissed. The employment tribunal held that he had been discriminated against through harassment based upon his sexual orientation. The employee was awarded £118 000.

The Act allows for the defence of genuine occupational qualification where being of a particular sexual orientation is a genuine requirement and where the employer is a religious organization and a particular sexual orientation contradicts the beliefs of the members of the particular religion.

7. *Acts of third parties* **(S.40)** An employer may well be liable where an employee is subjected to unwanted conduct amounting to harassment by persons not under his control. This could be another employee, customer, client, delivery driver or any visitor to the employer's premises. The Act introduces a 'three strike' criteria by requiring that the unwanted conduct occurs on at least three occasions to the knowledge of the employer. It is not a requirement that the acts be committed by the same person it could be three separate occasions by three separate individuals. The employer is required to take *reasonable steps* to prevent the unwanted conduct. The affected employee may also have an action under the *PROTECTION FROM HARASSMENT ACT 1997* – this would be heard in the county court not an employment tribunal. In *BURTON v RHULE DE VERE HOTELS (1997)* here an entertainer hired by the hotel verbally abused two waitresses on duty at the time. The tribunal found that the employer had control over the event and could have stopped the abuse. Under the *EQUALITY ACT 2010* this could well be harassment by a third party if it happened on three previous occasions – with potentially three different perpetrators – with the employer's knowledge. The protection from third party harassment will apply to all of the *protected characteristics* except pregnancy and maternity.

8. *Collective Agreements* Any term in a collective agreement or in an employer's rules for his employees which would result in a breach of the Act will be void. The same applies to any rule made by an organization of employers or workers or trade association or body which confers qualifications. The voiding of discriminatory terms and rules will not impair employees' rights under their contracts of employment.

9. *Gathering Information* To allow for the gathering of information by a claimant from an employer, the *Equality (Obtaining Information) Order Regulations 2010* provides for questionnaires to be used setting out questions for an alleged discriminator with a section for their responses.

10. *EC Directive 2000/43* This directive extends the European Union's involvement in promoting equal treatment to race or ethnic origin requiring that there be equal treatment between persons irrespective of racial or ethnic origin. This will allow UK courts and tribunals to be subject to scrutiny by the Commission and ultimately the European Court of Justice. Previously, promoting equal treatment between different races and ethnic minorities had been left to Member States.

SELF TEST QUESTIONS

Self Test Questions No. 52 (for Answers see Appendix 1):

1 Outline the broad purposes of the *EQUALITY ACT 2010*

2 Explain each of the various forms of discrimination:

direct

indirect

harassment

victimization.

3 What is: associative, perceptive and dual or combined discrimination?

4 Briefly explain the nature of each of the protected characteristics under the Act, namely:

ageism

disability

gender reassignment

race

religion or belief

sex

sexual orientation.

(Pregnancy and maternity are covered in Chapter 54.)

5 What are genuine occupational qualifications?

6 What is the liability of an employer to his employees for harassment by third parties?

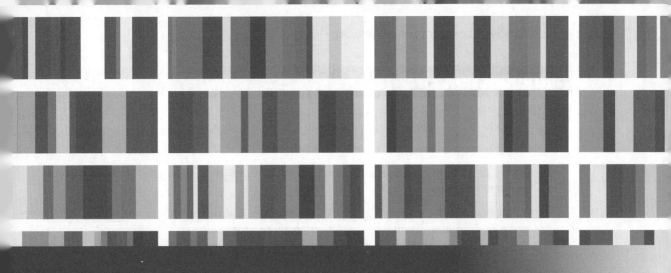

TERMINATION OF CONTRACTS OF EMPLOYMENT

56

Learning Outcomes At the end of this chapter you should be able to:

- Explain the various forms the termination of a contract of employment can take.

- Understand the meaning of *constructive dismissal*.

- Outline the remedies available under common law for a *wrongful dismissal*.

- Explain the stages of statutory *unfair dismissal*:

  - who qualifies for protection

  - the requirement of a *dismissal*

  - *admissible reasons*

  - *employer reasonableness*

  - *procedural fairness*

  - remedies.

INTRODUCTION

1. Termination of a contract of employment can arise in several ways:

    a. By agreement between the employer and employee.

    b. By an act of either party of sufficient gravity to terminate the contract without notice i.e. *gross misconduct*.

    c. By operation of the law, e.g. death, dissolution of a partnership, appointment of a receiver, compulsory winding-up of a company or frustration.

    d. By an act of either party terminating the contract with notice.

    In this chapter we will consider termination with notice, termination by operation of the law, wrongful dismissal and unfair dismissal.

TERMINATION WITH NOTICE

2. The usual method of terminating a contract is for the employer to give a period of notice, determined as follows:

    a. Where the contract is for a fixed term – on completion of that term.

    b. It may be ascertained by custom of the trade.

    c. The contract may state the period – subject to the minimum under *S.86. EMPLOY-MENT RIGHTS ACT 1996*.

NOTICE – S.86 EMPLOYMENT RIGHTS ACT 1996 (ERA)

3. The notice required to be given by an employer to terminate the contract of employment of a person who has been continuously employed for 4 weeks or more shall be:

    a. Not less than 1 week if his period of continuous employment is less than 2 years.

    b. Not less than 1 week for each year of continuous employment if his period of employment is 2 years or more but less than 12 years, and

    c. Not less than 12 weeks if his period of continuous employment is 12 years or more.

4. The employment must be of a continuous nature; periods of sickness are reckonable, but not periods of strikes.

5. The following categories of employee have no right to the statutory minimum period of notice:

    a. Employees engaged in work wholly or mainly outside Great Britain. However, such periods, whilst not counting towards service, do not break its continuity.

    b. Employees in employment under a contract made in contemplation of the performance of a specific task which is not expected to last for more than 3 months and which in fact lasts no longer than that time.

    c. Certain seamen.

6. The employee, in the absence of any other term in the contract, is required to give 1 week's notice after he has been employed for 4 weeks or more. When an employee has contracted to give a longer period of notice and fails to do so, the employer cannot seek a court order to compel him to continue working. However, in rare cases, an employer may claim damages for any loss caused by the employee's premature departure.

7. Any employer may generally pay wages in lieu of notice unless the employee's reputation is involved (*CLAYTON & WALLER v OLIVER (1930)*).

BY OPERATION OF THE LAW

8. a. *Death*. Death of either the employer or the employee will end the contract.

   b. *Dissolution of a partnership*. Such an event will end a contract of employment and may give rise to wrongful dismissal, but:

   In *BRACE v CALDER (1895)* P was employed by a partnership. There was a change in the membership of the partnership which automatically results in dissolution. The claimant was offered re-engagement on the same terms by the remaining partners but refused. It was held that he was entitled to nominal damages as he had failed to mitigate his loss.

   c. *Sale of a business*. As contracts of employment (i.e. of personal service) cannot be assigned, the sale of a business constitutes the 'death' of one employer and the 'birth' of another. An employee cannot be transferred to the new employer against his will.

   If he wishes to treat the contract as terminated he will only be awarded nominal damages for dismissal. It is because of this fundamental principle of English law that statutory rules have been devised to safeguard the continuity of employment and other statutory rights of employees in the event of the transfer of a business, or the transfer of an employee to an associated employer. (See *Transfer of Undertakings (Protection of Employment) Regulations 2006*, 27.d below)

   d. *Liquidation of a company*. An order for compulsory winding-up will operate to terminate the contracts of employment of all the company's employees (employees may have a right to claim damages for wrongful dismissal). However, a resolution for voluntary winding-up does not automatically terminate employees' contracts of employment. The liquidator may carry on the business or he may close it down and thus terminate the employment contracts. In these circumstances an employee has no right to terminate his contract without notice and claim damages unless it is obvious that the company will be unable to fulfil its obligation under the contract.

   e. *Bankruptcy*. Bankruptcy or insolvency of either party will terminate the contract if the solvency of the party concerned is an essential element of the relationship.

   f. *Frustration*. A contract of employment will be frustrated when either party is incapable of performing his part of the contract due to circumstances beyond his control. Frustration is not dependent upon the conduct of the parties to the contract and therefore there is no dismissal. The employee cannot claim wrongful or unfair dismissal. Frustrating events are:

i. *Illness.* Sickness may be a frustrating event if it renders future performance impossible or fundamentally different from that envisaged by the parties when they entered into the contract:

In *CONDOR v BARRON KNIGHTS (1966)* P was the drummer in a pop group. Owing to illness he was forbidden by his doctor from performing more than a few nights per week. Since the nature of the work required him to be present 7 nights a week the contract was held to be frustrated.

Contrast *STOREY v FULHAM STEEL WORKS (1907)* where a manager on a 5-year contract was absent owing to illness for 5 months and was dismissed. It was held that in this case the period of illness did not frustrate the contract because of the nature of the contract. However, an employer would not be expected to keep a job open indefinitely.

Further indication as to the criteria to be applied in deciding whether or not a contract of employment is frustrated has been given in more recent cases, as follows:

In *MARSHALL v HARLAND & WOLFF LTD (1972)* the Court held that the employment tribunal should take the following points into account when considering whether or not a contract of employment is frustrated by sickness or injury:

(a) Terms of the contract (including sick pay).

(b) Duration of the contract in the absence of sickness.

(c) Nature of the employment.

(d) Nature of the incapacity, its duration and the prospects of recovery.

(e) Period served in employment up to the time of the sickness.

In addition, when considering whether it is reasonable for an employer to keep open an employee's position the following should be taken into account (*EGG STORES (STAMFORD HILL) LTD v LEBOVICI (1977)*):

(a) The need for the work to be done and the requirement for a replacement.

(b) Whether wages have continued to be paid.

(c) The acts and statements of the employer, including dismissal or failure to dismiss the employee.

(d) Whether it is reasonable for the employer to wait longer before replacing the employee.

ii. *Imprisonment.* A contract of employment may be frustrated by a period of imprisonment, dependent on the length of service and the nature of employment.

In *HARE v MURPHY BROS LTD (1974)* P received a 12-months' prison sentence for an assault not connected with his employment. It was held that although the offence may not be a frustrating event (being self-induced) the prison sentence frustrated the contract, being an unforeseen event and delaying return to work for so long that the contract was brought to an end.

The contract is frustrated from the time of the sentence regardless that the employee appeals against the sentence and even if the appeal is successful.

WRONGFUL DISMISSAL

9. If an employee is unjustifiably dismissed he has a claim in damages at common law. A claim for wrongful dismissal may be carried on concurrently with a claim for unfair dismissal under the *Employment Rights Act 1996*.

10. ***Contract of Indefinite Duration*** Where a contract is of an indefinite duration it may be terminated by notice on either side. Notice must be at least as long as that laid down in the *Employment Rights Act 1996 S.86* (see 3. above). If the parties intend the period of notice to be greater than the statutory period and this is not expressly stated in the contract, the courts may decide on what is reasonable in the circumstances. This depends on, e.g., the status, skills and length of service of the employee. Some examples of court decisions in the past in this respect are: 12 months for the chief engineer of an ocean liner (***SAVAGE v BRITISH INDIA STEAM NAVIGATION CO LTD (1930)***), 6 months for a journalist (***BAUMAN v HULTON PRESS LTD (1952)***), 3 months for a company director (***JAMES v THOS H KENT & CO LTD (1951)***) and 1 month for an advertising and canvassing agent (***HISCOX v BATCHELOR (1867)***).

11. If the employer dismisses an employee without notice the employee may take action for wrongful dismissal, unless the dismissal results from certain actions of the employee.

12. ***A Fixed-Term Contract*** A contract of employment will be regarded as one of a fixed term if it states the maximum duration of the contract, even if provision is made for notice to be given before this by either party. It is not a fixed contract if it has no definite end, i.e. based upon some uncertain future event. A contract for the completion of a particular task is not a fixed-term contract.

13. ***Action by the Employee*** The employer may terminate a contract of employment without notice if the employee acts in such a manner as to show repudiation of the contract. The circumstances can be summarized as being:

    a. *Misconduct*. Where the conduct of the employee interferes with the proper performance of his duties, even outside working house, e.g. drunkenness, immorality, insubordination.

    b. *Disobedience*. Disobedience of a lawful order may justify dismissal, but this may be mitigated if it is only a single act which is not a wilful flouting of authority.

    c. *Negligence*. Negligence, to warrant dismissal, must be a single act of a serious nature or habitual minor acts.

    Details of the above circumstances, with case law, are outlined in Chapter 51.

    Since the introduction of statutory unfair dismissal employees must be given a clear indication of the type of conduct which the employer regards as warranting summary dismissal. Moreover the misconduct must be gross or grave, seen in the light of all the circumstances of the case.

    In ***MARTIN v YORKSHIRE IMPERIAL METALS LTD (1978)*** dismissal was for tying down one of two levers (designed as a safety device to occupy both hands of an operative) which activated a machine. The operative admitted to being aware that interference with the safety device would lead to dismissal without warning. It was held that the dismissal was fair.

Contrast *LADBROKE RACING LTD v ARNOTT (1979)* where the Employment Appeal Tribunal (EAT) held that warning of liability to summary dismissal could not be justification for summary dismissal for a minor offence.

CONSTRUCTIVE DISMISSAL

14. A contract of employment may be terminated by an employer's repudiatory conduct. For there to be a repudiation by the employer he must by his act or omission be guilty of either a fundamental breach of the contract or a breach of a fundamental term of the contract. The term may be express or implied:

In *MARRIOTT v OXFORD AND DISTRICT CO-OPERATIVE SOCIETY LTD (1970)* P (an electrical supervisor) was informed that because of a reduction in the size of his department his post had been made redundant and his salary and status would be reduced. P protested but continued to work under the new conditions for a few weeks until he found alternative employment. It was held that his contract had been terminated unilaterally by his employer. The fact that he had stayed on for a few weeks did not signify his agreement to the change.

In *COLEMAN v BALDWIN (1977)* the buyer in a greengrocery business had the bulk and the most interesting part of his work removed from him, which left only repetitive and boring duties. This occurred without any agreement. It was held that there was a fundamental breach of contract entitling the employee to leave. It was unfair because no attempt had been made to negotiate with him.

15. For the purposes of redundancy and unfair dismissal the *EMPLOYMENT RIGHTS ACT 1996 (S.95)* gives statutory force to the doctrine of constructive dismissal by declaring that an employee shall be treated as dismissed by his employer if the employee terminates the contract, with or without notice, in circumstances such that he is entitled to terminate it without notice by reason of the employer's conduct. Examples of the courts' interpretation are given below:

In *WESTERN EXCAVATING (EEC) LTD v SHARP (1978)* an employee left his employment because his employer would not give him an advance of pay. It was held that this was not a fundamental breach of contract. The employee could not leave on some 'equitable test' based on the employer's 'unreasonable conduct'.

However, in *BRITISH AIRCRAFT CORPORATION LTD v AUSTIN (1978)* it was suggested that a term might be implied in a contract of employment that employers shall act in accordance with good industrial relations practice.

In *WIGAN BOROUGH COUNCIL v DAVIES (1979)* D, an employee at an old peoples' home was 'sent to Coventry' by fellow employees following her impropriety. It was not possible to move her to another job. D left and claimed constructive dismissal. It was held that the employer had been in breach of the contractual obligation to give her support to enable her to carry out her duties free from harassment.

In *ISLE OF WIGHT TOURIST BOARD v COOMBES (1976)* a director made a remark to his secretary about another employee that she was an intolerable bitch on a Monday morning. The employee left and claimed constructive dismissal. It was held that there was a fundamental alteration to the trust and respect the relationship required.

REMEDIES FOR WRONGFUL DISMISSAL

16. *Damages* To claim damages for wrongful dismissal the employee must prove that:

    a. He was engaged on a fixed term – and that he was dismissed before the expiry of the term.

    b. The contract stipulates a period of notice – and that the dismissal was without such notice.

    c. The notice given was less than that required by the *EMPLOYMENT RIGHTS ACT 1996*.

    d. Dismissal was without just cause.

17. *Assessment of Damages*

    a. Damages should cover such loss as may be fairly considered to arise naturally from the breach and also for any loss which was reasonably foreseeable as likely to arise from the breach. Generally the amount awarded should compensate for the monetary loss for the period of notice entitlement.

    b. The amount should cover the following:

        i.   Wages.

        ii.   Gratuities.

        iii. Commission.

        iv.   Publicity and reputation (Actors etc.).

        v.   Difficulty in obtaining future employment in cases where narrow specialization has occurred.

        Damages have traditionally not been recoverable for what are termed 'non-economic losses', such as the manner in which the dismissal took place (*ADDIS v GRAMO-PHONE CO (1909)*), or for hurt feelings, in *BRITISH GUIANA CREDIT CORPN v DA SILVA (1965)* the employee unsuccessfully claimed additional damages in respect of 'humiliation, embarrassment and loss of reputation'. This was later confirmed in *NORTON TOOL CO V TEWSON (1973)*. However, in *JOHNSON v UNISYS LTD (2001)* Lord Hoffman took the view that there was no reason why damages for hurt feelings should not be awarded. The Court of Appeal in *DUNNACHIE v KINGSTON – UPON – HULL CITY COUNCIL (2004)* ruled that *S.123* of the *EMPLOYMENT RIGHTS ACT 1996* which deals with compensation awards for *unfair dismissal* (see 20. below) was wide enough to cover an award of damages for non-economic loss, but that such awards should be for 'real injury' to self-respect. In the case an award of £10 000 in damages was made which took account of extreme workplace bullying which management knew about but failed to address. However on appeal, the House of Lords (now the Supreme Court) ruled that in *unfair dismissal* claims (see 20. below) compensation for non-economic loss should not be allowed as it was outside of *S.123 EMPLOYMENT RIGHTS ACT 1996*.

18. *Deductions from Damages* A dismissed employee must mitigate his loss (*BRACE v CALDER (1895)*). In assessment of damages the court would take the following into account:

a. Income tax liability.

b. Unemployment benefit received by the employee.

c. National insurance contributions payable.

d. Unfair dismissal compensation received.

e. Redundancy payment received.

19. *Other Remedies* Other remedies, apart from damages are:

a. *Quantum meruit* (as much as he has earned). This is an equitable remedy compelling the defendant to pay for performance done and already accepted.

b. *Injunction.* A court will not normally grant an injunction which has the effect of requiring specific performance of a contract for personal services owing to the voluntary nature of contracts of employment and the difficulty of the supervision of the enforcement of this remedy.

In *PAGE ONE RECORDS v BRITTON (1968)* an injunction was sought against a pop group (the 'Troggs') which would require the group to honour a promise to employ a certain person as manager. The injunction was refused as it was held that a manager had duties of a 'personal and fiduciary' nature and in this particular case the pop group had lost confidence in the person.

However, sometimes an injunction will be granted restraining an employee from working for a rival employer, e.g. *WARNER BROTHERS v NELSON (1937)* (see Chapter 21.11).

An injunction may be granted in exceptional cases:

In *HILL v C.A. PARSONS LTD (1972)* the court granted the employee an injunction restraining his employer from terminating his employment. The employer had been influenced by union pressure to dismiss the employee, and the court considered it a 'highly exceptional case'.

UNFAIR DISMISSAL

20. The law relating to unfair dismissal is contained in the *S.94, EMPLOYMENT RIGHTS ACT 1996 (ERA)*. The rights apply to those working on a contract of service i.e. employees, it does not extend to the self-employed.

21. *Excluded Categories*

Employees with less than 1-year's continuous service are excluded from unfair dismissal protection.

22. *Pre-hearing* (*S.9*)

In order to assess the merits and likely success of a claim to an employment tribunal, the chair of the tribunal – referred to as a 'judge', sitting alone, can require a deposit of £500 from a potential claimant, as a condition of the claim proceeding where it is felt that the claim has no reasonable prospect of success or that to pursue it would be frivolous vexatious or otherwise unreasonable. The *S.22 EMPLOYMENT ACT 2002*, also provides the awarding of costs and expenses against representatives – persons who charge for their services – such as lawyers, instead of the parties where it is felt a claim is vexatious or there is inappropriate behaviour. This could mean that a representative is unable to claim fees and expenses from the client and may even have to pay the other party's costs themselves. Also, the section allows a tribunal to award costs associated with the time and expense of preparing the case, to the other party – usually the employer – where it is felt the action was unreasonable.

23. *The Meaning of 'Dismissal'* 'Dismissal' is deemed to have occurred in the following situations *(S.95)*:

   a.   The employee's contract of employment is terminated, with or without notice (i.e. voluntary resignation is not 'dismissal').

   b.   The employee is employed under a fixed-term contract which is not renewed.

   c.   The employer is in breach of contract, in circumstances such that the employee is entitled to regard the contract as repudiated, i.e. *constructive dismissal* (see 14. above).

   d.   Failure to permit a female employee to return to work after confinement.

   Note: The employee must prove 'dismissal'.

24. *Compensation for Unfair Dismissal* The right not to be 'unfairly' dismissed is applicable regardless of whether or not the employer has given the statutory amount of notice. The concept of unfair dismissal goes some way towards acknowledging the property right an employee has in his job.

   The onus is on the employer to prove that the dismissal was fair. He must satisfy the tribunal that there was a valid *admissible reason* for the dismissal, i.e. any one of the following reasons:

   a.   *Lack of capability or qualifications.* Capability is assessed by reference to skill, aptitude, health or any other physical or mental quality. Qualification refers to any degree, diploma or other academic, technical or professional qualification relevant to the position which the employee held.

      In *WINTERHALTER GASTRONOM v WEBB (1973)* a sales director was held to have been fairly dismissed where his employers established that he had not achieved the standard of sales which the company was entitled to expect from its sales director, notwithstanding the difficulties under which he was working.

      Contrast *EARL v SLATER & WHEELER (AIRLYNE) LTD (1972)* where a planning and estimating engineer was dismissed, after several warnings, for inadequate performance. He was dismissed after a spell of absence when it was discovered that contracts were behind time. On his return to work he was handed a letter dismissing him summarily. The court found the dismissal to be unfair as the employee was not given an opportunity to explain the deficiencies in his work.

      Generally an employee should be given an opportunity to state his case, but failure to do so does not necessarily render dismissal unfair:

      In *TAYLOR v ALIDAIR LTD (1978)* an airline pilot made one single but serious mistake on landing his aircraft. His dismissal was held to be fair even though he had been given no opportunity to state his case prior to dismissal.

   b.   *The conduct of the employee.* Examples of misconduct which have been held to justify dismissal include: dishonesty (even suspected dishonesty), breach of safety regulations, conviction for a criminal offence, sexual aberrations, fighting with fellow employees, disclosing information to a competing firm and rudeness to customers.

In *NEEFJES v CRYSTAL PRODUCTS CO LTD (1972)* the employee assaulted a fellow employee and was dismissed. He had been warned in writing several months earlier that he would be dismissed in the event of further complaints as to his conduct. It was held that he was fairly dismissed. For crimes committed outside of employment the employer would have to show some damage to the organization. In *POST OFFICE V LIDDIARD (2001)*, an employee was involved in football violence overseas, he was dismissed. A tribunal found the dismissal unfair, there was no evidence of any adverse effect on the business of the employer.

An employee may refuse to obey an unreasonable order:

In *MORRISH v HENLYS (FOLKESTONE) LTD (1973)* a stores driver objected when the manager altered the record of the amount of diesel oil drawn by the employee. The manager explained that alteration of the record was done in order to cover any discrepancies in the account. He was dismissed when he continued to object. It was held that the dismissal was unfair, as his objection to the falsification of the account was not unreasonable.

Conduct outside working hours may also amount to a valid reason for dismissal if it affects his employer's business adversely:

In *SINGH v LONDON COUNTY BUS SERVICES LTD (1976)* the employee drove a one-man-operated bus. He was convicted of offences of dishonesty committed outside his employment. It was held that misconduct does not have to occur in the course of employment, or at the employee's place of work, or even connected with work to justify dismissal, so long as it somehow affects the employee when he is doing his work or is thought likely to do so.

In *CREFFIELD v BBC (1975)* a film cameraman was dismissed following his conviction of indecently assaulting a 13-year-old girl. His dismissal was held to be fair as the employer could not be selective in allocation of assignments to the employee, and might justifiably fear a recurrence of the employee's behaviour.

c.   *If the employee is redundant.* Provided there is no unfair discrimination and the proper procedures are carried out, an employee who is dismissed because of redundancy will not succeed in a claim for unfair dismissal.

In *HEATHCOTE v NORTH WESTERN ELECTRICITY BOARD (1974)* the employee held the position of driver's mate, classed as a labourer. He was dismissed for redundancy because the board decided there was no longer any need for drivers' mates. Selection was made on the basis of last in, first out. However, selection was confined to the transport section and not the whole of the business. It was held that this was not the correct approach. As the employee was in a class of lesser-skilled worker selection should have been made from the whole concern.

d.   *If the employee could not continue to work in that position without contravening a statutory restriction.*

In *FEARN v TAYFIELD MOTOR CO LTD (1975)* the employee was engaged as a vehicle supervisor, part of his duties including the requirement to drive vehicles. He was convicted of careless driving and failing to stop after an accident and was disqualified from driving for 12 months. His dismissal was held to be fair as he could no longer legally do the job he was employed to do.

e. *Some other substantial reason.* In considering the case of **RS COMPONENTS LTD v IRWIN (1973)** it was said

'There are not only legal but also practical objections to a narrow construction of "*some other reason*". Parliament may well have intended to set out the common reasons for a dismissal but can hardly have hoped to produce an exhaustive catalogue of all the circumstances in which a company would be justified in terminating the services of an employee.'

Some examples are:

i. Where personality conflicts gave rise to hostility and tension between employees began to have a detrimental effect on the employer's business **TREGANOWAN v ROBERT KNEE & CO LTD (1975)**.

ii. Failure to accede to a request by the employer to work at times other than those provided in the contract **KNIGHTON v HENRY RHODES LTD (1974)**.

iii. Where an employee refuses to sign an undertaking that on leaving the employment he would not compete with the employer **GLENDINNING v PILKINGTON BROS LTD (1973)**.

iv. Where an employee moves to an unreasonable distance from his work, despite a company rule that employees must live within reasonable travelling distance **FARR v HOVERINGHAM GRAVEL LTD (1972)**.

v. When an employee is a danger to other workers **MORTIBOY v ROLLS ROYCE (1983)**.

25. *Employer Reasonableness* Even if the employer can show that an employee was dismissed for any of the above reasons, or some other substantial reason he must have acted 'reasonably' in dismissing the employee.

The decision is left to the tribunal which would take into account all circumstances including the size and administrative resources of the undertaking, and decide the question on the grounds of equity and the substantial merits of the case. The tribunal's assessment of whether a particular employer has acted reasonably or not will require that he be compared with what a similar employer might reasonably have done in a similar situation. This was laid down in **ICELAND FROZEN FOODS v JONES (1983)** where the Court held that if a tribunal found that a similar employer might reasonably dismiss, then the dismissal is fair, it is not for the tribunal to decide alone. This has been referred to as the 'range of reasonable employer response' test. In **FOLEY V POST OFFICE AND HSBC BANK V MADDEN (2000)**, The Court of Appeal reaffirmed the approach to the assessment of reasonableness. Tribunals were not to approach the matter of reasonableness or unreasonableness of a dismissal by reference to their own judgement of what would have been done if they had been the employer. A tribunal should conclude that a dismissal is fair if it is within the *range of reasonable responses* an employer might make, even though the tribunal would not have regarded the response of an employer as reasonable.

With regard to the *admissible reason of conduct*, a crime committed within employment will usually amount to gross misconduct justifying instant (summary) dismissal. In **FRANCIS v BOOTS THE CHEMIST LTD (1998)** an employee was observed loading boxes into the boot of his car at night, he was summarily dismissed. The Employment Appeal Tribunal found the employer acted reasonably and that the dismissal was fair, even though the employer could not prove any loss of stock. The employer had a reasonable belief based upon reasonable grounds and that was sufficient. Theft from the employer, however low the value, will constitute gross misconduct. In **TESCO STORES LTD v KHALID (2001)** an employee was dismissed for taking cigarettes from his employer's stock. His dismissal was held to be fair even though the stock was damaged and was due to be returned to the manufacturer; his dismissal was within the *range of reasonable employer responses.*

Crime committed outside of employment is not so clear. Whilst, as seen, the employer is required to act reasonably within the *range of reasonable employer responses* it appears that the crime would need to impact in some way on the employment relationship. For example, the treasurer of a cricket club caught stealing could well be dismissed from his employment if his job were an accountant working for a local authority. In **POST OFFICE v LID-DIARD (2001)** an employee was dismissed from his job after being involved in football violence. The tribunal found the dismissal to be unfair. If the employee had been a teacher for instance, the dismissal might well be found to be fair.

26. *Procedural Fairness*

In determining whether or not an employer has acted reasonably or not the tribunal may examine the procedures followed by the employer. Guidance as to the fairness of a procedure can be obtained from the *ACAS CODE OF PRACTICE ON DISCIPLINARY AND GRIEVANCE PROCEDURES.* The Code is a guide with the purpose of promoting good industrial relations. If an employer fails to observe any provision of the codes he will not be thereby liable to any proceedings, but the employment tribunal can take the codes into account in any proceedings brought against the employer. Procedural fairness requires the employer to:

a.   A set of rules attempting to set out the circumstances that may give rise to disciplinary procedures.

b.   Employees must be made aware of the likely consequences of breaking the rules. They should in particular clearly identify those acts which can result in dismissal without notice.

c.   Disciplinary procedures should not be seen as primarily a means of imposing sanctions; they should help and encourage an improvement in performance.

d.   Due regard should be paid to the rules of natural justice, that is:

   i.   Advanced warning to the employee of the hearing and allegations alleged with evidence.

   ii.   An opportunity to challenge the allegations and evidence before a decision is reached.

   iii.   A right of appeal against the decision.

   iv.   Provision for a brief period of suspension with full pay, where relationships have broken down or there is a risk to property, should be available.

   v.   Conditions applying for oral or written warnings should be clearly stated.

   The *EMPLOYMENT RELATIONS ACT 1999* introduced the right for employees to be accompanied by a single person if the employee requests it.

27. *Presumption of Unfair Dismissal* Dismissal is presumed to be unfair in the following circumstances:

a.   The employee was selected for redundancy whilst other employees in a similar position were retained and either:

   i.   Selection was in contravention of an agreed or customary arrangement relating to redundancy (e.g. last in, first out), or

    ii.   Reason for the selective dismissal was in connection with the trade union membership or activities of the employee.

b.   *Dismissal on the grounds of pregnancy and childbirth.* An employee shall be treated as unfairly dismissed if the reason, or principal reason is:

    i.   Pregnancy or a reason connected with pregnancy.

    ii.   Maternity leave period is ended by dismissal and the reason is that she has given birth to a child.

    iii.   She took or availed herself of the benefits of maternity leave.

    iv.   Before the end of maternity leave she notified her employer that by reason of disease or bodily or mental disablement she would be incapable of work after the end of her leave, or her contract was terminated within 4 weeks of the end of her leave when she continued to be incapable of work and the reason for dismissal was that she had given birth to a child.

    v.   Her maternity leave is ended by dismissal on account of redundancy and the employer has not complied with the statutory requirements (offer of alternative employment).

c.   If the employee was selected for dismissal on grounds of race or sex.

d.   *TRANSFER OF UNDERTAKING (PROTECTION OF EMPLOYMENT) REGULATIONS 2006.* When an undertaking is transferred from one person to another every contract of employment is automatically transferred. A relevant transfer will be found where, pre-transfer, there is an undertaking consisting of an organized group of employees which has as its principal purpose the carrying out of the activities concerned on behalf of the transferor, and the transferee carries out the same activities. However, an organized grouping of employees will include a single employee. There has to exist an *economic entity* by which is meant an organized grouping of resources (including employees) which has the objective of pursuing an economic activity, whether or not that activity was central or ancillary to the employer. The Regulations will not apply where there exists a single specific event or task of short-term duration. Where the Regulations apply, if either the transferor or transferee dismisses any employee for a reason connected with the transfer the dismissal is unfair. Dismissal, however, will not be unfair if it is caused by economic, technical or organizational reasons incidental to the transfer and these reasons entail changes in the workforce of either the transferor or transferee. On the other hand an employee need not accept a transfer if there is a substantial change in his working conditions or the change of employer leads to a significant change, to the detriment of the employee.

In **SHIPP v D.J. CATERING LTD (1982)** dismissal in order to reduce manning levels under new management was held by an industrial tribunal to be fair – the dismissal being economic grounds for changes in the workforce.

e.   *Dismissal for claiming a statutory right.* It will be an automatic unfair dismissal where an employee is dismissed for bringing proceedings against the employer to enforce a statutory right.

f.   *Cases of health and safety.* Dismissals will be automatically unfair where the reason for dismissal was an employee carrying out health and safety duties.

g. *Working time.* Dismissal will be automatically unfair where the reason for the dismissal is an employee insisting on his rights under the *WORKING TIME REGULATIONS 1998.*

h. Dismissal for a spent conviction under the *REHABILITATION OF OFFENDERS ACT 1974.*

28. **Dismissal in Other Circumstances** The following are the rules of unfair dismissal in other situations:

a. *Unfair dismissal in connection with trade union membership or activities.*

The dismissal of an employee shall be regarded as unfair if the reason for dismissal is that the employee:

i. Was or proposed to become a member of an independent trade union, or

ii. Had taken part or proposed to take part in the activities of an independent trade union, or

iii. Was not a member of any trade union or had refused or proposed to refuse to become or remain a member.

b. *Dismissal during a strike.* If an employee is dismissed for taking part in a strike the tribunal has no jurisdiction to decide whether the dismissal was fair or unfair unless it was a case of selective dismissal, i.e.

i. Others taking the same action were not dismissed, or

ii. Any of the strikers has, within 3 months, been offered re-engagement, but the complainant has not been offered re-engagement, and the reason is the complainant's membership or non-membership of a trade union or union activities.

Note: There may be selective dismissal of employees taking part in an unofficial strike or other unofficial action.

c. *Dismissal during a lock-out.* Dismissal following a lock-out is fair if the employee is offered re-engagement from the date of resumption of work, and refuses. Dismissal is unfair if re-engagement is not offered.

d. *Industrial pressure.* If an employer dismisses an employee because of threats of strike action by other employees no account shall be taken of this factor in deciding whether the dismissal was fair or unfair.

e. Dismissal on grounds of health and safety (see Chapters 61.42–61.44).

29. **Written Statement of Reasons for Dismissal** Employees with 1-year's service have a right to a written statement of the reasons for their dismissal, subject to the following conditions (*S.92*):

a. The entitlement to a statement does not depend on whether or not the dismissal is fair.

b. It must be supplied by the employer within 14 days of the request.

c. Failure to provide a statement within 14 days, or the provision of one with 'inadequate or untrue' reasons gives the right of a complaint to an industrial tribunal within 3 months of dismissal.

d. The statement has the protection of 'qualified privilege', i.e. the employer will not be liable for defamatory statements unless malice can be proved.

REMEDIES FOR UNFAIR DISMISSAL

30. *Conciliation* and *Arbitration*

If either party to a potential claim request it, a conciliation officer from the Advisory, Conciliation and Arbitration Service (ACAS) will try to settle the dispute. If unsuccessful the complaint will proceed with all matters relating to discussions in that informal conciliation process, not being admissible before a tribunal.

ACAS also provides an arbitration service whereby the parties can agree to be bound by the outcome of an arbitration process conducted by a conciliation officer.

31. *Reinstatement and Re-engagement* An unfairly dismissed employee has the right to state whether he wishes to be reinstated or re-engaged. In reinstatement the employee is treated in all respects as if he had not been dismissed. Any pay, pension and seniority must be restored to him and he must be given any pay arrears and any other lost benefits. In re-engagement the employee may be employed in a different job provided it is suitable. The terms and conditions may differ from the previous ones. Re-engagement may be by a new employer, e.g a successor to the former employer. Damages may be awarded in respect of loss of benefits arising between the dismissal and re-engagement (*S.117–118*).

32. The tribunal may make a recommendation to reinstatement taking into account the extent to which the employee contributed to his own dismissal and the practicability of reinstatement (e.g. his fellow-employees' attitude). Alternatively the tribunal can recommend re-engagement.

33. If an employer fails to comply with a recommendation for reinstatement or re-engagement he may be liable to pay 'punitive' compensation in addition to compensation based on actual loss suffered by the employee.

34. *Compensation* Any compensation which may be awarded is based on the following factors:

   a.   The immediate loss of wages, if any.

   b.   Compensation for future loss of wages.

   c.   The loss of statutory protection from unfair dismissal and redundancy as the employee will need to complete a further 2 years with another employer to qualify again for such protection.

35. Compensation may be reduced if there is contributory fault on the part of the employee:

In ***ROBERTSON v SECURICOR TRANSPORT LTD (1972)*** an employee was dismissed for carelessness in signing a receipt for a missing container. It was held that he was unfairly dismissed as his employer had not acted reasonably by treating this one act of negligence as sufficient to justify dismissal. However, the employee's compensation was reduced by 50% because of his contributory fault.

36. *Reduction in Basic Award* There are two circumstances under which a tribunal could reduce the basic award of compensation:

   a.   Where the employee has unreasonably refused an offer of reinstatement which would have had the effect if accepted of reinstating him in all respects as if he had not been dismissed.

b. Where the tribunal considers that the employee's conduct before the dismissal was such that it would be just and equitable to reduce the basic award. The conduct referred to was not the reason for the dismissal, but came to light afterwards.

In ***DEVIS & SONS LTD v ATKINS (1977)*** the employee was dismissed for alleged incompetence, receiving 6-weeks notice and £6000 compensation. Afterwards, it came to light that he had been accepting secret commissions. His employers refused to pay the compensation and treated him as summarily dismissed. It was held that this was unfair dismissal as only information known at the time of dismissal is relevant to determine whether it is fair.

37. *Amount of Compensation*

a. *The basic award.* This is calculated on a formula set out in the Act (*S.119*). It is based upon an employee's length of service up to a maximum of 20 years.

It is calculated on a normal week's pay excluding overtime, unless there is a contractual term entitling the employee to work over time. There are limitations on the overall amount claimable; firstly, only a maximum of 20-years service can be claimed; secondly, the amount of weekly pay is a maximum of £430, making the maximum basic award £12 900.

The basic award can be reduced where:

i. Re-engagement or reinstatement is offered and unreasonably refused by the claimant.

ii. The conduct of the employee before the dismissal makes it reasonable to do so.

iii. Where it is found that the true reason for the dismissal was redundancy, the redundancy entitlement will be reduced from the basic award.

b. *Compensatory award.* This is an amount left to a tribunal to determine based upon what it considers to be just and fair, the current maximum under this head is £72 300. (In cases of dismissal founded upon discrimination, there is no upper limit.) Factors covered here will include:

i. Immediate and future loss of earnings.

ii. Expenses and loss of statutory rights.

iii. Loss of pension rights.

iv. Failure of the employer to go through a laid down appeal procedure.

The employee is required to mitigate his loss and the amount awarded will be reduced where he or she fails to do so.

c. *Additional award.* Where an employer unreasonably refuses to re-engage or reinstate an employee an additional award may be made; this will be between 13 and 26 weeks' pay, but if dismissal is on grounds of sex or race this will increase to 26 and 52 weeks' pay. (The week's pay being subject to the £430 maximum.)

35. **Complaints to Employment Tribunals** An employee who considers that he has been unfairly dismissed may complain to an employment tribunal from the time he receives notice. An appeal lies from an industrial tribunal on a point of law to the Employment Appeal Tribunal. Appeals lie from the EAT to the Court of Appeal, and from there to the Supreme Court.

36. *Interim Relief for Unfair Dismissal* An employee may apply to a tribunal for interim relief. He must apply within a period of 7 days following termination of employment. The tribunal must notify the employer of the application, and time of the hearing within 7 days.

The tribunal will announce its findings and ask the employer if he will reinstate or re-engage the employee and treat him as if he had not been dismissed. If the employer will not comply with the tribunal's request or the employee reasonably refuses to accept re-engagement on the employer's terms, the tribunal will make an order for continuance of the employee's contract of service. This is for the purposes of pay and other benefits derived from employment and his period of continuous employment. This order will also specify the amount to be paid by the employer between the date of dismissal and final determination of the complaint. The sums paid will be taken into account in discharging the employer's liability for breach of contract for that period.

SELF TEST QUESTIONS

Self Test Questions No. 54 (for Answers see Appendix 1):

1   How can a contract of employment be terminated?

2   What is *wrongful dismissal*?

3   What is a *constructive dismissal*?

4   What remedies are available for a wrongful dismissal?

5   What is unfair dismissal?

6   Explain each of the stages of an unfair dismissal claim, that is:

who qualifies for protection

the requirement for a dismissal

admissible reasons

employer reasonableness

procedural fairness

remedies.

57 REDUNDANCY

Learning Outcomes At the end of this chapter you should be able to:

- State who is covered by statutory redundancy.

- The requirements for a dismissal to be redundancy.

- Explain how redundancy payments are calculated.

- Outline the requirements for consultation.

INTRODUCTION

1. In certain circumstances an employee may receive compensation for the loss of his job. The amount of compensation is related to the age, length of service and average weekly earnings of the redundant employee. The purpose of the redundancy payments scheme is to compensate for loss of security and to encourage employees to accept redundancy without damaging industrial relations. A Redundancy Fund is established, financed by contributions collected with the employers' National Insurance payments. The fund is used to make redundancy payments in the event of an employer being unable to pay due to insolvency. Disputes about entitlement to payment etc are settled by employment tribunals. The law relating to redundancy payments is contained in the *EMPLOYMENT RIGHTS ACT 1996 S.135*. References in this chapter are to the ERA unless otherwise stated.

CONDITIONS FOR PAYMENT

2. For a person to be entitled to redundancy payment he must have been:

   a. An employee.

   b. Continuously employed for the requisite period.

   c. Dismissed, and

   d. Dismissed by reason of redundancy.

3. *'Employee'* is defined as 'An individual who has entered into or works under (or, where the employment has ceased, worked under) a contract of employment.' In cases where the employer disputes that the applicant was an employee, it is for the applicant to prove that he was in fact an employee.

4. ***Continuous Employment for the Requisite Period*** The applicant must have been continuously employed for a period of 2 years ending with the relevant date. The following events do not break continuity:

   a. *Change in job with the same employer.*

   b. *Change in ownership of the business.* When a business that is wholly or partly carried on in the UK is transferred from one person to another the *TRANSFER OF UNDERTAKINGS (PROTECTION OF EMPLOYMENT) REGULATIONS 2006* impose the following obligation on the transferor and transferee:

      i. Every contract of employment is automatically transferred to the transferee employer. Thus the employee cannot claim that he has been dismissed or made redundant.

      ii. Dismissal by reason of the transfer of the business will be unfair unless it is caused by economic, technical or organizational reasons (ETO) incidental to the transfer. A true redundancy situation might well establish grounds for an ETO justification (See Chapter 56.27.d).

   c. *Engagement by an associated employer.* Where an employee is taken into the employment of an associated company his period of employment with the first company counts as a period of employment with the associated company. Two companies are associated if one has control (directly or indirectly) of the other or if both are controlled (directly or indirectly) by a third person.

      In ***ZARB v BRITISH & BRAZILIAN PRODUCE CO LTD (1978)*** P was a canteen worker employed by Total Staff (Recruitment) Ltd. D took over the running of the canteen and P became employed by them. It was held that the two companies were associated employers. The same two people controlled more than 50 per cent of shares in each company. The case brought out the fact that a group of persons who act together can share control.

   d. *Absence.* Periods of absence from work for reasons of sickness, injury, absence due to pregnancy or confinement of less than 26 weeks, or temporary cessation of work count as periods of employment. Additionally, where an employee exercises her right to return to work after an absence due to pregnancy or confinement, the whole period of absence will count as continuous employment notwithstanding that it is longer than 26 weeks.

e. *Strikes.* The continuity of employment is not destroyed by participation in a strike. However, any week during any part of which the employee is on strike is not counted in the computation of the number of weeks of employment.

f. *Lock-outs.* A period in which an employee is locked out by his employer does not break continuity of employment.

g. *Working temporarily abroad.* An employee may work abroad temporarily for up to 26 weeks without breaking his contract of employment, but the time abroad does not count towards computation of the length of continuous service.

h. *Dismissal followed by reinstatement or re-engagement.* Where an employer reinstates or re-engages an employee after he has been dismissed the continuity of employment is maintained if the action was taken as a result of an application to an industrial tribunal by the employee or as a result of an agreement brought about by a conciliation officer.

The 'relevant date' is generally the date on which the employee actually ceased to work. However, where less than the statutory minimum period of notice is given, the relevant date is calculated as the date on which the minimum period of notice would have expired had it been given. If an employee is given pay in lieu of notice the relevant date is the day of dismissal.

But an employer cannot prevent an employee from having the necessary qualifying period by dismissing him without notice, or with pay in lieu of notice, where to have given him proper notice would have given him the qualifying length of employment. Additionally, an employee exercising her right to return to work after a pregnancy will be deemed to have been continuously employed up to her notified date of return if she is not permitted to return to work by the employer.

Temporary cessation of work is a matter of fact in each case:

In *BENTLEY ENGINEERING CO LTD v CROWN (1976)* C was employed by X Co. from 1948 to 1963 when he became redundant. He obtained employment elsewhere. In 1965 he became employed by Bentley Eng. Co. (an associated company of X Co.) C was subsequently made redundant again and claimed payment on the basis of continuous employment from 1948. It was held that the period 1963 to 1965 should be regarded as temporary cessation of work. Regard was especially taken of the length of service before and after the cessation.

Contrast this with *WISHART v NATIONAL COAL BOARD (1974)* where P was employed by D. He left and subsequently returned. During his absence he remained a member of D's pension scheme (for D employees only). It was held that P was regarded as in D's employment by custom or arrangement for the purposes of the pension scheme. He was therefore to be regarded as in continuous employment for redundancy payments.

5. *The Meaning of Dismissal* By *S.136* an employee will be taken to be dismissed by his employer if:

a. The contract under which he is employed by the employer is terminated by the employer, whether it is terminated by notice or not, or

b. Where under that contract he is employed for a fixed term which expires without being renewed under the same contract, or

c. The employee terminates the contract with or without notice where his employer's conduct is such as to justify the employee leaving without notice (constructive dismissal).

There is no dismissal, and therefore no redundancy payment where an employee leaves voluntarily or where the contract is frustrated:

In *MORTON SUNDOUR FABRICS LTD v SHAW (1966)* S was employed in the company's velvet department. He was notified that his job in that department was likely to end in some months time. S found a job elsewhere and left MSF Ltd. It was held that S was not entitled to a redundancy payment as he had left voluntarily without having had notice from his employer.

6. *Redundancy Must be the Reason for Dismissal* Redundancy is defined by *S.139* as the dismissal of an employee wholly or mainly on account of:

   a. The fact that his employer has ceased, or intends to cease, to carry on the business for the purposes of which the employee was employed by him, or he ceased, or intends to cease, to carry on that business in the place where the employee was so employed, or

   b. The fact that the requirements of that business for employees to carry out work of a particular kind in the place where he was so employed, have ceased or diminished or are expected to cease or diminish.

7. The following cases illustrate how the statutory definition of 'redundancy' has been interpreted:

   In *EUROPEAN CHEFS v CURRELL LTD (1971)* a pastry cook was dismissed because the requirement for his speciality (eclairs and meringues) had ceased and there became a requirement to produce continental pastries, for which another person was taken into employment. It was held that the pastry cook was entitled to redundancy payment as *the need for a cook of his type had ceased*.

   In *VAUX & ASSOCIATED BREWERIES v WARD (1969)* a quiet public house was converted into a discotheque. The landlord dismissed the 57-year-old barmaid as he required a younger person (a 'Bunny Girl') to attract customers. It was held that there was no entitlement to redundancy payment as there had been no change in the nature of the particular work being done.

   In *LESNEY PRODUCTS & CO LTD v NOLAN (1977)* a reorganization entailed elimination of the night shift. The night shift employees received redundancy payments. A double day shift system was introduced and all day shift workers were offered employment on it. Those who refused the offer were dismissed. It was held that they were not entitled to redundancy payments as *there had been no diminution in requirement for a type of worker, just a reorganization in the interests of efficiency*.

   In *UK ATOMIC ENERGY AUTHORITY v CLAYDON (1974)* the employee was obliged by his contract to move anywhere in the UK as required by his employer. *The need for fewer employees at one plant did not constitute a diminution at his place of employment* as his place of employment was 'anywhere in the UK'.

   In *NORTH RIDING GARAGES v BUTTERWICK (1967)* B had been employed at a garage for 30 years as a workshop manager, which mainly involved a mechanic's work. When the garage came under new ownership B was required to deal with administrative as well as technical matters. B found that he could not adapt to the new situation, and was dismissed. He claimed redundancy payment but failed as it was held that there had been no diminution in requirement for a workshop manager.

   In *HINDLE v PERCIVAL BOATS LTD (1969)* P was dismissed on the grounds that his work was too thorough to be economical. He was a highly skilled carpenter who had spent his working life building boats and his employer's business had moved from wooden hulled to fibreglass boats. The company still employed woodworkers to install wooden furniture. It was held that dismissal was not due to redundancy as the employers still required woodworkers.

In *O'HARE v ROTOPRINT LTD (1980)* in anticipation of increased sales the employers took on additional personnel. The increased work failed to materialize and the staff was reduced back to its original level. It was held that *there was no cessation or diminution of work*, and a redundancy payment was inadmissible.

In *CHAPMAN v GOONVEAN AND ROSTOWRACK CHINA CLAY CO LTD (1973)* the company provided free transport for employees living 30 miles from the works. The transport was discontinued when demand fell so as to make it uneconomical. Employees who could not then get to work gave notice. It was held that there was no redundancy as the *requirement for employees had not diminished.*

In *BROMBY & HOARE LTD v EVANS (1972)* the company's business had been increasing but found it more economical to use self-employed workers rather than its own men. As a consequence two workers were dismissed. It was held that they were entitled to redundancy payments as the company's need for employees had diminished.

In *EXEC. OF EVEREST v COX (1980)* a canteen manageress of a firm with a concession at a police station was offered suitable employment elsewhere when the concession came to an end. She refused because the company taking over the work led her to believe she would be employed by them, but in the event she was not. It was held that she was entitled to redundancy payment as her conduct was not unreasonable at the time she took the decision.

In *J. STOTT & SON LTD v STOKES (1971)* the employee, an alleged troublemaker was sacked for absenting himself from a site when he should have been working. He claimed it was a cover-up for redundancy. It was held that as it was proved the dismissal was due to conduct entitling the employer to sack him summarily, then even though a redundancy situation existed, the employee was not entitled to redundancy pay.

In *HIGH TABLE LTD. v HORST (1997)* the question arose as to whether an employee could truly be regarded as being redundant where there was an express term in the contract of employment stating that the employee could be required to work anywhere within the UK (a mobility clause). The employer claimed that the employees were no longer needed at the place where they worked and were therefore, redundant. The employees claimed that they could have been relocated to another branch. The Court of Appeal ruled that the correct approach was a factual investigation into whether employees had in fact been required to work at one location and not what the strict contractual terms stated.

In *SAFEWAY STORES PLC v BURRELL (1997)* a petrol station manager was dismissed following a reorganization of the workforce; a new post, at a reduced salary, of petrol station controller was introduced. There were insufficient vacancies in the new post and redundancies were inevitable. The claimant argued that he had not been made redundant as the new post was essentially the same as his old job. The court laid down a three stage test as to whether a redundancy situation existed:

a. Was the employee dismissed? if so

b. Had the requirements of the employer's business for employees to carry out work of a particular kind ceased or diminished?

c. Was the dismissal of the employee caused wholly or mainly by the state of affairs identified at stage ii?

Whether the claimant was no longer needed was to be assessed by reference to the needs of the business; here the claimant was no longer required and was redundant. This statutory test approach was affirmed in a recent House of Lords decision (*MURRAY v FOYLE MEATS (1999)*). The current situation now appears to be that the employer only needs to show some reduction in the need for work of a particular kind in his business and that this situation led to the dismissal of the claimant. For example, an employer who employs two chefs and one receptionist may show redundancy where the requirements of the business for chefs is reduced (as in a fall in demand) and selects the receptionist for redundancy (being the last to join the business) and gives that job to one of the chefs (sometimes referred to as 'bumping').

SPECIAL CONDITIONS FOR LAY-OFF AND SHORT-TIME

In *NEEPSEND STEEL & TOOL CORPN v VAUGHAN (1972)* in order to cancel the effect of lay-offs or short time an employee must be offered work of a kind he is employed to do. This is not a case of a 'suitable alternative offer' of work.

EXCLUSIONS FROM THE RIGHT TO A REDUNDANCY PAYMENT

8. The following employees are not entitled to a redundancy payment:

    a. Employees who have not completed at least 2-years' continuous employment with their employer.

    b. Civil servants and other public employees.

    c. Persons employed as a domestic servant by someone to whom they are related.

    d. Share fishermen.

    e. Persons on a fixed-term contract who have agreed in writing to exclude any right to a redundancy payment. (This is the only circumstance in which the statutory right to a redundancy payment may be excluded by a term in the contract of employment.)

    f. Employees who are summarily dismissed for misconduct or if notice is given and is accompanied by a statement in writing that the employer would be entitled to terminate the contract without notice by reason of the employee's conduct. This provision does not apply where the dismissal is for taking part in a strike.

    g. Employees who, after having been given notice of dismissal for redundancy, accept oral or written offers of further employment on the same or similar conditions.

    h. Employees who unreasonably refuse oral or written offers of further employment on the same or similar conditions. Where the offer of continued employment is on different terms and conditions, the employee must be permitted a trial period of up to 4 weeks in which to decide whether the job is suitable.

    i. Persons outside Great Britain on the relevant date, unless they are ordinarily employed in Great Britain.

    j. Persons ordinarily employed outside Great Britain unless they are at the relevant date in Great Britain in accordance with their employer's instructions.

(The non-entitlement to persons outside Great Britain does not apply to persons employed as master or seamen in a British ship who are ordinarily resident in Great Britain.)

Note: *Suitable Alternative Offer and Reasonable Rejection.* Whether an offer of alternative employment is suitable or not must be determined objectively. If an employee's wages or status are considerably reduced, this will not normally amount to a suitable alternative. Even if the offer is suitable, an employee may not be barred from compensation if he can show that his refusal to accept it was not unreasonable in the circumstances. The latter is a subjective test, and may depend on personal or financial circumstances.

In *TAYLOR v KENT COUNTY COUNCIL (1969)* P was headmaster of a boys' school. The school was amalgamated with a girls' school and new head appointed over the combined school. P was offered employment in a pool of teachers, standing in for short periods in understaffed schools. He would retain his current salary. It was held that P was entitled to redundancy pay as he was being offered something substantially different, particularly in regard to status.

CALCULATION OF REDUNDANCY PAYMENTS

9. The amount of the payment is related to the employee's length of continuous employment, age and gross average wage.

10. *Continuous Employment* This is employment on a contract of employment excluding the following:

   a.   Any week when the employee was on strike.

   b.   Any week before the employee's 18th birthday.

   c.   Any week when the employee was employed outside Great Britain and no employer's contribution was payable in respect of that week.

11. *Term of Employment* The amount of redundancy payment is calculated in the same way as the basic award for unfair dismissal (see Chapter 56.36).

NOTIFICATION OF REDUNDANCIES UNDER TRADE UNION AND LABOUR RELATIONS CONSOLIDATION ACT 1992 *(TULRCA)*

12. *Introduction* The employer has a duty under the EPA to notify both recognized trade unions and the Secretary of State for Employment of forthcoming redundancies.

13. *Notification to Trade Unions* An employer proposing to dismiss as redundant any employee of a class in respect of a trade union recognized for collective bargaining purposes must consult with the representatives of that union at the earliest opportunity, and in any event comply with the following timings:

   a.   Where it is proposed to dismiss 100 or more employees at one establishment within a period of 90 days or less, notification must be given at least 90 days before the first of the dismissals takes effect.

b.   Where it is proposed to dismiss 10 or more, but less than 100 within a period of 30 days or less, notification must be given at least 30 days before the first of the dismissals takes effect.

The employer must begin consultations with the trade union representatives before giving individual notices of dismissal.

In *NATIONAL UNION OF TEACHERS v AVON COUNTY COUNCIL (1978)* the employers issued dismissal notices to some of their teachers on 28 October 1976. Consultation over redundancies with the recognized independent union was not started until 29 October 1976. It was held that the employer failed to comply with the rules, in that individual notices of dismissal should not have been issued before consultations begin.

14. *Consultation* When the employer is planning redundancies involving 20 or more employees, there is an obligation to consult with any recognized trade union or other employee representatives (*S.188–198 TULRCA*). For the purposes of consultation, the employer must disclose in writing to the trade union representatives or employee representatives the following:

a.   Reasons for the proposed redundancies.

b.   Number and description of the employees involved.

c.   Total number in that category employed at the establishment.

d.   Proposed method of selection for redundancy.

e.   Proposed method of carrying out the dismissals.

The employer must consider any representations made by the trade union or employee representatives, reply to those representations and where he rejects any of them, state his reasons. The requirement is to begin the consultation process when the employer is *contemplating* redundancies, which suggests consultation should begin as soon as is reasonably practicable. In *R v BRITISH COAL CORPORATION, EX PARTE VARDY (1993)* it was held that consultation should begin when the employer first believes there may be a need to make redundancies. And, in *JUNK v KUHNEL (2005)* the European Court of Justice (ECJ) held that this should be when the employer forms an intention to make redundancies and not when the notices of dismissal are sent to employees.

TULRCA S.188 states that consultation should take place:

i.   Where between 20 and 99 employees are to be made redundant and the minimum consultation period is 30 days before the first dismissal.

ii.   Where over 100 employees are to be made redundant – the minimum period is 90 days before the first dismissal.

When an employee has been informed they are to be made redundant, they are entitled to time off work to attend training courses and attend interviews (*S.52 EMPLOYMENT RIGHTS ACT 1996*).

Failure to consult may render the employer liable to a claim for unfair dismissal and a complaint by the trade union to an employment tribunal.

15. *The Protective Award* Where a trade union makes a complaint, which is upheld by the tribunal, the tribunal may make a protective award. In this case the employer will have to pay remuneration to the specified employees for a protected period. This is the period beginning with the date on which the first of the dismissals take effect, or the date of the award whichever is the earlier.

The maximum awards permitted are:

a.   Up to 90 days' pay where a minimum of 90 days' notice should have been given.

b.   Up to 30 days' pay where a minimum of 30 days' notice should have been given, or

c.   Up to 28 days' pay in any other case.

In *JOSHUA WILSON & BROS. v USDAW (1978)* the EAT made a protection award of 40 days because it found that on 31 January 1977 the employees were told that they were being made redundant as from 26 February, since the warehouse in which they were working was closing down. The employers recognized the independent union for collective bargaining purposes and there were no special circumstances in which the employers could claim exemption from their duty to consult the union.

Any payment of wages made by an employer to an employee in respect of any period covered by a protective award will offset the protective award.

An employer who fails to consult with the trade union may use as a defence that special circumstances existed which made it impracticable to consult. Nevertheless he must show that he has taken steps to comply as are reasonably practicable. An employee himself cannot apply for a protective award but may complain to an industrial tribunal if he fails to receive full payment of any such award.

16. *Notification to the Department for Business Innovation and Skills* The employer also has a duty to notify the DOBIS when redundancies are proposed. Employers proposing to dismiss over 100 employees are required to notify the Department at least 90 days before the first redundancy takes place (*S.193 TULRCA*) between 20 and 100, at least 30 days before dismissals. The requirements are as for trade unions. Failure to notify the Department is a criminal offence and may lead to a fine (*S.194 TULRCA*).

MISCELLANEOUS PROVISIONS

17. *Death of Employer* Where the employer dies the employee is deemed to be dismissed and may claim a redundancy payment from his employer's personal representative, unless the business is carried on and re-engagement is offered and takes effect within 8 weeks.

18. *Death of Employee* Where the employee dies, any unresolved claims which are pending will survive him.

19. *Insolvency of Employer* A redundant employee may claim payment out of the Redundancy Fund where his employer is unable to make payment on the grounds of insolvency.

20. *Employee Leaving Before Expiry of Notice* A redundant employee wishing to leave before expiry of his notice may do so if he notifies his employer in writing and the employer has no objection. If the employer objects he must notify the employee of his objection and his intention to contest the redundancy payment.

21. *Strikes During Notice* If, whilst serving notice due to redundancy, an employee is dismissed for going on strike he is still entitled to a redundancy payment. The employer may require him to return to work to complete the days lost due to the strike.

22. *Written Statement* On making any redundancy payment, except as a result of a tribunal decision, the employer must give the employee a written statement indicating how the payment has been calculated.

23. *Time Limit for Claims* Employees are not entitled to a redundancy payment after 6 months from the date of redundancy unless:

 a.   The payment has been agreed and paid.

 b.   The employee has made a claim for payment in writing.

 c.   A question as to the right of the employee to the payment, or to the amount, has been referred to an industrial tribunal.

 d.   A complaint of unfair dismissal has been presented by the employee to an industrial tribunal.

 An industrial tribunal may order a redundancy payment in respect of a late claim if it considers it 'just and equitable'. However, after 1 year has elapsed a claim will not be considered.

24. *Exemption Orders* The Secretary of State for Employment may exempt employers from liability to make redundancy payments under the *EMPLOYMENT RIGHTS ACT 1996* where they have similar or more advantageous agreements with their employees or with trade unions representing them.

SELF TEST QUESTIONS

Self Test Questions No. 55 (for Answers see Appendix 1):

1   Who is covered under statutory redundancy?

2   What is meant by the term, *dismissal*?

3   How is redundancy defined?

4   How is redundancy pay calculated?

5   What are the requirements for employer consultation?

58 INDUSTRIAL INJURIES: EMPLOYER'S LIABILITY

Learning Outcomes At the end of this chapter you should be able to:

- Outline the position at common law for injuries caused to employees through fault of the employer.

- State the statutory duties on the employer.

- Understand the limitation periods for bringing a legal action.

- Explain how the assessment of damages is determined.

INTRODUCTION

1. An employer has a responsibility for the safety of his employees whilst at work. This responsibility includes common law and statutory duties. If an employee suffers injury at work he may be entitled to claim compensation from his employer. In this chapter we consider the courses and remedies open to an employee injured at work, and an employer's defences. In addition the subjects of fatal accidents and limitation of action by lapse of time are covered.

COMMON LAW

2. *Action by an Employee* If an employee suffers injury as a result of the failure of his employer's common law duties of safety the employee must prove the following if he wishes to claim damages:

   a. There was a duty imposed on the employer, ie, the common law duty to provide a safe system of work, safe premises, etc., and

   b. The employer failed to carry out his duties in a reasonable manner. This action is on the grounds of negligence, and

   c. The employee suffered an injury as a *direct* result of the breach. It is possible that an injury suffered by an employee may not be as a direct result of his employer's breach of duty, i.e. the fault may lie with the employee (*McWILLIAMS v SIR WILLIAM ARROL (1962)*) or the chain of causation may have been broken *QUINN v BURCH BROTHERS LTD (1966)*. A breach of contract to supply plant to a sub-contractor was not a 'cause' of the sub-contractor being injured by using makeshift equipment, but just the 'opportunity' or 'occasion'.

   If there are several reasons for the occurrence of an accident the court will single out the root cause and base judgement on this.

3. *Employer's Defences* An employer may attempt to refute his employee's action by raising the following defences:

   a. *Deny the breach of duty.* For example, the employer may show that the claimant was acting outside the course of employment when injured, e.g. he was on 'a frolic of his own'. Or he may show that he had used all reasonable care, e.g. in making all efforts to persuade his employee to use safety equipment (*WOODS v DURABLE SUITES LTD (1933)*).

   b. *Plead 'Volenti non fit injuria'.* Literally this means 'That to which a man consents cannot be considered an injury.' The nature of this defence is that in a dangerous employment situation the employee is not only aware of the risk, but freely takes the risk. This defence is normally applicable to jobs with high inherent dangers. There must be no pressure on the employee to take the risk (e.g. the threat of loss of his job), and the employer must prove that the employee willingly agreed to the risk.

      BOWATER v ROWLEY REGIS CORPORATION (1944) (see Chapter 24.3c).

      Contrast *BOLT v WM MOSS & SONS LTD (1966)* where a workman, expressly informed of the danger, persisted in performing a task in a dangerous manner (having a painter's moveable scaffold moved whilst remaining on it). It was held that volenti was a good defence because the task was undertaken entirely with full knowledge of the risk.

      ICI LTD v SHATWELL (1965) (see Chapter 24.3.b).

   c. *The injury was the sole fault of the employee.* It is a good defence if it can be shown that the employee was solely responsible for his injury. In *BROPHY v BRADFIELD & CO (1955)* the body of a lorry driver was discovered in a boiler house. He had been overcome by fumes. The employer knew of no reason why the driver should have been there and could not have known of his presence. The employer was not liable.

   d. *Plead contributory negligence.* This defence, whilst admitting a breach of duty, attempts to secure a reduction in any damages awarded because of the employee's own negligence.

'Contributory negligence' was introduced by the *LAW REFORM (CONTRIBUTORY NEGLIGENCE) ACT 1945*. This is not merely carelessness or inadvertence as an employer has a greater degree of responsibility for the employee's safety than he does for himself. It is more in the nature of a deliberate flouting of safety regulations.

In awards of contributory negligence the motive would be taken into account, e.g. if the employee was acting in the employer's best interest the negligence attributable to the employee would tend to be lower.

In *SHILTON v HUGHES-JOHNSON (1963)* an employee was injured whilst investigating a fault in a press without first switching off the machine, as to do so would have stopped all production. It was held that the employee was contributorily negligent, but as he had acted in the best interest of the employer by not causing a stoppage of production, the amount of contributory negligence was reduced.

e. *Deny the existence of an employer/employee relationship.* This would generally be a good defence unless the injury arose as a result of the employer's breach of duty of common care to visitors, as the occupier of premises.

f. *Rely on an exemption clause in the contract of service.* This would be extremely rare, relating only to very risky jobs, e.g. circus acts. An exemption clause for accidents which are no fault of the employer is still valid. However, a clause which purports to exempt an employer for liability for an accident caused by his own or the employee's negligence is invalid under the *UNFAIR CONTRACT TERMS ACT 1977*. The Act states that liability for personal injury through negligence cannot be excluded or restricted by any contract term or notice.

g. *Stress-related personal injury.* Recent case law, to be now considered, allows the employer to show that he took all reasonable steps to manage risk associated with stress at work.

The Court of Appeal in *HATTON V SUTHERLAND (2002)* set out guidance for employers which if followed, would lead to a defence against any claim for alleged stress related illness at work. These are:

i. Employers are not obliged to make searching inquiries to establish whether an individual is at risk.

ii. Where an employee voluntarily agrees to stay in a stressful job, then without more he will bear the burden of any subsequent stress related harm.

iii. Any impending harm arising from workload must be clearly foreseeable by the employer.

iv. There are no occupations that should be regarded as intrinsically harmful to mental health.

v. Employers who offer confidential counselling services with access to treatment are unlikely to be found in breech.

vi. Any illness must be caused by the employer breaching his duty and not be just occupational stress.

vii. Any compensation awarded must take account of any pre-existing condition or factors indicating that an employee would have become ill anyway.

More recently the House of Lords (now the Supreme Court) endorsed the above principles in *BARBER V SOMERSET COUNTY COUNCIL (2004)*.

STATUTE

4. In order to claim damages for an employer's breach of a statutory duty, e.g. under the *HEALTH & SAFETY AT WORK ACT 1974* (HSAW), the employee must prove:

   a. The employer failed to comply with the statutory duty, e.g. failure to fence a dangerous piece of machinery.

   b. The employee was injured as a result of the breach, and

   c. The injury was of a class the duty was designed to prevent.

   Generally statutory duties are specific and well defined, and are thus easier to prove than breaches of common law duties. In some cases statutory duties of care are 'absolute' whereas the common law duties tend to require only 'reasonable' care.

5. *The Employer's Defences* An employer may bring the following defences to counter an allegation of breach of statutory duty:

   a. Deny the breach.

   b. Allege contributory negligence.

   c. Deny employer/employee relationship. This defence would not be valid against all breaches of statutory duty as some sections of, e.g., the *FACTORIES ACT 1961* make an employer liable to 'all persons working on the premises', i.e. including independent contractors.

      i. The employer cannot exclude statutory duties in a contract of service.

      ii. The statutes exist to protect the employee, therefore *volenti non fit injuria* cannot be pleaded.

FATAL ACCIDENTS

6. The *FATAL ACCIDENTS ACT 1976* (amended by the *ADMINISTRATION OF JUSTICE (MISCELLANEOUS PROVISIONS) ACT 1985*) gives certain rights to the dependants in the circumstances where an employee dies due to an employer's breach of duty such as would have given the deceased employee a right to an action for damages if he had lived.

7. *Definition of 'Dependant'*

   In the Act a dependant means:

   a. The wife or husband of the deceased.

   b. The parent or grandparent of the deceased.

   c. A child or grandchild of the deceased.

   d. A brother, sister, aunt or uncle of the deceased.

   e. A son or daughter of the brother, sister, aunt or uncle of the deceased.

The Act also includes stepchildren and illegitimate children.

8. *Persons Entitled to Bring the Action* In the first place action should be taken by the executor or administrator of the deceased. In the event of there being no executor or administrator or if the action is not commenced within 6 months after death the action may be taken by, and in the name of, all or any of the dependants. However, only one action may be taken in respect of the subject matter of the complaint.

9. *Assessment of Damages*

   a.   Damages awarded may be divided amongst the dependants as directed.

   b.   In the case of damages awarded to a widow, no account shall be taken of her remarriage or her prospects for remarriage.

   c.   Damages may be awarded in respect of funeral expenses.

   d.   Damages may be awarded in respect of bereavement, which may only be paid for the benefit of the wife or husband of the deceased or in the case of an unmarried child, his parents.

   e.   Damages will not be reduced by any financial benefits received by the dependants on account of insurance money, pensions, or benefits received in respect of social security or payment by a trade union or friendly society.

   f.   Any saving to the injured person attributable to his maintenance at public expense in a hospital or other institution shall be set off against loss of income attributable to his injuries.

   Note: The estate may claim for other than loss of earnings under the *LAW REFORM (MISCELLANEOUS PROVISIONS) ACT 1934*, e.g., pain and loss of amenities. However, any damages awarded under this Act would be subject to reduction for contributory negligence.

THE LIMITATION ACT 1980

10. The *LIMITATION ACT 1980* lays down time limits and other rules for the bringing of actions in respect of wrongs causing personal injuries or death.

    a.   No action may be brought after the expiration of 3 years from:

         i.   The date on which the cause of action arose, or

         ii. The date of the plaintiff's knowledge, if the extent of the injury is not immediately apparent.

    b.   If a claim is made under the *FATAL ACCIDENTS ACT 1976* no action may be brought after the expiration of 3 years from:

         i.   The date of death, or

         ii. The date of knowledge of the person for whose benefit the action is brought, whichever is the later.

11. Reference to a plaintiff's date of knowledge is a reference to the date on which he first had knowledge of the following facts:

    a.   The injury was significant (sufficiently serious to justify proceedings).

b. The injury was attributable to the act of alleged negligence or breach of duty.

c. The identity of the defendant (e.g., in the case of vicarious liability or, for example, a 'hit and run' driver).

A person's knowledge includes his own observable knowledge or facts ascertainable with the help of medical or other expert advice.

12. The court may override the time limit if it considers it equitable to do so, taking into account, e.g the reasons for the plaintiff's delay, e.g. the nature of the injury being such that the plaintiff is incapable of making judgements.

ASSESSMENT OF DAMAGES

13. Damages may be awarded under two general headings, i.e. Special and General damages.

a. *Special damages.* These are awarded on the basis of an estimated loss of earnings. This includes not only loss of present earnings, but an estimate of future loss. It would take into account the employee's age, his position and his earnings potential.

b. *General damages.* These are at the discretion of the court and include such things as, loss of expectation of life, pain and suffering, expenses, loss of faculties and loss of enjoyment of life. In past cases general damages have been awarded where an employee has become sexually impotent due to an accident, and where an employee has lost the ability to enjoy his recreational pursuits, e.g., darts playing or dancing.

14. Any damages awarded will be reduced by, e.g., contributory negligence, a proportion of any benefits received under the Social Security Acts and an estimated amount of income tax which would have been payable on future earnings.

SELF TEST QUESTIONS

Self Test Questions No. 55 (for Answers see Appendix 1):

1   What are the rights of an employee for harm caused by the employer under common law?

2   What is the position under statute?

3   What are *fatal accidents* and what are the legal implications?

4   What are the limitation periods for bringing a claim?

5   How are damages assessed?

Learning Outcomes At the end of this chapter you should be able to:

- Explain the general duties on employers, employees and others under the *HEALTH AND SAFETY AT WORK ACT 1974*.

- Be aware of the role and function of health and safety inspectors.

- State the various offences under the *Act*.

- Understand the role and function of safety representatives and safety committees.

- Explain the nature and content of the *HEALTH AND SAFETY AT WORK REGULATIONS 1992*.

- Understand the relevant provisions regarding smoke-free premises.

INTRODUCTION

1. This chapter deals with two pieces of legislation, namely, the *HEALTH & SAFETY AT WORK ACT 1974* and the *HEALTH & SAFETY AT WORK REGULATIONS 1999*. The former lays down a requirement for reasonable safety at all places of work and is couched mainly in general terms. The intention is that most of the health and safety legislation will be replaced

by a system of Regulations and Codes of Practice. The *HEALTH AND SAFETY AT WORK REGULATIONS 1999* introduce more detailed rules with appropriate Codes of Practice.

HEALTH & SAFETY AT WORK ACT 1974 *(HSAWA)*

2. *Introduction* The *HEALTH AND SAFETY AT WORK ACT 1974* is to provide for reasonable safety at all places of employment. The Act covers not only persons at work (including self-employed) but also the general public. The only excluded category is that of domestic employment.

GENERAL DUTIES OF EMPLOYERS TO THEIR EMPLOYEES

3. *Health, Safety and Welfare* Under *S.2* of the Act it is the duty of an employer to ensure, so far as is reasonably practicable the health, safety and welfare at work of all his employees. This duty covers the following aspects:

   a. The provision of plant and systems of work that are safe and without risks to health.

   b. Arrangements for ensuring safety and absence of risks to health in connection with the use, handling, storage and transport of articles and substances.

   c. The provision of such information, instruction, training and supervision as is necessary to ensure the health and safety at work of his employees.

   d. With regards to any place of work under the employer's control. He must maintain it in a safe condition and without risks to health, and provide safe means of access to and egress from his premises.

   e. The provision and maintenance of a working environment that is safe, without risk to health and with adequate facilities and arrangements for his employees' welfare.

   The above duties are not absolute but require the employer to exercise 'reasonable care'. Thus they accord with an employer's common law duties toward his employees.

4. *Information and Consultation* An employer must comply with the following provision with regard to the supply of information and consultation with trade unions:

   a. Provide a written statement of safety policy, e.g., accident procedure, action on outbreak of fire, safety training. An establishment with fewer than five employees is exempt from this provision.

   b. Where the appointment is made of a safety representative by a recognized trade union or other employees he shall represent the employees in consultations with the employer.

   c. The employer must consult any such representatives with a view to the making and maintenance of arrangements for enabling their effective co-operation in promoting, developing and monitoring measures to ensure the health and safety at work of the employees.

   d. Appoint a safety committee on the request of two or more safety representatives.

DUTIES TO PERSONS OTHER THAN EMPLOYEES

5. The following duties are imposed on employers and self-employed persons for the safety and health of their employees *(S.3)*:

   a. An employer and a self-employed person shall conduct his undertaking in such a manner that persons other than employees are not exposed to risks to their health or safety.

   b. They also have the duty to give information to persons other than employees, who may be affected by the way the business is carried out. Such information will detail aspects of the way in which the business is carried out which may affect their health or safety.

DUTIES OF PERSONS IN CONTROL OF PREMISES (S.4. AND S.5)

6. *Health and Safety* The Act provides that a person who has control of any work premises owes a general duty of care to persons other than his employees who are working there.

7. His duty shall be to ensure, as far as is reasonably practicable that the premises and means of access to and egress from, and any plant or substance in the premises are safe and without risks to health.

   Similar provisions are laid down in the *OCCUPIERS' LIABILITY ACT 1957*. However, contravention of the Occupiers Liability Act is a civil offence, contravention of the *HSAWA* is a criminal offence.

8. *Harmful Emissions* A person who has control of a business where noxious or offensive fumes are involved must do his best to prevent these fumes from entering the atmosphere, and to render them harmless if they are emitted.

DUTIES OF MANUFACTURERS AND INSTALLERS (S.6)

9. The Act requires anyone who designs, manufactures, imports or supplies an article or substance for use at work to ensure that such article or substance is safe when used in accordance with the instructions issued by them.

10. The duty extends to the provision of instructions for the user and the carrying out of any necessary testing, inspection and research to ensure compliance with the obligations of safety.

11. Those who install plant have a duty to ensure it is safely installed.

DUTIES OF EMPLOYEES (S.7)

12. An employee has the following duties:

   a. To act, in the course of employment, with due care for the health and safety of himself, other workers and other persons who may be affected by his acts or omissions at work (i.e. the general public).

b. To observe the provision of the Act insofar as it concerns him and is under his control.

c. To co-operate with his employer to enable compliance with the requirements of the Act.

GENERAL DUTIES

13. The Act makes provision for the following general duties:

a. No person shall interfere with or misuse anything provided under any statutory provision in the interests of health, safety and welfare, e.g. safety clothing, washing facilities *(S.8)*.

b. An employer shall not levy a charge on his employees for anything provided to meet the legal requirements *(S.9)*.

HEALTH AND SAFETY COMMISSION (S.10–14)

14. The Act made provision for the setting up of two corporate bodies, the Health and Safety Commission and the Health and Safety Executive.

15. *Composition of the Commission* The Commission comprises a Chairman and not less than six but not more than eight members appointed by the Secretary of State: three after consultation with employers' organizations, three after consultation with the Trades Union Congress (TUC) and two others appointed from local authorities.

16. *Composition of the Executive* The Executive will consist of three persons: the Director is appointed by the Commission and approved by the Secretary of State and the two others are appointed by the Commission after consultation with the Director.

The Commission and the Executive are now merged into one organization.

17. *Functions of the Commission* The Commission has the following functions:

a. To ensure provision for the health, safety and satisfactory working environment of persons during the course of work. This excludes domestic and agricultural operatives work and certain activities of transport workers.

b. To secure provision against hazards to the safety and health of the public from industrial etc. activities.

c. To advise Government Departments and to promote safety education and training.

d. To prepare and enforce regulations and codes.

e. To investigate any hazardous situation, accident or occurrence.

f. To delay inquests pending investigation of fatal accidents, to authorize a representative to be present at inquests, with the power to examine witnesses and request a report from the coroner.

g. To charge fees, e.g. for providing advisory work.

h. To appoint independent persons or committees if considered necessary, to assist and advise the Commission in its work.

18. *Functions of the Executive* The Executive has the following duties:

   a. To exercise the Commission's functions as it delegates to it.

   b. To make adequate arrangements for the enforcement of the relevant statutory provisions except insofar as the Secretary of State has conferred the duty of enforcement upon some other authority.

REGULATIONS AND CODES OF PRACTICE (S.16–S.17)

19. The Secretary of State, after consultation with the Commission, has the power to make 'health and safety regulations'. Such regulations may:

   a. Repeal any of the existing statutory provisions, e.g. the *FACTORIES ACT 1961.*

   b. Exclude or modify any of the foregoing duties, or statutory provisions.

   c. Impose requirements by reference to the approval of the Commission.

   d. Provide for exceptions from any of the relevant statutory provisions.

   Note: see *HEALTH AND SAFETY AT WORK REGULATIONS 1992* (42.–48. below).

20. If a person does not observe any particular approved code of practice it does not mean he will be open to criminal proceedings, but a relevant code of practice is admissible as evidence where there are criminal proceedings.

21. *Authorities Responsible for Enforcement* The Secretary of State may make local authorities responsible for enforcement of the Act, including the current Acts, scheduled for replacement *(S.18)*.

22. Local authorities already have safety and health enforcement duties under existing regulations.

23. Guidance will be given by the Commission. Where technical assistance is required it will be provided, as far as possible by the central organization.

24. Provision is made for closer and more effective co-operation between the health and safety organization and other bodies, i.e. the local authorities, the fire authorities and the local planning authorities.

HEALTH AND SAFETY INSPECTORS

25. Enforcing powers have authority to appoint inspectors, who have the following powers *(S.19–20)*:

   a. To enter (accompanied by any person he considers necessary) any place where it is considered the Act will apply. This includes any premises on which he has reason to believe activities are being carried out which could endanger public safety.

   b. To inquire into the causes and assist inquiries on any safety situation. He can demand either oral or written information.

   c. If a qualified medical practitioner he may carry out medical examinations he considers necessary.

d. To examine, search any premises, plant, materials, equipment, records or any other documents and take samples, measurements, recordings, copies and conduct tests.

e. To demand facilities and assistance from any person if it is considered necessary.

26. *Enforcement* An inspector is empowered to issue:

a. *Improvement notices.* These are to meet a situation where there is contravention of a regulation but no imminent, serious risk of injury is involved. They require remedial action to be taken within a specified time, to comply with the requirements of the Act or to implement non-statutory codes and standards where the inspector considers this to be appropriate.

b. *Prohibition notices.* An inspector may serve a prohibition notice upon a person who is in control of activities which, in the inspector's opinion, involve a risk of serious personal injury. The prohibition notice will state the inspector's opinion that there is a risk of this nature, specify the matters which in his opinion give rise to the risk, and direct such that the activities to which the notice relates shall not be carried on, by or under the control of the person on whom the notice is served unless the matters specified in the notice have been remedied. A direction contained in a prohibition notice when the risk of personal injury is imminent shall take effect:

i. At the end of the period specified in the notice, or

ii. If the notice so declares, immediately.

27. **Right of Appeal** There is a right of appeal against an improvement or prohibition notice. This should be made to an industrial tribunal within 21 days. Pending the appeal, improvement notices will be held in abeyance but prohibition notices will remain in force unless the employer satisfies the tribunal by an application prior to the hearing that it should not do so *(S.24)*.

OFFENCES (*S.33*)

28. It is an offence for a person:

a. To fail to discharge a duty as outlined in paragraphs 4 to 14 above.

b. To wilfully interfere with anything provided for health, safety and welfare.

c. To contravene any health and safety regulation.

d. To contravene any requirement imposed by an inspector.

e. To contravene any requirements made by an improvement or prohibition notice.

f. To intentionally obstruct an inspector in the performance of his duties.

g. To intentionally make a false entry in any book, notice or document required to be kept by law.

29. *Penalties* For most of the offences the penalty is a fine. However, some offences are triable by the Crown Court and a convicted person is liable to imprisonment for a term not exceeding 2 years or an unlimited fine or both.

30. **Offences Due to the Fault of Another Person** Where a person is accused of an offence, but this is due to another person, the other person shall be guilty of the offence *(S.36)*.

31. *Offences by a Body Corporate* Where an offence committed by a body corporate is proved to have been committed with the consent, agreement or neglect of any company officer, then the officer as well as the body corporate shall be guilty of the offence *(S.37)*.

32. *Onus on Proving Limits of 'Practicability'* If a person is accused of an offence involving failure to comply with statutory provisions of the Act as far as is reasonably practicable he has to prove that it was not practicable to do more than he had done in the situation and he had been as practicable as possible to meet the duty, i.e. the onus is on the employer *(S.40)*.

SAFETY REPRESENTATIVES

33. *Appointment* A recognized trade union:

    a.   Appoints safety representatives where one or more members are employed. Normally more than 2-years' service with the company or with a similar industry is required.

    b.   Notifies the employer in writing of the names.

    c.   Notifies employers when an appointment is terminated.

34. *Functions* The functions of a safety representative are:

    a.   To represent employees in discussions with management.

    b.   Investigate potential hazards.

    c.   Investigate complaints.

    d.   Inspect the workplace at 3-monthly intervals, or more often after agreement with the employer.

    e.   Carry out inspections after an accident, dangerous occurrence or notifiable industrial disease.

    f.   Receive information from Health and Safety Inspectors.

    g.   Attend meetings of safety committees.

35. *Inspections* Safety representatives have the authority to inspect the workplace:

    a.   After giving the employer reasonable written notice and a 3-month interval has passed.

    b.   If there has been a substantial change of work within the 3-month interval.

    c.   If there has been a notifiable accident, dangerous occurrence or industrial disease in the workplace.

    d.   Inspect any document which is required to be kept by law except a medical examination report of an identifiable employee.

36. *Notifiable Accidents, Dangerous Occurrences and Notifiable Diseases*

    a.   An immediate inspection takes place when there has been a notifiable accident or dangerous occurrence.

    b.   Written or verbal notification to be given to management by the safety representative.

   c.   Employer shall provide all facilities.

   d.   Although independent inspections are allowable, nothing shall prevent the employer or his representative from being present at the workplace.

Note: '*Accident and Dangerous Occurrences*'. Accidents and dangerous occurrences are those which are listed in the *NOTIFICATION OF ACCIDENTS AND DANGEROUS OCCURENCES REGULATIONS 1980*, and which are notifiable to the Health and Safety Executive. They include, inter alia, accidents involving personal injury which result in employees being absent for more than 3 days, and such occurrences as the overturning of cranes, boiler explosions, building collapses, explosions or fires causing damage and leading to suspension of work for at least 5 hours, and gassing accidents.

37. *Information from an Employer* Safety representatives have the right to inspect any relevant document kept under the Act for health, safety and welfare. The exceptions are:

   a.   Information against the interests of national security.

   b.   Information relating specifically to an individual without his consent.

   c.   Information, the disclosure of which, for reasons other than health and safety at work could cause substantial injury to the employer's undertaking.

   d.   Information obtained for legal proceedings.

38. *Payments and Time Off for Safety Representatives* An employer shall permit a safety representative to take such time off with pay during the employee's working hours as shall be necessary to enable the safety representative to:

   a.   Perform his functions under the Act.

   b.   Undergo training to enable him to perform these functions.

39. *Industrial tribunals* Complaints may be made to an industrial tribunal if the safety representative is not paid or is not given time off for safety matters. The complaint must be made within 3 months of the date the failure took place. If the complaint is justified, the tribunal can order the employer to pay compensation.

SAFETY COMMITTEES

40. *Establishment* An employer must establish a safety committee conforming to these requirements:

   a.   Safety representatives have been appointed and at least two request a safety committee in writing.

   b.   Employer and safety representatives and trade union representatives consult to determine the composition of the committee.

   c.   A notice must be posted in a place where it can be read.

   d.   The committee shall be formed within 3 months.

41. *Functions* The committee will meet for discussion. Topics for discussion may include:

   a.   The investigation of individual accidents and cases of notifiable diseases.

b.   The study of accident statistics and trends.

c.   Examination of safety audit reports.

d.   Consideration of safety representatives' reports.

e.   Assist in the development of works safety rules and safe systems of work.

f.   Periodic inspection of the workplace, its plant, equipment and amenities.

g.   Publicity and communication effectiveness.

h.   Keeping adequate records of the proceedings and activities of the committee.

HEALTH & SAFETY AT WORK REGULATIONS 1992

42. ***Introduction*** The *HEALTH & SAFETY AT WORK REGULATIONS 1992* implement EC directives on health and safety at work. They are part of a continuing modernization of existing UK law and part of the European Commission's programme of action on health and safety. They have been developed under Article 118A which has been added to the *TREATY OF ROME 1957* for this purpose. The duties outlined in the regulations clarify and make more explicit the current health and safety law. Much old law is repealed by the new regulations. The emphasis is on sound health and safety management and duties to assess risk and choose matching protective measures. The regulations cover: General Health & Safety Management, Work Equipment Safety, Manual Handling of Loads, Workplace Conditions, Personal Protective Equipment and Display Screen Equipment. For each of these regulations the Health and Safety Executive has issued a Code of Practice. The Regulations came into effect on 1 January 1993. In this Chapter the regulations are covered in outline only. Copies of the full regulations and Codes of Practice may be obtained from HMSO bookshops.

43. ***Health & Safety (General Provisions) Regulations*** The Health and Safety (General Provisions) Regulations set out some broad general duties which will apply to almost all kinds of work. They are aimed mainly at improving health and safety management.

The regulations will require the employer to:

a.   Assess the risk to the health and safety of his employees and to anyone else who may be affected by his work activity. This is so that the necessary preventive and protective steps can be identified. Employers with five or more employees will have to write their risk assessments down. (The same threshold is already used in the HSAWA. Employers with five or more employees have to prepare a written safety policy.).

b.   Make arrangements for putting into practice the preventive and protective measures that follow from his risk assessment. They will have to cover planning, organization, control, monitoring and review, i.e. the management of health and safety. Again, employers with five or more employees will have to put their arrangements in writing.

c.   Carry out health surveillance of his employees where it is appropriate.

d.   Appoint competent people to help him to devise and apply the protective steps shown to be necessary by the risk assessment.

e.   Set up emergency procedures.

f.   Give his employees information about health and safety matters.

g. Work together with other employers when he shares a workplace.

h. Make sure that his employees have adequate health and safety training and are capable enough at their jobs to avoid risk, and

i. Give some particular health and safety information to temporary workers, to meet their special needs.

The regulations will also:

j. Place duties on employees to follow health and safety instructions and report danger, and

k. Extend the current law which requires an employer to consult employees' safety representatives and provide facilities for them.

44. *Provision and Use of Work Equipment Regulations* These regulations are designed to consolidate the laws governing equipment used at work. Instead of piecemeal legislation covering particular kinds of equipment in different industries they will:

a. Place general duties on employers, and

b. List minimum requirements for work equipment to deal with selected hazards whatever the industry.

In general, the regulations will make explicit what is already somewhere in the law or is good practice. Some older equipment may need to be upgraded to meet the minimum requirements.

'Work equipment' is broadly defined to include everything from a hand tool, through machines of all kinds, to a complete plant such as a refinery. 'Use' will include starting, stopping, installing, dismantling, programming, setting, transporting, maintaining, servicing and cleaning.

The general duties will require an employer to:

a. Take into account the working conditions and hazards in the workplace when selecting equipment.

b. Make sure that equipment is suitable for the use that will be made of it and that it is properly maintained; and give adequate information, instruction and training.

Specific requirements will cover:

c. Guarding of dangerous parts of machinery (replacing the current law in the *FACTORIES ACT 1961*).

d. Maintenance operations.

e. Danger caused by equipment failure.

f. Parts and materials at high or very low temperatures.

g. Control systems and control devices.

h. Isolation of equipment from power sources.

i. Stability of equipment.

j. Lighting, and

k. Warnings and markings.

The regulations implement an EC directive aimed at the protection of workers. There are other directives setting out conditions which much new equipment (especially machinery) will have to satisfy before it can be sold in EC member states. They will be implemented in the UK by regulations made by the Department of Trade and Industry. Equipment which satisfies those other directives will satisfy many of the specific requirements listed above.

45. *Manual Handling Operations Regulations* The regulations apply to any manual handling operations which may cause injury at work. Those operations will be identified by the risk assessment carried out under the Health and Safety (General Provisions) Regulations. They include not only the lifting of loads, but also lowering, pushing, pulling, carrying or moving them, whether by hand or other bodily force.

An employer has to take three key steps:

a. Avoid hazardous manual handling operations where reasonably practicable. Consider whether the load must be moved at all. And it must, whether it can be moved mechanically, for example, by fork-lift truck.

b. Assess adequately any hazardous operations that cannot be avoided. An ergonomic assessment should look at more than just the weight of the load. He should consider the shape and size of the load; the way the task is carried out (e.g. the handler's posture); the working environment (e.g. is it cramped or hot?); the individual's capacity (e.g. is unusual strength required?). Unless the assessment is very simple a written record of it will be needed.

c. Reduce the risk of injury as far as reasonably practicable. A good assessment will not only show whether there is a problem but will also point to where the problem lies. That is the starting point for improvements. For example, if the load is bulky or heavy it may be possible to use mechanical handling aids or break down the load. If handlers have to adopt an awkward posture he may be able to rearrange the task. Additional training may be required.

46. *Workplace (Health, Safety and Welfare) Regulations* These regulations replace much old law including parts of the *FACTORIES ACT 1961* and the *OFFICES, SHOPS AND RAILWAY PREMISES ACT 1963*.

The regulations cover many aspects of health, safety and welfare in the workplace. Some of them are not explicitly mentioned in the current law though they are implied in the general duties of the *HEALTH & SAFETY AT WORK ACT 1974*. The regulations will apply to all places of work except: means of transport, construction sites, sites where extraction of mineral resources or exploration for them is carried out and fishing boats. Workplaces on agricultural or forestry land away from main buildings will also be exempted from most requirements.

The regulations will set general requirements in four broad areas:

a. *Working environment*

   i. Temperature.

   ii. Ventilation.

   iii. Lighting including emergency lighting.

   iv. Room dimensions.

   v. Suitability of workstations.

   vi. Outdoor workstations (e.g. weather protection).

b. *Safety*

   i. Safe passage of pedestrians and vehicles (traffic routes, for example, must be big enough and marked where necessary, and there must be enough of them).

    ii.   Windows and skylights (safe opening, closing and cleaning).

    iii.   Glazed doors and partitions (use of safe material and marking).

    iv.   Doors, gates and escalators (safety devices).

    v.   Floors (construction and maintenance, obstructions and slipping and tripping hazards).

    vi.   Falls from heights and into dangerous substances.

    vii.   Falling objects.

c.   *Facilities*

    i.   Toilets.

    ii.   Washing, eating and changing facilities.

    iii.   Clothing storage.

    iv.   Seating.

    v.   Rest areas (and arrangements in them for non-smokers).

    vi.   Rest facilities for pregnant women and nursing mothers.

d.   *Housekeeping*

    i.   Maintenance of workplace, equipment and facilities.

    ii.   Cleanliness.

    iii.   Drainage.

An employer will have to make sure that any workplace within his control complies with the regulations. Other people concerned with the workplace, such as the owner of a building which is leased to one or more employers or self-employed people, will also have to make sure that requirements falling within their control are satisfied.

47. ***Personal Protective Equipment (PPE) at Work Regulations*** Personal protective equipment is defined as all equipment designed to be worn or held to protect against a hazard. It includes most types of protective clothing and equipment such as eye, foot and head protection, safety harnesses, life jackets and high visibility clothing. There are some exceptions, for example ordinary working clothes and uniforms (including clothing provided for food hygiene).

Personal protective equipment (PPE) should be relied upon only as a last resort. But where risks are not adequately controlled by other means an employer will have a duty to provide suitable PPE, free of charge, for employees exposed to those risks.

The regulations say what is meant by 'suitable' PPE, a key point in making sure that it effectively protects the wearer. Personal protective clothing will be suitable only if it is appropriate for the risks and the working conditions; takes account of workers' needs and fits properly; and gives adequate protection. An employer will have to assess the risks and the PPE he intends to issue to make sure that these conditions are satisfied.

An employer will also have duties to:

a.   Maintain, clean and replace PPE.

b.   Provide storage for PPE when it is not being used.

    c.   Ensure that PPE is properly used, and

    d.   Give training, information and instruction on its use to his employees.

New PPE will also have to comply with an EC directive on design, certification and testing. It will be implemented in the UK by regulations made by the Department of Trade and Industry. PPE brought before these regulations came into force may still be used.

48. ***Health and Safety (Display Screen Equipment) Regulations*** Unlike some of the other regulations the Health and Safety (Display Screen Equipment) Regulations will not replace old legislation but will cover a new area of work activity for the first time. Work with display screen equipment is not generally high risk, but it can lead to muscular and other physical problems, eye fatigue and mental stress.

The regulations apply to display screens where there is a 'user', that is, an employee who habitually uses display screen equipment as a significant part of normal work. They cover equipment used for the display of text, numbers and graphics regardless of the display process used. There are some specified exclusions, such as systems on board a means of transport, systems mainly for public use, portable systems, cash registers and window typewriters.

An employer will have duties to:

    a.   Assess display screen equipment workstations and reduce risks which are discovered.

    b.   Make sure that workstations satisfy minimum requirements which are set for the display screen itself, keyboard, desk and chair, working environment and task design and software.

    c.   Plan display screen equipment work so that there are breaks or changes of activity, and

    d.   Provide information and training for display screen equipment users.

Display screen equipment users will also be entitled to appropriate eye and eyesight tests, and to special spectacles if they are needed and normal ones cannot be used.

49. ***Smoke-free Premises*** The Health and Safety Executive is not responsible for enforcing the legislation in this area, enforcement is by local authority officers. Relevant legislation includes:

    a.   *Health And Safety at Work Act 1974*, identifies exposure to environmental tobacco smoke (ETS).

    b.   Management of *Health and Safety at Work Regulations 1999* (as amended). These impose the requirement for employers to carry out risk assessments and as ETS is known to have risks associated with exposure to it, this should be included in any risk assessment with appropriate measures to deal with the risk.

    c.   *Workplace (Health, Safety and Welfare) Regulations 1992.* Here, designated rest areas must be made available to non-smokers without discomfort of ETS exposure.

    d.   *Employment Rights Act 1996* places a general duty on the employer to protect employees from risk. Where an employee is exposed to ETS they could resign and claim constructive dismissal.

    e.   *Smoke-free (Premises and Enforcement) Regulations 2006* bans smoking in any enclosed public space, including the workplace. Company vehicles must also be non-smoking if they are likely to be used by more than one person. A breach of the Regulations is a fixed penalty fine of £50.

SELF TEST QUESTIONS

Self Test Questions No. 57 (for Answers see Appendix 1):

1   What are the general duties under the *HEALTH AND SAFETY AT WORK ACT 1974*?

2   What is the role of the Executive and Commission?

3   What do health and safety inspectors do?

4   What are the offences under the *Act*?

5   Explain the nature and content of the *HEALTH & SAFETY AT WORK REGULATIONS 1992*.

6   What are the legal rules pertaining to smoke-free premises?

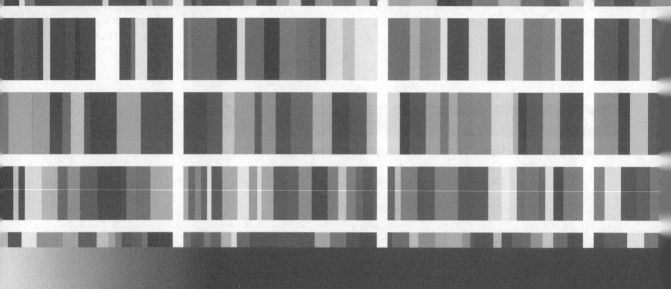

60 INSTITUTIONS AND TRIBUNALS

Learning Outcomes At the end of this chapter you should be able to:

- Outline the role of ACAS, the CAC, the CO and Commissioner for the Rights of Trade Union Members.

- Understand the structure of tribunals and the right of appeal.

INTRODUCTION

1. The *EMPLOYMENT PROTECTION ACT 1975 (EPA)* set up a number of statutory bodies described as the 'machinery for promoting the improvement of industrial relations'. The constitution and functions of these statutory bodies, which are now set out in the *TULR(C)A 1992* as amended by the Trade Union and Labour Relations Act 1992 (TUR) *and* Employment Protection Act (EPA) 1992, are explained in this chapter. The jurisdictions of the Employment Tribunal and the Employment Appeal Tribunal are also explained for the purpose of completing the students' overall view of the machinery available for settling employment disputes. The *TRIBUNALS, COURTS and ENFORCEMENT ACT 2007* introduced a new structure for all tribunals.

THE ADVISORY, CONCILIATION AND ARBITRATION SERVICE (ACAS)

2. The Advisory, Conciliation and Arbitration Service (ACAS) is charged with the general duty of promoting the improvement of industrial relations, and in particular of encouraging the extension of collective bargaining and the development and, where necessary, reform of collective bargaining machinery. ACAS is directed by a council appointed by the Secretary of State for Employment. The council consists of a full-time chairman and nine other members. In appointing six of the nine members the Secretary of State is required to consult employers' organizations as regards three appointments and workers' organizations as regards three. This ensures that a balance between workers' and employers' interests is maintained.

3. *Principal Functions* ACAS has five principal functions:

   a. *Conciliation*:

      i.   Where a trade dispute exists or is anticipated, ACAS may offer to assist in bringing about a settlement either with or without the consent of the parties.

           To achieve this, ACAS may either appoint an independent person or one of its own officers as a Conciliation Officer. No charge may be made for such assistance. Moreover, during the course of conciliation the parties should be encouraged to use any existing procedures for the resolution of the dispute.

      ii. Conciliation Officers appointed by ACAS are required to endeavour to promote a settlement of any complaint presented to an employment tribunal in respect of:

           (a) Unfair dismissal.

           (b) Age, disability, gender reassignment, pregnancy and maternity, race, religion or belief, sex, and sexual orientation.

           (c) Itemized pay statements.

           (d) Guarantee payments.

           (e) Medical suspension payments.

           (f) Trade union membership and activities.

           (g) Time off work.

           (h) Written statement of reasons for dismissal.

           (i) Redundancy consultations.

           (j) Protective awards.

           Where a conciliation officer succeeds in bringing about an agreement between the parties, it is recorded in writing and is legally binding on the parties. The Court of Appeal has held that where the conciliation officer has formally recorded any agreement and the parties have signed it, the employee is precluded from presenting a complaint to an employment tribunal (*MOORE v DUPORT FURNITURE PRODUCTS LTD AND ACAS (1980)*).

   b. *Arbitration.* The *EMPLOYMENT PROTECTION ACT 1978* provides for ACAS, at the request of one or more parties to a dispute and with the consent of all the parties in dispute, to refer any or all of the matters in dispute for settlement by arbitration of:

i.   An independent arbitrator who may not be an officer or servant of ACAS, or

ii. The Central Arbitration Committee.

It is the duty of ACAS to ensure that existing conciliation procedures have been exhausted before referring a matter for arbitration, unless there is some special reason which justifies arbitration. The report of the arbitrator may be published by ACAS providing all the parties consent.

c.   *Advice.* ACAS has the discretionary power to offer advice to employers, workers and their organizations on any matter concerned with industrial relations or employment policies, including the following:

i.   The organization of workers or employers for the purpose of collective bargaining.

ii.   The recognition of trade unions by employers.

iii. Machinery for the negotiation of terms and conditions of employment, and for joint consultation.

iv.   Procedures for avoiding and settling disputes and workers' grievances.

v.   Questions relating to communication between employers and workers.

vi.   Facilities for officials of trade unions.

vii. Procedures relating to the termination of employment.

viii. Disciplinary matters.

ix.   Manpower planning, labour turnover and absenteeism.

x.   Recruitment, retention, promotion and vocational training of workers.

xi.   Payment systems, including job evaluation and equal pay.

Such advice may be given either on the initiative of ACAS itself or upon the request of an interested party. The advice so given may be published by ACAS without the consent of any other party, but it must be of a general nature and without reference to specific employers or employees.

d.   *Inquiry.* ACAS may, if it thinks fit, inquire into any question relating to industrial relations generally or to industrial relations in any particular industry or in any particular undertaking or part of an undertaking. The findings of such an inquiry published in ACAS may consider publication to be desirable for the improvement of industrial relations, but only after consulting all the parties concerned and taking account of their views.

e.   *Codes of Practice.* The original Code of Practice was published by the Secretary of State for Employment under powers conferred by the *INDUSTRIAL RELATIONS ACT 1971* with the specific purpose of giving practical guidance upon the four general principles set out in Section I of that Act, namely:

i.   Freely conducted collective bargaining.

ii.   Orderly procedures for settling disputes.

iii. Free association of workers and employers.

iv.   Freedom and security for workers.

This Code of Practice has been retained, and in addition the following codes have been issued by ACAS, under the Employment Protection (Consolidation) Act.

i.   Disciplinary practice and procedures in employment.

ii. Disclosure of information to trade unions for collective bargaining purposes.

iii. Time off for trade union duties and activities.

Additionally ACAS has a general power to issue Codes of Practice to give practical guidance for promoting the improvement of industrial relations. The Secretary of State is also empowered, after consulting ACAS and gaining the approval of both Houses of Parliament, to issue Codes of Practice. Two codes have been issued by the Secretary of State on:

i.   Picketing, and

ii. The closed shop.

Codes issued under the *HEALTH & SAFETY AT WORK ACT 1974* are:

i.   Time off work with pay for safety representatives to carry out their statutory functions and undergo training.

ii. Disclosure of relevant information to safety representatives on matters such as dangers relating to machinery used at work.

The provisions of a Code of Practice are not legally binding upon employers. Failure to observe provisions cannot of itself lead to a criminal penalty or civil liability. Nevertheless, in any proceedings before an industrial tribunal or the Central Arbitration Committee a Code of Practice is admissible in evidence. The employer's compliance or otherwise is taken into account.

THE CENTRAL ARBITRATION COMMITTEE (CAC)

4. The Secretary of State is responsible for appointing the members of the Central Arbitration Committee (CAC) and its chairman and deputy chairman. ACAS must be consulted with regard to the appointment of the chairman and his deputies. ACAS nominates persons as members who are experienced in industrial relations, ensuring that both employers' and workers' representatives serve on the Committee.

5. *Jurisdiction* The main jurisdictions of the CAC are as follows:

   a. Voluntary jurisdiction in matters referred by ACAS in connection with a trade dispute. An award under this jurisdiction will only be binding upon the parties insofar as it is incorporated into individual employment contracts with the agreement of the parties.

   b. Statutory jurisdiction regarding a complaint that an employer has failed to disclose to a trade union information under the EPA in respect of the findings of a Statutory Joint Industrial Council.

   c. Statutory jurisdiction derived from the EPA in respect of the findings of a Statutory Joint Industrial Council.

   d. Jurisdiction arising from various statutes where financial assistance or licence is provided by central or local government.

6. *Appeals* There is no procedure for appeal against an award made by the CAC but if it can be shown to have exceeded its powers or acted in breach of natural justice, its decisions may be challenged in the High Court.

THE CERTIFICATION OFFICER (CO)

7. The Certification Officer (CO) is appointed by the Secretary of State and its principal functions are:

   a. Duties in connection with the listing and certification of independent trade unions and the monitoring of their annual returns and accounts.

   b. The exercise of powers concerning the political fund rules of trade unions.

   c. The handling of complaints relating to amalgamations of trade.

   Provision is made for appeal from certain decisions of the CO to go before the Employment Appeal Tribunal (see 17. below).

COMMISSIONER FOR THE RIGHTS OF TRADE UNION MEMBERS

8. The Secretary of State appoints the Commissioner, who holds office for 5 years, and then is eligible for reappointment. An annual report of the Commissioner's activities will be laid before Parliament.

9. The Commissioner is empowered to assist a trade union member who is taking (or contemplating) the following types of action against his trade union:

   a. An application to the court in respect of:

      i.   Failure to call a ballot on industrial action.

      ii. Failure to permit the member to examine the union's accounts etc.

      iii. Unlawful application of the union's property by trustees.

      iv. Failure to hold a ballot on the use of the union's funds for political purposes.

   b. That a trade union has failed to bring or continue proceedings to recover funds or property used unlawfully to indemnify an individual.

   c. Failure to hold a secret ballot for election to the principal executive committee.

   d. To restrain the use of trade union funds for unlawful political purposes.

   e. Proceedings arising out of an alleged breach or threatened breach of a union's rules in relation to:

      i.   Appointment or election of a person to, or removal from, any office.

      ii. Disciplinary proceedings by the union (including expulsion).

      iii. Authorizing or endorsing industrial action.

      iv. The balloting of members.

> v.   Application of union funds or property.
>
> vi.   In respect of any levy for the purposes of industrial action.
>
> vii.   The constitution or proceedings of any committee conference or other body.

10. Assistance in respect of e. above may only be given if the breach in question affects a member of the union other than the applicant.

11. In determining whether or not to grant the application for assistance, the Commissioner may consider:

    a.   Whether the case raises a question of principle.

    b.   Whether it is unreasonable, with respect to the complexity of the case, to expect the applicant to deal with it unaided, and

    c.   Whether the case involves a matter of substantial public interest.

    The Commissioner is not empowered to provide assistance in the making of an application to the CO, in industrial tribunals or before the EAT.

EMPLOYMENT TRIBUNALS

12. Employment tribunals were established for the purpose of resolving disputes between employers and Training Boards arising out of the liability to pay a training levy. Since 1964 the industrial tribunal has assumed many other statutory jurisdictions and have emerged as 'labour courts'. The tribunals have some 30 separate statutory jurisdictions covering virtually every individual employment right which has been created by statute, such as social security, employment, immigration and mental health.

13. *Advantages* The advantages of bringing a case before an employment tribunal are:

    a.   The procedure is far simpler than for a case in the County Court.

    b.   The interval of time between commencing proceedings and the hearing is much shorter in comparison with ordinary courts.

    c.   The formality of tribunals is considerably relaxed being designed to put the parties at ease; procedural rules are interpreted flexibly and the rules of evidence which apply in the ordinary courts are not binding on the tribunal.

    d.   They are relatively inexpensive, in comparison with the ordinary courts since legal representation is not encouraged by the rule that costs may only be awarded the losing party where the complaint is frivolous or vexatious.

14. *Claims* A person wishing to bring a claim before an employment tribunal is called the 'applicant' and he commences proceedings by lodging an Originating Notice of Application at the Central Offices of employment tribunals (COET). The COET then serves a copy of the application on the defendant who is known as the Respondent who has 14 days in which to return his answer in the form of a Respondent's Notice of Appearance. The COET is also required to notify Conciliation Officers CO's, designated by ACAS, of the claim. These officers have a statutory duty to endeavour to promote a settlement even in the absence of a request from either party, providing there is a reasonable prospect of success. In cases where

the CO has been unable to achieve a settlement, the tribunal chairman has powers to order the giving of particulars by one party to the other, the attendance of witnesses and the production of documents. A tribunal may order an applicant to pay a deposit of up to £1000 as a condition of proceeding with his claim. The *EMPLOYMENT TRIBUNALS (CONSTITUTION & RULES OF PROCEDURE) REGULATIONS 2001* in attempting to speed up tribunal claims and reduce the number of frivolous claims puts the parties under a duty to assist the tribunal in ensuring that both parties deal on an equal footing, saving expense and dealing with cases in a way that is proportionate to the issues. In addition tribunals have the power to award costs (up to £10 000) where they believe that a party has acted 'vexatiously, abusively, disruptively or otherwise unreasonably, or the bringing or conducting of the proceedings has been misconceived'.

15. *Composition* Employment tribunals sit in about 80 different centres through Britain, each tribunal consisting of a chairman, who must be a barrister or solicitor of not less than 7 years' standing, and two panel members one representing employees' interests and the other employers' interests. Panels of each category of member are nominated; the chairman being appointed by the Secretary of State after consultation with employers' and employees' organizations.

16. *Reform of the Tribunal System* The *TRIBUNALS, COURTS AND ENFORCEMENT ACT 2007* introduced a new simplified statutory framework for all tribunals. There are now two levels of tribunal:

   a. *First Tier Tribunal* deals with:

      i. Social entitlement.

      ii. General regulatory.

      iii. Health.

      iv. Education and social care.

      v. Taxation and land.

      vi. Property and housing.

   b. *Upper Tier Tribunal* deals with:

      i. Administrative appeals.

      ii. Finance and Tax.

      iii. Land.

Each level is organized into groups of tribunals called Chambers headed by a Chamber President. The Administrative Justice and Tribunals Council will keep the whole system under review.

EMPLOYMENT APPEAL TRIBUNAL (EAT)

17. The EAT was established to hear appeals from industrial tribunals. An appeal to the EAT may be made on a *question of law* not on a finding of fact, arising from any decision of an employment tribunal.

Additionally, the EAT hears appeals on questions of law from decisions of the CO concerning the political fund rules and amalgamations and on questions of fact and law under the

TULR(C)A 1992 (relating to listing and independence of trade unions), and unfair exclusion or expulsion from a trade union.

20. *Appeals* An appeal generally lies only on an error of law. In order to succeed the appellant must show:

    a.   The tribunal misdirected itself in law, or misunderstood the law or misapplied the law, or

    b.   That there is no evidence to support the tribunal's findings of fact, or

    c.   That the decision was 'perverse' (i.e. no reasonable tribunal could have reached such a decision).

21. *Composition* The EAT is composed of High Court and Court of Session Judges and appointed members who must have industrial relations knowledge or experience. Each appeal is heard by one judge and between two and four appointed members.

22. *Further Appeals* A decision of the EAT may, with leave, be appealed to the Court of Appeal, and with further leave, to the Supreme Court. Such appeals must, however, be on a point of law. On some matters, e.g. sex and racial discrimination, cases may be referred to the European Court of Justice.

23. *The Employment Rights (Dispute Resolution) Act 1998* Under this Act, Employment Tribunals are to be allowed to determine proceedings without a hearing and in private where the parties give their written consent. ACAS conciliation officers may be used for statutory redundancy claims. The Act seeks to facilitate compromise agreements outside of ACAS, encouraging employer 'in-house' disciplinary and grievance procedures to be used, with power given to tribunals to reduce or increase compensation awards where an employee refuses to use them or an employer denies access to them.

SELF TEST QUESTIONS

Self Test Questions No. 58 (for Answers see Appendix 1):

1   What is ACAS and what does it seek to do?

2   What is the role and function of the Central Arbitration Committee, the Certification Officer and the Commissioner for the Rights of Trade Union Members?

3   What are the advantages of the use of tribunals and what are the reforms introduced by the *TRIBUNALS, COURTS AND ENFORCEMENT ACT 2007*

4   What is the Employment Appeal Tribunal?

61 TRADE UNIONS

Learning Outcomes At the end of this chapter you should be able to:

- Define what a trade union is – its legal capacity and liability in tort.
- Outline the requirements for *listing* a trade union.
- Outline the requirements for a trade union ballot.
- State the law regarding trade union rules.
- Explain what a *collective agreement* is.

INTRODUCTION

1. In this chapter we shall consider the status of trade unions and the liabilities and rights of unions and their members under current legislation which is the *TRADE UNION AND LABOUR RELATIONS (CONSOLIDATION) ACT 1992* (TULR(C)A) as amended.

DEFINITION

2. A trade union is an organization (whether permanent or temporary) which either:

   a. Consists wholly or mainly of workers and is an organization whose principal purposes include the regulation of relations between workers and employers or employers' associations, or

   b. Consists wholly or mainly of:

      i. Constituent or affiliated organizations which fulfil the conditions specified in a. above, or

      ii. Representatives of such constituent or affiliated organizations; and in either case is an organization whose principal purposes include the regulation of relations between workers and employers or between workers and employers' associations, or include the regulation of relations between its constituent or affiliated organizations.

LEGAL CAPACITY

3. A trade union is not a body corporate but nevertheless has been given some characteristics of legal personality, so that it can:

   a. Make contracts.

   b. Own property, though it must be vested in trustees.

   c. Sue or be sued in its own name in proceedings relating to property or founded in contract or tort or any other cause of action (subject to statutory immunity in tort).

   d. Be subject to judgements, orders or awards, in proceedings brought against it.

LIABILITY IN TORT

4. Action in tort may be brought against a trade union if a person suffers loss due to unlawful industrial action organized by its officials. It will be liable for actions inducing breach of contract (or threats to do so) or actions for conspiracy not in contemplation or furtherance of a trade dispute if that action is authorized or endorsed by a responsible person of the union, i.e. the principal executive committee, any other person empowered by the rules of the union to authorize or endorse such action, the president or general secretary, an employed official, or any committee to whom an employed official regularly reports. The Act makes provision for exemption from liability if the action is repudiated.

TRADE UNION AFFAIRS

5. *Listing of Trade Unions* An association of employees which falls within the statutory definition of a trade union is entitled to have its name entered on a list of trade unions. This list is

maintained by the Certification Officer (CO) (see Chapter 60.7). In order to be listed a trade union must:

a. Pay the requisite fee.

b. Submit a copy of its rules.

c. State the address of its head or main office.

d. Submit a list of its officers, and

e. State the name under which it is known.

6. The CO has the following powers in relation to the list, subject to a right of appeal on questions of both fact and law to the Employment Appeal Tribunal (EAT):

a. To prevent the use of a misleading name.

b. Removal of a trade union if it no longer appears to be a union within the statutory definition.

c. Removal of a trade union from the list upon the specific request of that union.

d. Removal where a trade union has ceased to exist.

e. The issue of a certificate of listing, which is evidence of trade union status.

7. The purpose of the certificate of listing is two-fold:

a. It is proof of the trade union's status without which it would be unable to obtain tax relief on its provident fund income, and

b. It is a prerequisite for obtaining a certificate of independence.

8. *Certificate of Independence* A listed trade union may apply to the CO for a certificate that it is independent. The certificate is conclusive evidence of a trade union's independence.

9. *Definition of Independence* An independent trade union is one which:

a. Is not under the domination or control of an employer or a group of employers or of one or more employers' associations, and

b. Is not liable to interference by an employer or any such group or association (arising out of the provision of financial or material support or by any other means) tending towards such control.

10. The importance of the certificate of independence lies in the statutory requirement that a union must be independent in order to:

a. Enforce rights to information.

b. Allow individuals to claim protection for trade union membership and activities.

c. Allow individuals to claim time off for union activities.

d. Claim consultation in respect of redundancies.

e. Obtain planning information under the *INDUSTRY ACT 1975*.

f. Appoint safety representatives under regulations issued under the *HEALTH & SAFETY AT WORK ACT 1974*.

g.   Be consulted about contracting out of occupational pension schemes.

h.   Take advantage of the financial assistance available for conducting union ballots.

i.   To be able to use employer's premises for the purpose of a secret ballot.

The absence of a certificate of independence will not in itself prevent a trade union exercising the above rights, but in the event of the union's independence being challenged any proceedings would be stayed until the CO had issued or refused a certificate.

11. Additionally, the CO may withdraw a certificate at any time if he is of the opinion that the union is no longer independent. The CO must, in coming to such a decision, take into account any relevant information submitted to him by any person. Appeal lies to the EAT.

12. The CO is also required to keep a register of independent trade unions which is open to inspection by the public, free of charge, at all reasonable hours.

RECOGNITION

13. For an independent trade union to exercise the rights set out in 10. a. c. d. g. h. and j. above, it must be one which is 'recognized' by the employer for the purposes of collective bargaining. Recognition must now be achieved voluntarily through the conciliation procedures of *S.2*, Employment Protection Act (EPA) may still be exercised by Advisory Conciliation and Arbitration Service (ACAS) on application of either party, or otherwise if in the view of ACAS it can achieve a settlement to a dispute.

14. Recognition for collective bargaining purposes may be either express or implied. For recognition to be implied the alleged acts of recognition must be clear and unequivocal and involve a course of conduct or a period of time (*NATIONAL UNION OF GOLD, SILVER AND ALLIED TRADES v ALBURY BROS (1979)*).

ANNUAL RETURNS AND ACCOUNTS

15. Detailed requirements with regard to the keeping of accounts, making of annual returns, appointment of auditors and the qualified examination of a report on members' superannuation schemes are contained in the *TULR (C)A 1992* (the Act):

a.   *Duty to keep accounting records.* Every trade union must keep proper accounting records so as to give a true and fair view of the state of its affairs and to explain its transactions, and in particular:

   i.   Cause to keep proper accounting records with respect to its transactions and its assets and liabilities, and

   ii. Establish and maintain a satisfactory system of control of its accounting records, its cash holdings and all its receipts and remittances.

b.   *The Annual Return.* A return must be made in each calendar year to the CO, containing:

   i.   Revenue accounts indicating the income and expenditure of the trade union for the period to which the return relates.

   ii.   A balance sheet as at the end of that period.

   iii. Other such accounts (if any) as the CO may require.

   iv. A copy of the rules of the trade union as in force at the end of the period.

   v.   A note of all changes in the officers of the union and any change in the address of the head or main office of the union during the period to which the return relates.

   vi. A copy of the auditors' report.

   vii. Details of the salary paid to and other benefits provided to each member of the executive, the president and general secretary by the trade union.

   viii. The number of names on the union register and the numbers not accompanied by an address.

  c.   *Appointment of auditors.* Trade unions must appoint auditors to audit the annual accounts. Generally, such auditors must be qualified to act as auditors of a company incorporated under the Companies Acts. The auditors are required to report on the accounts stating whether, in their opinion, the accounts give a true and fair view of the matters to which they relate.

  d.   *Members' superannuation schemes.* Before such a scheme is commenced:

    i.   The proposals for the scheme must have been examined by an appropriately qualified actuary, and

    ii. A copy of a report made to the trade union by the actuary on the results of his examination, signed by the actuary, must have been sent to the CO.

The CO must keep available for public inspection copies of all annual returns. Every trade union must, on the request of any person supply a copy of its rules and latest annual return, for which it may make a reasonable charge.

AMALGAMATION

16. There are two methods by which a merger of trade unions can be achieved:

  a.   By an agreed instrument of amalgamation must contain certain matters (a guidance pamphlet is available from the CO) and obtain a simple majority of the members of each union voting by ballot.

  b.   By a transfer of engagements which involves the transference by one union of all its obligations and assets to the other whilst still retaining its nominal identity. In this method only the members of the transfer union are required to vote and a simple majority of those voting by ballot will suffice.

17. The Act lays down procedural requirements, which in some cases must first be approved by the CO, for the notice informing members of the proposals and for the conduct of the ballot. Additionally there are grounds for complaint, by any member of the unions concerned, to the CO and a right of appeal on questions of law to the EAT. Union merger ballots are to be fully postal and subject to an independent scrutineer. The notice sent out with voting papers for union merger ballots must not make a recommendation or express an opinion about the proposed merger.

THE POLITICAL FUND

18. The procedure for the maintenance and conduct of a political fund, for the protection of the minority is as follows:

    a. There must be a secret ballot of the membership of the trade union to approve the establishment of a political fund.

    b. Any trade union which has adopted a political fund resolution must pass a new resolution by means of a secret ballot of all its members if it wishes to spend money on political matters. The ballot must be carried out at intervals of not more than 10 years.

    c. It is the duty of the union to provide the independent scrutineer with an up-to-date copy of the membership register and the duty of the scrutineer to inspect it.

    d. The union must also ensure an independent count of the votes on the ballot and safekeeping of the ballot papers.

    e. The fund must be financed by a political levy and in no other way.

    f. After approval by a simple majority of those voting in the ballot at a. the union must incorporate in its rules special rules, approved by the CO for the conduct of the fund.

    g. Members of the union must have the right to contract out and to suffer no discrimination by doing so, except in the control of the fund.

    h. The political fund may only be used to promote certain political objects:

        i. Payment of expenses incurred by a candidate or prospective candidate for election to Parliament or any other public office.

        ii. Holding of meetings and the distribution of literature in support of such candidates or prospective candidates.

        iii. Maintenance of a person who is a Member of Parliament or holds any other public office.

        iv. Registration of electors or the selection of a candidate for Parliament or any other public office.

        v. Holding of political meetings of any other kind or the general distribution of political literature, unless the main purpose of these is the furtherance of the statutory objects of the union.

        vi. Complaints regarding any breach of the political fund provisions are dealt with by the CO with a right of appeal to the EAT.

TRADE UNION BALLOTS

19. Specific provision is made for the financing and holding of secret ballots by trade unions:

    a. *Financial assistance in respect of secret ballots.* The Secretary of State is empowered to make regulations providing for financial assistance to be given to independent trade unions holding a secret ballot within the following purposes:

   i.   Obtaining a decision or ascertaining the views of members as to the calling or ending of a strike or other industrial action.

   ii.   Carrying out an election provided for by the rules of the union.

   iii.   Electing a worker who is a member of a trade union to be a representative of other members also employed by his employer.

   iv.   Amending the rules of a trade union.

b.   *Secret ballots for election of principal executive committees.* The Act requires that all voting members of a trade union's executive committee will be elected by secret postal ballot at least once every 5 years. All members of the trade union in question must be given a voting entitlement except those who are precluded by the union rules and those in the following classes:

   i.   Members who are not in employment.

   ii.   Members in arrears with union subscriptions.

   iii.   Apprentices, trainees, students or new members.

c.   *Workplace ballot.* Alternatively a workplace ballot may be allowed if it is:

   i.   Secret and free from interference or constraint.

   ii.   Provides a convenient method of voting to members without incurring cost to themselves (e.g. by forfeiting overtime in order to vote).

   iii.   Voting is by ballot paper and votes are fairly and accurately counted.

d.   *Secret ballot before industrial action.* A trade union must hold a secret ballot not more than 4 weeks before taking strikes or other industrial actions to ascertain the wishes of the majority of their members. In the event of failure to do so the union will lose any immunity in tort. The ballot must be conducted by post and involve the marking of a ballot paper. The ballot must be secret and followed by announcement of the voting figures to the members concerned. Entitlement to vote must be given equally to trade union members who it is believed will be called upon to take industrial action, and to no others. Written notice of intent to ballot must be given to an employer at least 7 days before the opening of the ballot. The notice includes details of the employees and includes a sample voting paper.

e.   *Secret ballots on employer's premises.* An employer with more than 20 workers, has a statutory duty to permit the use of his premises, so far as is reasonably practicable, for the purpose of giving those workers employed by him and who are members of the union, a convenient opportunity of voting. This duty only exists where the request is made by an independent trade union recognized by the employer for the purpose of collective bargaining and where the ballot is in respect of at least one of the questions set out in a. above. Moreover, the proposals for the conduct of the ballot must be such as to secure so far as reasonably practicable, that those voting may do so in secret. Where an employer is in breach of this duty the trade union concerned may complain to an employment tribunal which has the power to award compensation to be paid by the employer to the union. Appeal on the question of law lies to the EAT.

20. *Postal ballot.* The regulations so far issued only provide for financial assistance to be given in the case of a postal ballot and contain detailed conditions to ensure that payment is not made if the CO is not satisfied that the ballot was properly and fairly held:

a. The ballot must be conducted so as to secure as far as reasonably practicable, that those voting may do so in secret.

b. Those voting must be required to do so by marking a voting paper.

c. Those voting must be required to return the voting papers individually by post to the union or to a person responsible for counting the votes.

d. The voting paper must contain only questions within the prescribed purposes. Moreover, as regards election of officers, only the positions of president, chairman, secretary, treasurer executive committee members or other positions whereby the person becomes an employee of the union are permitted.

e. Payments under the scheme will generally cover the cost of printing stationery and postage and will be made by the CO upon application of the union after the expenditure has been incurred.

TRADE UNION MEMBERSHIP

21. *Rules* The statutory regulation of trade union rules is as follows:

a. No rule of a trade union shall be unlawful or unenforceable by reason only that it is in restraint of trade.

b. Where a union membership agreement exists, an actual or prospective employee is entitled not to have his application for union membership unreasonably refused, and not to be unreasonably expelled from the union. This right is in addition to any common law right that may exist. The question as to whether the trade union has acted reasonably is to be tested in accordance with equity and the substantial merits of the case. Compliance with the rules does not of itself establish reasonableness, nor does a breach automatically demonstrate unreasonableness.

22. *Compensation for Unreasonable Exclusion or Expulsion* In addition to any common law action a complaint may be made to the employment tribunal in a situation where a person is unreasonably excluded or expelled from a trade union in circumstances where he either is, or is seeking to be, employed by an employer who has entered into a union membership agreement and it is the practice for the employees to belong to a union in accordance with that agreement. The ultimate remedy of the industrial tribunal will of course be compensation since a person could not be forced upon any particular trade union.

23. When a tribunal finds an applicant's case well founded it makes a declaration that the exclusion or the expulsion was unreasonable. There is a right of appeal from the tribunal's decision to the EAT on the question of both law and fact.

24. For the applicant to obtain compensation a further application to either the employment tribunal or the EAT must be made at least 4 weeks after and within 6 months after the declaration as follows:

a. *Employment Tribunal.* If at the time of the application for compensation the applicant has been admitted or readmitted to membership of the union against which he made the complaint, the employment tribunal may award such amount as it considers appropriate for the purpose of compensating the applicant for the loss sustained by him in consequence of the exclusion or expulsion which was the subject of the complaint. Such compensation is payable by the trade union concerned and may not exceed an amount equal to 30 times the current maximum amount of a week's pay for the purposes of calculating the basic award in unfair dismissal cases plus an amount equal to the current maximum compensatory award.

b. *Employment Appeal Tribunal.* On the other hand, if the applicant has not been admitted or readmitted to trade union membership at the time of the application for compensation it will be made to the EAT which can award compensation of such amount as it considers just and equitable in all the circumstances. The maximum compensation that the EAT can award is the limit of the industrial tribunal plus a sum equal to 52 times the maximum amount of a week's pay for the purposes of calculating additional awards of compensation in unfair dismissal cases.

25. ***Exclusion or Expulsion from Membership*** An individual may not be excluded or expelled from a trade union unless it is for a permitted reason. These are:

a. Not qualified because the union's rules restrict membership to a specified trade or industry, of a particular occupation or in possession of specified qualifications or work experience.

b. The individual's conduct.

Any individual who claims to have been unreasonably excluded or expelled from a trade union has the right of complaint to an employment tribunal.

26. ***Participation in Trade Union Affairs*** The right of the individual member to participate in the affairs of his trade union may be conveniently classified under two headings.

a. *Positive rights.* Other than the two statutory rights (of voting where a trade union proposes to establish a political fund and where it proposes to amalgamate with another trade union) the positive right of the trade union member to participate in his trade union affairs by attending meetings, voting, seeking office, attending delegate conferences, etc, is merely a matter of construction of the contract established by the rules of the trade union.

In ***BREEN v AEU (1971)*** the claimant sought a declaration that the decision of a union's district committee to refuse to endorse his election as a shop steward was void as being contrary to the requirements of natural justice. The union claimed that natural justice was inapplicable as the committee's function was not judicial. It was held that natural justice, i.e. the need to act fairly was applicable. However, in this particular instance the facts indicated that the committee's decision was not biased.

b. *Negative rights.* The member also has a right to restrain any trade union action which is not permitted by its constitution subject to the rule in ***FOSS v HARBOTTLE (1843)***, which provides for a minority to restrain a trade union action where it is acting beyond its powers. The courts, however, will not permit a minority action to proceed where the action is within the powers of the union though lacking some formality which can be ratified by the appropriate body.

This again is a question of the individual enforcing his right under the contract of membership to prevent the trade union acting in breach of its rules.

In ***EDWARDS v HALLIWELL (1950)*** a resolution beyond the capacity of the constitution of the union to increase members' subscriptions was successfully challenged.

In *HODGSON v NALGO (1972)* an executive council instruction to delegates attending a TUC conference to vote in favour of Britain joining the EEC contrary to NALGO policy was disallowed.

COLLECTIVE AGREEMENTS

27. ***Statutory Definition*** A collective agreement as any agreement is defined or arrangement made by or on behalf of one or more trade unions and one or more employer or employers' association and relating to one or more of the following matters:

    a. Terms and conditions of employment, or the physical conditions in which any workers are required to work.

    b. Engagement or non-engagement, or termination or suspension of employment or the duties of employment, of one or more workers.

    c. Allocation of work or the duties of employment as between workers or groups of workers.

    d. Matters of discipline.

    e. The membership or non-membership of a trade union on the part of a worker.

    f. Facilities for officials of trade unions, and

    g. Machinery for negotiation or consultation, and other procedures, relating to any of the above matters, including the recognition by employers or employers' associations of the right of a trade union to represent workers in any such negotiation or consultation or in the carrying out of such procedures.

28. ***Enforceability*** A collective agreement shall be presumed not to have been intended by the parties to be a legally enforceable contract unless the agreement is in writing, and contains a provision which (however, expressed) states that the parties intended that the agreement shall be a legally enforceable contract.

29. If a collective agreement contains a provision which states that the parties intend that only one or more parts of the agreement shall be a legally enforceable contract, then it will have this effect.

30. The extent to which a collective agreement may be enforced by or against those workers who are covered by it is a question of whether it has been expressly incorporated, in whole or in part into the contract of employment.

31. ***The Collective Agreement and Common Law*** The collective agreement is the product of a generally voluntary system of negotiation of terms, and conditions of employment. This is reflected in the presumption as to non-enforceability unless the parties take positive steps to make the agreement legally binding. This presumption, however, applies only to those agreements which fall within the statutory definition. The common law will apply in the case of agreements not conforming to the statutory definition, but it is uncertain what provision is made under common law. There are two possibilities:

    a. It is suggested that there is a general presumption of legal enforceability as there is with any other commercial agreement.

    b. There is the view that collective agreements are not enforceable because the parties do not intend to create legal relations.

It rather suggests that collective agreements are of such a divers nature that it is impossible to adopt a universal rule and that each must be considered on the facts at the time. More-over, some collective agreements do not fulfil a contractual function, and others are too vague to be enforceable.

32. *'No Strike' Clauses* Any terms of a collective agreement which prohibit or restrict the right of workers to engage in a strike or other industrial action, or have the effect of prohibiting or restricting that right, shall not form part of any contract between any worker and the person for whom he works unless the agreement:

    a.   Is in writing, and

    b.   Contains a provision expressly stating that those terms shall or may be incorporated in such a contract, and

    c.   Is reasonably accessible at his place of work to the worker to whom it applies and is available for him to consult during working hours, and

    d.   Is one where each trade union which is a party to the agreement is an independent trade union; and unless the contract with the worker expressly or impliedly incorporates those terms in the contract.

33. The effect of this provision is that no court shall, whether by way of an order for specific performance or an injunction restraining a breach of, or threatened breach of a contract of employment, compel an employee to do any work or attend at any place for the doing of any work.

34. The effect of a 'no strike' clause complying with the statutory provisions is therefore limited to circumstances where, for example, procedural requirements like consultation must be exhausted before taking strike action. In such circumstances an injunction could be granted in order that the proper procedure be followed.

35. Right to challenge the validity of the terms of a collective agreement. An employee may present a complaint to an employment tribunal that a term in a collective agreement is void as being discriminatory under the terms of the Equality Act 2010 if he has reasons to believe that:

    a.   The terms may at some future time have effect in relation to him, and

    b.   An act provided by the term may at some time be done in relation to him and the act would be unlawful.

36. *The Present Law Relating to Immunity in Tort* An act done by a person in contemplation or furtherance of a trade dispute shall not be actionable in tort on the ground only:

    a.   That it induces another person to break a contract or interferes or induces any other person to interfere with its performance, or

    b.   That it consists of a threat that a contract (whether one to which he is a party or not) will be broken or its performance interfered with, or that it induces another to break or interfere with a contract's performance.

Note: An agreement or combination by two or more persons to do or procure the doing of any act in contemplation or furtherance of a trade dispute shall not be actionable in tort if the act is one which, if done without any such agreement or combination, would not be actionable in tort.

37. *Trade Dispute* This is defined as a dispute between workers and their employer which is connected with one or more of the following:

a.   Terms and conditions of employment, or the physical conditions in which any workers are required to work.

b.   Engagement or non-engagement, or termination or suspension of employment or the duties of employment, of one or more workers.

c.   Allocation of work or the duties of employment as between workers or groups of workers.

d.   Matters of discipline.

e.   The membership or non-membership of a trade union on the part of a worker.

f.   Facilities for officials of trade unions, and

g.   Machinery for negotiation or consultation, and other procedures, relating to any of the above matters, including the recognition by employers or employers' associations of the right of a trade union to represent workers in any such negotiation or consultation or in the carrying out of such procedures.

38.   *Acts in Contemplation of Furtherance of a Trade Dispute* The statutory immunity only applies where industrial action is taken in contemplation or furtherance of a trade dispute. This is traditionally called the '*Golden Formula*' and has been subjected to considerable scrutiny by the courts. The following criteria must be satisfied in order to gain the protection of the golden formula:

a.   There must be a dispute.

In *BBC v HEARN (1977)* the refusal of technicians to transmit television pictures of the FA Cup Final to South Africa was held not to be a trade dispute.

b.   The dispute must fall within the statutory definition of a trade dispute (see 37. above).

In *J.T. STRATFORD & SONS LTD v LINDLEY (1965)* the plaintiffs hired out barges. A trade union imposed an embargo on the company because one of the company's subsidiaries refused to recognize the union. Members of the union would not return the barges which had been hired out thus rendering the hirers in breach of contract. The company's business was brought to a standstill. The company was granted an injunction against the union as no trade dispute as then defined was shown to exist.

c.   The dispute must be between the parties mentioned in 37. above – *BEAVERBROOK NEWSPAPERS LTD v KEYS (1980)*.

d.   The action must be in contemplation or furtherance of the dispute – *EXPRESS NEWS-PAPERS LTD v MACSHANE (1980)*.

39.   *Strikes* A strike is defined for the purpose of computing continuous employment as a cessation of work by a body of persons employed acting in combination, or a concerted refusal of any number of persons employed to continue to work for an employer in consequence of a dispute, done as a means of compelling their employer or any person or body of persons employed, or to aid other employees in compelling their employer or any person or body of persons employed, to accept or not to accept terms or conditions of or affecting employment.

40.   In *TRAMP SHIPPING CORPN v GREENWICH MARINE INC (1975)* Lord Denning defined a strike as a concerned stoppage of work by men done with a view to improving their wages or conditions of employment, or giving vent to a grievance or making a

protest about something or other, or supporting or sympathizing with other workmen in such endeavour.

41. There is no right to strike recognized by British law, though immunity from the consequences is conferred under the law, provided the strike is for a proper purpose. There would seem little argument to contradict the view that a strike is merely one form of industrial action.

42. *Picketing* Lawful picketing must be:

  a.   In contemplation or furtherance of a trade dispute, and

  b.   Only at the following specified places:

   i.   At or near his own place of work, or

   ii.   If his last employment was terminated in connection with a trade dispute, at or near his former workplace, or

   iii. If he does not work at any one place or if the place is in a location such that attendance there for picketing is impracticable, any premises of his employer from which he works or from which his work is administered, or

   iv.   If he is an official of a trade union, at or near the place of work or former place of work of a member of that union whom he is accompanying and whom he represents, and

  c.   For the purpose only of peacefully obtaining or communicating information or peacefully persuading any person to work or abstain from working.

43. Where picketing extends outside the legal limits the persons concerned may not claim the immunity from actions in tort.

44. Additionally, even where picketing falls within the conditions described in 42. above, immunity will only be effective if:

  a.   The picketing does not constitute secondary industrial action, or

  b.   The employer of the pickets is a party to the trade dispute, or, if not, the actions of the pickets fall within the rules of lawful secondary action.

45. *Secondary Action* Immunity from legal proceedings in tort is not available when the industrial action consists of secondary action which is not lawful picketing. There is secondary action in relation to a trade dispute when a person:

  a.   Induces another to break a contract of employment or interferes or induces another to interfere with its performance, or

  b.   Threatens that a contract of employment under which he or another is employed, will be broken or its performance interfered with, or that he will induce another to break a contract of employment or to interfere with its performance if the employer under the contract of employment is not a party to the trade dispute. Contracts of employment include self-employed and persons employed from an employment agency.

In *MARINA SHIPPING LTD v LAUGHTON AND ANOTHER (1981)* a blacking action by officials of the International Transport Workers Federation against a Maltese ship was declared unlawful in the Court of Appeal. The court held that for such secondary action to be lawful under the then *Employment Act (EA)* 1980 a contract would have to exist between the shipowners and the port authority supplying the services. No such contract had been entered into by the owners, or by the ship's master on their behalf.

In *SHAH v SOGAT 82 (1984)* members of SOGAT picketed the premises of the 'Stockport Messenger' a place which was not the pickets' place of work. It was held that the action was unlawful secondary picketing and an injunction was imposed. The plaintiff also successfully claimed damages for loss of revenue.

46. *Acts to Compel Trade Union Membership* There is no immunity from liability in tort:

   a. Where a person induces or threatens to induce an employee to break his contract of employment, or interferes with or threatens interference with performance by an employee of his contract of employment, for the purpose of compelling workers to join a particular trade union, where the workers being compelled are employed neither by the same employer nor at the same place of work as that employee.

   b. Any term in a contract for the supply of goods or services is void insofar as it purports to require that the whole or part of the work is to be done by persons who are members of a trade union. Thus, union-only or non-union-only labour contracts are void.

47. *Employers' Remedies* The rights and remedies of an employer who is or has been the target of industrial action are discussed under the following headings:

   a. *Remuneration of employees.* Industrial action by employees may constitute a breach, termination or suspension of the contract of employment dependent upon the terms of the contract. Similarly, the giving of notice of intention to take industrial action may be construed as anticipatory breach or repudiatory action or merely as an intention to suspend the contract. In any event it would seem that the employer has no duty to remunerate employees participating in industrial action unless he has expressly or impliedly contracted to do so.

   b. *Dismissal of employees.* Where industrial action may be construed as a breach of the contract of employment, the employer may dismiss all employees participating in the industrial action. For unfair dismissal provision see Chapter 56.20.

   c. *Damages.* The employer may have a right to claim damages in tort against workers participating in industrial action for which immunity is not provided by statute. Moreover, a claim for damages in tort may also be impossible against trade unions and their officials. Damages may be awarded against trade unions for certain torts. The limits depend on the total membership of a particular union, e.g., £10 000 for less than 5000 members to £250 000 for 100 000 or more. These limits do not apply in cases of personal injury caused by negligence, nuisance or breach of duty, nor for breach of duty connected with the ownership, occupation, possession, control or use of property.

   d. *Injunction.* Where the industrial action is not in contemplation or furtherance of a trade dispute the employer can seek an injunction to restrain such action. The courts, however, will not grant an injunction where its effect is to compel employees to work.

   e. *Conciliation.* In the interests of promoting good industrial relations the best solution to industrial action that the employer can have available is conciliation and if necessary with the assistance of ACAS.

48. *Effect of Industrial Action on Employees' Rights* The consequences for employees participating in industrial action (whether or not in furtherance of a trade dispute) are discussed under the following headings:

a. *Remuneration.* As indicated in the preceding paragraph the employee loses his right to receive remuneration during the industrial action.

b. *Social security benefits.* An employee is not entitled to unemployment benefit for any period during which he is participating in industrial action. He may, however, be entitled to supplementary benefit in respect of his dependants.

c. *Guarantee payments.* Employees engaged in industrial action are not entitled to guarantee payments under the terms of the *EMPLOYMENT RIGHTS ACT 1996.*

d. *Unfair dismissal.* An employee dismissed because of his participation in industrial action will only be considered as unfairly dismissed in the circumstances outlined in Chapter 56.20.

e. *Continuous employment.* For the purposes of redundancy and unfair dismissal, absence due to participation in a strike does not break the continuity of employment, but the period of absence does not count in the computation of the period of continuous employment.

SELF TEST QUESTIONS

Self Test Questions No. 59 (for Answers see Appendix 1):

1 Define a trade union?

2 Outline the position of a trade union with regard to its liability in tort.

3 What are the requirements for a trade union to be listed?

4 What are the procedures governing a trade union ballot?

5 What are the rules governing membership?

6 What is a collective agreement?

REFLECTION AND CONSOLIDATION VI

For answers go to the student digital support resources for the book (see page xxv).

Reflection

Key areas of study

Employee/self-employed distinguished

The contract of employment – formation and contents

Common law duties on employee and employer

Wages

Maternity rights

Equality

Termination of the contract of employment

Redundancy

Industrial injuries

Health & safety at work

Tribunals

Trade unions.

Consolidation

The following are practice assessment exercises; you will find the answers and guidance by going to the student digital support resources for the book (see page xxv).

MULTIPLE CHOICE QUESTIONS

1 Which ONE of the following statements is **correct**?
   A   An employer is obliged to provide a careful and honest reference
   B   An employer is obliged to provide a safe system of work
   C   An employer is obliged to provide employees with smoking facilities during authorized breaks at work
   D   An employer with fewer than 20 employees is obliged to provide an itemized written pay statement

2 An employer must provide an employee with a written statement of particulars of the employment
   A   Within 1 month of the employment commencing
   B   As soon after the commencement of employment as possible
   C   Within 2 months of the employment commencing
   D   Within a reasonable time of the employment commencing

Typical Examination Questions

3 (a) Ronald, a male employee at Mac's Garage Ltd, left his job without giving any notice to his employer. He had been employed for 51 weeks. He has confided to you that the reason he left was because of persistent, and sometimes dangerous, practical jokes against him by a number of employees. Despite addressing his grievances to Mac, the garage owner, the problem had persisted for a further 6 months without any direct action by Mac.
   Mac is threatening to sue Ronald for breach of contract, and Ronald seeks your advice as to whether he has a claim against the garage, or whether he is liable for breach of contract.
   Advise Ronald.

(*8 marks*)

(b) You have been asked by the board of directors to prepare a report regarding the proposed redundancy of some 50 employees.
   Your report should consider the procedures they need to follow: selection criteria, entitlement based on age and length of service, and whether re-deployment is to be considered.

(*12 marks*)
(20 marks)
ICSA, November 2004

4 Explain in detail the main duties owed by employers to employees under legislation, and those implied, in the context of health and safety in the workplace.

(20 marks)
ICSA, November 2004

5 Explain the aim and broad content of the *Equality Act 2010*.

(20 marks)

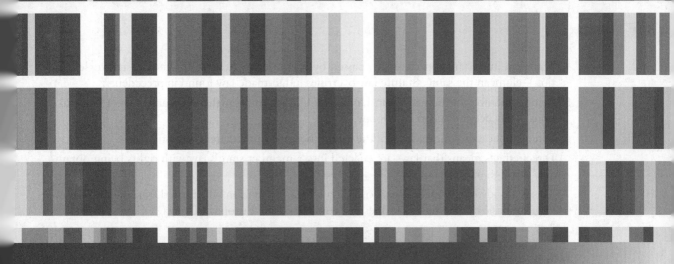

APPENDIX 1
ANSWERS TO SELF TEST QUESTIONS

No. 1

1. Law is defined as a set of rules to regulate human behaviour.

2. Morality differs from law in that, natural or moral law is enacted as a part of English law but is accepted by a particular society as being correct. Law and justice are not always the same, what is just might not be achievable in law due, for example, to a lack of sufficient evidence.

3. Differences between civil and criminal law:

   - Crime is a wrong to the state, the accused being punished if found guilty.
   - Civil law deals with wrongs between individuals, seeking to compensate the claimant for damage caused.

No. 2

1. The means by which law is brought into existence.

2. Judicial precedent is law found in past cases which bind future decisions where the basis of the claim is the same under existing rules.

3. Past decisions in higher courts will bind judges in lower courts. Main advantages are:

   - Provides a degree of certainty.
   - Law evolves on a 'case by case' basis.
   - The law is flexible.

   Disadvantages:

   - Law becomes rigid.
   - Grows slowly.
   - Can become large and complex.

4. The most important source of law, passed by Parliament – Acts of Parliament, statute, legislation – all mean the same. Statute law overrules judge-made law found in precedent.

5. Being a member of the European Union the UK is bound by the decisions of the EU institutions. They become a part of UK law.

6. Direct applicability means laws of the Union become immediately part of UK law.

   Direct effects means that laws are enacted into a member state's law with rights being obtainable through national courts.

7. This is a body of law made a part of UK law by a convention which the UK signed up to setting out basic human rights. It does not come from the European Union/EC Law.

No. 3

1. Equity was developed to address certain problems/defects in the common law. Both are found within case law and work side by side.

2. Equity.

No. 4

1. a. show
   - European Court of Justice
   - Supreme Court
   - Court of Appeal – Civil
   - High Court
   - County Court.

   b. show
   - European Court of Justice
   - Supreme Court
   - Court of Appeal – Criminal
   - High Court – Queen's Bench
   - Crown Court
   - Magistrates Court.

2. D

No. 5

1. Disputes are referred to an agreed person by the parties in dispute. They are not brought before the formal courts. It is more informal and less costly.

2. *Advantages*
   - Allow for specialist knowledge and experience to be used.
   - They are informal.
   - Less expensive.
   - Disputes settled more quickly.

Disadvantages
- Decisions can be inconsistent – tend to be based on particular facts of the dispute. Often no reason for decisions are given.
- No presence of professional lawyers.

No. 6

1. *Solicitors*
   - Often the first point of contact in civil or criminal matters.
   - They instruct and work with, where needed, barristers.

   Barristers
   - Specialize in a particular field of law.
   - Have certain rights of audience in the higher courts.
2. • To apply existing rules of law to a case before them.
   - Carry out certain administrative functions.
3. Juries hear cases and decide upon guilt or innocence.
   - *Arguments for*: Involves laymen in the law bringing reality to it, maintains public support.
   - *Arguments against*: Selection can lead to some persons not being intellectually capable of reaching a decision, can be biased e.g. against authority figures, police, etc., can be led by skilled advocates, often unpopular with some in that they lose money attending.

No. 7

1. • Plaintiff becomes claimant.
   - Writ becomes claim form.
   - Pleading is now statement of case.
   - Affidavit now a statement of truth.
2. Pre-action protocols
   - Alternative Dispute Resolution
   - Payments into court
   - Designated tracks for case to follow
3. A claim is served
   - Respondent acknowledges claim
   - Exchange of statements takes place
   - Documents are prepared for trial
   - Trial takes place
   - Conclusion by judicial enforcement

No. 8

1. A person having full legal capacity; potentially subject to any rule of law.
2. *Nationality*. This is the relationship between a person and state. There are three categories:
   - British citizen
   - Citizenship of British dependencies
   - British overseas citizenship.

Domicile: The country a person is resident in. Three types of domicile:

- Domicile of origin
- Domicile of choice
- Domicile of dependence.

Residence: A question of fact to be determined by the courts.

No. 9

1. *Real property*: Freehold; *personal property*: chattels-leasehold and interest in land, and chattels in personal possession.
2. Legal *estates:* Fee simple absolute in possession and term of years absolute (leasehold).
3. *Ownership*: Sum total of a person's rights over property he owns. *Possession*: is the means of exercising control over things held.
4. A *chose in action* is personal property the right to which can only be enforced by legal action.

No. 10

1. It legally binds the parties.
2. It must be clear and certain.
3. An invitation to treat is an inviting of the other party to make the offer.
4. • By its withdrawal – revocation.
   - A refusal or a counter-offer.
   - Failure to meet a condition the offer is subject to.
   - Death of the offeree.
5. • Oral or in writing.
   - Must be unconditional/unqualified.
6. Consideration is a promise to act or give something of value at the time of the offer – executory consideration or executed consideration.
7. There must be an intention presumed or expressed, that the agreement is to be a legal relationship.

No. 11

1. A minor is someone who has not reached the age of 18. Necessaries are goods or services deemed necessary for the minor, who must pay i.e. is legally bound.
2. A contract of service/employment will bind a minor if deemed by the court to be beneficial.
3. Binds unless the minor chooses to avoid the contract.
4. The minor is not bound to pay.
5. Loans to minors are not binding. However, if there is a guarantor of a loan to a minor, he will be liable.
6. They will have no capacity to contract, the contract will be void, unless necessaries.

No. 12

1. A conveyance or transfer of a legal estate in land. A deed must be:

- In writing.
- Signed by the parties.
- Witnessed.
- Delivered formally to both parties.

2. No.

3. Requires written evidence – usually in the form of a signature.

4. Is for the above and other legal formalities to take place electronically.

No. 13

1. A term is a legally enforceable part of the contract, a representation is a statement relating to a term it is not a part of the contract; breach of term = breach of contract, an untrue representation = action for misrepresentation.

2. A condition is a vital important term of a contract; a warranty is a less important term.

3. All of the terms must be discernable and not vague and unclear.

4. These are pre-printed forms with standard terms and conditions stated.

5. This is a term put into the contract by someone other than the parties, usually the court or legislation.

6. This seeks to limit or exclude liability of terms for a breach.

7. The Unfair Contract Terms Act seeks to control exemption clauses where they are deemed unreasonable.

8. Liability for death or personal injury cannot be excluded. In standard forms, the terms must be reasonable which will be determined by the courts. Fundamental breach is the breaking of a key term of the contract and any exemption clause will have to be clear in covering the precise nature of the breach.

No. 14

1. Most contracts are valid irrespective of mistakes as to quality.

2. Mistake at common law is:
   - Mistake as to the existence of the subject matter
   - Mistake as to the identity of subject matter
   - Mistake as to identity of contracting party
   - Mistake as to the terms.

3. Equity will grant limited relief: rescission, rectification, I did not do it (*non est factum*).

4. An untrue statement of fact which induces the other party to contract:
   - Fraudulent and innocent misrepresentation.

5. Contract is voidable.

6. • Contracts for the commission of something wrong.
   - Contracts illegal by statute.
   - Contracts illegal for reasons of public policy.

No. 15

1. • Performance.

- Precise payment of debt.
- Goods comply with the terms.
- Performance of all parts.

2. • Severable contracts.
  - Acceptance of part performance.
  - Prevention of performance.
  - Substantial performance.

3. • Bilateral discharge.
  - Unilateral discharge.
  - Novation.
  - Condition subsequent.

4. Occurrence of an event outside the control of the parties causing performance to be impossible or radically different.

5. Failure by one of the parties to perform and anticipatory breach.

No. 16

1. Remoteness of damage and amount of monetary compensation.

2. Arising naturally from a course of events or within the reasonable contemplation of the parties.

3. Actual loss which is not too remote taking account of inconvenience and annoyance.

4. A claimant must seek to reduce or avoid losses.

5. Unliquidated damages assessed by the court, liquidated damages set by the contract.
   Equitable remedies include: specific performance and injunction.

6. Six years for a simple contract, 12 years for a deed.

No. 17

1. No one can sue or be sued unless they are a party to the contract.

2. • Statute.
  - Equity.
  - Covenants.
  - Assignment.
  - Collateral contracts.

3. The Act gives, in certain circumstances, rights to third parties to enforce a contract. These are:
  - Where the contract expressly provides.
  - Intention of the parties as to benefits to third parties.
  - Third party must be expressly identified.
  - Third party has rights as if a party to the contract.

No. 18

1. A breach of duty fixed by law.

2. • *Contract* – obligations arise by agreement between the parties.
   • *Trust* – the duty is only recognized in equity, not common law.
   • *Crime* – the object is to punish the offender not compensate the victim.
3. The defendant's motives are irrelevant.

No. 19

1. Mere knowledge is insufficient. The claimant must appreciate both the nature of the risk and consent to that risk.
2. There is not sufficient closeness to the acts of the respondent and the harm caused to the claimant.
3. Harm caused has to be sufficiently closely linked to the respondent's acts.
4. No liability as eventual harm was not foreseeable.
5. • *Mistake* – the general rule is mistake is no defence. Exceptions are: False imprisonment and malicious prosecution.
   • *Inevitable accident* – respondent being utterly without fault.
   • *Act of God* – no human foresight can guard against.
   • *Self-defence* – use of reasonable force to defend oneself.
   • *Necessity* – harm suffered in order to avoid a greater loss to the respondent.
   • *Statutory authority* – a thing done expressly authorized by statute.
   • *Illegality* – cause of action cannot be maintained if claimant is seeking to rely on conduct that is illegal.

No. 20

1. Liability of a person for the wrongs of another, e.g. employer for employee.
2. An employer is generally not liable for the acts in tort of an independent contractor.
3. The possibility that more than one person could be held liable for the same tort.

No. 21

1. • Duty of care.
   • Breach.
   • Damage.
2. A duty of care is owed to any person who we can reasonably foresee will be injured by our acts or omissions.

   The court will substitute the 'person' – the respondent, with the *reasonable man/woman* and ask the question, 'Would a reasonable man/woman have foreseen the potential for some injury to the claimant?' If yes, a duty will be owed.
3. Financial loss is generally not recoverable.
4. A negligent statement must result in some physical injury.
5. Ordinary grief and sorrow will not amount to nervous shock, there must be some identifiable psychiatric illness.
6. Did the respondent exercise the care a reasonable man would have exercised?

7. The court may take account of 'desirable activities' that are in the public interest.

8. The facts/thing, speaks for itself.

9. • Damage must result from the respondent's acts or omissions.
   • Must not be too remote.
   • Must be physical injury to person or property.
   • Must be reasonably foreseeable.
   • Where appropriate, the finding of a 'special relationship'.

10. Where the claimant contributed to the cause of the accident.

11. A duty is owed to lawful visitors.

12. Yes, albeit a lesser duty.

No. 22

1. Liability is incurred without any fault or negligence on the part of the respondent.

2. A person who brings onto his land anything likely to do harm if it escapes, will be liable.

3. An action will lie unless a statute expressly prohibits it.

4. The Act introduces strict liability on a manufacturer for defective goods which cause harm to the claimant, consumer safety and for misleading price indications.

5. • The product contained a defect.
   • The claimant suffered damage.
   • Damage was caused by the product.
   • The respondent was a producer, 'own brander' or importer of the product.

6. Criminal sanctions with civil liability.

No. 23

1. The unlawful interference with a person's use and enjoyment of his land.

2. • Extent to which acts are unusual or excessive.
   • Duration.
   • Respondent's intention.
   • Character of the neighbourhood.
   • Sensitivity of claimant.
   • Respondent's lack of care.

3. The person creating the nuisance and the person in possession of land.

4. • *Volenti non-fit injuria* (see Chapter 21.2).
   • Statutory authority.
   • Nuisance caused by a stranger.
   • Long use.
   • Public interest.

5. An unlawful act or omission which endangers the health, safety or comfort of the public.

6. Criminal prosecution, injunction or damages.

No. 24

1. • *The person* – intentional interference with the person or liberty of another.
   • *Land* – direct interference with the possession of another person's land without lawful authority.
   • *Goods* – direct interference with the possession of goods.
2. Conversion is dealing in a claimant's goods which deny him the right to possess those goods.

No. 25

1. A false statement that tends to injure the claimant's reputation, or cause him to be shunned by ordinary members of society.
2. • *Slander* – a statement lacking permanence.
   • *Libel* – a statement in permanent form.
3. Would the words tend to lower the claimant in the estimation of right thinking members of society generally?
4. No requirement that claimant named, just that the statement referred to him.
5. Communicated to at least one person.
6. • Justification.
   • Honest belief.
   • Fair comment.
   • Absolute privilege.
   • Qualified privilege.
   • Unintentional.
7. An innocent publication, where statement does not appear defamatory and the publisher was not negligent.
8. • Apology.
   • Proof of provocation.
   • Evidence of a bad reputation.

No. 26

1. A sum of money payable by the respondent.
2. • Loss of amenity.
   • Pain and suffering.
   • Loss of expectation of life.
   • Loss of income.
3. *Nominal damages.* Are a small amount awarded where the tort is shown but no actual loss.
   Exemplary damages. Given in rare cases to punish a respondent.
4. Equitable remedy. *Mandatory injunction* – order of the court commanding that something be done. *Interlocutory injunction* – a temporary order pending the case being heard.
5. • Recovery of land – 12 years.
   • Personal injury – 3 years.

No. 27

1. An agent is a person who enters into a contract on behalf of a principal, with a third party.

2. • Express agreement.
   • Implication.
   • Necessity.
   • Ratification.

3. Duties of the agent:
   • Carry out instructions of his principal.
   • Exercise reasonable care.
   • Act in good faith.
   • Not make a secret profit.
   • Not misuse confidential information.
   • Employees – such as directors – can be seen as agents of the employer company.
   • Breach may result in loss of right to remuneration.
   • Must not delegate his duties.
   • Must not mix his financial affairs with those of the principal.

   Duties of the principal:
   • Pay commission.
   • Indemnify the agent.

4. Express; implied or apparent authority.

5. Unless the parties state otherwise:
   • The agent incurs no rights or liabilities under the contract entered into on behalf of the principal.
   • The agent may be sued and may sue under the contract.
   • Both principal and agent are liable together for any tort committed.

6. • Auctioneers.
   • Mercantile agents.
   • Brokers.
   • Stockbrokers.
   • Del credere agents.

7. • By the acts of the parties.
   • By operation of law.
   • By completion of the agency agreement.

No. 28

1. • Where a seller in the course of a business delivers goods which do not conform with the contract of sale, it is presumed that the lack of conformity existed at the time of delivery if discovered within the first 6 months.
   • The consumer is entitled to a repair or replacement free of charge.
   • The consumer is entitled to either, a reduction in price, or rescission.

2. A contract of sale is a contract whereby the seller transfers or agrees to transfer the property in goods to the buyer for a money consideration called the price.

3. Goods means all chattels (meaning any property other than freehold land – see Chapter 11) and money.

4. Where goods are sold to a minor, a person lacking mental capacity or through drunkenness/drugs, they only have the capacity to contract and pay a reasonable price for *necessaries*.

5. This is the person who owns the goods and so has the right to sell them and pass on title to another.

6. This is where the sale of goods is based upon their description by the seller. They must be as they are described.

7. Where goods are sold in the course of a business there is an implied term (see Chapter 15.6) that the goods will be of satisfactory quality.

8. • *Unascertained goods* – property passes when the goods become ascertained
   • *Specific or ascertained goods* – property passes when the parties intend it to pass
   • Where there is no definite intention, property will pass where:
     • *Rule 1* – goods are specific and in a deliverable state; at the time of the contract.
     • *Rule 2* – goods are specific but seller has to put them into a deliverable state; when put in a deliverable state and the buyer informed.
     • *Rule 3* – goods are specific and in a deliverable state, but seller has to weigh, measure, test the goods, when that is done and the buyer is informed.
     • *Rule 4* – goods are delivered on sale or return, or on approval; when the buyer indicates acceptance, or does anything consistent with him being the owner – e.g. sells the goods.
     • *Rule 5* – goods are unascertained or future goods by description; when goods are in a deliverable state and appropriated to the contract.

9. Title/ownership/property cannot pass to the buyer. The goods remain the property of the original owner.

10. By delivery or by instalments if agreed to.

11. • Hold the goods until paid – a *lien* (see Chapter 41).
    • Stop if in transit.
    • Where a reservation of title clause – reclaim the goods.

12. • Action in contract for damages.
    • Repudiate the contract.
    • Sue for specific performance.
    • Seek compensation.

13. Certain implied terms are created:
    • Seller has the right to sell.
    • Goods will correspond with description.
    • Goods will be of satisfactory quality.
    • Goods supplied by sample will correspond with the bulk.

No. 29

1. Unfair commercial practice is where it contravenes the requirements for *professional diligence* and *distorts the economic behaviour of the average consumer.*

2. Commercial activity is misleading if it is untruthful and deceptive which causes, or is likely to cause, a consumer to make a transactional decision they would not otherwise make.

3. Misleading omissions are where a trader omits important information on a product.

4. Aggressive commercial practices are where a trader engages in behaviour amounting to harassment, coercion or undue influence which significantly impairs the average consumer's freedom of choice.

5. Automatic unfair commercial practices are:

   - Claiming to be a signatory to a code of conduct when *you* are not.
   - Claiming some form of public body approval which is not correct.
   - Inviting the purchase of goods having no reasonable grounds for thinking they can be supplied.

6. The trader must be shown to have, knew or was reckless as to whether a contravention of professional diligence had occurred. The maximum penalty is an unlimited fine or 2-years' imprisonment.

7. Due diligence is a defence where the trader can show:

   - A mistake.
   - Reliance on information supplied.
   - Act or default of another.
   - Accident.
   - Some cause beyond his control.
   - Took all reasonable precautions and exercised due diligence.

8. Enforcement is through the Office of Fair Trading and local authority Trading Standards Services.

No. 30

1. Open and fair competition through a regulation of the market.

2. - *Article 81* prohibits agreements between organizations that restrict or distort competition.
   - *Article 82* prohibits abuse of a dominant position.
   - Competition Act 1998.

3. - To hear appeals against decisions of the Office of Fair Trading.
   - Investigate the conduct of companies or mergers and takeovers.

No. 31

1. - The Consumer Credit Act 1974 (as amended).
   - EU Consumer Credit Directive 2008.
   - Statutory Regulations on:
     - Total Charge for Credit.
     - Disclosure of Information.
     - Agreements.
     - Amendments.
     - Advertisements.

2. - *Consumer credit* – an agreement by which the creditor provides the debtor with credit of not more than £25 000.
   - *Consumer hire agreements* – where the hirer pays regular amounts to hire goods which are then purchased through an option to buy term.

3. • *Conditional sale* – an agreement whereby price is paid in instalments and ownership remains with the seller until full payment.
   • *Credit sale* – agreement whereby price paid in five or more instalments, ownership passes immediately.
   • *Credit card/token* – holder pays for goods and services using the card with a set credit limit
   • *Loan* – money lent by a bank to customers.
   • *Overdraft* – where a bank agrees for customers to spend up to a certain amount above what they have in their account.
   • *Shop budget/revolving or running credit-facility* offered by large retail outlets whereby customers pay in a set amount per month and can spend set multiples of that amount.

4. A *debtor creditor supplier agreement* is where the supplier of credit is also the supplier of the goods.

5. Is where goods are hired, leased, rented or bailed to a consumer.

6. The seller is allowed to hold the goods – bailed – with an option to purchase at the end of the agreement. If he sells before that time he cannot pass title to another.

7. Full details of the agreement to be given, including:
   • Legible wording.
   • All terms included.
   • Comply with regulations re format.
   • Details of any right to cancel.

8. A credit broker is a person who acts as an intermediary between creditor and debtor.

9. • To take delivery of goods.
   • To take reasonable care of goods.
   • To pay the instalments.

10. • Rate of interest.
    • Fees charged.
    • Total amount of credit.
    • Actual percentage rate.
    • Cash price.
    • Duration of agreement.
    • Total amount payable.
    • Amount of each instalment.

11. The creditor is required to assess the credit rating of a borrower before entering a new agreement.

12. • Explanations of defined *certain matters*.
    • Allow borrower to see all information.
    • Give opportunity for borrower to ask questions.
    • Provide a point of contact for a borrower to ask later questions.

13. A borrower may cancel within 14 days of the agreement being signed. Notice to cancel must be in writing. The agreement is treated as if it had never been entered into.

14. • Borrower entitled to receive another copy of the agreement.
    • Annual statements must be provided where appropriate.

15. • If card given to third party with borrower consent – borrower is fully liable.

    • Where card is lost or stolen – limit of £50 maximum for the borrower.

16. *Enforcement orders* – this is an order of the court permitting enforcement.

    Time orders give the borrower more time to pay.

17. The Consumer Credit Act 2006 allows the court to assess the overall fairness of a credit agreement and to modify the agreement accordingly.

No. 32

1. A contract whereby the insurer, in return for a sum of money called the premium, contracts with the insured to pay a specified amount upon some event happening.

2. • *Good faith* – contract is voidable for non-disclosure of any material fact.

   • *Insurable interest* – subject of the insurance must be owned by the insurer or benefit or be prejudiced by its destruction.

   • *Indemnity* – covers the insured for loss up to a certain amount.

   • *Subrogation* – the insurer has the right to take over rights associated with a loss from the insured.

   • *Contribution* – where two policies cover the same loss, the insured may recover from one.

   • *Risk* – loss resulting from negligence.

3. • *Life insurance* – insurer agrees to pay persons named to benefit from the life insured.

   • *Fire insurance* – indemnity over a set period for loss due to fire.

   • *Motor vehicle insurance* – under statute motorists must insure against liability for injury to third parties.

   • *Insurance against theft* – same principles as apply to life and fire insurance.

   • *Accident insurance* – covers personal injury to the policy holder.

No. 33

1. A new property right created under statute.

2. *Patents* – protect an inventor from others exploiting his invention.

   • It must be capable of industrial application.

   • The invention must be new.

   • It must involve an *inventive step*.

   • *Infringement* occurs:

     • Where the invention is a product; by disposing, using or importing it or keeping the product for another.

     • Where a process; by using or offering its use, when he knows or should know this would be an infringement. Also, disposing, using, importing or keeping products using the process.

     • Supplies the means necessary for putting an invention into effect.

Copyright – protects the skill, labour and effort expended in producing work. There is no requirement to register. It is not a monopoly it is a right against copying. Duration is the life of the creator plus 70 years.

Works eligible for copyright protection are:

- Literary, dramatic, musical or artistic works.
- Sound recordings, films, broadcasts or cable programmes.
- Typographical arrangement.
- Paintings, drawings, sculptures, engravings, photographs.
- Architecture.
- Works of artistic craftsmanship.
- *Infringements* occur by:
  - Copying.
  - Reproducing the work.
  - Publishing the work.

Trade marks – used on goods or services to indicate a connection between the goods or services and the person having the right to use the mark. It distinguishes goods and services from a competitor. A trade mark can be renewed indefinitely.

- *Infringement* occurs when a person, without permission, uses in the course of business a mark identical or similar to a registered trade mark.

3. *Passing-off* is where a person attempts to sell goods or services as being supplied by another.

No. 34

1. • *Data* – information being processed or recorded for use by equipment operating automatically, or is part of a relevant filing system or is a health, education or publicly accessible record.
- *Rights conferred* – the right of access to personal data.
- *Data protection principles*:
  - Processing should be fair and lawful.
  - Obtained for lawful purposes.
  - Adequate and not excessive.
  - Accurate.
  - Not kept for longer than stated purpose.
  - Processed under the Act.

2. The Act creates three criminal offences dealing with the misuse of computers:
- Unauthorized access to computer material.
- Unauthorized access to commit an offence.
- Unauthorized modification of computer material.

No. 35

1. Sole practitioners and investment firms are brought within one statutory framework. The principle is one of self-regulation within the framework. The overall aim of the Act is to protect private investors.

2. *Investments* include:
- Company shares.
- Debentures.

- Government and local authority securities.
- Warrants entitling investment.
- Certificates conferring rights to acquire.
- Units in collective investment schemes.
- Option to acquire or dispose of certain investments.
- Futures.
- Contracts for differences.

3. The regulatory body for investments. An authorized investment business is anyone providing any form of investment service.

4. A computerized database of investment firms.

5. *Rules for regulation of investment businesses:*
   - Act in the best interests of the client.
   - Comply with requirements as to advertising.
   - Disclose information about fees, commissions, etc.
   - Separation of salesman from advisor.
   - Money kept separate from client's.
   - Have a customer agreement.
   - Prohibition of unsolicited visits or calls.
   - Have a complaints procedure.
   - Advice to be fair and not misleading.

6. It exists to:
   - Provide support for its subsidiary bodies.
   - Promote good financial reporting.
   - Make representations to government.
   - Provide guidance.

7. To facilitate the buying and selling of shares.

8. The *FRAUD ACT 2006* identifies three offences:
   - Fraud by false representation.
   - Fraud by failing to disclose information.
   - Fraud by abuse of position.

No. 36

1. • Responsible for all debts.
   - Makes all decisions, takes all profits and losses.
   - No formalities.
   - Death ends the business.

2. • An unincorporated association.
   - Relations that subsist between persons carrying on a business in common with a view to profit.

3. • No formalities.
   - Maximum number 20 partners.

- Trade under any name.
- Partnership agreement dealing with:
  Name
  Place of business
  Date of commencement
  Proportion of capital provided
  Bank account details
  Management of the business
  How profits and losses shared
  Keeping of accounts
  Consequences upon death
  Limitations of competing with partnership
  Property
  Insurance
  Arbitration.

4. Every partner has implied authority to bind the business.
5. Partners are *jointly and severally liable*.
6. Partnership ends:
   - Defined time.
   - Completion of venture.
   - Death or bankruptcy of a single partner, unless provided otherwise in the partnership agreement.
   - Illegality.
   - Notice of a partner – subject to partnership agreement.
   - Order of the court.
7. One formed under the Limited Liability Partnership Act 2000. Partners enjoy limited liability.

No. 37

1. • Chartered companies.
   - Statutory companies – namely:
     - Private and public companies limited by shares.
     - Companies limited by guarantee.
     - Unlimited companies.
     - Partnership companies.
2. • Process of registration.
   - Expense of formation.
   - Artificial legal entity.
   - Shares in public companies are freely tradable.
   - One member required.
   - Members/shareholders may not take part in the management of the company *as shareholders*.

- Shareholder/member is not an agent of the company.
- Liability of shareholder/member is limited.
- Powers and duties regulated by Companies Act 2006.
- Compliance with formalities – keeping registers etc.
- Public access to affairs of the company.
- Requirement that certain capital be maintained.

3. Once formed it is a legal person in its own right separate from those associated with it e.g. directors, shareholders, parent and subsidiary companies.

4. When the court goes behind the separate legal entities existence, and examines the relationships and liabilities of those associated with it. It is an occasion of an exception to the company maintaining its own separate existence.

5. Public companies may issue and trade in shares on the Stock Exchange, a private company must not offer its shares to members of the public generally.

6. Application to Registrar of Companies for certificate of incorporation, requiring:
   - Articles of association.
   - Registration fee.

7. Persons who first form a company as named in the articles.

8. Contracts before incorporation do not bind the company once incorporated unless ratified by the company.

No. 38

1. • Name.
   - Registered office.
   - Objects.
   - Limitation of liability.
   - Affairs of the company re members and directors and dealings with outsiders.

2. A model set of articles.

3. The official address of the company.

4. The purposes for which the company is formed.

5. Shareholders' liabilities for the debts of the company are limited to the amount of money paid for shares held.

6. By a special resolution – 75% majority, that must be bona fide for the benefit of the company.

7. S 33 Companies Act forms a contract between the company and its members/shareholders.

No. 39

1. A private company – through the members of the bank: public companies listed on the Stock Exchange – through the issuing of shares.

2. • Capital.
   - Share capital.
   - Loan capital.

3. A certain sum of money representing the capital of the company be maintained in order that assets remain available to balance that capital maintained.

4. A special resolution – 75% – enables a company to reduce its capital.

5. Profits paid to shareholders on a so much per share basis.

6. • Preference shares.

    • Ordinary shares.

7. Contract law governs the process; the prospectus is an *invitation to treat* with the subscriber making the *offer* which the compnay may accept or reject through a resolution of its board of directors.

No. 40

1. There is an implied power for a company, once registered, to borrow money and give security for loans.

2. *Shares:* Shareholders own a bundle of rights in the company.

    Debentureholders: Have a claim against the company rather than an interest in it.

3. • *Fixed charge.*

    • *Floating charge.*

    • *Reservation of title clause.*

4. Charges must be registered within 21 days of their creation.

5. • Legal fixed charges.

    • Floating charge.

6. It is a charge on some or all of the present and future assets of a company which changes from time to time.

7. The charge will be avoided if the company was solvent at the time.

8. A register of all its charges kept by a company. Failure to register does not effect the validity of a charge.

9. • Sue creditors for arrears of interest.

    • Petition to wind up the company.

    • Apply for the appointment of a receiver.

No. 41

1. When his name is registered on the Register of Members. Minors – persons under 18 – may become members.

2. The name and address of each member with a statement of shares held, amount paid, date of entry on the register and date of cessation of membership.

3. Where a wrong is done to a company the proper claimant is the company itself, no one else.

4. Minority shareholders may not sue on behalf of the company, with exceptions.

5. • Ultra vires act.

    • Where the company acts on an ordinary resolution which should have been a special resolution.

    • Infringement of individual shareholder rights.

    • Fraud.

6. Occurs where the affairs of the company are being conducted in a manner which is unfair and prejudicial to the interest of members.

No. 42

1. Directors manage the affairs of the company. A director is similar to an agent and trustee.

2. First directors appear in the statement of directors. Subsequent directors are appointed by general meeting of shareholders by ordinary resolution.

3. Powers are defined in the articles.

4. Directors must disclose any conflict of interest.

5. A fiduciary is a person who is in a special position of trust and must not abuse that trust; statutory fiduciary duties:

   - Act within the powers conferred for a proper purpose.
   - Promote the success of the company.
   - Exercise independent judgment.
   - Exercise reasonable care and skill.
   - Avoid conflicts of interest.
   - Not to accept bribes or secret profits.
   - Declare any conflicts of interest.

6. Insider dealing is where a person has inside information not generally available and who deals in shares using that share price sensitive information.

7. • Did not expect the dealing to result in a profit.
   - Did not believe the information was 'insider' information.

No. 43

1. At the general meeting directors are required to present audited accounts.

2. Exemptions from the statutory audit are for companies with a turnover under £90 000 and who qualify as a small company.

3. First auditors are appointed by directors; subsequent auditors are appointed by the general meeting of shareholders.

   - Auditors may be removed before the expiry of their appointed period. The Registrar of Companies must be notified within 14 days.
   - Removed auditor is entitled to attend the general meeting at which it is proposed to remove him.
   - Auditors may resign by serving notice at the company's registered office; the copy must send a copy to the Registrar of Companies.

4. • Presentation of a report.
   - Carry out such investigations as will enable the opinion to be formed that proper accounting procedures have been complied with.
   - Auditors have the power to access all books and accounts of the company.
   - It is a criminal offence for an officer of the company to make an untrue statement to the auditor
   - Auditors must be fit and proper persons.
   - The duties of the auditor are owed to the company.

5. • Upon a request by 200 members minimum, or members holding at least 10% of the issued shares.
   - An order of the court.

No. 44

1. Except for private companies passing an elective resolution not to do so, every company must hold an AGM of shareholders every year or not more than 15 months.

2. • *Ordinary resolution* – simple majority of votes of those attending meeting or through proxies.
   • *Special resolution* – as above but with 75% majority.

3. Disclosure of a company's affairs is a fundamental principle of company law. This is obtained primarily through:
   • Publication in the *Gazette*.
   • Registration of documents with Registrar.
   • Keeping of certain registers.
   • Making of annual returns.

4. Kept at the company's registered office:
   • Register of directors and secretaries.
   • Director's names on all stationary.
   • Register of director's interests.
   • Register of substantial shareholdings.

5. • Address of registered office.
   • Summary of share capital.
   • Type of company and business activities.
   • List of members.
   • Particulars of directors and secretaries.
   • Any elective resolutions for the private company.

6. Every company must keep accounting records which show:
   • The financial position of the company.
   • A balance sheet giving a true and fair view.

7. • General provisions.
   • Dividends and reserves.
   • Assets.
   • Political and charitable donations.
   • Details of directors.
   • Employees shares acquired.

8. Through the Combined Code of Practice – a *remuneration committee* and publication of director's pay.

No. 45

1. • *Merger* occurs when two companies join together.
   • *Takeover* – acquisition of sufficient shares to control a company.

2. Merger
   • Must pass a special resolution.

- Second special resolution putting company into voluntary liquidation.
- Assets of transferee company become assets of transferor.

Reconstruction

- Shares are transferred from one company to another.

3. Used to effect any compromise or arrangement.

- Company, creditor or member ask court to convene a meeting of creditors.
- Notice of special meeting to be sent out.
- Ordinary resolution of 75% in value required.
- Court approval.

4. Where creditors agree to take a proportion of what is owed to them.

5. Informal guidelines. Code is supervised by the Panel on Takeovers. There is an Appeals committee. Aim is that directors act in the best interests of shareholders.

No. 46

1. Liquidation is the process by which the life of a company is brought to an end with its assets 'liquidated' that is, turned into cash or cash equivalent, and monies used to pay creditors and be shared amongst members.

2. Someone who is a member of a professional body who is permitted by its rules to act as an insolvency practitioner.

3. • The company is unable to pay its debts as defined in the *IA S.123*.
   - Just and equitable grounds.

4. • Official Receiver appointed.
   - Any disposition is void unless approved by the court.
   - No legal action can be commenced or proceeded.
   - Directors' powers cease.
   - Employees automatically dismissed.
   - Floating charges crystallize.
   - Assets remain the property of the company.

5. • *Fraudulent trading* – company has been carrying on business with an intent to defraud creditors.
   - *Wrongful trading* – a person knew or ought to have concluded that there was no reasonable prospect that the company would avoid insolvent liquidation.

6. • Winding-up costs.
   - Preferential debts.
   - Floating charge holders.
   - Unsecured creditors.
   - Members.

7. Two types: *Voluntary* members and creditors.
   - *Members*: Directors or a majority of directors make a *declaration of solvency*. Process is controlled by the company

- *Creditors:*
  - Meeting of creditors is called.
  - Assets and liabilities made known.
  - Creditors appoint a committee of inspection.
8. An order freezing a company's assets and assisting an administrator save the company or better realize its assets.
9. Appointed by a debentureholder to liquidate assets the subject of the debenture and re paying off the loan.
10. A CVA:
  - Nominee's statement made.
  - Moratorium issued.
  - Where members and creditors disagree, court can impose wishes.
  - Advertise the CVA and inform Registrar.
  - Attempts to obtain credit could be a criminal offence.
  - Assets may be disposed of only if a benefit to the company.
  - Charged goods may be sold.
  - Criminal offences created.

No. 47

1. Certain obligations on the employer where there is an employee that is not the same as those that are self-employed.
2. • Control Test.
   - Integration Test.
   - Multiple Test.
   - Mutuality of Obligation Test.
3. Must not be treated less favorably than full-time employees.

No. 48

1. Same as for other contracts:
   - Offer and acceptance.
   - Consideration.
   - Capacity.
   - Legality.
2. Written statement of terms detailing:
   - Names of parties.
   - Date of commencement.
   - Pay and intervals of pay.
   - Hours of work.
   - Holidays.
   - Sick pay schemes.

- Pensions.
- Length of notice required.
- Job title.
- Place of work.
- Any collective agreements.

3. Basic rule: Cannot be varied without consent of both parties. However, can be various implied terms based in:

- Custom and practice.
- Law.
- Collective agreements.

No. 49

1. • Indemnity.
- Misconduct.
- Personal service.
- Loyalty and good faith.
- Not to compete with the employer.
- Careful service.
- Account for property and gain.
- Trade secrets – note 'whistle blowing'.
- Inventions.
- Obedience.
- Notice.

No. 50

1. • To provide work.
- To pay wages.
- Indemnify the employee.
- Provide safe premises and equipment.
- Provide a disciplinary and grievance procedure.

2. Standard of reasonableness is required – i.e. so far as is reasonably practicable.

3. To ensure so far as is reasonable, law visitors.

4. An employer may be held liable for harm caused by persons employed by him.

5. • Trade union duties and activities.
- Public duties.
- Look for work or training.
- Safety representatives duties.
- Antenatal care.

6. Information without which a trade union representative would be materially impeded in carrying on collective bargaining.

No. 51

1. • Deductions from pay.
   • Setting of a minimum hourly rate of pay.
2. • To pay reasonable wages.
   • Pay for availability for work.
   • No obligation to pay where no work available.
   • Payment for overtime.
   • Payment during illness.
   • Power to suspend without pay where express term authorizes.
3. Any deduction not authorized under statute. In retail trade any deductions to pay for lost stock is limited to 10%.
4. • Eliminating discrimination between men and women with regard to pay.
   • Entitles equal pay where:
     • There is like work.
     • Of a broadly similar nature.
     • Rated equal under a job evaluation exercise.
     • Work is of equal demands to that of a man.
   An equality clause is written into every contract of employment.
5. These ensure that employees who are laid-off will receive some payment.
6. • Gross amount of wages.
   • Deductions.
   • Total fixed deductions.
   • Net wages payable.

No. 52

1. Automatically an unfair dismissal.
2. There are three elements:
   • Ordinary.
   • Compulsory.
   • Additional.
3. Upon giving 28 days notice, after *ordinary maternity leave*, employee is entitled to return to the job she previously did.
4. Suspension from work on maternity grounds is acceptable where it is:
   • A requirement of statute.
   • A code of practice.
   • Under the Health & Safety At Work Act 1974.
5. Pregnant employees are entitled to time off during working hours to attend antenatal clinics.

No. 53

1. Brings together statutes on inequality giving a single legal framework for all.

2. • *Direct* – where an employer deliberately treats a person less favorably because of a *protected characteristic.*

   • *Indirect* – applies a provision, criterion or practice which leads to a particular group with a protected characteristic to be treated less favorably.

   • *Harassment* – unwanted conduct based upon a protected characteristic.

   • *Victimization* – a person is treated less favorably because they brought an action under the Act.

3. • *Associative* – where action brought by a person who is treated less favorably because of their association with another who has a protected characteristic.

   • *Perceptive* – where less favorable treatment given because an employer thinks a person has a protected characteristic.

   • *Dual* – action brought where there are two or more protected characteristics involved.

4. This is where less favorable treatment is given based upon a person's:
   Ageism – age
   Disability – substantial and long-term impairment
   Gender-reassignment – medical process to change sex
   Pregnancy – being pregnant
   Race – being of a particular race
   Religion or belief – holding a particular faith or belief
   Sex – being a man or a woman
   Sexual orientation – showing a particular sexual preference.

5. A defence, where the employer can show a protected characteristic is a genuine requirement of the job.

6. Where an employee suffers unwanted conduct by others.

No. 54

1. • By agreement.
   • Conduct of the parties.
   • Operation of law.

2. Dismissal at common law based in contract.

3. Where the actions of the employer justify the employee terminating his employment.

4. Damages.

5. Dismissal under statute.

6. • Who qualifies for protection – 1-year continuous employment.
   • A dismissal must have occurred.
   • The reason must be an admissible reason.
   • The employer must act reasonably.
   • Employer to follow any disciplinary or grievance procedures.
   • Remedies – return to employment or compensation.

No. 55

1. Persons with 2-years continuous employment.

2. • Notice given by either party.

- Ending of a fixed-term contract.
- Constructive dismissal.

3. *S.139 ERA*:
   - Cessation of business.
   - Diminished requirement for employees doing work of a particular kind.

4. Same as the Basic Award for unfair dismissal (see Chapter 56.33).

5. Where 20 or more employees to be made redundant the employer is required to consult employees and trade unions.

No. 56

1. An action in negligence (see Chapter 23).

2. Action under Health & Safety At Work Act 1974 – a successful prosecution can be used in a civil action for negligence.

3. Death following an accident. Under the Fatal Accidents Act 1976, the deceased has a right of action as if still alive.

4. Three years.

5. • *Special damages* – based on estimated loss of future earnings.
   - *General damages* – at the discretion of the court.

No. 57

1. To ensure, so far as is reasonably practicable, the health, safety and welfare at work of his employees (*S.2 HSAW*).

2. To ensure a healthy working environment for employees through inspection and inquiries.

3. Enforce health and safety law.

4. • Failure to discharge a duty under the Act.
   - Willfully interfere with anything associated with health, safety and welfare.
   - Contravene a regulation.
   - Contravene a requirement of an inspector.
   - Obstruct an inspector.
   - Make false entries in health and safety records.

5. They implement EC Directives setting out broad general duties and requirements for risk assessment.

6. Smoking be taken account of in any risk assessment and the banning of smoking in all places of work including vehicles.

No. 58

1. A body charged with promoting the improvement of industrial relations.

2. To arbitrate and make binding decisions on the parties when requested.

3. Procedures are cheap, quick and informal. There are now First Tier and Upper Tier tribunals under one uniform structure.

4. An appeal court hearing appeals from employment tribunals.

No. 59

1. An organization of workers seeking to regulate relations between worker and employer.

2. Action in tort can be brought by persons suffering loss through unauthorized industrial action.

3. That it is a recognized independent trade union.

4. Special provisions exist for the financing and holding of secret ballots by trade unions.

5. Rules shall not be unlawful or unenforceable and no employee shall have his application to join unreasonably turned down.

6. Any agreement made on behalf of one or more trade unions and one or more employers.

INDEX